CorelDRAW! 2
Made Easy

Emil & Sybil Ihrig
and
Martin S. Matthews
& Carole Boggs Matthews

Osborne **McGraw-Hill**

Berkeley   New York   St. Louis   San Francisco
Auckland   Bogotá   Hamburg   London   Madrid
Mexico City   Milan   Montreal   New Delhi   Panama City
Paris   São Paulo   Singapore   Sydney
Tokyo   Toronto

Osborne **McGraw-Hill**
2600 Tenth Street
Berkeley, California 94710
U.S.A.

Osborne **McGraw-Hill** offers software for sale. For information on software, translations, or book distributors outside of the U.S.A., please write to Osborne **McGraw-Hill** at the above address.

CorelDRAW!® 2 Made Easy

567890 DOC 9987654321

ISBN 0-07-881726-9

Acquisitions Editor: Liz Fisher
Technical Reviewer: Michael Katz
Project Editor: Janis Paris
Copy Editor: Paul Medoff
Proofreading Coordinator: Nancy Pechonis
Cover Design: Bay Graphics Design, Inc.
Production: Peter F. Hancik and Erick J. Christgau

Contents

Acknowledgments

After two editions of this book and the Ihrigs' and the Matthews' work on other computer books, these authors have found one thing to be abundantly clear: Corel Systems has the finest customer support service in the industry!

Vivi Nichol, manager, and super support gurus Andrew Knox and Shawn Greenberg all provided an incredible responsiveness, great depth of knowledge, and an understanding and patience that is almost unheard of in the industry. They are responsible for making the book much more accurate and complete and the examples easier to produce. Anyone who has wrestled to get a bit of information out of a customer service department will understand what a joy it can be to work with Corel Systems.

Introduction

Since its initial release in January of 1989, CorelDRAW! has become the most talked-about graphics software package for IBM-compatible PCs. It's easy to understand why the program has received many major industry awards and received so much favorable attention. Quite simply, no other drawing software offers so many powerful drawing, text-handling, autotracing, color separation, and special effects capabilities in a single package.

About This Book

CorelDRAW! 2 Made Easy is a step-by-step training guide to CorelDRAW! that leads you from elementary skills to more complex ones. Each chapter contains hands-on exercises that are richly and clearly illustrated so that you can match the results on your computer screen.

This book makes few assumptions about your graphics experience or computer background. If you have never used a mouse or worked with a drawing package, you can begin with the exercises in the early chapters and move forward as you master each skill. On the other hand, if you have experience in desktop publishing, graphic design, or technical illustration, you can concentrate on the chapters that cover more advanced features or features that are new to you. Even the basic chapters contain exercises that stimulate your creativity, however, so it is worth your while to browse through each chapter in order to gain new design ideas.

How This Book Is Organized

CorelDRAW! 2 Made Easy is designed to let you learn by doing, regardless of whether you are a new, intermediate, or advanced user of CorelDRAW!. You begin to draw right away, and as the book proceeds, you continue to build on the skills you have learned in previous chapters.

The organization of this book is based on the philosophy that knowing how to perform a particular *task* is more important than simply knowing the location of a tool or menu command. The body of the book therefore contains step-by-step exercises that begin with basic drawing skills and progresses to advanced skills that combine multiple techniques. The appendixes at the end of the book contain handy reference material that you can turn to when you need to review what you have learned.

The organization of each chapter will help you locate quickly any information that you need to learn. Each section within a chapter begins with an overview of a particular skill and its importance in the context of other CorelDRAW! functions. In most chapters, every section contains one or more hands-on exercises that allow you to practice the skill being taught.

Chapters 1 through 5 of *CorelDRAW! 2 Made Easy* help you become familiar with the software interface and with basic drawing skills. Chapter 1, "Getting Acquainted with CorelDRAW!," gives you a guided tour of the CorelDRAW! screen and introduces you to the menus, tools, and mouse techniques of the software. Chapter 2, "Drawing and Working with Lines and Curves," introduces you to the Pencil tool and shows you how to create straight lines, polygons, curves, and closed curve objects. Chapter 3, "Drawing and Working with Rectangles and Squares," and Chapter 4, "Drawing and Working with Circles and Ellipses," introduce the Rectangle and Ellipse tools respectively. Chapter 5, "Adding Text," shows you how to enter text on the CorelDRAW! page and define the font, point size, alignment, and spacing for text.

Chapters 6 and 7 describe how you can customize the CorelDRAW! screen to enhance your drawing power. Chapter 6, "Using Magnification and View Selection," acquaints you with the Magnification tool and with the five ways you can define a limited or expanded viewing area. In Chapter 7, "Previewing Your Graphics," you will learn how the screen can show you your graphics just as they will look when you print them.

Chapters 8 through 12 show you how to *edit* objects and text and combine them into more complex images. Chapter 8, "Selecting, Moving, and Arranging Objects," teaches you how to select objects in order to perform further work on them and how to group, combine, move, and change the relative order of objects on the screen.

Chapter 9, "Transforming Objects," describes how to stretch, scale, rotate, and skew objects, how to create mirror images in any desired direction, and how to leave a copy of the original object as you transform it.

Chapter 10, "Shaping Lines, Curves, Rectangles, and Ellipses," shows you how to use the Shaping tool to turn rectangles into rounded rectangles, circles or ellipses into wedges or arcs, and lines or curves into any shape you desire.

Chapter 11, "Shaping and Editing Text," introduces a variety of special effects (such as word pictures) that you can achieve when you edit text with the Shaping tool.

Chapter 12, "Cutting, Copying, and Pasting Objects and Pictures," describes how to use the Windows clipboard to transfer objects between CorelDRAW! pictures or between CorelDRAW! and other applications. This chapter also covers CorelDRAW! techniques for duplicating objects and repeating operations and suggests ways to exploit the special-effects potentials of these techniques.

Chapters 13, 14, and 15 cover an especially rich topic: the process of defining outlines and fills for objects within a drawing. In Chapter 13, "Defining the Outline Pen," you will learn how to create calligraphic outlines and define line styles for existing and new objects.

Chapter 14, "Defining Outline Color," lets you practice assigning spot color, process color, or gray shades to any object's outline and defining outlines that contain special PostScript halftone screen patterns. In Chapter 15, "Defining Fill Color," you learn how to fill the interior of any object with process or spot color, shades of gray, or special-effects fountain fills.

Chapters 16 through 18 cover skills and special topics that go beyond drawing and editing techniques. The ability to use CorelDRAW! in conjunction with other graphics applications is discussed in Chapter 16, "Importing and Exporting Files."

Chapter 17, "Printing and Processing Your Images," reviews how to set up your printer and lets you experiment with printing color separations with crop marks and registration marks, printing to a file, and defining a variety of printing parameters.

In Chapter 18, "Creating Special Effects," you will find out how to use the powerful special effects introduced with CorelDRAW! Version 2.0. These effects, which work with text as well as other graphic objects, include using an envelope to shape an object, putting an object into multidimensional perspective, extruding an object to make a three-dimensional image, and blending two objects to make a new one.

Chapter 19, "Combining CorelDRAW! Features," allows you to integrate all the skills taught in the earlier part of the book. It contains several lengthy exercises that let you review many techniques and design a variety of drawings.

The Appendixes at the back of the book provide easy reference information. To benefit from suggestions for getting the most from your software, turn to Appendix A, "Installing CorelDRAW!." Use Appendix B, "Keyboard and Mouse Shortcuts," when you need to look up the use of a special key combination quickly. For information on using third-party fonts or clip art, or for help in using WFNBOSS to convert other manufacturers' fonts to CorelDRAW! format and vice versa, see Appendix C, "Corel Connectivity: Clip Art and Fonts." Finally, Appendix D, "Tracing Bitmapped Images," lets you practice techniques for tracing imported bitmaps manually or automatically. You will also learn how to trace single or multiple bitmaps rapidly, using the sophisticated new CorelTRACE! batch autotracing utility.

Note

The exercises in this book were designed with a VGA display adapter and screen driver in mind. If the screen driver that you installed for Windows has a lower or higher resolution (for example EGA or 800 X 600), you may need to adjust viewing magnification or rulers for some of the exercises.

Conventions Used in This Book

CorelDRAW! 2 Made Easy uses several conventions designed to help you locate information quickly. The most important of these are:

- Terms essential to the operation of CorelDRAW! appear in *italics* the first time they are introduced.

- The first time an icon or tool in the CorelDRAW! toolbox or interface is discussed, it appears as a small graphic in the text; for example, the Pencil tool ✐. A small icon also appears in the text the first time you are asked to use or refer to a given tool or icon within a chapter.

- You can locate the steps of any exercise quickly by looking for the numbered paragraphs that are indented from the left margin.

- Names of keys appear as small graphics that look similar to the actual keys on your computer's keyboard (for example, (CTRL)).

- Text or information that you must enter using the keyboard appears in this book in **boldface**.

1

Getting Acquainted with CorelDRAW!

Welcome to CorelDRAW!. You have selected one of the most innovative and advanced graphics tools available for the IBM personal computer. CorelDRAW! will sharpen your creative edge by allowing you to edit any shape or character with ease and precision, fit text to a curve, autotrace existing artwork, create custom color separations, explore calligraphic "pens" and fountain fills, and more. You can combine CorelDRAW!'s features to achieve many different special effects, such as placing a line of text or an object in perspective; folding, rotating, or extruding a line of text or an object; blending two lines of text or two objects; and creating mirror images, masks, and 3-D simulations. CorelDRAW! makes these and other capabilities work for you at speeds far surpassing those of other graphics programs.

To support your creative and technical endeavors, CorelDRAW! has a large number of fonts and clip-art libraries at your disposal. If the more than 150 fonts provided with CorelDRAW! fail to meet your needs, you can use the WFNBOSS utility (provided with version 1.1 or later) to access thousands of commercial fonts. Your software also supplies over 3000 symbols and over

750 clip-art images, and you can obtain thousands more from industry vendors. (For more information on fonts and clip art, see Appendix C, "Corel Connectivity: Clip Art and Fonts.")

If you haven't installed CorelDRAW!, turn to Appendix A, "Installing CorelDRAW!" before continuing with this chapter.

Starting CorelDRAW!

To start CorelDRAW!, first turn on your computer. Next, you may or may not need to start Windows. If you do *not* automatically load Windows, use the first two instructions below for that purpose. If you already have Windows up on your screen, skip to the paragraph following the second step.

1. Change to the drive and directory of the hard disk in which you have installed Windows. If you are not in the correct drive, you need to change the drive by typing the drive letter followed by a colon. For example, type **c:** and press (ENTER). To then change the directory to the Windows directory, type **cd windows** or **cd***yourname*, if you have named the directory something else, and press (ENTER).

2. Type **win** and press (ENTER) to start Windows. After an introductory screen and a few seconds, the Program Manager window appears on the screen, as shown in Figure 1-1.

Depending on how you or someone else last left Corel on your computer, the Corel Applications window (representing the group of Corel Applications) may be open, as shown in Figure 1-1, or you may see an icon at the bottom of the screen. If you don't see an open window with the title "Corel Applications," look for an icon with that name that looks like this:

If you don't see either the Corel Applications window or icon, open the

Corel Applications

Window menu and look there.

3. *Click* on "Window" in the menu bar of the Program Manager window (with your mouse, place the mouse cursor on top of the word "Window" and press and release the left mouse button). The Window menu should open and look like this:

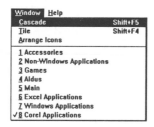

4. If you see "Corel Applications" in the Window menu, click on it (place the mouse cursor on top of the phrase "Corel Applications" and press and release the left mouse button). Your Corel Applications group window should open.

Figure 1-1.   *The Program Manager window with the Corel Applications group window open*

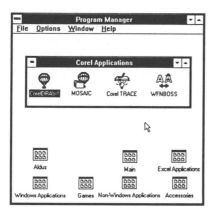

Caution

If you don't see "Corel Applications" in the Window menu you need to turn to Appendix A and install CorelDRAW!. Do that now and then return here.

If "Corel Applications" is an icon, open it now.

5. *Double-click* on the Corel Applications group icon (place the mouse cursor on the icon and press and release the left mouse button twice in rapid succession). The Corel Applications group window should open.

6. To start CorelDRAW!, double-click on the CorelDRAW! application icon (place the mouse cursor on the icon and press and release the left mouse button twice in rapid succession).

After a moment, an information screen is displayed, then the CorelDRAW! screen appears.

The CorelDRAW! Screen

You will see references to the various screen components of CorelDRAW! many times throughout the book. Take a moment now to familiarize yourself with these terms and their functions within the program. Figure 1-2 shows the location of each screen component.

Window Border   The Window border marks the boundaries of the CorelDRAW! window. By placing your mouse pointer on and dragging the border, you can scale this window. Refer to your *Microsoft Windows User's Guide* for full details on how to scale a window.

Title Bar   The title bar shows the name of the program you are working in and the name of the currently loaded image. All files in CorelDRAW! format have the file extension .CDR directly after the filename. When you first load CorelDRAW!, the screen hasn't been saved yet, so the title bar reads "UN-TITLED.CDR."

Minimize Button   You will find the minimize button ▼ at the upper-right corner of your screen. Click on this button to turn the CorelDRAW! window

1

into an icon—a small picture of a balloon. When running as an icon, CorelDRAW! frees up memory that you can use to run another application. To restore CorelDRAW! to its previous size, position the mouse over the icon, and double-click.

Maximize Button   If you want to make the CorelDRAW! window fill the entire screen, click on the maximize button ▲ located next to the minimize button. This button then turns into the restore button ⬍. You can return the CorelDRAW! window to its previous size by clicking on this button once more.

Control-Menu Box   You can use the Control-menu box ⊟ as another easy way to move, minimize, maximize, or otherwise change the size of the CorelDRAW! program window. To use the Control-menu box, simply click on the small bar inside the box, or press (ALT)-(SPACEBAR) and the Control menu will appear. Select the command you want by clicking on it. When you have finished, click anywhere outside the Control menu to close it. The Control menu is a Windows feature that is not needed by CorelDRAW!.

Figure 1-2.   *The CorelDRAW! screen*

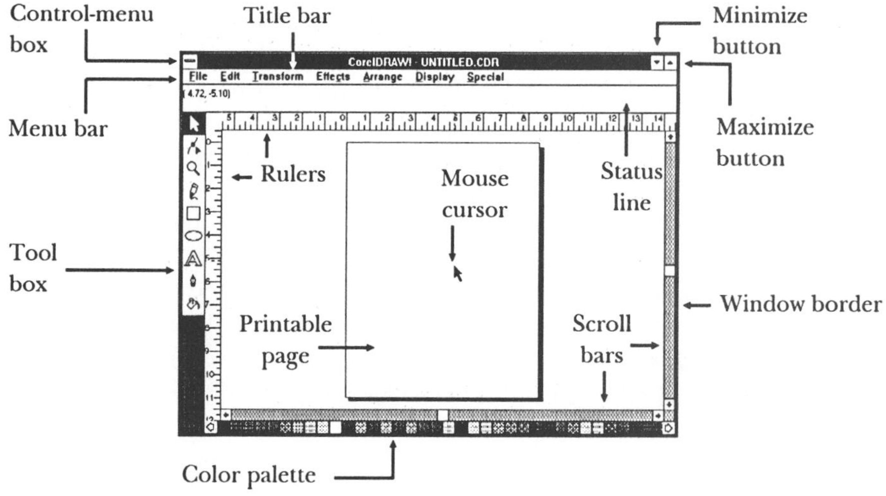

Menu Bar   The menu bar contains seven menus that you pull down by clicking on one of the menu names. See the section "The CorelDRAW! Menus" later in this chapter for a brief summary of the command options in each menu.

Status Line   The status line contains a rich source of information about the image you have on your screen. When you first load CorelDRAW!, this line contains only a pair of numbers—the coordinates of the mouse cursor. When you are drawing or editing images, however, it displays information such as the number, type, and dimensions of objects you select and the distance you travel when moving these objects. The exact nature of the information displayed depends on what you are doing at the time. The status line offers invaluable aid to technical illustration or to any work that requires precision.

Printable Page Area   You create your images in the printable page area. The exact size of the page depends on the printer or other output device that you installed when you set up Microsoft Windows, as well as on the settings you choose through the Page Setup command in the File menu. When you first load CorelDRAW!, the screen displays the total printable page area. Once you learn about magnification in Chapter 6, "Using Magnification and View Selection," you can adjust the area of the page that is visible at any one time.

Scroll Bars   The scroll bars are most useful when you are looking at a magnified view of the page. Use the horizontal scroll bar to move to the left or right of the currently visible area of the page; use the vertical scroll bar to move to an area of the page that is above or below the currently visible area. You will find more information on how to use the scroll bars in Chapter 6.

Rulers   The horizontal and vertical rulers that appear in Figure 1-2 may not appear on your screen. These are optional and must be specifically turned on by selecting Show Rulers from the Display menu. A dashed line in each ruler shows you where the mouse cursor is. You can see such lines at about 4.7 on the horizontal ruler and about 5.1 on the vertical ruler. These are the same as the coordinates in the status line. The rulers allow you to judge the relative sizes and placements of objects quickly and accurately.

Color Palette   The color palette at the bottom of the CorelDRAW! window in Figure 1-2 allows you to apply shades of gray on a monochrome screen or shades of gray and colors on a color monitor. Like the rulers, the color palette can be turned on or off in the Display menu. In CorelDRAW!, shading and color can be applied to either a character's or object's outline or its body.

Toolbox   The toolbox contains tools that carry out the most important and powerful drawing and editing functions in CorelDRAW!. Click on a tool icon to select a tool. The tool icon now appears in reverse video—white images on a black background. Other changes to the screen or to a selected object may also occur, depending on which tool you have selected. For a brief explanation of the function of each tool, see the section, "The CorelDRAW! Tool" later in this chapter.

With a basic understanding of the screen elements, you can get around the CorelDRAW! window easily. The next three sections of this chapter explore three types of interface elements—menus, dialog boxes, and tools—in greater depth.

The CorelDRAW! Menus

When you pull down a menu, some commands appear in boldface, while others appear in gray. You can select any command that appears in boldface, but commands in gray are not available to you at the moment. Commands become available for selection depending on the objects you are working with and the actions you perform on them.

This book is a tutorial rather than a reference manual. As such, it organizes information about CorelDRAW! according to the task you want to perform and not by menu. You'll learn to use program menus by working with particular functions of CorelDRAW!. This section briefly describes the major purposes of each menu. These menus are shown in Figure 1-3.

The File Menu   The File menu in Figure 1-3(a) is similar in all Windows applications. Most of the commands in the File menu do not apply to the process of drawing. Instead, they cover program functions that deal with entire files at a time or with running the program as a whole. Examples of such functions are loading, saving, importing, exporting, and printing a file, and exiting CorelDRAW!. If you select the About CorelDRAW! command in

Figure 1-3. *The CorelDRAW! menus*

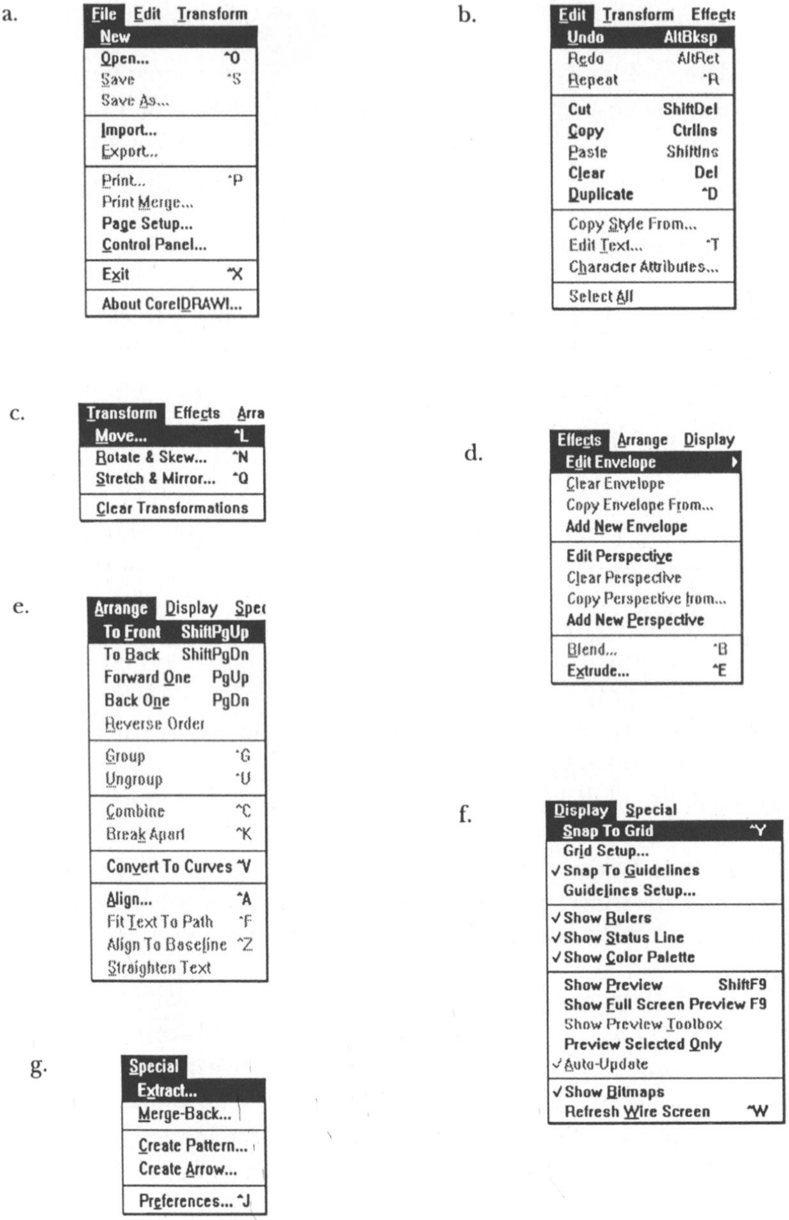

a.

File Edit Transform
New
Open...   ^O
Save   ^S
Save As...

Import...
Export...

Print...   ^P
Print Merge...
Page Setup...
Control Panel...

Exit   ^X

About CorelDRAW!...

b.

Edit Transform Effects
Undo   AltBksp
Redo   AltRet
Repeat   ^R

Cut   ShiftDel
Copy   CtrlIns
Paste   ShiftIns
Clear   Del
Duplicate   ^D

Copy Style From...
Edit Text...   ^T
Character Attributes...

Select All

c.

Transform Effects Arra
Move...   ^L
Rotate & Skew...   ^N
Stretch & Mirror...^Q

Clear Transformations

d.

Effects Arrange Display
Edit Envelope   ►
Clear Envelope
Copy Envelope From...
Add New Envelope

Edit Perspective
Clear Perspective
Copy Perspective from...
Add New Perspective

Blend...   ^B
Extrude...   ^E

e.

Arrange Display Spec
To Front   ShiftPgUp
To Back   ShiftPgDn
Forward One   PgUp
Back One   PgDn
Reverse Order

Group   ^G
Ungroup   ^U

Combine   ^C
Break Apart   ^K

Convert To Curves ^V

Align...   ^A
Fit Text To Path   ^F
Align To Baseline ^Z
Straighten Text

f.

Display Special
Snap To Grid   ^Y
Grid Setup...
√ Snap To Guidelines
Guidelines Setup...

√ Show Rulers
√ Show Status Line
√ Show Color Palette

Show Preview   ShiftF9
Show Full Screen Preview F9
Show Preview Toolbox
Preview Selected Only
√ Auto-Update

√ Show Bitmaps
Refresh Wire Screen ^W

g.

Special
Extract...
Merge-Back...

Create Pattern...
Create Arrow...

Preferences...   ^J

the file menu, a message box like the one shown here pops up on the screen, displaying information about the current version of CorelDRAW! and other information:

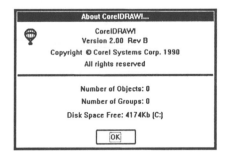

When you are finished reading the message, click on OK to exit and return to the program.

The Edit Menu   The Edit menu in Figure 1-3(b) is also similar to other Windows applications. Use the commands in this menu to copy, cut, and paste objects or images, to undo the last action you performed, and to copy or change attributes of objects and text.

The Transform Menu   The commands in the Transform menu, shown in Figure 1-3(c), allow you to edit the shape of selected objects and text. A more direct way to perform these functions is to use the Select and/or Shape tools, which you'll learn about in Chapters 8 through 11.

The Effects Menu   The Effects menu, shown in Figure 1-3(d) is new to CorelDRAW! 2.0 and contains some of its most powerful features. The Effects menu allows you to place text or an object in an envelope and then shape that envelope—make text or an object appear to be in perspective or extruded. It also allows you to blend two lines of text or two objects. A more detailed discussion will be presented in Chapter 18, "Creating Special Effects."

The Arrange Menu   The commands in the Arrange menu, shown in Figure 1-3(e), all have to do with the relative placement of objects within an image. Select the commands in this menu to move a selected object or group of objects to the forefront or background of an image, to combine, group, ungroup, or break apart selected objects, and to align objects and text. You will find more details about the Arrange menu commands in Chapter 8, "Selecting, Moving, and Arranging Objects."

The Display Menu   The Display menu in Figure 1-3(f) has one very clear function: to help you customize the user interface and make the CorelDRAW! screen work the way you do. Use the commands in this menu to display or hide the rulers and the status line, to set up grids for precision drawing, and to choose whether and how to display fully accurate, WYSIWYG (What-You-See-Is-What-You-Get) previews of your images.

The Special Menu   The Special menu in Figure 1-3(g) has three main functions. First, it allows you to bring text into CorelDRAW! from an external word processing program or to export text from CorelDRAW! to edit in a word processing program. Second, you can use the Special menu to create patterns and line endings. Finally, it lets you fine-tune many different program parameters using the Preferences command. Discussions about these options, which apply to a wide range of functions, appear in their respective contexts.

Dialog Boxes

Some menu commands are automatic: Click on them, and CorelDRAW! performs the action immediately. Other commands are followed by three dots (an ellipsis), indicating that you must enter additional information before CorelDRAW! can execute the command. You enter this additional information through dialog boxes that pop up on the screen when you click on the command. This section introduces you to the look and feel of typical dialog boxes in CorelDRAW!.

Dialog boxes contain several kinds of controls and other ways for you to enter information. Compare the following descriptions with the screen elements in Figures 1-4 and 1-5 to familiarize yourself with operations in a dialog box. Look at Figure 1-4 first.

Circular *option buttons* like those in Figure 1-4 present you with mutually exclusive choices. In a group of option buttons, you can select only one at a

Figure 1-4.   *Representative controls in a dialog box*

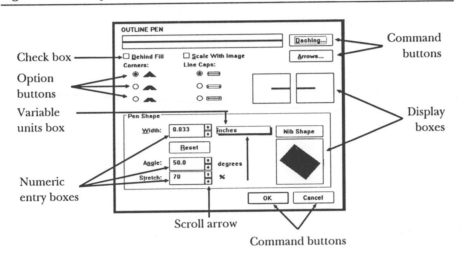

Figure 1-5.   *Additional dialog box controls*

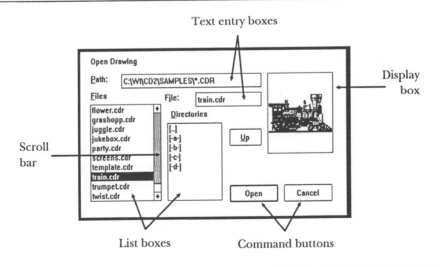

time. When you click on an option button to select it, the inner circle becomes black.

Square *checkboxes* in a dialog box offer you choices that are not mutually exclusive, so you can select more than one option simultaneously. Checkboxes behave like light switches; you turn them on or off when you click to select or deselect them. When you turn on or enable an option in a checkbox, an "X" fills it. When you turn off or disable the option, the "X" disappears.

The larger rectangles in a dialog box are *command buttons*. When selected, a command button is highlighted temporarily, and usually CorelDRAW! performs the command instantly. When you click on a command button that has a label followed by three dots, you open another dialog box that is nested within it.

A rectangle that contains numeric entries and that is associated with up and down scroll arrows is a *numeric entry box*. You can change the numeric values in three ways. To increase or decrease the value by a single increment, click on the up or down arrow respectively. To increase or decrease the value by a large amount, press and hold the mouse button over one of the scroll arrows. You can also click on the value itself to select it, erase the current value, and then type in new numbers.

Rectangles containing units of measurement represent *variable unit boxes* that are valid only for the associated option and dialog box. Click on the variable unit box as many times as necessary to change to the unit of measurement you prefer.

Some dialog boxes contain *display boxes* that show you just how your current selection will look after you exit the dialog box. You do not perform any action on the display box itself; instead, its contents change as you change your selections in the dialog box.

Figure 1-5 shows an example of a dialog box that contains different types of controls. Use the *text entry boxes* available in some dialog boxes to enter strings of text. Depending on the dialog box involved, text strings might represent filenames, path names, or text to appear in an image. To enter new text where none exists, click on the text entry box and type the text. To edit an existing text string, click on the string, then use the keyboard to erase or add text. You will become familiar with the specific keys to use as you learn about each type of text entry box.

The *list boxes* within a dialog box list the names of choices available to the user, such as filenames, directory and drive names, or typestyle names. Drive and directory names within a list box appear in boldface and in all capital letters, while filenames do not. You can tell drive names from directory names because the former are surrounded by both brackets and hyphens, [-a-], while the latter are, at most, surrounded by brackets only, [coreldrw]. Click on a name in the list box to select it.

Scroll bars accompany text entry boxes or list boxes when the contents of those boxes exceed the visible area in the dialog box. You can use the scroll bar to access the portions of the list that are outside of the currently visible area. To move up or down one name at a time, click on the up or down arrow of the scroll bar respectively. To move up or down continuously, press and hold the mouse button over the up or down arrow of the scroll bar. Alternatively, you can click on the scroll bar itself, drag the scroll box, or press (PGUP) or (PGDN) to move up or down the list box in large increments.

Some options in a dialog box appear in gray, indicating that you cannot select them at the moment. On the other hand, a command button within a dialog box may appear in boldface, indicating that you can select it, and also may have a bold outline around it. This command button represents the default selection. You can simply press (ENTER) to activate that selection, exit the dialog box, and return to your graphic. The OK command button is normally the default. The OK button accepts and processes the entries you made in the dialog box. You can leave most dialog boxes without changing any settings by clicking on the Cancel button or pressing (ESC).

You will learn more about operating within dialog boxes in the context of each chapter in this book. The following section will acquaint you with the toolbox, the portion of the interface most vital to the operation of CorelDRAW!.

The CorelDRAW! Toolbox

One of the features that makes CorelDRAW! so easy to work with is the economy of the screen. The number of tools in the CorelDRAW! toolbox (Figure 1-6) is deceptively small. Several of the tools have more than one

Figure 1-6. *The CorelDRAW! toolbox icons*

Select tool

Magnification tool

Rectangle tool

Text tool

Fill tool

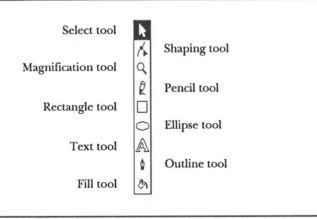

Shaping tool

Pencil tool

Ellipse tool

Outline tool

function, and nested submenus *fly out* when you select them. This method of organization reduces screen clutter and keeps related functions together.

The tools in the CorelDRAW! toolbox perform three different kinds of functions. Some allow you to draw objects, others let you edit the objects you have drawn, and a third group permit you to alter the appearance of the screen so that you can work more efficiently. This section describes each tool briefly in the context of its respective function.

Drawing Tools

CorelDRAW! allows you to create or work with nine different types of objects as shown in Figure 1-7. Because you use the same tools and techniques for some of the objects, however, there are actually only five different *classes* of objects. These classes, and the kinds of objects you can design in each, are

- Lines, curves, and polygons
- Rectangles and squares
- Ellipses and circles
- Text

1

- Bitmapped (pixel-based) images imported from a scanner or paint program

Does nine seem like a small number? Professional artists and graphic designers know that basic geometrical shapes are the building blocks on which more elaborate images are constructed. After you "build" an object using one of the four drawing tools, you can use one or more of the editing tools in the CorelDRAW! toolbox to reshape, rearrange, color, and outline it.

The four drawing tools—the Pencil tool, the Rectangle tool, the Ellipse tool, and the Text tool—are all you need to create eight of the nine object types in CorelDRAW!. You work with the last object type, a bitmapped image, after importing it. (See Chapter 16 "Importing and Exporting Files," and Appendix D, "Tracing Bitmapped Images," for a fuller discussion of this subject.)

The Pencil Tool The Pencil tool ✐ is the most basic drawing tool in the CorelDRAW! toolbox. This single tool allows you to create lines, curves, curved objects, and polygons. CorelDRAW! 2.0 has changed the Pencil tool

Figure 1-7. *The nine types of objects*

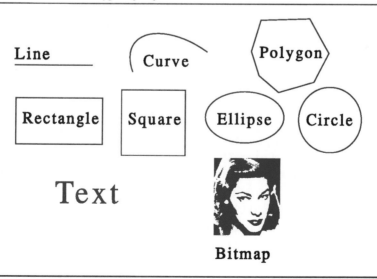

from a single-mode freehand drawing instrument to a more sophisticated dual-mode instrument by adding the ability to create Bézier lines and curves. Freehand mode is the default and is used for less precise work. Bézier mode is selected with the Lines and Curves option of the Preferences command in the Special menu and is used for smooth, precise curves, even when magnified or distorted. Chapter 2, "Drawing and Working with Lines and Curves," guides you through a series of exercises that teach you all the basic CorelDRAW! skills for using this tool in both modes.

To select the Pencil tool, press (F5) or click on the Pencil icon once, and then move the mouse cursor into the white space on the page. When you select this tool, the mouse cursor takes the shape of a crosshair ⊞, the Pencil tool icon becomes highlighted, and the message "Drawing in Freehand mode..." appears on the status line.

The Rectangle Tool   The Rectangle tool ▢ lets you draw rectangles and squares. You'll create your own rectangles and squares in Chapter 3. To round the corners of a rectangle, however, you need to use the Shaping tool ▨, one of the editing tools in the CorelDRAW! toolbox.

To select the Rectangle tool, press (F6) or click on the Rectangle icon once, and then move the mouse cursor into the white space on the page. The Rectangle icon becomes highlighted, the mouse cursor becomes a crosshair, and the message "Rectangle" appears in the status line.

The Ellipse Tool   The Ellipse tool ◯ allows you to design ellipses and perfect circles. You can learn more about using the Ellipse tool in Chapter 4.

To select the Ellipse tool, press (F7) or click on the Ellipse icon once, and then move the mouse cursor into the white space on the page. The Ellipse icon becomes highlighted, the mouse cursor becomes a crosshair, and the message "Ellipse" appears in the status line.

The Text Tool   The Text tool 𝔸 gives you access to more than 150 Corel Systems fonts and (if you use the WFNBOSS utility described in Appendix C) to thousands of other commercial fonts as well. Chapter 5 teaches you how to enter text in CorelDRAW!.

To select the Text tool, press (F8) or click on the Text icon once, and then move the cursor into the white space on the page. The Text icon becomes highlighted, the mouse cursor becomes a crosshair, and the message "Text" appears in the status line.

1

Tip

If you "scribbled" on the page while trying out any of the drawing tools, clear the screen before proceeding. To do this, click on the File menu name and select the New command. A dialog box appears with the message:

UNTITLED.CDR Has Changed, Save Current Changes?

Select the No command button to exit the message box and clear the screen.

Editing Tools

Once you have created objects on a page with the drawing tools, you use a different group of tools to move, arrange, reshape, and manipulate the objects. The editing tools include the Select tool, the Shaping tool, the Outline tool, and the Fill tool.

The Select Tool   The Select tool ▣ is really two tools in one. In the *select mode*, you can select objects in order to move, arrange, group, or combine them. In the *transformation mode*, you can use the Select tool to rotate, skew, stretch, reflect, move, or scale a selected object. This tool does not let you change the basic shape of an object, however. Chapters 8 and 9 introduce you to all the functions of the Select tool.

The Shaping Tool   The Shaping tool ▣ allows you to modify the shape of an object. Use this tool to smooth or distort any shape, add rounded corners to rectangles, convert a circle into a wedge or arc, modify a curve, or kern individual characters in a text string. Chapters 10 and 11 cover the basics of using this tool.

The Outline Tool   The Outline tool ▣, like the Select tool, functions in more than one way. Use the Outline tool and its associated fly-out submenu to choose a standard or custom outline color, or to create a custom outline "pen" for a selected object. Chapters 13 and 14 instruct you in the use of this tool.

The Fill Tool   Use the Fill tool ▣ and its associated fly-out submenu to select a standard or custom fill color for selected objects or text. As you'll learn in Chapter 15, your options include custom colors, PostScript screens, fountain fills, and PostScript textures.

Tools for Customizing
The CorelDRAW! Screen

The third group of tools helps you customize the CorelDRAW! interface so that it works the way you do. Only one of these tools, the Magnification tool 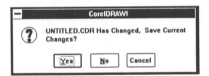, is visible in the CorelDRAW! toolbox. The Magnification tool and its associated fly-out menu let you control just how much of your picture you will view at one time. Use this tool when you need to work on a smaller area in fine detail, or when you need to zoom in or out of a picture. Chapter 6 will discuss the Magnification tool and its fly-out menu in more detail.

Other screen adjustment tools are available, but you can access them only when you use the preview window (see Chapter 7) to view your graphic just as it would appear when you print it.

Quitting CorelDRAW!

Now that you are familiar with the screen components, exit CorelDRAW! and return to the Program Manager. You can use the mouse, the keyboard and mouse, or the keyboard alone to quit CorelDRAW!.

Using the mouse, double-click on the Control-menu box in the upper-left corner, or display the File menu by moving the mouse cursor to the File menu name and then click once. Then, select the Exit command by clicking on it once.

Using both mouse and keyboard, display the File menu by clicking on the menu name. Then, with the File menu displayed, type **X**.

Using the keyboard alone, you can either press (ALT)-(F) to display the File menu and then type **X** or press (CTRL)-(X).

If you have attempted to draw during this session, a screen message like the one shown here appears:

1

Select the No command button to abandon your changes.

If you are like most CorelDRAW! users, you will want to begin drawing immediately. This book encourages you to draw. In Chapter 2 you will use the Pencil tool to begin drawing lines and curves.

2

Drawing and Working with Lines and Curves

The Pencil tool ✐ is the most versatile tool in the CorelDRAW! toolbox. By using this tool in two different ways, you can create both straight and curved lines, and from these simple building blocks you can construct an almost infinite variety of polygons and irregular shapes. Work through the exercises in this chapter to become thoroughly familiar with this most basic CorelDRAW! tool.

Freehand vs. Bézier Mode

The Pencil tool has two modes of drawing: *Freehand* mode where curves mirror the movements of your hand on a mouse, and Bézier mode where curves are precisely placed between two or more points you identify. Drawing straight lines is very similar in the two modes, but drawing curves is very different. In the remaining sections of this chapter, Freehand mode, the default, will be discussed first, and then Bézier mode.

Drawing Straight Lines

In the language of the CorelDRAW! interface, *line* refers to any straight line, while the term *curve* refers to curved lines, irregular lines, and closed objects you create with such lines. Drawing a straight line requires that you work with the mouse in a different way than when you draw a curved or irregular line. To draw a straight line in CorelDRAW!,

1. Load CorelDRAW! if it isn't running already.

2. Position the mouse cursor over the Pencil tool icon ✐ and click once. The cursor changes to a crosshair ⊞ and the Pencil tool icon appears in reverse video.

3. Position the crosshair cursor at the point where you want a line to begin. This can be anywhere inside the printable page area.

4. Press *and immediately release* (*click*) the left mouse button, and then move the crosshair cursor toward the point where you want to end the line. A straight line appears and extends as far as you move the crosshair cursor, as in Figure 2-1. You can move the line in any direction, or make the segment longer or shorter.

5. When you have established the length and direction you want, complete the line by clicking and releasing the mouse button. As Figure 2-2 shows, a small rectangular *node* appears at each end of the line to show that the line is complete and can be selected for further work.

6. Press (DEL) to clear the line off the screen.

Tip

When you begin to draw a line, be sure to release the mouse button as soon as you press it. If you continue to hold down the mouse button while drawing, you create a curve instead of a straight line.

Figure 2-1. *Extending a straight line*

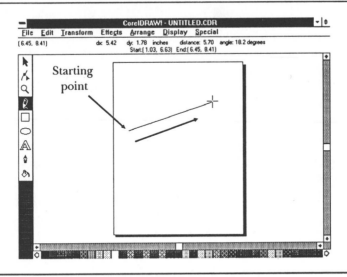

Figure 2-2. *Nodes on a completed line*

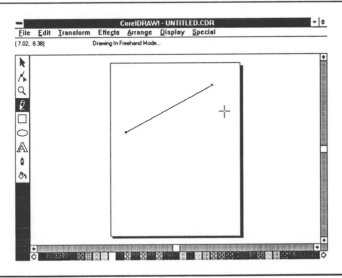

Using the Status Line to Improve Precision

Chapter 1 introduced you briefly to the status line and its potential for helping you draw with precision and accuracy. In the next exercise, pay attention to the useful information that appears on the status line.

1. With the Pencil tool still selected, begin another line by clicking the mouse button at a point about halfway down the left side of the page. The coordinates on the left side of the status line should be *about* 1.0, 5.5 (absolute precision is not important).

2. Move the mouse toward the right side of the page. Don't click a second time yet.

3. Notice that as soon as you clicked once and began to move the mouse, a message appeared on the status line as shown here:

CorelDRAW! - UNTITLED.CDR
File   Edit   Transform   Effects   Arrange   Display   Special
(5.91, 8.13)   dx: 4.91   dy: 2.58   inches   distance: 5.55   angle: 27.7 degrees
Start:(1.00, 5.55) End:(5.91, 8.13)

Look more closely at the status line. It includes the following information about the line you are drawing:

dx   The *dx* code refers to the *x-coordinate* or horizontal location of your line on the page relative to the starting point. The number following this code identifies how far your line has traveled (in other words, its distance) from that starting point along the X or horizontal axis. A positive number (one with no minus sign in front of it) indicates that you are extending the line to the right of the starting point, while a negative number indicates reverse.

dy   The *dy* code refers to the *y-coordinate* or vertical location of your line on the page relative to the starting point. The number following this code identifies how far your line has traveled (in other words, its distance) above or below that starting point along the Y or vertical axis. A positive number indicates that you are extending the line above the starting point, while a negative number indicates that you are extending it below the starting point.

inches The unit of measurement for the current *dx* and *dy* position indicators appears on the status line as well. The CorelDRAW! default is inches, but you can change it to centimeters or picas and points using the Grid Setup command in the Display menu. You'll gain experience with the grid later in this chapter.

distance The number following this text indicates the length of your line relative to the starting point.

angle The number following this text indicates the angle of the line relative to an imaginary compass, where 0 degrees is at the 3 o'clock position, 90 degrees is at the 12 o'clock position, 180 degrees is at the 9 o'clock position, and –90 degrees is at the 6 o'clock position.

Start and End The pairs of numbers following each of these items represent the coordinates of the start and end points of the line.

4. Choose an end point for the line and click again to freeze the line in place. Note that the status line indicators disappear as soon as you complete the line, just as they did in Figure 2-2.

5. Press (DEL) to delete the line before going further.

As you may have noticed, information appears on the status line only when you are performing some action on an object. This information makes CorelDRAW! especially powerful for applications requiring great precision, such as technical illustration.

Erasing Portions of a Line

In the following exercise, you'll practice erasing part of a line that you have extended but not completed. You can always backtrack and shorten a line in CorelDRAW!, as long as you have not clicked a second time to complete it.

1. With the Pencil tool still selected, choose a starting point for another line.

Figure 2-3.   *Extending a line using the status line indicator*

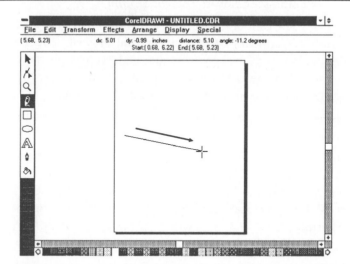

2. Move the cursor downward and to the right until the *dx* indicator reads about 5.00 inches and the *dy* indicator reads about –1.00 inches, as in the example in Figure 2-3.

3. Without clicking the mouse button a second time, backtrack upward until the *dx* indicator reads 4.00 inches. Notice that the line you have drawn behaves flexibly and becomes shorter as you move the mouse backward.

4. Click a second time to freeze the line at *dx* 4.00 inches.

5. Before going any further, delete the line by pressing (DEL).

Constraining a Line to an Angle

You need not rely on the status line alone when seeking to control the precision of your drawing. You can also use the (CTRL) key while drawing to *constrain* (force) a line to an angle in increments of 15 degrees. In the following exercise, you'll create a series of seven straight lines this way.

1. With the Pencil tool still selected, press *and hold* (CTRL) and click the mouse button to choose a starting point for the line.

2. Release the mouse button, but continue holding (CTRL) as you extend the line outward and downward from the starting point. Try moving the line to different angles in a clockwise direction; as the angle indicator in the status line shows, the line does not move smoothly, but instead "jumps" in increments of 15 degrees.

3. Now, extend the line straight outward, so that the angle indicator on the status line reads 0 degrees. While still holding down (CTRL), click the mouse button a second time to freeze the line at this angle.

4. Release (CTRL). (Remember always to click the mouse *before* you release (CTRL). If you release (CTRL) first, the line doesn't necessarily align to an angle.)

5. Draw six more lines in the same way, each sharing a common starting point. Extend the second line at an angle of 15 degrees, the third at an angle of 30 degrees, the fourth at an angle of 45 degrees, the fifth at an angle of 60 degrees, the sixth at an angle of 75 degrees, and the seventh at an angle of 90 degrees. When you are finished, your lines should match the pattern shown in Figure 2-4.

Clearing the Screen

Before going any further, clear the screen of the lines you have created so far.

1. Click on the File menu to pull it down.

2. Select the New command.

3. A message box appears with the message:

   UNTITLED.CDR Has Changed, Save Current Changes?

Figure 2-4.   *Constraining lines to angles in 15-degree increments*

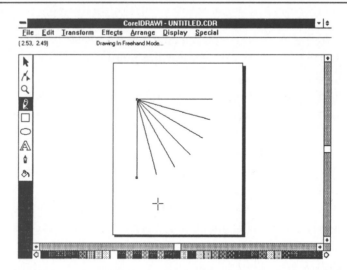

Click on the No command button to exit the message box and clear the screen. The Select tool in the tool box is highlighted by default, just as when you first loaded CorelDRAW!.

Drawing Multisegment Lines

With CorelDRAW!, you can easily draw several straight lines in sequence so that each begins where the previous one left off. Use this technique both for drawing open-ended line figures and for constructing polygons. In the present exercise, you will construct a series of peaks and valleys.

1. Select the Pencil tool using a shortcut—press the (F5) function key. Then click to choose a line starting point. Extend a line upward and to the right.

2. When you reach the desired end point for the line, freeze it in place with a *double click* rather than a single click of the mouse button.

3. Move the mouse downward and to the right, without clicking again. The flexible line follows the crosshair cursor automatically.

4. Double-click again to freeze the second line in place.

5. Continue zig-zagging in this way until you have created several peaks and valleys similar to those in Figure 2-5.

6. When you reach the last valley, click once instead of twice to end the multisegment line.

7. Press (DEL) to clear the screen before proceeding.

If you make a mistake while drawing, you can erase the last line segment you completed in one of two ways. You either press (ALT)-(BACKSPACE) *or select the Undo command in the Edit menu. Don't press* (DEL) *when drawing a multisegment line, or you will erase all of the segments you have drawn so far.*

Tip

Drawing a Polygon

A *polygon* is a closed two-dimensional figure bounded by straight lines. You create polygons in CorelDRAW! by drawing multisegment lines and then

Figure 2-5. *Drawing multisegment lines*

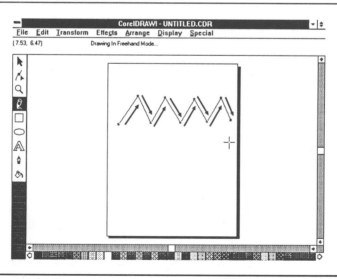

connecting the end point to the starting point. In the following exercise, you'll create a polygon figure like the one in Figure 2-6.

1. Draw the first line, double-clicking at the line end point so that you can continue drawing without interruption.

2. Draw four additional lines in the same way, following the pattern in Figure 2-6. End the last line segment with a single click at the point where the first line segment began.

Did your last line segment "snap" to the beginning of the first? Or does a small gap remain between them? If you can still see a small gap, don't worry. In the section "Joining Lines and Curves Automatically" later in this chapter, you'll learn how to adjust the level of sensitivity at which one line will join automatically to another. For now, clear the screen and begin the next exercise.

Figure 2-6.   *Drawing a polygon*

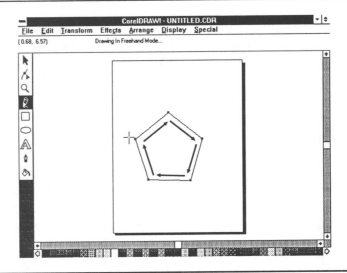

Straight Lines in Bézier Mode

The Bézier mode of drawing is to identify end points or *nodes* and place lines or curves between them. Therefore, drawing straight lines in Bézier mode is very similar to drawing straight lines in Freehand mode. Try it next and see for yourself.

Selecting Bézier Mode

To use Bézier mode, you must first select it from the Lines and Curves option of the Preferences command in the Special menu. Use these instructions for that:

1. With the mouse (it doesn't matter which tool is selected) click on the Special menu. The Special menu will open.

2. Click on "Preferences" at the bottom of the menu. The Preferences dialog box will open.

3. Click on the Lines and Curves command button in the lower left of the dialog box. The Lines and Curves dialog box will open as shown in Figure 2-7.

4. Click on the Bézier option on the left just below center.

5. Click OK twice or press (ENTER) twice to return to your drawing.

6. If your Pencil tool is not selected, press (F5) or click on the tool in the Toolbox.

Your status line should now include the words "Drawing in Bézier Mode..."

Drawing Single Lines in Bézier Mode

Now draw a single line segment as you did earlier in Freehand mode.

1. Click on a starting point in the middle left of the page, immediately release the mouse button (if you hold down the mouse button,

CorelDRAW! will think you are drawing a curve), and move the mouse cursor to the upper right of the page.

Notice that the starting point is a solid black square. This starting point is a *node*, a point on a line that is used to define the line. When you start the line, the starting point is selected and is therefore black. Also, there is no line connecting the starting point and the mouse cursor, and no information in the status line except the coordinates of the mouse cursor. A line does not appear and there is no information in the status line because a Bézier line is not defined until you have placed at least two nodes.

2. Click on an end node. A straight line is drawn between the two nodes as shown in Figure 2-8, and information now appears in the status line. The line segment, however, is called a "curve."

Drawing a Polygon in Bézier Mode

Unlike Freehand mode, you can continue to add line segments after clicking on an end node only once in Bézier mode. Do that next to build a

Figure 2-7.   *Lines and Curves dialog box*

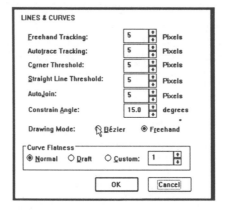

2

polygon (your screen should still be as you left it after drawing the first Bézier line segment).

1. Click on two more nodes, one toward the lower right and the other toward the lower left. Lines will be added connecting the nodes.

2. Position the mouse cursor on top of the original starting node and click one final time. The result is a four-sided polygon like the one shown in Figure 2-9.

As you can see, there are many mechanical similarities between Freehand and Bézier drawing of straight lines. The results are virtually the same, but the screen looks very different during the creation of the lines. For straight lines there is little reason to use Bézier over Freehand.

Like Freehand mode, you can move the mouse cursor in any direction, including backward, over the path already traveled to "erase" the object *before* clicking on a node. After clicking on a node you can use Undo (either (ALT)-(BACKSPACE) or choose Undo from the Edit menu) to erase the previous line (or curve) segment. If you want to delete the entire object (line or polygon) while it is still selected (you can see all of the nodes), press (DEL).

Figure 2-8.   *Bézier straight line segment*

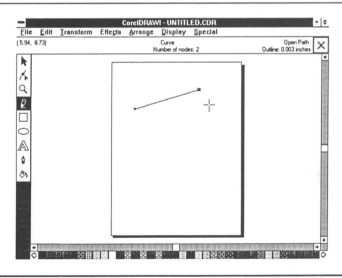

Figure 2-9.   *Bézier polygon*

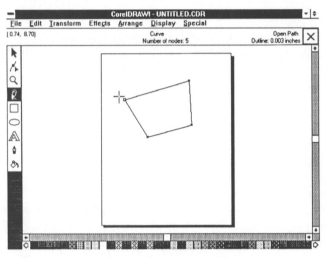

If you want to draw two or more Bézier line segments that are not connected, press the (SPACEBAR) twice, then draw your second line.

3. Press (DEL) to clear your drawing. To return to Freehand mode, click on the Special menu, the Preferences command, the Lines and Curves command button, and the Freehand option button. Click on OK twice or press (ENTER) twice to return to your drawing, in Freehand mode, and begin working with curves.

Drawing Curves

The Pencil tool has a twofold purpose in CorelDRAW!; you can use it to draw curved or irregular lines as well as straight lines. This section introduces you to the basics of drawing a simple curve, closing the path of a curve to form a closed curve object, and erasing unwanted portions of a curve as you draw.

To draw a simple curve:

1. Select the Pencil tool if it is not still selected.

2. Position the crosshair cursor at the point on the page where you want a curve to begin and then press *and hold* the mouse button. The Start and End coordinates appear on the status line.

3. Continue to hold the mouse button and *drag* the mouse along the path where you want the curve to continue. Follow the example in Figure 2-10.

4. Upon completing the curve, release the mouse button. The curve disappears momentarily while CorelDRAW! calculates exactly where it should go. Then the curve reappears with many small square nodes, as in Figure 2-11. Note that when you have finished, the word "Curve" and the number of nodes appear in the middle of the status line and the message "Open Path" appears at the right side of the status line. "Open Path" indicates that you have drawn a curved line, not a closed figure.

5. Press (DEL) or select the Undo command in the Edit menu to clear the curve you have just drawn.

Figure 2-10.   *Drawing a curve*

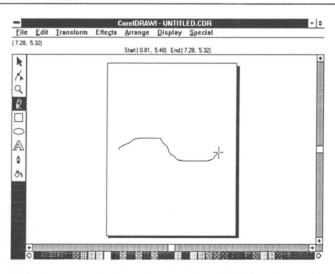

Figure 2-11.   *A completed curve with nodes*

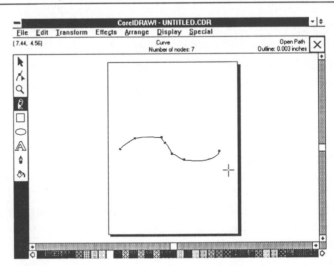

Tip

To draw a straight line, click and release the mouse button. To draw a curve, press and hold the mouse button and drag the mouse along the desired path.

Erasing Portions of a Curve

Should you make a mistake while drawing a curve, you can backtrack and erase what you have drawn, as long as you have not yet released the mouse button. You use (SHIFT) to erase the portion of a curve that you no longer want.

1. Begin another curve by pressing and holding the mouse button over the point at which you want the curve to start.

2. Drag the mouse as desired. Do not release the mouse button yet.

3. While still holding down the mouse button, press and hold (SHIFT) and backtrack over as much of the curve as you wish to erase.

4. After you have erased a portion of the curve, release (SHIFT) and continue to draw by dragging the mouse in the desired direction.

5. Release the mouse button to finalize the curve. Delete the curve by pressing (DEL).

6. Clear the screen by selecting New from the File menu. Do not save your changes.

Drawing Multisegment Curves

Just as you drew multisegment lines, you can also draw multisegment curves. You can join two successive curves together automatically if the starting point of the second curve is within a few pixels of the end point of the first curve. Refer to Figure 2-12 for this exercise.

1. Select a starting point for the first curve and begin dragging the mouse.

2. Complete the curve by releasing the mouse button. Do not move the mouse cursor from the point at which your first curve ends.

3. Draw the second curve and complete it. The second curve should "snap" to the first, as in Figure 2-12.

Figure 2-12.   *Drawing two curves that "snap" together*

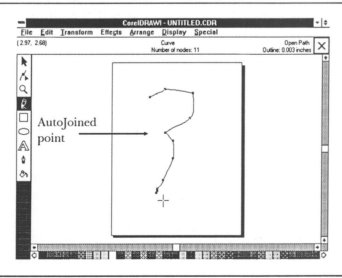

If the two curved lines didn't snap together, you moved the cursor farther than five pixels away before starting the second curve. Don't worry about it at this point. CorelDRAW! has a default value of five pixels distance for automatic joining of lines and curves. In the "Joining Lines and Curves Automatically" section of this chapter, you will learn how to adjust the sensitivity of this AutoJoin feature.

Closing an Open Path

When you drew your first curve, the message "Open Path" appeared at the right side of the status line. This message indicates that your curved line is not a closed object, and therefore that you cannot fill it with a color or pattern (see Chapter 15, "Defining Fill Color"). You can create a closed curve object with the Pencil tool, however. Refer to Figure 2-13 to create a closed outline of any shape for this exercise. You'll draw this shape as a single curve.

1. Before beginning the exercise, select New from the File menu to clear the screen. When a message box appears and asks whether you want to save your changes, select No.

2. Select the Pencil tool.

3. Start the curve about midway across the page area.

4. Continue dragging the mouse creating the closed shape. Your drawing doesn't have to look exactly like the one in Figure 2-13. If you make a mistake, press (SHIFT), backtrack and erase the portions of the curve that you do not want.

5. When you return to the point at which you began make sure you are over your starting point and then release the mouse button. After a few seconds, the object reappears with many square nodes along the path.

Note that the message in the middle of the status line now reads "Curve" and the number of nodes. At the right side of the status line, the message "Fill:Black" appears, followed by a representation of a solid black color. This indicates that you now have a closed curve object and that you have filled it with the default color, black. You can't yet see the fill for this object, because

Figure 2-13. *Drawing a closed curve object*

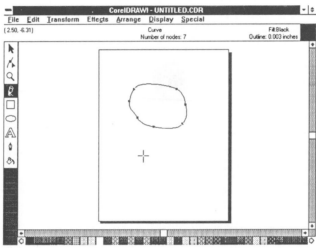

you haven't begun to work with the preview window that allows you to see your graphic just as you would print it. You'll become familiar with the preview window in Chapter 7, "Previewing Your Graphics."

Drawing Curves in Bézier Mode

If you are like most people, drawing smooth curves in Freehand mode is very difficult, if not impossible. Of course, as you'll see in Chapter 10, "Shaping Lines, Curves, Rectangles, and Ellipses," CorelDRAW!'s Shaping tool allows you to clean up messy artwork very quickly. As an alternative, though, the Bézier mode of drawing allows you to draw smooth curves to start with—after a little practice.

The principle of Bézier drawing is that you place a node, set a pair of control points that determine the slope and the height or depth of the curve, and then place the next node. The method is to move the crosshair to where you want a node, press and hold the mouse button while you drag the control points until you are satisfied with their positioning, release the mouse button, and go on and do the same thing for the next node. When you have two or more nodes, curves appear between them reflecting your settings. This is very different from Freehand mode drawing and will take some getting used to. Dragging the mouse with the button depressed moves the control points in two dimensions and only indirectly identifies the path of the curve. Understanding how to handle control points, though, will help you use the Shaping tool in Chapter 10.

The only way to really understand Bézier drawing is to try it.

1. Clear your screen by selecting New from the File menu and choosing No in answer to the Save Changes message.

2. Select Bézier from the Lines and Curves dialog box reached through the Preferences command of the Special menu.

3. Select the Pencil tool if it isn't already selected.

4. Move the mouse cursor to where you want to start the curve and press and hold the left mouse button.

5. Move the mouse in any direction while continuing to hold the left mouse button and you should see the *control points* appear—two small black boxes on dashed lines connecting them to the larger node, as shown here:

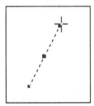

There are three principles involved in moving the mouse to set the control points:

• Begin by dragging a control point in the direction that you want the curve to leave the node.

• Drag the control point away from the node to increase the height or depth of the curve and drag the control point toward the node to decrease the height or depth.

2

- Rotate the control points about the node to change the slope of the curve. The slope follows the rotational movement of the control point.

6. Drag the control point out away from the node toward 2 o'clock and swing it in an arc about the node. Notice how the two points move in opposite directions. Continue to hold the left mouse button.

7. Drag the control point in toward the node until it is about a half inch away from the node and swing it until the control point you clicked on is pointing at 2 o'clock. Your node should look like this:

8. Release the mouse button and move the mouse cursor to where you want the second node to be—about two inches to the right and in line with the first node.

9. Again press and hold the left mouse button to set the node.

10. Drag the control point toward 5 o'clock so it is about a half inch away from the node.

11. Release the mouse button. A curve segment is drawn between the two nodes that should look like this:

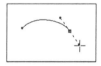

12. Move the mouse cursor and press and hold the mouse button to set a third node about an inch below and in the middle of the first two nodes.

13. Drag the control point so it is about a quarter of an inch to the left of the node, at 9 o'clock.

14. Release the mouse button. A second curve segment will appear as shown here.

15. Move the mouse cursor until it is on top of the first node you set and press and hold the mouse button.

16. Drag the control points until they are about a half inch away from the node and the top control point is aimed at 2 o'clock, like this:

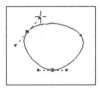

17. Release the mouse button. A third curve segment appears completing a curved triangle.

Practice drawing other Bézier objects. Notice how moving the control points both in and out from the node and in an arc around the node can radically change the curve segment to its left (behind the node) and to a lesser extent, the curve segment to the right (ahead of the node). Also, notice how the number of nodes can affect the finished object. As a general rule the fewer nodes the better, but there are some minimums:

A continuous curve like a circle should have a node every 120 degrees or three nodes on a circle like this:

A curve that changes direction like a sine wave needs a node for every two changes in direction, as shown here:

2

A curve that changes direction in a sharp point (called a *cusp*) needs a node for every change in direction like this:

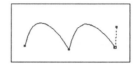

18. Return to Freehand mode by opening the Special menu, choosing the Preferences command, and selecting the Lines and Curves option, as before.

Increasing Precision

CorelDRAW! has three features that aid in precision drawing in addition to the mouse cursor coordinates and the other line and curve data displayed in the status line. These are an adjustable grid that underlays the drawing surface and assists in aligning points and objects, a pair of rulers to give you a visual reference to where you are, and the ability to place nonprinting guidelines on the page for purposes of alignment.

The grid and the guidelines can optionally be given a magnet-like property that causes points or objects that are placed near them to be drawn to them. These are called *Snap To Grid* and *Snap To Guidelines*. The Snap To property can be turned on and off, like the rulers, through the Display menu. You can also turn the Snap To Grid on and off by pressing (CTRL)-(Y). The Display menu also provides access to Setup dialog boxes for Grids and Guidelines. The Grid Setup dialog box allows you to display the grid on the screen (as a series of faint dots) and, if so, to determine the horizontal and vertical spacing of the grid. The Guideline Setup dialog box allows you to place guidelines with a very high degree of precision. You can also place guidelines by dragging them out of either ruler and placing them by visually aligning them in the opposite ruler.

This section shows you how to use the rulers and the grid to draw with greater precision. Guidelines will be used and discussed further in a later section.

Setting the Grid and Displaying Rulers

You will next make several changes to the settings for the grid and turn on the Snap To property. Then you will turn on the display of both the grid and the rulers.

1. Select the New command from the File menu to clear the screen of the shape you drew in the last exercise and don't save any changes.

2. Select the Grid Setup command from the Display menu. The dialog box in Figure 2-14 appears. The settings in your software may be different from the ones in the figure.

Figure 2-14.   *The Grid Parameters dialog box*

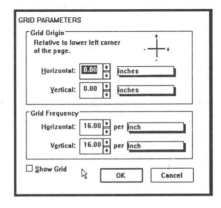

2

3. Adjust both horizontal and vertical grid frequencies to 16.00 per inch, if necessary. To change the value in the numeric entry box, press and hold the mouse button over the up or down scroll arrow until the number changes to 16.00. Alternatively, you can click on the numeric value itself and type in the new number. To change the unit of measurement in the rectangular units box, just click on it until the word "inch" appears.

4. Click on Show Grid to turn on its display and then adjust the Grid Origin so the Vertical position of the lower-left corner is at 11 inches. (Some versions of CorelDRAW! use the upper-left corner as the point of reference, in which case a vertical position of 0 is correct.) Click on OK to save these settings and close the dialog box.

5. Look at the Snap To Grid command in the Display menu. If no check mark appears in front of it, select it to make the grid active. If a check mark already appears in front of it, you don't need to do anything.

6. Select the Show Rulers command from the Display menu. Since you have set the grid size to inches, the rulers will also display in inches, as in Figure 2-15. Notice that the zero point for both the horizontal

Figure 2-15. *Displaying the rulers*

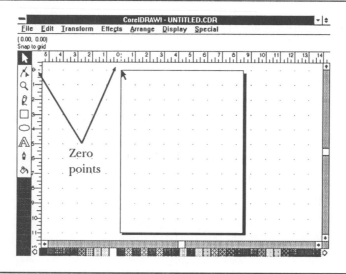

and vertical rulers begins at the upper-left corner of the page area, as shown by the cursor arrow in the figure. This is a convenient way to set the rulers so that you can measure everything relative to that corner.

Joining Lines and Curves Automatically

CorelDRAW! has a feature called AutoJoin which causes lines and curves to "snap" together automatically when their end points are separated by a preset number of *pixels* (the smallest element on a screen—the "dots" with which everything is built). You can adjust the threshold number of pixels through the Preferences command in the Special menu.

Literal joining of two end points is important because CorelDRAW! classifies an object as being either *open* or *closed*. If an object is open, you cannot fill it with a color or shade. Try out the AutoJoin feature and then change the AutoJoin threshold and see the effect.

1. Select the Pencil tool, then move the crosshair cursor to a point 1 inch to the right of the zero point on the horizontal ruler and 2 inches below the zero point on the vertical ruler. Notice that as you move the mouse, dotted "shadow" lines in each ruler show you the exact location of your cursor.

2. Click once at this point to begin drawing a line. The parameters in the status line appear.

3. Using the rulers and the status line to help you, extend the line 4 inches to the right. The *dx* and distance parameters on the status line should read 4.0 inches, as in Figure 2-16. Click a second time to freeze the line in position. Notice how both the grid display and the grid's Snap To feature help you do this.

4. Move the crosshair cursor exactly 1/4 inch to the right of the end point of the line. Use the rulers to help you.

5. Press and hold the mouse button at this point and drag the mouse to form a squiggling curve.

6. Release the mouse button to complete the curve. If you began the curve 1/4 inch or more to the right of the line end point, the curve

Figure 2-16. *Extending a line (dx=4.00 inches, distance=4.00 inches)*

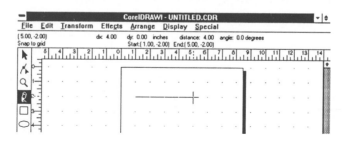

remains separate from the line and does not snap to it, as in Figure 2-17. In order to make a curve snap to a line automatically at this distance, you'll need to adjust the AutoJoin threshold value in the Preferences dialog box. (You'll become familiar with this process in the next section.)

Figure 2-17. *Curve failing to snap to a line (AutoJoin value too low)*

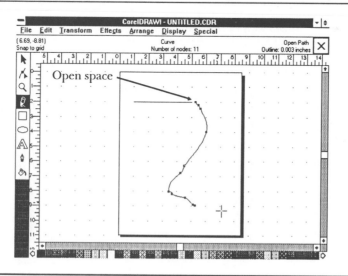

7. Select the New command from the File menu to clear the screen before proceeding. Do not save any changes.

Adjusting the AutoJoin Threshold

The AutoJoin feature determines how far apart (in pixels) two lines or curves have to be for them to join together automatically. If the setting in the Lines and Curves dialog box is a small number, such as 3 or less, lines snap together only if you draw with a very exact hand. Use this lower setting when you want to *prevent* lines from joining accidentally. If your technique is less precise, you can set the AutoJoin threshold value to a number higher than 5 pixels so that lines will snap together even if you don't have a steady hand.

1. Select the Lines and Curves option from the Preferences command in the Special menu. The Lines and Curves dialog box in Figure 2-18 appears. The default setting for most of the features in the Lines and Curves dialog box is 5 pixels. You'll use some of the other settings later on, when you learn skills for which these settings are

Figure 2-18.   *Auto Join in the Lines and Curves dialog box*

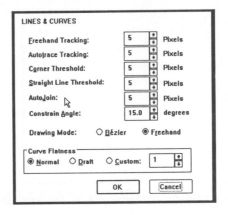

2

useful. For now, you will concern yourself only with the AutoJoin setting.

2. Set the AutoJoin value to 10 pixels by clicking several times on the up scroll arrow.

3. Select OK twice to save the new value and return to the drawing.

4. Now you can redraw the line and make the curve snap to it. With the Pencil tool selected, redraw a straight line as you did in steps 7 through 9 of the previous section.

5. Move the crosshair to a point 1/4 inch to the right of the end point of the line and then press and hold the mouse button to begin drawing a curve. The horizontal ruler on your screen displays only four markings per inch, not eight as you would find on an actual ruler.

6. Drag the mouse and draw the squiggling curve as you did in step 5 of the previous section.

7. Release the mouse button. This time, the curve joins automatically to the line, as shown in Figure 2-19.

Figure 2-19.   *Curve snapping to a line (AutoJoin value high)*

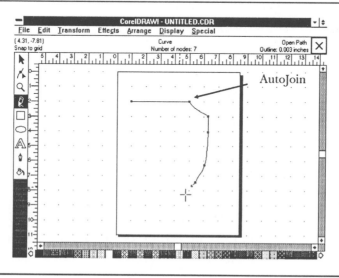

8. Select New from the File menu to clear the screen before going further.

The AutoJoin feature has other uses in addition to allowing you to connect lines and curves. You can also use it to accomplish the following:

- Join lines to lines or curves to curves.
- Add a curve or line to the end of an existing curve, line, or object that you have selected.
- Create closed curve objects and polygons by starting and ending a curve (or a series of line segments) at the same point.

Creating a Drawing Using Lines, Curves, and Polygons

You have learned to create all of the simple objects—line, curve, closed curve, and polygon—that you can make with the Pencil tool. In this exercise, you'll bring together all of the skills you have learned by drawing a kite that consists of lines, curves, and a polygon. Use Figures 2-21 through 2-28 as a guide to help you position the start and end points of the lines and curves.

1. Turn on the rulers and show the grid (if they do not appear onscreen already) by selecting Show Rulers from the Display menu and Show Grid from the Grid Setup dialog box reached from the Display menu.

2. Also from the Display menu, select Snap To Guidelines. You have now turned on all of CorelDRAW!'s precision enhancement features.

Guidelines, nonprinting lines placed on a drawing by either dragging on a ruler or via a dialog box, are used like the grid to align objects in a drawing. Guidelines have two major benefits over the grid: They can be placed anywhere, not just on a ruler mark and, since they are continuous dotted lines, they provide a better visual reference than the grid dots. When a guideline is near a grid line, the guideline always takes priority. This allows you to place a guideline very near a grid line and have objects snap to the guideline. Neither guidelines nor grid lines affect objects on a drawing retroactively—turning on Snap To Grid, for example, will not move objects already on the drawing.

Since the drawing you are doing here only uses major ruler coordinates, you could very easily do it without guidelines. Use the guidelines anyway to see how they work and to use them as a visual reference.

3. With any tool, from any point on the horizontal ruler at the top of the drawing area, drag a horizontal guideline down to 7 inches below the zero point on the vertical ruler. (Move the mouse cursor to the horizontal ruler, press and hold the left mouse button while moving the mouse cursor and the dotted line that appears, down to 7 inches; then release the mouse button.) You'll see that the Snap To Grid helps you align the guideline. Your screen should look like this as you are dragging the guideline:

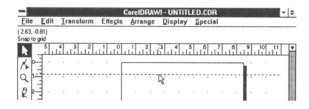

4. As you did in step 3, drag two more horizontal guidelines down to 3 inches and 1 inch respectively, below the zero point on the vertical ruler.

If you misplace a guideline, move the mouse cursor to it, press and hold the left mouse button until a four-headed arrow appears, then drag the line into proper position. You can drag a guideline off the page to get rid of it. Also, you can double-click on a guideline and get the Guideline Setup dialog box. From there you can move a guideline precisely or delete it.

5. Again like step 3, drag three vertical guidelines to the right from the vertical ruler and place them at 6, 4, and 2 inches to the right of the zero point on the horizontal ruler.

Figure 2-20.   *Guidelines in place*

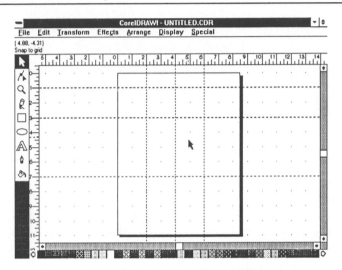

When you are done placing all of the guidelines, your screen should look like the one shown in Figure 2-20.

6. Select the Pencil tool.

7. Move to a point 2 inches to the right of the zero point on the horizontal ruler and 3 inches below the zero point on the vertical ruler and then click once to start a line.

8. Extend the line upward and to the right until you reach a point 4 inches to the right of the horizontal zero point and 1 inch below the vertical zero point. Use the status line information to help you and refer to Figure 2-21. Double-click and release the mouse button at this point. With the intersections of the guidelines at each of these points, the lines you are drawing jump to these points if you get anywhere near them.

9. Extend the next line segment downward and to the right as shown in Figure 2-22, until you reach a point 6 inches to the right of the horizontal zero point and 3 inches below the vertical zero point. Double-click at this point to add on another line segment.

2

Figure 2-21. *Drawing a kite: the first line segment*

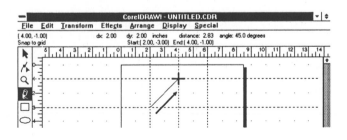

10. Extend another line segment horizontally to the left until you reach the starting point. Double-click at this point. The last line segment will connect to the first line segment and form a triangle, as shown in Figure 2-23.

11. From this point, extend another line segment downward and to the right until you reach a point 4 inches to the right of the horizontal zero point and 7 inches below the vertical zero point, as shown in Figure 2-24. Double-click at this point to complete this segment.

Figure 2-22. *Drawing a kite: the second line segment*

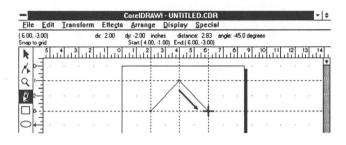

Figure 2-23.   *Drawing a kite: the third line segment*

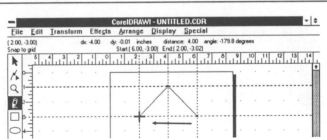

12. Now, extend a segment upward to the lower-right corner of the original triangle, as in Figure 2-25. Click just once to finish the line and complete the basic kite shape.

13. Next, add a vertical crosspiece to the kite. Since this line must be absolutely vertical, begin by pressing and holding (CTRL) and then clicking once at the top of the kite.

Figure 2-24.   *Drawing a kite: the fourth line segment*

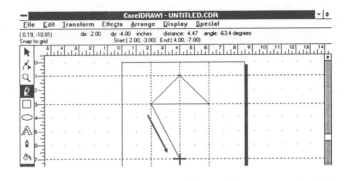

2

Figure 2-25. *Completing the basic kite shape*

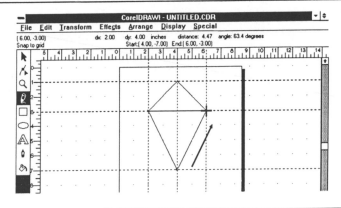

14. Extend this new line to the base of the kite as shown in Figure 2-26 and then click once. You are going to attach a curve to this line.

15. To attach a curve to the line, press and hold the mouse button and then draw a kite tail similar to the one in Figure 2-27. Release the mouse button to complete the curve.

16. Finally, add a string to the kite. Click on the point at which the crosspieces meet and extend a line diagonally downward and to the left until you reach the margin of the printable page area. Use Figure 2-28 as a guide. Click once to complete the line.

17. Your kite should now look similar to the one in Figure 2-28. Leave the kite on your screen for the concluding section of this chapter.

Saving Your Work

As you work on your own drawings, save your work frequently during a session. If you don't save often enough, you could lose an image in the event of unexpected power or hardware failures.

In order to save a new drawing, you must establish a filename for it.

Figure 2-26.   *Drawing the vertical crosspiece*

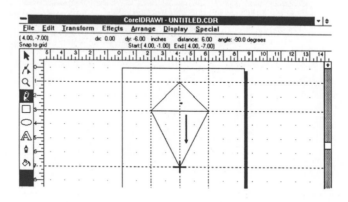

Figure 2-27.   *Drawing the kite "tail" (a curve)*

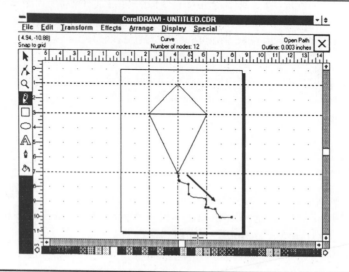

Figure 2-28.   *Adding a string and completing the kite*

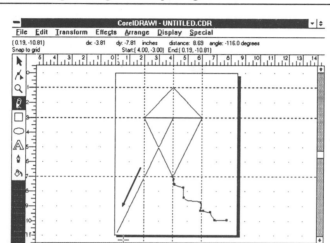

To save the kite you just drew,

1. Select the Save As command from the File menu to display the Save Drawing dialog box in Figure 2-29. If you installed the sample drawings with CorelDRAW!, the directory indicator shows that you are in the SAMPLES directory of your hard drive. (Path names may vary, depending on how and where you installed the software.) If you cannot see your full path name, click anywhere in the Path text entry box, and then press (END). To return to the beginning of the text line, press (HOME).

2. If the Path text entry box shows some other path, or if you want to save the drawing in a different drive and/or directory, for example \DRAW as suggested in Appendix A, change to the correct drive and directory by double-clicking on the correct entries in the Directories list box. When you double-click, the selected path name will appear in the Path text entry box. If the drive or directory name you want is not visible in the Directories list box, position the mouse

Figure 2-29.   *The Save Drawing dialog box*

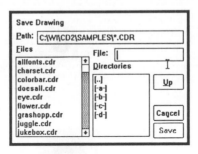

cursor over the up or down arrow in the scroll bar, and then press and hold the mouse button until the path name becomes visible. You can then select the drive or directory name.

3. Name the drawing by clicking in the File: text entry box, and then typing the desired name of your file. Use no more than eight characters; CorelDRAW! adds the .CDR extension for you when you select the Save command button. In this case, type **KITE**. The Save command button, which was gray before, now becomes available for selection.

4. Save the file by clicking on the Save command button or pressing (ENTER). CorelDRAW! adds the extension .CDR to the file. You exit the Save File dialog box and return to your drawing. Notice that the title bar now contains the name of your drawing, KITE.CDR.

5. Select New from the File menu to clear the screen before continuing. Since you have just saved a picture, the Save Changes warning box doesn't appear.

The foregoing procedure applies only the first time you save a drawing. To save a drawing that has already been saved, either select the Save command from the File menu, or press (CTRL)-(S).

Retrieving a File

2

To open a drawing that you have saved, use the following procedure. In this exercise, you'll open the KITE.CDR file you just saved.

1. Select Open from the File menu. The Open Drawing dialog box appears, as in Figure 2-30. Its layout is very similar to the Save As dialog box.

2. If you saved your file in a directory other than the default directory (the SAMPLES directory), select the drive and/or directory name from the Directories list box. Use the scroll bar if necessary.

3. If you can't see the file KITE.CDR in the Files list box, position the mouse cursor over the down arrow in the scroll bar and then press and hold it until the filename becomes visible.

4. Click once on the filename KITE.CDR. The name appears in reverse video (white lettering on black background) and displays in the File text box. Also, you will see a miniature of the drawing in the display box.

Figure 2-30.   *The Open Drawing dialog box*

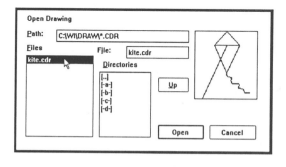

5. To open the file, select the Open command or press (ENTER). After a moment, the file displays in the window and its name appears in the title bar.

6. Exit CorelDRAW! by pressing (CTRL)-(X), or by selecting Exit from the File menu.

Tip

There's a shortcut to opening a file once you are in the Open File dialog box. Instead of clicking once on the filename and then selecting Open, you can simply double-click on the filename.

That's all there is to it. You have created a complete drawing using the Pencil tool, saved it, and loaded it again. Along the way, you have learned how to do both freehand and Bézier drawing of both lines and curves and to use the rulers, grid, guidelines, and status line to help you work.

3

Drawing and Working with Rectangles and Squares

The rectangle is a basic shape that underlies many complex man-made forms. In this chapter, you will begin to use the Rectangle tool to create both rectangular and square shapes. As you work your way through the exercises in this book, you will apply a host of CorelDRAW! special effects, fills, and shaping techniques to rectangles and squares to make them come alive.

Drawing a Rectangle

Using the Rectangle tool in the CorelDRAW! toolbox, you can initiate a rectangle from any of its four corners, as well as from the center outward. Having this degree of freedom and control over the placement of rectangles saves you time and effort when you lay out your illustrations.

Drawing from Any Corner

You can start a rectangle from any of its four corners. The corner that represents the starting point always remains fixed as you draw; the rest of the outline expands or contracts as you move the cursor diagonally. This flexibility in choosing a starting point allows you to place a rectangle more quickly and precisely within a drawing. Perform the following exercise to become familiar with how the CorelDRAW! interface reacts when you use different corners as starting points.

1. Load CorelDRAW! if you are not running it already.

2. Select the Rectangle tool by placing the mouse cursor over the Rectangle icon ▢ and clicking once, and then moving the mouse out of the toolbox and to the right. The mouse cursor turns into a crosshair ⊞ , and the Rectangle icon is selected.

3. Position the cursor anywhere on the printable page area, press and hold the left mouse button, and drag the mouse *downward* and to

Figure 3-1.   *Drawing a rectangle*

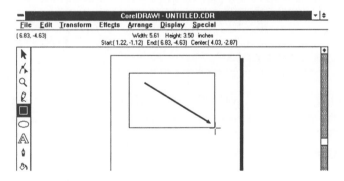

the *right* along a diagonal path, as shown in Figure 3-1. When you draw in this direction, the width and height indicators on the status line display as positive numbers.

4. Experiment with different widths and heights until you achieve the shape you want. You can easily modify the shape of the rectangle by redirecting the movement of the mouse. Notice that the upper-left corner, which was your starting point, remains fixed.

5. When the rectangle is the shape and size you want, release the mouse button. This action freezes the rectangle in place. Four nodes appear at the corners of the rectangle, and the status line changes to display the messages "Rectangle" and "Fill:" followed by a solid black square, as in Figure 3-2. You will learn more about fills in Chapter 15, "Defining Fill Color."

6. Press and hold the mouse button at a new starting point, and then move the cursor along a diagonal path *downward* and to the *left*. This time, the width indicator on the status line displays a negative number, and the height indicator displays a positive number.

Figure 3-2.   *Completing a rectangle*

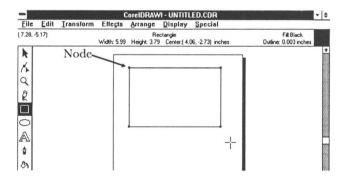

3

Release the mouse button when the rectangle has the dimensions you want.

7. Press and hold the mouse button at a different starting point, and then move the cursor along a diagonal path *upward* and to the *right*. This time, the width indicator displays a positive number and the height indicator displays a negative number. Release the mouse button when the rectangle has the dimensions you want.

8. Move to another new starting point, and then press and hold the mouse button and move the cursor along a diagonal path *upward* and to the *left*. When you use the lower-right corner as your starting point, both of the dimension indicators in the status line display as negative numbers. Release the mouse button when the rectangle has the dimensions you want.

   You can get rid of a rectangle while it is selected—has nodes on the corners—by selecting the Clear command from the Edit menu or pressing (DEL).

9. While the last rectangle you drew is still selected, choose Clear from the Edit menu to remove it.

10. Clear the rest of the page by choosing New from the File menu and not saving the changes.

The type of information appearing in the status line reflects the kind of object you are drawing. When you create a line, the status line displays the x- and y-coordinates, the distance (d) traveled, and the angle of the line. When you create a rectangle, the status line displays the width, and height, start, end, and center.

Keep in mind that while you are drawing, the width and height indicators always show you the direction of the rectangle relative to the starting point.

- A positive width indicator means you are drawing from left to right.

- A negative width indicator means you are drawing from right to left.

- A positive height indicator means you are drawing from top to bottom.

- A negative height indicator means you are drawing from bottom to top.

Drawing from the Center Outward

CorelDRAW! allows you to draw a rectangle from the center outward. Using this technique, you can place rectangular shapes more precisely within a graphic, without having to pay close attention to rulers or grid spacing. The width and height indicators display the exact dimensions of the rectangle as you draw. Draw a rectangle now, using the center as its starting point.

1. With the Rectangle tool selected, press and hold both (SHIFT) and the mouse button at the desired starting point. Keep both (SHIFT) and the mouse button pressed as you move the mouse. As with any rectangle, you can draw in any direction; the width and height indicators in the status line reflect that direction. You can tell that the rectangle in Figure 3-3 is being drawn from the center to the

Figure 3-3.   *Drawing a rectangle from the center outward*

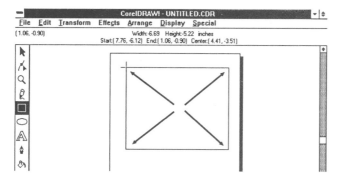

upper-left corner because both of the indicators display negative numbers.

2. Release both (SHIFT) and the mouse button to complete the rectangle.

3. Press (DEL) to clear the rectangle from the screen.

Drawing a Square

In CorelDRAW!, you use the same tool to produce both rectangles and perfect squares. The technique is identical, except that you bring (CTRL) into play when creating a square.

Drawing from Any Corner

Follow these steps to draw a square. As with a rectangle, you can use any corner as your starting point.

1. With the Rectangle tool selected, position the cursor at the point where you want to begin the square.

2. Press and hold both (CTRL) and the mouse button and then draw diagonally in any direction. Note that the status line indicators show that the width and the height of the shape are equal, as in Figure 3-4.

3. To complete the square, release the mouse button first, and then release (CTRL). If you release (CTRL) first, you might draw a rectangle with unequal sides rather than a square.

4. Press (DEL) to clear the square from the screen.

Drawing from the Center Outward

To draw a square in any direction, using the center as a starting point, you must use both (CTRL) and (SHIFT) as well as the mouse button.

1. With the Rectangle tool selected, position the cursor at the point where you want to begin the square.

2. Press and hold (CTRL), (SHIFT), and the mouse button simultaneously, and draw diagonally in any direction.

3. To complete the square, release the mouse button first, and then release (CTRL) and (SHIFT). If you release (CTRL) and (SHIFT) first, you might draw a rectangle with unequal sides, and the center might turn into a corner.

4. Press (DEL) to clear the square from the screen.

Practicing with the Grid

If your work includes design-oriented applications such as technical illustration, architectural renderings, or graphic design, you may sometimes

Figure 3-4.   *Drawing a square*

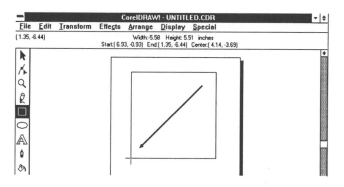

find it necessary to align geometrical shapes horizontally or vertically in fixed increments. In this section, you can practice aligning rectangles and squares while drawing; Chapter 8, "Selecting, Moving, and Arranging Objects," will introduce you to techniques for aligning shapes *after* you have drawn them.

Tip

As you learned in the previous chapter, the grid in CorelDRAW! can either be invisible or a pattern of dots on the screen. Objects are aligned to the grid because of the Snap To feature that is similar to a magnetic attraction.

One way to align objects while drawing is to take advantage of the Grid Size and Snap To Grid commands in the Display menu. The process of aligning new objects to a grid consists of four steps:

- Adjusting the grid spacing
- Displaying the grid
- Displaying the rulers
- Enabling the Snap To Grid feature

1. Pull down the Display menu and select the Grid Setup command. The Grid dialog box in Figure 3-5 will display.

2. Adjust both the Horizontal and Vertical Grid Frequency values to 2.00 per inch. To do this, press and hold the mouse button over the lower scroll arrow until the number 2.00 appears. Alternatively, you can drag on the current value, and type **2.00**. Use Tab to go from Horizontal to Vertical. If the selected unit of measurement is something other than inches, click on the units box until the word "inch" appears.

3. Click on Show Grid and click on OK to save these settings, and exit the dialog box.

4. Display the rulers (if they do not already appear on the screen) by selecting the Show Rulers command in the Display menu. A checkmark will appear next to the command, indicating that the rulers are now active.

5. Pull down the Display menu once more to see if the Snap To Grid feature is currently selected. If a checkmark appears next to the Snap To Grid command, it is already active, and you can align and place

Figure 3-5. *Adjusting Grid Frequency to 2.00 per inch*

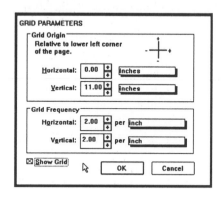

objects automatically at the specified increment. If a checkmark does not appear, select this command to activate the feature. Once the Snap To Grid feature is on, a message appears to that effect in the lower-left corner of the status line.

6. Next, select the Rectangle tool and position the cursor at the 1-inch mark relative to both the horizontal and vertical rulers. Even if you place the cursor inexactly, the corner of the rectangle will align perfectly to the 1-inch marks when you begin to draw.

7. Press and hold the mouse button and draw a rectangle 4 inches wide and 3 inches deep.

8. Draw a second rectangle the same size as the first beginning at a point 1/2 inch to the right and 1/2 inch below the first. The shadow rulers align exactly with the 1/2-inch marks on both rulers. The grid setting prevents you from "missing the mark."

9. Draw a third rectangle from a starting point 1/2 inch below and 1/2 inch to the right of the second. Your three rectangles should align like the ones in Figure 3-6.

Figure 3-6.   *Drawing rectangles at 1/2-inch intervals*

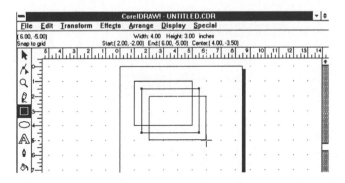

10. Select New from the File menu to clear all of the rectangles from
     the screen. When the Save Changes message box appears, select No.

Now that you have practiced drawing all possible types of rectangles, you
are ready to build a drawing with rectangular and freehand elements.

Creating a Drawing Using Rectangles and Squares

In the following exercise, you will integrate all the skills you have learned
so far by creating a teacup that includes rectangles, squares, and freehand
drawing elements. In the process, you will also learn how to adjust the relative
smoothness of curved lines you draw with the Pencil tool. The adjustment
involves a feature called Freehand Tracking, which controls how closely
CorelDRAW! follows the movements of your mouse cursor when you draw
curves.

To prepare for this exercise, select the Grid Setup command from the Display menu and adjust both the Horizontal and Vertical Grid Frequency to 8.00 per inch. Both Show Grid and Show Rulers should still be selected, and Snap To Grid should be turned on. Refer to the steps in the preceding section if necessary. When you are ready to create the drawing, proceed through the following steps, using the numbers in Figure 3-7 as a guide. If you wish, use the rulers as an aid in laying out your work.

1. Draw a rectangle (1) to represent the body of the teacup. It should be higher than it is wide.

2. Position your cursor at the right side of this rectangle and attach a rectangular handle (2) to the body of the teacup. The handle should touch the edge of the teacup but not overlap it; the grid settings you have chosen will prevent overlapping.

3. Draw a smaller rectangle (3) inside the one you just created (2) to make the opening in the handle.

Figure 3-7.   *A teacup using rectangles, squares, and freehand elements*

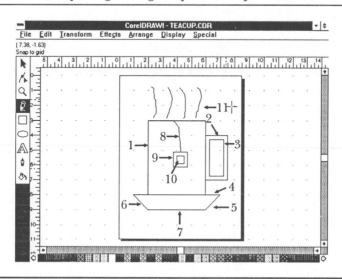

4. Now select the Pencil tool ⧉ and add a straight line (4) to the base
   of the teacup. (Freehand mode should be selected, not Bézier. If you
   need to change the drawing mode, use the Lines and Curves dialog
   box from the Preferences command in the Special menu.) This
   represents the top of the saucer. Remember to press and hold (CTRL)
   while drawing to ensure that the line remains perfectly horizontal;
   use the information in the status line if you need guidance.

5. Extend a diagonal line (5) and (6) down from each end of the top
   of the saucer. Check the status line indicators as you draw: The angle
   for the diagonal line to the left (6) should read –45 degrees, while
   the angle for the diagonal line to the right (5) should read –135
   degrees. Be sure to make both lines the same length. Each line snaps
   to the saucer base to form a multisegment line, as you learned in
   Chapter 2.

6. Now add another straight line (7) to form the bottom of the saucer.
   Remember to constrain the line using (CTRL). The saucer base snaps
   to the other line segments to form a single object, a polygon.

7. With the Pencil tool still selected, press and hold the mouse button
   and draw a curve (8) to represent the string of a tea bag. Does your
   string appear excessively jagged? If it does, you can adjust the
   Freehand Tracking setting in the next set of steps.

8. Before adjusting the Freehand Tracking value, erase the tea bag
   string you have just drawn by selecting Undo from the Edit menu.

9. Select the Lines and Curves option from the Preferences command
   in the Special menu to display the Lines and Curves dialog box, as
   shown in Figure 3-8. You used this same dialog box in Chapter 2 to
   adjust the AutoJoin values. The default value in the numeric entry
   box next to Freehand Tracking is 5 but you are going to adjust it to
   a higher number to facilitate smoother curves.

10. Using the scroll arrow, adjust the sensitivity level in the Freehand
    Tracking option to 10 pixels. This is the highest number possible
    and causes CorelDRAW! to smooth your curved lines as you draw.
    Lower numbers, on the other hand, cause the Pencil tool to track
    every little dip and rise as you move the mouse.

Figure 3-8. *Adjusting the Freehand Tracking value for smoother curves*

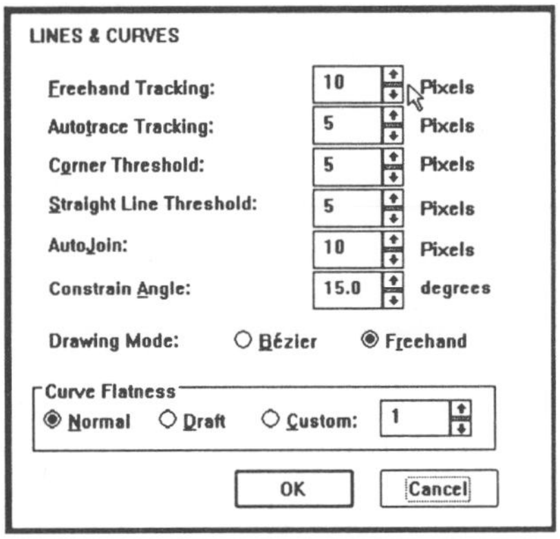

LINES & CURVES

Freehand Tracking:	10	Pixels
Autotrace Tracking:	5	Pixels
Corner Threshold:	5	Pixels
Straight Line Threshold:	5	Pixels
AutoJoin:	10	Pixels
Constrain Angle:	15.0	degrees

Drawing Mode: ◯ Bézier ⦿ Freehand

Curve Flatness
⦿ Normal ◯ Draft ◯ Custom: 1

OK   Cancel

11. Select OK twice to exit the dialog box and save your setting.

12. Now draw the tea bag string a second time. Your curve should be somewhat smoother now, more like the one in Figure 3-7.

13. Next, attach a tag to the string: Select the Rectangle tool again, position the cursor just below the bottom of the string, press and hold (CTRL) and (SHIFT) simultaneously and draw a square (9) from the center outward.

14. To add a center label to the tag, create a square (10) inside the first square. Select one of the corners as the starting point for this smaller square.

15. To add a finishing touch to your drawing, create some steam (11) by selecting the Pencil tool and drawing some curves. Since you have set Freehand Tracking to a higher number of pixels, you can create more effective "steam."

Figure 3-9.   *Saving the drawing as TEACUP.CDR*

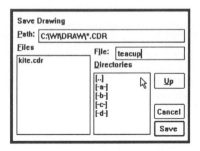

16. Finally, save your drawing. Select the Save As command from the
    File menu and **teacup** as shown in Figure 3-9. When you click on the
    Save command button, CorelDRAW! adds the extension .CDR
    automatically.

4

Drawing and Working with Ellipses and Circles

The ellipse and the circle are basic shapes that underlie more complex forms in nature and in man-made artifacts. The Ellipse tool in CorelDRAW! allows you to create both ellipses and perfect circles. For added convenience in placement, you can choose to initiate ellipses and circles either from any point on the rim or from the center outward.

Follow the exercises in this chapter to begin creating ellipses and circles of many different shapes and sizes using CorelDRAW!. In later chapters, you will expand your skills and apply a rich variety of special effects and shaping techniques to these basic geometrical forms.

Drawing an Ellipse

All versions of CorelDRAW! allow you to start an ellipse from any point on the rim. You can also draw an ellipse from the center point outward by using the (SHIFT) key. This second method allows you to place ellipses precisely within a graphic.

Using the Rim as a Starting Point

You can initiate an ellipse from any point on its rim. This flexibility in choosing your starting point allows you to position an ellipse easily within a drawing, without sacrificing precision.

When you began creating rectangles in Chapter 3, you saw how the status line width and height indicators displayed positive or negative numbers, depending on the starting point you chose and the direction in which you moved the mouse. You cannot use a corner as a starting point for ellipses and circles, but you can still use the width and height indicators as guides. Keep in mind that a positive width indicator means you are drawing from left to right, while a negative width indicator means you are drawing from right to left. Similarly, a positive height indicator means you are drawing from top to bottom, and a negative height indicator means you are drawing from bottom to top.

CorelDRAW! gives you an additional visual cue when you are drawing ellipses and circles. If your starting point is on the upper half of the rim, CorelDRAW! places the node at the uppermost point of the ellipse; if your starting point is on the lower half of the rim, CorelDRAW! places the node at the bottommost point of the ellipse. Perform the following exercises to become familiar with how the Corel DRAW! interface reacts when you choose different points on the rim as starting points for an ellipse.

1. Load CorelDRAW! if you are not running it already. Your rulers and Snap To Grid should be displayed, and the Snap To Grid should be turned on.

2. Select the Ellipse tool ⊘ by positioning the mouse cursor over the Ellipse icon and clicking once. Move the mouse to the right, out of the toolbox. The mouse cursor turns into a crosshair and the Ellipse icon appears highlighted.

3. Position the cursor anywhere on the printable page area, press and hold the mouse button, and drag the mouse downward and to the right along a diagonal path, as shown in Figure 4-1. The indicators

---

Figure 4-1. *Drawing an ellipse from top to bottom*

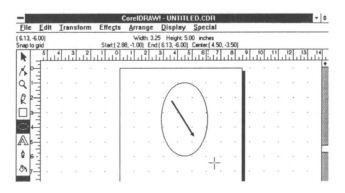

4

---

on the status line display the width and height of the ellipse as positive numbers.

4. When the ellipse is the shape you want, release the mouse button. This action completes the ellipse and freezes it in place. As in Figure 4-2, a single node appears at the uppermost point of the ellipse, and the status line changes to display the messages "Ellipse" and "Fill:" followed by a solid black rectangle. The "Fill:" message indicates that the ellipse has a default interior color of black. Press (DEL) to clear the page.

5. Choose a new starting point and draw an ellipse from bottom to top. Press and hold the mouse button at a desired starting point anywhere on the bottom half of the rim and then move the cursor *upward* in a diagonal direction. This time the height indicator on the status line displays negative numbers.

6. When the ellipse has the dimensions you want, release the mouse button. Note that the node is now at the bottom of the ellipse, as in Figure 4-3.

7. Press (DEL) to clear this ellipse from the screen.

Figure 4-2.   *A completed ellipse showing the node at the top*

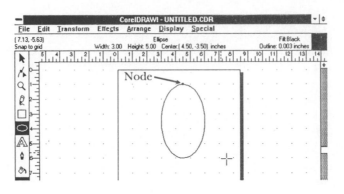

Figure 4-3.   *A completed ellipse drawn from bottom to top (node at bottom)*

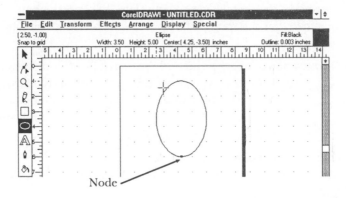

Drawing from the Center Outward

CorelDRAW! allows you to draw an ellipse from the center outward, just as you did with rectangles and squares in the previous chapter. This feature offers you a more interactive method of working, without sacrificing precision. The width and height indicators continue to display the exact dimensions of the ellipse as you draw. Practice drawing an ellipse using the center as a starting point.

1. With the Ellipse tool selected, press and hold both (SHIFT) and the mouse button at the desired starting point. Keep both (SHIFT) and the mouse button depressed as you move the mouse. As with any ellipse, you can draw in whichever direction you choose; the width and height indicators in the status line reflect that direction, as shown in Figure 4-4, in which an ellipse was drawn from its center, downward and to the right.

2. Release the mouse button and then release (SHIFT) to complete the ellipse. Be sure to release the mouse button *before* you release (SHIFT)

4

Figure 4-4.   *Drawing an ellipse from the center outward*

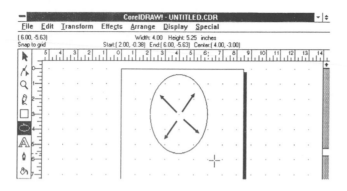

or the ellipse may "snap" away from the center point you have chosen and your center point will be treated as a rim point.

3. Clear the ellipse from the screen by pressing (DEL).

Drawing a Circle

In CorelDRAW! you use a single tool to produce both ellipses and perfect circles, just as you used the same tool to produce rectangles and squares. The technique is identical; you use (CTRL) to constrain an ellipse to a circle. As with ellipses, you can choose either the rim or the center of the circle as a starting point.

Using the Rim as a Starting Point

Perform the following exercise to create a perfect circle, starting from the circle's rim.

1. With the Ellipse tool selected, position the cursor at a desired starting point.

2. Press and hold both (CTRL) and the mouse button and draw diagonally in any direction. As you can see in Figure 4-5, the status line indicators show that both the width and the height of the shape are equal.

3. To complete the circle, release the mouse button and then (CTRL). Be sure to release the mouse button *before* you release (CTRL) or your circle may turn into an ordinary ellipse of unequal height and width.

4. Clear the circle from the screen by pressing (DEL).

Because of the way CorelDRAW! works, you are actually creating an imaginary rectangle when you draw an ellipse or circle. That is why the status line indicator for a perfect circle displays width and height instead of diameter. The ellipse or circle fits inside this rectangle, as you will see more

Figure 4-5. *Drawing a circle using* (CTRL)

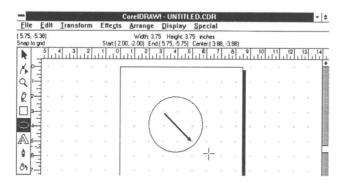

clearly when you begin to select objects in Chapter 8, "Selecting, Moving, and Arranging Objects."

Drawing from the Center Outward

In the following brief exercise, you will draw a circle using the center as a starting point.

1. With the Ellipse tool selected, position the cursor at the point where you want to begin the circle.

2. Press and hold (CTRL), (SHIFT), and the mouse button simultaneously and draw in any direction.

3. To complete the circle, release the mouse button and then (CTRL) and (SHIFT). If you release the keys before you release the mouse button, you may jeopardize both your circle and its central starting point.

4. Clear the circle from the screen by pressing (DEL).

Now that you have created some circles and ellipses using all of the available techniques, you can integrate these shapes into an original drawing. Continue with the next section to consolidate your skills.

Creating a Drawing Using Ellipses and Circles

The following exercise brings together all the skills you have learned so far. You will create a drawing (of a house and its environment) that will include ellipses, circles, rectangles, squares, and freehand drawing elements. The grid can assist you with some of the geometrical elements of the drawing; other elements you can draw freehand. Since this drawing will be wider than it is high, you will also learn how to adjust the page format from portrait (the default vertical format) to landscape (horizontal format). The first few steps get you into the habit of anticipating and preparing for your drawing needs before you actually begin to draw, so that you can draw quickly and without interruption. Use the numbers in Figure 4-6 as a guide in performing this exercise.

1. To prepare for the geometrical portion of the drawing, select the Grid Setup command from the Display menu and adjust both the Horizontal and Vertical Grid Frequencies to 4.00 per inch. If you need help, refer to the section of Chapter 3 entitled "Practicing with the Grid."

2. Change the page setup so that your page is wider than it is long. To do this, select the Page Setup command from the File menu. When the Page Setup dialog box in Figure 4-7 appears, select the Landscape option button to set the Orientation option to Landscape. Exit by selecting the OK command button.

3. Select Lines and Curves option from the Preferences command in the Special menu and set both the Freehand Tracking and the AutoJoin options to 10 pixels, if they are not already. As you recall from the previous chapter, a high Freehand Tracking setting lets you draw smoother curves and a high AutoJoin setting causes lines and

Figure 4-6. *A drawing using ellipses, circles, rectangles, and freehand elements*

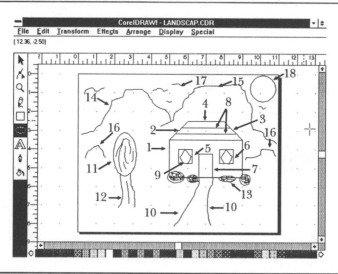

Figure 4-7. *The Page Setup dialog box*

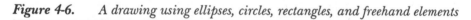

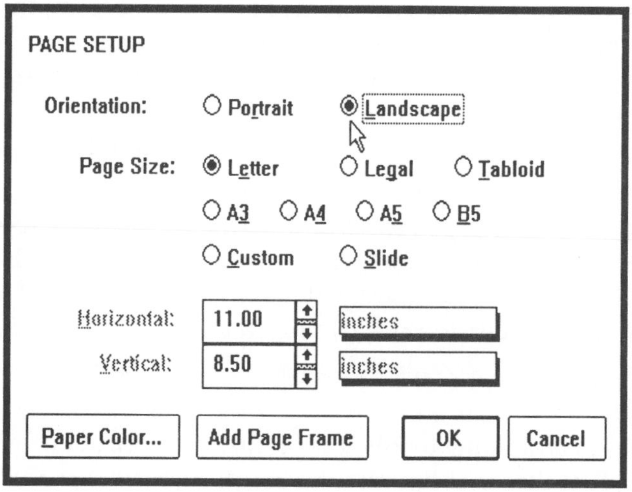

curves to snap together even when their end points are a few pixels apart. Click on the OK command button twice to exit both dialog boxes.

Tip

When you changed the page setup from Portrait to Landscape, the vertical ruler went back to its default of zero being in the lower-left corner. (You may remember that you moved the vertical zero to the upper-left corner in Chapter 2.) Change this again for this drawing to provide a more normal reference.

4. Select Grid Setup from the Display menu, press (TAB) to get to the vertical ruler origin, type **8.5**, and click on OK to return to the drawing. Zero should now be in the upper-left corner on both the vertical and horizontal rulers.

5. Select the Rectangle tool □ and position the cursor at the 5-inch mark on the horizontal ruler and the 3 1/2-inch mark on the vertical ruler. Draw a rectangle that extends from this point to the 9-inch mark on the horizontal ruler and to the 5 1/2-inch mark on the vertical ruler. This rectangle will compose the main element of the house (1).

6. Designing the roof of the house requires three steps involving constrained lines and automatic joining of lines to form a polygon. Select the Pencil tool ✐ and position your cursor at the upper-left corner of the "house." Extend a line (2) upward and to the right at a 45-degree angle. Remember to press (CTRL) while drawing to constrain this line to the correct angle automatically. End the line at the 6-inch mark on the horizontal ruler and the 2 1/2-inch mark on the vertical ruler.

7. Extend a line (3) upward and to the left at a 135-degree angle. Remember to press (CTRL) while drawing to constrain this line to the control angle automatically. When you reach the 8-inch mark on the horizontal ruler and the 2 1/2-inch mark on the vertical ruler, end the line with a double-click so you can continue with another line segment.

8. While continuing to hold (CTRL), extend a horizontal line (4) back to the first diagonal line (2) and single-click to end it. The two line

segments should snap together and form a polygon that constitutes the "roof" of the house.

9. You will need smaller grid increments when drawing the next few objects. Select the Grid Setup command from the Display menu again and set both the Horizontal and Vertical Grid Frequencies to 8.00 per inch. Select OK to save this setting and return to your drawing.

10. Create two square windows for the house. To create the first window, select the Rectangle tool and begin a square (5) near the left side of the house, a little below the "roof." Practice drawing a square from the center outward using the (CTRL)-(SHIFT) key combination. Notice the dimensions of your square just before you complete it, so that you can draw a square of the same size in the next step. If you do not like the first square you draw, press (DEL) immediately to erase it and try again.

11. Create a second square window (6) near the right side of the house. Make sure this square is the same size as the first and that it begins and ends on the same horizontal plane. The grid settings should help you place it correctly.

12. Make a rectangular door (7) for the house about halfway between the two windows. Use the rulers to help guide your movement. If you make a mistake, press (DEL) or select Undo in the Edit menu to delete the rectangle and try again.

Change both the horizontal and vertical grid frequencies to 6.00 since you are trying to divide an inch into three equal parts in the next step.

Tip

13. To create planes of shingles for the roof, select the Pencil tool, press and hold (CTRL), and draw two perfectly horizontal lines (8) across the roof.

14. Add asymmetrical curtains for the house by drawing some diagonal freehand curves (9) inside the windows. Remember to press and hold the mouse button as you draw to create curves instead of lines.

15. Draw a freehand sidewalk (10) that widens as it approaches the foreground of your picture.

4

16. Select the Ellipse tool and draw an elongated ellipse (11) to the left of the house. This represents the foliage of a poplar tree.

17. Select the Pencil tool and form the trunk of the poplar by adding some freehand vertical curves (12) beneath it. If you wish, you can add some small lines to the "foliage" of the poplar.

18. Select the Ellipse tool again and draw a series of "bushes" (13) immediately in front of the house. Use ellipses for the outlines of the bushes; create detail in the bushes by inserting a few ellipses and circles inside each one. Insert more ellipses to create a denser bush. (You can practice this technique on the poplar tree, too.)

19. Select the Pencil tool and create a mountain (14) behind and to the left of the house. Use curved instead of straight lines. Your mountain doesn't have to look exactly like the one in the figure.

20. Before creating the second mountain, select the Lines and Curves option from the Preferences command in the Special menu and set Freehand Tracking to 1 pixel. This will make the outline of your subsequent freehand curves more jagged. Select OK twice to exit the dialog boxes and save the new setting.

21. Draw the second mountain (15) behind the house. Notice that the outline of this mountain looks rougher than the outline of the first mountain.

22. Continue by using freehand curves to add a little landscaping (16) beneath the mountains and, if desired, a few birds (17).

23. Select the Ellipse tool and create a sun (18) by drawing a circle from the center outward at the upper-right corner of the picture.

24. Finally, save your drawing by selecting the Save As command from the File menu. When the Save As dialog box appears, type **Landscap** and select Save. CorelDRAW! adds the .CDR extension automatically.

Congratulations! You have mastered the Ellipse tool and created another masterpiece with CorelDRAW!

5

Adding Text

CorelDRAW!'s advanced text-handling features let you turn text into a work of art. You can rotate, skew, reshape, and edit a character or a *text string* (a group of characters) just as you would any other object. You can perform these feats on Corel Systems typefaces and on the extensive library of typefaces available from other manufacturers. The more than 150 Corel Systems fonts provided with your software look similar to standard industry typefaces and will print on any printer with which CorelDRAW! is compatible. If you already have a favorite typeface manufacturer, you can use the WFNBOSS utility discussed in Appendix C, "Corel Connectivity: Clip Art and Fonts," to convert popular fonts to the CorelDRAW! format.

In this chapter, you will learn how to insert text into a drawing and select the typeface, typestyle, point size, alignment, and spacing attributes of your text. You will also learn how to enter special foreign language or symbolic characters. After you have completed the exercises in this chapter, you will be ready to tackle more advanced techniques for reshaping your text (Chapter 11, "Shaping and Editing Text") and converting other manufacturers' typefaces to a format that you can use in CorelDRAW! (Appendix C).

Entering Text

The Text tool ▣ , the last of the four basic drawing tools in CorelDRAW!, is represented by a stylized capital letter "A." You use the text tool to insert text into your pictures, just as you use the Ellipse or Rectangle tool to insert geometrical objects. The process of inserting text into a drawing can involve up to eight steps:

1. Select the Text tool.
2. Choose between a text string and a paragraph.
3. Select an insertion point.
4. Enter text in the text window.
5. Choose the point size of your text.
6. Set the alignment for the text.
7. Select a typeface and typestyle.
8. Adjust the spacing between the letters, words, and lines of your text.

The sections that follow treat each of the preceding steps in greater detail. Since most of this chapter consists of exercises, however, the order in which you perform these steps may vary slightly from this list.

Selecting the Text Tool

You use the Text tool in CorelDRAW! to enter new text on a page. When you first load CorelDRAW!, the Select tool is highlighted; in order to enter text, you must activate the Text tool. In the following brief exercise, you will adjust the page format, and then activate the Text tool.

1. If the printable page area is in portrait format (vertical instead of horizontal), select Page Setup from the File menu and select Land-scape format. If you did the drawing exercise at the end of Chapter 4, the printable page area is already in landscape format. This is

because CorelDRAW! always "remembers" the page setup you used the last time you created a new drawing.

2. Select the Text tool Ⓐ by positioning the mouse cursor over the Text icon and clicking once. The Text tool is highlighted and the mouse cursor turns into the familiar crosshair.

Text Strings and Paragraphs

CorelDRAW!, in versions 2.0 and later, has two modes of entering text. The first is designed to enter shorter *text strings,* such as titles, captions, and notes that can be up to 250 characters long. The second is designed for longer *paragraphs* for, say, a brochure that can be up to 4000 characters long.

You make a distinction between text strings and paragraphs through the initial use of the Text tool. For text strings, you simply click the Text tool at the point on the page you want text to begin. For a paragraph, you drag a *bounding box* from where you want text to start to where you want text to end.

Paragraph text provides many of the attributes of word processing. Text will automatically wrap at the end of a line; text can be justified, as well as left-aligned, right-aligned, and centered; text can be cut and pasted to and from the Clipboard; you can adjust the space between paragraphs in addition to adjusting the space between characters, words, and lines; and you can create up to eight columns with a *gutter* (space between columns) you define. Also, you can import ASCII (American Standard Code for Information Interchange) text files created outside of CorelDRAW!.

Selecting an Insertion Point

The *insertion point* is the point on the printable page where you want a text string to begin. Text aligns itself relative to that point. In CorelDRAW!, you cannot enter text directly on the page; instead, you type it in a special dialog box, where you also select its attributes. To select an insertion point and prepare for the other exercises in this chapter, follow these steps:

5

1. Make sure that Snap To Grid is on and set both the Horizontal and Vertical Grid Frequencies to 2 per inch. If your screen does not already display rulers and/or the grid, select Show Rulers from the Display menu and Show Grid from the Grid Setup dialog box.

2. Position the mouse cursor at the top center of the page area at 5 1/2 inches horizontal and 1 inch vertical and click once. After a few seconds the Text dialog box displays, as shown in Figure 5-1.

The Text Dialog Box

Using the elements of the Text dialog box, you can enter text and then customize it in five different ways. Take a moment to become familiar with the layout of this dialog box and the way the keyboard functions within it.

Figure 5-1.   *The Text dialog box*

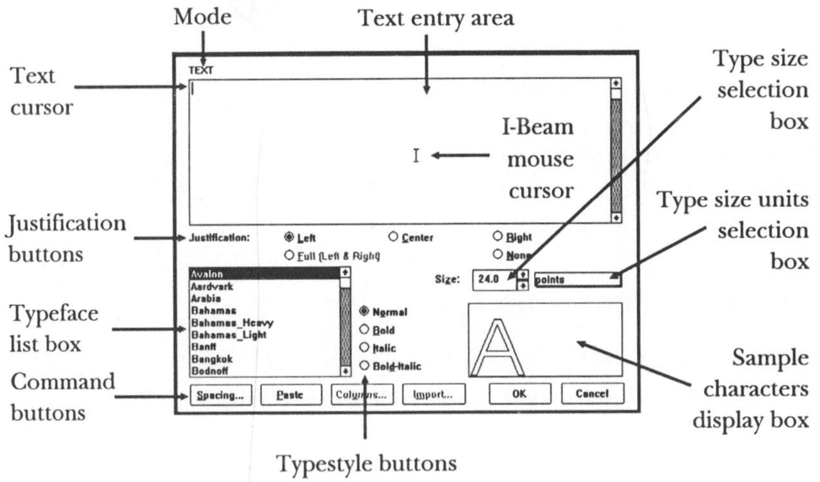

The following are the components of the Text dialog box and their respective functions. Figure 5-1 points out the major components. The word "TEXT" in the top left of the dialog box indicates that you are in Text String mode. If you use Paragraph mode you will see "PARAGRAPH TEXT" in the upper-left corner.

Text Cursor   A flashing text cursor appears in the text entry window when you first call up this dialog box. Type your text string, or series of characters, in this window. A text string can include up to 250 characters. You can include an unlimited number of text strings in a single file.

Justification Buttons   Use the justification buttons to align your text relative to the insertion point. The default setting for this text attribute is Left. The dimmed Full (Left & Right) justification is for justified paragraphs and is available only in Paragraph mode.

Typeface List Box   The typeface list box contains the names of all the CorelDRAW! typefaces from which you can choose. If you prefer, you can customize this list and rename the typefaces to their industry equivalents, such as "Times" or "Helvetica." See the "Renaming CorelDRAW! Typefaces" section later in this chapter.

Sample Characters Display Window   When you select a typeface, the first two characters you type will be displayed in the sample characters display window. This gives you a true WYSIWYG example of that typeface.

Typestyle Buttons   Once you choose a typeface, use the typestyle buttons to specify the typestyle in which you want the typeface to appear. In the graphics industry, *typeface* refers to an entire character set that shares the same basic design, regardless of the size (for example, 10 points) or weight (for example, bold or italic). A *typestyle* is narrower in scope. One typestyle includes only a single weight (roman or normal, bold, italic, or bold italic) for a particular typeface. Although there are four possible typestyles, some typefaces are not available in all four styles and the unavailable styles are therefore dimmed.

Type Size Selection Box   Use the type size selection box to choose the size for the text you enter. The default setting for this attribute is 24 points, but you

5

can change this value by adjusting the scroll arrows at the right side of the dialog box (see "Selecting a Type Size" later in this chapter).

Type Size Units Selection Box   Click on the type size units box to change the unit of measuring type sizes from points (the default) to inches, millimeters, or picas and points.

Spacing Button   The Spacing button gives you access to an additional dialog box where you can specify spacing between characters, words, or, if you are in Paragraph mode, paragraphs. See the "Adjusting Text Spacing" section in this chapter for detailed instructions on how to adjust spacing.

Paste Button   Clicking on the Paste button transfers the contents of the Windows Clipboard to the text entry window. If the Clipboard contains more than 250 characters in Text String mode or 4000 characters in Paragraph mode, the excess will be cut off and not brought into CorelDRAW!.

Columns Button   If you are in Paragraph mode, the Columns button lets you divide text into columns—up to eight of them—and specify the gutter (width of the space between the columns) in inches, millimeters, points, or picas and points. See "Working with Paragraphs" later in this chapter.

Import Button   The Import button allows you to import a text file into CorelDRAW! if you are in Paragraph mode. The file can be no more than 4000 characters (any excess will not come into CorelDRAW!) and needs to be unformatted ASCII text. Most word processing programs have a command for saving a file without formatting. Use that command for exporting to CorelDRAW!. Also, you should not use tabs or indents. These get translated into spaces and will then probably be incorrectly spaced in CorelDRAW!. The file can have any extension to the filename, but CorelDRAW! initially looks for .TXT files.

OK and Cancel Buttons   Press the OK button to save your attribute settings and display, on screen, the text you have entered. To exit the Text dialog box without entering any text, press the Cancel button.

Using the Keyboard and Mouse

You can use both the mouse and the keyboard to move between attributes and between attribute settings in the Text dialog box. The only exception is the type size units box or if you have a CorelDRAW! version earlier than 1.1, in which case you can enter the typeface list box only with the help of the mouse.

If you are using a mouse to move around in the Text dialog box, you can select a text attribute in two different ways: by clicking on an option button or by scrolling with a scrollbar or scroll arrow. You work with option buttons to choose alignment and typestyle, and you use scrollbars or scroll arrows to choose the typeface, point size, and spacing attributes.

If you prefer to use the keyboard in the Text dialog box, you can select most text attributes using (TAB), (SHIFT)-(TAB), and the four arrow keys on your cursor pad. (If you have CorelDRAW! version 1.11 or later, you can select all text attributes this way.) When you first enter the dialog box, the text cursor appears in the text entry window; pressing (TAB) moves you from one attribute to the next, while the (SHIFT)-(TAB) key combination moves you between attributes in the reverse order. The order in which you can move between attributes depends on which version of CorelDRAW! you have. If you are using version 1.11 or later, you can access the typeface list box using the keyboard alone. If you have an earlier version, you must use the mouse to select a typeface.

Now you are familiar with how to get around in the Text dialog box. In the following sections you will learn how to set text attributes for yourself.

Entering Text in the Text Window

When you first enter the Text dialog box, the text entry window is automatically selected, as you can see by the text cursor in Figure 5-1. (On your monitor, the text cursor is flashing.) If you are not in the text entry window because of the previous exercises, click in the window now to return

5

there or press (TAB) or (SHIFT)-(TAB) until you get there. To enter a maximum of 250 text characters, simply begin typing. For this exercise, enter text in the following way:

1. Type **CorelDRAW!** at the flashing text cursor. Notice how the "Co" from "CorelDRAW!" appears in the sample character display window in the current typeface.

2. Press (ENTER) to begin a new line, type **Made**, and press (ENTER) again.

3. On the third line, type **Easy**.

Your text entry window should now look like this:

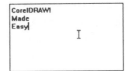

Using Keys to Move Around

The way you use your computer keys to move around in the CorelDRAW! text entry window may differ from the way you use them in a word processor. Whenever you have several lines of text in the text entry window, you can use the following keyboard commands:

- Press (ENTER) to start a new line within the text entry window and begin entering text into it. The window will hold as many lines of text as you generate, as long as you do not exceed the 250-character limit.

- Press (↓), the down arrow key, to move the text cursor down one line. (This does not apply if you are already on the last line of text.)

- Press (PGDN) to move the text cursor down the last line of text. The text in the previous two lines may "jump" out of visual range, like this:

```
┌─────────────┐
│ Easy        │
│             │
│             │
└─────────────┘
```

- Press ⟨↑⟩, the up arrow key, to move the text cursor up one line. (This has no effect if you are already on the top line of text.)
- Press ⟨PGUP⟩ to move the text cursor up to the first line of text.
- Press ⟨HOME⟩ to move the cursor to the beginning of the current line.
- Press ⟨END⟩ to move the cursor to the end of the current line.
- Press ⟨→⟩, the right arrow key, to move the cursor one letter at a time to the right.
- Press ⟨←⟩, the left arrow key, to move the cursor one letter at a time to the left.
- Press ⟨BACKSPACE⟩ to delete the character immediately preceding the text cursor.
- Press ⟨DEL⟩ to delete the character immediately following the text cursor.

Using the Mouse

You can also perform some text entry operations using the mouse:

- Use the scroll bar at the right side of the text entry window to locate a line of text that is not currently visible.
- If you want to insert text at a given point, click at that point.
- To select one or more characters in a text string, position the text cursor at the first character you want to select and then drag the mouse across the desired characters. The characters appear highlighted, as shown here:

- You can delete a text string that you have selected in this way by pressing ⟨DEL⟩.

When you have finished experimenting with the keyboard controls, press ⟨TAB⟩ or ⟨SHIFT⟩⟨TAB⟩ until you select the numeric value in the point size box and it becomes highlighted.

Aligning Text

The next exercise involves deciding how you want to align the text. You have four choices: Left, Center, Right, and None. In Paragraph mode, you also have Full (both Left and Right) justification.

Left Justification

Left is the default justification setting. When you choose this setting, text will align on the page as though the insertion point were the left margin.

1. Using the mouse, select Left justification by positioning the mouse cursor over the Left button and clicking once. To select Left justification using the keyboard, press (TAB) until you reach the Justification line, and then press (→) or (←) until the Left option button is selected. The center of the Left option button darkens when you select it.

2. Select OK to exit the Text dialog box. The text that you entered displays on the page in the default typeface, left-aligned at the 5 1/2-inch mark, as in Figure 5-2. The text string actually has a default fill of black like other closed objects in CorelDRAW!, but you see it only in outline form. (When you work with the

Figure 5-2.   *Left-justified text*

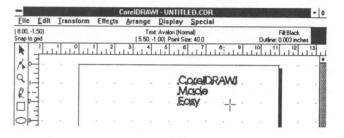

Preview window in Chapter 7, "Previewing Your Graphics," your text will be displayed with its appropriate fill.) The small rectangles at the base of each letter are nodes that help you edit text shape and attributes, as you will learn in Chapter 11.

3. Leave this text on the page and select another insertion point, at the 3-inch vertical mark and the 5 1/2-inch horizontal mark, just below the first text string. The Text dialog box displays again.

Center Justification

When you select Center justification, the insertion point becomes the midpoint of any string you type. Perform these steps to compare center alignment with left alignment:

1. Type **CorelDRAW!** on one line, **Made** on the next, and **Easy** on the third line, as you did in the last section.

2. Using the mouse, change to Center justification by positioning the mouse cursor over the Center button and clicking once. To select Center justification using the keyboard, press (TAB) until you reach the Justification line, and then press (→) or (←) until the Center option button is selected.

3. Select OK to return to the page. The text you entered appears in the default font, center-aligned with respect to the 5 1/2-inch mark. Your page should now look like Figure 5-3.

4. Leave this text on the page. Return to the Text dialog box by selecting a third insertion point, this time at the 5-inch vertical mark and the 5 1/2-inch horizontal mark, just below the center-aligned text. The Text dialog box displays again.

Right Alignment

When you select Right alignment, the text aligns on the page area as though the insertion point were the right margin. Perform these steps to compare right alignment with left and center alignment:

5

1. Type **CorelDRAW! Made Easy** on three lines as you did in the previous exercises.

2. Using the mouse, change to Right alignment by positioning the mouse cursor over the Right button and clicking once. To select Right alignment using the keyboard, press (TAB) until you reach the Justification line, and then press (←) or (→) until the Right option button is highlighted.

3. Select OK to return to the page. The text you entered appears in the default font, right-aligned with respect to the 5 1/2-inch mark. Your page should now look like Figure 5-4.

4. Leave this text on the page. Return to the Text dialog box one more time by selecting a fourth insertion point, this time at the 7-inch horizontal and 5 1/2-inch vertical mark. The Text dialog box displays once more.

No Justification

When you select None for justification, text displays on the page exactly as you enter it. This selection is useful when you want to add unusual spacing

Figure 5-3.   *Center-justified text added*

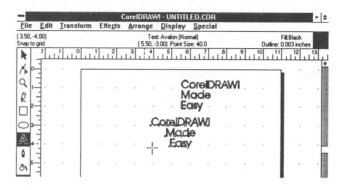

Figure 5-4. *Right-aligned text added*

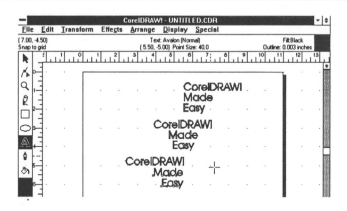

at the beginning of a line in a text string. Perform these steps to compare text with no alignment to text with Left, Center, and Right justification:

1. Type **CorelDRAW!** on the first line of the text entry window and press (ENTER).

2. On the second line, indent two spaces, type **Made**, and press (ENTER) again.

3. On the third line, indent four spaces and type **Easy**.

4. Using the mouse, change the justification to None by positioning the mouse cursor over the None button and clicking once. To change alignment to None using the keyboard, press (TAB) until you reach the Justification line, and then press (→) or (←) until the None button is highlighted.

5. Select OK to return to the page. The text that you entered appears in the default font, with the spacing exactly as you typed it. Your page should now look like Figure 5-5.

6. Clear the page of text by selecting New from the File menu. Do not save the changes.

5

Figure 5-5.   *Unjustified text added*

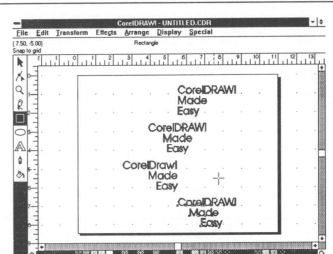

Selecting a Type Size

Normally, you will select alignment and typeface settings for a text string before you specify the type size, which is measured in *points* (72 points make up an inch). For this exercise, however, you will want to see results on the full page in a larger size than the default value of 24 points. You can change the default point size in either of two ways, depending on whether you want to use the mouse or the keyboard.

To change the type size from 24 to 40 points using the mouse,

1. Position the cursor over the upper scroll arrow next to the Points box and depress and hold the mouse button. As you scroll, the numerical value in the Points size box increases.

2. Release the mouse button when the value in the Points size box reaches 40.0.

To change the type size from 24 to 40 points using the keyboard,

1. Tab out of the text entry window and into the Points size box by pressing (TAB) or (SHIFT)-(TAB) until you select the Points size box. Again, the value in the Point Size box appears highlighted when you select it.

2. Type **40.0**. As you type, the "24.0" is replaced.

Selecting a Type Design

So far, you have used only the Avalon typeface, which is the default typeface in CorelDRAW! because it appears first in the typeface list box. In this section, you will have the opportunity to experiment with some of the different typefaces and typestyles supplied with your software.

Selecting a Typeface

Many books and trade magazines offer guidelines for selecting appropriate typefaces. A thorough discussion of the subject is beyond the scope of this book; however, when choosing the typeface you will use in a CorelDRAW! graphic, you should consider the tone and purpose of your work, as well as your intended audience. Look at the two fonts in Figure 5-6, for example. You probably would not choose an elaborate, flowery font such as Paradise for a graphic that you would present to a meeting of civil engineers; a typeface such as Frankfurt Gothic might prove a better choice.

Practice selecting typefaces in the following exercise.

1. Select the Text tool and then select an insertion point that is at the 1 1/2-inch mark on the horizontal ruler and the 1-inch mark on the vertical ruler. The Text dialog box appears, with the sample letter A for the default Avalon typeface in the sample character window.

2. Type **Paradise** in the text entry window.

5

Figure 5-6.   *Comparing the "tone" of typefaces*

3. Select the Paradise typeface from the typeface list box. You can select a typeface in one of four ways:

Click directly on the typeface name if it is visible in the list box. When you do this, the typeface name becomes highlighted and a faint dotted outline surrounds it. If the typeface you want is not visible, use one of the following techniques.

Scroll continuously up or down the list: Position the mouse cursor on the up or down scroll arrow and then depress and hold the mouse button until the desired typeface comes into view. Click on the typeface name to select it.

Scroll up or down the list one line at a time: Position the mouse cursor on the up or down scroll arrow at the top or bottom of the scroll bar in the typeface list box. Click repeatedly until the name of the typeface you want comes into view. Select that typeface name by clicking on it. This is the same as using ⊙ or ⊙ with the typeface list box selected.

Scroll up or down the list one list box at a time: Position the mouse cursor in the scroll bar, not on a scroll arrow, either above or below the scroll box, and click. The list will move up or down by the height of the list box. This is the same as using (PGUP) or (PGDN) with the typeface list box selected.

4. Set the type size to 100 points, using either the mouse or keyboard technique described earlier in this chapter.

5. Set Justification to Left.

6. Select OK to return to the page, where you will see the Paradise text string with the selected attributes, as shown in Figure 5-7. Although too small to be seen here, on your screen nodes will appear between each letter.

7. Select another insertion point at the 1 1/2-inch mark on the horizontal ruler and the 3-inch mark on the vertical ruler.

8. When the Text dialog box appears, type **Avalon** in the text entry window.

9. Select the Avalon typeface in the typeface list box.

10. Select OK to return to the page, where you will see the Avalon text string beneath the Paradise text string, as in Figure 5-8.

11. Select a third insertion point at the 1 1/2-inch mark on the horizontal ruler and the 5-inch mark on the vertical ruler.

12. When the Text dialog box displays, type **Aardvark** into the text entry window.

13. Select the Aardvark typeface from the list box.

14. Select OK to exit the Text dialog box. Your page now looks like Figure 5-9.

15. Select a fourth insertion point at the 1 1/2-inch mark on the horizontal ruler and the 7-inch mark on the vertical ruler.

5

Figure 5-7.   *A text string using the Paradise typeface*

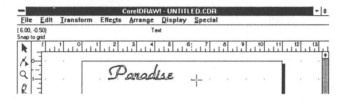

Figure 5-8.   *Text strings using Paradise and Avalon*

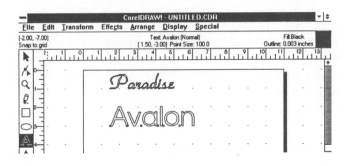

16. When the Text dialog box displays, type **Dixieland** in the text entry window.

17. Select the Dixieland typeface from the list box and notice that a nonalphabetic symbol, rather than a letter, appears in the sample character window. This typeface, like the Geographic Symbols, Greek/Math Symbols, and Musical Symbols typefaces, consists of symbols rather than letters. You see only letters when you type, however, because CorelDRAW! does not display these characters in the text entry box. See Appendix C for a complete list of all CorelDRAW! typefaces and the character sets for each.

Figure 5-9.   *Comparing Paradise, Avalon, and Aardvark typefaces*

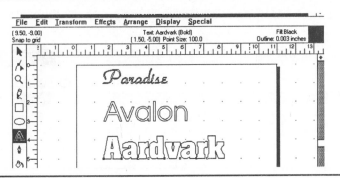

Figure 5-10. *Adding a text string from a nonalphabetic (symbol) typeface*

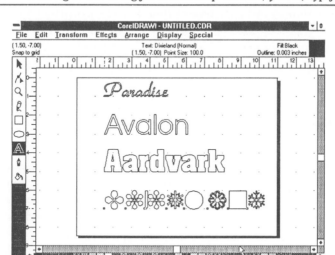

18. Select OK to see the text on the page. Your page now resembles Figure 5-10. You will notice that even though you have entered all of the text strings at the same point size, some appear larger than others. Each typeface has its own characteristic width and height.

19. Clear the screen by selecting New from the File menu. Do not save any changes.

Practice trying out different typefaces. When you are ready for the next section, clear the screen by selecting New from the File menu. You are ready to learn how to select one of the four available typestyles for a given typeface.

Renaming CorelDRAW! Typefaces

CorelDRAW!'s proprietary typefaces closely resemble standard industry typefaces from well-known manufacturers. In fact, Corel Systems has named the typefaces to remind you of their existing counterparts. If you already use

some of these counterparts with other programs, or if you find it easier to
remember common industry names than Corel's proprietary ones, you can
rename the typefaces. Then each time you call up the Text dialog box, the
standard industry names will appear in the typeface list box. Refer to
Appendix C for full instructions on how to rename typefaces.

Selecting a Typestyle

While you were experimenting with typefaces in the foregoing exercise,
you may have noticed that the appearance of the typestyle option buttons to
the right of the typeface list box kept changing. This is because some typefaces
have only one or two typestyles available, while others have three or four.
When a typestyle is not available for a specific typeface, it displays in gray and
you cannot select it.

Perform the following exercise to practice selecting available typestyles
for the CorelDRAW! typefaces.

1. Select the Text tool and then choose an insertion point that is at the
   1 1/2-inch mark on the horizontal ruler and the 1 1/2-inch mark on
   the vertical ruler. The Text dialog box displays.

2. Type **Frankfurt Gothic** in the Text entry window.

3. Change the point size to 75.0 points.

4. Select Frankfurt Gothic from the typeface list box.

5. Select the Italic typestyle. A dark dot fills the center of the option
   button beside "Italic" and the letters in the sample character window
   change their appearance.

6. Select OK to display the resulting text on the page, as in Figure 5-11.
   Leave this text on the page for now.

7. Select another insertion point at the 1 1/2-inch horizontal and
   3-inch vertical ruler marks to display the Text dialog box once more.
   The Frankfurt Gothic typeface is still selected; CorelDRAW! remembers the last typeface you selected during the current session.

8. Type **Frankfurt Gothic** in the text entry window again.

Figure 5-11. *Text string in Frankfurt Gothic italic*

9. Select Bold from the typestyle list and watch the characters in the sample character window change to reflect this choice.

10. Select OK to display the resulting text on the page, as in Figure 5-12.

11. Select a third insertion point at the 1 1/2-inch horizontal and the 4 1/2-inch vertical ruler marks.

12. When the Text dialog box displays, type **Frankfurt Gothic** in the text entry window.

13. Select Bold Italic from the typestyle list. A dotted outline surrounds the typestyle name, the center of the associated option button darkens, and the characters in the sample character window change to reflect the new choice.

Figure 5-12. *Comparing italic and bold typestyles*

Figure 5-13.   *Comparing italic, bold, and bold italic typestyles*

14. Select OK to display the resulting text on the page. Your screen should resemble Figure 5-13.

15. Select New from the File menu to clear the screen before continuing with another exercise.

Take a few moments to practice selecting typestyles for other typefaces. When you have finished, continue with the next section to learn how to adjust spacing when you enter a new text string.

Adjusting Text Spacing

The Spacing command button in the lower-left corner of the Text dialog box may be easy to overlook, but it can give you enormous control over text. When you select this button, the Spacing dialog box appears, which allows you to control the spacing between characters, words, and lines of text.

In this chapter, you are working with attributes only as you enter text. However, CorelDRAW! also allows you to adjust text spacing *interactively*. This means that even after text displays on the page, you can change the spacing of one character, several characters, or an entire text string without going back to the Text dialog box. You will learn more about how to change spacing attributes for existing text in Chapter 11.

Setting Up the Exercise

In the following exercise, you will have the opportunity to review what you have learned thus far about setting all of the attributes in the Text dialog box. If you have forgotten how to perform any of these functions, go back to the relevant section and review it.

1. Select the Text tool if it is not selected already.

2. Select an insertion point near the top of the page, aligned to the 5 1/2-inch horizontal and 1-inch vertical marks on the rulers.

3. When the Text dialog box displays, enter four lines of text in the text entry window. Type your name on the first line, your address on the second, your city, state, and zip code on the third, and your telephone number on the fourth.

4. Change the type size to 50.0 points.

5. Select Center alignment.

6. Select Gatineau as the typeface and Normal as the typestyle. The Text dialog box should now look like Figure 5-14, except that the actual text you have entered into the text entry window will differ.

5

Figure 5-14.   *Settings: Gatineau normal, Center justification, 50 points*

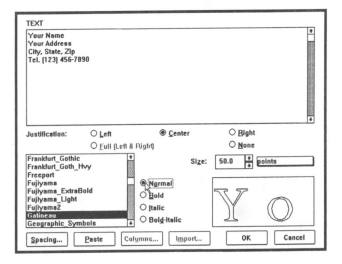

7. Select the Spacing command button by clicking on it once. The Text
   Spacing dialog box in Figure 5-15 appears. If you had not entered
   text into the text entry window, CorelDRAW! would display an error
   message and not permit you to enter the Text Spacing dialog box.

The Text Spacing Dialog Box

The Text Spacing dialog box features four options for adjusting spacing:
Inter-Character, Inter-Word, Inter-Line, and Inter-Paragraph. You will not
change them at this point in the exercise, but take a moment to become
familiar with your options.

Inter-Character   The Inter-Character option controls spacing between each
pair of characters within each word of the text. The default value is 0.00 ems.
In other words, CorelDRAW! inserts no space at all between characters unless
you change that value. An *em* is a unit of measurement that is equal to the
width of the capital letter "M" for the current point size of the selected typeface
and typestyle. This measurement is relative, because the width of a capital M
varies, not only among different typefaces, but also among different styles
and sizes of the same typeface. You can adjust the value of intercharacter
spacing in increments of .10 ems automatically using the scroll arrow, or in
increments of .01 ems if you type the value manually.

Figure 5-15.   *The Text Spacing dialog box*

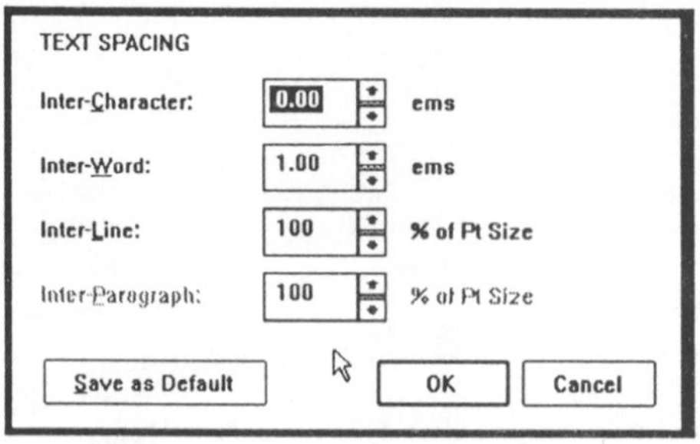

Inter-Word   The Inter-Word option controls spacing between each word of the text that you enter. The default value is 1.00 em. You can adjust the value of interword spacing in increments of .10 ems automatically using the scroll arrow, or in increments of .01 of an em if you type the value manually.

Inter-Line   When your text contains more than one line, the Inter-Line option controls the amount of space between each line. In the printing industry, this type of spacing is also known as *leading*. The default value is 100% of the type size, which means that if your text size is 10 points, the total amount of space between two lines is exactly 10 points and no more. You can adjust interline spacing in increments of 1%.

Inter-Paragraph   If you are in Paragraph mode, and you have more than one paragraph, the Inter-Paragraph option controls the amount of space between each pair of paragraphs. The default value is 100% of the type size. If your text size is 10 points, the space between paragraphs will be 10 points. You can adjust the interparagraph spacing by increments of 1%.

You can adjust the values in the Text Spacing dialog box in two ways: by scrolling with the mouse or by using the keyboard.

To adjust values using the mouse only,

1. Position the mouse cursor on the up or down scroll arrow. If you want to increase the value, position it on the up arrow; if you want to decrease the value, position it on the down arrow.

2. Press and hold the mouse button until the value you want displays in the adjoining box, and then release the mouse button.

To adjust values using the keyboard,

1. Use TAB or SHIFT-TAB to go from item to item in the dialog box. When you reach one of the spacing number boxes, the entire number will be highlighted. This means that if you type a new number, you will completely replace the original number.

2. Type in the value you want. To go to the next setting, press TAB or SHIFT-TAB.

Leave the spacing options at their default settings for the current text
string and select OK twice. You exit the Text Spacing dialog box, and the text
that you typed in the text entry window now appears on the page. Your text
string has the default settings of 1.00 em spacing between words, no spacing
between characters, and no extra leading between lines, as shown in Figure 5-16.

Adjusting and Comparing Text Spacing

Now that you are acquainted with the way the Text Spacing dialog box
works, you will create another text string, identical to the first except that its
spacing values differ. You can then visually compare the results of your
spacing adjustments.

1. Select an insertion point at the 5 1/2-inch mark on the horizontal
    ruler and the 4-inch mark on the vertical ruler, just beneath the last
    line of text on the page.

2. When the Text dialog box displays, type your name, street address,
    city, state, and zip, and telephone number on four separate lines.
    Leave all of the other attribute settings just as they are.

3. Select the Spacing command button to display the Text Spacing
    dialog box.

4. This time, adjust the spacing in the Inter-Character number box to
    0.50 ems, Inter-Word to 2.00 ems, and Inter-Line to 130%. This
    means that the space between characters will equal the width of half
    a capital "M," the space between words will equal the width of two

Figure 5-16.   *Address text string with default spacing attributes*

capital "M" 's, and the space between lines will equal 1.3 times the height of the typeface itself.

5. Select OK twice to save these settings and exit to the page. The second text string now displays beneath the first. Your page resembles Figure 5-17.

6. Select New from the File menu to clear the screen. Do not save any changes.

Working with Paragraphs

So far in this chapter, all of your work has been in Text mode. This is fine for titles, captions and other pieces of text that are only a few short lines. If you are creating a brochure, a flyer, or other documents where you need large blocks of text, you should use Paragraph mode. Paragraph mode offers

5

Figure 5-17.   *Comparing default and custom spacing attributes*

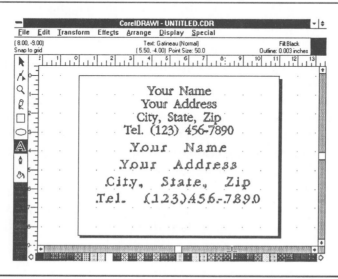

several features that are valuable for large blocks of text and are not available in Text String mode. Among these features are:

- An increase in the character limit from 250 characters to 4000 characters
- Automatic word wrap at the end of each line
- Variable line length controlled by a bounding box or frame whose dimensions can be changed
- Full (Left and Right) justification
- The ability to define up to eight columns with variable intercolumn spacing
- The ability to paste text into the text entry window or onto the page from the Windows Clipboard
- The ability to import ASCII text created with a word processor
- Adjustable interparagraph spacing

Try out Paragraph mode now with these steps:

1. Select the Text tool and place the mouse cursor at 1 on both the horizontal and vertical rulers.
2. Press and hold the mouse button while dragging the mouse cursor to 10 on the horizontal ruler and 7.5 on the vertical ruler as shown in Figure 5-18.
3. Release the mouse button and the Paragraph Text dialog box will be displayed.

   As you can see in Figure 5-19, the Paragraph Text dialog box has a few differences. The title now reads "Paragraph Text"; Full (Left & Right) justification and the Columns and Import buttons are now turned on; and if you look at the Spacing dialog box you will see that interparagraph spacing can now be set.
4. Type several paragraphs such as those shown in Figure 5-20. It doesn't matter what you type as long as you have two or more paragraphs about as long as those shown. Press (ENTER) only at the

Figure 5-18. *Forming the Paragraph mode bounding box or frame*

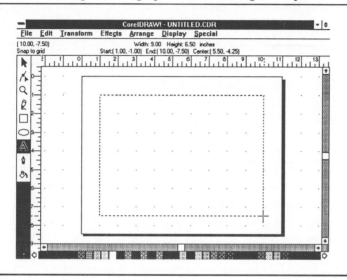

Figure 5-19. *Text dialog box in Paragraph mode*

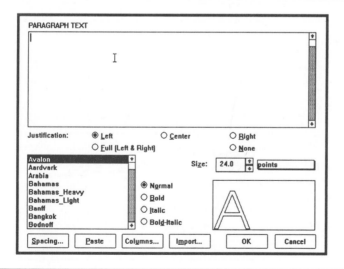

end of the paragraphs and let CorelDRAW! automatically wrap the text at the end of each line. Put an extra line between the two paragraphs by pressing (ENTER) a second time.

5. When you are done typing, click on Full justification, adjust the size to 24 points, select the Palm Springs typeface and Normal style.

6. Click on the Spacing command button, change the interline spacing to 120% and the interparagraph spacing to 90%. Click OK twice to return all the way out to the page.

When you return to the page, a box will form where you drew the bounding box and, after a moment, the text will appear. It will not be terribly readable, as shown in Figure 5-21, because of the nodes on each of the characters. In Chapter 6, "Using Magnification and View Selection," you will see how to magnify a portion of the page to be able to read it better.

To preserve the typing you have done, save this file.

7. From the File menu select Save As, type **paratext** in the filename text box and press (ENTER) or click on OK.

Figure 5-20.   *Two paragraphs entered into the Text window*

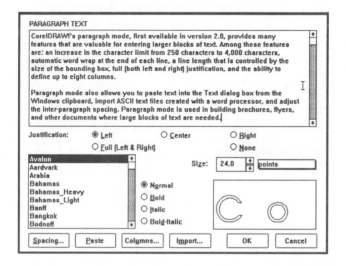

Figure 5-21.   *Paragraph text as it is displayed on the page*

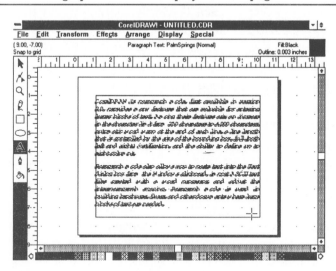

Extracting Text from CorelDRAW!

CorelDRAW!, in versions 2.0 and later, includes a feature that allows you to extract text from CorelDRAW! in a format that is usable in a word processing program. You can modify the text in the word processor and then merge the text back into CorelDRAW! automatically reattaching all of the formatting, such as typeface, size, and style that was originally attached to the text. (In the word processing program you will not see any of the formatting.)

In this section you will extract the text you entered, bring that text into a word processor, modify it, save it, save it again as a plain text file, and place it on the Windows Clipboard. In the next section, you will use each of these items in CorelDRAW!.

Start by extracting the text from CorelDRAW!. The text you typed should still be on the screen with the nodes as shown in Figure 5-21. That is, the text you want to extract should be selected.

1. From the Special menu, select Extract. The Extract dialog box will open.

2. Type **extrpara** in the Filename text box and click on Extract. You have now written an ASCII text file containing the paragraphs you entered. Next, switch out of CorelDRAW! without closing it, open Windows Write, and edit that file. (Almost any word-processor could be used in place of Windows Write.)

3. Open the Control menu in the upper-left corner and select Switch.

4. From the Task list, double-click on Program Manager. The Program Manager window will open.

5. Open the Accessories group (if necessary) and double-click on Write. The Write word processing program will open.

6. Select Open from the File menu, type **extrpara.txt** in the Filename text box, and click on OK.

7. A dialog box will open asking, "Convert to Write format?" Click on No Conversion to preserve the ASCII text format. The text you entered in CorelDRAW! will appear on the Windows Write screen as shown in Figure 5-22.

   The first two lines and the last two lines of text (the last line is blank) are reserved for CorelDRAW! to use in merging the text back in. It is, therefore, very important that you do not change these four lines or CorelDRAW! will not be able to merge this file. You can change all other parts of the file except the first two and last two lines.

8. Modify any of the text you entered. In this exercise, it doesn't matter what you modify as long as you can recognize the change when you get back to CorelDRAW!.

9. When you complete modifying the text, open the File menu and save the file under its original file name, EXTRPARA.TXT. This is the file that will be used to merge back in to your CorelDRAW! PARATEXT.CDR file.

   Now that you have saved the merge file, you can remove the first two and last two lines to make another text file that you can import into CorelDRAW!. Also, you will copy the remaining text to the Windows Clipboard and paste it into CorelDRAW!.

Figure 5-22. *Paragraph text in Windows Write*

10. Delete the first two and last two lines of the file so you only have left the text you entered (select the lines by dragging over them with the mouse and press (DEL)).

11. From the File menu, select Save As, type test.txt, and click on OK. This is the file you will import.

12. Select all of the text you entered and now have modified by dragging over it with the mouse, and then from the Edit menu select Copy. This places a copy of the text on the Windows Clipboard.

13. Double-click on the Control menu to close Windows Write and then open the Program Manager's Control menu and select Switch.

14. Double-click on CorelDRAW! to switch to that program. CorelDRAW! will reappear on the screen.

Merging, Importing, and Pasting Text into CorelDRAW!

You now have four copies of the text you entered: the original file you saved in PARATEXT.CDR, the modified merge file EXTRPARA.TXT, the clean text file TEST.TXT, and finally the copy on the Windows Clipboard. Use each of the last three of these copies to see how CorelDRAW! merges, imports, and pastes text from outside CorelDRAW!.

1. From the Special menu, select Merge-Back. The Merge-Back dialog box will open.

2. Double-click on EXTRPARA.TXT in the Files list box. After a moment you will see the revised text displayed on the page. The copy of PARATEXT.CDR in memory has now been revised with the changes you made in Windows Write. All of the formatting in the original file has been maintained. Had you had some graphic elements in the file they would also remain unchanged. Only the words and their positions have changed.

3. Select New from the File menu to clear your screen. Save the revised file if you wish.

4. Select the Text tool and draw a paragraph bounding box from 1 on both the horizontal and the vertical rulers to 10 on the horizontal and 7.5 on the vertical ruler. The Text dialog box will open. Note that your text settings, typeface, size, and style are still set.

5. Click on Import and then double-click on TEST.TXT. The revised text will be brought into the Text dialog box as shown in Figure 5-23.

6. Click on Cancel to throw away the imported text.

7. Draw another bounding box from 1 on both the horizontal and vertical rulers to 10 on the horizontal and 7.5 on the vertical rulers. The Text dialog box will again open.

8. Click on the Paste command button. Once again the revised text will come into the Text dialog box, this time from the windows clipboard.

Figure 5-23. Bottom portion of text imported into the Text dialog box

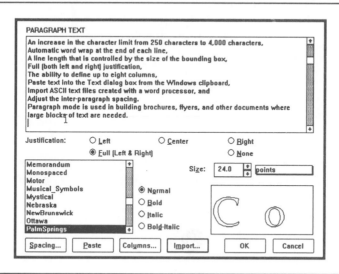

You have now seen how you get text out of CorelDRAW! and how you can bring text back in to CorelDRAW! in three different ways. Now look at how you can use columns in CorelDRAW!.

Putting Text in Columns

Many brochures, flyers, and other documents appropriate for CorelDRAW! put text into multiple columns instead of one wider column in a effort to make the text easier to read. CorelDRAW! 2.0 added this feature for Paragraph mode text. Try it here. You should still be in the Text dialog box with the revised paragraphs you pasted into the text window.

1. Click on the Column command button. The Column dialog box will open as shown here:

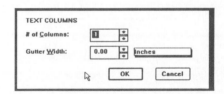

2. Type 2 for the number of columns, press (TAB) to move to the Gutter number box, type **.5**, and press (ENTER) to close the Column dialog box and return to the Text dialog box.

3. Click on OK to close the Text dialog box and return to the page layout. After a moment the text will appear in a two-column format as shown in Figure 5-24.

4. Select New in the File menu to clear the page and answer No to saving the current contents.

Figure 5-24.   *Text in a two-column format*

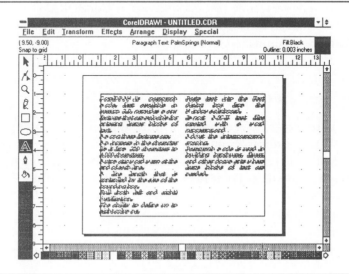

Using the Symbol Library

CorelDRAW!, beginning with version 2.0, includes a library of over 3000 symbols that are stored and retrieved like characters in a font using the Text tool. The symbols are simple, but effective, drawings that are stored as *vector images* (unlike most clip art, which is stored as *bitmapped* images). As a result, the symbols can be enlarged, stretched, rotated, and edited like any other CorelDRAW! objects without any loss in the quality of the image. Also, they take very little room to store. To use the symbols, you must have installed them on your hard disk. CorelDRAW!'s Install program will do this for you as discussed in Appendix A, "Installing CorelDRAW!".

The symbols are organized into 39 categories like Animals, Borders, Holidays, Space, and Weather. These categories are like typefaces. You first select a category, and then from that category you select a particular symbol. The number of symbols in a category varies from 30 to 208, with the average around 80. Corel includes with CorelDRAW! a catalog of all of the symbols, giving each a number within a category. If you know this number, once you have selected a category you can enter the number and get the symbol. Also, as you will see in a moment, you can select a symbol from a display box that shows ten symbols at a time, once you have decided on a category.

Try this feature now by selecting several symbols.

1. Select the Text tool and move the mouse cursor to 2 on both the horizontal and vertical rulers.

2. Press and hold (SHIFT) while you click the mouse button. The Symbols dialog box will open as shown in Figure 5-25.

3. Click on several categories in the list box in the upper-right corner. For example, click on Computers. Look at the ten images that appear in the display box across the bottom for each category you click on. Use the vertical scroll bar on the list box to see more categories.

4. Click on the horizontal scroll bar under the display box of symbols to see additional symbols.

   Use steps 3 and 4 to look at a number of symbols. Notice on the left above the display box there is a number box where you can specify the initial size of a symbol when it is placed on the page. In

5

Figure 5-25.   *Symbols dialog box*

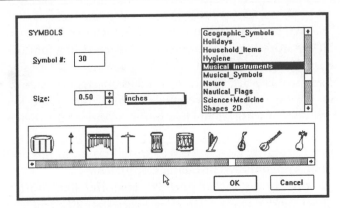

future chapters you will see how you can also size symbols that have already been placed on the page.

5. Change the size to 1 inch and then click on a symbol in the display box to put on the page.

6. Move the mouse cursor to 4 on the horizontal ruler and 2 on the vertical ruler, press (SHIFT) and click, choose another symbol, and click on it to put that symbol on the page.

7. Move the mouse cursor to first 6 and then 8 on the horizontal ruler, and repeat step 6. When you are done, you should have a string of symbols like Figure 5-26.

The Symbol Library provides a good source of quick art that can be used for many purposes.

Entering Special Characters

CorelDRAW! includes five different proprietary character sets beyond the standard alphabet and characters that appear on your computer key-

Figure 5-26.   *Sampling of symbols on the page*

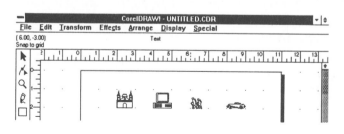

board. You enter special characters in the text entry window of the Text dialog box, and can adjust alignment, type size, and spacing for these special characters, just as you can for alphabetic characters. The five character sets are Corel, Dixieland, Greek/Math, Musical, and Geographic.

- The Corel character set includes all keyboard characters, foreign language characters, currency symbols, and copyright and other popular commercial symbols. This character set applies to 71 of the 75 typefaces you have available in CorelDRAW!.

- The character set in the Dixieland typeface includes decorative and directional symbols and callouts.

- The character set in the Greek/Math typeface includes a variety of scientific and mathematical symbols.

- The character set in the Musical typeface contains common musical notes and notations.

- The character set in the Geographic typeface includes geographical, military, and industrial symbols.

A complete listing of the contents of each character set appears in Appendix C and on the Character Reference Chart provided with your software. Also, the Dixieland, Musical, and Geographic character sets are available as symbols in the Symbol Library. Each of the typefaces is a category in the list box and each of the characters is a symbol.

No matter which of the five character sets you are using, characters above ASCII 128 are not accessible by pressing a single key on your keyboard. To

type one of these special characters, depress and hold (ALT) and then type the
appropriate number on your numeric keypad. Be sure to include the "0" that
precedes each number. For example, to type the character "u" in the Corel
character set, type **0129**.

Caution

*The Corel character set differs in some respects from the standard Windows character
set, which is common to many Windows applications. For instance, the four symbol
typefaces provided with CorelDRAW! have nothing in common with the Windows
character set. As a result, the text you enter in the Text dialog box may not always
match what displays on the screen.*

Always refer to your CorelDRAW! Character Reference Chart or to
Appendix C of this book when you are entering special characters.

6

Using Magnification and View Selection

Until now, you have done all your work in CorelDRAW! using the full-screen view. This is the default view when you load CorelDRAW! or open a file, but it has obvious limitations if you need to edit images or do fine detail work. The Magnification tool, however, can customize the viewing area of your screen any way you wish. As you become familiar with this tool, you will experience greater drawing convenience and ease in editing.

The Magnification Tool

The Magnification tool [Q] , the third tool in the CorelDRAW! toolbox, resembles a small magnifying glass. Unlike the Pencil, Rectangle, Ellipse, and Text tools, the Magnification tool is not a drawing tool. It could be called a view adjustment tool, because it allows you to zoom in or out of the viewing

Figure 6-1.   *The five viewing options for the Magnification tool*

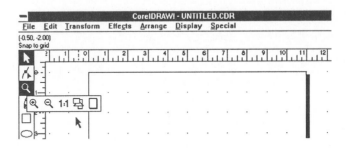

area in a variety of different ways. Because the Magnification tool gives you complete control over the content of the viewing area, it helps enhance every object you draw and increases the usefulness of every tool in the CorelDRAW! toolbox.

The Magnification tool is five tools in one. When you select this tool, the fly-out menu shown in Figure 6-1 appears, giving you five options for adjusting your viewing area.

Zoom-In   The Zoom-In tool ⌖ allows you to zoom in on any area of a drawing that you select.

Zoom-Out   The Zoom-Out tool ⌖ either zooms out of your current image by a factor of two or, if your screen currently shows a zoom-in view, returns you to the previous view.

Actual Size   Selecting the Actual Size icon 🔳 lets you see your drawing in the actual size it will be printed.

Fit-In-Window   Selecting the fit-in-window icon 🔳 fits all of the current graphic, everything you have placed on the page, into your viewing window.

Show Page   The Show Page icon ⬚ returns you to the default full-page view of your graphic.

In order to have something to magnify, switch to the Samples directory, probably a subdirectory to your CorelDRAW! directory, and open the file GRASHOPP.CDR that was provided with your software. When you have the grasshopper on your screen, perform these steps.

1. Select the Magnification tool by positioning the mouse cursor over the Magnification tool icon in the toolbox and clicking once. The menu containing the five viewing options flies out below and to the right of the Magnification tool.

2. Select an icon from the fly-out menu using either the mouse or your keyboard. To select an icon using the mouse, simply click on it or drag the mouse cursor until you highlight the tool and then click. To select an icon using the keyboard, you must use individual function keys for each of the magnification tools (the Actual Size tool ⅛ is not available through the keyboard). The function keys and the magnification tools they activate are:

    - F2 Zoom-In
    - F3 Zoom-Out
    - F4 fit-in-window
    - SHIFT F4 Show Page

All of the five Magnification tools except the Zoom-In tool perform their functions automatically when you select them. The following sections discuss each Magnification tool and present hands-on exercises that allow you to practice using these tools.

The Zoom-In Tool

The Zoom-In tool icon ⌕ looks like the main Magnification tool icon, except that it is smaller and contains a plus sign. The Zoom-In tool is the most versatile of the five Magnification tools, because it lets you define precisely

6

how much of your picture you want to view at once. It is therefore invaluable for drawing fine details or editing small areas of a picture.

Defining the Viewing Area

Unlike the other Magnification tools in the fly-out menu, the Zoom-In Tool does not perform its function automatically. You have to define the zoom-in area in a series of four general steps. Try this yourself now on the grasshopper:

1. Select the Zoom-In tool by first activating the Magnification tool and then selecting the Zoom-In tool icon from the fly-out menu or press F2. The cursor changes to an image of a magnifying glass containing a plus sign 🔍.

2. Position the cursor at any corner of the area you want to magnify; usually it is most convenient to start at the upper-left corner.

3. Press and hold the mouse button at that corner and then drag the mouse diagonally towards the opposite corner of the area on which you want to zoom in. A dotted rectangle (the *marquee*) will follow your cursor and "lasso" the zoom-in area, as in the example in Figure 6-2.

4. When you have surrounded all of the objects on which you want to zoom in, release the mouse button. The screen redraws as in Figure 6-3, and the viewing window now contains a close-up view of only the objects you lassoed.

You can zoom in on successively finer areas of the screen using the Zoom-In tool. You must re-select the Zoom-In tool each time you wish to magnify further, however, for as soon as you have redrawn the screen, CorelDRAW! automatically returns to the Select tool. Simply select the Zoom-In tool again and lasso another area, as in Figure 6-4. The number of times you can zoom in depends on the type of monitor and display adapter you use. Try zooming in on progressively smaller areas; eventually, you reach a point where you are unable to zoom in any further. When this occurs, you have reached the maximum magnification possible for your monitor and display adapter. At that point, 1 pixel on the screen represents approximately

Figure 6-2. *Lassoing an area with the marquee*

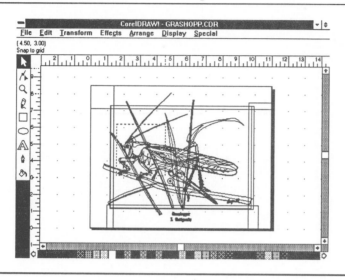

Figure 6-3. *A close-up view of the lassoed area*

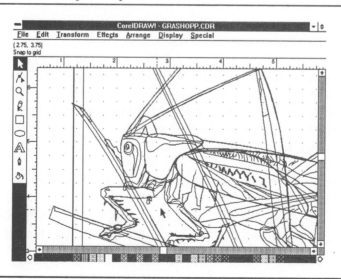

Figure 6-4.   Zooming in a second time

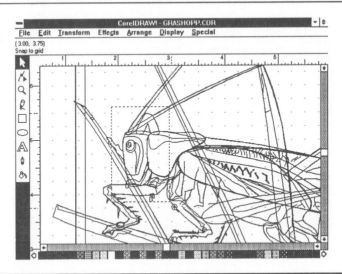

1/1000 of an inch. You must use another magnification tool first before you can use the Zoom-In tool again.

Zooming In and Editing TEACUP.CDR

The following exercise lets you practice using the Zoom-In tool on the teacup illustration you created in Chapter 3, "Drawing and Working with Rectangles and Squares." You will edit this illustration by entering text inside a tiny area of the drawing, a function you couldn't perform without using the Magnification tool. This exercise also allows you to practice the text entry skills you learned in Chapter 5, "Adding Text."

1. Select Show Rulers from the Display menu if the rulers do not already appear on the screen.

2. Make sure that a checkmark appears in front of the Snap To Grid command in the Display menu. If a checkmark does not appear, select this command.

Figure 6-5. *Lassoing the tea tag*

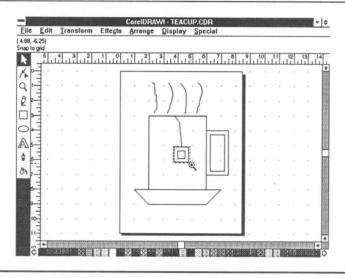

3. Select Grid Setup from the Display menu and set both Horizontal and Vertical Grid Frequency to 16 per inch and make sure Show Grid is checked.

4. Select Open from the File menu, select the file TEACUP.CDR, and click on the Open button.

5. Select the Magnification tool, and then select the Zoom-In tool from the fly-out menu. The cursor changes into a replica of the Zoom-In tool as soon as you move into the drawing window.

6. Zoom in on the tag for the teabag: Position the cursor at the top left corner of the tag, press the mouse button, and drag the mouse diagonally downward until you have surrounded the tea tag, as in Figure 6-5.

7. Release the mouse button. The screen redraws and displays only the tea tag and its immediate environment, as in Figure 6-6. Notice that in magnified view, the scale of the ruler changes from 1/4 inch to 1/16 inch.

8. Select the Text tool. The mouse cursor turns into a crosshair.

Figure 6-6.   *A close-up view of the tea tag*

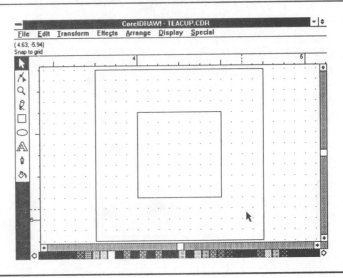

Figure 6-7.   *Selecting a text insertion point*

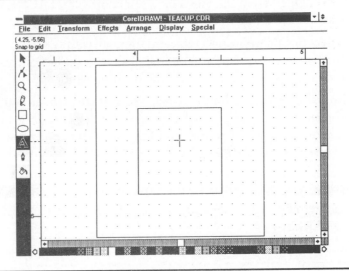

9. Position the cursor near the top center of the inner tea tag square and align it with a horizontal ruler marker, as in Figure 6-7.

10. Click once to select this point as the insertion point.

11. When the Text dialog box displays, type **JASMINE TEA** in all capital letters on two separate lines in the text entry window. Then select the following text attributes: Center justification, Fujiyama Normal, 10.0 points. The Text dialog box should look like Figure 6-8.

12. Select the Spacing button within the Text dialog box and change the values to Inter-Character: 0.30 ems, Inter-Word: 1.00 ems, Inter-Line: 125% of type size.

13. Select OK twice to return to the magnified display window. The text you typed now appears within the tea tag label, as in Figure 6-9.

14. Finally, select the Save As command from the File menu. When the Save As dialog box appears, type **teacup2** in the File text entry box, and then select Save.

6

Figure 6-8. *Text attributes for JASMINE TEA*

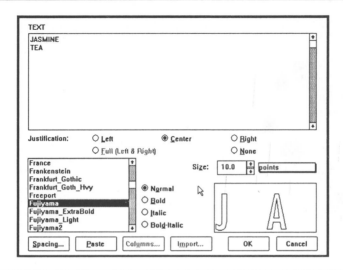

Figure 6-9.   *Entering text in close-up view*

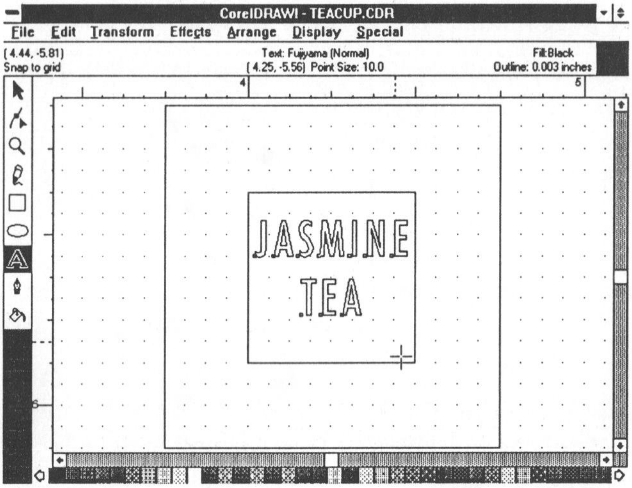

The Zoom-Out Tool

The Zoom-Out tool ⌐ looks like the main Magnification tool, except that it is a little smaller and contains a minus sign. As soon as you select this tool, it defines the zoom-out area for you automatically in one of two ways:

- If you are currently in an Actual Size, Fit In Window, or Show Page viewing magnification, selecting the Zoom-Out tool causes your current viewing area to zoom out by a factor of two.

- If you are currently in a Zoom-In viewing magnification, selecting the Zoom-Out tool causes you to return to the previously selected view. You can therefore use the Zoom-Out tool to back out of successive zoom-ins one step at a time.

The maximum zoom-out you can achieve is a full view of the page at 50% of the original size.

To use the Zoom-Out tool, select the Magnification tool, and click on the Zoom-Out tool icon or press (F3). The cursor does not change shape when you select this tool, but the screen redraws according to the preceding rules.

In the following simple exercise, you will practice using both the Zoom-In and Zoom-Out tools while editing the LANDSCAP.CDR file that you created in Chapter 4, "Drawing and Working with Ellipses and Circles." Remember the few extra circles and ellipses you drew inside the bushes of that picture? Now that you can see the bushes up close, you can add even more detail. Turn Snap To Grid off before you begin.

1. Select Open from the File menu and open the file called LANDSCAP.CDR that you created in Chapter 4. The image first appears in full-page view.

2. Select the Magnification tool and then click on the Zoom-Out tool icon to select the Zoom-Out tool. You can still see the full page, but it now appears at half size, as in Figure 6-10.

Figure 6-10.   *Zooming out to a 50% page view*

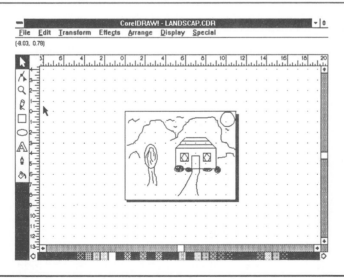

3. Select the Zoom-Out tool again. This time, you zoom out only a little further. You cannot zoom out further than this.

4. Select the Zoom-In tool and then lasso the house and bushes. The screen redraws to include just these objects.

5. Select the Zoom-In tool again and magnify the bushes only.

6. Select the Zoom-In tool once more and lasso a single bush.

7. Select the Ellipse tool ⬭ and add detail to the bush by inserting small ellipses and circles, as shown in Figure 6-11.

8. Now, select the Zoom-Out tool. The screen displays the view you magnified in step 5 but the bush you worked on has more detail.

9. Select the Zoom-Out tool again. This time, the screen displays the view you selected in step 4.

10. Select the Zoom-Out tool a third time. This time, the screen displays the full page at 50% of its size, as in step 2. The bush you edited probably looks denser than the others because of the detail you have added.

Figure 6-11.   *Adding detail to a magnified view*

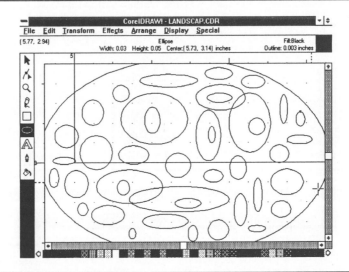

11. Select the Save As command from the File menu. When the Save As dialog box appears, type **LANDSCA2** in the File text entry box, and then select Save or press (ENTER).

12. Select New from the File menu to clear the screen.

You have seen how the Zoom-In and Zoom-Out tools work well together when you are interested in editing a picture in minute detail. In the next section, you will learn how to achieve the kind of view that is useful when you want to print your image.

Viewing at Actual Size

When you want to see approximately how large your image will look when printed, use the Actual Size tool ⌐1:1⌐ in the Magnification fly-out menu. At a 1:1 viewing magnification, 1 inch on your screen corresponds to about 1 inch on the printed page. The amount of the page you see at this magnification may vary, depending on the way Microsoft Windows works with your monitor.

To achieve actual-size viewing magnification, select the Magnification tool and click on the 1:1 icon. You can practice using this tool on the TEACUP2.CDR image that you edited earlier in this chapter.

1. Open the file TEACUP2.CDR using the Open command from the File menu. Unless you have a full-page, 19-inch, or 24- inch monitor, the full-page view of the image is too small to allow you to read the text you entered earlier in this chapter.

2. Select the Actual Size tool. The screen redraws to display an area of your image similar to Figure 6-12. The actual area may vary because of the variety of monitors and display adapters available. At this viewing magnification, your text still appears small but it is legible.

3. Select the Zoom-In tool and lasso the tea tag with the marquee. The screen redraws to display only this portion of the image.

4. Select the Zoom-Out tool. Since you were in a 1:1 view previously, you zoom out by a factor of two.

5. Clear the screen by selecting New from the File menu.

6

Figure 6-12.   *Viewing an image at actual size*

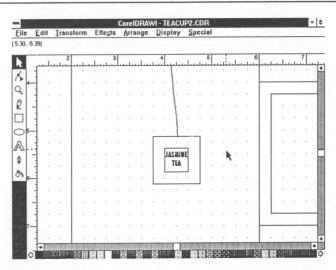

The next section shows you how to fit an entire image within the viewing window. This is a different type of magnification than the 1:1 ratio.

Fitting a Graphic in a Window

When the pictures you draw extend all the way to the edge of the page, they already fit within the viewing window. The fit-in-window tool is not of much use to you in such cases. When some blank space exists, however, you can use the fit-in-window tool to view everything you have drawn, but no more. This can be especially useful for small designs, such as logos.

To select the fit-in-window tool, first select the Magnification tool, then click on the fit-in-window or press (F4). The screen redraws to fill the entire viewing area with the graphic image. Practice using this tool on one of the sample CorelDRAW! files in the following exercise.

Figure 6-15. *The parts of the scroll bar*

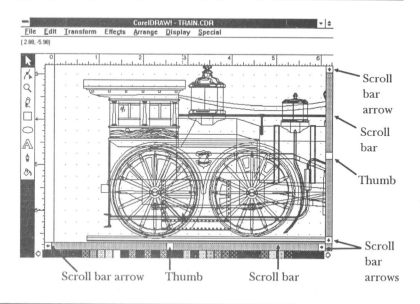

- To pan in large increments, click on either side of the blank box, or *thumb,* located in the middle of the horizontal and vertical scroll bars. Once again, the image appears to move in the opposite direction from where you clicked. This method has only limited usefulness for editing, because the movement of the screen is rather jumpy and unpredictable.

- To control the exact distance that you pan, position the cursor over the thumb and drag it across the scroll bar in the direction that you want to pan. Release the mouse button when you reach the desired area.

Now that you are familiar with all of the magnification tools and with the scroll bars, you have complete control over the portion of your picture that you display at any one time. In Chapter 8, you will put this new skill to work to help you select, arrange, and move objects and text.

7

Previewing Your Graphics

When you first open a file in CorelDRAW!, only a skeleton view of the image appears on the screen. You can see the basic shapes of objects and text, but not the custom outlines or fill colors with which you flesh them out. (You will begin working with outlines and fills in Chapters 13, 14, and 15.) This "bare bones" view is designed for speedy editing, but it doesn't give you as much visual information or accuracy as you would see in an actual printout of the image. For example, if an image contains several layers of objects, the editing view doesn't make it easy to tell which objects are in the foreground and which are in the background. The advantage of this stripped-down view is that it allows you to edit an image rapidly and conveniently. The disadvantage is that when you are moving, shaping, or editing objects, or working with colors, you need to see a true WYSIWYG display of your pictures to work efficiently.

Fortunately, WYSIWYG graphic displays are always available in CorelDRAW!. Just invoke the *preview window* and a second, more accurate view of your image appears either full screen or next to the editing window. This preview image redraws automatically every time you make a change to a selected object in the editing window. You can edit an image and then check the results immediately. Frequent redrawing of the preview image can lower the performance speed of your software, so use this feature sparingly.

Like the Magnification tool discussed in Chapter 6, the preview window helps you customize the user interface of CorelDRAW! in many different ways. You can decide just how much of the screen you want the preview window to occupy, where you want to place the preview window on the screen, and even how much of your image you want shown in the preview window at any given moment. Follow the exercises in this chapter to make the preview window suit the way you work.

The Preview Window

In this exercise, you will open one of the sample images that came with your software. Because this image contains several colors and multiple layers of objects, it can show you the benefits of working with the preview window. Prepare for the exercise by setting up the CorelDRAW! window as follows:

1. Select the Display menu. If a checkmark appears in front of the Snap To Grid command, click on it to turn this feature off.

2. Select the Display menu again and turn off the Show Rulers command by clicking on it.

3. From the Display menu select Grid Setup, click on Show Grid to turn it off, and click on OK to return to the drawing page. The dots representing the grid should disappear.

You can choose to display or conceal the preview window at any time while editing an image. Practice turning the preview window on and off now, using the TRUMPET.CDR sample file.

4. Select Open from the File menu and open the file TRUMPET.CDR. The image appears on the screen in skeletal form, as in Figure 7-1. Notice that the multiple layering of objects makes it difficult for you to tell objects apart or to guess which objects are in the foreground.

Figure 7-1. Skeletal image for speedy editing

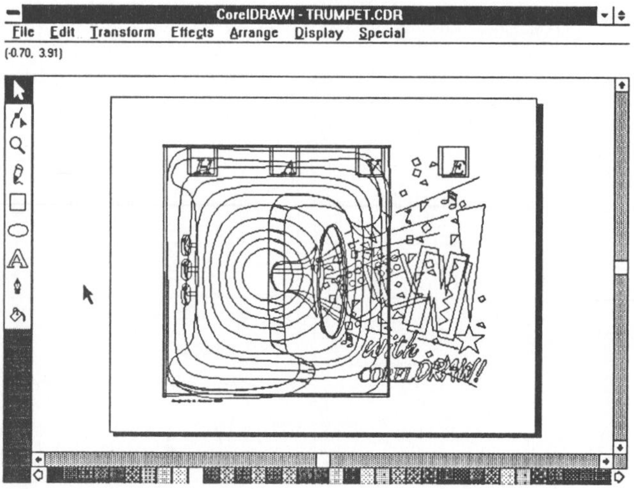

5. Pull down the Display menu and select the Show Preview command, or press the (SHIFT)-(F9) key combination as a shortcut. The skeletal, or editing, view of the image now takes up only the left half of the screen, while a second view apppears on the right, as shown in **Figure 7-2.** If you have a color display adapter and monitor, this second image appears in color.

What a difference! The preview window shows you the outlines, fill colors, and layering of each object in the picture—all information that the default editing window does not provide. Also, you can see which objects lie closer to the foreground of the picture and which lie behind other objects. In the preview window, the template clearly falls between the compass and the triangle, but you couldn't be sure just from looking at the editing window.

6. To turn the preview window off, select the Show Preview command from the Display menu once more or just press (SHIFT)-(F9) again. The preview window disappears and you are left with the editing window only.

7

Figure 7-2.   *Comparing the editing and preview windows*

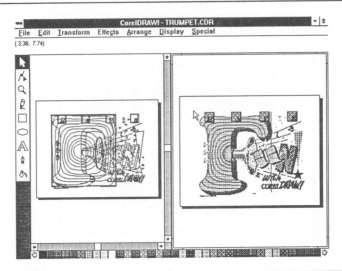

Full-Screen Preview

The preview window you just experienced shared the screen with the editing window, the toolbox, the menus, and the scroll bars. CorelDRAW!, beginning with version 2.0, also has a full-screen preview. This allows you to utilize the entire screen to see what your finished drawing will look like. While you can't edit and look at this screen at the same time, you see the largest preview image possible. Try it next.

1. Press (F9) or select Show Full-Screen Preview from the Display menu. The screen will clear and, over a few moments, the Trumpet drawing will be created in all its glory as shown in Figure 7-3.

2. When you are done, press any key to return to the editing window.

Tip

Full-screen preview is so useful that Corel has included the option of setting the right mouse button to toggle between Full-screen preview and the editing window. If you want to use the right mouse button to do this (Full-screen preview is one of five

Figure 7-3. *Full-screen preview*

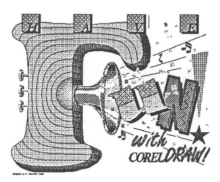

options), select the Mouse option from the Preferences command in the Special menu and choose Full-screen preview.

Limitations of the Preview Window

Since the preview window lets you see the results of editing a picture immediately, you may prefer to leave it turned on most of the time. The preview window does have two important limitations, however, and these make it advisable to turn it off under certain circumstances.

PostScript Effects

The first limitation of the preview window applies if you plan to output your images to a PostScript laser printer or imagesetter. CorelDRAW! includes many advanced features that make use of PostScript graphics capabilities, but not all of them are visible onscreen. To see how such features really look, you must print the files that contain them. CorelDRAW! cannot

7

display Custom PostScript textures and PostScript halftone screens with true WYSIWYG accuracy in the preview window.

You will learn about these features when you create custom outlines and fills for objects and text in Chapters 13 through 15.

Screen Redraw Time

Another limitation of the preview window applies to all CorelDRAW! users and involves screen redraw time, the time needed for all details of the WYSIWYG image to redisplay in the preview window. Select the Show Preview command to turn on the preview window for TRUMPET.CDR again and note that the screen redraws the preview image more slowly than the skeletal image. The preview contains much more visual information and is therefore more memory intensive. Also, the screen redraw occurs every time you make changes to the picture in the editing window. Fortunately, you can overcome this limitation in several different ways; see the "Improving Preview Speed" section near the end of this chapter. The following sections show you how to change the size and shape of the preview window to suit your needs.

Sizing the Preview Window

Since the shapes and sizes of pictures vary, you sometimes need to adjust the preview window to match the format of a picture. In addition to filling the screen, you can place the preview window beneath or beside the editing window and make it broad or long. The more closely you make the preview window fit the size and shape of your picture, the more control you have over the editing process.

Sizing with the Two-Way Arrows

To move or resize the preview window, you need only click on one of the window's boundaries and drag it to the desired position. Look again at the preview window and notice the narrow gray frame, or boundary, that surrounds it. When you move the mouse cursor to any part of the preview window boundary, a white two-way arrow appears, indicating which boundary you have approached and the direction in which you can drag the preview window from this point. With the file TRUMPET.CDR open and the preview window displayed, move the mouse cursor as follows:

1. Move the cursor to any point along the upper boundary of the preview window. A vertical two-way white arrow appears, like this:

This arrow indicates that from this point, you can move the preview window upward or downward.

2. Move the mouse to the upper-left corner of the preview window. Now, the two-way arrow points diagonally, indicating that you can drag the preview window diagonally from the corner:

3. Finally, move the cursor to any point along the left side of the preview window. The two-way arrow becomes horizontal, which tells you that you can drag the preview window back and forth in a horizontal direction:

In the following exercises, you can experiment with changing the size or shape of the preview window.

7

Top-to-Bottom Format

The first time you display the preview window, it appears automatically at the right side of the normal editing window, as it did in Figure 7-2. Sometimes a side-by-side format is inconvenient to work with. If you are editing a graphic that is wider than it is long, for example, you could see the graphic better if you positioned the preview window *below* the editing window.

1. Open the file DOESALL.CDR and then select the Show Preview command from the Display menu. The two windows appear side by side, as in Figure 7-4. This picture has a horizontal orientation.

Figure 7-4.   *Previewing DOESALL.CDR*

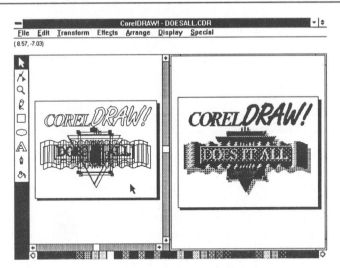

2. Select the Magnification tool and then select the Zoom-In tool and lasso the words "CorelDRAW" at the top of the editing window, as shown in Figure 7-5. Release the mouse button when you have surrounded the entire section. Both the editing window and the preview window redraw to show the magnified area (Figure 7-6). You can see some of the graphic below the specified zoom-in area as well, because CorelDRAW! adjusts the zoom to the proportions, or *aspect ratio*, of the page. To obtain a better view, you must change the arrangement of the preview and editing windows.

3. Position the mouse cursor along the upper boundary of the preview window. The two-way vertical arrow appears, as shown in Figure 7-6.

4. Press and hold the mouse button and drag the upper preview boundary downward until it is below the midpoint of the screen, so it occupies only the bottom 1/3 of the column.

5. Release the mouse button. CorelDRAW! adjusts the windows so that the preview window appears below the editing window, as in Figure 7-7. Now you can see exactly the area you zoomed in on and no

Figure 7-5. *Magnifying the upper portion of the picture in the editing window*

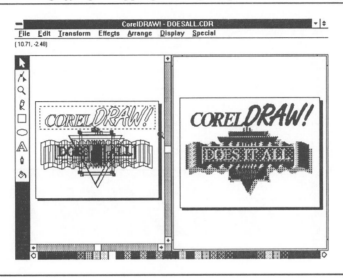

Figure 7-6. *Redraw screen showing magnified view in both windows*

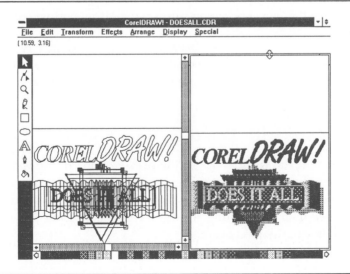

7

Figure 7-7.   *Preview window in top-to-bottom format*

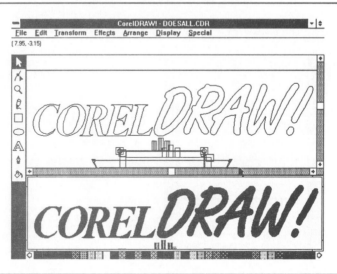

more, because you have tailored the aspect ratio of the editing and preview windows to the dimensions of the zoom-in area.

6. Leave the two windows in this top-to-bottom format for now.

Tip

You can also place the preview window below the editing window by dragging the diagonal boundary instead of the vertical boundary. To do so, drag the diagonal boundary first downward and then to the left. The result is the same.

Changing Size with Top-to-Bottom Format

You can alter the relative size of the preview and editing windows once you have them in a top-to-bottom format. If you wanted to see large, clear results of an edit involving color or outline, you could make the preview window larger than the editing window. Practice altering the size of the preview window in the next exercise.

1. With the DOESALL.CDR image still in top-to-bottom format on the screen, move the mouse cursor to the top boundary of the preview window until the vertical two-way arrow appears.

2. Drag this boundary upward until it covers approximately 75% of the screen and release the mouse button. The two windows redraw, with the preview window taking up most of the display area, as in Figure 7-8.

3. Take this sizing a step further. Drag the upper boundary of the preview window until you reach the top of the screen, and then release the mouse button. The preview window now fills the entire display area, crowding out the editing window entirely.

4. Drag the upper boundary back to a point more than halfway down the screen. The preview and editing windows return to a top-to-bottom format.

CorelDRAW! doesn't allow you to edit anything but the skeletal image in the editing window. You cannot edit the preview image.

Note

Figure 7-8.   *Increasing the size of the preview window (top-to-bottom format)*

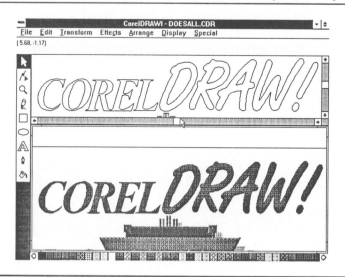

7

When you have finished checking the results of your edits using a full-screen preview window, return the display to either a top-to-bottom or side-by-side format to continue editing.

Side-by-Side Format

In this section, you will change back to the side-by-side placement of the editing and preview windows.

1. Move the mouse cursor to any point along the left boundary of the preview window; a two-way horizontal arrow appears.

2. Press and hold the mouse button and drag the left preview boundary toward the right until you have passed the halfway point of the screen.

3. Release the mouse button. CorelDRAW! redraws the screen so that both the preview and editing windows are side by side in vertical format, as shown in Figure 7-9.

4. Leave this image on the screen for now.

Figure 7-9.   *Preview window back to side-by-side format*

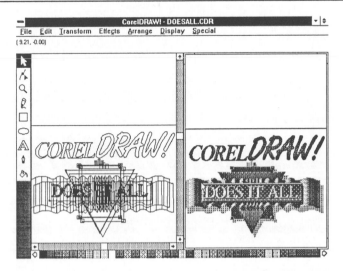

Another way to change from a top-to-bottom to a side-by-side format is to drag the diagonal boundary of the preview window instead of the horizontal one. To do this, drag the diagonal boundary first to the right and then upward. Similarly, to change from a side-by-side to a top-to-bottom format, drag the diagonal boundary first downward and then to the left.

Tip

Changing Size with Side-by-Side Format

You can alter the relative size of the preview and editing windows once you have them in a side-by-side format. Make the preview window larger than the editing window if you want to view results more clearly; make the editing window larger if you want to concentrate on manipulating the image.

1. With the DOESALL.CDR image still on the screen, move the mouse cursor to the left boundary of the preview window so that the horizontal two-way arrow appears.

2. Drag this boundary to the left until it covers approximately 75% of the screen, and then release the mouse button. The two windows redraw, with the preview window taking up most of the display area, as in Figure 7-10.

3. Now drag the boundary of the preview window about 75% of the way to the right and then release the mouse button. This time, the editing window takes up most of the display area.

4. Take this sizing a step further by dragging the left boundary of the preview window all the way to the left edge of the screen and then releasing the mouse button. The preview window fills the entire display area, crowding out the editing window entirely.

5. Select New from the File menu to clear the screen before proceeding.

Changing the format of the preview window manually is convenient, especially since it takes only a second to alter the relative size of the editing and preview windows. By dragging the appropriate two-way arrow, you can change both the format and the sizing of the preview window. If you prefer

7

Figure 7-10.   *Increasing the size of the preview window in side-by-side format*

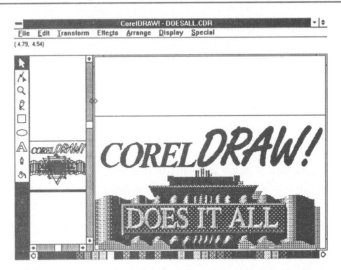

to switch preview window format (not size) automatically, however, you can activate the preview toolbox.

The Preview Toolbox

The preview window has its own toolbox, which you can turn on or off using the Show Preview Toolbox command in the Display menu. Unlike the regular toolbox for the editing window, the preview toolbox contains no drawing tools. The sole function of its tools is to customize the format or content of the preview window relative to the editing window. Using this toolbox, you can choose between top-to-bottom and side-to-side preview format and magnify custom areas of the preview window.

When the preview toolbox is turned on, the preview window does not update itself automatically to match changes made in the editing window.

Caution

Perform the following brief exercise to display the preview toolbox and adjust the format of the preview window automatically.

1. Open the file JUGGLE.CDR and press (SHIFT)-(F9) to show the preview window.

2. Select the Show Preview Toolbox command from the Display menu. At the right side of the preview window, three icons appear, as in Figure 7-11. The top icon, the Magnification tool, works exactly like the Magnification tool for the editing window. The second icon allows you to arrange the editing and preview windows in a side-by-side format. The third icon allows you to arrange the editing and preview windows in a top-to-bottom format.

3. Click anywhere on the second icon in the preview toolbox to return the preview window to a side-by-side display. Note that the preview and editing windows occupy equal areas of the screen. You can adjust the relative size of the two windows by manually dragging the left boundary of the preview window, just as you did earlier.

Figure 7-11.   *Displaying the preview window toolbox*

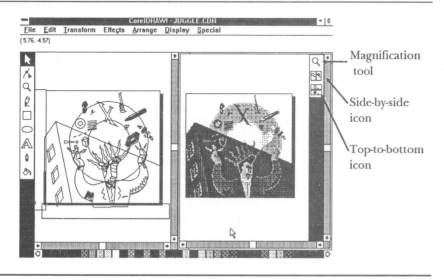

4. Change to a top-to-bottom arrangement of the two windows by clicking anywhere on the third icon in the preview toolbox. Your screen should now look like Figure 7-12. Again, the preview and editing windows occupy equal areas of the screen.

5. To conceal the preview toolbox, click on the Show Preview Toolbox command from the Display menu once more. Leave the JUGGLE .CDR image on the screen for the next exercise.

Magnification in the Preview Window

The Magnification tool in the preview toolbox contains the same five icons (Zoom-In, Zoom-Out, Actual Size, fit-in-window, and Show Page) as its counterpart in the editing window. Both Magnification tools work the same way—but they work independently. The Magnification tool in the preview toolbox controls only the content of the preview window, so you can look at

Figure 7-12.   *Returning to a top-to-bottom format*

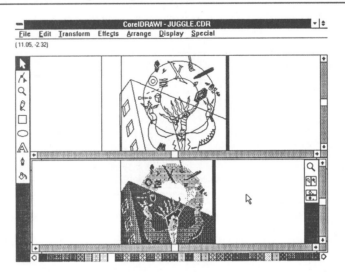

different sections of the same image in each window. Perform the following brief exercise for a quick example of the potential of this feature.

1. With the JUGGLE.CDR file on the screen, drag the left boundary of the preview window to the right and adjust the windows to a side-by-side format.

2. In the editing window, select the Magnification tool and then select the Zoom-In tool and lasso the head only. Both windows redraw automatically, as in Figure 7-13.

3. Select Show Preview Toolbox from the Display menu. Notice that as soon as you activate the preview toolbox, scroll bars appear along the bottom and right boundaries of the preview window. You can now adjust the preview window magnification using the same techniques you learned in Chapter 6.

4. In the editing window, select the Magnification tool and the Zoom-In tool again. Zoom in again on the head. As Figure 7-14 shows, the editing window redraws to show the new magnification, but the preview window does not redraw. Whenever the preview toolbox is turned on, the preview window no longer changes magnification automatically; you must change it yourself using the preview Magnification tool.

5. Select the Text tool A in the editing window toolbox and then select an insertion point in the middle of the man's forehead.

6. When the Text dialog box appears, type **X** in the text entry window. Set the text attributes to Left justification, Avalon Normal, 4 points.

7. Select OK to confirm these settings. The letter "X" now appears in both the editing and preview windows, as in Figure 7-15, but in the preview window you see it in perspective, among all the surrounding objects, and with a default fill color of black.

8. To practice varying the magnification in the preview window, click on the Magnification tool in the preview toolbox and again on the Zoom-In icon. Lasso the head in the preview window; the screen redraws to show approximately the same area that appears in the editing window. The other icons in the Magnification tool fly-out

7

Figure 7-13.   *Automatic magnification of both windows (preview toolbox off)*

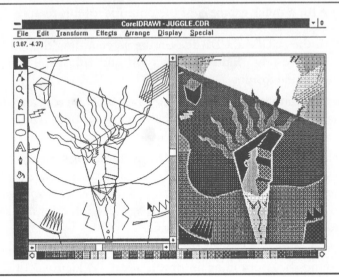

Figure 7-14.   *Different magnification in each window (preview toolbox on)*

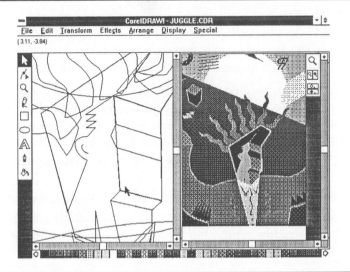

menu of the preview toolbox work just like their counterparts in the editing window, too.

9. Turn the preview toolbox off by selecting the Show Preview Toolbox command from the Display menu once more.

10. Select New to clear the screen. Do not save the changes you made to the picture in this exercise.

You have mastered all of the basic techniques for customizing the preview window to best view your images. The next section of this chapter contains tips on advanced techniques for reducing the amount of memory and time that is needed to redraw the preview window.

Improving Preview Speed

If you allow CorelDRAW! to redraw the preview window whenever you edit a picture, you can spend a lot of potential drawing time waiting, especially

Figure 7-15.   *Previewing edits with different magnification in each window*

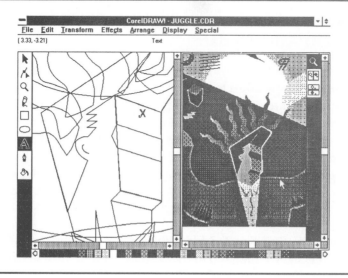

7

if you are working on a complex image. Fortunately, you can slash redraw time while still retaining all the most important editing benefits of the preview window. Just use any of these four techniques:

- Interrupt the screen redraw before it has finished.
- Turn off the Auto-Update feature so the preview will no longer redraw automatically every time you make a change.
- Turn off the display of bitmaps in the editing window.
- Use the Preview Selected Only command so the screen will display only those objects on which you are currently working.

The following sections describe each of these techniques and offer suggestions for their use.

Interrupting the Screen Redraw

You can interrupt the redraw of the preview window at any time before it is finished. Simply begin another operation using the mouse button. CorelDRAW! senses the signals from the mouse and stops redrawing the preview as soon as the object it is currently redrawing is complete. This means that if the object that is currently being redrawn is a complex one, your interruption of the process may take effect only after a few seconds.

Turning Off Auto-Update

One of the most effective ways to speed up CorelDRAW! operation while retaining the preview window is to turn off the Auto-Update feature, controlled by the Auto-Update command in the Display menu. This feature is turned on by default, so that the preview window redraws with every change you make to the editing window. To turn this feature off, click on the Auto-Update command in the Display menu, and the checkmark in front of the command should disappear. This prevents the preview window from redrawing unless you click on any point in the preview window. Practice this technique by performing the following brief exercise:

1. Open the PARTY.CDR file. When the image appears, click on the Auto-Update command in the Display menu to turn off this feature.

2. Embellish the editing window any way you like. For example, select the Pencil tool and draw an "X" on one of the diamonds or add geometric shapes. The preview window does not redraw at any time.

3. When you have finished doodling in the editing window, click anywhere on the preview window. In a few seconds, you see the results of your actions. If your "doodles" do not appear in the preview window and you have drawn a line or curve, click on the Outline tool ⬚ and again on the second or third line width in the first row of the fly-out menu. This ensures that the outlines of your lines and curves are visible. Then draw the same doodles over again. You will learn more about the Outline tool in Chapter 13, "Defining the Outline Pen."

4. Select New from the File menu and answer No to clear the screen.

You can see why toggling the Auto-Update command on and off is a favorite work habit of seasoned CorelDRAW! users. If you use this method most of the time, you will always have the preview handy, while avoiding its potential drawbacks.

Concealing Bitmaps in the Editing Window

Bitmapped images take a long time to redraw, even in the editing window, as you will learn when you work with bitmapped images and autotracing in Appendix D, "Tracing with Bitmapped Images." A useful technique is to leave the Show Bitmaps command in the Display menu turned off. This command, which you can turn on and off like the Auto-Update command, is normally turned off and doesn't have a checkmark in front of it. When it is turned off, bitmapped images display in the editing window as an empty rectangle, but continue to appear in the preview window. Turn Show Bitmaps and Auto-Update off when you are finished cropping and editing bitmaps; this will allow you to work at maximum speed and still check the results of your edits.

Previewing Selected Objects Only

When your main concern is to view the specific object or objects you are editing, you can select the Preview Selected Only command in the Display menu. Invoking this command causes CorelDRAW! to redraw only the object(s) you have selected. This is a particularly useful technique when you

7

object(s) you have selected. This is a particularly useful technique when you are trying to figure out which objects are in the foreground and which are in the background. Chapter 8, "Selecting, Moving, and Arranging Objects," introduces the Select tool and gives you ample opportunity to practice displaying selected objects in the preview window.

8

Selecting, Moving, and Arranging Objects

In order to change the appearance or position of any object or text string, you must first *select* it. Once you have selected an object, you can move and rearrange it, stretch, scale, rotate or skew it, give it a custom outline, or fill it with a color or pattern. Learning how to select an object is therefore an important prerequisite to mastering most of the skills in CorelDRAW!.

You use the Select tool , the first tool in the CorelDRAW! toolbox, to select objects and text. When you first load CorelDRAW!, the Select tool is automatically active and remains active until you choose a different tool. If you are already working with one of the other tools, you can activate the Select tool by clicking on the Select tool icon in the toolbox.

Pressing the spacebar once is more efficient. This is a time-saving shortcut that allows you to switch back and forth between tools quickly. To reactivate the tool you were working with before you selected the Select tool, press the spacebar again. Use this

Tip

shortcut often when you want to draw objects, immediately move, rearrange, or transform them, and then continue drawing.

The Select tool performs more than one function; it has both a select mode and a transformation mode. The select mode includes all those functions—selecting, moving, and arranging—that do not require you to change the size or structure of the object. The transformation mode allows you to stretch, scale, rotate, skew, or reflect objects. This chapter covers the functions of the select mode; Chapter 9, "Transforming Objects," will acquaint you with the use of the Select tool in the transformation mode.

Selecting and Deselecting Objects

You can select objects only when the Select tool is active. This tool is always active when you first open a picture, when you begin a new picture, and immediately after you save your work. To activate the Select tool when you're using the Shaping tool or one of the drawing tools, you either press the spacebar or click on the Select tool icon once.

Once the Select tool is active, you can select one or more objects by clicking on their outlines, by using (SHIFT) with the mouse, or by lassoing the objects. The technique you choose depends on the number of objects you are selecting, the placement of the objects within the graphic, and whether it's more convenient to select objects with the mouse or with the keyboard shortcuts.

The CorelDRAW! screen gives you three visual cues to let you know that an object is selected. First, a *highlighting box* consisting of eight small rectangles, called *boundary markers,* surrounds the object. These markers allow you to stretch and scale the object, as you'll learn in Chapter 9. Second, one or more tiny hollow nodes appear on the outline of the object or group of objects. The number of nodes displayed depends on the type and number of objects selected. The nodes are the means by which you can change an object's shape, as you'll learn in Chapters 10 and 11. Finally, the status line tells you the type of object you have selected (rectangle, ellipse, curve, and so on) or the number of objects you have selected if you have selected more than one. Figure 8-3 will identify each of these aids.

Single Objects

Any time you activate the Select tool while working on a graphic, it automatically selects the last object you created. If you want to select a different object, simply click once anywhere on the object's *outline*. Clicking on the inside of a rectangle or ellipse, or on an open space inside a letter, has no effect. Also, you must click on a point unique to that object; it cannot share that point with the outline of any other object. Only when an object is the same type and size as another object on top of it does it have no unique selection point available. For information on how to select superimposed objects without unique selection points, see the "Cycling Through Objects" section of this chapter.

To *deselect* an object or text string so that the tools or menu commands you use no longer affect it, click in any open area on the page. Alternatively, you can select a different object and thereby automatically deselect the previously selected object.

When you click twice on an object instead of once, arrows surround the object in place of the boundary markers. These arrows indicate that you have enabled the rotate and skew functions of the Select tool. This can happen to you accidentally, since the Select tool covers transformation mode as well as select mode functions. If you enable the transformation mode accidentally at any time, just click on the object's outlines again to toggle back to the select mode.

Tip

In the following exercise, you will practice selecting and deselecting single objects in the LANDSCA2.CDR file that you edited in Chapter 6. You will use the spacebar to select objects that you have just drawn and the mouse to select other objects.

1. Make sure that the Show Status Line command in the Display menu is turned on and the Snap To Grid command is turned off.

2. Open the LANDSCA2.CDR file. Note that when the picture displays on the screen, the Select tool is already active.

3. Select the Magnification tool 🔍 and then select the Zoom-In tool from the fly-out menu and lasso the lower-right quarter of the picture. The screen redraws an area of the image similar to that in Figure 8-1.

8

Figure 8-1.   *Magnifying the lower-right quarter of the file LANDSCA2.CDR*

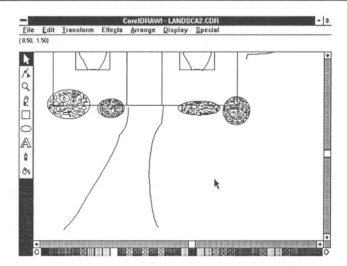

4. Select the Pencil tool and use the mouse to draw a large pond in the lower-right corner of the picture. Be sure to connect the starting point to the finish point, so that the curve representing the pond becomes a closed path that you can fill later. Notice that as soon as you finish drawing this object, nodes appear all along the path of the curve, as in Figure 8-2.

5. As soon as the pond appears, press the spacebar to activate the Select tool. Since the pond is the last object you drew, CorelDRAW! automatically selects it. A highlighting box surrounds the pond and the status line indicates "Curve" as in Figure 8-3.

6. Click on the outlines of the curve object again. As Figure 8-4 shows, black two-way arrows replace the boundary markers of the highlighting box. Your second click has enabled the rotate and skew functions of the Select tool. Click on the object's outlines again to toggle back to the select mode.

7. Now, zoom out of your magnified view using the Zoom-Out tool in the Magnification tool fly-out menu. Practice selecting objects that

Figure 8-2. Adding a pond to the drawing

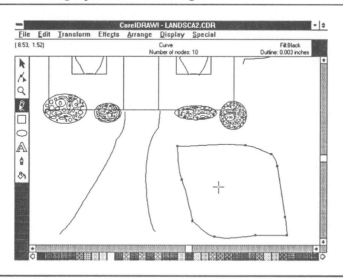

Figure 8-3. Using the spacebar to select the last object drawn

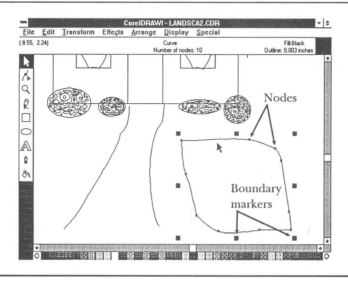

8

Figure 8-4.   *Enabling the transformation mode of the Select tool*

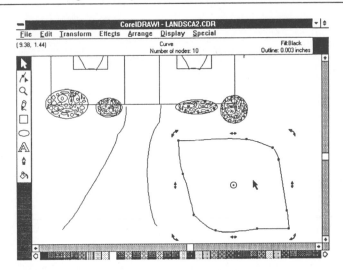

you drew in previous sessions. For example, click on one of the
curves that form the branches of the poplar tree. Each time you
select a new object, the previously selected object becomes
deselected; the highlighting box disappears from the previously
selected object and surrounds the new one instead. The name of the
currently selected object type always appears in the status line. If you
select any objects within other objects (the detail inside one of the
bushes, for example), you may notice that the highlighting box is
sometimes much larger than the object itself. If several objects of
the same type are crowded closely together, it may be difficult to tell
which one you have selected. Use the Zoom-In tool to magnify a
small portion of a crowded area before you attempt to select single
objects.

8. When you have practiced enough to feel comfortable with selecting
   objects, select Save As from the File menu and type **landsca3.cdr** to
   save the file.

9. Select New from the File menu to clear the screen.

Multiple Objects

It's often more convenient to perform an operation on several objects simultaneously than to perform the same operation on a series of single objects individually. Assume, for example, that you want to move the tree in the LANDSCA3.CDR file to another location within the picture. Since the tree consists of several separate objects, moving each component object individually would be tedious and might even lead to inaccurate placement.

CorelDRAW! gives you three alternative solutions to this type of problem. The first solution, simply *selecting* the objects, is appropriate when you want to keep multiple objects together only temporarily, without merging them into a single entity. For example, you might want to fill a certain number of objects in a picture with the same color or pattern or move them all by the same distance. You can select multiple objects by using the mouse and (SHIFT) key, by drawing a marquee around them, or by using the Select All command in the Edit menu. Your choice of technique depends on both the number of objects you want to select and their location within the graphic.

If the multiple objects are components of a larger whole and should remain together at all times, you might choose to *group* them, as you will learn to do later in this chapter. CorelDRAW! will still remember that grouped objects have separate identities. If the multiple objects belong together and contain many curves, you can choose to *combine* them into a single object. Combining objects, unlike grouping them, reduces the amount of memory they require and also allows you to reshape the entire resulting object.

You will learn more about the uses of grouping and combining multiple objects in the "Arranging Objects" portion of this chapter. The following group of sections lets you practice common methods of selecting multiple objects.

8

Selecting with the (SHIFT) Key

When you want to select a few objects at a time, you can conveniently select them one after another using the mouse and (SHIFT) together. The (SHIFT) key method is especially useful when the objects you want to select are not next to one another within the graphic. Practice selecting multiple objects using this method:

1. Select the first object by clicking on its outline.

2. Depress and hold (SHIFT) and select the next object.

3. Continue selecting objects in this way, holding down (SHIFT) continuously.

4. When you have selected all desired objects, release (SHIFT).

To deselect one or more of the objects you have selected in this way, hold down (SHIFT) and click again on that object's outline. This action affects only that object; other objects in the group remain selected. To deselect all of the selected objects simultaneously, click on any free space.

Each time you select another object using (SHIFT), the highlighting box expands to surround all the objects you have selected so far. Objects that you did not select also may fall within the boundaries of the highlighting box, making it difficult for you to see just which objects you have selected. The following exercise shows how you can use the status line information and the preview window as aids in selecting multiple objects with (SHIFT).

1. Open the TEACUP2.CDR file that you edited in Chapter 6.

2. Use the Maximize button to enlarge the size of the working area. Magnify the area that extends from the upper-left corner of the picture to the bottom of the tag on the teabag.

3. Click on the leftmost wisp of "steam" above the teacup to select it. A highlighting box surrounds the object, and the status line indicates that you have selected a curve.

4. Depress and hold (SHIFT) and click anywhere on the outlines of the text "JASMINE TEA." The message in the status line changes to "2 objects selected," but the highlighting box shown in Figure 8-5 seems to surround many more objects. It is difficult to tell whether you have selected the text string or one of the rectangles on the tea tag surrounding it. To find out, you need help from the preview window.

5. Press (SHIFT)-(F9) to display the preview window. Do not be concerned at this point that all of the objects in your drawing seem to blend into a solid black mass. You will learn how to edit the outlines and colors of individual objects in Chapters 13, 14, and 15.

6. Select Preview Selected Only from the Display menu. This command, first introduced in Chapter 7, causes only the currently

selected objects to appear in the preview window. The text string is too small to read clearly but, as Figure 8-6 shows, you can now be certain that you selected the correct objects. Or did you?

If you cannot see the "steam" when it is selected, click on the Outline tool *and again on the first or second line width in the first row of the fly-out menu. This action ensures that selected lines and curves have a visible outline.*

Tip

7. If you accidentally selected one of the tea-tag rectangles instead of the text string, deselect the incorrect object by holding (SHIFT) while clicking again on that object. When the highlighting box no longer surrounds that object, continue to hold down (SHIFT) and select the text string instead.

8. Still holding down (SHIFT), select the rightmost wisp of "steam" and add it to the group of selected objects. The status line now displays the message "3 objects selected," and the preview window displays all three objects. Again, if you can't see the steam when it is selected,

Figure 8-5.   *Selecting nonadjacent objects using* (SHIFT)

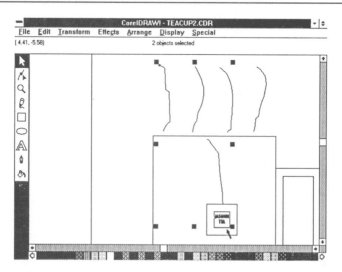

8

Figure 8-6.   *Using Preview Selected Only to confirm object selection*

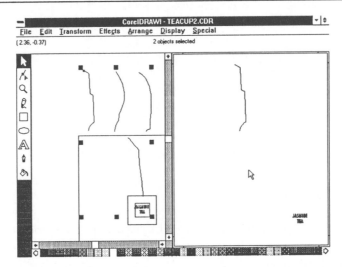

click on the Outline tool and click again on the first or second line
width in the fly-out menu.

9. Click on the Preview Selected Only command in the Display menu
   again to turn off this feature, and then select New from the File menu
   to clear the screen.

Selecting with the Marquee

If you need to select a large number of objects at once, using the mouse
and (SHIFT) can be tedious. A quick shortcut is to draw a marquee around all
of the desired objects with the Select tool. Perform the following exercise to
practice using a marquee:

1. Position the mouse cursor just above and to the left of the first object
   you want to select. (You can begin from any corner of the group of
   objects, but the upper-left corner is usually most convenient.)

2. Depress the mouse button and drag the mouse diagonally in the
   direction of the other objects you want to select. A dotted rectangle

(the marquee) follows the cursor. Make sure that every object you want to select falls completely within this rectangle, or CorelDRAW! will not select it.

3. When you have enclosed the last object you want to select within the marquee, release the mouse button. The highlighting box appears, encompassing all of the objects within the selected area.

If you want to exclude some of the objects that fall within the selected area, you can deselect them using (SHIFT). Lasso the entire group of objects first, depress and hold (SHIFT), and click on a particular object's outline to deselect that object. You can also use the status line and preview window as "quality control" aids to guide you in selecting exactly the objects you want.

Perform the following exercise to gain skill at selecting objects quickly with the marquee. Use magnification, status line information, and the preview window to make the selection process more efficient. Use (SHIFT) to fine-tune your selection and add or subtract objects to or from the group you selected with the marquee.

1. Open the file LANDSCA3.CDR. Note that the poplar tree you drew in an earlier lesson contains several objects: the ellipse that forms the main body of the foliage, a few curves that form the branches, and curves that make up the trunk. Since all of these objects are adjacent to one another, the tree is a perfect example of the types of multiple objects you can select easily with the marquee.

2. Select the Magnification tool and then select the Zoom-In tool from the fly-out menu. Zoom in to display the left half of the picture. As soon as you have magnified this area, the Select tool becomes highlighted again.

3. If necessary, press (SHIFT)-(F9) to turn on the preview window. Do not be concerned that many of the objects seem to be solid black; you can practice giving them different outline and fill colors after you work with Chapters 13, 14, and 15.

4. Select Preview Selected Only. The preview window now appears blank.

5. Position the mouse cursor above and to the left of the poplar tree. Drag the mouse downward and to the right until the marquee

8

surrounds all of the component objects of the tree completely and release the mouse button. The highlighting box appears and the status line indicates the number of objects you have selected, as in Figure 8-7. However, the preview window displays the foliage of the tree as a solid elliptical mass, without the detail of the curves you have entered inside it. You cannot distinguish between objects because the foliage curves and the ellipse have the same fill color.

6. Depress and hold (SHIFT) and then click once anywhere on the outline of the ellipse that makes up the main body of the foliage. CorelDRAW! deselects it and the status line shows there is one less selected object. You can now see the internal details in the preview window, as shown in Figure 8-8. As in the previous exercise, if you cannot see the foliage curves when they are selected, click on the Outline tool and click again on the first or second line width in the fly-out menu.

7. Click on any white space to deselect all of the objects, and then select New from the File menu to clear the screen.

Selecting All Objects in a Graphic

If you want to perform an operation on all the objects in the graphic, you can select them by drawing a marquee. A quicker way to select all objects is simply to invoke the Select All command in the Edit menu. Using this command, you can be sure that you haven't left out any objects.

You now know several methods for selecting single and multiple objects. Most of the time, selecting objects is a straightforward process in CorelDRAW!. But what if your graphic contains many small objects or you want to select an object that may have several other layers of objects on top of it? The next section makes that process easy for you.

Cycling Through Objects

The object selection techniques you have learned so far in this chapter are adequate for most applications. However, when working with complex drawings containing many objects or superimposed objects, you may find it

Figure 8-7. *Selecting all component objects of the tree*

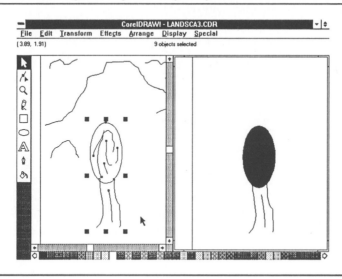

Figure 8-8. *Deselecting one object in a group of selected objects*

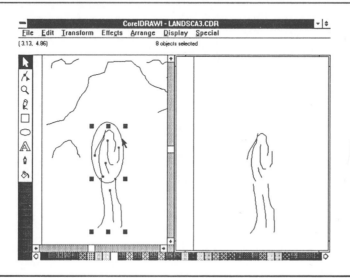

8

more convenient to cycle through the objects using (TAB). The following exercise summarizes this technique:

1. Select an object near or on top of the object you want to select.

2. Press (TAB). CorelDRAW! deselects the first object and selects the next object in the drawing. The "next" object is the one that was drawn just prior to the currently selected object. Each time you press (TAB), CorelDRAW! cycles backward to another object. If you press (TAB) often enough, you eventually select the first object again, and the cycle begins once more.

The following sections show you two different situations in which you might choose to cycle through objects in a drawing. The first section provides an example of objects that have other objects superimposed on them. The second section demonstrates how to locate and select small objects in a complex drawing.

Cycling Through Superimposed Objects

You may recall that in order to select an object in CorelDRAW!, you must click on a unique point on its outline, a point not shared by any other object. This limitation does not apply to most superimposed objects, because you can usually see separate outlines in the preview window. The only exception is when two or more objects are the same size and shape and overlay one another exactly.

Why might you choose to create two identical overlapping objects? You could achieve interesting design effects by varying the color and thickness of their respective outlines and fills, as shown in the example in Figure 8-9. The preview window shows that what appears to be a single rectangle in the editing window is actually two separate rectangles, each with its own outline color, outline thickness, and fill color. In Chapters 13, 14, and 15, you will learn more about outlines and fill colors. For now, you need only know that to select the object in the background, you can select one object and then press (TAB), checking the preview window for confirmation.

Cycling Through Many Objects

There is another, more common use for (TAB) when selecting objects in CorelDRAW!. Clip art, technical illustrations, and other complex drawings

Figure 8-9.   *An example of objects exactly superimposed*

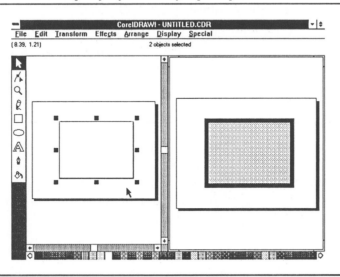

often contain many small objects close together. Even in magnified view, trying to select one or more of these with the mouse can be difficult at best. To ease the process, you can select one object, and then press (TAB) repeatedly until the fine little detail you are looking for is selected. CorelDRAW! cycles backward through the objects, selecting them in the reverse order to which you drew them. To cycle forward through the objects in a drawing, press (SHIFT)-(TAB). Perform the following brief exercise to gain a clearer understanding of how the (TAB) key method of selection works.

1. Open the file TRAIN.CDR. Turn on the preview window (if it isn't already on) by pressing (SHIFT)-(F9), and select Preview Selected Only from the Display menu.

2. Choose the Select All command from the Edit menu. The status line shows you that there are 214 separate objects that have not been grouped or combined.

3. Click on any white space to deselect all the objects, and then select the cowcatcher as shown in Figure 8-10. Notice the status line says "Group of 4 objects" so you have actually selected a group of objects,

8

not a single object. You'll learn more about this later in this chapter under "Grouping and Ungrouping Objects."

4. Press (TAB) several times. CorelDRAW! cycles through the objects layered below the cowcatcher, displaying each of the front wheels and other details each time you press (TAB).

5. Press (SHIFT)-(TAB) several times. Now CorelDRAW! selects objects in the opposite order, eventually selecting objects layered above the cowcatcher.

6. If you have the patience to cycle through all 214 objects, keep pressing (TAB) or (SHIFT)-(TAB) until CorelDRAW! selects the cowcatcher again.

7. Select New from the File menu to clear the screen before you proceed.

Now you are familiar with all of the available techniques for selecting any number of objects. In the next portion of this chapter, you will begin moving selected objects to other areas within the illustration.

Figure 8-10.   *Cycling through multiple objects in a complex drawing*

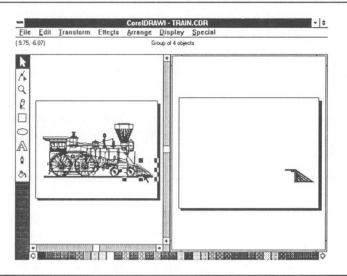

Moving Objects

Once you have selected an object, you can move it by positioning the cursor over any point on its *outline* (not on the highlighting box) and then dragging the mouse along with the object to the desired location. The status line provides you with precise, real-time information about the distance you are traveling, the x and y components of that distance, and the angle of movement. You can achieve precision worthy of the most demanding technical illustrations if you choose to work with the status line and grid.

Factors such as the number of objects you want to move, whether you want to constrain movement to a 90-degree angle, and whether you want to make a copy of the object determine your choice of technique. The following sections provide examples and exercises that show how to move objects in specific situations.

Moving a Single Object

The appearance of an object undergoes several changes during the process of moving it. Try the following simple exercise to become familiar with those changes.

1. If you have done the exercises earlier in this chapter, your drawing page is in landscape orientation and your preview window is turned on. Change both of these by choosing Portrait in the Page Setup dialog box reached from the File menu and by pressing (SHIFT)-(F9) to turn off the preview window.

2. Select the Ellipse tool ⬭ and draw an ellipse in the upper area of the page.

3. Activate the Select tool and select the ellipse. (Recall that you can simply press the spacebar to select the last object you have drawn.) The highlighting box surrounds the ellipse.

4. Move the mouse to any point on the outline of the ellipse, press and hold the mouse button, and begin dragging the mouse downward and to the right. The screen does not change immediately, because

8

CorelDRAW! has a built-in, 3-pixel safety zone; you must drag the mouse at least 3 pixels away from the starting point before the object begins to "move." As soon as you pass the 3-pixel safety zone, the cursor changes to a four-way arrow, and a dotted replica of the highlighting box follows the cursor, as shown in Figure 8-11. This dotted box represents the object while you are moving it; as you can see in the figure, the object itself seems to remain in its original position.

5. When you have dragged the dotted box to the lower edge of the page, release the mouse button. The ellipse disappears from its original position and reappears in the new location.

6. Press (DEL) to clear the screen before proceeding.

These are the basic steps involved in moving an object, but CorelDRAW! offers you additional refinements as well. The next three sections provide details on moving multiple objects, constraining an object to move at a 90-degree angle, and retaining a copy of an object while moving it.

Figure 8-11.   *Dragging the dotted move box to move an object*

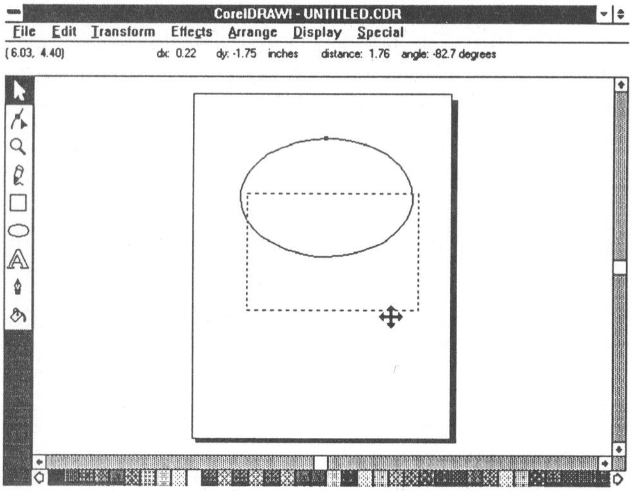

Moving Multiple Objects

The technique for moving multiple, selected objects differs very little from the way you move single objects. When more than one object is selected, you simply press and hold the mouse button on the outline of *any one* of the objects within the selected group. The entire group moves together as you drag the mouse. Complete the following exercise to practice moving multiple objects in the LANDSCA3.CDR file.

1. Open the file LANDSCA3.CDR. The Select tool is automatically activated when you open a new picture.

2. Draw a marquee and lasso the entire poplar tree in the front foreground of the picture to select it. The status line displays the number of selected objects. If you are not sure whether you have selected all of the objects that make up the tree, get confirmation by turning on the preview window and selecting Preview Selected Only from the Display menu.

3. Position the cursor over any of the outlines in the tree, and then drag the mouse until the dotted move box reaches the extreme right of the picture, as shown in Figure 8-12.

4. Release the mouse button. The tree disappears from its original location and reappears in the new location. The tree is now in part of the pond, so you will move the pond next.

5. Select the pond and move it to the left side of the picture where the poplar tree formerly stood.

6. Select the Zoom-In tool from the Magnification tool fly-out menu and magnify the area around the leftmost bush in front of the house. Your viewing area should look similar to Figure 8-13.

7. With the Select tool, select (lasso) the entire bush, including the detail you drew inside it, and then move the bush a little to the left of the house.

8. Zoom out to full-page view. Your picture should now resemble Figure 8-14.

9. Save this altered picture as LANDSCA4.CDR and leave it on the screen.

8

Figure 8-12.   *Moving multiple objects to a new location*

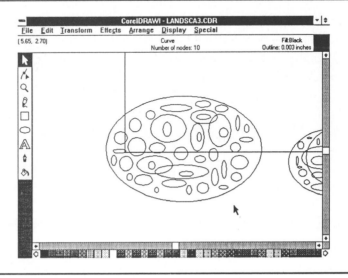

Figure 8-13.   *Magnifying the area around the leftmost bush*

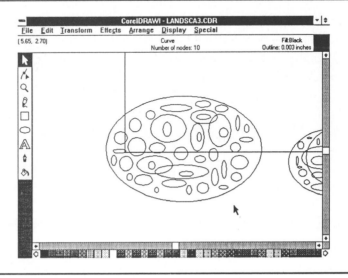

Figure 8-14. *LANDSCA3.CDR after moving the multiple-object bush*

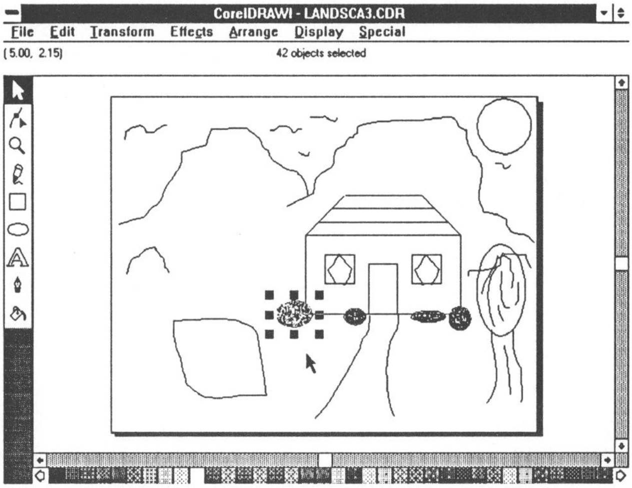

Moving at a 90-Degree Angle

The techniques you have learned so far in this chapter apply to moving objects in any direction. But what if the nature of your drawing requires that you move objects straight up or down or directly to the right or left? You could, of course, use the coordinates information in the status line to reposition the object precisely. But CorelDRAW! also offers you a more intuitive method of moving objects at an exact 90-degree angle using (CTRL). This is a convenient method for obtaining precision without slowing your drawing pace. Perform the following exercise to practice constraining the movement of objects vertically or horizontally.

1. With the LANDSCA4.CDR file still displayed, select one of the birds at the top of the picture.

2. Press and hold (CTRL) and then drag the bird to the right. Even if you don't have a steady hand, the bird remains at exactly the same horizontal level of the picture. The information on the status line

verifies the steadiness of your movement: both the *dy* indicator and the angle indicator remain at zero, as in the following illustration:

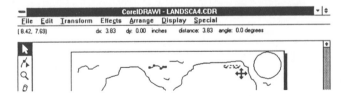

Release the mouse button first and then release (CTRL) to reposition the bird at the new location. If you release (CTRL) first, the selected object is no longer constrained and can move up or down relative to the starting point.

3. Press and hold (CTRL) and the mouse button a second time. This time, drag the bird to the left of its current location. Again, the bird remains at the same horizontal level and the *dy* indicator remains at zero. This time the angle indicator displays 180 degrees:

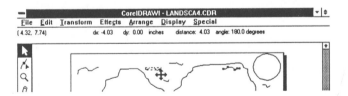

Release the mouse button and (CTRL) when you reach a satisfactory location.

4. Press and hold (CTRL) and the mouse button again and drag the bird directly downward. This time, the *dx* indicator remains at zero, and the angle indicator displays –90 degrees:

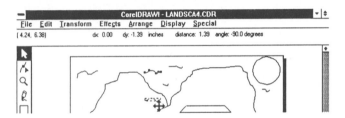

Release the mouse button and then (CTRL) to reposition the bird at the new vertical location. If you accidentally release (CTRL) first, the selected object is not constrained, and you can move it both horizontally and vertically relative to the original location.

5. Continue to depress both (CTRL) and the mouse button and drag the bird directly upward. The *dx* indicator remains at zero, but the angle indicator reads 90 degrees:

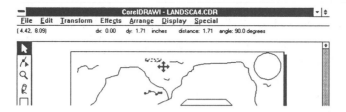

6. Continue practicing this technique with other objects in the picture. When you are finished, select New from the File menu but do not save any changes.

Moving Objects with the Keyboard (Nudge)

As you moved objects in the preceding exercises, you probably found that it was difficult to move an object in very small increments with any precision—most people repeatedly overshoot the mark.

CorelDRAW!, version 2.0 and on, has a feature called *Nudge* which allows you to use the arrow keys on your keyboard to move the selected object(s) by as little as 0.01 inch. The amount by which you move an object each time you press an arrow key and the unit of measure are determined in the Preferences dialog box reached from the Special menu. The default increment is 0.10 inch. Also, since you only have arrow keys pointing in 90-degree increments, nudging is always constrained to 90-degree increments.

1. If you don't have a currently selected object, reselect one of the birds and practice nudging it.

2. Open the Preferences dialog box from the Special menu and verify that the Nudge increment is set to 0.10 inch.

8

3. Press (→) three times and then press (↓) three times. The bird you selected should move to the right and down by 0.3 inch in each direction.

Practice this on your own for several minutes. Nudging can be very useful.

Copying an Object While Moving It

You may recall that while you are moving an object, it seems to remain in place and you appear to be moving only a dotted rectangular substitute. CorelDRAW! lets you take this feature a step further; you can make an identical copy of the object as you move it. The copy remains at the initial location while you move the original to a new location. This handy technique has interesting design possibilities, as you can discover for yourself by performing the next exercise.

1. Select the Grid Setup command in the Display menu, set both the Horizontal and Vertical Grid Frequencies to 2.0 per inch, set the Vertical Origin to 8.5 inches, and turn on Show Grid. Activate the Snap To Grid and Show Rulers commands in the Display menu. Since you just finished working on a picture in Landscape (horizontal) mode, the blank page area is also in this mode. (If you worked on something else in the meantime, change to Landscape mode now, using the Page Setup command in the File menu.)

2. Select the Text tool Ⓐ and then select an insertion point at the 1-inch mark on both the horizontal and vertical rulers. When the Text dialog box appears, type the word **Arrow** in upper- and lowercase in the text entry box. Set the text attributes to Bangkok normal, left-aligned, 100 points. Select OK to exit the dialog box. The word "Arrow" displays in the upper-left corner of the page.

3. Press the spacebar to activate the Select tool and select the text string. Press and hold the mouse button over the outline of any letter and begin to drag downward and to the right. Since you have set grid spacing in large units, the dotted move box travels and snaps in visibly discrete increments.

4. Continue holding down the mouse button. When the upper-left corner of the dotted move box snaps to a point half an inch below and to the right of the starting point (about midway down and across the letter "A"), press and release the ⊙ key in the numeric keypad or click the right mouse button in version 2.01 and on. At the right of the status line, the message "Leave Original" appears, as in Figure 8-15. The ⊙ key in CorelDRAW! is also called the Leave Original key.

5. Release the mouse button. An exact copy of the object appears at the starting point and the original appears at the new location.

6. Make four more copies of the text string in the same way, using the ⊙ key or right mouse button and moving the text object in 1/2- inch increments downward and to the right. You should now have a total of six identical text strings.

7. Change the direction in which you move the text object. Make five additional copies as you move the text object downward and to the left in 1/2-inch increments. When you are finished, 11 identical text strings form an arrowhead shape.

8. If the Preview Selected Only command is active, click on that command again to deselect this feature. Activate the full-screen preview by pressing (F9). Your screen should look like Figure 8-16. This gives you a good view of how your design really looks.

9. Press (F9) to return to your drawing, select Save As from the File menu, and save this picture under the name ARROW1.CDR.

Figure 8-15.   *Copying an object while moving it*

8

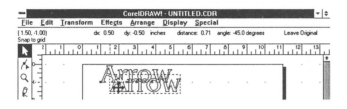

Figure 8-16.   *A preview of the arrow design*

Using the preceding exercise as an example, you can probably think up additional design ideas for copying single or multiple objects as you move them. Go on to the final portion of this chapter to discover ways of changing the relative order of objects within a drawing.

Arranging Objects

In CorelDRAW!, you can change the order of superimposed objects, group and combine separate objects, and align objects relative to one another. All of these techniques are ways of arranging objects on the page. The Arrange menu contains all of the commands you will use in this chapter, plus a few others (such as Fit Text To Path) that are discussed in Chapter 19, "Combining CorelDRAW! Features." The next four sections demonstrate the most common methods of arranging selected objects.

Reordering Superimposed Objects

When you draw a series of objects, CorelDRAW! always places the object you drew *last* on top of all of the other objects. If you could look at the

ARROW1.CDR file in 3D, for example, you would see that the first text string you created is beneath all of the others you subsequently copied.

You can change the order of objects at any time by applying one of the first five commands in the Arrange menu—To Front, To Back, Forward One, Back One and Reverse Order—to a selected object or group of objects. The To Front, To Back, Forward One, and Back One commands rearrange the selected objects *relative to* the other objects on the page, but they do not rearrange objects within a selected group. The Reverse Order command, on the other hand, rearranges the objects *within* a selected group, but it does not alter the relationship between the selected objects and the other objects in the picture. Practice working with these commands now, using the sample file PARTY.CDR that came with your software.

1. Select the Open command from the File menu and open the file PARTY.CDR.

2. Press (SHIFT)-(F9) to activate the preview window and display the object in color.

3. Press (F2) to select the Zoom-In tool and magnify just the center, "PARTYTIME," portion of the image. The preview window also redisplays automatically, but the aspect ratio in both windows is inappropriate for the magnification you have chosen.

4. Drag the preview window down below the halfway point on the screen to display it underneath the editing window. Now both windows should display a close-up of "PARTYTIME" in horizontal format, as in Figure 8-17.

5. In the editing window, select the word "PARTYTIME." When it's selected, you'll see it's a group of 23 objects.

6. Pull down the Arrange menu and select the To Back command. The entire group of selected objects disappears behind the background objects, as shown in Figure 8-18. When you apply this command to a group of objects, however, the relative order of the objects *within* the group does not change.

7. With the same group of objects still selected, select the To Front command in the Arrange menu. Now the objects reappear in their original order, in front of the background objects.

8

Figure 8-17.   *"PARTYTIME" and preview window in horizontal format*

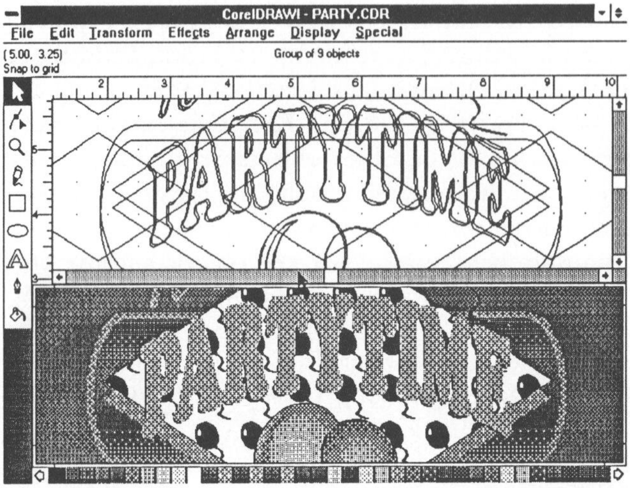

Figure 8-18.   *Using the To Back command on selected objects*

8. Leave these objects selected and select the Back One command from the Arrange menu. This command moves the selected objects back behind the first layer beneath them. As the preview redraws, you can see each layer appear. The stylized rectangles appear last of all as shown in Figure 8-19.

9. Select the Forward One command to return the objects to their original order on the screen. Leave this drawing on the screen for the next exercise.

Grouping and Ungrouping Objects

Selecting multiple objects with the marquee or (SHIFT) key is fine if you want to apply certain commands or operations to them on a one-time basis only. However, most drawings contain subsets of objects that belong together, such as the elements of a logo on a business card. If you want the same set of objects to form a single entity at all times, consider *grouping* them instead of merely selecting them.

Figure 8-19.   *Using the Back One command on selected objects*

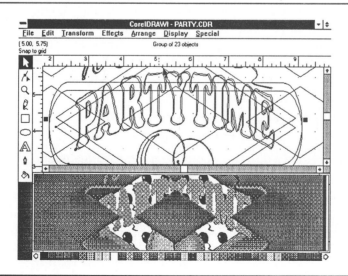

To group multiple objects, you first select them and then apply the Group command in the Arrange menu. Thereafter, the group responds to any operation collectively. You can move, align, color, and outline them together, without individually selecting each component of the group. However, CorelDRAW! still "knows" that the component objects have separate identities. As a result, you cannot apply the Reverse Order command to a group or reshape the group using the Shaping tool. You can also create groups within groups, and then use the Ungroup command to break them down into their component objects again.

Continue working with the PARTY.CDR file to become familiar with the basics of grouping and ungrouping objects.

1. Drag the preview window to the right and rearrange the preview and editing windows into a side-by-side format. Most of the page should be visible now.

2. The group made up of the word "PARTYTIME" should still be selected. The status line should display the message "Group of 23 objects selected."

3. Select the Ungroup command in the Arrange menu. The status line message changes immediately from "Group of 23 objects selected" to "23 objects selected," as shown in Figure 8-20.

4. Select the Reverse Order command from the Arrange menu. The 23 objects that used to form the group are now reversed in order— what was on the top is now on the bottom relative to the other 22 items in the group. The rectangles and other background objects that were originally behind the group are still behind the group. The only change is *within* the group.

5. Select the Reverse Order command again from the Arrange menu. The original order returns.

6. Select the Group command from the Arrange menu. The message in the status line changes back to "Group of 23 items selected."

7. Press and hold the mouse button at any point along the outline of any of the letters in "PARTYTIME" and drag the mouse with the selected objects to the bottom of the screen. The entire group moves

Figure 8-20.   *Grouping multiple objects*

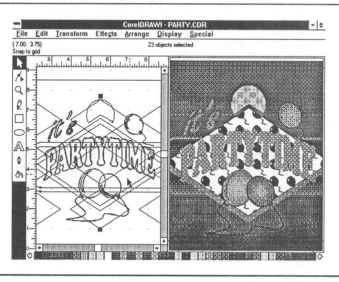

together and relocates when you release the mouse button as shown in Figure 8-21.

8. Practice moving the group around, ungrouping, forming new groups, rearranging the layers, and moving various objects in relation to one another.

   Before and after grouping objects and text strings, look at the menus to see how grouping affects which commands you can and cannot select.

9. When you are done, select New from the File menu to clear the screen before proceeding. Do not save any changes to this picture.

Combining and Breaking Objects Apart

The Arrange menu contains two sets of commands that seem almost identical in content, but are actually two different operations: Group/Un-

Figure 8-21.   *Moving the entire foreground group*

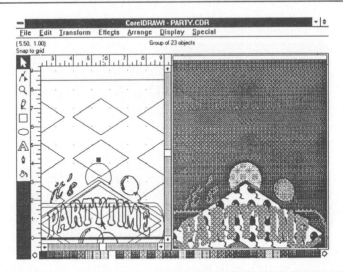

group and Combine/Break Apart. Combining objects differs from grouping them in several complex respects that are beyond the scope of the current chapter; you will gain more experience with the Combine command in Chapter 19. In general, however, you use Combine in the following situations:

- When you want multiple objects to *become* a single object that you can reshape with the Shaping tool

- When the objects contain many nodes and curves and you want to reduce the total amount of memory they consume

- When you want to create special effects such as transparent masks, behind which you can place other objects.

In these situations, simply grouping objects would not yield the desired results.

Later chapters contain several examples of creative uses for the Combine command. There is one interesting use of Combine, however, that you can practice in this chapter. Recall that when you first activated the preview window in Chapter 7, you couldn't distinguish the component objects of the

TEACUP2.CDR file because they all contained a default fill of black. If you combine objects with other objects contained within them, however, the net result is a reverse video effect that makes alternating objects transparent and creates contrast. For a clearer understanding of how this works, try the following exercise.

1. Open the TEACUP2.CDR file, activate the preview window, and zoom in on the area immediately surrounding the "handle" of the cup, as shown in Figure 8-22. The preview window displays a solid black mass because you haven't yet applied different fill colors or outlines to separate objects.

2. Select both the larger rectangle that forms the outline of the handle and the inner rectangle. Use either the marquee or the (SHIFT) key method. When you are done, the status line should say "2 objects selected."

3. Select the Combine command from the Arrange menu. The inside of the inner rectangle becomes transparent, as shown in Figure 8-23. This "special effect" comes about because the Combine command causes all overlapping areas in a graphic to appear transparent. Notice that the status line now refers to the combined object as a single curve object.

4. Zoom out to full-page view. Because of the hollow areas you created when you selected the Combine command, you can now distinguish the handle from the rest of the cup.

5. Save this file under the new name TEACUP3.CDR.

6. Select the newly combined handle if it is not still selected, and then select the Break Apart command from the Arrange menu. All objects revert to their previous state and become black again.

7. Clear the screen using the New command in the File menu. Do not save any changes.

Aligning Objects

Earlier in this chapter, you saw how you can move objects precisely using the (CTRL) key as a substitute for the grid. The Align command in the Arrange

8

Figure 8-22.   *Magnifying the handle of the teacup*

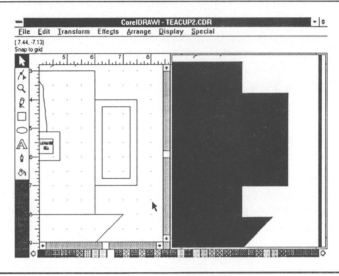

Figure 8-23.   *Using the Combine command to create a hollow inner region*

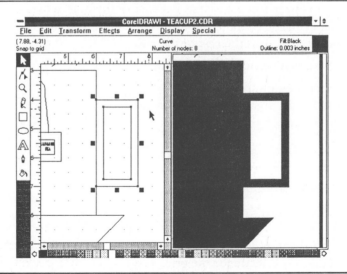

menu offers you another quick and easy method for aligning selected objects without having to spend all of your drawing time measuring. To align objects, you simply select the objects, click on the Align command, and then adjust the horizontal and vertical alignment settings in the Align dialog box.

You could try to memorize the abstract effects of all 15 possible settings, but experiencing those settings for yourself might be more meaningful. In the following exercise, you will create the surface of a billiard table complete with six pockets, combine all the elements of the table into one object, and then add a billiard ball and apply various alignment settings to the ball and the table.

1. Start with the page in Landscape orientation with the rulers and grid displayed, the Snap To Grid turned on, and both the horizontal and vertical grids set to 16 per inch. Select the Rectangle tool and draw a rectangle 9 inches wide and 4 inches deep. This rectangle represents the surface of the billiard table.

2. Magnify the area of the page that contains the rectangle, select the Pencil tool, and draw six billiard "pockets," as shown in Figure 8-24. You can draw the pockets either as curved or multisegment lines, as you wish.

If you want to draw the billiard pockets as curves, set Freehand tracking in the Preference dialog box to 10 pixels and then magnify each area as you draw a pocket in it. The smaller the area in which you are drawing, the smoother your curves become. Zoom out when you have finished drawing the fine details.

Tip

3. Activate the Select tool and draw a marquee around the billiard table to select both the table and the pockets and then apply the Combine command in the Arrange menu. This combines the pockets and the table surface into a single object to prevent accidental realignment of the pockets later on in this exercise.

4. Select the Ellipse tool, press and hold (CTRL), and draw a perfectly circular "ball" in the center of the table.

5. Press the (SPACEBAR) to switch to the Select tool and select the ball, next select the table, and then select the Align command in the Arrange menu. The Align dialog box in Figure 8-25 appears. The dialog box contains two rows of option buttons; the settings in the

8

Figure 8-24.   *A billiard "table" with six "pockets"*

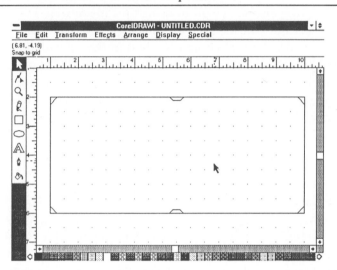

top row pertain to the relative *horizontal* alignment of the selected objects, while the settings in the bottom row pertain to their relative *vertical* alignment. You can set horizontal and vertical alignment independently of each other or mix them, for a total of 15 possible settings. When multiple objects are selected and you choose the Horizontal Left, Horizontal Right, Vertical Top, or Vertical Bottom

Figure 8-25.   *The Align dialog box*

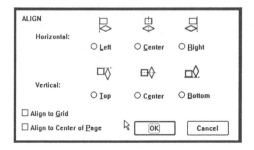

alignment option, CorelDRAW! repositions all but one of the objects. The object *last selected* remains in place. All other objects are moved to carry out the desired alignment. When you select Horizontal Center or Vertical Center alignment, however, CorelDRAW! repositions all of the selected objects, unless one of them is already in the desired location.

6. Select Horizontal Left and then click on the OK command button. The billiard ball reappears in position (1) in Figure 8-26, aligned to the left edge of the table.

   If your screen does not look like Figure 8-26—you can see only half of your table, your table moved, and the ball stayed stationary—then you selected your table first and the ball last. The last object selected stays stationary and previously selected items are moved the first time you do an alignment.

7. Select the Align command repeatedly and choose each of the numbered settings in the following list, one at a time. As you select each setting, check the location of the billiard ball against the corresponding callout numbers in Figure 8-26. Six of the following settings will cause your ball to "go" into one of the billiard table pockets.

   (1)   Horizontal Left
   (2)   Horizontal Center
   (3)   Horizontal Right
   (4)   Vertical Top
   (5)   Vertical Center
   (6)   Vertical Bottom
   (7)   Horizontal Left–Vertical Top
   (8)   Horizontal Left–Vertical Center
   (9)   Horizontal Left–Vertical Bottom
   (10)   Horizontal Center–Vertical Top
   (11)   Horizontal Center–Vertical Center
   (12)   Horizontal Center–Vertical Bottom
   (13)   Horizontal Right–Vertical Top
   (14)   Horizontal Right–Vertical Center
   (15)   Horizontal Right–Vertical Bottom

8

Figure 8-26.   *Results of Align dialog box settings*

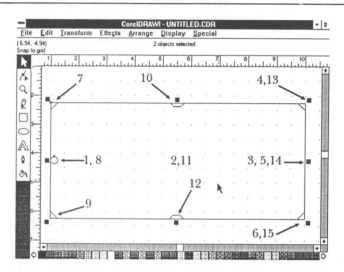

If you do the above alignments without reselecting the ball and the table, you will notice that the first time you do the alignment to the horizontal left, the ball moved as you would expect. The second alignment, the table moved, the third time, the ball moved again and so on, switching back and forth between objects. If you want the table to remain stationary, you must reselect first the ball and then the table before each pair of alignments.

The Align dialog box has two additional options, Align to Grid and Align to Center of Page. When used, you want to set either of these options before setting the horizontal and/or vertical alignments. Try both of these options now.

1. Open the Align dialog box and click on Align to Center of Page. Notice that the Center Horizontal and Center Vertical alignment have also been selected as a default. Click on OK. The ball returns to the center of the table and both objects are positioned in the center of the page as they were when you started this exercise.

2. Again select Align to Center of Page from the Align dialog box. Then click on Left Horizontal and Top Vertical and click on OK. The ball

moves to the upper-left corner of the table and the upper-left corner of the table moves to the center of the page as shown in Figure 8-27.

In Align to Center of Page, the objects first position themselves in accordance with the Horizontal and Vertical alignment instructions, and then the common point of alignment is positioned in the center of the page.

1. Click on anything other than the ball or the table to deselect them both, then click on the table to select only it.

2. In the Grid Setup dialog box reached from the Display menu, set both the Horizontal and Vertical Grid Frequencies to 2.

3. Using the arrow keys, nudge the table so that it is away from grid lines in both directions.

4. Select Align to Grid in the Align dialog box, click on Left Horizontal and Top Vertical, and click on OK. The table will move to the nearest grid point that is up and to the left of the table's original position.

Figure 8-27.   *Upper-left corner aligned to center of page*

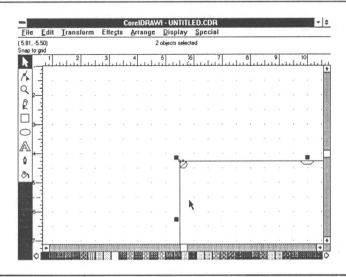

8

The Align to Grid command does not position objects in relation to each other but rather it individually aligns objects (all that are selected) in relation to the nearest grid point in the direction specified by the horizontal and vertical alignment commands.

Experiment on your own, perhaps with other objects in drawings you have already created. Other objects may align in a slightly different way, depending on the order in which you select alignment settings.

By now, you have had an opportunity to practice all of the functions of the Select tool that do not require you to change the size or structure of selected objects. In Chapter 9, "Transforming Objects," you will explore the transformation mode of the Select tool and learn to stretch, scale, rotate, skew, and mirror a selected object or group of objects.

9

Transforming Objects

In Chapter 8, you learned how to use the Select tool to select, move, and arrange objects. In this chapter, you will use the Select tool to *transform* the size or shape of selected objects.

When you transform an object with the Select tool, you do not alter its fundamental shape; a rectangle continues to have four corners and an ellipse remains an oval. (This is not the case when you *reshape* an object using the Shaping tool, which you will learn about in Chapters 10 and 11.) The five basic transformation techniques you will learn in this chapter enable you to stretch, scale, mirror, rotate, and skew an object in any direction. You will also learn how to retain a copy of the original object, repeat transformations automatically, and return an object to its original format even if you have transformed it several times.

The exercises in this chapter introduce not only the basic skills that make up the art of transformation, but also the alternative ways you can practice them. CorelDRAW! lets you customize the way you work when transforming objects. If you like to work interactively, you can carry out these functions using the mouse and keyboard alone. For a little extra guidance, you can look to the status line and rulers. And, if you have to render a technical illustration that requires absolute precision, you can specify transformations using the commands and dialog boxes in the Transform menu.

Throughout most of this chapter, you will practice each skill using a sample text string that you create in the following section. However, the stretch, scale, rotate, and skew functions of CorelDRAW! work exactly the same way with multiple selected objects as with single ones. In later exercises, you can practice combining transformation operations with other skills you have learned in previous chapters.

Stretching and Mirroring an Object

As you discovered in Chapter 8, a rectangular highlighting box, made up of eight black boundary markers, surrounds an object when you select it. These boundary markers, shown in Figure 9-1, have special functions in CorelDRAW!; you use them to stretch and scale objects. When you *stretch* an object, you change its *aspect ratio* (the proportion of its width to its height), because you lengthen or shorten it in one direction only. When you *scale* an object, you change the object's length and width at the same time, so the aspect ratio remains the same. To stretch an object, you must drag one of the four *middle* boundary markers, as shown in Figure 9-1. To scale an object, you drag one of the four boundary markers in the *corners* of the highlighting box.

This section covers all of the available techniques for stretching objects. You have the additional option of creating a mirror image or making a copy of the original object as you stretch it. The exercises in this section introduce you to both the interactive and menu-assisted methods for stretching, mirroring, and copying objects.

If you prefer to work interactively, bypassing menu commands and dialog boxes, you can stretch a selected object using the mouse and keyboard alone. You do not sacrifice precision when you work this way, for the status line assists you in setting precise values as you stretch an object. Practice stretching a text string interactively in the following sections.

Figure 9-1.   *A selected text object showing boundary markers*

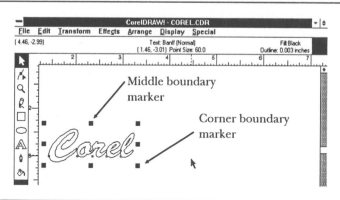

Stretching Horizontally

You can stretch an object in either a horizontal or vertical direction. In the following exercise, you will create a text string and stretch it toward the right.

1. Make sure your page is in portrait format before you begin. If it is not, choose the Page Setup command from the File menu and select the Portrait and letter option buttons.

2. Select the Magnification tool [Q] and choose 1:1 from the fly-out menu. Turn on the Show Rulers command and make sure that the Snap To Grid command is inactive and Show Grid is turned off.

3. Select the Text tool [A] and select an insertion point at the 1-inch mark on the horizontal ruler and the 5-inch mark on the vertical ruler.

4. When the Text dialog box appears, type **Corel** in the text entry box. Set text attributes to Banff, 60 points, Left justification, and then select OK. The text appears on your screen.

9

5. Select the Save As command from the File menu and type **corel.cdr**.

6. Press the spacebar to activate the Select tool ▣. A highlighting box surrounds the text string immediately, since it was the last object you drew. Your screen should resemble Figure 9-1.

7. Position the cursor directly over the center right boundary marker of the highlighting box. The mouse cursor changes to a crosshair like the one in Figure 9-2.

8. Depress and hold the mouse and drag the boundary marker to the right. The original object seems to stay in the same place, but a dotted rectangular box follows the cursor, which turns into a two-way horizontal arrow as shown in Figure 9-3. As you drag, the status line displays the message: "x scale:" followed by a numeric value and a percent sign. This value tells you by how much you are stretching the selected object in increments of 1/10 of a percentage point.

9. After you have stretched the object to the desired size, release the mouse button. Corel redraws a horizontally stretched version of the original object, like the one in Figure 9-4.

10. Select the Undo command from the Edit menu to return the text string to its original size. The original text string remains selected for the next exercise.

To stretch a selected object to the left instead of to the right, drag the middle boundary marker at the *left* side of the highlighting box. Practice stretching the text string from the left side if you wish, but select Undo after you are finished so that the original text string remains on the screen.

Stretching Vertically

You can also stretch an object in a vertical direction. The mouse cursor and status line information change to reflect the direction of your stretch.

1. Select the "Corel" text string if it is not selected already.

2. Position the mouse cursor directly over the middle top boundary marker of the highlighting box. The mouse cursor changes to a crosshair.

Figure 9-2. *Preparing to stretch a selected object horizontally*

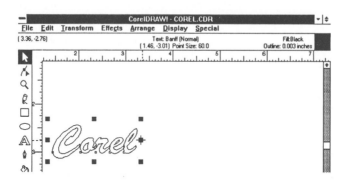

3. Depress and hold the mouse and drag the boundary marker upward. The original object seems to stay in the same place, but a dotted rectangular box follows the cursor, which turns into a two-way vertical arrow, as shown in Figure 9-5. As you drag, the status line displays the message: "y scale:" followed by a numeric value and a percent sign. This value tells you by precisely how much you are stretching the selected object in increments of 0.1%.

Figure 9-3. *Stretching an object horizontally to the right*

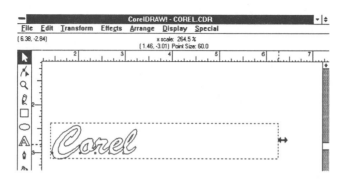

9

Figure 9-4.   *A text object stretched horizontally*

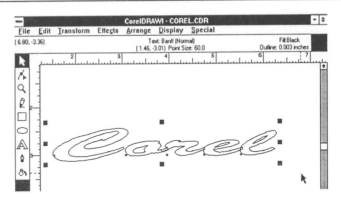

4. After you have stretched the object to the desired size, release the mouse button. Corel redraws a vertically stretched version of the original object.

5. Select the Undo command from the Edit menu to return the text string to its original size.

If you wish, practice stretching the text string downward in a vertical direction. When you are finished, undo your changes to the original object and then proceed with the next exercise.

Stretching in Increments of 100%

In previous chapters, you saw how to use (CTRL) to constrain your drawing or moving operations to fixed increments or angles. The same holds true when you are stretching a selected object. To stretch an object in fixed increments of 100%, press and hold (CTRL) as you drag the boundary marker in the desired direction. The status line keeps track of the increments in which you are stretching the object. As always, remember to release the mouse button *before* you release (CTRL), or the object may not stretch in exact

Figure 9-5. *Stretching an object vertically and upward*

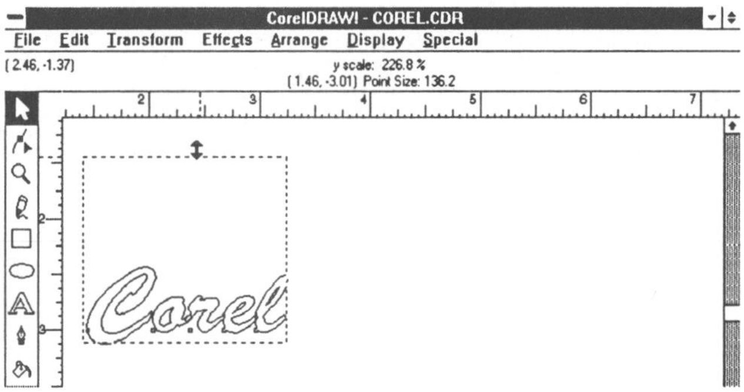

increments. In the following exercise, you will triple the width of the original object using (CTRL).

1. Select the text string if it is not selected already.

2. Press and hold (CTRL) and then drag the middle-right boundary marker to the right. Notice that the dotted rectangular outline does not follow the two-way arrow cursor continuously; instead, it "snaps" outward only when you have doubled the width of the object.

3. When the status line displays the message, "x scale: 300.0%" as shown in Figure 9-6, release the mouse button first and then (CTRL). The text string redisplays at triple its original width.

4. Select the Undo command from the Edit menu to revert to the original unstretched object.

Retaining a Copy of the Original Object

A useful design technique is to make a copy of the original object as you stretch it, so that both the original and the stretched objects appear on the screen. To retain a copy of the original object, just press the (.) key or click the right mouse button once as soon as you begin the stretching, when the outline box appears.

9

Figure 9-6.   _A horizontal stretch constrained to 300% original size_

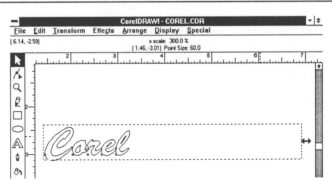

You can also retain a copy of the original object when using (CTRL). Try this technique now:

1. Select the text string "Corel" if it is not already selected. Position the mouse cursor over the bottom middle boundary marker and begin to drag this marker downward.

2. As soon as the dotted outline box appears, press the (·) key on your numeric keypad or press the right mouse button once. The message "Leave Original" appears at the right side of the status line.

3. Press and hold (CTRL) and continue to drag the bottom middle boundary marker downward until the status line reads "y scale: 200.0%."

4. Release the mouse button and then (CTRL). The screen displays both the original and stretched object, as in Figure 9-7.

5. Undo your changes to the original text string before continuing.

If the stretched object does not appear in the correct proportions, you either failed to press and hold (CTRL), or you released (CTRL) before releasing the mouse button. Keep practicing until you feel comfortable with the technique, but remember to undo your changes. In the next exercise, you will create mirror images of both the original and stretched text strings.

Figure 9-7.   *Retaining a copy of the original object while stretching it*

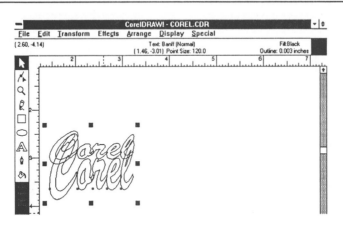

Creating a Mirror Image

Using the middle boundary markers on the highlighting box, you can create a horizontal or vertical mirror image of an object. You have several choices of technique, depending on your needs. If, for example, you choose to retain a copy of the original object, you need to use the (.) key or click the right mouse button. If you choose to make the size of the mirror image an exact multiple of the original, you need to use (CTRL). You can just as easily decide not to copy the original object, or make the mirrored object a custom size. In every case, however, you will drag the *opposite* center boundary marker until it "flips" in the direction in which you want the mirror image to appear.

The following exercise assumes that you want to create a perfect horizontal mirror image of an object, like the one in Figure 9-8. In this figure, the original object is retained but neither the original nor the mirrored object is stretched. At the end of the exercise are suggestions for obtaining other results.

1. Select the text string "Corel" if it isn't selected already.

2. Position the mouse cursor over the left middle boundary marker and begin to drag this marker to the right.

9

Figure 9-8.   *Retaining a copy of the original object while mirroring it*

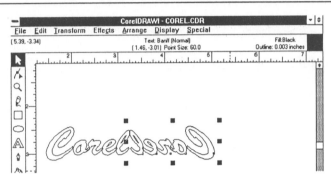

3. As soon as the dotted outline box appears, press the ⊙ key on your numeric keypad or click the right mouse button once. The message "Leave Original" appears at the right side of the status line.

4. Press and hold (CTRL) and continue to drag the marker to the right. The (CTRL) key ensures that the size of the mirrored object will be an exact multiple of the original, in this case the identical size (100%).

5. When the dotted outline box "snaps" beside the original object and the status line reads "x scale: -100.0%," as in Figure 9-9, release the mouse button and then (CTRL). CorelDRAW! redraws the screen showing both the original and the mirrored object, as in Figure 9-8. The mirrored object is selected. If your text strings look different, select Undo and try the exercise again.

6. Press (ALT)-(BACKSPACE) for Undo and to return the text string to its original unmirrored state.

You can vary this exercise to achieve different results. For example, to create a vertical mirror image that appears beneath the object, drag the upper middle boundary marker downward. To make the mirror image double or triple the size of the original, keep stretching the mirror object using (CTRL). To make the mirror image a custom size, just drag the boundary marker *without* using (CTRL). If you want to create a mirror image only, without retaining the original object, do not use the ⊙ key or the right mouse button.

Figure 9-9. *Creating a perfect horizontal mirror image of an object*

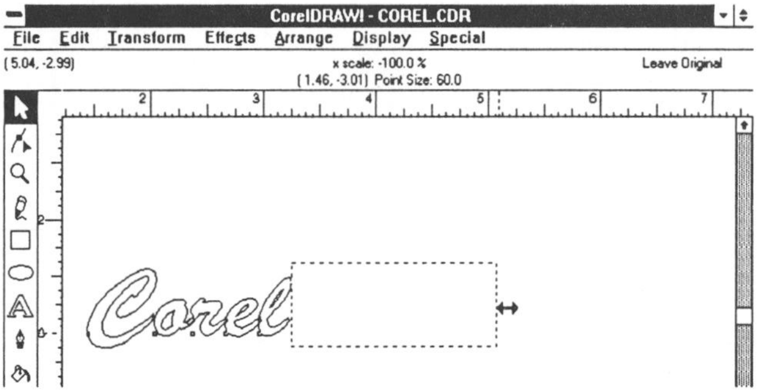

If you want to create a mirror image appearing at a diagonal to the original object, you first need to be familiar with how to scale an object. See the section "Scaling an Object" later in this chapter for instructions.

The Stretch & Mirror Command

If you find the use of the mouse and the keyboard controls inconvenient, you can perform all of the possible stretch operations using the Stretch & Mirror command in the Transform menu. The dialog box that opens when you select this command allows you to choose the direction of the stretch, specify the exact amount of stretching, retain a copy of the original object, and create horizontal or vertical mirror images.

Stretching an Object

Take another look at the COREL.CDR file that you created in the first part of this chapter. Then try the following exercise to become familiar with the Stretch & Mirror command.

1. Select the "Corel" text string and then click on the Stretch & Mirror command from the Transform menu. The dialog box shown in Figure 9-10 appears. The controls in the center of the dialog box let you specify the direction and amount of stretch in increments of

9

Figure 9-10.   *The Stretch & Mirror dialog box*

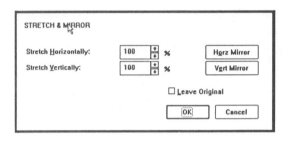

1%. The controls at the right allow you to mirror the object horizontally or vertically. The Leave Original checkbox determines whether
you make a copy of the original object as you stretch or mirror it.

2. Set the numeric value next to Stretch Vertically to 175%, using either
    the scroll arrow or the keyboard, and then select OK. The text string
    has increased in height. Notice, however, that when you stretch an
    object using the Stretch & Mirror dialog box instead of the mouse,
    the stretched object is centered on the same position as the original.
    If you want it to appear in another location, click on the object's
    outline and drag it to the desired location.

3. Select the Clear Transformations command from the Transform
    menu to return the object to its original size. (You can also use
    Undo.)

4. Select the Stretch & Mirror command again, set the Stretch Hori-
    zontally value to 175%, and then select OK. This time, the text string
    increases in width.

5. Clear the current transformation by selecting the Clear Transforma-
    tions command in the Transform menu. Then select Stretch &
    Mirror again. This time, you will constrain the stretch of the image
    to an exact multiple of the original, as you did using (CTRL) and the
    mouse button.

6. Set the Stretch Vertically value to 300% and then click on the Leave Original checkbox to retain a copy of the original object.

7. Select OK to exit the dialog box. CorelDRAW! redisplays the original object against a vertically stretched image three times the size of the original. Notice that when you use the Stretch & Mirror dialog box for these operations, the stretched object is superimposed on the original and both objects share a common center point as shown in Figure 9-11. If you want the stretched object to appear above, below or to the side of the original, you must drag its outline to the desired location.

8. To erase the transformed copy of the object so that only the unaltered original remains, select the Undo command from the Edit menu.

If you desire to erase the copy of the original object after a transformation, use the Undo command rather than the Clear Transformations command. If you use the Clear Transformations command, the transformed object on the top layer is not erased, but instead becomes an exact copy of the original. The transformation is cleared, but not the object itself. As a result, what looks like one object on the screen is actually two, superimposed, objects.

Caution

Figure 9-11. *300% vertical transformation sharing same center with original*

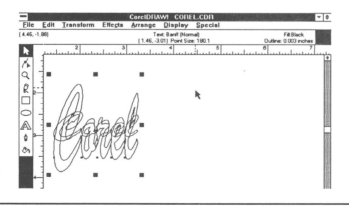

9

Mirroring an Object

The following exercise shows you how to create a vertical or horizontal mirror image using the Stretch & Mirror command instead of the mouse and keyboard. Once you create a mirror image, you can choose whether or not to retain a copy of the original object. You should continue working in actual size viewing magnification for this exercise.

1. With the text string in the COREL.CDR file selected, select the Stretch & Mirror command from the Transform menu.

2. Click on the Vert Mirror command button in the Stretch & Mirror dialog box. Notice that the value next to Stretch Vertically becomes a negative number automatically. Leave this value at –100%.

3. If a checkmark appears in the Leave Original checkbox, click on the checkbox again to remove it. Then select OK to exit the dialog box. A vertical mirror image of the object replaces the original, as shown in Figure 9-12.

4. Select Clear Transformations to return the object to its original state.

5. Select the Stretch & Mirror command again, but this time click on the Horz Mirror command button. Notice that the Stretch Horizontally value becomes a negative number automatically.

6. Select OK to exit the dialog box. A horizontal mirror image of the original text appears.

7. Select Clear Transformations to return the image to its original state.

You can customize the settings in the dialog box to achieve different results. If you want to merge a copy of the original object with the mirrored version, for example, just click on the Leave Original checkbox. If you want to make the mirror image larger or smaller than the original, set the Stretch Horizontally value accordingly. Remember that this value must always be a negative number if it is to result in a mirror image.

Keep in mind, too, that when you use the Stretch & Mirror dialog box instead of the mouse to create a mirror image, the mirror image occupies the same position as the original. If you want the mirrored object to appear above, below or to the side of the original, you must drag its outline to the desired location.

Figure 9-12. *A vertical mirror image of the original object*

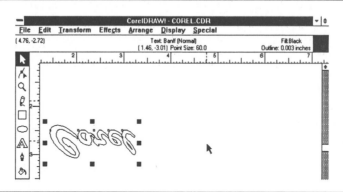

Scaling an Object

As you have just seen, stretching an object involves changing its size in one direction (horizontal or vertical) only. When you *scale* an object, you change its size horizontally and vertically at the same time, thereby maintaining the same proportions and aspect ratio. You can scale an object interactively using the keyboard and mouse, or you can scale an object using the Stretch & Mirror dialog box instead. If you prefer to work more spontaneously, without menus and dialog boxes, you can scale an object using the mouse and keyboard controls. Recall that when you stretch an object, you drag it by one of the *middle* boundary markers. Scaling an object is similar, except that you drag one of the *corner* boundary markers instead.

To practice scaling objects interactively, try this exercise:

1. Open the COREL.CDR file if it is not open already and select the "Corel" text string.

2. Position the mouse cursor directly over one of the corner boundary markers. You can scale from any corner but, for the sake of this exercise, use the lower-right corner marker. The cursor changes to a crosshair, just as when you prepared to stretch an object.

9

3. Drag the lower-right boundary marker diagonally downward. As you drag, the cursor changes to a four-way arrow, similar to the move arrow except that it is rotated diagonally, as in Figure 9-13. The original object appears to stay in the same place, but a dotted outline box follows the scaling cursor. The scaling cursor increases or decreases in size, depending on the direction in which you drag the marker. Figure 9-13 shows an object increasing in scale from the lower-right corner marker. Note that the status line displays the message "scale:" followed by a percentage value. This value tells you precisely how much larger or smaller you are making the object.

4. When the dotted outline box is the size you want the text string to be, release the mouse button. The selected object reappears in a scaled version.

5. Select Clear Transformations in the Transform menu or Undo in the Edit menu to return the object to its original size.

Figure 9-13.   *Dragging the scaling cursor to scale an object*

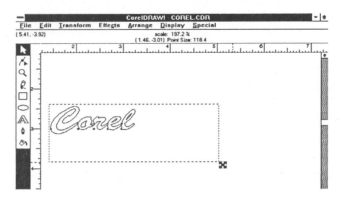

Scaling in Increments of 100%

To scale an object in increments of 100% of its size, all you need to do is press and hold (CTRL) while scaling the object. Just as when you stretched objects using (CTRL), the dotted outline box does not move smoothly but instead "snaps" at each 100% increment. Likewise, the message in the status line changes only when you reach the next 100% increment. Remember to release the mouse button *before* you release (CTRL), or the increments will not be exact.

Keep in mind, too, that an object scaled to 200% of its original size takes up four times the area of the original object, not twice as much, because you are increasing both the height and width of the object by a factor of two.

Retaining a Copy While Scaling

To retain a copy of the object in its original location as you scale it, just press and release the (·) key on the numeric keypad or click the right mouse button as soon as you begin to scale the object. The status line displays the message, "Leave Original," just as when you leave a copy while stretching an object.

Creating a Diagonal Mirror Image

Using the corner boundary markers on the highlighting box, you can create a mirror image that appears at a *diagonal* to the original object. You have several choices of technique, depending on your needs. If you choose to retain a copy of the original object, you need to use the right mouse button or the (·) key. If you choose to make the size of the mirror image an exact multiple of the original, you need to use (CTRL). You can just as easily decide not to copy the original object or to make the mirrored object a custom size. In every case, however, you drag the *opposite* corner boundary marker until it "flips" in the direction in which you want the mirror image to appear.

The following exercise assumes that you are going to create a perfect diagonal mirror image of an object like the one in Figure 9-14. In this figure, the original object remains, but neither the original nor the mirrored object is scaled beyond the original size. At the end of the exercise you will find suggestions for obtaining other results.

1. Select the text string "Corel," if it is not selected already.

9

2. Position the cursor over the boundary marker in the upper-left corner of the highlighting box and begin to drag the marker downward and to the right.

3. As soon as the dotted outline box appears, click the right mouse button or press the (.) key on your numeric keypad once to leave a copy of the original object. The message "Leave Original" appears at the right side of the status line, as shown in Figure 9-14.

4. Press and hold (CTRL) and continue dragging the boundary marker until the dotted outline box "snaps" at a diagonal to the original object and the status line reads "scale: -100.0%." (The (CTRL) key ensures that the size of the mirrored object will be an exact multiple of the original, in this case 100%.)

5. Release the mouse button and then (CTRL). CorelDRAW! redraws the screen showing both the original and the mirrored object, as in Figure 9-15. The mirrored object is selected. If your text strings do not match this figure, try the exercise again.

6. Select Undo from the Edit menu or press (ALT)-(BACKSPACE) to return the object to its original unmirrored state.

Figure 9-14.   *Creating a diagonal mirror image of an object while scaling*

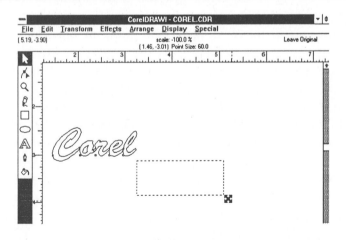

Figure 9-15.   *An original object with a diagonal mirror image*

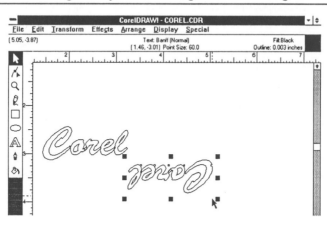

You can vary this exercise to achieve different results. For example, to place the mirror image at the upper-right corner of the original object, drag from the lower-left corner marker upward. To make the mirror image double or triple the size of the original, keep stretching the mirror object using (CTRL). To make the mirror image a custom size, just drag the opposite boundary marker without using (CTRL). If you want to create a mirror image only, without retaining the original object, do not use the right mouse button or the ⊙ key.

Scaling with the Stretch & Mirror Command

If you find the use of the mouse and keyboard controls inconvenient, you can perform all of the scaling operations precisely, using the Stretch & Mirror command in the Transform menu. You can specify the amount of scaling desired, retain a copy of the original object, and create mirror images that appear at a diagonal to the original. Work through the following exercise to become familiar with using the Stretch & Mirror command to scale an object.

9

1. With the COREL.CDR file open and in an actual size viewing magnification, select the "Corel" text string, and then select the Stretch & Mirror command from the Transform menu.

2. To scale an object, you need to set both the Stretch Horizontally and the Stretch Vertically values to the same number. Set both of these values to 150%, using either the scroll arrow or the keyboard.

3. Make certain that a checkmark does not appear in the Leave Original checkbox, and then select OK. The text string has increased in both height and width. Notice, however, that a scaled object created with the Stretch & Mirror command appears in the same location as the original and has the same center point. If you want the scaled object to appear elsewhere, move it to the desired location.

4. Select the Clear Transformations command from the Transform menu to return the object to its original size.

Retaining a Copy While Using Stretch & Mirror

It is easy to make a copy of the original object from the Stretch & Mirror dialog box. Simply place a checkmark in the Leave Original checkbox before you exit the dialog box.

1. Select the text string "Corel" and then select the Stretch & Mirror command. This time, you will constrain the stretch of the image to an exact multiple of the original, as you did using (CTRL) and the mouse. You will also leave a copy of the original object in its original location.

2. Set the Stretch Vertically and Stretch Horizontally values to 200% and then click on the Leave Original checkbox to retain a copy of the original object.

3. Select OK to exit the dialog box. CorelDRAW! redisplays the original object along with a scaled text string four times the size of the original. Again, notice that when you copy and scale an object using the Stretch & Mirror dialog box, the scaled object is superimposed on the original and the two objects share a common center

point. If you want the stretched object to appear elsewhere, you must move it by dragging its outline.

4. To erase the transformed copy of the object so that only the unaltered original remains, select the Undo command from the Edit menu. If you have moved the copy of the original, select it and press (DEL) to clear it.

Stretching and Scaling from the Center

In the previous exercises of stretching and scaling using the mouse, the object was modified in one dimension (stretching) or two dimensions (scaling) from a fixed opposite side or sides. In other words, when you dragged the right side of the object to the right, the left side remained fixed and was in the same position as was the right side of the modified object. Similarly, when you dragged the lower-right corner down and to the right, the top and left sides remained fixed and had the same horizontal and vertical position as the modified object.

When you used the Stretch & Mirror dialog box and modified an object in one or two dimensions, the opposite sides moved proportionally. That is, with the dialog box, the object was being modified from a fixed center point instead of a fixed side or sides. When you changed the horizontal and vertical percentages, all four sides changed, leaving the same center point as the original object.

CorelDRAW!, in versions 2 and above, has the capability to stretch and scale an object from the center point with the mouse by pressing (SHIFT) while dragging. This is the same as drawing an ellipse or rectangle from the center by pressing (SHIFT) while dragging with the ellipse or rectangle tool.

Recall how you stretched and scaled with the mouse originally and see how this changes when you press (SHIFT):

1. The COREL.CDR text object should be selected on your page in an actual size view.

2. As you did in an earlier exercise, drag the middle boundary marker on the right side to the right several inches. Notice how the left side remains fixed. Release the mouse button and press (ALT)-(BACKSPACE) to undo the modification with the Undo command.

9

3. Press and hold (SHIFT) while dragging the right middle boundary marker to the right an inch or so. Notice how the left side now moves a proportionate amount—the left and right sides are moving outward in equal amounts. Release the mouse button and press (ALT)-(BACKSPACE) to undo the modification.

4. Again, as you did before, drag the lower-right corner boundary marker down and to the right several inches. Notice how the left and top sides remain fixed. Release the mouse button and press (ALT)-(BACKSPACE) to undo the modification.

5. Press and hold (SHIFT) while dragging the lower-right corner boundary marker down and to the right an inch or so. Notice how the top and left sides are now moving proportionately with the right and bottom sides. Release the mouse button and press (ALT)-(BACKSPACE) to undo the modification.

The ability to stretch or scale an object from the center allows you to more easily fill a regular enclosing space.

Rotating an Object

When you click on an object once using the Select tool, you can move, arrange, stretch, or scale it. In addition, the Select tool can *rotate* and *skew* an object. Rotating involves turning an object in a clockwise or counterclockwise direction, at an angle that you define. When you skew an object, on the other hand, you slant it toward the right, left, top, or bottom in order to create distortion or three-dimensional effects.

As with stretching and scaling, you can rotate an object interactively, using the mouse and keyboard, or you can use the Rotate & Skew command in the Transform Menu. If you feel more comfortable working with dialog boxes than with the mouse and keyboard, you can select the Rotate & Skew command after clicking on an object only once. To rotate an object interactively, however, you must either click on a selected object a second time, or double-click on an object that you have not yet selected.

Practice entering the interactive rotate/skew mode now, using the text string in the COREL.CDR file.

1. With the COREL.CDR file open and displayed at the Actual Size viewing magnification, click once on the outline of the text string. The normal highlighting box with its eight black boundary markers appears.

2. Click on the outline of the text string a second time. CorelDRAW! replaces the eight boundary markers with eight two-way arrows, as shown in Figure 9-16. You can drag any one of the corner arrows to rotate the object but, for the sake of this exercise, you will work with the upper-right corner arrow.

3. Position the mouse cursor over the two-way arrow in the upper-right corner of the rotate/skew highlighting box. When the cursor becomes a crosshair, press and hold the mouse button and drag the mouse in a counterclockwise direction. As soon as you begin to drag, the mouse cursor changes to an arc with arrows at either end. A dotted outline box representing the text string begins to rotate in a counterclockwise direction, as in Figure 9-17. Notice that the status line displays the angle of rotation as a positive number.

4. Continue to drag the corner highlighting arrow in a counterclockwise direction until you have rotated the object more than 180 degrees. At that point, the status line begins to display a negative number for the angle of rotation, and the number begins to decrease

Figure 9-16. *A selected object in rotate/skew mode*

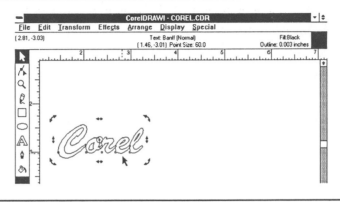

Figure 9-17.   *Rotating an object in a counterclockwise direction*

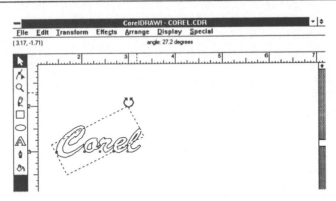

from −180. Use the number on the status line to inform yourself how far you have rotated a selected object.

5. Continue rotating the text object until the number becomes positive again. Release the mouse button when the status line indicates an angle of 17 degrees. CorelDRAW! redisplays the object at the selected angle of rotation, as shown in Figure 9-18.

6. Select the Clear Transformations command from the Transform menu to return the object to its original angle.

7. Drag the highlighting arrow in the upper-right corner again, but in a clockwise direction. The angle indicator on the status line displays a negative number until you rotate the text string more than 180 degrees. At that point, the number becomes positive and begins to decrease from 180 degrees downward.

8. Release the mouse button to redisplay the object at the new angle of rotation.

9. Select the Clear Transformations command from the Transform menu to return the object to its original angle.

Figure 9-18. A selected object after rotation

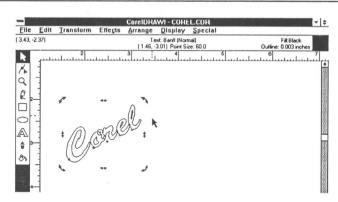

You may sometimes rotate an object several times in succession. The angle of rotation displayed in the status line, however, refers to the amount of the current rotation, not to the cumulative angle.

Note

Continue with the next section to find out how you can constrain rotation of an object to increments of 15-degree angles.

Rotating in Increments of 15 Degrees

As in almost every drawing or editing function of CorelDRAW!, you can use (CTRL) to constrain movement in the rotation of objects. Simply press and hold (CTRL) while dragging a corner arrow of the rotate/skew highlighting box, and the object rotates and "snaps" to successive 15-degree angles. The status line keeps track of the angle of rotation. As always, remember to release the mouse button before you release (CTRL), or you will not constrain the angle of rotation. You will use the constrain feature in the following exercise.

1. Double-click on the text string if it is not selected already or click once on its outline if it is selected. The two-way arrows appear to show that you are in the rotate/skew mode.

2. Position the cursor over the upper-right corner highlighting arrow until the cursor turns into a crosshair. Press and hold the (CTRL) key

9

and the mouse button and drag the highlighting arrow in the desired direction. Notice that the dotted rectangular box does not follow the rotation cursor continuously; instead, it "snaps" each time you reach an angle that is a multiple of 15 degrees.

3. When you reach the desired angle, release the mouse button first, and then release (CTRL). The object redisplays at the new angle of rotation.

4. Select Clear Transformations from the Transform menu to return the object to its original angle.

Retaining a Copy While Rotating

If you like to experiment with design, you may find it useful to make a copy of the original object as you rotate it. Figure 9-19 illustrates one design effect you can achieve easily. This text pinwheel, suitable for desktop publishing applications, was created by rotating a text string in increments of 30 degrees and copying the original each time.

You can also retain a copy of the original object using (CTRL), but this operation requires a bit more coordination. Try this technique now:

1. With the COREL.CDR file open and in an actual size viewing magnification, click on the text string "Corel" if it is already selected, or double-click if it is not selected. The rotate/skew highlighting arrows appear.

2. Position the mouse cursor over the upper-right highlighting arrow marker and begin to drag this marker upward. As soon as the dotted outline box appears, click the right mouse button or press the (·) key on your numeric keypad once to leave a copy of the original.

3. Press and hold (CTRL) and continue dragging the arrow marker upward until the status line reads "angle: 30 degrees."

4. Release the mouse button and then the (CTRL) key. The screen displays both the original and the rotated object, as shown in Figure 9-20.

5. Continue copying and rotating the text strings four more times at the same angle to create the design shown in Figure 9-19. Then undo your changes to the original text string before going further.

Figure 9-19. *A text pinwheel created by repeatedly rotating and retaining a copy of a text string*

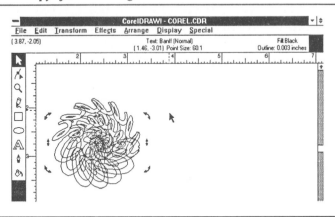

Changing an Object's Rotation

Look at an object on your screen when it is in rotate/skew mode. In the center of the object is a small dot surrounded by a circle. This graphic aid appears every time you activate the rotate/skew mode and represents the

Figure 9-20. *Retaining a copy of the original object while rotating*

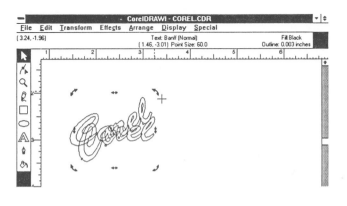

9

center of rotation of an object. The object turns on this axis as you rotate it. The center of rotation does not have to be the center of the object, however. If you want the object to rotate on a different axis, you can alter the center of rotation freely by dragging the center of rotation symbol to the desired location using the mouse. In the following exercise, you will create a simple text design that involves changing the center of a text string's rotation.

1. Select the text string if it is not selected already and move it to the center of the display. Click on its outlines again to access the rotate/skew mode.

2. When the rotate/skew highlighting box appears, position the mouse cursor over the center of rotation symbol until it becomes a cross. Drag the rotation symbol to the upper-right corner of the rotate/skew highlighting box, as shown in Figure 9-21. Then release the mouse button.

3. Position the mouse cursor over any one of the corner highlighting arrows and begin dragging the arrow in a clockwise direction. As

Figure 9-21.   *Relocating an object's center of rotation to a corner of the highlighting box*

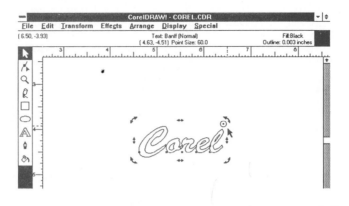

soon as the dotted outline box appears, click the right mouse button or press the ⊙ key on your numeric keypad once to leave a copy of the original. Notice that because you have changed the center of rotation, the text string turns on its end rather than on its center point.

4. Press and hold (CTRL) and continue dragging the marker until the status line shows that you have rotated the text string by –90 degrees.

5. Release the mouse button first, and then (CTRL). Both the original object and the rotated object display at 90-degree angles to one another.

6. Repeat this process two more times, until you have a text design similar to the one in Figure 9-22. To make all the text strings behave as though they were one object, click on the Select All command in

Figure 9-22. *A text design created by rotating and copying an object with an altered center of rotation*

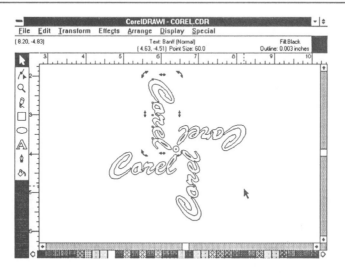

the Edit menu, group the text strings, and then reposition the group to the center of the display.

7. Save this figure as 4CORNERS.CDR.

8. Clear the screen by selecting New from the File menu.

Your new center of rotation does not have to be a highlighting arrow; you can relocate the center anywhere within the highlighting box. But a corner or boundary of the selected object often proves to be a convenient "handle" when you are performing rotations.

Rotating with the Rotate & Skew Command

If you find the use of the keyboard controls inconvenient, you can perform all of the preceding rotation operations with precision using the Rotate & Skew command in the Transform menu. You can select this command regardless of whether the normal highlighting box or the rotate/skew highlighting box is visible around a selected object. Perform the following brief exercise to familiarize yourself with the workings of the Rotate & Skew dialog box.

1. Open the COREL.CDR file and set the viewing magnification to 1:1. Click once on the text string to select it.

2. Select the Rotate & Skew command from the Transform menu. The Rotate & Skew dialog box appears as in Figure 9-23.

3. Enter a number in the numeric entry box next to "Rotation Angle:". You can enter a number either by scrolling in increments of 5 degrees or by clicking on the numeric entry box and typing in a number in increments of 1/10 of a degree. Note that as soon as you enter a number in this box, the Skew Horizontally and Skew Vertically entry boxes become unavailable for selection. You cannot skew and rotate an object at the same time.

4. If desired, click on the Leave Original checkbox to make a copy of the original object as you rotate it.

Figure 9-23.   *The Rotate & Skew dialog box*

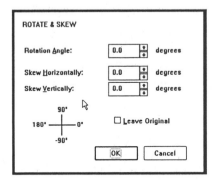

5. Select OK to exit the dialog box and see the results of your settings. When you are finished, select Undo to return the original object to its former angle. Leave this image on the screen for the next exercise.

That's all there is to rotating an object at the angle and axis of your choice. You can leave a copy of the original object while rotating it, just as when you copy an object that you are stretching or scaling. In the next section, you will practice skewing an object to achieve interesting distortion effects.

Skewing an Object

When you *skew* an object, you slant and distort it a horizontal or vertical angle, thus warping its appearance. This technique can be useful for creating three-dimensional or surrealistic effects. As with the other techniques you have learned in this chapter, you can skew an object either interactively or by using the controls in the Rotate & Skew dialog box.

9

1. With the COREL.CDR file open and in an actual size viewing magnification, select the "Corel" text string. Then click a second time anywhere on its outline to enter rotate/skew mode.

2. To begin skewing the object horizontally, position the mouse cursor directly over the upper-middle highlighting arrow and drag it to the right. The mouse cursor changes to two half arrows pointing in opposite directions, and a dotted outline box slants to the right, the direction you are moving your mouse, as shown in Figure 9-24. The status line keeps track of the current angle of horizontal skew.

3. When you reach the desired skewing angle, release the mouse button. CorelDRAW! redisplays the object as you have skewed it, as shown in Figure 9-25.

4. Select Clear Transformations from the Transform menu to return the object to its original unskewed state.

5. Practice different angles of horizontal skewing. You can skew an object up to 75 degrees to the right or left. If you drag one of the middle highlighting arrows along the left or right *side* of the highlighting box, you can skew the object in a vertical direction.

Figure 9-24.   *Skewing an object to the right*

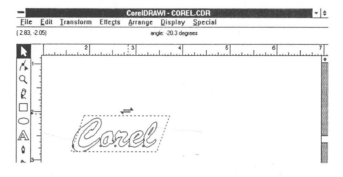

Figure 9-25. *An object skewed horizontally to the right*

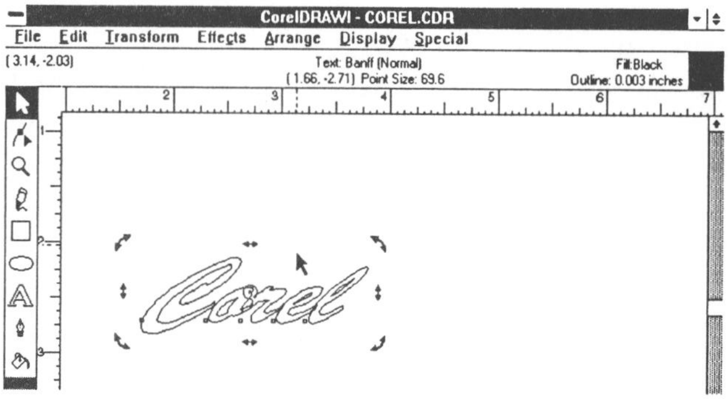

6. When you feel comfortable with basic skewing operations, select Clear Transformations from the Transform menu. Leave the text string on the screen for the next exercise.

Skewing in Increments of 15 Degrees

Once again, you can use (CTRL) to introduce an extra measure of precision to the interactive transformation of objects. When skewing an object, pressing and holding (CTRL) forces the object to skew in increments of 15 degrees. Try using this constraint feature now.

1. Select the text string "Corel" and enter the rotate/skew mode.

2. Position the mouse cursor over the upper-middle highlighting arrow, press and hold (CTRL), and begin dragging the mouse to the right or left as desired. The mouse cursor changes to the skew cursor, and the dotted outline box "snaps" in the desired direction in increments of 15 degrees.

3. When you reach the desired angle, release the mouse button first, and then release (CTRL). If you release (CTRL) first, you might not constrain the skewing operation to a 15-degree increment.

9

4. Select Clear Transformations from the Transform menu to return the skewed object to its original state. Leave the text string on the screen.

Retaining a Copy While Skewing

For an interesting design effect, you can skew an object and then make a copy of the original. As you will see in the following exercise, you can then position the skewed object behind the original to make it seem like a shadow.

1. Select the "Corel" text string and enter rotate/skew mode.

2. Position the mouse cursor over the upper-middle highlighting arrow and begin dragging the arrow to the right. As soon as the dotted outline box appears, press the ⊙ key on your numeric keypad or click the right mouse button to leave a copy of the original.

3. Press and hold (CTRL) and continue dragging the marker until the status line shows a –60-degree skewing angle.

4. Release the mouse button first and then release (CTRL). The skewed object, which is selected automatically, appears on top of the copy of the original, as in Figure 9-26.

5. Select the To Back command from the Arrange menu to position the skewed object behind the unskewed original.

6. You can manipulate the skewed object like any other object. Click once on its outline to toggle back to the select mode, and then scale it to a smaller size by dragging the upper-right corner boundary marker of the highlighting box.

7. Adjust the viewing magnification to fit-in-window and activate the preview window to obtain a WYSIWYG display of the original object and its skewed "shadow." Your preview should look roughly similar to Figure 9-27. When you learn about filling objects in Chapter 15, "Defining Fill Color," you can refine the appearance of skewed background images to create a clearer "shadow" than this one.

8. To remove the transformed copy of the object so that only the unaltered original remains, select the Clear command from the Transform menu. Also, turn off the preview window.

Figure 9-26. *Retaining a copy of an object while skewing*

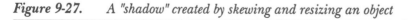

Skewing with the Rotate & Skew Command

If you find the use of keyboard controls inconvenient, you can perform all of the possible skewing operations using the Rotate & Skew command in the Transform menu. You can select this command regardless of whether the

Figure 9-27. *A "shadow" created by skewing and resizing an object*

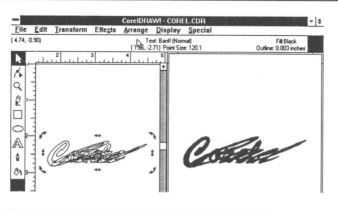

9

normal highlighting box or the rotate/skew highlighting box is visible around a selected object. Perform the following brief exercise to familiarize yourself with using the Rotate & Skew command to skew an object.

1. Open the COREL.CDR file and set the viewing magnification to ⊡. Click once on the text string to select it.

2. Select the Rotate & Skew command from the Transform menu. The Rotate & Skew dialog box appears.

3. First, skew the text object horizontally. Enter a number in the numeric entry box next to "Skew Horizontally:". You can enter a number either by scrolling in increments of 5 degrees or by clicking on the numeric entry box and typing in a number in increments of 1/10 of a degree. Only values between –75 and 75 degrees are valid. You will recall that a positive number results in skewing to the left, while a negative number results in skewing to the right.

4. If desired, click on the Leave Original checkbox to make a copy of the original object as you rotate it.

5. Select OK to exit the dialog box and see the results of your settings. When you are finished, select Undo to return the original object to its former angle (and erase the copy, if you have made one).

6. Select the Rotate & Skew command from the Transform menu once more. This time, enter a number in the numeric entry box next to "Skew Vertically:". You can adjust this value in the same way that you adjusted the "Skew Horizontally:" value in step 3.

7. Select OK to exit the dialog box and see the results of your settings. When you are finished, select Clear Transformations from the Transform menu to return the original object to its former angle.

In the final section of this chapter, you will have the opportunity to combine additional transformation techniques and apply your most recently performed operation to other objects in a drawing.

Repeating a Transformation

CorelDRAW! stores the most recently performed transformation in memory until you quit the current session. You can save design and drawing time by automatically repeating your most recent stretch, scale, rotate, or skew operation on a different object or set of objects. Just remember that the second object, the one on which you wish to repeat the transformation, must exist on the screen *before* you perform the transformation the first time. If you perform a transformation and then create another object and try to repeat that transformation on it, nothing happens. Perform the following brief exercise to see how this feature can work for you.

1. With the COREL.CDR file open and in actual size viewing magnification, select the Ellipse tool ⬭ and draw a long, narrow ellipse next to the "Corel" text string.

2. Press the spacebar to activate the Select tool. Select the "Corel" text string and then scale the text string to 200% using the lower-right corner boundary marker and (CTRL). Leave a copy of the original using the ⊕ key or click the right mouse button, as described earlier in this chapter.

3. Select the ellipse that you drew next to the text string.

4. Select the Repeat command from the Edit menu or press the shortcut keyboard combination (CTRL)-(R). CorelDRAW! scales the ellipse to 200%, leaving a copy of the original, as shown in Figure 9-28. If the objects extend beyond your viewing window, adjust viewing magnification to fit-in-window.

5. Select New from the File menu to clear the screen. Do not save any changes to your work.

9

Figure 9-28.   *Repeating a transformation on a different object*

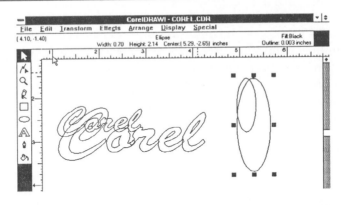

You have seen how stretching, scaling, rotating, and skewing objects can lead to creative ideas for advanced designs. Continue practicing some of the techniques you have learned and see what original ideas you can come up with on your own. Chapters 18 and 19, "Creating Special Effects" and "Combining CorelDRAW! Features," will expand on these and other techniques and provide additional stimulation for your imagination.

10

Shaping Lines, Curves, Rectangles, and Ellipses

The power to reshape any object to the limits of the imagination is at the very heart of CorelDRAW! Using the Shaping tool, you can change any type of object into an image that can showcase your creativity.

The Shaping tool ⬙, the second tool in the CorelDRAW! toolbox, allows you to change the underlying shape of an object. Although the Select tool, in transformation mode, allows you to resize, rotate, or skew an object, it leaves the fundamental shape of the object intact. When you edit an object with the Shaping tool, however, it becomes something quite different from what you originally drew.

You can apply the Shaping tool to all object types: lines and curves, rectangles and squares, ellipses and circles, text, and pixel-based (bitmapped) graphics. Shaping functions for text and bitmapped graphics, however, is part of a broader range of editing functions that apply specifically to those object types. You will find information specifically about shaping text in Chapter 11, "Shaping and Editing Text," and about shaping curves to fit traced bitmaps in Appendix D, "Tracing Bitmapped Images." This chapter covers techniques for shaping lines, curves, rectangles, and ellipses.

About the Shaping Tool

The Shaping tool performs several different functions, depending on the kind of object to which you apply it. You take advantage of the most powerful capabilities of the Shaping tool when you use it to edit curves, but it has specific effects on other object types as well.

When you are working with lines and curves, the Shaping tool is at its most versatile. You can manipulate single curve points (nodes) interactively, move single or multiple curve segments, control the angle of movement, and add or delete curve points in order to exercise greater control over the degree of curvature. You can break apart or join segments of a curve and change one type of node into another. You can even convert curves to straight lines and back again.

When you apply the Shaping tool to rectangles and squares, you can round the corners of a rectangle and turn rotated, stretched, or skewed rectangles into near-ellipses and circles. When you apply the Shaping tool to ellipses and circles, you can create pie-shaped wedges or arcs. If these shaping options for rectangles and ellipses seem limited, you will be pleased to learn that you can convert any object in CorelDRAW! to curves—and then proceed to apply the most advanced shaping techniques to it.

Selecting with the Shaping Tool

You must select an object with the Shaping tool before you can edit it. CorelDRAW! allows you to select only one object with the Shaping tool at a time. Although the Shaping tool affects each type of object in a different way, the basic steps involved in editing are similar with all object types. To select an object for editing,

1. Activate the Shaping tool B by clicking on it. The cursor turns into a thick arrowhead A as soon as you move it away from the toolbox and toward the page area.

2. If the object you want to work with is already selected, its nodes enlarge in size automatically as soon as you select the Shaping tool, and the highlighting box around the object disappears. The number of nodes may vary, depending on the object type and (in the case of curves) the way your hand moved when you drew it. If the object you want to work with is not selected, click on any point of the object's outline with the arrowhead cursor. Enlarged nodes appear on the object, while the status line shows the object type and information about the nodes on the object. If the selected object has multiple nodes, the first node appears larger than the others, as in the example in Figure 10-1. The first node is the one closest to where you started drawing the object. Often this is the farthest to the left on lines and curves, the one at the top left corner in rectangles, and at the topmost point on ellipses.

3. Refer to the chapter that covers your object type for more help on how to edit the shape of that object.

Figure 10-1.   *Selecting an object with the Shaping tool*

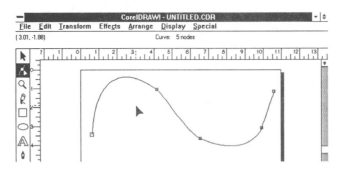

10

If multiple objects are selected when you activate the Shaping tool, CorelDRAW! automatically deselects all of them, and you must select a single object to edit with the Shaping tool. If you try to apply the Shaping tool to grouped objects, the outlines of the objects become dotted and your mouse actions have no effect. The only time you can edit more than one object simultaneously is when you *combine* the objects prior to selecting the Shaping tool. You will see examples of editing combined objects in the "Shaping Lines and Curves" section of this chapter.

To deselect an object that you are editing with the Shaping tool, either click on the outline of a different object, or select another tool from the CorelDRAW! toolbox.

The following sections show you how to use the Shaping tool to edit specific types of objects. These sections follow the order of the drawing tools in the CorelDRAW! toolbox: lines and curves, rectangles, and ellipses.

Shaping Lines and Curves

The Shaping tool is at its most powerful when you use it to edit a curve. Ways in which you can reshape a curve include moving, adding, or deleting nodes, changing node shape, breaking nodes apart or joining them together, and manipulating the control points that define the shape of a curve segment.

You may recall that every object in CorelDRAW! has nodes, which appear when you first draw an object and become enlarged when you select it with the Shaping tool. Nodes on a curve (shown in Figure 10-1) are the points through which a curve passes, and each node is associated with the curve segment that immediately precedes it. The *control points* that appear when you select a single node with the Shaping tool (see Figure 10-5) determine the curvature of the node and of the curve segments on either side of it. You can use the Shaping tool to manipulate both nodes and curves.

Your options for shaping straight lines with the Shaping tool are much more limited than for curves; lines have no angles of curvature and, therefore, no control points that you can manipulate. When you edit a line segment with the Shaping tool, you can only move the nodes or stretch or diminish the length of the line segment. In the course of creating and editing a complex curve object, however, you often need to fuse curve and line segments, change curves into lines, or turn lines into curves. The Shaping tool allows you to do all of these things, and so a discussion of shaping both kinds of freehand objects belongs together.

Selecting a Line or Curve

You must select a line or curve with the Shaping tool before you can begin to manipulate its nodes. The status line provides you with information about the number of nodes in the object.

In the following exercise, you will draw a straight line and a freehand curve and then select each object in turn. Turn off the Snap To Grid option before you begin this exercise.

1. Activate your Magnification tool C and zoom in on the upper half of your page. Then, select the Pencil tool G and draw a straight horizontal line across the top half of the screen, as shown in Figure 10-2.

Figure 10-2.   *Displaying the number of nodes in a curve*

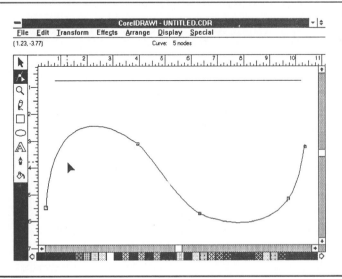

10

2. Below the line, draw a Freehand curve in a horizontal "S" shape. Small nodes appear on the curve.

3. Select the Shaping tool. The cursor turns into an arrowhead, and the S-curve is automatically selected, because it was the last object you drew. The nodes of the S-curve increase in size, and the status line displays the number of the nodes in the curve, as shown in Figure 10-2. The number of nodes in your curve may differ from the number in the figure. Notice that the node farthest to the left is probably larger in size than the others, because it is where you started drawing the curve.

4. To deselect the S-curve and select the line, simply click on any point of the line with the Shaping tool. Only two nodes appear on the line, one at each end. Again, the node farthest to the left is probably larger. The status line displays the message, "Curve: 2 nodes," as shown in Figure 10-3. (As far as the Shaping tool is concerned, every line has the potential of becoming a curve.)

5. Clear the screen before continuing by selecting New from the File menu. Do not save your work.

Figure 10-3.   *Displaying the number of nodes in a line*

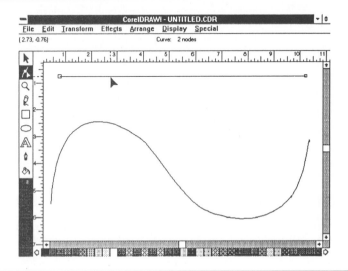

Your next step in shaping a selected line or curve is to select one or more of its nodes. Continue with the next section to explore the choices open to you.

Selecting Nodes of a Line or Curve

Although you can shape only one curve or line at a time, you can select and shape either single or multiple nodes. The shaping options available to you depend on whether you select one node or several. You can reshape a single curve node interactively in one of two ways: by dragging the node itself or by dragging the control points that appear when you select the node. Moving a node stretches and resizes the associated curve segment(s) but does not allow you to change the angle of curvature. Dragging the control points, on the other hand, allows you to change both the angle of curvature at the node and the shape of the associated curve segment(s). When you select multiple nodes, you can move only the nodes, not their control points; as a result, you reshape all of the selected segments in the same way.

In general, you should select single nodes when you need to fine-tune a curve, and multiple nodes when you need to move or reshape several segments in the same way without changing their angle of curvature.

The exercises in the following sections guide you through the available techniques for selecting nodes in preparation for moving or editing them. Along the way, you will become familiar with the different types of nodes that CorelDRAW! generates and how they indicate the shape of a particular curve.

Nodes of a straight line segment are always cusp nodes and contain no control points. They become important only when you begin adding or deleting nodes or changing a line into a curve. You will concentrate on working with curves in the next few sections.

Tip

Selecting and Deselecting Single Nodes and Identifying Node Type

When you click on a single curve node, the status line provides information about the type of node you have selected. There are three node types: cusp, smooth, and symmetrical. Each type of node indicates what will happen

10

when you drag the control points to reshape a curve. In the following exercise, you will practice selecting and deselecting single nodes.

1. Using the Pencil tool, at Actual Size (1:1) magnification, draw a curve object that looks roughly like Figure 10-4. The object should have sharp curves, gentle curves, and some in between. Don't worry if it doesn't look exactly like Figure 10-4.

2. Select the Shaping tool and click anywhere on the outline of the curve object. The status line indicates that this curve object contains 20 nodes (yours may be different).

3. Click on the node farthest to the left on the selected curve object. The node becomes a black-filled square, and two control points, tiny black rectangles connected to the node by dotted lines, pop out, as shown in Figure 10-5. (You will also see a control point extending from each of the nodes on either side of the selected node.) The messages "Selected node: Curve" and "Cusp" appear on the status line. "Cusp" refers to the node type, which you will learn about shortly.

Figure 10-4.   *Magnifying the curve object*

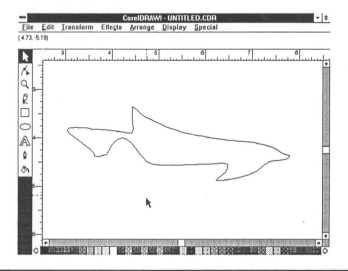

Figure 10-5. *Selecting a single node and displaying control points*

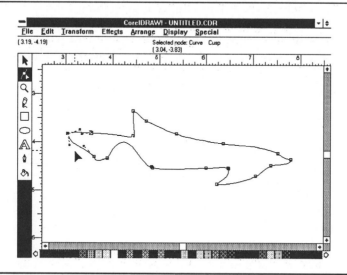

4. Click on each node in turn to select it and deselect the previous node. Each time you select a node, control points pop out, and the status line tells you what type of node you have selected. Notice that some of the nodes are cusp nodes, while others are smooth.

5. Leave this object on the screen for the next exercise.

CorelDRAW! generates three different kinds of nodes when you draw lines and curves: cusp nodes, smooth nodes, and symmetrical nodes. These names describe both the curvature at the node and, in the case of curve objects, the way you can shape the node. Straight lines contain only cusp nodes, while curves can contain all three node types.

Cusp Nodes Cusp nodes occur at the end point of a line or curve or at a sharp change of direction in a curve. When you edit the control points of a cusp node, you can alter the curvature of the segment that precedes the node without affecting the segment that follows it.

Smooth Nodes Smooth nodes occur at smooth changes of direction in a curve. When you edit a smooth node, you alter the shape and direction of

10

both the segment preceding and the segment following the node. The curvature of the two segments does not change in identical degrees, however.

Symmetrical Nodes   Symmetrical nodes occur where the segments preceding and following the node curve in identical ways. (Symmetrical nodes occur less frequently than other node types in freehand drawing but you can change any node type to symmetrical using the Node Edit menu, which you will learn about shortly.) When you edit a symmetrical node, you alter the shape and direction of the curve segments before and after the node in identical ways.

You can always change the node type by using the pop-up Node Edit menu, as you will see shortly. But you can also control whether the majority of nodes you generate during the freehand drawing process are smooth or cusped. To generate mostly cusped nodes (and create more jagged curves), select the Lines & Curves option from the Preferences command in the Special menu and set the Corner Threshold option in the Preferences dialog box to 3 pixels or lower. To generate mostly smooth nodes and create smoother curves, set the Corner Threshold option to 8 pixels or higher.

You will become familiar with techniques for moving control points in a moment. First, finish the next section to learn how to select more than one node at a time.

Selecting and Deselecting Multiple Nodes

You select multiple nodes with the Shaping tool in the same way that you select multiple objects with the Select tool, using either (SHIFT) or the marquee technique. When multiple nodes are selected, you are unable to move control points to shape your object. You can only move the nodes and reshape their associated curve segments in a more limited way. Review the selection techniques in the following brief exercise.

1. Select the node that the cursor is pointing to in Figure 10-6. While pressing and holding (SHIFT), select two additional nodes to the left of the first node. As in Figure 10-6, the nodes turn dark but display no control points, and the status line changes to show the total number of nodes you have selected.

2. Deselect the node farthest to the right of the selected group by pressing and holding (SHIFT) and then clicking on the node with the Shaping tool. The other nodes remain selected.

Figure 10-6. *Curve with multiple nodes selected*

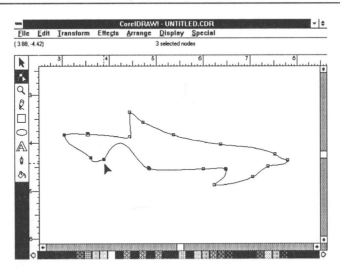

3. Deselect all of the selected nodes by clicking on any white space. The curve object itself remains selected for further work with the Shaping tool, however.

4. Select the six nodes at the left side of the object by drawing a marquee around them, as shown in Figure 10-7. The selected nodes turn dark after you release the mouse button, and the status line tells you how many nodes you have selected.

5. Deselect one node at a time using (SHIFT) and the mouse button, or deselect all of the nodes by clicking on any other node or on any white space.

6. When you have finished, clear the screen by selecting New from the File menu. Do not save the changes you have made.

Now that you are familiar with how to select nodes, you are ready to begin editing a curve object. You can edit a curve by moving nodes and control points interactively or by selecting options in a pop-up Node Edit menu. The next portion of the chapter discusses the first of these methods.

10

Figure 10-7.   *Selecting multiple nodes with the marquee*

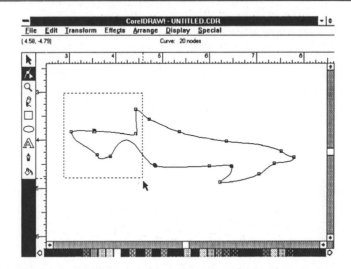

Moving Nodes and Control Points

You can reshape a curve interactively in one of two ways: by moving one or more nodes or by manipulating the control points of a single node. You can move any number of nodes, but in order to work with control points, you can select only one node at a time.

You move nodes when your aim is to stretch, shrink, or move the curve segments on either side of a node. The angle of curvature at selected nodes doesn't change as you move them, because the control points move along with the nodes. The end result of moving nodes is a limited reshaping of the selected area of the curve object.

In general, your best strategy when reshaping curves is to move the nodes first. If just repositioning the nodes does not yield satisfactory results, you can fine-tune the shape of a curve by manipulating the control points of one or more nodes. When you drag control points to reshape a curve, you affect both the angle of curvature at the node and the shape of the curve segment on one or both sides of the node. The effects of this kind of reshaping are much more dramatic. The way you move control points is determined by the type of node you select.

Try the exercises in each of the following sections to practice moving single or multiple nodes, manipulating control points, and constraining node movement to 90-degree increments.

Moving a Single Node

To move a single node, you simply select the curve and then select and drag the node in the desired direction. In the following exercise, you will draw a wave-form curve, select a node, and move the node to reshape the curve.

1. To prepare for the exercise, make sure that the Snap To Grid and Show Rulers options are turned off. Check to see that all of the settings in the Lines & Curves option of the Preferences command are at 5 pixels. (This will result in curves with a fairly even distribution of cusp and smooth nodes.) Set viewing magnification to an Actual Size (1:1) ratio.

2. Select the Pencil tool and draw a waveform curve similar to the one in Figure 10-8. Don't be concerned if your curve is shaped a little differently.

3. Select the Shaping tool and then select a node near the crest of one of the curves. Elongate this curve by dragging the node (not the

Figure 10-8.   *Drawing a waveform curve*

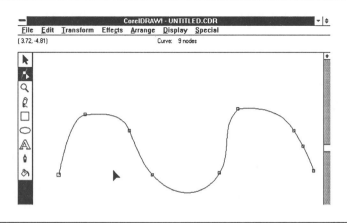

Figure 10-9.   *Moving a single selected node*

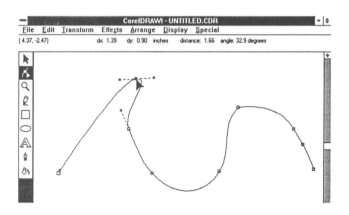

control points) upward and to the right, as shown in Figure 10-9. As you begin to move the node, the status line provides information about *dx-* and *dy-*coordinates, the distance you have traveled, and the angle of movement relative to the starting point. Release the mouse button when you are satisfied with the stretch of your curve.

4. Select Undo from the Edit menu to return the curve to its original shape. Leave this curve on the screen for now. You can use it to move multiple nodes in the next exercise.

Moving Multiple Nodes

There are many cases in which you might choose to move multiple nodes instead of a single node at a time. You might move multiple adjacent nodes, for example, if you need to reposition an entire section of a curve at one time. Or you might select nonadjacent nodes and move them all in the same direction for special design effects. Whatever the case, all you need do is select the nodes and drag them.

1. Using the mouse button and (SHIFT), select one node near the beginning of your waveform curve and one near the end. Again, do not be concerned if the nodes in your curve are in different positions

Figure 10-10. *Moving multiple selected nodes*

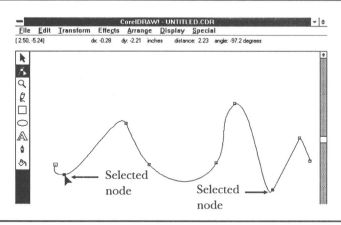

from the nodes in the figure. The process of freehand drawing is so complex that two people rarely produce the same results.

2. Drag one of the nodes downward and to the right. Even though the two selected nodes are separated by several others, they move at the same angle and over the same distance, as shown in Figure 10-10.

3. Release the mouse button when you are finished. Select Undo from the Edit menu to return the curve object to its former shape.

If you prefer to draft even the most "creative-looking" freehand curves with precision, you may wish to exercise greater control over the angle at which you move nodes. The next section will show you how to move nodes with precision.

Constraining Node Movement to 90-Degree Angles

You have the option of moving nodes and their associated curve segments in increments of 90 degrees relative to your starting point. You use the now-familiar (CTRL) key to achieve this kind of precise movement.

1. Select the same two nodes you worked with in the preceding section, press and hold (CTRL), and drag one of the nodes to the left. At first the two nodes do not seem to move at all; then, they "snap" at a

10

the two nodes do not seem to move at all; then, they "snap" at a 90-degree angle from their starting point. The status line on your screen reflects this precise angle of movement, as in Figure 10-11.

2. Release the mouse button when you reach the desired angle. Select New from the File menu to clear the curve from the screen. Do not save your changes.

What if you have moved one or more nodes every which way but you are still not satisfied with the shape of the curve segments on either side of the node? In the next section you will fine-tune your curves by manipulating the control points of a node.

Moving Control Points

By moving one or both control points of a node, you can control the shape of a curve segment more exactly than if you move just the node itself. The effect of moving control points varies, depending on the type of node—cusp, smooth, and symmetrical. Figure 10-12 (a through d) illustrates this difference.

The control points of cusp nodes are not in a straight-line relationship to one another. This means that you can move one control point and change the shape of one curve segment at a time, without affecting the other

Figure 10-11.   *Moving multiple nodes by increments of 90 degrees*

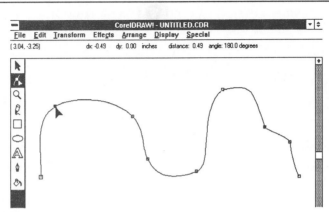

are in a straight line relative to one another. If you move one control point of a smooth node, you affect the curvature of both line segments at once, though not to the same degree. Finally, the control points of a symmetrical node are at an equal distance from the node. When you move one control point of a symmetrical node, the curvature of both associated curve segments changes in exactly the same way. Your waveform curve may not have a symmetrical node, because due to the steadiness of hand required, symmetrical nodes rarely occur naturally in freehand drawing. You can practice moving the control points of smooth and cusp nodes, however, by following the steps in the next exercise.

1. Select the Pencil tool and draw a curve similar in shape to the one in Figure 10-12a. Don't be concerned if your curve has a slightly different shape. You should draw part of the curve with a steady hand and part using more jagged movements. This will result in an even distribution of node types.

2. Select individual nodes on your waveform curve until you find a cusp node. You will know what type of node you have selected by referring to the status line. Do not use one of the end nodes, however; end nodes have only one control point, because only one curve segment is associated with them. If you can't find a cusp node, redraw the curve to be more jagged, and then try again. For your reference, Figure 10-12a shows the waveform curve with no nodes selected and no control points moved.

3. Drag one of the cusp node's control points outward as far as you can without extending it beyond the viewing window. The farther you drag the control point outward from the node, the more angular the curvature of the associated segment becomes. Note also that the curve segment associated with the other control point does not change.

4. Drag the other control point in any direction you choose. The angle of the second curve segment associated with the node changes, independently of the first one. If you have extended both control points independently, you will see a sharp change in curve direction at the node, as in Figure 10-12b.

10

Figure 10-12.   *Moving control points of a cusp, smooth, and symmetrical node*

a.

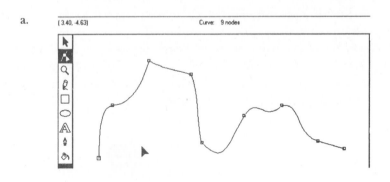

b.

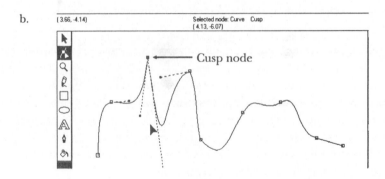

c.

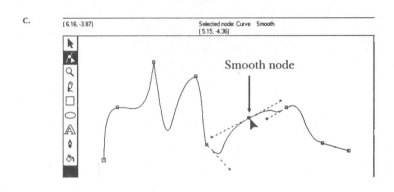

Figure 10-12. *Moving control points of a cusp, smooth, and symmetrical node (continued)*

d.

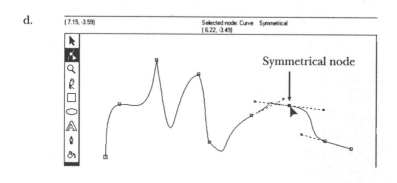

5. When you have played with this technique to your satisfaction, find and select a smooth node. Note that the two control points of this node lie along a straight line.

6. Drag one of the control points of the smooth node outward, and notice that the curvature of *both* of the segments associated with the node changes. As shown in the example in Figure 10-12c, however, the two segments do not change in exactly the same way. (The curvature of your curve segments may differ from those in the example, depending on how you drew the curve.)

7. If your waveform curve contains a symmetrical node, select it and move the control points. If you do not have a symmetrical node, observe the curvature changes in Figure 10-12d when the control points of a symmetrical node are moved. The curvature of these segments changes by an identical angle.

8. When you have played with control points to your satisfaction, activate the Select tool A and press (DEL) to delete the waveform curve from the screen.

Now you have a working knowledge of all the possible interactive techniques for moving and editing curves. It may sometimes happen, however, that even these techniques are not enough to shape your curve just as you

10

it. What if you are working with a cusp node and just can't make it smooth enough? Or what if you need an additional node at a certain point to enable you to fit a curve to an exact shape? For these and other node-editing tasks, you can call up the Node Edit menu. Using this menu to edit curves is the subject of the remaining sections on shaping lines and curves.

Editing Nodes

Selecting a curve object and moving nodes and control points are interactive operations that you can perform without invoking a special command or menu. There are times, however, when you need to *edit* the nodes themselves: to change their shape, or to add nodes, delete nodes, join nodes together, or break them apart. Editing nodes requires that you use a special Node Edit menu that pops up when you double-click on a node or on the curve segment that immediately precedes it.

Working with the Node Edit Menu

To call up the Node Edit menu, you double-click on the node you wish to edit. Alternatively, you can double-click on the curve or line segment that immediately precedes the node. As the example in Figure 10-13 shows, double-clicking on a node or curve segment causes that segment to thicken temporarily. The Node Edit menu appears exactly at the selected node. If multiple nodes are selected, their associated curve segments thicken.

The commands in the Node Edit menu allow you to add or delete selected nodes, join two nodes or break them apart, convert lines to curves and curves to lines, change the node type or align sets of nodes on two separate subpaths. Not all commands are available to you for every node, however. Some commands appear in gray and are unavailable, depending on the number and type of node(s) you have selected. See the section pertaining to the relevant Node Edit command for more information about why particular commands are not available at certain times. To select commands that are available, click once on the command name.

Figure 10-13.   *Invoking the Node Edit menu*

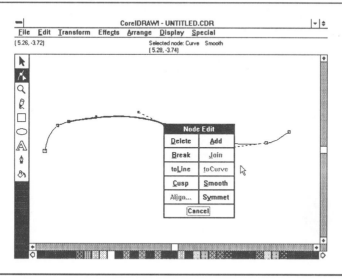

The underlined letters in the command names of the Node Edit menu allow you to select a command by pressing ALT and the underlined letter.

Tip

   If the Node Edit menu conceals an area of a curve that you want to view, just click on the title and drag the entire menu out of the way. Figure 10-14 shows the Node Edit menu from Figure 10-13 moved to the left of its original location.

   Except for the Align command, as soon as you select any command from the Node Edit menu, the menu disappears, and CorelDRAW! immediately applies the command to the selected node(s). If you accidentally invoke the Node Edit menu at any time, select Cancel to remove it from the display.

   Try the exercises in each of the following sections to become familiar with using the commands in the Node Edit menu.

Adding a Single Node

   If you have moved nodes and manipulated control points to the best of your ability but still cannot achieve the exact shape you want, consider adding

10

Figure 10-14.   *The Node Edit menu moved away from the selected node(s)*

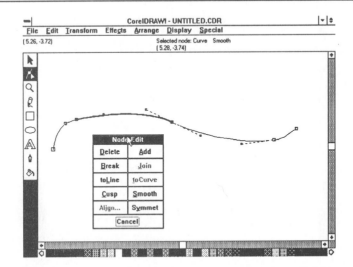

one or more nodes where the curvature seems most inadequate. You can add a single node or multiple nodes, depending on how many nodes are selected.

If the node you have selected is the first node of a line or curve, you cannot add a node to it. In CorelDRAW!, a first node can never have a node or segment preceding it.

The following exercise furnishes the necessary steps to add a single node between two existing nodes. Set the viewing magnification to Actual Size (1:1). Make sure that the Snap To Grid and Show Rulers commands are turned off for this and all of the other exercises in the "Editing Nodes" portion of this chapter.

1. Select the Pencil tool and draw a waveform curve similar to the one shown in Figure 10-15a. Activate the Shaping tool to select the curve for editing. Your curve may contain a different number of nodes from the one in Figure 10-15a.

2. Double-click with the Shaping tool on either the node or the curve segment immediately in front of the point at which you want to add

a node. The Node Edit menu appears, with its left side on the selected node, as shown in Figure 10-15b.

3. Select the Add command from the Node Edit menu. A new node appears on the curve or line segment preceding the selected node, as shown in Figure 10-15c. If you first deselect all of the selected nodes by clicking on any white space, you can move this added node or manipulate its control points just like any other node.

4. Leave the current curve on your screen for use in the next exercise.

If you add a node to a straight line segment instead of to a curve, then move the new node, you effectively add a new line segment.

Adding Multiple Nodes

Perform the following brief exercise to add several nodes to a curve at one time. The technique is the same as when you add a single node, except that multiple nodes must be selected.

1. You should have a waveform curve on your screen in Actual Size magnification, and the Shaping tool should be selected as shown in Figure 10-16a (your curve may look different and may have more or fewer nodes).

2. Select two or more nodes using either (SHIFT) or the marquee method. You will add nodes in front of each of these selected nodes. All of the squares that mark the selected nodes blacken.

3. Using the Shaping tool, double-click on any of the selected nodes or segments. The Node Edit menu appears at the node on which you double-clicked, as in Figure 10-16b.

4. Click on the Add command of the Node Edit menu. A new node appears in front of each of the selected nodes, as shown in Figure 10-16c. If you deselect all of the currently selected nodes, and then select the added nodes, you can move any or all of them. If you select the new nodes individually, you can manipulate their control points to suit your drawing needs.

5. Again, leave the current curve on your screen for use in the next exercise.

10

Figure 10-15.   *Adding a single node*

a.

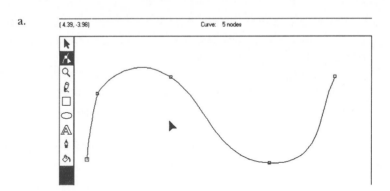

b.

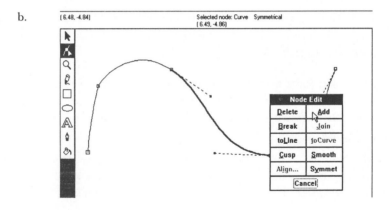

c.

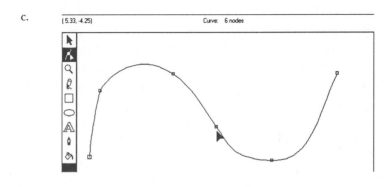

Figure 10-16. *Adding multiple nodes*

a.

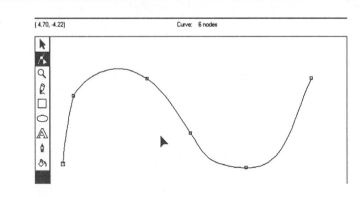

b.

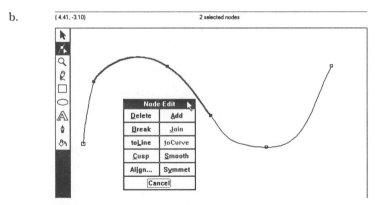

c.

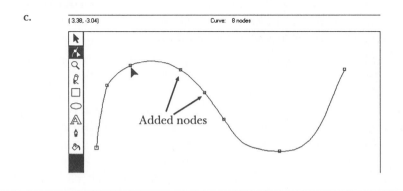

Added nodes

The counterpart to adding nodes is deleting them. Continue with the next sections to practice deleting one or more nodes from a curve.

Deleting a Single Node

When you draw freehand curves, it is often difficult to control mouse movement completely. Changing the Freehand Tracking, Corner Threshold, and AutoJoin settings in the Lines and Curves dialog box may help, but erratic movements while you execute a curve still can produce occasional extraneous nodes. You can smooth out an uneven curve quickly and easily by deleting single or multiple extraneous nodes.

Caution

Always use the Delete command in the Node Edit menu with caution. Deleting a node at random, without checking to see if other nodes are nearby, can radically alter the shape of a curve in ways that are not always predictable.

Perform the following exercise to delete a single node from a curve.

1. You should still have a waveform curve on your screen in Actual Size magnification, and the Shaping tool should be selected as shown in Figure 10-17a (your curve may look different).

2. Using the Shaping tool, double-click on either the node or segment that you want to delete. The Node Edit menu appears, as in Figure 10-17b.

3. Select the Delete command from the Node Edit menu. CorelDRAW! deletes the node that you selected and redraws the curve without it, as in Figure 10-17c. The shape of your redrawn curve could be quite different from your original one; just how different it is depends on the location of the node you selected for deletion.

4. Continue to use the curve for the next example as shown in Figure 10-18a.

Keep in mind that if you delete one of the end nodes of a curve, you delete the associated curve segment as well. If you try to delete either node of a straight line, you delete the entire line in the process.

Tip

As a shortcut to deleting a node, you can select a node and press (DEL) *instead of invoking the Node Edit menu.*

Figure 10-17. *Deleting a single node*

a.

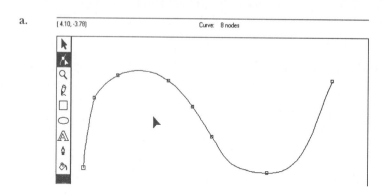

b.

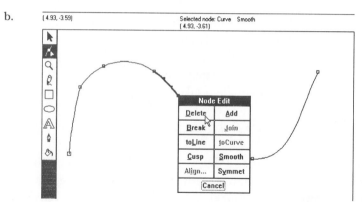

c.

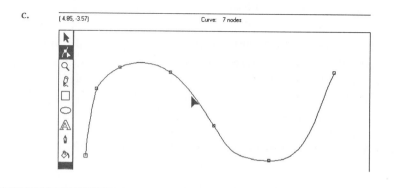

Deleting Multiple Nodes

You can delete multiple nodes as well as single nodes from a curve, as long as all of the nodes you want to delete are selected. To delete multiple nodes,

1. With the previous curve still on screen (see Figure 10-18a), select the nodes you want to delete, using either (SHIFT) or the marquee method; Figure 10-18b shows three nodes selected—the blackened squares. Keep in mind that if you try to delete an end node, you will delete the associated curve segment along with it.

2. Double-click with the Shaping tool on one of the nodes or curve segments in the selected group. The Node Edit menu appears, as in Figure 10-18b.

3. Select the Delete command in the Node Edit menu. CorelDRAW! immediately deletes the selected nodes from the screen and redraws the curve without them, as in Figure 10-18c. The shape of the curve can change subtly or dramatically between node positions; the extent of the change depends on the original positions of the selected nodes.

4. Keep the curve for the next example.

You have learned to add and delete nodes when you need to reshape a curve more than the existing nodes allow. Sometimes, though, you may want your curve to flatten to the extent that you need to replace a curve segment with a straight line segment. You accomplish this by converting one or more curve segments to straight lines.

Converting a Single Curve Segment to a Straight Line Segment

CorelDRAW! allows you to convert curve segments to line segments. Before you convert a curve to a line, you need to be able to identify whether a selected segment is a curve or a straight line. Some important guidelines to follow are

- A curve segment has two control points; a straight line segment has none.

Figure 10-18. *Deleting multiple nodes*

a.

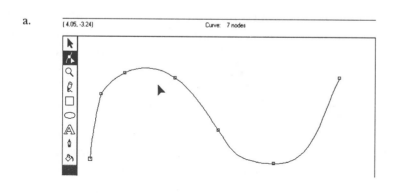

b.

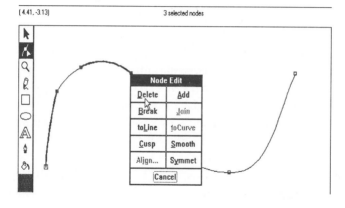

c.

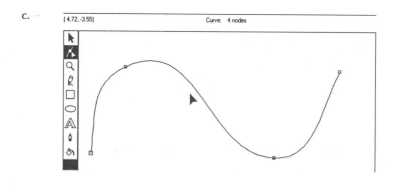

- When you select the segment or its node, the status line indicates whether the segment is a line or curve.

- The shape of the *selected* node identifies the type of segment that precedes it. A black fill in the selected node signifies a curve segment, while a hollow selected node signifies a straight line segment.

Perform the following exercise to gain experience in converting a single curve segment into a straight line segment.

1. Again, use the curve from the previous example. If your curve has only a couple of nodes left, add a node using the steps you recently learned, so that there is a curve segment that is a good candidate for a straight line as shown in Figure 10-19a.

2. Using the Shaping tool, double-click on a segment or node of a curve that you want to convert to a straight line. The Node Edit menu appears, as in Figure 10-19b.

3. Now, select the toLine command in the Node Edit menu. The two control points related to the selected curve disappear and the curve segment becomes a straight line segment, as shown in Figure 10-19c. You can reposition, stretch, or shorten this line segment by using the Shaping tool to drag the nodes at either end.

Converting Multiple Curve Segments to Straight Line Segments

Continue with the next exercise to practice converting multiple curve segments to straight lines.

If you want a curve object in your drawing to be more angular, you can change its appearance by selecting multiple nodes or curve segments and converting them to straight lines. To convert multiple curve segments to straight line segments,

1. Press (ALT)-(BACKSPACE) to undo making the curve segment a line and, if necessary, add a node, so that there are at least two curve segments that are good candidates for straight lines as shown in Figure 10-20a.

2. Select the curve segments or nodes you want to convert to straight lines, using either (SHIFT) or the marquee technique.

Figure 10-19.   *Converting a curve segment to a straight line segment*

a.

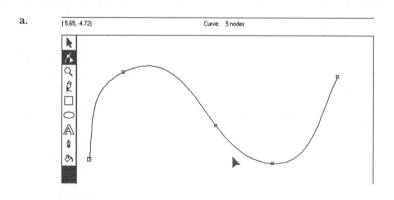

b.

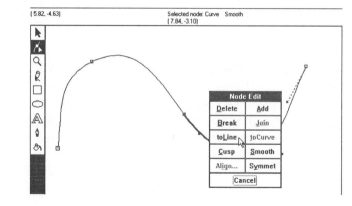

c.

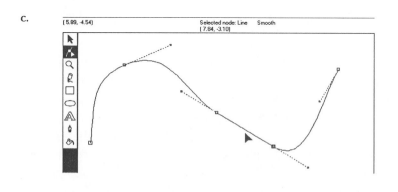

10

3. Using the Shaping tool, double-click on any one of the selected nodes or curve segments. The Node Edit menu appears, as shown in Figure 10-20b.

4. Select the toLine command in the Node Edit menu. The selected curve segments convert to straight lines and all associated control points are eliminated (straight lines do not include control points). The object becomes much more angular, as in Figure 10-20c. You can now reposition, stretch, or shrink any or all of the line segments by dragging the node(s).

5. Select New from the File menu to clear the screen. Do not save your work.

If your object consists of angular line segments but you want to give it much smoother contours, you can convert line segments to curves. The next section shows you how.

Converting a Single Straight Line Segment to a Curve Segment

With CorelDRAW! you can convert straight line segments to curve segments through the Node Edit menu. Before you convert a line segment to a curve segment, you need to identify whether a selected segment is a straight line or a curve. If you are uncertain about identifying segments, review the guidelines in the last section before you proceed.

Try the following exercise to practice converting a single line segment into a curve segment.

1. Set magnification to Actual Size, and then select the Pencil tool and draw a straight line. Double-click and drag the mouse to continue with a waveform curve, as shown in Figure 10-21a.

2. Activate the Shaping tool to select the curve object. Your drawing may show a different number of nodes from the one in the figure.

3. Using the Shaping tool, double-click on the straight line segment of the object or on the *second* node of the straight line. The Node Edit menu appears, as in Figure 10-21b. (If you select the first node of the line segment, you will not be able to convert it to a curve.)

4. Now, select the toCurve command in the Node Edit menu. CorelDRAW! turns the selected straight line segment into a curve,

Figure 10-20. *Converting multiple curve segments to line segments*

a.

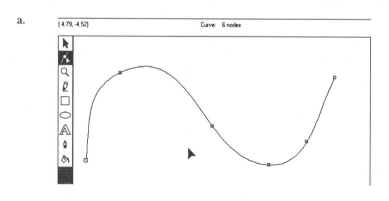

b.

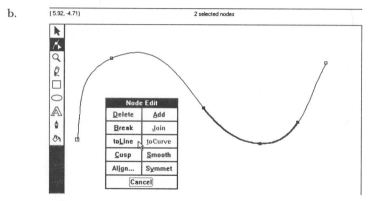

c.

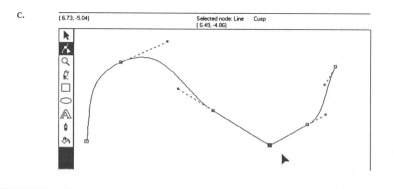

Figure 10-21.   *Converting a line segment to a curve segment*

a.

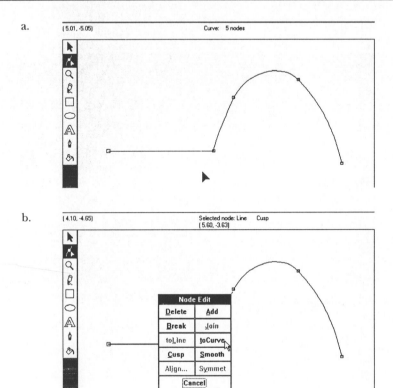

c.

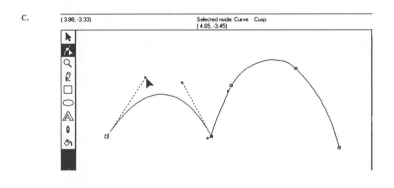

causing two control points to appear on the line segment. Drag these control points up, as shown in Figure 10-21c.

5. Select New from the File menu to clear the screen.

Converting Multiple Straight Line Segments to Curve Segments

You can turn several straight line segments into curve segments at the same time, as long as they are part of the same object. Try the following exercise to convert multiple straight line segments to curves.

1. At Actual Size magnification, select the Pencil tool and draw a multisegment "sawtooth" shape line like the one in Figure 10-22a. Remember to double-click as you complete each line segment in order to attach the next one to it.

2. Activate the Shaping tool to select the multisegment line for editing.

3. Select the line segments or nodes you want to convert to curves, using either (SHIFT) or the marquee technique.

4. Double-click with the Shaping tool on one of the selected straight line segments or on the node that follows it. The Node Edit menu appears, as in Figure 10-22b.

5. Select the toCurve command in the Node Edit menu. The selected straight line segments convert to curve lines. On the surface, the segments do not appear to have changed. However, if you deselect all nodes and then select any one of the converted nodes, two control points appear. You can reshape the peaks and valleys like any other curve, as in the example in Figure 10-22c.

6. Experiment with the nodes and control points of the converted segments to prove to yourself that you really are working with curves now. When you are finished, select New from the File menu to clear the screen before continuing.

You have experimented with adding and deleting nodes, and with changing lines to curves and curves to lines. Another group of commands in the Node Edit menu allows you to change the type of single or multiple nodes. These commands are Cusp, Smooth, and Symmetrical and are the subject of the next several sections.

10

Figure 10-22.   *Converting multiple line segments to curve segments*

a.

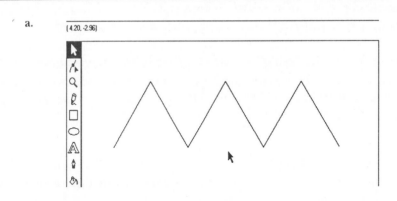

b.

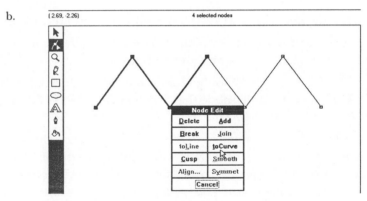

c.

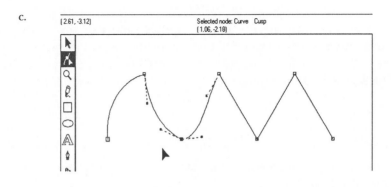

Cusping Single or Multiple Nodes

When you work with a cusp node, you can move either of its control points independently of the other. This makes it possible to independently control the curvature of both of the curve segments that meet at the node, without affecting the other segment. Cusp nodes are especially desirable when you want to render an abrupt change in direction at a node.

The following exercises show you how to turn a single smooth or symmetrical node into a cusped node.

1. Set magnification to Actual Size, then activate the Pencil tool and draw a waveform curve similar to the one shown in Figure 10-23a.

2. Activate the Shaping tool to select the curve automatically. It is not important if your node count does not match the one in the figure. Find a smooth or symmetrical node that you want to cusp.

3. Using the Shaping tool, double-click on the node you want to cusp. Select any node except an end node; CorelDRAW! designs all end nodes as cusp nodes.

4. When the Node Edit menu appears as in Figure 10-23b, select the Cusp command. The appearance of the curve will not change. However, if you manipulate the control points of this node as shown in Figure 10-23c, you will find that you can move one control point without affecting the curve segment on the other side of the node.

When you want a curve object to have a relatively jagged appearance but you do not want to turn your curves into straight lines, the next best solution is to change multiple smooth or symmetrical nodes into cusp nodes. You can then shape the cusped nodes to create a more angular appearance for the affected portions of the object.

1. Select two or more smooth or symmetrical nodes, using either (SHIFT) or the marquee technique. All of the selected nodes blacken as shown in Figure 10-24a.

2. Double-click with the Shaping tool on any of the nodes or segments of the curves you selected for cusping. The Node Edit menu appears, as shown in Figure 10-24b.

10

Figure 10-23. *Cusping a single node*

a.

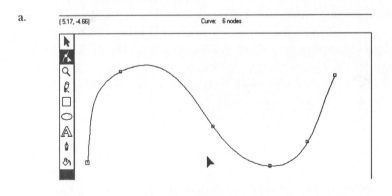

b.

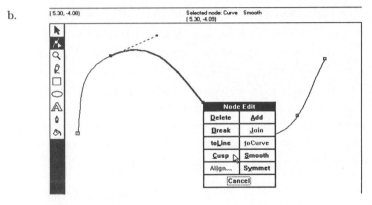

c.

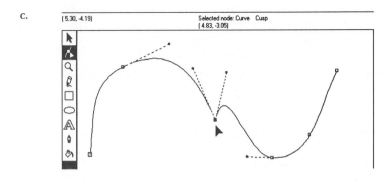

Figure 10-24.   *Cusping multiple nodes*

a.

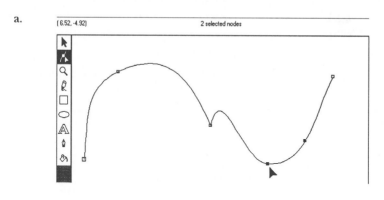

b.

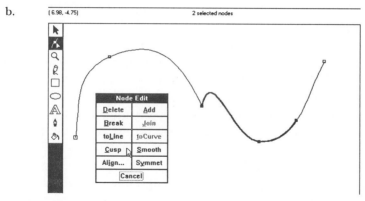

c.

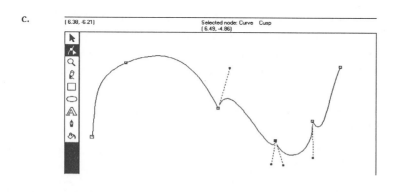

10

3. Select the Cusp command in the Node Edit menu. The curves selected for cusping will not change in appearance. However, if you select each cusped node separately and manipulate its control points (Figure 10-24c), you can move one control point without affecting the curve segment on the other side of the node.

4. Select New from the File menu to clear the screen. Do not save your work.

In the next section, you will become familiar with changing cusped or symmetrical nodes into smooth nodes.

Smoothing Single or Multiple Nodes

In the previous section, you saw that cusp nodes are desirable when you want to create a rougher, more jagged appearance for an object. When you want to make an object's curves smoother, however, you seek out the cusped nodes and turn them into smooth ones.

A smooth node can be defined as a node whose control points always lie along a straight line. A special case exists when a smooth node is located between a straight line and a curve segment, as in Figure 10-25a. In such a case, only the side of the node toward the curve segment contains a control point, and you can only move that control point along an imaginary line that follows the extension of the straight line. This restriction maintains the smoothness at the node.

In the next exercise, you will convert a single cusp node that lies at the juncture between a straight line and curve segment into a smooth node.

1. Set viewing magnification to Actual Size. Then select the Pencil tool and then draw a straight line connected to a curve segment, as shown in Figure 10-25a. Remember to double-click at the end of the line segment to attach it to the curve segment automatically.

2. Activate the Shaping tool. Your curve object may not include the same number of nodes as the one in this figure, but that is not important for the purpose of this exercise.

3. Using the Shaping tool, double-click on the cusp or symmetrical node that you want changed to a smooth node. When the Node Edit menu appears (Figure 10-25b), select the Smooth command. The

Figure 10-25.   *Smoothing a single cusp node*

a.

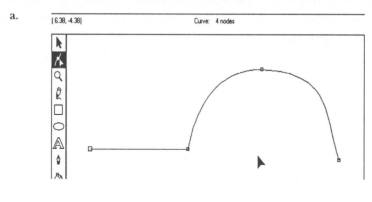

b.

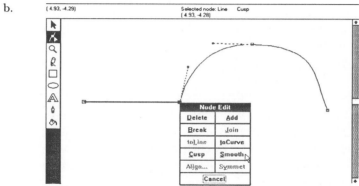

c.

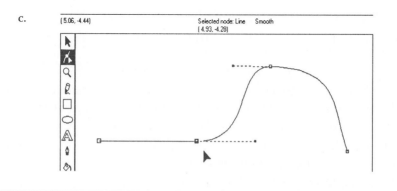

curve passing through the selected node is smoothed, like the one in Figure 10-25c, and will remain smooth when you move either the node itself or its control points. The straight line segment does not change, of course.

4. Select New from the File menu to clear the screen.

To smooth multiple nodes, you simply select multiple nodes and then repeat the steps for smoothing a single node.

1. Set magnification to Actual Size, then select the Pencil tool and draw a waveform curve with several peaks and troughs, like the one in Figure 10-26a. Attempt to draw each curve with sharp peaks in order to see final smoothing results.

2. Activate the Shaping tool and select two or three cusp nodes at the peaks of the curve object, using either (SHIFT) or the marquee.

3. Using the Shaping tool, double-click on any of the selected nodes. The Node Edit menu appears, as in Figure 10-26b.

4. Select the Smooth command. The selected curves convert to smooth curves and pass through the nodes smoothly, similar to the curves in Figure 10-26c.

5. Deselect all of the nodes by clicking on any white space. Then select each node that you smoothed and play with its control points to see how the control points of a smoothed node behave.

6. Clear the screen by selecting New from the File menu.

Go on to the next section to learn how you can turn smooth or cusp nodes into symmetrical nodes and how this affects the drawing process.

Making Single or Multiple Nodes Symmetrical

Symmetrical nodes share the same characteristics as smooth nodes, except that the control points on a symmetrical node are equidistant from the node. This means that the curvature is the same on both sides of the symmetrical node. As with the smooth nodes, when you move one of the control points, the other control point moves. In effect, symmetry causes the two control points to move as one.

Figure 10-26. Smoothing multiple cusped nodes

a.

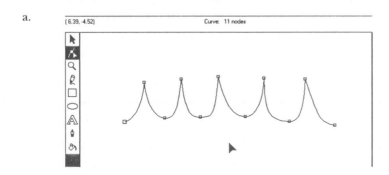

b.

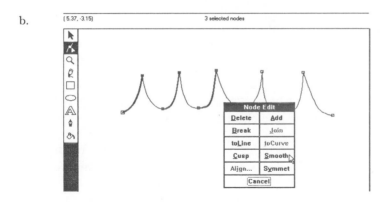

c.

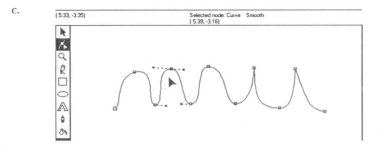

Another important point to remember is that you cannot make a node symmetrical if it connects to a straight line segment. The node must lie between two curve segments in order to qualify for a symmetrical edit.

Perform the following brief exercise to convert a single cusp node to a symmetrical node.

1. Set viewing magnification to Actual Size, then select the Pencil tool and draw a curve similar to the one in Figure 10-27a.

2. Activate the Shaping tool to select the curve. Your curve may contain a different number of nodes from this figure but this is not important for the purposes of this exercise.

3. Find a cusp node that you want to make symmetrical and then double-click on it. The Node Edit menu appears, as in Figure 10-27b.

4. Click on the Symmet command. The selected node is now converted to a symmetrical node and CorelDRAW! redraws the curve so that it passes through the node symmetrically, as in Figure 10-27c.

5. Move the control points of this node until you have a satisfactory understanding of how symmetrical nodes work. Then select New from the File menu to clear the screen.

Making multiple nodes symmetrical is just as easy as making single nodes symmetrical. The only difference is that you select more than one node at a time, using either (SHIFT) or the marquee method.

1. Set viewing magnification to Actual Size, then select the Pencil tool and draw a curve as shown in Figure 10-28a.

2. Activate the Shaping tool to select the curve. Your rendition of the curve may have a different number of nodes.

3. Find and select several cusp and smooth nodes that you want to make symmetrical.

4. Use the Shaping tool to double-click on one of the nodes or related curve segments. The Node Edit menu appears, as in Figure 10-28b.

5. Select the Symmet command. As in Figure 10-28c, CorelDRAW! converts all of the selected nodes to symmetrical nodes and the curve changes to pass through the nodes symmetrically. If you want to see

Figure 10-27. *Making a cusp node symmetrical*

a.

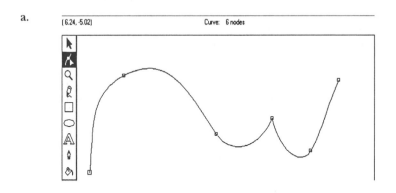

b.

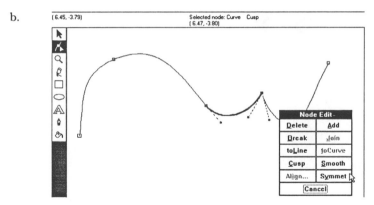

c.

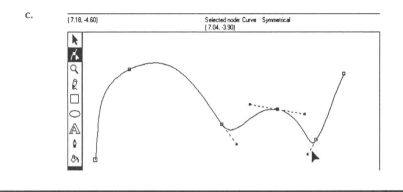

10

Figure 10-28.   *Making multiple nodes symmetrical*

a.
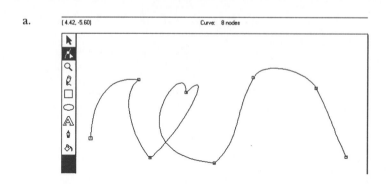

b.
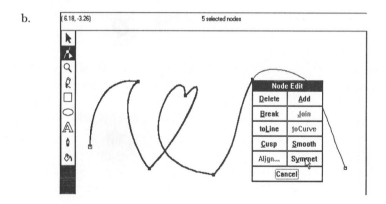

c.
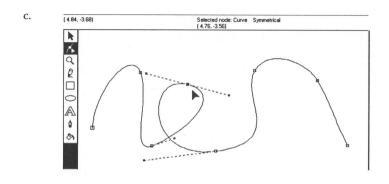

how the converted symmetrical nodes behave, deselect all of them, then select them one at a time and move their control points. When you move the control points of these nodes, you affect both associated line segments in the same way.

6. Select New from the File menu to clear the screen.

In the next sections, you will find out how to master the art of breaking nodes apart and joining them together—and why you might choose to do so.

Breaking Curves at Single or Multiple Nodes

Breaking a node involves splitting a curve at a selected node, so that two nodes appear where before there was one. Although you can move the separate sections of a broken node as though they were separate curves, CorelDRAW! does not regard them as separate. These split segments actually constitute different *subpaths* of the same curve. Breaking a node into separate subpaths gives the impression of spontaneous freehand drawing, yet it allows you to keep separate "drawing strokes" together as one object. Breaking curves at the nodes is also a useful "trick" when you need to delete a portion of a curve and leave the rest of the curve intact.

Keep in mind that you cannot break a curve at an end node, because there is no segment on the other side of the end point with which to form a separate subpath.

When you break a node, it becomes two unconnected end nodes. You are then free to move either end node and the entire subpath to which it is connected. The two subpaths remain part of the same object, however, as you can see when you select either subpath with the Select tool. In the following exercise, you will draw another curve, break it at a single node, and then observe how CorelDRAW! handles the two resulting subpaths.

1. Select the Pencil tool and draw a waveform curve similar to the one in Figure 10-29a.

2. Activate the Shaping tool to select the curve and then select a node in the trough of the curve.

3. Double-click on the selected node to cause the Node Edit menu to pop up, as in Figure 10-29b.

10

4. Select Break from the Node Edit menu. The single node splits into two nodes. Since they are close together, however, the change is not visible until you begin to move the new end nodes.

5. Move the left end point away from the subpath to the right as shown in Figure 10-29c, and then deselect both nodes. The object itself remains selected for editing, and the status line informs you that the curve now has two subpaths.

6. Press the spacebar to activate the Select tool. Notice that the Select tool treats these two subpaths as a single object, even though they look like separate curves. There may be times when you want to make subpaths into truly separate objects, so that you can manipulate and edit them independently. As the next step shows, CorelDRAW! provides a means for you to turn the subpaths into independent curves.

7. To separate the two subpaths into two truly distinct objects, leave the Select tool active and then select the Break Apart command from the Arrange menu. This command is available only when multiple subpaths of a single curve object are selected.

8. Select New from the File menu to clear the screen.

In this brief exercise, you have seen some applications for breaking a curve at a node. For example, you can create two separate objects from a single object, or create separate subpaths that move together as a single object.

Caution

If you break a closed curve object at a node, you will not be able to fill the object with a color or pattern.

When you break a curve at multiple nodes, the result is multiple subpaths, which still remain part of the same object. To break your own curve at multiple nodes, perform the following exercise.

1. Set magnification to Actual Size, then select the Pencil tool and draw a waveform curve like the one in Figure 10-30a.

2. Activate the Shaping tool to select the curve and then select three or four nodes using (SHIFT). Do not select one of the end nodes; as

Figure 10-29. *Breaking a curve at a single node*

a.

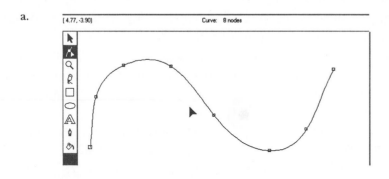

b.

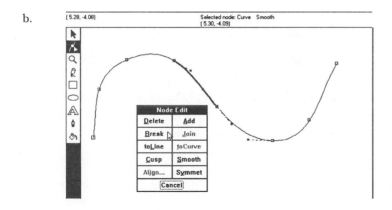

c.

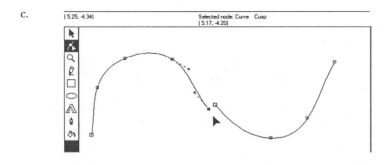

10

previously mentioned, you cannot break an end node into separate subpaths.

3. Double-click on any of the selected nodes to call up the Node Edit menu, as shown in Figure 10-30b.

4. Select Break from the Node Edit menu. The status line displays the message, "*xx* selected nodes on *x* subpaths," indicating how many subpaths you have created and how many nodes the entire curve object contains.

5. Move the end points of the subpaths away from each other until the subpaths look like separate curves, as in Figure 10-30c.

6. Press the spacebar to activate the Select tool. All of the subpaths are selected automatically as a single object.

7. Select Break Apart from the Arrange menu. Now each subpath constitutes a separate object.

8. Select New from the File menu to clear the screen before going on to the next exercise.

The reverse of breaking curves apart is joining them together. In the next section, you will find out when you can and cannot join nodes together, as well as some reasons why you might want to do so.

Joining Nodes

By now, you have probably noticed that the Join command is rarely available for selection when you invoke the pop-up Node Edit menu. You can join nodes only under very specific conditions.

- You can join only two nodes at a time, so only two nodes can be selected.

- The two nodes must be either end nodes of the same object or end nodes of separate subpaths of the same object.

- You cannot join an end node of an open curve to a closed object such as an ellipse or a rectangle.

When might you want to join two nodes, then? The two chief occasions are when you want to close an open path, or when you want to make a single continuous curve from two separate paths.

Figure 10-30. *Breaking a curve at multiple nodes*

a.

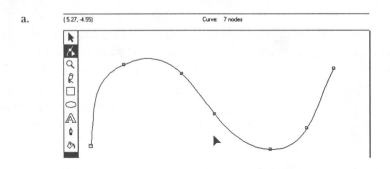

b.

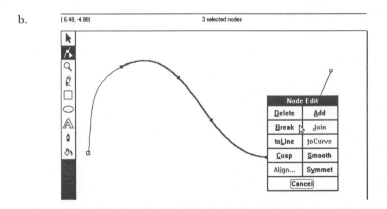

c.

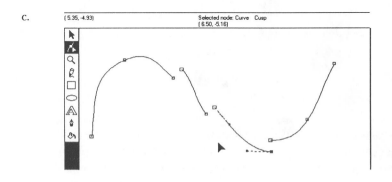

10

Joining Nodes to Close an Open Path   An open path, as you will recall from your previous freehand drawing experience in CorelDRAW!, is a curve object whose end points do not meet and which therefore cannot be filled with a color or pattern. To prevent open paths, you can set the AutoJoin option in the Preferences dialog box to a higher number and make it easier for end nodes to snap together as you draw. There are still times, however, when you might choose to join end points after drawing an open curve. In such cases, you use the Join command in the pop-up Node Edit menu. The following exercise presents a situation in which you could use the Join command to make the drawing process easier.

1. Set magnification to Actual Size. Select the Pencil tool and draw a more or less oval curve, but do not finish the curve at a point close to where you started it. See Figure 10-31a for an example.

2. Activate the Shaping tool to select this curve object, and then select both of the end nodes using the marquee or (SHIFT) key technique.

3. Double-click on either of the selected end nodes to call up the Node Edit menu, as shown in Figure 10-31b.

4. Select the Join command in the Node Edit menu. CorelDRAW! redraws the curve as a closed path, like the one in Figure 10-31c. You can then fill this path with a color or pattern, as you will learn in Chapter 15.

5. Select New from the File menu to clear the screen before going further.

It is easy to close an open path with the Shaping tool. Joining nodes from separate curves, however, is a bit trickier. Read on to learn how to combine the curves so that you can join the nodes.

Joining Nodes on Separate Subpaths to Form a Continuous Curve
(Combined Objects)   You can also join two end nodes if they are on two subpaths of the same curve. The two subpaths then become a single, continuous curve segment. A special case exists when you have two separate curve objects (not two subpaths of the same curve) and want to make them into a single curve. Knowing that you cannot join nodes from two separate objects, what do you do? Your best option is to combine the curves using the Select

Figure 10-31. *Joining nodes to close an open path*

a.

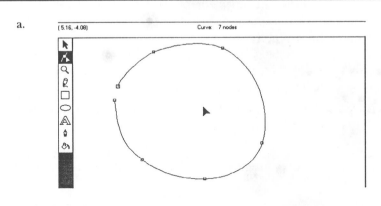

b.

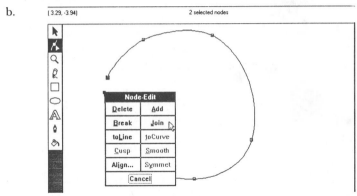

c.

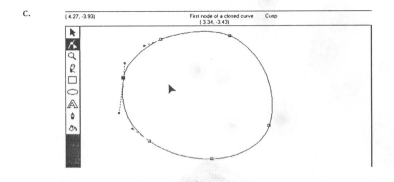

10

Select tool and the Combine command in the Arrange menu. Even though the curves continue to look like separate objects, from the standpoint of the software they become two subpaths of a single curve. You can then join their end nodes to unite the subpaths.

1. Select Actual Size magnification and with the Pencil tool draw four separate curve segments as shown in Figure 10-32a.

2. With the Select tool, draw a marquee around all four curve segments to simultaneously select them.

3. From the Arrange menu, select Combine to make a single, broken curve out of the four segments. The result of this is shown in Figure 10-32b.

4. With the Shaping tool, select the curve and then select each of the three pairs of end points to be joined, double-click on one of the end points in each of the pairs to get the Node menu, and select Join. Repeat this for the two remaining pairs. The result is a single continuous curve as shown in Figure 10-32c.

Tip

The only trick to this is to first combine the curve segments with the Select tool and the Arrange menu before trying to join the segments with the Shape tool.

5. Select New from the File menu, but do not save the changes you have made.

Going through this process is a good way to familiarize yourself with all the steps involved in both joining and breaking nodes apart. Perhaps you have some new ideas for using the Join command for some of your own original drawings.

Aligning Nodes

If you want two objects to share a common edge, like two pieces in a puzzle, the Align command in the Node menu can accomplish it for you. The two objects must first be combined with the Arrange menu, and you must add or delete nodes until there are the same number of nodes in each object in roughly the same location. Once you have completed aligning the two objects, you can break them apart.

Figure 10-32. *Joining nodes to form a continuous curve*

a.

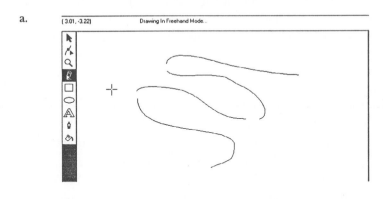

b.

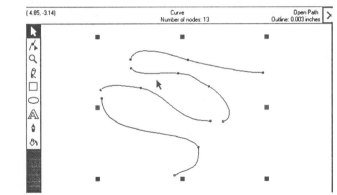

c.

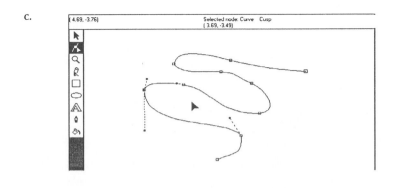

10

Objects can be aligned vertically or horizontally and they can literally share a common border by aligning the control points. If you want to superimpose one object on the other, you would align them both horizontally and vertically and align their control points. The latter is the default.

The following exercise will allow you to experiment with the Align command in the Node menu.

1. At Actual Size (1:1) magnification and with the Pencil tool, draw two curve objects similar to those shown in Figure 10-33a.

2. With the Select tool, draw a marquee, around both objects to select them. Then, from the Arrange menu, select Combine.

3. With the Shaping tool, add or delete nodes until the two objects have the same number of nodes in roughly the same position as shown in Figure 10-33b.

4. For each pair of nodes you want to align, perform these steps with the Shaping tool in the order given:

   a. Select the node to be *realigned* (moved).

   b. Press (SHIFT) and select the node to *align* to (move to).

   c. Double-click on one of the nodes to open the Node menu.

   d. Select Align. The Node Align dialog box will open as shown here:

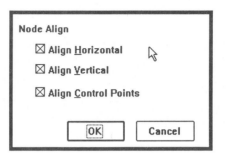

   e. Click on OK to choose the default of all three options, which will superimpose the nodes and align the control points.

Figure 10-33.   *Aligning the nodes of two curve objects*

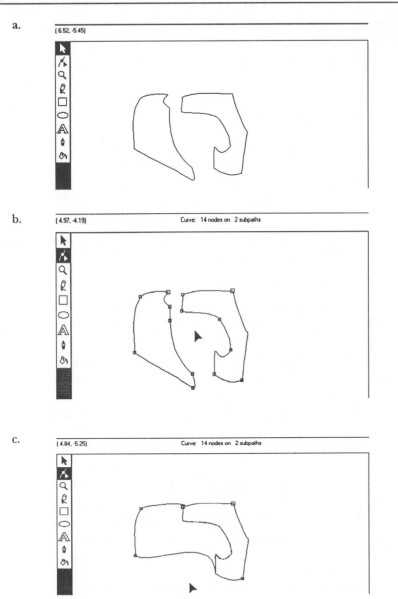

(continues on next page)

10

Figure 10-33.   *Aligning the nodes of two curve objects (continued)*

d.

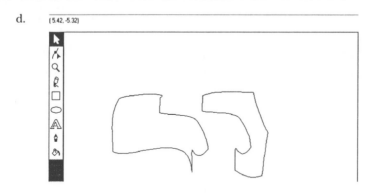

When you have aligned all of the node pairs you want to align, you should have a single curve segment shared by both objects whose shape is the same as the object to which you aligned, as shown in Figure 10-33c.

5. With the Select tool, select the combined object and choose Break Apart from the Arrange menu.

6. Still with the Select tool, click on white space to deselect the combined object and then select and drag one of the original objects until you can see the two individual objects again. Now the two objects, though, have a common, although mirror-image, shape on one side as shown in Figure 10-33d.

Edit Cancellation

If you invoke the Node Edit menu by accident or change your mind about editing a node once the Node Edit menu has appeared, simply select the Cancel command. The Node Edit menu disappears from the screen but the selected node or nodes remain selected for further work.

This concludes your exploration of the techniques for shaping lines and curves. In the remaining sections of this chapter, you will have a hands-on opportunity to explore techniques for shaping rectangular and elliptical objects.

Shaping Rectangles and Squares

The Shaping tool has a specific function when you apply it to rectangles and squares in CorelDRAW!. It rounds the corners of a rectangle, thus creating a shape separate from a rectangle or square. The status line keeps track of the radius of the rounded corner as you drag. You can control the degree of rounding either interactively or by using the grid to ensure exactness.

For interesting distortions, you can stretch, rotate, or skew the rectangle or square before rounding its corners.

Rounding the Corners of a Rectangle

Complete the following exercise to practice rounding rectangles and squares using the Shaping tool. You will begin by rounding corners interactively; later, you will use the grid to perform the same work.

1. For the beginning of this exercise, make sure that the Snap To Grid and Show Rulers commands are inactive and that you are working in an Actual Size viewing magnification. Then select the Rectangle tool and draw a rectangle of unequal length and width.

2. Activate the Shaping tool and select a node at one of the corners of the rectangle. As shown in Figure 10-34a, the status line indicates that the corner radius of this rectangle is 0.00 inches. The corner radius helps you measure the degree to which you have rounded the corners of a rectangle or square with the Shaping tool.

3. Position the Shaping cursor at this node and begin to drag the corner slowly toward the nearest other corner. As shown in Figure 10-34b, each corner node separates into two separate nodes, with each node moving farther away from the original corner as you drag. The status line also informs you just how much of a corner radius you are creating. The further you drag the nodes from the corners, the rounder the corners become and the more the corner radius increases.

10

Figure 10-34.   *Rounding the corners of a rectangle*

a.

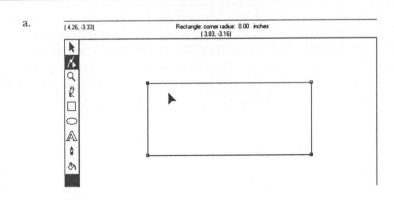

b.

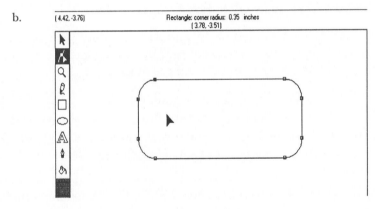

c.

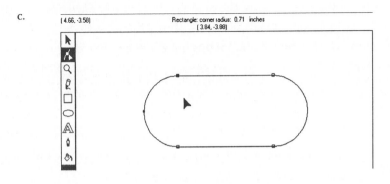

Figure 10-35.   *Rounding the corners of a square*

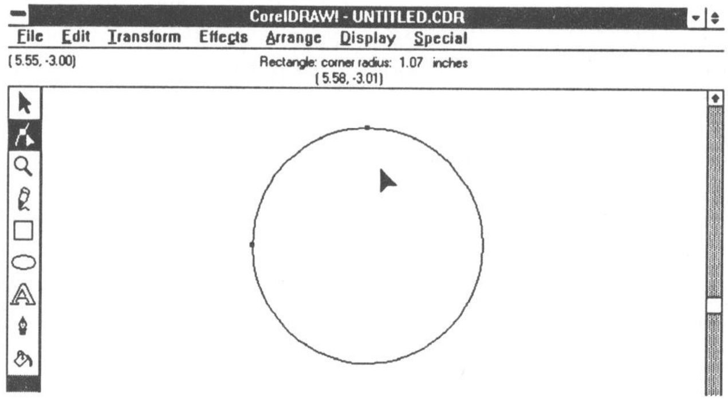

4. Continue dragging the mouse until you reach the logical limit of rounding: when the nodes from adjacent corners meet at the sides of the rectangle. At this point, your rounded rectangle has become almost an ellipse, similar to the rectangle shown in Figure 10-34c.

5. Begin dragging the selected node from the middle of the line back to the former corner. As you do so, the corner radius diminishes. You can return the rectangle to its original shape by dragging the nodes all the way back to the corner.

6. Delete the rectangle from the screen, then draw a square and repeat steps 2 through 5. Notice that when you begin with a square and then round the corners to the logical limit, the square becomes a nearly perfect circle rather than an ellipse, as in Figure 10-35.

7. Press (DEL) to clear the screen of the square turned circle.

Although the status line information helps you round corners precisely, you can gain even greater precision using the grid and rulers. The next exercise guides you through the process of rounding corners of a rectangle or square with the help of these aids.

1. Activate the Snap To Grid command, set the grid spacing to 4 per inch, and then display the rulers and the grid.

10

2. Draw a rectangle 2 inches wide by 1.25 inches deep. Activate the Shaping tool and select one of the corner nodes of the rectangle.

3. Drag this corner node away from the corner to round the rectangle. This time, the corner radius changes in increments of 0.25 inches because of the grid setting.

4. Draw a square and round its corners. The radius of the square also changes in increments of 0.25 inches.

5. When you have finished experimenting with the rectangle and the square, select New from the File menu to clear the screen.

In the next section, you will see what can happen when you stretch, rotate, or skew a rectangle or square before attempting to round its corners.

Stretched, Rotated, or Skewed Rectangles and Squares

When you transform a rectangle or square by stretching, rotating, or skewing it with the Select tool and then round its corners, the value of the corner radius may be distorted. The corner radius indicator on the status line is followed by the word "distorted" in parentheses. As Figure 10-36 shows, the final shape of such a rounded rectangle may also be distorted; in extreme cases it can resemble a skewed flying saucer or rotated ellipse. Figure 10-37 shows a skewed square whose corners have been rounded.

Practice this technique on your own and then go on to the final section on shaping rectangles. In this next section, you will find out how to turn a rectangle into a curve so that you can shape it in an infinite number of ways.

Converting a Rectangle to a Curve Object

If the shaping options for rectangles or squares seem limited to you, don't worry. You can convert any rectangle or square into a curve object and, from that point onward, you can turn a formerly four-cornered object into anything at all. The technique is simple, as you will see in the following brief exercise.

1. Set magnification to Actual Size (1:1) and turn off the ruler, the grid, and Snap To Grid in preparation for this exercise.

Figure 10-36. *Rounding the corners of a skewed rectangle*

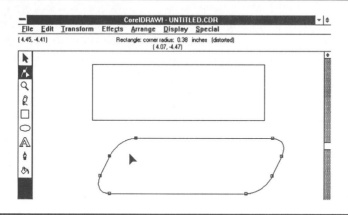

2. Select the Rectangle tool if it is not selected already and then draw a rectangle of any size or shape.

3. Activate the Select tool, select the rectangle, and select the Convert To Curves command from the Arrange menu. The status line message changes from "Rectangle" to "Curve." Note that the new

Figure 10-37. *Rounding the corners of a skewed square*

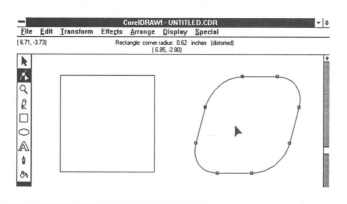

10

four-cornered "curve" still has the same number of nodes as when it was a rectangle.

4. Activate the Shaping tool and then select and drag one of the nodes in any direction. As the example in Figure 10-38 shows, dragging the node no longer forces the associated line/curve segment to move parallel to the other line segments.

5. Continue warping the shape of this rectangle-turned-curve in a variety of ways. For example, you could add nodes, convert line segments to curves, create symmetrical nodes, or even turn the former rectangle into a candy cane or other hybrid object.

6. Press (DEL) to clear the screen before going further.

Now that you have mastered the art of shaping rectangles and squares, you are ready to apply the Shaping tool to Ellipses and Circles for some quite different effects.

Shaping Ellipses and Circles

When you shape ellipses or circles with the Shaping tool, you can create either an open arc or a pie wedge. You can even shift back and forth between these two shapes as you draw, depending on whether the tip of the shaping cursor lies inside or outside the ellipse or circle. You also have the option of constraining the angle of an arc or pie wedge to 15-degree increments.

Creating an Open Arc

To turn an ellipse or circle into an arc, you position the tip of the shaping cursor just *outside of* the rim at the node and then drag the node in the desired direction. Make certain that the tip of the cursor remains outside the rim of the ellipse as you drag, or you will create a wedge instead of an arc. The status line provides information about the angle of the arc as you draw. Practice creating arcs from both ellipses and circles in the following exercise.

1. Turn off the Snap To Grid command if it is active and set the viewing magnification to actual size.

2. Select the Ellipse tool and draw a perfect circle.

3. Activate the Shaping tool to select the circle automatically.

4. Position the tip of the Shaping tool exactly at the node but just outside the rim of the circle, and then drag the node downward slowly in a clockwise direction. As Figure 10-39 shows, the single node separates into two nodes, with the second node following your cursor as you drag. If the circle seems to be turning into a pie wedge instead of an arc, the tip of your mouse cursor is inside the rim of the circle. Move it outside of the rim and try again.

Note that the status line provides information about the angle position of the first and second nodes and about the total angle of the arc. This information is based on a 360-degree wheel, with 0 degrees at 3 o'clock, 90 degrees at 12 o'clock, 180 degrees at 9 o'clock, and 270 degrees at 6 o'clock.

Figure 10-38.   *Editing a rectangle that has been converted to curves*

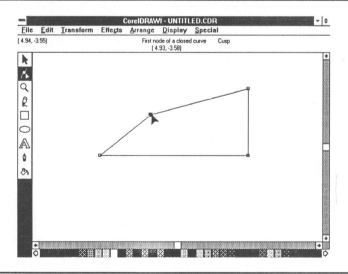

Figure 10-39.   *Creating an arc from a circle*

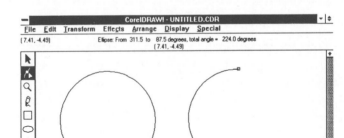

5. Continue to drag the shaping cursor, but now press and hold the (CTRL) key as well. The angle of the arc snaps in increments of 15 degrees. Release the mouse button when your arc has the angle you want.

6. Select the Ellipse tool and draw a perfect circle. Then repeat steps 4 and 5, completing this arc at a 105-degree angle. If you use an ellipse instead of a circle, the "total angle" information on the status

Figure 10-40.   *Selecting an arc for alignment purposes*

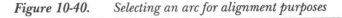

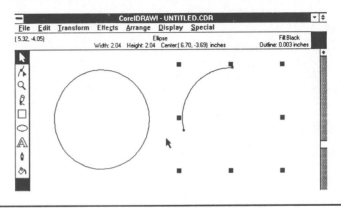

line is followed by the message "distorted" in parentheses. This message occurs because Corel DRAW! bases its calculation of an arc on a perfect circle rather than on an ellipse with different height and width. The angle assignments for arcs created from an ellipse are therefore approximate.

7. Press the spacebar to activate the Select tool and select the newly created arc. Notice that the highlighting box, like the one in Figure 10-40, is much larger than the arc itself; in fact, it seems to surround the now invisible but complete original ellipse. The purpose of this large highlighting box is to make it easy for you to align an arc or wedge concentrically, using the Align command in the Arrange menu. The disadvantage of this large highlighting box is that when you are selecting objects with the marquee, you must make certain that your marquee surrounds the entire highlighting box.

8. Select New from the File menu to clear the screen before going further.

Creating a wedge shape from an ellipse is just as easy as creating an arc, as you will see in the next section.

Creating a Pie Wedge

The only difference between creating an arc and creating a pie wedge is that in the latter case, you position the tip of the shaping cursor *inside* the ellipse or circle as you drag. Perform the following exercise to see the difference for yourself.

1. Set magnification to Actual Size, and then select the Ellipse tool and draw a circle. Activate the Shaping tool to select it for editing.

2. Position the tip of the shaping cursor inside the circle exactly at the node, and then begin dragging the node downward in a clockwise direction. The two nodes separate as before, but this time the circle turns into a shape like a pie missing a piece, suitable for pie charts and wedges, as shown in Figure 10-41.

10

Figure 10-41.   *Creating a pie wedge from a circle*

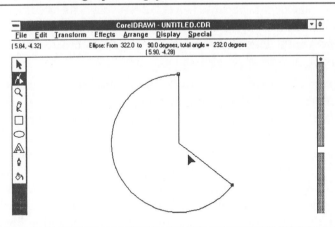

3. Press and hold (CTRL) and continue dragging the mouse. The angle of the wedge shape now moves in fixed increments of 15 degrees. Release the mouse button when you have obtained the desired angle.

4. Just as you did with the arc, press the spacebar to activate the Select tool and select the wedge. Notice the oversized highlighting box once more. Make sure to surround this highlighting box completely whenever you attempt to select a wedge with a narrow total angle.

5. Press (DEL) to clear the screen.

That's all there is to creating arcs and wedges from ellipses and circles. If these shaping techniques are not flexible enough for you, you can always convert the arc or wedge to a curve object, as you will see in the next section.

Converting Ellipses and Circles to Curve Objects

If the shaping options for ellipses and circles seem limited to you, don't worry. You can convert any ellipse, circle, arc, or wedge into a curve object and, from that point onward, you can add and delete nodes, drag nodes and control points, or change node types. In the following exercise, you will create

Figure 10-42. *A wedge created from an ellipse, with a total angle of 240 degrees*

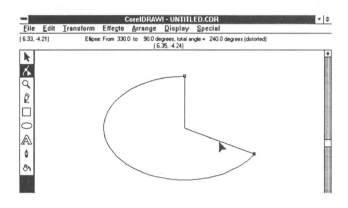

a wedge from a circle, convert the wedge to curves, and then reshape the new curve object into the body of a baby carriage.

1. Select the Ellipse tool and draw an ellipse that is wider than it is high, starting from the upper-left area of the rim and moving downward as you drag.

2. Activate the Shaping tool and position the arrowhead cursor over the node of the circle. Drag the node downward, keeping the tip of the shaping cursor inside the rim, and create a wedge with a total angle of 240 degrees, as shown in Figure 10-42.

3. Press the spacebar to activate the Select tool and select the wedge, and then select the Convert To Curves command from the Arrange menu. Notice that because of the shape of the wedge, the new curve object has five nodes, whereas the circle had only one node.

4. Reactivate the Shaping tool and drag the node furthest to the right upward and outward, as shown in Figure 10-43. Since the segment next to this one is a straight line, the selected node has only one control point. Moving this node upward and outward has the effect of stretching the straight line.

10

Figure 10-43.   *Dragging a node to form the top of a carriage*

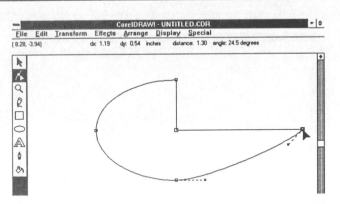

5. The curvature of the segment associated with the node you just moved is not adequate to round out the bottom of the "carriage." To remedy this, double-click on the curve segment and select Add from the Node Edit menu. A new node appears between the selected node and the one below and to the left of it, as shown in

Figure 10-44.   *Adding a node to obtain better curve control*

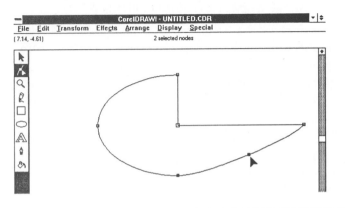

Figure 10-45. *Rounding out the bottom of the carriage*

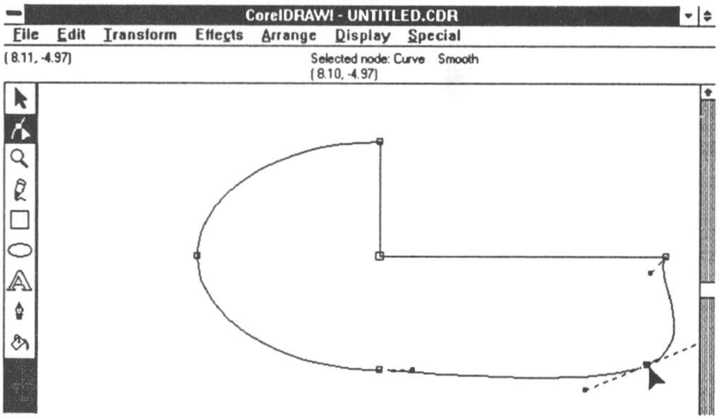

Figure 10-44. It's a smooth node because of the existing curvature and because the object originated as an ellipse.

6. Select and drag this newly added smooth node downward and to the right, until it forms a nicely rounded bottom to the "carriage" body, as shown in Figure 10-45.

Perhaps the example in the preceding exercise will stimulate your imagination to create any number of complex objects from the basic objects available to you through the drawing tools. The Shaping tool makes it all possible!

10

11

Shaping and Editing Text

Text can be an important design element, whether you specialize in original art, graphic or industrial design, technical illustration, or desktop publishing. Every choice you make concerning typeface, typestyle, spacing, alignment, type size, and placement can affect how your intended audience receives your work. You should have the option of editing text attributes at any time, not only when you first enter text on a page.

With CorelDRAW!, you do have that option. Using the Select tool and the Shaping tool, you can edit existing text in ways that enhance both its typographic and pictorial value. You already edited text as a graphic element in Chapters 8 and 9 by using the Select tool to rotate, stretch, scale, skew, and reflect text strings. In this chapter, you will concentrate on editing the *typographical* text attributes (such as typeface and type size) of individual characters, groups of characters, and complete text strings. You will also learn to customize your text picture even further by converting a text string to a set of curves and then reshaping each curve. The Select and Shaping tools share these editing functions between them.

Editing Attributes for a Text String

Remember the Text dialog box you used to select attributes when you first entered a text string? You can also use this dialog box to change attributes for text that already exists: Simply click on the text string with the Select tool and then select Edit Text from the Edit menu. This menu option is available only when you have selected a text string with the Select tool and the changes you make apply to every character in the text string. To change attributes for selected characters within a text string, you need to use the Shaping tool as described in the section entitled "Selecting and Editing with the Shaping Tool."

In the following exercise, you will create a short text string that you will use in many different exercises throughout this chapter. Then, you will select the text string and change some of its attributes using the Edit Text command from the Edit menu.

1. Set your viewing magnification to Actual Size and turn the Show Rulers, Show Grid, and Snap To Grid commands off for this portion of the chapter.

2. Select the Text tool Ⓐ and then select an insertion point midway down the left edge of your viewing window. When the Text dialog box appears, type the following text string on three separate lines:

   Doing
   what comes
   naturally

3. Use the default text attributes in the dialog box: Avalon Normal, 24.0 points, and Left Justification. Adjust your dialog box if it shows other settings.

4. Select OK to exit the dialog box and display the text on the page.

5. Press the spacebar to activate the Select tool ⓚ and select the text string. A highlighting box surrounds the text string.

Figure 11-1. Editing attributes in the Text dialog box

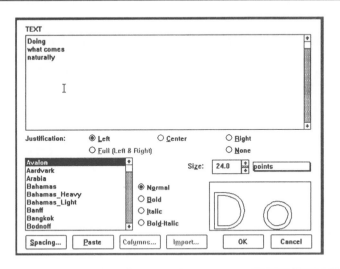

6. Select Edit Text from the Edit menu. The Text dialog box shown in Figure 11-1 appears. This dialog box is the same one you use when you enter a new text string.

7. Change the text attributes to Cupertino Italic, 65.0 points, and Center Justification; then select OK. Because you have changed the alignment, some of the text may not appear within viewing range. If this is the case, drag its outlines until it fits within the viewing window, as shown in Figure 11-2.

8. Deselect the text string and save your work as the file named DOINWHAT.CDR. Leave the text on the screen for the next exercise.

You can change attributes for a text string as often as desired. However, as long as you use the Select tool to select text, any attribute changes you make will affect the entire text string. If your work requires highly stylized text

Figure 11-2.   *Changing typeface, typestyle, justification, and type size*

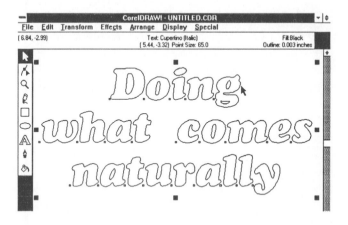

designs, where attributes must be decided on a character-by-character basis, you need to use the Shaping tool.

Selecting and Editing with the Shaping Tool

When the Shaping tool is active, you can select any number of characters within a text string and edit their typographical attributes. Depending on how you prefer to work, you can edit attributes either interactively or with the Character Attributes command in the Edit menu. Some of these attributes, specifically typeface, typestyle, and type size, overlap with the attributes in the Text dialog box. Others, including horizontal and vertical shift and character angle, are adjustable only through the Character Attributes dialog box. And you can move letters and adjust spacing and kerning interactively, without using menu commands or dialog boxes. If all these adjustments fail to give your text the desired look, you can gain more editing control by converting text to curves and then manipulating its nodes and control points.

Before you can edit text attributes on a character-by-character basis, you must first use the Shaping tool to select the text string in which the characters are located. This is similar to selecting a curve object as a prerequisite to selecting one or more of its nodes. After you select a text string, you can select a specific character, multiple adjacent or non-adjacent characters, or all characters in the text string. Practice selecting different combinations of characters in the following exercise.

1. Open the DOINWHAT.CDR text file that you created in the last exercise, if it is not open already. If the Select tool is active, make sure that the text string is not selected; it should not be surrounded by a highlighting box.

2. Activate the Shaping tool ▣ and click once on the outline of any character in the text string. A square node appears at the base of each letter in the text string, and vertical and horizontal arrow symbols appear at the lower-left and lower-right corners of the text string, respectively:

You will become acquainted with the meaning of these symbols in a moment. For now, it is enough to recognize that this change in the text string's appearance indicates that you have selected it for editing with the Shaping tool. The status line shows that you have selected all 23 characters.

3. Select a single character in the text string, the letter "n" in "naturally." Do this by clicking *once* on the node of this character. The status line now contains the message "1 character(s) selected," and the node at the bottom left of the letter turns black, like this:

4. Deselect the letter "n" by clicking anywhere outside the text string. Notice that the string itself remains selected, however.

5. Select the initial letter of each word. Click once on the node for the "D" in "Doing." Then press and hold the (SHIFT) key and click on the node for the initial letter of each of the other words. Check the status line to keep track of the number of characters you select.

6. To deselect these characters, either click on any white space, or press and hold (SHIFT) and click on each selected character node one by one.

7. Select the entire word "Doing" by lassoing its nodes with a marquee:

Your marquee does not have to surround the characters completely, as long as it surrounds the nodes. All the nodes of this word become highlighted after you release the mouse button.

8. Deselect these characters, and then draw a marquee that surrounds all of the text string. All of the characters are now selected for editing.

9. Deselect all of the characters by clicking on any white space. Leave the text on the screen, with the text string selected for editing with the Shaping tool, but with no individual characters selected.

You may be wondering, "Why should I bother to select all the characters with the Shaping tool, when I could activate the Select tool and change attributes for the entire text string?" You can control *some* attributes that way, but the Character Attributes dialog box, which you can access only when the Shaping tool is active, offers you even more options for altering the appearance of text. Read on to find out how those additional attributes can enhance the design of text in CorelDRAW!.

The Character Attributes Dialog Box

When you use the Character Attributes dialog box, you can control other characteristics of selected characters besides typeface, typestyle, and point size. You can tilt characters at any angle, shift them up, down, or sideways, or make them into small subscripts and superscripts. Practically the only thing you can't do is change the characters themselves. In this section, you will learn how to access this dialog box and work with each of the controls in it. As you work through the exercises, you will learn about useful applications for each type of attribute. By the end of the section, you will have altered the design of the DOINWHAT.CDR text string substantially.

You can access the Character Attributes dialog box either by double-clicking on a selected character node, or through the Edit menu. Any attributes that you alter in this dialog box apply only to the characters you have selected. Make sure, then, that you have selected all of the characters you want to edit before accessing the Character Attributes dialog box.

1. With the Shaping tool active, select the node in front of the letter "n" in "naturally."

2. Access the Character Attributes dialog box in the way that is most convenient for your working habits. If you prefer to use menu commands, select the Character Attributes option from the Edit menu. If you like using the mouse best, double-click on any of the selected nodes. The Character Attributes dialog box shown in Figure 11-3 appears.

Take a moment to become familiar with the options available to you in this dialog box and with the significance of each attribute.

Reviewing the Dialog Box

The options in the Character Attributes box in Figure 11-3 allow you to control eight different types of text attributes: typeface, typestyle, type size

Figure 11-3.   *The Character Attributes dialog box*

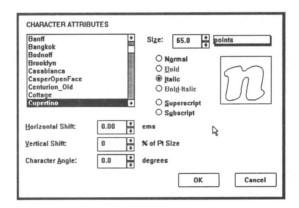

and its unit of measure (in points), horizontal shift, vertical shift, character angle, superscript, and subscript. You are familiar with the first three attributes, but the concepts behind horizontal and vertical shifts, character angle, superscript, and subscript may be new to you. If so, browse through this section to find out more about these attributes.

Horizontal Shift   The Horizontal Shift option controls the distance, in ems, by which selected characters shift to the right or left of their original location. You may recall from Chapter 5 that one em equals the width of the capital letter M in the current typeface. This unit is therefore variable, depending on the typeface of the selected characters.

Vertical Shift   The Vertical Shift option controls the distance by which selected characters shift above or below their starting location (baseline). CorelDRAW! expresses this distance as a percentage of the point size of the selected characters. This distance is therefore variable, too.

11

Character Angle   The Character Angle option allows you to tilt the selected characters in any direction and at any angle. You can turn characters upside down, sideways, or anywhere in between.

Superscript and Subscript   The Superscript and Subscript options let you place selected characters above or below the rest of the text respectively. Superscript text bottom-aligns with the imaginary line at the top of surrounding text (example: the "2" in $E=mc^2$). Subscript text top-aligns with the baseline of surrounding text, for example the "2" in H_2O. The term baseline refers to the imaginary straight line to which text is normally anchored and with which it aligns.

The values that display in the Character Attributes dialog box depend on how you invoke the dialog box. If you access this dialog box by double-clicking on a character, you will see the settings assigned to that character, even if you have selected other characters at the same time. If you call up the dialog box by selecting the Character Attributes command, the values displayed correspond to the first character in the selected group.

Tip

You can move between options in the Character Attributes dialog box either by using the mouse, or by pressing the (TAB) or (SHIFT)-(TAB) and cursor keys. With (TAB) or (SHIFT)-(TAB) you can get to the currently selected typestyle. To change typestyles, use one of the arrow keys ((←) and (↑)) move the cursor up the list, while (→) and (↓) move the cursor down the list. To select Subscript or Superscript, press (↓) to get to the option you want and then press (TAB) to move on. To deselect Subscript or Superscript, use (↑) to select the Normal typestyle, then if you want to select Italic or Bold, do so. Of course, using the mouse is much simpler!

In the next five sections, you will have the opportunity to redesign text imaginatively, using all of the options in the Character Attributes dialog box.

Editing Typeface and Typestyle

In the following exercise, you will assign a different typeface and/or typestyle to each letter in the word "naturally." You selected the first letter of the word before entering the dialog box, so you will alter the letter "n" first of all.

1. Select the Aardvark typeface in the typeface list box and then select OK. Your text string redisplays on the screen, but now the letter "n" looks quite different from the surrounding letters.

2. Double-click on the character node of the "n" once more. When the dialog box appears this time, it shows the current typeface of the *selected* character or characters. (See the tip in the previous section.) Select Cancel to exit the dialog box.

3. Select each of the other letters in the word "naturally" in turn. Assign typefaces and typestyles to them in the following order: Paradise Normal, Frankfurt Gothic Bold Italic, Cupertino Normal, Renfrew-Normal, Switzerland Italic, Unicorn Normal, USA Black Italic, Banff Normal. When you are finished, the word "naturally" displays an interesting patchwork of fonts:

4. Save the changes you have made by pressing (CTRL)-(S), and leave your work on the screen for the next exercise. Note that whenever you save the picture you are working on, CorelDRAW! activates the Select tool automatically.

Go on to the next section to apply different point sizes to the letters whose typefaces and typestyles you have already altered.

Editing Type Size

When you changed typefaces for each letter in the word "naturally," you left the type sizes unaltered, yet the letters do not appear to be the same size. You have probably guessed by now that different typefaces have different heights and widths and that point size is only one way to measure text size.

In the following exercise, you will make the letters in this word closer to one another in actual size.

1. Activate the Shaping tool again and then double-click on the character node of the first letter "a" in "naturally." When the Character Attributes dialog box appears, change the point size for this letter to 140.0 and then select OK. Even though you have more than doubled its point size, this letter only now approximates the height of its neighbors. Type point size measures from the baseline of one line to the baseline above it and is not necessarily a measure of the actual type.

2. In the same way, select the first letter "l" and change its type size to 75.0 points.

3. Finally, select the letter "y" and change its point size to 90.0. Now, all of the letters seem more uniform in height and size:

4. Save your work by pressing (CTRL)-(S), leaving the text string on screen.

To edit the word "naturally" so that it conveys a sense of a more natural state, you can shift some of the characters up or down relative to the baseline and move others sideways. In the next exercise, you will practice moving individual characters.

Horizontal and Vertical Shift

When you shift selected characters horizontally, you move them to the right or left of their starting position, causing them to overlap with other characters on the same line. You can use this technique to convey a sense of being rushed or crowded, or simply to adjust spacing between letters precisely. When you shift characters vertically, they fall above or below the baseline, which can create a feeling of spontaneity or excitement.

In the next exercise, you will shift some of the characters in the word "naturally" to enhance the sense of spontaneity and a natural look in the text.

1. Activate the Shaping tool and then double-click on the character node for the letter "n" in the word "naturally" to enter the Character Attributes dialog box. Set Horizontal Shift to -0.50 ems and then select OK. Because you set the value to a negative number, the letter shifts to the left of its original position.

2. Select the character node for the next letter "a" and set Vertical Shift to 20% of point size. When you select OK, the position of the letter shifts above the baseline.

3. Select the following letters in turn and change the shift settings for each as follows. Change "r" to Vertical Shift -25%, the second "l" to Vertical Shift 10%, and the "y" to Horizontal Shift .40 ems and Vertical Shift 25%. Notice that a negative value for Vertical Shift causes the selected character, "r," to reposition itself below the baseline. The resulting text should now look like this:

4. Save your changes and leave this text on the screen.

So far, you have edited attributes for one letter at a time. In the next section, you will select a group of characters and practice positioning them as superscripts and subscripts.

Creating Superscripts and Subscripts

Perform the following exercise to simulate a superscript and subscript.

1. Reactivate the Shaping tool and then select the character nodes of all of the letters in the word "comes" except the letter "c." Double-click on the node in front of "o" to access the Character Attributes dialog box.

2. Click on the Superscript option button and then select OK. The selected letters have become small and appear as a superscript to the letter "c," like this:

3. Select the Undo command in the Edit menu to return the selected characters to their original position.

4. Select the same characters again and return to the Character Attributes dialog box by double-clicking on the "o" node. This time, click on the Subscript option button. When you select OK, the letters display as a subscript to the letter "c."

5. Press (ALT)-(BACKSPACE) to return the selected characters to their original position.

In the next section, you will complete the last exercise pertinent to the Character Attributes dialog box. You will practice tilting the characters in the word "naturally" to different angles.

Editing Character Angle

You can tilt selected characters at any angle using the Character Angle setting in the Character Attributes dialog box. Values between 0 and 180 degrees indicate that you are tilting the characters above an imaginary horizon, in a counterclockwise direction. Values between 0 and –180 degrees indicate that you are tilting the characters below an imaginary horizon, in a clockwise direction. At a 180-degree angle, the characters are upside down. Practice adjusting character angle in the following exercise.

1. With the Shaping tool active, select the character nodes of the letter "n," the letter "u," and the letter "y" in the word "naturally." Double-click on one of these nodes to access the Character Attributes dialog box. Set Character Angle to –15 degrees and then select OK. The selected characters now appear tilted toward the right.

2. Deselect these three letters and select the letter "t," the second letter "a," and the second letter "l." Double-click on one of these nodes to access the Character Attributes dialog box. Set Character Angle to 15 degrees and then select OK. These characters appear tilted toward the left. The word "naturally" now seems to fly off in all directions:

3. Save your changes and then select New from the File menu to clear the screen.

This concludes the tutorial on the use of the settings in the Character Attributes dialog box. No doubt you have come up with a few creative ideas of your own while practicing on the exercises in the preceding sections. When you are ready to proceed, continue through the next portion of this chapter, where you will learn some convenient ways to kern text and adjust spacing interactively.

Kerning Text Interactively

Kerning, simply defined, is the art of adjusting the space between individual pairs of letters for greater readability. There are many possible letter pair combinations in the 26 letters of the English alphabet, but most typeface manufacturers provide automatic kerning for only a few hundred commonly used pairs. Occasionally you will see too much or too little space between adjacent letters. You can kern these letter pairs by moving one of the letters subtly to the right or left.

Using kerning as a design element can enhance the power of your message. For instance, you will draw more attention to your text when you kern letters to create special effects, such as expanded letter spacing in selected words of a magazine or newspaper headline.

The exercises in this section offer more extreme examples of kerning than you are likely to find in most text, but they will help you become familiar with the concept of kerning. Follow the steps in each exercise to learn how to kern single or multiple characters. Integrated within the exercises is information on using constraint and alignment techniques to kern more easily and precisely.

Kerning Single Characters

The following exercise lets you practice adjusting spacing between any two text characters. As you work through the steps, you will learn how to ensure that characters align properly with the surrounding text after you move them. Before starting the exercise, adjust viewing magnification to actual size. Turn on Snap To Grid, Show Rulers, Show Status Line, and Show Grid, and set both the Horizontal and Vertical Grid Frequency to 8 per inch. Retain these settings for both exercises on kerning.

1. Select the Text tool and then select a text insertion point at the 1-inch mark on the horizontal ruler and the 4 1/2-inch mark on the vertical ruler.

2. After the Text dialog box appears, type the word **Kerning** in upper-
   and lowercase letters. Leave a space after the "K" and another after
   the "e." Press (ENTER) to begin a new line and type the word **Text** on
   this line. Leave one space after the letter "T," one space after the "e,"
   and two spaces after the letter "x."

3. Set the justification to None, the type size to 80.0 points, the typeface
   to Bodnoff, and click on OK.

4. After the text string appears on the screen as in Figure 11-4, select
   the Shaping tool. Since the text string was the last object you created,
   the Shaping tool selects it automatically. A node appears next to
   each character in the text string; vertical and horizontal spacing
   control handles appear at each end of the last line of the text string.

5. You will need to bring the letter "e" in "Kerning" much closer to the
   "K" and the letters "rning" closer to the "e." To adjust the spacing
   between "K" and "e" so that the text will appear more uniform, press

Figure 11-4.   *Text in need of kerning*

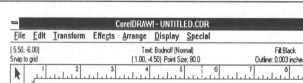

11

and hold the left mouse button on the node in front of the letter "e." When you begin to move the mouse, the cursor turns into a four-headed arrow. Drag the letter 0.75 inches to the left, as shown in Figure 11-5. A dotted outline of the letter follows the cursor as you drag. When you release the mouse button, the letter itself appears in this location.

6. If the "e" is not aligned with the rest of the text, snap this letter back to its original position by selecting the Straighten Text command in the Arrange menu, and then repeat step 5. This command erases any previous kerning information, so use it only when you want to return text to its original location. Alternatively, you can select the Align To Baseline command, also in the Arrange menu. When you accidentally position a character above or below the baseline, this command forces the character to align with the baseline again. Unlike the Straighten Text command, the Align To Baseline command does not erase any previous kerning information.

Figure 11-5.   *Kerning a single letter*

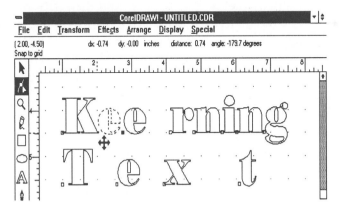

7. Save your kerned text as KERN1.CDR and leave it on the screen for the next exercise.

Tip

If you require a high degree of precision in the placement of kerned text, zoom in on the character(s) you want to move. Alternatively, you can press and hold (CTRL) *while moving the characters, thereby constraining the text to align with the nearest baseline. Be sure to release the mouse button before you release* (CTRL) *to make certain of proper alignment.*

Kerning Multiple Characters

In this section, you will learn how to move and kern multiple characters within a text string simultaneously. In practice, your most common use for this feature will be to move the remaining characters of a word closer to another letter that you have already kerned. However, you can select and reposition any group of characters, including nonadjacent characters, to another location in the same way.

1. With the KERN1.CDR file displayed in an Actual Size viewing magnification, select the Shaping tool and draw a marquee around the letters "rning."

2. Click on the node for the letter "r" and then drag the mouse 1.37 inches to the left. Refer to the status line for assistance. All the letters in the selected group follow, as shown in Figure 11-6. If the selected characters do not line up with the adjoining text when you release the mouse button, review step 6 in the previous exercise. You may want to use the Align To Baseline and Straighten Text commands. Deselect the letters "rning" when you have them in the desired location.

3. Use (SHIFT) to select the "e" and the second "t" in "Text." Click on the node in front of the letter "e" and drag it 0.60 inches to the left as shown in Figure 11-7a. Both selected letters should move together across the screen without disturbing the "x." After you release the mouse button the letters "e" and "t" will appear, as shown in Figure 11-7b.

Figure 11-6. *Kerning multiple adjacent letters*

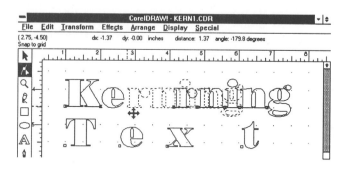

4. As you can see, the letters "x" and "t" still are not close enough to the "e." Experiment by moving these two letters on your screen until the text string appears normal.

5. Save your changes to the file by pressing (CTRL)-(S). Then select New from the File menu to clear the screen.

Kerning is not the only text attribute that you can adjust interactively with the Shaping tool. In the next section, you will learn how to adjust spacing between characters, words, and lines for an entire selected text string.

Adjusting Spacing Interactively

There are two ways to edit intercharacter, interword, and interline spacing of existing text in CorelDRAW!. The first way, as you will recall, is to select the text string with the Select tool and then invoke the Text dialog box using either (CTRL)-(T) or the Edit Text command in the Edit menu. Using this method, you can click on the Spacing command button in the Text dialog

Figure 11-7.   *Kerning multiple nonadjacent letters*

a.
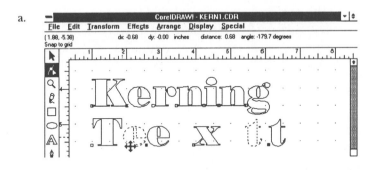

b.
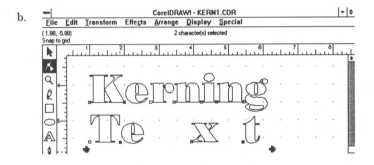

box and set spacing in the sub-dialog box provided. You enjoy the advantage of precision but experience the disadvantage of going through a series of additional steps.

If you prefer to work more spontaneously, CorelDRAW! offers you an interactive method of spacing as well. This method involves selecting the text string with the Shaping tool and then dragging one of the two stylized arrows that appear at the text string's lower boundary. Keep in mind, however, that you adjust spacing for *all* of the characters in the text string when you use this technique. To adjust spacing between two individual characters, see the "Kerning Single Characters" section of this chapter.

To alter intercharacter spacing interactively, you drag the horizontal arrow at the lower-right boundary of the text string. To alter interword spacing, you drag the same arrow while holding down (CTRL). And to alter interline spacing, you drag the vertical arrow at the lower-left boundary of the text string.

The next three sections provide a short tutorial on altering each of the three types of spacing interactively.

Adjusting Intercharacter Spacing

In the following exercise, you will create a text string and adjust the intercharacter spacing, observing the changes in the CorelDRAW! interface as you work.

1. Set viewing magnification to Actual Size, then activate the Text tool and select an insertion point near the upper-left corner of your viewing window.

2. When the Text dialog box appears, type **Running out of** on the first line of the text entry window and **space** on the second. Set text attributes to Fujiyama Normal, Left Justification, and 75.0 points, and then select OK. The text displays in your viewing window. If the text string is not completely visible on the display, select the text string and move it to the location shown in Figure 11-8.

3. Activate the Shaping tool. Each character node increases in size, and stylized vertical and horizontal arrows appear at the lower-left and lower-right boundaries of the text object, just as in Figure 11-8.

4. Position the Shaping cursor directly over the horizontal arrow at the lower-right boundary of the text object, until the cursor turns into a crosshair. Then, drag this arrow to the right. Notice that, just as in the example in Figure 11-9, the characters do not seem to move immediately; instead, you see a dotted outline following the two-way arrow cursor. As you drag, the status line displays the message

Figure 11-8.   *Displaying the spacing adjustment arrows*

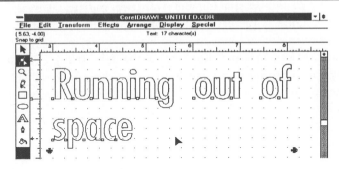

"Inter-Character," followed by information about the horizontal distance by which you are increasing the size of the text boundary.

5. When the right boundary of the text string (represented by the dotted outline) reaches the desired point, release the mouse button.

Figure 11-9.   *Adjusting intercharacter spacing*

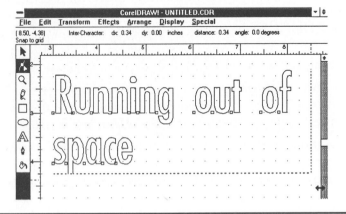

Figure 11-10. *Increasing intercharacter spacing*

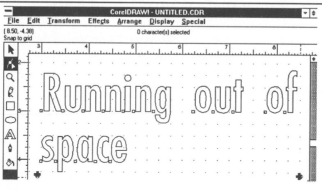

The text repositions itself to align with that boundary, and the space between each character increases proportionally, as shown in Figure 11-10.

6. If you would like to know the exact intercharacter spacing measurement you have obtained, select the text string with the Select tool and access the Text and Spacing dialog boxes. This is a good way to check for precision.

7. Select the Undo command from the Edit menu to return the text to its former position. Then *decrease* the space between characters by dragging the horizontal arrow to the left instead of to the right. If you decrease the space drastically, letters may even overlap each other, like this:

8. Select Undo once more to return the characters to their original positions. Leave this text on the screen for now.

This method is useful when you want to fit text into a defined space within a drawing, without changing the point size or other attributes. Go on to the next section to practice changing interword spacing independently of the spacing between characters.

Adjusting Interword Spacing

Suppose that you don't need to change the spacing between letters but your design calls for increased or decreased spacing between words. To adjust interword spacing interactively, you drag the same horizontal arrow that you used for intercharacter spacing. The difference is that you also hold down CTRL at the same time. Try the following exercise, using the text string you created in the previous section.

1. With the Shaping tool active and the text string selected, position the cursor over the horizontal arrow until the cursor turns into a crosshair. Then press and hold CTRL and drag the two-way arrow cursor to the right. The status line displays the message "Inter-Word," followed by the horizontal distance by which you are stretching the text boundary.

2. When the outline that you are dragging has the desired width, release the mouse button first, and then CTRL. (If you release CTRL first, you will adjust the intercharacter rather than the interword spacing.) The text redisplays with increased space between each word, as shown in Figure 11-11.

3. Select the Undo command in the Edit menu to return the text to its original interword spacing.

4. Try decreasing the amount of interword spacing by dragging the horizontal arrow to the left instead of the right. When you are finished experimenting, select the Undo command once more. Leave this text on the screen for the next exercise.

Figure 11-11. *Increasing interword spacing*

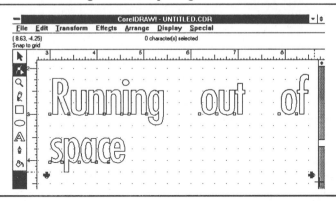

You can change the spacing between lines of a text string, as well as between words or characters. The next section gives you hands-on practice in editing interline spacing.

Adjusting Interline Spacing

To edit interline spacing with the Shaping tool, you drag the vertical arrow located at the lower left of the text boundary. Try increasing and decreasing the space between lines now, using the same text string you have been working with for the past two sections. Note that if your text string contains only one line, dragging the vertical arrow has no effect.

1. With the Shaping tool active and the text string selected, position the mouse cursor directly over the vertical arrow that appears at the lower-left text boundary and drag this arrow downward. The cursor turns into a two-way vertical arrow. Simultaneously, the status line displays the message "Inter-Line," followed by the vertical distance measurement, which tells you how much you have increased the size of the text boundary.

2. When you have increased the boundary by the desired size, release the mouse button. The text repositions itself to fit the new boundary; as in Figure 11-12, only the spacing between lines changes, not the length or size of the text itself.

3. To see the precise amount of interline spacing that you have added, activate the Select tool and select the Edit Text command in the Edit menu. Then, click on the Spacing command button to see the Spacing dialog box. When you are finished, select Undo from the Edit menu to return the text string to its former interline spacing.

4. Reduce the interline spacing of the text string by dragging the vertical arrow upward instead of downward. When you are finished, select Undo to return the text to its former spacing.

5. Select New from the File menu to clear the screen before beginning the next section.

By now, you have explored all of the possible text attributes that you can change using the Select and Shaping tools. If you need to give your text an even more customized look, however, you have the option of converting text to a curve object and then editing its nodes. This is the topic of the next and final section of this chapter.

Figure 11-12.   *Increasing interline spacing*

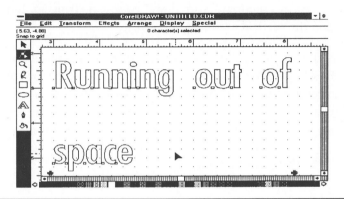

Reshaping Characters

Graphic designers and desktop publishers often have need of stylized text characters that give their messages extra flair, but which just don't exist in standard typefaces. CorelDRAW! can help you create such "text pictures" easily. All you have to do is select text attributes that approximate the effect you want to achieve, and then convert the text string to curves. You can then reshape the text using the Select and Shaping tools.

The following exercise contains a simple step-by-step example of how to create stylized text pictures. Carry out the steps and give your own imagination a boost!

1. To prepare for this exercise, turn off Show Rulers, Snap To Grid, and Show Grid, and set the viewing magnification to actual size.

2. Activate the Text tool and select an insertion point about midway down the left edge of your viewing area. The Text dialog box appears.

3. Type **Snake** in upper- and lowercase letters in the text entry box. Test each of the typefaces in the typeface list box against the sample display character. The capital "S" of the Gatineau typeface bears a fairly strong resemblance to a snake, so set text attributes to Gatineau Bold Italic, 150.0 points, and Left Justification. Select OK to exit the Text dialog box and display your text on the page, as shown in Figure 11-13.

4. Activate the Shaping tool and double-click on the node for the letter "S" to open the Character Attributes dialog box.

5. Your aim is to increase the size of the letter "S" and make it a *drop cap*—a first capital letter that falls below the baseline of the remaining text. To achieve this aim, set the type size for the letter "S" to 250.0 points and set Vertical Shift to –25% of type size. Select OK to make these changes take effect. Your text should now look like Figure 11-14.

6. Activate the Select tool to select the entire text string, and then click on the Convert To Curves option in the Arrange menu. The text redisplays with many little nodes, indicating that it has become a

Figure 11-13.   *"Snake" text: Gatineau Bold Italic, 150.0 points*

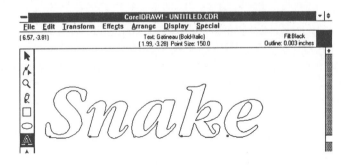

curve object. If you activate the Shaping tool again, the status line
displays the message, "Curve: 66 nodes on 8 subpaths." This message
indicates that CorelDRAW! now considers this text string to be one
object with eight combined segments.

Figure 11-14.   *Increasing the size of the letter "S"*

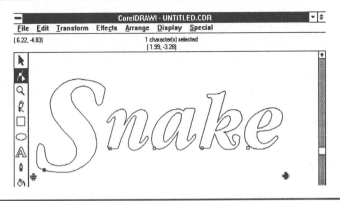

Figure 11-15. *"S" converted to curves and reshaped with the Shaping tool*

7. Activate the Select tool again and select the Break Apart command in the Arrange menu. Each letter is now a separate object.

8. Deselect all of the letters and then click on the letter "S" with the Select tool. Stretch the letter vertically by dragging the middle boundary markers on the upper and lower sides of the highlighting box. Your goal is to elongate the letter, thereby enhancing the "snake-like" appearance.

9. Now, activate the Shaping tool and manipulate the nodes of the "S" so that you achieve the general look of Figure 11-15. Make some areas of the "snake" narrower and others broader. You will want to reshape and move the snake's head, too. Make the "tail" of the snake narrower, as well.

10. You can try to match the results in Figure 11-15 exactly or develop your own creative enhancements utilizing all of the skills you have learned at this point in the book. When you are satisfied with the appearance of the snake, save the image under the filename SNAKE.CDR.

11. Select New from the File menu to clear the screen.

As you can see, the possibilities for creating custom characters for text are virtually endless. If you find yourself fired up with new ideas for your own projects, experiment until you design a word picture that best enhances your message.

12

Cutting, Copying, and Pasting Objects and Pictures

So far, you have learned how to select, move, rearrange, transform, and reshape objects within a single graphic. An equally important part of the editing process involves the *transfer* of image information within a graphic, between pictures, or between CorelDRAW! and other Windows applications. The editing functions that allow you to transfer image data include copying, cutting, and pasting objects and pictures, deleting or duplicating objects, and copying object attributes. You access these operations using the Cut, Copy, Paste, Clear, Duplicate, and Copy Style From commands in the Edit menu.

These editing functions have many uses that will save you time and design effort. You don't have to start from scratch each time you need to duplicate an object or its style attribute. You can simply transfer image information, using the editing commands. You perform some of the transfer operations within a single picture; others allow you to transfer information between

CorelDRAW! files, and even between CorelDRAW! and other Windows applications.

Starting with Version 1.1, CorelDRAW! allows you to transfer objects to and from the Windows clipboard. This means that you can copy or cut objects between different image files in CorelDRAW!, or from CorelDRAW! to a file in another Windows application. Conversely, you can copy or cut objects from files in other Windows applications and paste them to the page of your choice in CorelDRAW!.

This chapter covers the use of the Windows clipboard, both within CorelDRAW! and between CorelDRAW! and other Windows applications. It also introduces you to some additional object and style copying functions in CorelDRAW! that complement the use of the Windows clipboard. You'll find out how to duplicate objects within a drawing and how to copy attributes from one object to another. You'll also review the difference between cutting objects from a file and deleting them permanently.

About the Windows Clipboard

If you haven't used Windows applications before, you may be wondering how the clipboard works. Think of the Windows clipboard as a temporary storage bin that can contain only one item at a time. When you select an object and then click on the Copy or Cut command in the Edit menu, you send a copy of the object to the clipboard. When you use the Paste command, you retrieve a copy of that object from the clipboard to place it in your drawing at the desired location. The copy you sent to the clipboard remains there until you overwrite it by copying or cutting another object, or until you exit Windows and end a session.

Windows creates its own file format, called a *metafile*, out of the information that you send to the clipboard. This standard metafile format allows you to share information between different applications that run under Windows. A metafile can be larger or smaller than the object you send to the clipboard, depending on the complexity of the information you are trying to transfer. Versions of Windows previous to 3.0 accept only 64K of data at a time into the clipboard. However, as you will see later in the chapter, this limitation does not always apply when you are simply transferring information between different CorelDRAW! files. As a rule of thumb, the more complex an object is in terms of its attributes, the more memory it requires when you send it to the clipboard.

Theoretically, all Windows applications should be able to trade information through the clipboard. In practice, however, some types of information in objects or files transfer better than others. When you have completed the basic exercises on copying, cutting, and pasting objects within CorelDRAW!, turn to the section entitled "Between Applications." There you will find tips for trouble-free transfer operations through the clipboard.

Copy, Cut, Duplicate, or Clear

In order to duplicate or delete one or more objects, or copy or cut them to the clipboard, you must first select the objects with the Select tool. The Edit menu commands and their keyboard shortcuts are unavailable to you unless one or more objects are already selected.

You can select a single object, multiple objects, or all objects in a graphic for any of the Edit menu operations discussed in this chapter. To select a single object for one of the transfer operations, just click on its outline once. To select multiple objects for a transfer operation, use (SHIFT) or the marquee method you first learned in Chapter 8. (You might also want to group the objects after you select them in order to avoid separating them from each other accidentally.) To select all of the objects in a graphic, click on the Select All command in the Edit menu.

Once you have selected one or more objects, you are ready to apply the commands in the Edit menu.

Copying and Pasting Objects

The Copy and Paste commands in the Edit menu enable you to copy CorelDRAW! objects and paste them to the same file, to another file in CorelDRAW!, or to another Windows application. When you *copy* an object to the clipboard, the original object remains in position on the page. When you *paste* the object, Windows makes another copy from the copy in the clipboard. The copy in the clipboard remains there until you overwrite it by copying or cutting another object or group of objects, or until you exit Windows.

To practice copying objects to the clipboard and pasting them to the same or different pictures, you will use a file that you created in Chapter 8, as well as two sample files provided with your software.

Copying and Pasting Objects Within a Picture

When you copy an object to the clipboard and then paste it to the same picture, the copy overlays the original object exactly. The copy is selected as soon as it appears on the page, however, so you can move it safely without displacing the original object.

A more convenient way to copy an object within the same picture is to use the Duplicate command. When you invoke this command, CorelDRAW! automatically offsets the copy of the object from the original by a fixed distance that you specify. As a result, you can see both the original and the copy at the same time. See the "Duplicating Objects" section of this chapter for more details.

1. Open the ARROW1.CDR file and group all of the text strings in the picture, using the Select All command in the Edit menu and then the Group command in the Arrange menu.

2. To copy the grouped objects to the clipboard, either select the Copy command from the Edit menu as shown in Figure 12-1, or press (CTRL)-(INS). The cursor turns into an hourglass until CorelDRAW! finishes copying the selected object to the clipboard. If the error message shown in Figure 12-2 appears, click on the OK command button to return to the drawing. In most cases, CorelDRAW! will actually have copied the selected objects to the clipboard in spite of the message. Check the Paste command in the Edit menu; if it is now available for selection, the objects have been successfully copied. If this command is not available, CorelDRAW! could not copy the selected objects.

Figure 12-1. *Selecting the Copy command*

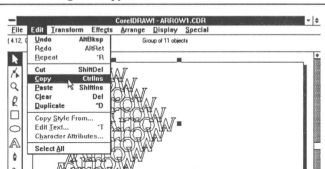

3. Select Paste from the Edit menu or press (SHIFT)-(INS). The screen redraws, with the pasted object selected. You will not notice anything different because the pasted object appears exactly on top of the original.

4. To move the pasted object away from the original, press and hold the mouse button directly over any outline of the selected object and drag it as desired. You can now scale, rotate, stretch, skew, or otherwise edit the pasted object.

5. Select New from the File menu to clear the screen before continuing. Do not save any changes to the ARROW1.CDR document.

Text is the most complex kind of object that CorelDRAW! copies to the clipboard. If you try to copy a text string that contains attributes such as

Figure 12-2. *The Windows clipboard "too large" error message*

custom calligraphic outlines (Chapter 13, "Defining the Outline Pen"), Post-Script halftone screens (Chapter 14, "Defining Outline Color"), or fountain fills (Chapter 15, "Defining Fill Color"), you are likely to see the "too large" error message, shown in Figure 12-2. The clipboard may accept an object in spite of the error message, however, as long as you remain in CorelDRAW! and do not go to another software application. Check the Edit menu to see whether the Paste command becomes available. If the Paste command is still gray, the object has not been copied. You may have to break it down into smaller components (such as a few characters) and then try to copy each component separately.

In the previous exercise, you copied a group of objects to the same picture. In the next section, you will copy an object to a different picture and use it as a design enhancement there.

Copying and Pasting Between Pictures

In the following exercise you will copy the text string from the DOINWHAT.CDR file and paste it to the KITE.CDR file.

1. Open the DOINWHAT.CDR file and select the text string.

2. Select Copy from the Edit menu or press (CTRL)-(INS) to copy the text to the clipboard. The cursor may temporarily turn into an hourglass until CorelDRAW! finishes copying the text string. This lets you know it's busy.

3. Open the KITE.CDR file and drag all of the guidelines off the screen.

4. From the Edit menu, choose Select All; then from the Arrange menu, select Group. The Status line should contain "Group of 4 objects."

5. Position the cursor at any of the four corner boundary markers of the group. Then drag the marker diagonally inward to scale down the kite to approximately 50% of its original size.

6. Drag the kite so it is approximately centered horizontally (and leaves about two-thirds of the vertical white space at the top). See Figure 12-3.

7. Select Paste from the Edit menu or press (SHIFT)-(INS). The text string will come into the center of the page.

Figure 12-3.   *Kite positioned to receive pasted text*

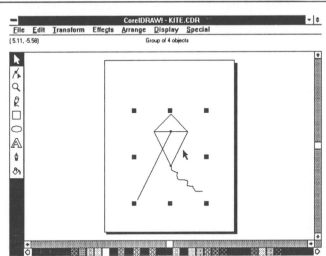

8. Drag the text to the top of the page to complete the image (to be produced here) as shown in Figure 12-4.

9. Select Save As from the File menu, type **kite2,** and select Save.

As you can see from the preceding exercise, you don't have to start from scratch to design an attractive picture. You can copy and paste existing objects and images to an illustration in progress, saving yourself work without sacrificing quality or originality. In the next sections, you will experiment with the Cut and Paste menu commands and see how their operation differs from that of Copy and Paste.

Cutting and Pasting Objects

When you select an object and then invoke the Cut command in the Edit menu, the object disappears and goes to the clipboard. When you then select the Paste command, Windows places a copy of the cut object on the page.

Figure 12-4.   *Copying and pasting an object to an existing image*

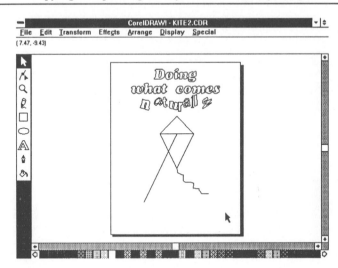

The original object that you cut remains in the clipboard until you overwrite it by cutting or copying another object, or until you end a Windows session.

To begin practicing cutting and pasting objects, you will use the LANDSCAP.CDR file you created in Chapter 6.

Cutting and Pasting Within a Picture

There are two ways to remove an unwanted object from a picture in CorelDRAW!. You can either cut it to the clipboard using the Cut command, or delete it from the program memory entirely by using the Clear command. Use the Cut command unless you are absolutely certain that you will never need the object again. If you delete an object using the Clear command, CorelDRAW! doesn't store a copy anywhere; unless you immediately select the Undo command, you won't be able to recover the object.

CorelDRAW! always pastes a cut or copied object as the top layer of the picture. Therefore, when you cut and paste objects within an image that contains several layers of objects, remember to restore the original object arrangement using the commands in the Arrange menu.

1. Open the LANDSCAP.CDR file that you created in Chapter 6.

2. With the Select tool, draw a marquee around the tree and its trunk to select it (make sure your marquee is large enough to completely enclose the boundary markers for the top of the tree).

3. From the Arrange menu, select Group.

4. Select Cut from the Edit menu or press (SHIFT)-(DEL). The tree disappears from the drawing as shown in Figure 12-5.

5. Select Paste from the Edit menu and the tree comes back onto the drawing in the same place it was originally.

   If the tree was not on the top layer of the drawing, it is after pasting. In that case it is not *exactly* where it was originally.

6. Select a bird and the select Clear from the Edit menu or press (DEL).

Figure 12-5. *The tree cut from LANDSCAP.CDR*

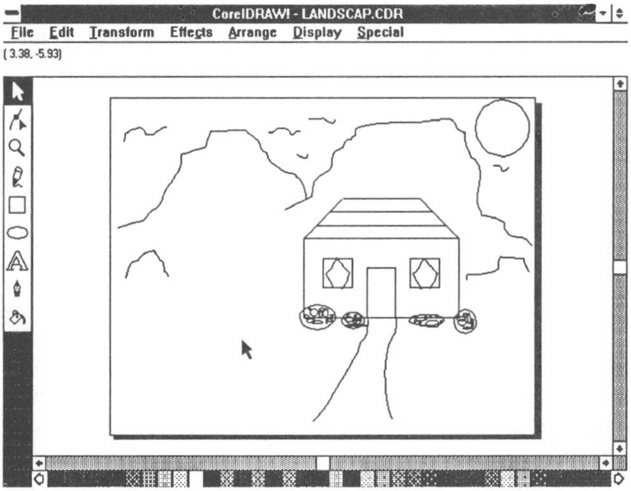

Once an object has been cleared or deleted from a drawing you can use Undo to restore it. If you do so, select Undo prior to doing anything else; otherwise the object is gone. Undo only remembers the last action.

7. Press (SHIFT)-(INS) or select Paste again. Another tree comes onto the drawing, not the bird—the bird is not on the clipboard; the tree still is. There will be a second tree because the second tree came in on top of the original tree. Drag the second tree off to one side to see the other tree. Press (DEL) to get rid of the second tree.

Go immediately on to the next section of this chapter because you will need to use the contents of the clipboard (the tree) in the next section, where you will cut and paste objects between different pictures in CorelDRAW!.

Cutting and Pasting Between Pictures

Earlier in this chapter, you created a poster by combining the kite you drew in Chapter 2 with some text you created in Chapter 11. In the following exercise, you will add two copies of the tree you cut from the LANDSCAP.CDR drawing and the word "CorelDRAW!" you will cut from a sample drawing that came with your copy of CorelDRAW!.

1. From the File menu, select Open. Answer No to saving changes to the LANDSCAP.CDR file and select KITE2.CDR as the file to open.

2. Press (SHIFT)-(INS) to paste the tree from the clipboard onto the kite poster. When the tree comes onto the drawing, drag it down about a quarter of an inch.

3. Again select Paste and drag the second tree to the right side of the poster and then approximately align it with the first tree. See Figure 12-6.

4. Save the file as KITE3.CDR and then, from your SAMPLES directory, open the DOESALL.CDR file.

5. With the Select tool, draw a marquee around the word "CorelDRAW!," select Group from the Arrange menu, and select Cut from the Edit menu.

Figure 12-6. 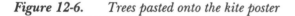 *Trees pasted onto the kite poster*

12

6. Select Open from the Files menu, answer No to saving the current file, and select KITE3.CDR.

7. Select Paste. The word "CorelDRAW!" appears in the middle of the drawing.

8. Drag "CorelDRAW!" to the bottom of the poster and, by dragging on one of the corner boundary markers, scale it to fit in the space available as shown in Figure 12-7.

9. Save the completed poster as KITE4.CDR and select New to clear your workspace.

Working with Different Applications

The number of software packages running under Microsoft Windows is increasing almost daily. These programs include such diverse applications as word processors, desktop publishing and presentation software, database

Figure 12-7.   *Completed poster with four pasted objects*

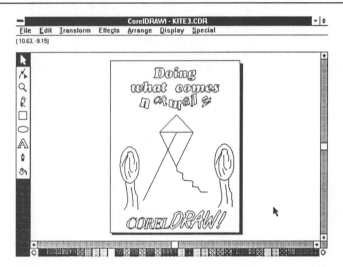

managers and forms generators, and, of course, paint and illustration software. If your other favorite Windows applications also support the Windows
clipboard, you should be able to transfer data back and forth between them
and CorelDRAW!.

Features and techniques differ with every application; however, as a
result, not all visual information transfers equally well between programs.
There are too many Windows applications to catalog what happens to each
file type as it transfers to or from CorelDRAW! through the clipboard.
However, the following sections should give you an idea of how the clipboard
handles graphic information that you transfer between CorelDRAW! and
some of the most popular software.

Clipboard Memory Limits

Microsoft Windows, not CorelDRAW!, determines just how much information you can transfer to the clipboard at one time. The limit for Microsoft

Windows 2.11 and earlier is 64K, while Windows 3.0 is theoretically unlimited. This number refers to the size of the Windows metafile (WMF) that is created when you send information to the clipboard; this is *not* the file size that you see in a DOS directory. Since you cannot predict exactly how large a metafile a certain object or group of objects will generate, it's not easy to define how many or which kinds of objects you can transfer easily. If the objects you want to place on the clipboard exceed the metafile limit, however, the error message box shown in Figure 12-2 appears. As previously mentioned, the clipboard may accept these large objects if you paste them to another file within CorelDRAW!, but if you leave CorelDRAW! and then try to paste the objects to another application, the clipboard will appear to be empty.

In general, you'll have the best chance of success when copying, cutting, and pasting CorelDRAW! objects that don't take advantage of too many advanced features at one time. An image that includes text, custom calligraphic outlines, PostScript fills, or fountain fills, for example, will be more difficult to transfer to the clipboard than an apparently complex geometrical image that contains none of these features.

Transferring Objects to Other Applications

When you copy or cut a CorelDRAW! object to the clipboard, you are transferring not only the shape of an object, but also its attributes. Attributes include outline, outline fill, object fill, and text characteristics. Some attributes do not transfer well in their original form, owing in some cases to the diversity of Windows applications and in others to the complexity of CorelDRAW! features.

Most problems with transferring CorelDRAW! objects into the clipboard have to do with the memory limit. The following tips should help you avoid clipboard memory or Windows metafile compatibility problems.

Fountain fills and PostScript fills (both discussed in Chapter 15) are extremely memory intensive from the standpoint of the Windows clipboard, and they may go through unpredictable changes when transferred to another program. For example, the following anomalies have been observed when transferring objects containing fountain and PostScript fills:

- With CorelDRAW! 2.0 and before, fountain fills tended to cover an area larger than the object that contained them. This was corrected in 2.01.

- Objects with PostScript fills may be represented by blank space when they are pasted into some applications. Even the outline disappears.

When an object with PostScript fill is transferred through the clipboard, you often get the outline and then either no fill, or the little "PS"s that you see on the CorelDRAW! screen. The PostScript fill itself is not transferred in any instance.

Text sent from CorelDRAW! files to the clipboard can be sensitive also. The greater the number of letters and/or attributes in a text string, the more likely that some information will not transfer properly. The specific program to which you want to send the text may further influence the transfer of information. As a general rule text comes in as a graphic object rather than as editable text.

On the positive side, a number of applications such as PageMaker can import CorelDRAW!-produced lines, curves, fills, fountain fills, and text, with all of their attributes, from the clipboard without a problem.

Transferring Objects from Other Applications

When you transfer objects from your other favorite Windows applications to CorelDRAW!, you may not always receive exactly what you sent to the clipboard. Sometimes this limitation depends on what the Windows clipboard can interpret; at other times, the apparent discrepancy is specific to the interaction between the other program and CorelDRAW!.

The clipboard, for example, has difficulty transferring special text kerning or text rotation information, pattern or flood fills, pixel-by-pixel manipulations, and combined pen colors from other Windows applications to CorelDRAW!.

Text that you import into CorelDRAW! from another Windows application comes in with the default text attributes. If you know the typeface, typestyle, alignment, and other attributes you want, set these before importing the text. You can import a maximum of 4000 text characters at a time.

Some features do not transfer well into CorelDRAW!. Bitmaps, for example, often don't transfer well. Text sent from other graphics applications (as opposed to word processors) often arrives in CorelDRAW! as curves. A fill or fountain fill from another program may transfer into CorelDRAW! as solid, or as an outline and separate fill object. Circles and ellipses may come in as connected line segments, while curves may become straight line segments. As CorelDRAW!, Microsoft Windows, and other Windows applications are constantly being upgraded, however, you can expect compatibility to improve. In the remaining sections of the chapter, you will learn about special commands in the CorelDRAW! Edit menu that make it easy for you to copy objects or their attributes within a CorelDRAW! file.

Duplicating Objects

As you saw earlier in the chapter, you can use the Copy and Paste commands in the Edit menu to make a copy of an object within a picture. This process can be somewhat time-consuming if you use it frequently, because you need two separate menu commands or keyboard combinations to perform one action. A more convenient way of achieving the same end is to use the Duplicate command in the Edit menu or its keyboard shortcut, (CTRL)-(D).

The Duplicate command causes a copy of the selected object or objects to appear at a specified *offset* from the original. In other words, the duplicate copy does not appear directly on top of the original, but at a horizontal and vertical distance from it, which you specify. This makes it easier to move the duplicate to a new location.

You can also use the Duplicate command alone or with the Combine command in the Arrange menu to achieve unusual logo or graphic designs, or special effects. In the next exercise, you will create and duplicate three different series of rectangles, each with a different specified offset. Then you will combine them to create the design shown in Figure 12-12.

1. Starting with a blank page, change the page format to Landscape using the Page Setup command from the File menu.

2. Select the Preferences command from the Special menu. Check the
    Place Duplicate settings at the top of the Preferences dialog box.
    The numeric entry and units boxes should each show the default
    value setting of 0.25 inches, as shown in Figure 12-8.

    If the values are correct, select OK and exit the dialog box. If you
    see a different setting, change it to 0.25 inches.

3. Select the Rectangle tool and draw a rectangle about halfway down
    the left edge of the page. The rectangle should be wider than it is
    long.

4. Press (CTRL)-(D) or select the Duplicate command from the Edit
    menu. An exact copy of the rectangle appears 0.25 inches to the
    right and above the original. Press (CTRL)-(D) repeatedly until you
    have created 14 copies of the rectangle, as in Figure 12-9.

5. Change the Place Duplicate setting in the Preferences dialog box to
    0.05 inches in both the Horizontal and Vertical numeric entry boxes.

Figure 12-8.   *Place Duplicate settings*

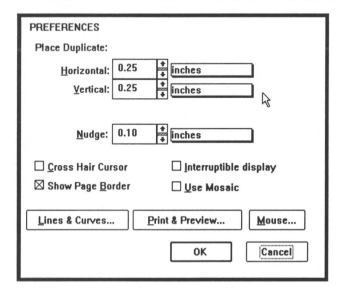

Figure 12-9. *Creating and duplicating the first set of rectangles*

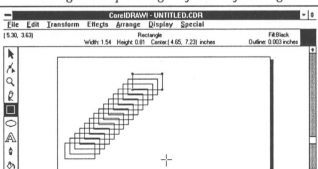

12

6. With the Rectangle tool still selected, draw another rectangle to the right of the first series. Then, press (CTRL)-(D) twenty (20) times in succession. This time, the duplicates appear at much shorter intervals, as shown in Figure 12-10, giving a smooth appearance to the transitions between the series of duplicated objects.

7. Refer to the Place Duplicate: setting in the Preferences dialog box one more time and change both values to – 0.10 inches. The negative

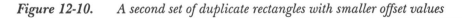

Figure 12-10. *A second set of duplicate rectangles with smaller offset values*

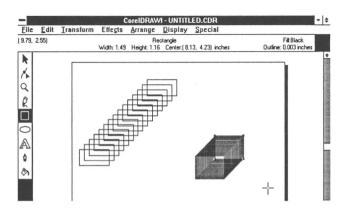

Figure 12-11.   *Creating and duplicating a third set of rectangles*

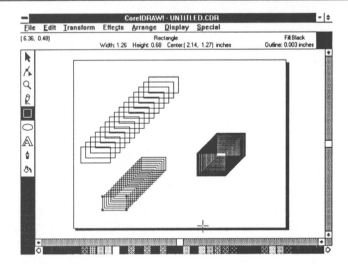

numbers indicate that the duplicates will appear below and to the
left of the original object.

8. Draw a third rectangle between the first and second series of
   rectangles and then press (CTRL)-(D) twenty (20) times in succession.
   This time, the duplicates appear to the left of and below the original
   object, as shown in Figure 12-11.

9. Turn on the preview window in side-by-side format and then activate
   the Select tool. Beginning with the first series of objects you created,
   select each series and apply the Combine command in the Arrange
   menu. You will recall from Chapter 8 that the use of the Combine
   command causes alternating objects in a group to become
   transparent.

10. When you have combined all three series of objects, adjust the
    preview window so that it fills the entire screen. As you can see from
    Figure 12-12, the various offset settings lead to different special
    effects when you combine each group of rectangles.

Figure 12-12. *Special effects created with the Duplicate and Combine commands (with full screen view)*

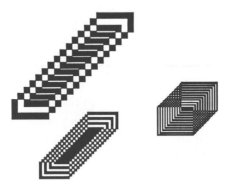

11. Save this file as DUPECOMB.CDR and then select New to clear the screen.

The preceding exercise shows you only one potential use for the Duplicate command. You can probably think of many others that will spark your creativity and enhance your design abilities, especially since you can apply this command to multiple or grouped objects as well as single objects. In the next section, you will see an example of another interesting CorelDRAW! copying technique—one that transfers attributes rather than the objects themselves.

Copying an Object's Style

Suppose that you have spent a lot of time designing an object, giving it a custom calligraphic outline, special fills, or a unique combination of text attributes. You would like to give the same set of attributes to another object, but you don't want to waste time setting up all those attributes from scratch. CorelDRAW! allows you to save time and enhance the design of your image by using the Copy Style From command in the Edit menu. You will practice using this command in the following exercise.

1. Select the Page Setup command in the File menu and change the page format to Portrait.

2. Adjust magnification to actual size (1:1), then activate the Text tool and select an insertion point near the top left of the page. When the Text dialog box appears, type **Corel** in the text entry window. Set text attributes to Aardvark bold, 100.0 points, and justification None. Click on the Spacing command button, change intercharacter spacing to 0.30 ems, and then select OK twice.

3. Select a second insertion point a little below the first one. This time, type **DRAW!** in the text entry window and set attributes to Avalon Italic, 50.0 points, and Left justification. Click on the Spacing command button, assure that the intercharacter spacing has automatically been reset to 0.00 ems, and then select OK twice. When

Figure 12-13.   *Preparing to copy text attributes from one text string to another*

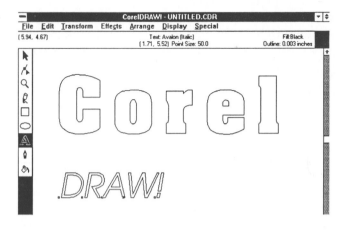

this text string appears, your screen should look similar to the one in Figure 12-13.

4. Activate the Select tool to select the second text string automatically, and then click on the Copy Style From command in the Edit menu. The Copy Style dialog box shown in Figure 12-14 appears. This dialog box contains four options—Outline Pen, Outline Color, Fill, and Text Attributes—each with its own checkbox. You can choose to copy any or all of these attributes to the selected object. If you use the Shaping tool instead of the Select tool to select your text, Text Attributes will be grayed-out and unavailable. Cancel and pick the Select tool. Since you haven't worked with the Outline or Fill tools yet, just click on the Text Attributes checkbox to place a checkmark in it. Notice that a message at the bottom of the dialog box instructs you to select the object from which you want to copy the attributes.

5. Click on the OK command button to exit to the page. The cursor turns into a thick arrow containing the word "From?" This reminds you to click on the object from which you want to copy attributes.

6. Select the "Corel" text string by clicking anywhere on its outlines with the tip of the arrow. The "DRAW!" text string immediately changes to reflect the same attributes as the "Corel" text string, as

Figure 12-14. *The Copy Style dialog box*

Figure 12-15.   *Selected object with attributes copied from adjoining object*

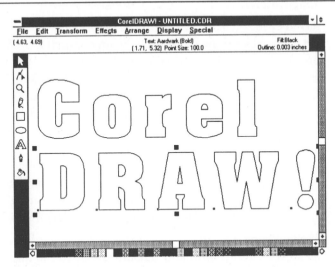

shown in Figure 12-15. If you miss the outline when you click, a dialog box comes up giving you the chance to try again.

7. Select New from the File menu to clear the screen. Do not save these changes.

You will have opportunities to use this dialog box again in Chapters 13 through 15. In the final section of this chapter, you will review techniques for deleting objects in CorelDRAW!.

Deleting Objects

As mentioned previously, you can delete objects from a CorelDRAW! drawing in one of two ways: by cutting them to the clipboard (SHIFT)-(DEL) or by selecting the Clear command from the Edit menu (keyboard shortcut: (DEL)). It is generally advisable to cut an object to the clipboard if you might want to paste it back to the same or to a different drawing later. Use the Clear command or its keyboard shortcut only if you are certain that you will not need the deleted object later, because CorelDRAW! doesn't save a cleared object anywhere in memory.

To delete a single object, select the object, and then apply the Clear command. You can also choose to delete multiple objects or all objects in the picture, using any of the multiple selection techniques you learned in earlier chapters.

You have experimented in this chapter with the available techniques for copying, cutting, and pasting objects and attributes within or between CorelDRAW! files, and between CorelDRAW! and other applications. In the next three chapters, you will learn about outline width, outline fill, and object fill—important attributes that you can assign to any new or existing object.

13

Defining the Outline Pen

In CorelDRAW!, all objects have outline pen, outline color, and object fill attributes. In addition, text has its own set of attributes, as you learned in Chapter 11. All of the objects you created and edited until now had standard black fills and fixed-width black outlines. In this chapter, however, you will start to modify outline attributes, using the CorelDRAW! Outline tool ⌕.

The Outline tool is actually two tools in one. In order to create an outline for any object, you need to define the *outline pen* and the *outline color* in two separate steps. Think of the Outline tool as a calligraphic pen having an almost infinite number of replaceable nibs. The outline pen, which you will explore in this chapter, represents the shape of the nib and emulates the possible ways you can slant your hand while drawing. And the outline color, which you will learn about in Chapter 14, "Defining Outline Color," represents the ink and textures that flow from the pen.

When defining an outline pen for any object, you can vary the width, line type, corner shape, line end styles, and nib shape of the pen. You can also control the placement of the outline relative to the object's fill color. Only CorelDRAW! allows you so great a degree of control over the shape and appearance of your drawings. With your first try, you can create ornate calligraphic effects and simulate a hand-sketched look electronically.

Defining Outline Pen Attributes

The method you use to define outline pen attributes depends on whether you are creating new objects with the current default settings, editing attributes for existing objects, or altering default outline settings. The following checklist summarizes the order of steps involved.

- To create an object with the current default outline pen attributes, you select the appropriate drawing tool and draw the object. You can then select the Outline tool to view the current default outline attributes (optional).

- To edit outline pen attributes for an existing object (including grouped or combined objects), you activate the Select tool, select the object, and then click on the Outline tool.

- To begin setting new outline pen default attributes, you click on the Outline tool and then on the desired icon.

Once you have selected the Outline tool, you can choose between defining a custom outline pen or selecting a preset outline width. In the remaining sections of this chapter, you will practice customizing outline pen attributes and selecting preset outline pen widths for both planned and existing objects.

Tip

Always work with the preview window turned on when you define outline pen attributes. The editing window doesn't show you how the outline pen really looks, but the WYSIWYG preview window lets you see the results of your settings instantly.

Customizing the Outline Pen

You have complete control over the attributes of the outline pen in CorelDRAW!, thanks to a dialog box that appears when you click on the outline pen icon in the Outline tool fly-out menu. By altering the settings in this dialog box, you can vary the outline's placement and width, change the shape of corners and line end styles, design custom nibs, and create an array of calligraphic effects.

The way you access this dialog box varies, depending on whether you are creating objects with default attributes, editing attributes for existing objects, or altering default attributes. In the following exercises, you will create an object with default outline pen attributes and become familiar with the settings in the Outline Pen dialog box. Then, you will edit outline pen attributes for existing objects in the sample files that came packaged with your software. Finally, you will set up new default outline pen attributes that will apply to objects you draw later.

If you simply want to specify outline width, without creating a custom outline pen, turn to the section "Selecting a Preset Outline Pen Width." There, you will find out how to alter the width of the outline pen quickly, without accessing a dialog box.

Creating Objects with Default Attributes

When you create a new object, CorelDRAW! applies the current default settings to it automatically. You can leave those settings as they are or edit them. When you edit outline pen settings for a newly created object, however, your changes apply only to that object. Other objects that you create continue to have the default outline pen attributes until you set new defaults.

In the exercise that follows, you will create a text string, select the Outline tool fly-out menu and access the Outline Pen dialog box, and observe the default outline pen attributes that are standard with CorelDRAW!.

1. Make sure that the Show Rulers, Show Grid, and Snap To Grid commands are turned off, select the Magnification tool ⟨Q⟩ and set magnification to Actual Size (1:1).

2. Activate the Text tool ⟨A⟩ and select an insertion point near the upper-left edge of the page. When the Text dialog box appears, type **outline pen** in the text entry box. Set text attributes to Gatineau Normal, 90.0 points, and Left Justification. Set intercharacter spacing to 0.10 ems, and then select OK twice.

3. When the text string appears, turn on the preview window and adjust the editing and preview windows to a top-to-bottom format. Magnify the text string only by using the Zoom-In tool ⌖ in the Magnification tool fly-out menu. You do not have to activate the Select tool to select the text string; the presence of the nodes indicates that as a newly drawn object, it's already selected.

4. The interior of the text string in the preview window is black. For the purposes of this exercise, you want to remove the fill color to clearly view your outline. To do this, click on the Fill tool icon ⬡ at the bottom of the CorelDRAW! toolbox and then select X from the fly-out menu that appears:

The text string in the preview window redisplays with just the outline. The center is hollow, as shown in Figure 13-1. (If your text seems to have vanished completely in the preview window, you will find a solution in the next step.)

5. Click on the Outline tool ⬡ . A fly-out menu appears:

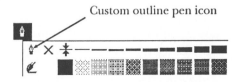

Custom outline pen icon

The Outline tool fly-out menu contains two rows of options. The top row consists of controls for the outline pen, which you will use throughout this chapter. The second row of the fly-out menu, which you will work with in Chapter 14, contains controls for the outline fill color. (If the text string has disappeared from your preview window, click on the solid black icon in the second row of this fly-out menu to make it reappear.)

6. Ignore all but the first (left most) control in the top row of the fly-out menu. The eleven controls after the first one allow you to quickly specify fixed outline widths (but no other attributes) for the outline pen. You will practice working with these eleven controls in the "Selecting a Preset Outline Pen Width" section of this chapter. For now, click on the first icon in the top row, the *Custom Outline Pen* icon. It looks just like the Outline tool icon, but it has the more specialized function of allowing you to specify all the possible attributes of the outline pen. The Outline Pen dialog box displays, as in Figure 13-2. Leave this dialog box on the screen for now.

The Outline Pen dialog box contains controls for nine outline pen attributes. The default settings on your screen should match the settings in Figure 13-2, unless you or another user has altered them since installing the software. If your dialog box shows different settings, adjust them to match the ones in the figure. Then, take a moment to become familiar with the attributes and how they function.

Figure 13-1.   *Outline text with fill removed*

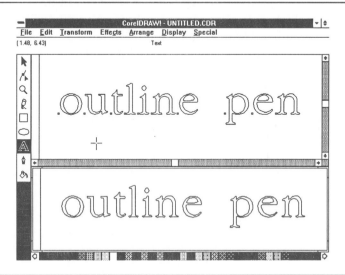

Figure 13-2.   *The Outline Pen dialog box*

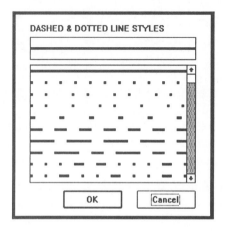

Line Style   At the top of the dialog box is a display box that shows the line style currently selected. To the right of this box is a command button labeled Dashing. This command button opens another dialog box that allows you to choose from a number of dotted and dashed line styles as you can see here:

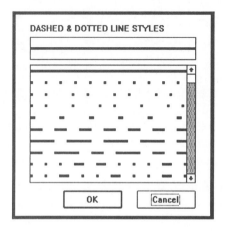

To choose a line style, use the scroll bar to display the style you want, click on that line style, and click on OK. You'll be returned to the Outline Pen dialog box, and the line style you choose will be in the display box. The solid line shown in Figure 13-2 is the default line style.

Arrows   Below the Dashing command button is the Arrows command button. The Arrows command button opens the Arrowhead Selection dialog box shown in Figure 13-3. This dialog box allows you to select or construct a line ending to go on either end of a line. These line endings are shown in the display boxes immediately below the Arrows command button in the Outline Pen dialog box and in the two display boxes in the Arrowhead dialog box. Figure 13-3 shows two selected line endings. To select a line ending, scroll through the boxes of line endings until you see the one you want. Click on the line ending you want with the left mouse button if you want the ending applied to the beginning of a line (normally the left end) or with the right mouse button if you want the ending applied to the end of a line (normally the right). If you don't know which end is the beginning, click on the line with the Shape tool and see which end has the larger node; the one that does is

Figure 13-3.   *Arrowhead Selection dialog box*

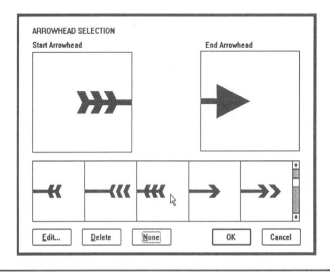

the beginning. If you want to get rid of a line ending from the list of line endings, select it and click on Delete. If you want to remove a line ending you previously selected, select None. After you have selected a head or tail shape, the Edit command button will be enabled. Clicking on it opens the Arrow Head Editor shown here:

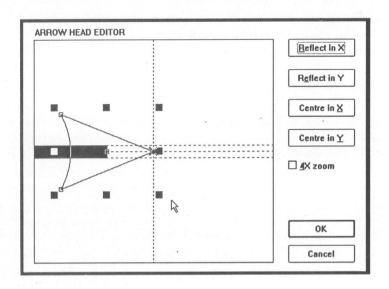

The Arrow Head Editor displays an enlarged arrowhead and allows you to move, scale, and stretch the arrowhead by dragging on it or one of its boundary markers; you can center the arrowhead relative to the X in the middle of the editor by selecting Centre in X to center horizontally or Centre in Y to center vertically; or you can flip the arrowhead horizontally with Reflect in X or vertically with Reflect in Y. Also you can magnify the arrowhead image by clicking on 4X zoom.

Behind Fill   The Behind Fill checkbox lets you specify whether the outline of an object should appear in front of or behind the object's fill. The default setting is in front of the fill (empty checkbox), but if you create objects with thick outlines, you will want to activate Behind Fill. This is especially advisable with text, where thick outlines appearing in front of the fill can obliterate empty spaces and cause text to appear smudged, like this:

outline pen

When you place an outline behind the fill, only half of it is visible. The outline therefore appears to be only half as thick as specified.

Scale With Image　When the Scale With Image checkbox contains an X, the width and angle of the outline change proportionally as you resize, rotate, or skew the object. CorelDRAW! automatically updates the width and angle settings in the Outline Pen dialog box when Scale With Image is active. When the Scale With Image setting is *not* active, the width and angle of an object's outline do not change, no matter how you stretch, scale, rotate, or skew the object. This can lead to some interesting but unintended changes in appearance when you define a calligraphic pen nib for the object, as you will see in the "Scaling the Outline with the Image" section of this chapter.

Corners　The Corners options pertain to objects that tend to have sharp corners: lines, open and closed curve objects, rectangles, and some angular typefaces. The three option buttons in this area of the dialog box allow you to choose just how CorelDRAW! shapes those corners. The first (default) option shows a sharp or *miter* corner, where the outer edges of two joining line or curve segments extend until they meet. By altering the Miter Limit setting in the Print and Preview dialog box under the Preferences command, you can control the angle below which CorelDRAW! flattens or bevels the edge of a sharp curve. When you choose the second option button, CorelDRAW! *rounds* the corners where two lines or curve segments meet. When you choose the third or *bevel* corner option button, corners of joining curve or line segments are flattened. The results of the Corners settings are usually subtle, unless you magnify an object or combine Corners settings with Pen Shape attributes for calligraphic effects.

Line Caps　The Line Caps options apply to lines and open curves, but not to closed path objects such as rectangles, closed curves, or ellipses. These settings determine the end styles of lines and curves. The first or default option is a *butt* line end style, where the line ends exactly at the end point.

The second option gives you *rounded* line end points. When you choose either the second or the third (*square* line end type), the line extends beyond the end point for a distance equal to half of the line thickness. When you select any of the line end caps, that style applies to both end points of the line or curve. If you have selected dashed lines as your line type for an object, each dash takes on the shape of the line end style you choose.

Width, Angle, and Stretch   The remaining three outline pen attributes— width, angle, and stretch—all help you define a custom pen shape, analogous to the *nib* or point of a calligraphic fountain pen. With default values of 0.014-inch width, a 0 degree angle, and 100% stretch, the pen shape is square, resulting in a plain outline. On their own, these settings will not create calligraphic effects. When you alter them in combination, however, they allow you to outline objects with varying thick and thin strokes at the angle of your choice. The Corners settings work with the Pen Shape settings to define the appearance of calligraphic strokes, as you will learn in the "A Pen Shape for Calligraphic Effects" section of this chapter.

Now that you are familiar with the functions of the attributes in the Outline Pen dialog box, exit the dialog box by selecting Cancel. Clear the screen by selecting New from the File menu before going further.

A Custom Outline Pen for New Objects

Different artists have different styles, and you may prefer to create most of your objects with outline pen styles that differ from the standard settings. If so, perform the exercise in this section to learn how to customize outline pen defaults. Objects that you create after changing the default attributes will then conform to the appearance that characterizes your working style.

Creating objects with new outline pen defaults is a three-stage process. First, you access the 'New Object' Outline Pen dialog box. Then you change the outline pen attributes. Finally, you create new objects, which automatically adhere to the new default attributes. The dialog box that you use to edit default settings is identical to the Outline Pen dialog box, except for its title and the way you access it.

1. Start with a blank page. (If you are in an existing drawing and want to change default settings, make sure that no object is selected.)

Then select the Outline tool and click on the Custom Outline Pen icon. Since no object is selected, the message box in Figure 13-4 appears.

2. Select OK to access the 'New Object' Outline Pen dialog box and have the defaults apply to all new objects. The contents of this dialog box are identical to the contents of the normal Outline Pen dialog box. Only the title is different, to remind you that you are changing default attributes for the outline pen.

3. For now don't change the defaults. As you go through this chapter you will exercise each of the options in this dialog box and become familiar with their effects and what your likes and dislikes are. When you are done with the chapter, you can come back here and set the defaults to what is right for you.

4. Select Cancel to close the dialog box without change and return to the work area.

Figure 13-4.   *'New Object' Outline Pen dialog box*

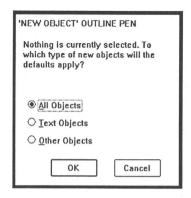

It's that easy to alter default settings for the outline pen. As with almost every other CorelDRAW! feature, customization is the key word. CorelDRAW! encourages you to create images according to your unique working habits and style.

On the other hand, if you are involved in technical illustration or your normal CorelDRAW! tasks are relatively uncomplicated, you may seldom require calligraphy or other special options in the Outline Pen and 'New Object' Outline Pen dialog boxes. The next section shows you how to change the outline pen width quickly and interactively, without the use of a dialog box.

Selecting a Preset Outline Pen Width

If Width is the outline pen attribute you change most frequently, CorelDRAW! offers a shortcut that saves you time and keeps you out of the Outline Pen dialog box. The first row of the fly-out menu that appears when you select the Outline tool, as shown in Figure 13-5, contains ten preset outline widths from which you can choose.

You can choose one of these options for a currently selected object, or you can set a fixed line width as a new default. When you choose a preset outline width for a selected object, you apply that width to the selected object only. When you click on one of these options without having first selected an object, however, CorelDRAW! assumes that you want to set the option as a new default width and the message box shown in Figure 13-4 pops up. Select OK to set the selected line width as a new default for objects that you draw in the future. If you meant to select an existing object first, click on the Cancel command button instead.

The first option next to the Custom Outline Pen icon on the left (see Figure 13-5) is an X; click on this option when you want a selected object to have no outline at all. When an object has no outline, an outline will appear in the editing window, but not in the preview window.

The next option, a thin line with two arrows, represents a hairline or a line 1/4 point wide. The preview window, however, does not display a true WYSIWYG representation of an outline this thin. The outlines in the editing

Figure 13-5.   *Preset outline widths available in Outline tool fly-out menu*

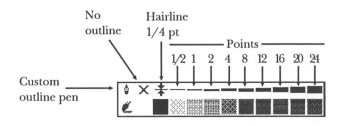

13

and preview windows appear to be the same width when you choose this option.

As Figure 13-5 shows, the remaining nine options in the fly-out menu represent fixed outline widths from 1/2 point to 24 points. Think of these options as "package deals," in which each width selection includes an angle of 0 degrees and a stretch value of 100% in the Outline Pen dialog box.

If you have altered any of the other default outline pen settings using the 'New Object' Outline Pen dialog box, they are still effective when you select a preset outline pen width. For example, if you previously had selected the Behind Fill or Scale With Image options as defaults, your outlines will exhibit these attributes even when you select a preset outline width. Since the Angle and Stretch settings are standardized for preset widths, however, you cannot achieve calligraphic effects.

Editing Outline Pen Attributes of Existing Objects

To define outline pen attributes for an existing (not newly created) object, you must select the object before you access the Outline tool fly-out menu. If you try to access the Outline Pen dialog box without having selected an object, CorelDRAW! assumes that you want to set new defaults for the outline pen, and any changes you make in the Outline Pen dialog box will not affect existing objects.

When you define outline pen attributes for an existing object that is selected, you are in effect *editing* its current outline style. The changes you make apply to that object only and have no effect on the default settings for objects you create later.

If you use the (SHIFT) method to select multiple objects in order to change their outline pen attributes, the Outline Pen dialog box displays the settings for the last object that you selected in the group. If you use the marquee method to select the objects, the dialog box displays the settings for the last object that you drew. Any changes you make will apply to all of the selected objects, however, so be very careful about changing outline pen attributes for more than one object at a time.

Each of the following sections concentrates on the effects of editing a specific attribute or related set of attributes in the Outline Pen dialog box. You will work with sample files that best demonstrate how changes to an attribute can alter the overall design and mood of a picture.

Adjusting Line Width

The line width you assign to an object's outline pen helps define the balance and weight of that object within a picture. In the following exercise, you will alter the line width for several elements in the sample drawing named DOESALL.CDR and observe how your changes affect it.

1. Open the file DOESALL.CDR and turn on the preview window in top-to-bottom format.

2. Activate the Preview Selected Only command in the Display menu, and then magnify just the area containing the word "CorelDRAW!".

3. Select the word "CorelDRAW!" by dragging a marquee around the word. The status line informs you that you selected ten objects. Your screen should now display an area similar to Figure 13-6.

Figure 13-6. DOESALL.CDR text as it starts out

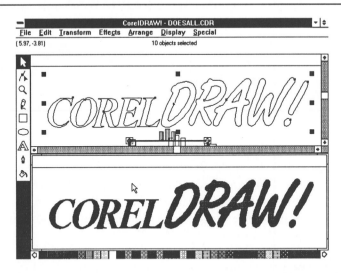

4. Select the Outline tool and click on the X to remove the outline. The word in your preview window should look like this:

5. Select the Outline tool again and click on the fourth line width after the X, a 2-point line. Now, the word "CorelDraw!" in your preview window should look like this:

6. Select the Outline tool a third time and click on the third line width from the right, a 16-point line. "CorelDRAW!" should now look like this:

7. Select the Outline tool and open the Outline Pen dialog box. Notice that outline width is at 0.222 inches, which is equivalent to 16 points (a point is 1/72 of an inch or 0.0389 inches) as shown in Figure 13-7. Remember that the default line width is 0.014 inches, which is one point—the third line width in the Outline tool fly-out menu.

As you can see, the variation in line width makes a big difference in how an object looks, and you can vary the line width either by selecting one of the

Figure 13-7. *Outline Pen dialog box with a 16-point line width*

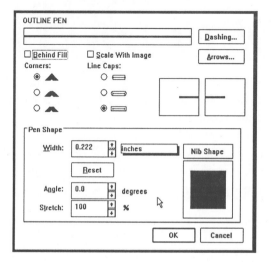

established options on the fly-out menu or entering a width of up to three decimal places in the Outline Pen dialog box.

Leave the dialog box open and the DOESALL.CDR drawing on your screen for further use. The next section explores the design possibilities of placing outlines of objects behind or in front of their fills.

Adjusting Placement of Outline and Fill

The Behind Fill setting in the Outline Pen dialog box determines whether the outline of a selected object is placed behind or in front of the object's fill. This attribute is most important when you are working with text. Thick outlines appearing in front of the fill can clog up the open spaces in letters, making the letters appear unclear as you saw in the 16-point example in the last exercise. In the following exercise, you will adjust outline placement for the letters in the DOESALL file that currently is open.

1. In the open Outline Pen dialog box, notice that the Behind Fill option is not selected.

2. Click on the Behind Fill check box to select it and then select OK to exit the dialog box. The word reappears with a much thinner outline as shown here:

Actually the outline is just as thick as before, but half of it is hidden behind the fill. You can see this if you watch the preview window redraw (unless you have a super-fast computer).

You have seen how the Behind Fill option affects the appearance of objects and can be especially useful with text. In the next section, you will observe how the Scale With Image setting impacts the appearance of resized or transformed objects.

Scaling the Outline with the Image

A wide outline, such as the 16-point width you applied in the last exercise, may be appropriate for large letters, say 75 points and above. When you scale that large type down to say 24 points, the wide border doesn't look good at all, as you can see.

The CorelDRAW! Outline Pen dialog box has an option to scale an outline's attributes with the image. If you select Scale With Image by clicking on the check box, an outline's attributes will be appropriately scaled as you change the image. The default, though, is to not scale the attributes, and you are likely to get something that looks like the last illustration.

1. With the DOESALL.CDR file still on the screen with a 16-point outline placed behind the fill, scale the image to about one-quarter its former size. You should get an image in your preview window that looks like that shown in the last illustration.

2. Press (ALT)-(BACKSPACE) to return the text to its original size.

3. Select the Outline tool, open the Outline Pen dialog box, click on the Scale With Image check box, and click on OK.

4. Again, scale the text image to about one-quarter its original size. You now get a much more usable image:

5. Clear the image from the screen by selecting New from the File menu and not saving the changes.

Setting Sharp (Miter), Rounded, or Beveled Outline Corners

The effect of changing corner attributes of the outline pen is so subtle that it is almost unnoticeable—unless the selected object has a thick outline as well as sharp corners. A thick outline enables you to see the shape of the object change as you cycle through the Corners options. Perform the following exercise to practice altering Corners settings for the letter E.

1. Select the Text tool, click anywhere on the page to open the Text dialog box, and type the capital letter **E**.

2. Select Avalon bold, 154 points, and click on OK.

3. Turn on the preview window, magnify the character until it fills the window, select the Outline tool and click on the 16-point line width (the third from the right), and select the Fill tool and click on the X to turn off the fill.

   When you have completed the above steps your screen should look like Figure 13-8. In the preview window you see the outline of the letter "E" with 12 corners on which to test the three corner styles. The default, the sharp or miter corner, is currently displayed and is shown in Figure 13-9a.

4. Select the Outline tool, open the Outline Pen dialog box, click on the rounded corner option button, and click on OK. You should see a distinct change in the corners as shown in Figure 13-9b.

5. Again open the Outline Pen dialog box, select the beveled corner option, and click on OK. Again the corners change as shown in Figure 13-9c.

Figure 13-8.   *The letter "E" set up to test the types of corners*

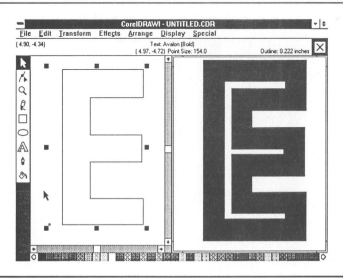

Figure 13-9.   *The letter "E" with (a) sharp or miter, (b) rounded, and*
                     (c) beveled corners

a.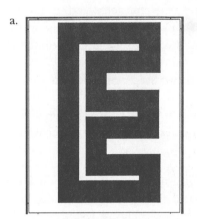

b.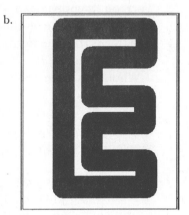

c.

6. Select New from the File menu to clear the screen. Do not save your changes.

In creating your own drawings, you will find the effects of the Corners options most dramatic when you assign thick outlines to objects that contain at least some cusp nodes. In the next section, you will explore when and how changes to the line end styles can alter an object's appearance.

Selecting Line End Caps

Line end options (*end caps*) apply only to straight lines and open-ended curves. It is difficult to see the difference between line end types unless you create very thick lines or magnify the line a lot—you'll do both here.

1. From the Display menu select Snap To Guidelines and Show Rulers.

2. Drag vertical guidelines from the ruler on the left to 2 and 4 inches.

3. Magnify the area from 1 horizontal and 2 vertical to 5 horizontal and 4 vertical and turn on the side-by-side Preview window ((SHIFT)-(F9)).

4. With the Pencil tool, draw two straight, vertical lines down the guidelines from 1.5 inches to 4.5 inches. These should be hairline width. If they don't appear in the Preview window to be hairline width, select both lines and then select the far left width from the Outline tool fly-out menu. Deselect these lines by clicking the Select tool any place in the work area except on one of the lines.

5. Select the Outline tool and click on the far-right line width, which is 24 points or .333 inches. Click on OK to apply this width to all new objects.

6. Draw three straight, horizontal lines from 2 to 4 inches on the horizontal ruler at 2.25, 3, and 3.75 inches on the vertical ruler. Your screen should look like Figure 13-10.

   The default line end cap, the *butt* end, is shown in the preview window in Figure 13-10. The lines end exactly at the termination of the line and are squared off.

7. Select the middle horizontal line, open the Outline Pen dialog box, select the middle or rounded line end cap, and click on OK. The line ends on the middle line are now rounded and project beyond

Figure 13-10.   *Lines prepared for testing line end caps*

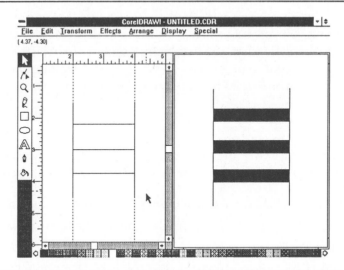

the termination of the line by one-half of the line width as shown
here:

8. Select the bottom horizontal line, open the Outline Pen dialog box,
   select the bottom or square line end cap, and click on OK. The line
   ends on the bottom line are now square and project beyond the
   termination of the line by one-half of the line width. Figure 13-11
   compares the three line end caps.

9. Clear the screen by selecting New from the File menu and turn off
   the rulers and Snap To Guidelines.

If an image contains many open-ended curves, selecting rounded line end
caps can soften the image, even if the lines are thin. Conversely, you can select

Figure 13-11. Butt, round, and square line end caps

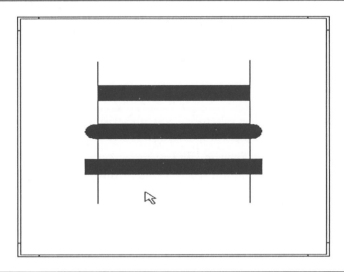

13

butt or square line end styles to give an object a more rough-hewn, sharp appearance.

Using Different Line Styles

So far in this book, all the lines you have drawn, including the lines in the characters you have typed, have been solid lines. Prior to CorelDRAW! version 2.0 you had the additional choices of a single dashed line or a single dotted line. With version 2.0 and beyond, you have a list box full of line styles and, if that is not enough, you can edit a file named CORELDRW.DOT and add more. Also, prior to version 2.0, the dotted and dashed lines were not visible on the screen and could only be printed on PostScript printers. With version 2.0 the lines are now visible in the preview window and can be printed with most printers.

In the following exercise you'll try out various line styles, look at them in various widths, and apply the different line end caps to them.

1. Select the Outline tool and click on the 1-point line width, the third from the left, and click on OK to apply this default to all objects.

You are starting with a 1-point line because a hairline (1/4-point) or a 1/2-point line is too small for demonstrating the different types of lines. The dots in a dotted line are the same height as the line is wide. Therefore, a dotted hairline has dots that are .003 inches high—three-thousandths of an inch! These will print on most laser and PostScript printers, but many other printers cannot print them, and the preview screen does not display them correctly without magnification.

2. Select Actual Size magnification and, with the Pencil tool, draw four straight horizontal lines, each about 3 1/2 inches long, at 2, 3, 4, and 5 inches on the vertical ruler.

3. Click the Text tool on the left side of the page at about 6 inches on the vertical ruler, type Corel, select Bodnoff normal, 60 points and click OK.

4. While the text is still selected, select the fill tool and click on X to turn off the fill. Your screen should look like Figure 13-12.

Figure 13-12.   *Lines and text prepared for testing line styles*

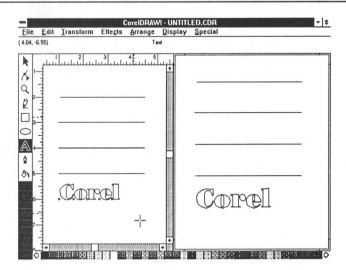

5. With the Select tool, click on the second line, open the Outline Pen dialog box and click on the Dashing command button. The Dashed & Dotted Line Styles dialog box will open as shown here:

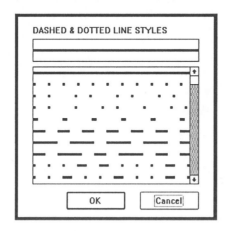

13

6. Select the second line type, a normal dotted line, and click on OK twice to return to the drawing.

7. Select the third line and then, from the Dashed & Dotted Line Styles dialog box, select the second dashed line (the sixth line type).

8. Select the fourth line and, from the Dashed & Dotted Line Styles dialog box, select the dash, double-dot line (the tenth line type).

9. Select the text and, from the Dashed & Dotted Line Styles dialog box, select the first dotted line. Your screen should now look like Figure 13-13.

Next, quickly look at how dotted and dashed lines look at various line widths and with various line end caps.

10. With the Select tool, draw a marquee around the four lines (not the text).

11. From the Outline tool fly-out menu, select first 4-point (fifth line width from the left) and then 12-point (fourth line width from the

right) line widths. Figure 13-14 compares the effects of 1-, 4-, and 12-point line widths on dotted and dashed lines.

12. Drag down the preview window frame below the middle to change to the top-to-bottom arrangement and magnify the second and third lines (the first dotted, the second dashed) so that they fill the screen.

13. Select each line individually, and then from the Outline Pen dialog box, select first the rounded end cap and then the square end cap to see the effect on dotted and dashed lines, as shown in Figure 13-15. Note that the end caps are placed on both ends of each dotted or dashed segment.

14. Select File New and No to clear the work area.

If you want to add additional dotted and/or dashed lines, leave CorelDRAW!, bring up an ASCII text editor such as Windows Notepad, and edit the file CORELDRW.DOT that is in the directory in which CorelDRAW! was installed. Instructions on adding line types are in the beginning of the file.

Figure 13-13.   *Using various line styles with 1-point lines*

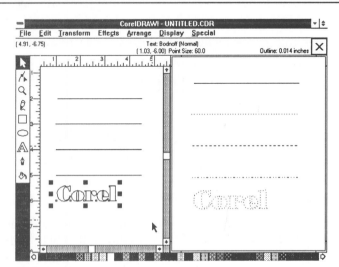

Figure 13-14.   *Effect of (a) 1-point, (b) 4-point, and (c) 12-point line widths on
dotted and dashed lines*

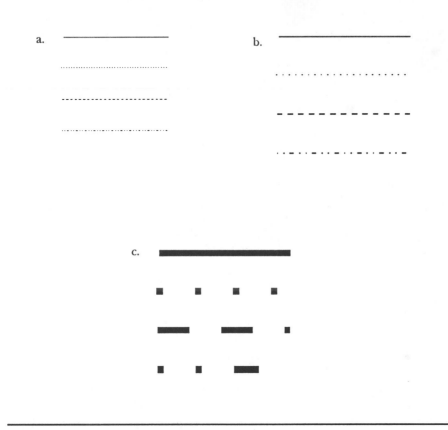

With CorelDRAW! 2.0 and later there is much variety in the styles, widths,
and ends you can use with lines. In the next section you will see how you can
further enhance a line with many different arrowheads and tail feathers.

Adding and Editing Arrowheads

In the section "Selecting Line End Caps," you saw one technique for
ending lines. In versions of CorelDRAW! prior to 2.0, this same technique
was used to add an arrowhead to a line end. In versions 2.0 and later,

Figure 13-15.   *(a) Butt, (b) rounded, and (c) square end caps on dotted and*
                        dashed lines

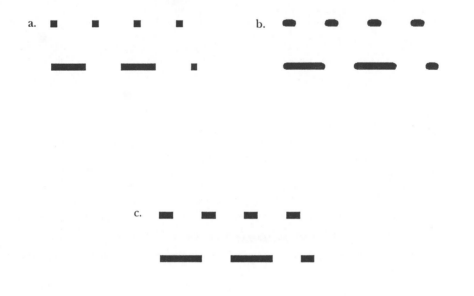

CorelDRAW! added a number of arrowhead and tail feather options that you
can place on the end of a line. You can also customize an existing arrowhead
with the Arrow Head Editor, and add new arrowheads to the Arrowhead
Selection dialog box. In this exercise you will add some arrowheads and then
customize one.

1. Select the Outline tool, click on the fourth (2-point) line width, and
   click on OK to apply this to all new objects.

2. Draw three horizontal lines about 2 inches long at 3, 4, and 5 inches
   on the vertical ruler. Be sure to draw the lines from left to right so
   the left end is the beginning of the line. Set the magnification to
   actual size.

3. With the Shaping tool, click on the first line and notice that the left end of the line has the larger node as shown here:

4. Change to the Select tool. The first line should automatically be selected.

5. From the Outline Pen dialog box, click on the Arrows command button. The Arrowhead Selection dialog box will open.

6. To put an arrowhead on the right end of a line, click the *right* mouse button on the second arrowhead in the graphic list of arrowheads at the bottom of the dialog box.

7. To add some tail feathers on the left end of the line, scroll the set of arrowhead display boxes by pressing the down scroll arrow five times and then click the *left* mouse button on the second set of tail feathers as shown in Figure 13-16.

8. Click on OK twice to return to your drawing. Your arrow should look like this:

9. In a similar manner, place line endings of your choice from the Arrowhead Selection dialog box on the second and third lines. Remember that the left mouse button places a line ending on the beginning of the line, in this case the left end of the line, and the right mouse button does the same on the other end of the line. One possible set of choices is shown in Figure 13-17.

10. With the Select tool, draw a marquee around the three lines and, from the Outline tool fly-out menu, set the line width, first, to 4 points (fifth from the left), and then to 8 points (fifth from the right). Figure 13-18 shows the three variations of line width with the line endings. Notice how the size of the line endings changes with the size of the line.

Figure 13-16.   *Arrowhead Selection dialog box with the initial settings*

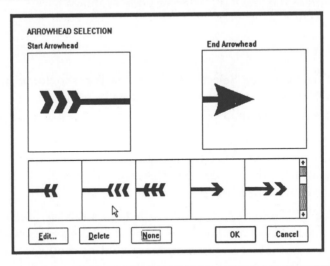

Figure 13-17.   *One possible set of line endings*

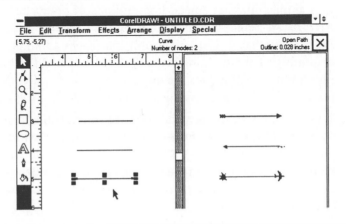

Figure 13-18.   *Arrows at (a) 2-point, (b) 4-point, and (c) 8-point line widths*

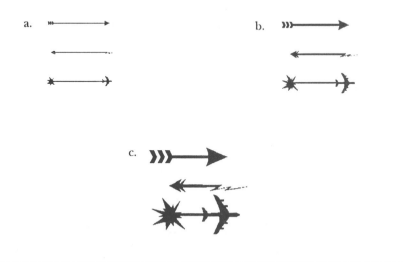

11. Select New from the File menu (and don't save the changes) to clear the work area.

Next, use the Arrow Head Editor to modify an existing arrowhead.

If, after modifying an arrowhead, you close the Arrow Head Editor and return to the drawing to see your handiwork, you will have permanently modified the arrowhead you are working on. You can again modify the arrowhead to try and re-create the original, but you may not get it exactly the way it was. The solution to this is to leave CorelDRAW!, go to the directory in which CorelDRAW! is installed, and make a copy of the file that contains the arrowheads–CORELDRW.END. Call the new file CORELDRW.EN1. Then you can modify arrowheads as you wish and when you are done, leave CorelDRAW! once again, and copy CORELDRW.EN1 back to CORELDRW.END to restore the original arrowheads.

Caution

12. At Actual Size magnification, draw a horizontal line in the middle of the page.

13. From the Outline fly-out menu, select the 4-point line width (fifth from the left).

14. Open the Outline Pen dialog box, select Arrows, click on the second arrowhead from the beginning of the list with the right mouse button, and click on Edit.

15. Using the eight boundary markers, modify the arrowhead by stretching out both the left and right ends and then reducing the height. In the latter operation it is likely that the arrowhead will get off center vertically. Use the Centre in Y command button to correct this. Try Reflect in X to see the effect of this, and use it again to return the arrowhead to its original orientation. When you are done, your dialog box should look like Figure 13-19.

Caution

If you click on OK and close the Arrow Head Editor, you will permanently modify the second arrowhead in the Arrowhead Selection dialog box. You can come back and move everything back to its original position (see the illustration under "Arrows" in the early part of this chapter to see how this should look). But, unless you want to do that, choose Cancel to exit the Arrow Head Editor.

16. If you don't mind permanently modifying the second arrowhead, click on OK to close the Editor and return to the Arrowhead Selection dialog box, click on the second arrowhead again to select your modifications, and click on OK twice to return to your drawing. Your arrow should look like this:

17. Select File New and No to clear the work area.

The Arrow Head Editor is used to stretch, scale, and position an existing arrowhead in relation to the line it will be applied to. If you want to create a new arrowhead, do so in CorelDRAW! like you would any other object (if you build an arrowhead with multiple objects, select them all and use Combine from the Arrange menu to make one object out of them), and then use the Create Arrow command in the Special menu to save the new arrowhead at

Figure 13-19. *Arrow Head Editor with modified arrowhead*

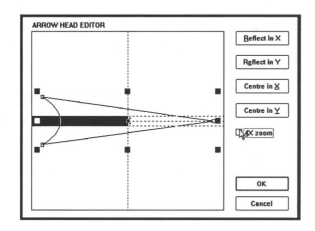

the end of the list of arrowheads. It does not matter if you have the relative size of the new arrowhead correct, because you can modify this with the Arrow Head Editor.

In the next section, you will begin working with the pen shapes—Width, Angle, and Stretch—that make calligraphic effects possible in CorelDRAW!.

A Pen Shape for Calligraphic Effects

The Width, Angle, and Stretch settings in the Outline Pen dialog box are in a separate enclosed area subtitled "Pen Shape." The Pen Shape options—Width, Angle, and Stretch—allow you to create variable calligraphic "nibs" that can be highly effective with freehand drawings and text. If you adjust all three of these settings in various combinations, you can approximate a freehand style of drawing.

In the following exercise, you will experiment with the Pen Shape settings, using some curves you will draw, to achieve both hand-sketched and comic-strip-style looks.

1. At Actual Size magnification (with the preview window on, but Preview Selected Only turned off, and the rulers turned off), draw an approximation of the objects shown in Figure 13-20.

2. Magnify the objects so they fill the window, select them all, group them using the Group command in the Arrange menu, set their Width to 2 points (the fourth width from the left), and turn off their fill by clicking on the X in the Fill tool's fly-out menu.

3. Save this image with the File Save As command and the name CURVES.

4. Activate the Outline tool and access the Outline Pen dialog box. The current Pen Shape settings for this object are Width 0.028 inch, Angle 0.0 degrees, and Stretch 100%.

5. Leave the Width value at 0.028 inch (2 points), but change the Angle and Stretch values to 42 degrees and 14% respectively. This translates into a thin outline and a relatively narrow nib with the "pen" held at a 42-degree angle. The effects are shown in Figure 13-21.

6. To vary line thickness, experiment with the stretch of the nib, expressed as a percentage of the nib width. Keep decreasing the

Figure 13-20.　　　*Objects on which to test the outline pen*

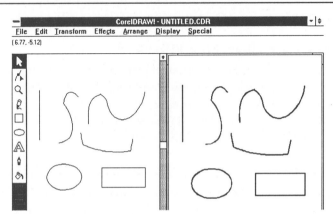

Figure 13-21.   *Outline Width of 0.028 inch, Angle of 42 degrees, and Stretch of 14%*

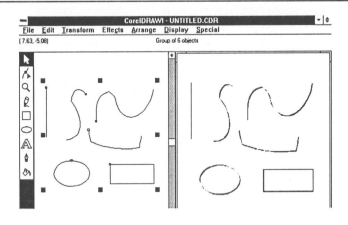

Stretch value all the way to 2%, and then select OK. There doesn't seem to be much change. As the value in the Stretch numeric entry box decreases, you effectively flatten the nib in one direction; the black symbol representing a pen nib in the Nib Shape display box flattens horizontally. The resulting nib is broad in one dimension and extremely narrow in the other, which makes more extreme calligraphic effects possible. If you were to increase the Stretch value all the way to 100%, the curves of the image would have the same thickness everywhere, and no calligraphic effects could result.

7. Access the Outline Pen dialog box once more. Return the stretch to 50% and adjust the Angle of the nib from 42 to 0 degrees. You will recall that the Angle setting is analogous to the way you hold a calligraphic pen in your hand; at a 0-degree setting, the Nib Shape display box alters to show you a perfectly vertical nib.

8. Select OK to exit the dialog box. Now the areas that display the thickest and thinnest lines have shifted by 42 degrees as shown in Figure 13-22. Adjusting the Angle value is therefore a convenient way to control where thick and thin lines appear on any selected object.

Figure 13-22.   *Outline Width of 0.028, Angle of 0.0 degrees, and Stretch of 50%*

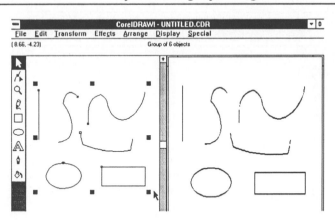

9. Access the Outline Pen dialog box again and click on the Reset button. This resets the Angle and Stretch settings (though not Width) to the default values of 0 degrees and 100%, respectively—a square nib with no variations in thickness. Now set Width to 0.06 inch, and then select OK. The curves are redrawn with a consistently thick outline, much like a cartoon character, as shown in Figure 13-23.

10. Experiment with Angle and Stretch settings at this Outline Width, too. For example, to obtain greater variation in line thickness, set Stretch at a reduced value, such as 4%. To change the placement of the thinner segments of the curve, try different angle settings.

11. Select New from the File menu and answer No to saving the changes to clear the screen.

The possibilities for creating custom calligraphic nibs should spark your imagination. An interesting use for an image sketched faintly at 0.01-inch width might be as a background illustration in a newsletter, where the text overprints the image without obscuring it totally. You have probably seen applications like this involving outlines of scanned photographs. Appendix D

Figure 13-23. *Outline Width of 0.06, Angle of 0.0 degrees, and Stretch of 100%*

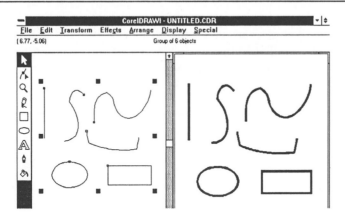

13

will give you more information on how to outline bitmapped and scanned images.

Avoid using 0.00-inch widths unless your draft printer is also the printer you will be using for your final output. As an Outline Width setting, 0.00 inch represents the thinnest line your printer is capable of printing. For PostScript printers, this is 1 pixel or 1/300 of an inch, but for a Linotronic or other high-resolution imagesetter, 0.00 inches could represent something even thinner. Because of the variations among printers, this setting does not truly represent a fixed width, and the preview window does not display a WYSIWYG representation of it.

Tip

Angle settings are especially useful to help you fine-tune the exact location of thick and thin lines within a drawing. With precise, degree-by-degree control available, you can make sure that thinner areas of a selected curve are positioned exactly where you want them.

The Stretch settings represent the relative squareness or roundness of the nib, with 100% representing a square nib and 1% representing a long and narrow nib. As the Stretch percentage value decreases, the variation in line thickness of a drawn object increases.

Outline Pen Hints

The range of choices available to you makes the outline pen one of the richer areas of CorelDRAW!. The following sections contain selected hints for making the most of your choices and coordinating your settings with the type of work you are doing.

Defining an Outline Pen for Text

Do you want text in your drawings to appear normally? Or are you aiming for exaggerated or stylized effects? For a clean-cut look, it's best to create text without an outline, using the X in the Outline tool fly-out menu. When text has a visible outline, some characters appear to be drawn thicker, with the result that spaces within letters (such as in a small "a" or "e") are partially or wholly filled in. This is especially the case when you create text in small point sizes.

If your design calls for outlined text, a good way to maintain readability in smaller point sizes is to activate the Behind Fill option in the Outline Pen dialog box. As mentioned earlier, Behind Fill causes the outline to appear half as thick as it really is, because the other half of the outline is hidden behind the object's fill.

In some cases, you may really prefer a slightly "smudgy" graphic look of text with thick outlines. Let the purpose and design of your illustration be your guide in choosing how to outline text.

Varying Your Calligraphic Style

Unless you have a prior background in calligraphy, the wealth of width, angle, stretch, and corners settings available to you in the Outline Pen dialog box can be confusing. The following hints should help put you on the right track if you know the effect you would like to achieve.

Desktop publishers can create faint background illustrations from original artwork or scanned photos and then overprint them with text. The result is a visible but not distracting piece of artwork that enhances the mood of an article or feature. Recommended settings for this kind of graphics effect are Width, 0.03 inch or less; Stretch, 14% or less; and a variable Angle according to your tastes. Keep in mind that if you reduce the Outline Width setting below 0.02 inch (or 1.2 fractional points), you will not be able to see an accurate representation of the calligraphy on your screen. The outline will still print according to your specifications, however.

Illustrators, cartoonists, and other artists seeking a traditional hand-sketched look should set Pen Shape options to achieve the desired variation in line thickness. For finer lines, outline pen width should be fairly thin, below 0.05 inch, and for blunter strokes, above 0.06 inch. Stretch should be set to 1 to 2% for the maximum variation in line thickness, and closer to 100% for minimal variation. The fine-tuning possible with angle settings permits illustrators to place thicker or thinner lines at exact locations. Miter corner settings promote a more angular look, while rounded corner settings create a smoother appearance.

For those who are interested in extremely broad calligraphic strokes, consider setting Stretch above 100%, removing the fill of an object, and then varying the Angle settings in the Outline Pen dialog box. The example text that follows has a three-dimensional look because it was created at a Width of 0.06 inch, at an Angle of 75 degrees, and with a Stretch of 225%:

outline pen

Copying Outline Styles

In Chapter 12, you transferred text attributes from one text string to another using the Copy Style From command in the Edit menu. You can do the same with outline pen attributes.

You can imagine how useful the Copy Style From command can be if you need to copy outline pen styles to, or from, even larger blocks of text or groups of objects.

14

Defining Outline Color

To define an object's outline completely in CorelDRAW!, you must define both the outline pen shape and the outline color attributes. You learned how to select attributes for the outline pen in Chapter 13; in this chapter, you will begin to define outline color. As you may recall, the outline pen allows you to draw with the characteristic style of a calligraphic pen, using "nibs" of various sizes. The outline color represents the colors and textures that flow from the pen.

CorelDRAW! offers you a choice between two different color systems—*spot color* and *process color*—for assigning color to an object's outline. In the spot color system, each color is assigned a unique name or number. The Pantone Color Matching System, which is the standard of the printing industry, has licensed its spot color specifications for use in CorelDRAW!. Spot color works best for images that contain only a few colors, such as headings in newsletters or single-color objects within black-and-white graphics. The process color system, on the other hand, specifies colors in terms of a mix of primary colors or color properties. Process color is more appropriate to use when you plan traditional four-color printing of images that contain a large number of colors. You will find more information concerning color

411

concerning color systems and color separation principles in Chapter 17, "Printing and Processing Your Images."

Your options for assigning outline colors do not end with spot and process colors, however. Unlike a hand-held pen, the CorelDRAW! pen not only dispenses "ink" in all colors of the rainbow, it can lay down an assortment of halftone screens for PostScript printing.

The exercises in this chapter will give you practice in specifying spot color, process color, gray shades, and halftone screen patterns for your object outlines. The preview window faithfully reproduces your settings, except in the case of halftone screens. Since you cannot preview an outline consisting of a halftone screen, you must print out your work on a PostScript printer in order to view it. See Chapter 17 for assistance with printing.

Defining an Object's Outline Color Attributes

Your first step in defining outline color attributes is to determine whether you want to define the attributes for existing objects or for objects not yet rendered. When defining outline color attributes for an existing object, you are in effect editing its current attributes. The changes you make apply to that object only, not to additional objects you may create later. When you define outline color attributes for a new object, on the other hand, you are changing default attributes. The next object or series of objects you draw will incorporate automatically the newly defined outline color attributes.

Tip

Always work with the preview window turned on when you alter outline color attributes. The editing window does not show you how the selected outline color looks, but for most attributes, the WYSIWYG preview window lets you see the results of your changes instantly.

An existing object can be either a newly created object or one that you have drawn previously. To begin the process of defining outline color attributes for an existing object, proceed as follows:

1. Activate the Select tool ▲ and select an object whose outline color attributes you wish to edit.

2. Click on the Outline tool 🖊. When the Outline tool fly-out menu appears, select the Custom Outline Color icon 🖌, the first icon in the second row, which looks like a paintbrush. The Outline Color dialog box appears, as shown in Figure 14-1. You will practice working with this dialog box later in this chapter; for now, click on Cancel.

Alternatively, if you have just drawn an object, it is selected automatically, as you will recall from Chapter 8. To invoke the Outline Color dialog box, follow step 1 above without activating the Select tool.

Tip

If you have an item selected, you can immediately open the Outline Color dialog box by pressing the shortcut keys (SHIFT)-(F12).

The next section explains the process of defining outline color attributes for objects that you haven't created yet.

Figure 14-1. *The Outline Color dialog box with default*

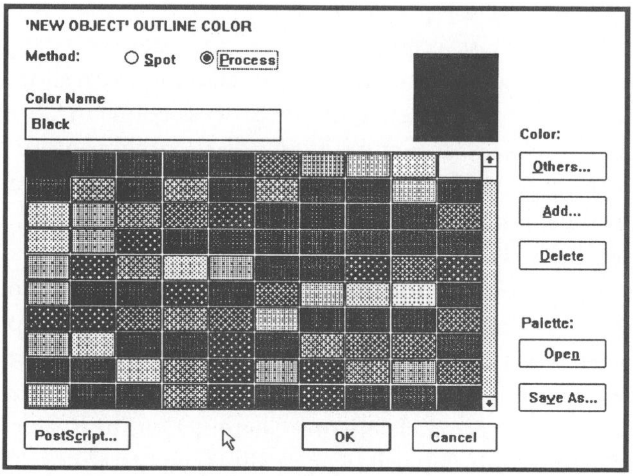

'NEW OBJECT' OUTLINE COLOR

Method: ○ Spot ◉ Process

Color Name

Black

Color:

Others...

Add...

Delete

Palette:

Open

Save As...

PostScript... OK Cancel

Setting New Outline Color Defaults

When you click on an option in the Outline tool fly-out menu without first having selected an object, CorelDRAW! assumes that you want to change the standard or default attributes for objects that you draw in the future. Here's how to begin the process:

1. Click on the Outline tool and then proceed to select the Outline Color tool. The message box shown in Figure 14-2 appears, asking you whether you want to change the default settings.

2. Click on OK. The 'New Object' Outline Color dialog box appears. The contents of this dialog box are the same as those of the Outline Color dialog box; only the title is different. For now, click on Cancel.

The next set of sections introduces you to the concept of spot color and lets you practice assigning a spot color to an existing or planned object. You gain access to the spot color display as soon as you invoke the Outline Color or 'New Object' Outline Color dialog box.

Outlining with Spot Color

If you work with a PostScript printer, you can create color separations for spot color and process color that are ready to take to a print shop. You should base your choice of a color system (spot or process color) in CorelDRAW! on the number of colors in your picture. If an image contains more than four or five colors, you would probably find spot color too expensive and time-consuming to produce, and should opt for process color instead. If an image contains fewer than six colors, and you require close color matching, you should use the spot color system to assign a unique Pantone color name to each color. Spot color is also the system to use with a PostScript printer, since it gives you access to special PostScript halftone screen patterns.

You define colors in CorelDRAW! using the Outline Color dialog box that you access when you click on the Custom Outline Color icon in the Outline tool fly-out menu. This dialog box allows you to choose between spot color and process color, to select a color from the palette (which is different

Figure 14-2. *The 'New Object' Outline Color dialog box*

depending on whether you choose Spot or Process), and to select from among several options. Two of the options, % tint and PostScript, are available only with Spot color. The third option, Others, allows you to define a color other than through the palette. The fourth and fifth options, Add and Delete, allow you to add and delete colors to and from the palette. The final options, Palette and Save As, allow you to bring in a new palette from disk and to save the current palette under a new name.

The colors you select using the spot color system are from the Pantone Matching System that is the standard for the printing industry. Since the colors that appear in the dialog box color display box are only approximations, you should use the Pantone Color Reference Manual to evaluate your choice of colors prior to printing. In addition, you can specify a percentage of the tint of any spot colors you select. The effect of settings below 100% is to render a lighter shade of the selected color on your monitor or color printout.

In the following set of exercises, you will learn how to specify spot colors for the outlines of your CorelDRAW! objects. If you are working with a color monitor, you will see your drawings come alive in vivid color. If you are working with a monochrome monitor, an exercise is included to show you how to set up your outlines in shades of gray. The exercises in these sections assume that you understand how to invoke the correct dialog box for either a planned object or an existing object. If you need to review this process, refer to the section of this chapter entitled "Defining an Object's Outline Color Attributes" before continuing.

Assigning Spot Color Outlines

To assign spot color to an object's outline, you select a color from the palette in the Outline Color dialog box. You access this dialog box by clicking on the Custom Outline Color icon in the Outline fly-out tool menu. This same dialog box allows you to assign process color to an outline, too, but the palette in the dialog box changes depending on which option you choose. In the following exercise, you will assign spot colors and shades of gray to the outline of an existing object.

1. From the Outline tool fly-out menu select the 2-point width (fourth from the left), click on OK to have it apply to all objects, then, at Actual Size (1:1) magnificaton, quickly draw several curves as shown here:

    When you are done, drag a marquee around all of the objects to select them and choose Group from the Arrange menu.

2. Activate the preview window in a side-by-side format. Make sure that Preview Selected Only is *not* active.

3. To begin editing the existing outline color attributes, select the curves, if they aren't already selected, and then click on the Outline tool and the Custom Outline Color icon or press (SHIFT)-(F12). The Outline Color dialog box appears. If you have not altered the default selections, the dialog box still looks like Figure 14-1. Click on the Spot option button to change from the default Process color.

4. Click on the fourth color in the top row. As shown in Figure 14-3, the selected color appears in a color display box at the top right of the dialog box. The % tint numeric entry box shows a value of 100% (the default value). The Pantone identification name or number for this color, in this case "PANTONE Rhodamine Red CV," displays above the palette. If you have the Pantone Color Reference Manual

Figure 14-3.   *Setting a new spot color for a selected object*

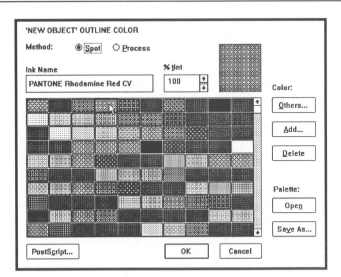

and have a color monitor, you can compare what you see on the
screen with what you see in the manual. There probably is a
difference since most color monitors are not perfectly calibrated.

5. Click OK in the dialog box. Notice that the curves have changed
   from black to Rhodamine Red. If you are not working with a color
   monitor, you'll see a dithered gray.

6. Invoke the Outline Color dialog box again. This time, click on the
   black color on the right and set the tint value to 51%. The color
   preview window in the dialog box now displays a 51% gray shade.

7. Click OK in the dialog box. If you have a VGA or Super VGA display
   card, you will see an actual representation of a 51% gray shade in
   the drawing, as shown in Figure 14-4. If you have an EGA display
   card, however, the outline appears not to have changed from pure
   black.

8. Access the Outline Color dialog box once more, reselect PANTONE
   Rhodamine Red (fourth color in the top row), and then return the

Tint value to 51%. You have just selected a lighter tint of Pantone Rhodamine Red.

9. Select OK to exit the dialog box with the new outline color setting. If you have a VGA color monitor, you will see an actual representation of the tint. If you have an EGA monitor, the outline color appears the same as if it were a 100% tint.

10. Save this as CURVES2 and clear the screen by selecting New from the File menu.

Note

If you have an EGA display card and monitor, the outline color functions of CorelDRAW! give you less than WYSIWYG displays in two respects. First, you cannot see an actual representation of less than 100% tints in the preview window. In addition, if you select a tint of any color of less than 51%, the outline in the preview window disappears completely. The object is still there, however, and you can print it normally. Should any selected object in a drawing not be visible, therefore, check its Outline Color settings. It could simply be that you have assigned a tint of 50% or less to that object.

In the next exercise, you will practice assigning new spot color outline default values. These values apply automatically to objects that you create after assigning the new defaults.

Figure 14-4.   *An outline at 51% gray shade*

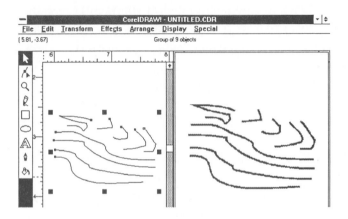

Setting New Spot Color Outline Defaults

When you access the Outline Color dialog box with no objects selected, CorelDRAW! assumes that you intend to change the default outline color values. If this is not the case, select Cancel and select an object before trying again. In the following exercise, you will change defaults for both the outline pen and outline spot color attributes, and then create new objects that exhibit those defaults automatically.

1. Begin with an empty page. Set the display magnification to 1:1.

2. Without creating or selecting any objects, click on the Outline tool and on the Custom Outline Pen icon in the first row of the fly-out menu. The message box that you saw in Figure 14-2 appears, asking whether you want to change default outline pen values. Click on OK to select All Objects and access the 'New Object' Outline Pen dialog box.

3. When the 'New Object' Outline Pen dialog box appears, set the outline pen attributes as follows: Type solid line, Corners sharp (miter), Line Caps butt, Width 0.15 inch, Angle −45 degrees, Stretch 10%. Do not check either Behind Fill or Scale With Image. Select OK to save these settings and exit the dialog box.

4. Still without selecting an object, click on the Outline tool and on the Custom Outline Color icon in the fly-out menu. As before, the "Nothing is currently selected" message box pops up, but this time it has the title 'New Object' Outline Color. Click on OK to signal that you wish to change the default outline color values. The 'New Object' Outline Color dialog box appears. This is identical to the Outline Color dialog box, except that the title and the purpose of each are different.

5. Set up the new object outline color attributes as follows: Spot Method, Pantone Process Blue CV (fourth box from the right in the top row), tint value 100%. Select OK to save these settings and exit the dialog box.

6. Activate the display rulers, turn on the preview window, and then click on the Text tool A. Click in the lower left of the edit window.

7. When the Text dialog box appears, type a capital **A** in the text entry window. Select the following text attributes: None Justification,

Banff Normal, 300.0 points. Select OK to exit the dialog box and display the text. If you followed all the steps up to this point, the text should have a default fill of black. Your screen should look like Figure 14-5, except that the color of the outline is blue. Remember that *all* of the new outline pen and color attributes you have selected apply to the new object automatically.

8. Clear the screen by selecting New from the File menu. Do not save your work.

If you create the same kinds of images regularly in your line of work, you probably have strong individual preferences for what you would like default outlines to look like. If you wish, start a new drawing on your own, setting up the outline pen and outline color default attributes that will apply to the basic elements in your drawing. You can edit settings for objects that should have different outline fills, by selecting them after you draw them and accessing the appropriate dialog boxes. If you are not satisfied with the results of your outline pen or outline color attribute settings, you can make any adjustments during the drawing process.

You may find selecting a particular spot color from the color palette difficult--it could be hard to find a particular Pantone color from the more

Figure 14-5.   *Letter created with new default Pantone spot color outline*

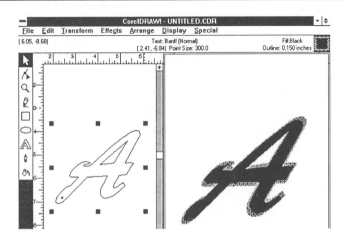

Figure 14-6. *Spot Outline Color dialog box listing spot colors*

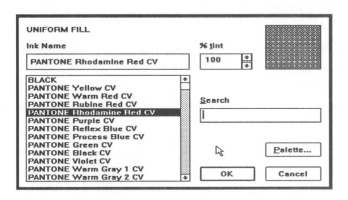

than 600 that are shown. If you have a Pantone Color Reference Manual and/or know the Pantone name or number of a particular color, CorelDRAW! provides another way to select a spot color by providing a list of the Pantone colors as shown in Figure 14-6. This list, in the Spot Outline Color dialog box, is reached by clicking on the Others command button in the Outline Color dialog box. When you select a color on the list, the color is displayed in the color display box to the right of the list. Also, you can enter a PANTONE number in the Search Text box and that number will be highlighted in the list and the color that number represents will be shown in the display box.

If you click on OK to leave the Spot Outline Color dialog box you are returned to your drawing and the next time you select the Custom Outline Color icon from the Outline fly-out menu, you will get the list of Pantone colors that you just left (Figure 14-6), not the Palette shown in Figure 14-3. If you want to return to the palette when you select the Custom Outline Color icon, select Palette to leave the Spot Outline Color dialog box. If you click on Palette to leave the Spot Outline Color dialog box, you are returned to the Outline Color dialog box and the color you chose is highlighted in the palette and shown in the display box just as if you had clicked on it in the palette.

If you own or use a PostScript printer, go on to the next section to learn how to assign a PostScript halftone screen as an outline color. This option is available only when you choose the spot color method, and it takes effect only if you have a PostScript printer.

Outlining with PostScript
Halftone Screen Patterns

If you work with a PostScript printer, you can elect to fill an outline with a *halftone screen pattern* of the currently selected spot color. This option is available only when you have selected spot color as your outlining color method. The preview window displays PostScript halftone screen patterns as solid colors only; to see the patterns, you must print the images on a PostScript printer.

The concept of a halftone screen is probably familiar to you already: it is a method of representing continuous tone or color by patterns of dots. Black-and-white and color photographs in newspapers and magazines are examples of halftone images that you see every day.

You define a PostScript halftone screen by clicking on the PostScript command button at the lower-left corner of the Outline Color or 'New Object' Outline Color dialog box. CorelDRAW! offers ten different types of halftone screen patterns. You can vary the frequency (number of occurrences per inch) and angle of any screen to achieve dramatic differences in outline appearance, even within a single pattern. To see how a PostScript halftone really looks, however, you must print it; the preview window cannot display these screens.

Defining a PostScript halftone screen outline requires the following steps:

1. Select the spot color (and tint, if desired) in which you want to print a screen pattern.

2. Click on the PostScript command button at the lower-left corner of the Outline Color or 'New Object' Outline Color dialog box.

3. Specify a halftone screen pattern from among the ten available patterns.

4. Select the frequency or number of occurrences of the pattern per inch.

5. Determine the angle at which the pattern should print. Since you cannot view the results of your selections in the preview window, this section does not feature any exercises. Following, however, are brief instructions for selecting a halftone screen pattern, frequency, and angle, and some guidelines you should keep in mind when

working with these patterns. You can refer to Chapter 17 for instructions on printing with PostScript printers.

Accessing the PostScript Halftone Screen Dialog Box

To begin defining a halftone screen outline, make sure you have selected the spot color and tint in which you want to print your outline. Then click on the PostScript command button at the lower-left corner of the Outline Color or 'New Object' Outline Color dialog box. The PostScript Halftone Screen dialog box shown in Figure 14-7 appears. This dialog box contains settings for pattern Type, Frequency, and Angle attributes.

Selecting the Halftone Screen Type

The Type option in the PostScript Halftone Screen dialog box features 10 halftone patterns that are available for your outline color work. Your choices are Dot (the default), Line, Diamond, Dot2, Grid, Lines, MicroWaves, OutCircleBlk, OutCircleWhi, and Star. To select a halftone pattern type,

Figure 14-7.   *The PostScript Halftone Screen dialog box with default settings*

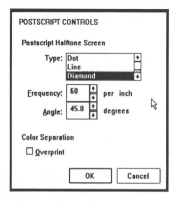

scroll through the list until you see the name of the desired pattern, and then click on the name to highlight it.

Selecting the Halftone Screen Frequency

The Frequency option in the PostScript Halftone Screen dialog box allows you to determine how many times per inch the pattern should occur within the outline. The available range is from 10 to 1000 per inch, and the default setting is 60. The number you should select depends upon the resolution of your ultimate output device; refer to Chapter 17 for more details on frequency settings for PostScript halftone screens.

Setting the Halftone Screen Angle

The third and last option in the PostScript Halftone Screen dialog box allows you to specify the angle of the screen pattern when you print it. Keep in mind that the halftone screen angle remains constant, no matter how you transform an object. If you stretch, scale, rotate, or skew an object after assigning it a halftone screen outline, you could alter its appearance significantly. If you do not want this to happen, remember to change the screen angle after performing a transform operation, to match the offset of the transformed object. You will achieve the best results by setting your screen angle at 0, 45, 90, and 180 degrees. In the next group of sections, you will begin defining process color outlines for objects in CorelDRAW!.

Outlining with Process Color

Process color is the term used for specifying color in terms of either a set of other colors or a set of color properties. CorelDRAW!, versions 2.0 and later, provide three methods or models for defining process color: CMYK (cyan, magenta, yellow, and black), RGB (red, green, and blue), and HSB (hue, saturation, and brightness). Prior to version 2.0, only CMYK was available.

Both CMYK and RGB define a color in terms of the constituent colors in the model while HSB defines a color in terms of color properties. For example, the color "brick red" is defined as 0% cyan, 60% magenta, 80% yellow, and 20% black in the CMYK model, or 80% red, 20% green, and 0% blue in RGB, or 15 degrees of hue, 100% saturation, and 80% brightness in HSB. You can use any of the three models you are most comfortable with, but CorelDRAW! will convert RGB and HSB to CMYK. Therefore, CMYK will be the primary focus of this book.

CMYK is the four-color standard for the printing industry. You can specify over 16 million colors by using various CMYK percentages. In general, you should specify process color instead of spot color when your drawing includes more than a four or five colors and you plan to reproduce it through the four-color printing process.

CorelDRAW! supports color separation for process as well as spot color if you send your work to a PostScript printer. When you specify color in CMYK terms, your printer generates only four sheets (one each for cyan, magenta, yellow, and black percentages) for every image page, no matter how many colors the image contains. When you specify in spot color terms, on the other hand, the printer generates a separate page for every single color used in the drawing. You will learn more about printing spot and process colors in Chapter 17.

To specify process colors for an existing object, you select or create the object, click on the Outline tool, and click again on the Custom Outline Color icon in the fly-out menu. When the Outline Color dialog box appears, you select the Process option button and then either select an established process color from the palette presented. Alternatively, you can click on the Others command and create a process color by defining a mixture of the constituent colors in a secondary Outline Color dialog box for creating process colors shown in Figure 14-8. For the sake of clarity, this will be called the Process Outline Color dialog box. There is a separate Process Outline Color dialog box for each of the three process color models, and a fourth for choosing a process color by name.

The Process Outline Color dialog box for the other two-color models is very similar to that shown in Figure 14-8 for CMYK. In the upper-left corner is a set of option buttons for selecting one of the color models or the list of names. Below the option buttons is a set of numeric entry boxes and scroll bars for entering or scrolling to a percentage of a constituent color or

Figure 14-8.   *CMYK Process Outline Color dialog box*

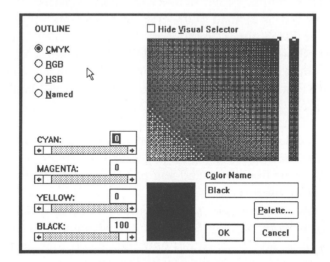

property. If you are using a color reference chart such as the one that came in the CorelDRAW! package, you can look for the process color you want in the chart and then enter the percentages that create that color.

In the upper-right corner of the dialog box is a visual selector that consists of two boxes (one circle and one box in the case of HSB) that are filled with varying shades of color. By dragging a marker in each box you can define a process color. The marker in the square box or circle can be moved in two directions (left or right and up or down) while the marker in the rectangular box can be moved only up or down. In the CMYK model the square defines percentages of cyan and magenta, while the rectangle defines the percentage of yellow (black is automatically defined). In the RGB model the square defines percentages of red and green while the rectangle defines blue. In the HSB model the circle defines the hue (it is specified in degrees from 0 to 360 around the circle) and the percentage of saturation (specified by the distance from the center) while the rectangle defines brightness.

Below the visual selector is a display box that shows you the color you are defining and its name, if any. Remember that on most monitors, the color is not totally accurate, so you need to use a color chart to see the exact color you are describing. The Palette command button sends you back to the primary Outline Color dialog box from which you started, while the OK and Cancel command buttons send you back to your drawing.

If you select the OK or Cancel command buttons, the next time you select the Custom Outline Color dialog box from the Outline tool fly-out menu, the Process Outline Color dialog box (shown in Figure 14-8) will open, not the Outline Color dialog box (shown in Figure 14-1). If you want the Outline Color dialog box with the palette to open, exit the Process Outline Color dialog box by clicking on the Palette command button and then on OK.

Tip

14

In the following exercise, you will specify both the outline pen and outline process color for a text string.

1. At Actual Size magnification with the rulers turned off, select the Text tool, click in the middle of the left side, and type **CorelDRAW!** in the Text dialog box.

2. Select Banff normal, no justification, 70-point type size, 0.3 em intercharacter spacing, and click on OK twice to return to the drawing.

3. From the Fill tool fly-out menu, click on X to turn off the fill. From the Outline tool fly-out menu, open the Outline Pen dialog box. Select rounded corners and enter 0.083 inches (6 points) for Width, 0 degrees for Angle, 14% for Stretch, and click on OK.

4. When you are back on the drawing, turn on the preview window and place it in top-to-bottom orientation. Your screen should look like Figure 14-9.

5. Your settings have resulted in a moderately thick text outline, and by the calligraphic Pen Shape, an "artistic" look. The rounded corners setting adds a more polished look to the outlines of corners of angular letters. The black color does not do it justice, so you will change it now.

6. With the text string still selected, click on the Outline tool once more. This time, select the Custom Outline Color icon in the second row of the fly-out menu to invoke the Outline Color dialog box. Notice that the current outline color is black.

Figure 14-9.   *Text for testing a color outline*

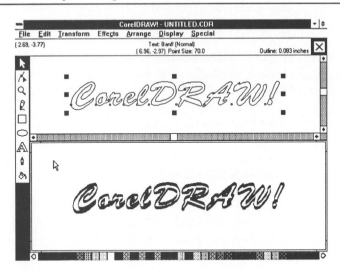

7. If necessary, click on the Process option button to switch color selection methods. The options in the dialog box change instantly. Take a moment to familiarize yourself with the process color palette by clicking on a number of the boxes. Across the top row are shades of black running from black on the left to white on the right. In the second row are the primary colors: blue, cyan, green, yellow, red, magenta, purple, orange, pink, and dark brown. As you move on down the palette you see variations on these colors: various blues, greens, yellows, reds, and so on. When you click on a color, you see it in the display box at the top right and its name on the top left.

8. Click on the Others command button. The Process Outline Color dialog box opens. This is where you can define your own process colors. Again take a moment to familiarize yourself with this dialog box. Move the markers in each of the visual selector boxes and notice how the color changes in the color display box as well as the percentages in the numeric entry boxes. Using the scroll bar or your mouse and keyboard, set the following color mix: Cyan 40%, Magenta 40%, Yellow 0%, and Black 60%. The color display box shows

Figure 14-10. *Magnified text string with a Deep Navy Blue outline*

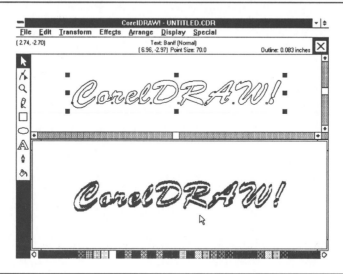

a real-time approximation of changes to the color as you scroll to or type in each specified value. When you have specified all of the values, the color display box shows a deep navy blue and the name confirms it.

9. Select OK to exit the dialog box. If you have a color monitor, the text string's outline displays as a deep navy blue, providing a contrast to the light background. This contrast is shown in Figure 14-10.

10. Press (SHIFT)-(F12) or click on the Custom Outline Color icon in the Outline tool fly-out menu. Notice that this time the Process Outline Color dialog box opens, not the Outline Color dialog box, since you returned to the drawing from the Process Outline Color dialog box.

11. Click on first RGB and then HSB and notice that the Deep Navy Blue has been defined in each of these models. Then type on Named. The Named Process Color dialog box has a list box of the color names as well as the standard display box and color name text box for the selected color. If you know a color name, look it up in the Named dialog box. Then you can go to one of the color models and see and possibly modify the color composition.

Next, define your own color and add it to the color palette. Leave the CorelDRAW! text string on your screen and the Process Color dialog box open. You can use the text string to test your new color.

Defining a New Color and Adding It to the Palette

The color palette in the Outline Color dialog box in Process mode displays a little more than 100 colors as it is shipped to you. This is a far cry from the more than 16 million possible colors available with the CMYK model. The Process Color dialog box is Corel's answer to this discrepancy. You have seen how you can define a new color with this dialog box when you want to apply it to an object. But if you want to use a color over and over, say a special corporate color you've defined, you will want to add this color to the Outline Color palette.

In the following exercise you will truly define a new color. In the last exercise the color you entered was already on the palette and in the name list. The new color you will define is Deep Royal Blue.

1. Click on the CMYK option button to open the CMYK Process Color dialog box.

2. Type in the numeric entry boxes, or use the scroll bars to define a color mix of 100% cyan, 55% magenta, 0% yellow, and 45% black. The color display box will show the color but the Color Name text entry box is empty because the color is not defined.

3. Click on the Color Name text entry box and type Deep Royal Blue. Your dialog box should look like that shown in Figure 14-11.

4. Click on OK to return to your drawing and see your new color. More important, clicking on OK defined your new color and added it to the color palette and the name list. See for yourself.

5. Press (SHIFT)-(F12) to reopen the CMYK Process Color dialog box and then click on the Palette command button. The Outline Color dialog box will open with a new color at the very end of the palette highlighted and the name Deep Royal Blue in the Color Name text entry box.

Figure 14-11. *Deep Royal Blue being defined*

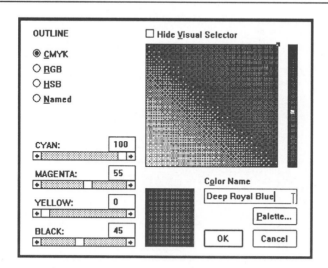

While it is nice to have a new color in the palette, having it at the very end of the palette is not very handy. CorelDRAW!, though, allows you to rearrange colors by dragging them around the palette. You can drag a color to any existing location and release the mouse button, and all the existing colors shift to the right to accommodate the new color.

6. Point on the new color you just defined, press and hold the mouse button while dragging the new color up to the second row displayed, third color from the right. When you are there, release the mouse button. Now Deep Royal Blue (your new color) is right next to Deep Navy Blue as shown in Figure 14-12.

7. Assure yourself that your newly defined color is in the list of named colors by clicking on the Others command button and, when the Process Outline Color dialog box opens, click on the Named option button.

8. After the Named Process Outline Color dialog box opens, click on the scroll bar below the scroll box until you see Deep Royal Blue. The list is alphabetical, so you should see it immediately after Deep Rose, as shown in Figure 14-13.

Figure 14-12.   *Result of dragging Deep Royal Blue up to Deep Navy Blue*

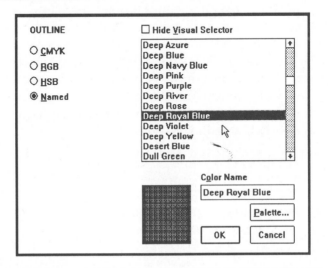

Figure 14-13.   *Newly defined color in named list of colors*

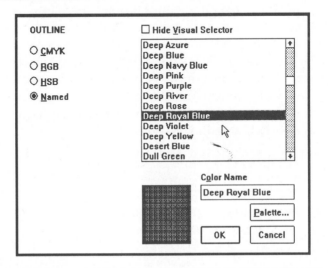

9. Click on OK to close the dialog box and return to the drawing. Leave the text string on your screen to use in the next exercise.

When specifying process colors, you can include as many colors in the picture as you like. When you finally print the image, the results will still be separated into no more than four sheets.

In the next section of this chapter, you will learn a shortcut to specifying outline color that will be useful if you usually print to a black-and-white printer.

Outlining with Black, White, or Gray

When you worked with the outline pen in Chapter 13, the first row of the Outline tool fly-out menu contained ten preset outline widths that you could select simply by clicking on the desired icon. The arrangement of the second row of the Outline tool fly-out menu is similar. Following the Custom Outline Color icon is a series of eleven symbols that let you select a preset outline color (gray shade) quickly, without having to set attributes in a dialog box. As Figure 14-14 shows, the eleven preset outline color options are white, black, and 10%, 20%, 30%, 40%, 50%, 60%, 70%, 80%, and 90% gray.

To select one of these preset outline colors for an existing object, you select the object, access the Outline tool fly-out menu, and then click on the appropriate icon. To select one of these options as the default outline color, you click on the desired icon in the Outline tool fly-out menu without first selecting an object.

In the following exercise, you will select several of the preset outline color options and apply them to the text string you created in the previous exercise.

1. Recreate the CorelDRAW! text string if you did not leave it on the screen after the last exercise. Magnify the area containing CorelDRAW! as before. Once again, turn on the preview window and place it beneath the editing window.

2. Select CorelDRAW!, and then select the Outline tool. When the fly-out menu appears, click on the black square in the second row

Figure 14-14.   *Preset black, white, and gray shades in the Outline tool fly-out menu*

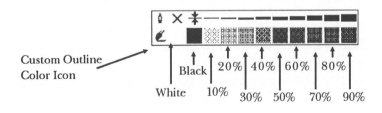

Custom Outline
Color Icon

Black   20%   40%   60%   80%

White   10%
          30%   50%   70%   90%

of the menu. The outline of the text string changes from dark blue to solid black.

3. Select the Outline tool again, and this time click on the 40% gray symbol (the fourth symbol after black in the second row). Now the text outline shows a much lighter color, as in Figure 14-15.

4. Experiment with different preset outline color settings. Leave the text string on the screen for the final exercise.

Figure 14-15.   *Magnified text string with preset outline of 40% gray*

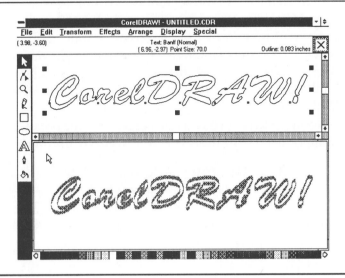

Remember that you are not limited to these preset shades of gray if you use a black-and-white printer. You can use either the spot color or the process color system to define custom shades of gray. To define custom shades of gray using the spot color method, access the Outline Color dialog box and set shades of gray by clicking on black and setting the % tint in increments of 1%. To define custom shades of gray using the process color method, define a percentage for black only, leaving cyan, magenta, and yellow all at 0%.

You can also use the preset shades of gray in the Outline tool fly-out menu in combination with the PostScript halftone screens.

Copying Outline Color and Pen Styles

In previous chapters, you have learned how to use the Copy Style From command in the Edit menu to copy text or outline pen attributes from one

Figure 14-16. *Rectangle with outline color and pen styles copied from text string*

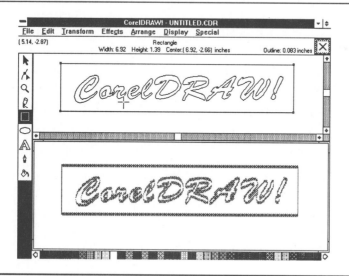

object to another. You use the same command to copy outline color attributes between objects, as you will see in the following exercise.

1. With the CorelDRAW! text string still on the screen from the previous exercise, zoom out to reduce the size enough to draw a rectangle around the string.

2. With the rectangle tool, draw a rectangle around the word "CorelDRAW!"; then turn off the fill by clicking on the X in the Fill fly-out menu. The result is a thin black rectangle around the text string.

3. Select the Copy Style From command in the Edit menu. When the Copy Style dialog box appears, click on both the Outline Pen and the Outline Color checkboxes, and then select OK. The cursor turns into an arrow containing the words "From?" to indicate that the next object you select will copy its outline attributes to the selected object.

4. Select the CorelDRAW! text string. The rectangle redisplays to show the same outline thickness and color as the text string, as shown in Figure 14-16.

5. Clear the screen by selecting the New command and not saving the changes.

For more practice with the Outline color tool, you could go back to the LANDSCA4.CDR or other landscape drawing that you created and edited in Chapters 4 through 8. The default outlines and fills of the objects in those files are black, but you can begin to differentiate objects by varying their outlines. You can give custom outlines to interior objects or copy outline styles to multiple objects at one time.

15

Defining Fill Color

In Chapters 13 and 14, you learned how to enhance your drawings by defining outline pen and outline color attributes for objects. The outline color attributes make up the "ink" that flows from a pen, while the outline pen is like the calligraphic pen or marker from which the ink flows.

This chapter introduces you to the CorelDRAW! Fill tool. The Fill tool ⬧, as its icon suggests, functions like a paint bucket with a limitless supply of paint, capable of filling the interior of any leakproof object. A leakproof object is any object that is a closed path; all CorelDRAW! objects are leakproof, except straight lines and open curves. If you have drawn a curve object in which the two end nodes do not join, the object remains an open path, and you cannot fill it. When you select such an object, the words "Open Path" appear at the right side of the status line. (You can close an open path by joining its end nodes, as you will recall from Chapter 10, "Shaping Lines, Curves, Rectangles, and Ellipses.")

The Fill tool is similar to the Outline Color tool in that it can dispense spot color, process color, and PostScript halftone screen patterns. It can also dispense other types of fills that the Outline Color tool does not provide: fountain fills in any combination of colors, Bitmap and Vector Pattern fills from the CorelDRAW! library, and 42 different gray-scale PostScript texture fills. You will learn more about these types of fills in the "Custom Fountain Fills," "Bitmat and Vector Fill Patterns," and "PostScript Fill Textures" sections of this chapter.

The exercises in this chapter give you practice in specifying spot or process color, gray shades, PostScript halftone screen patterns, fountain fills, bitmap fills and vector pattern fills, and PostScript fill textures for objects. The preview window faithfully reproduces your settings, unless you have chosen a PostScript halftone screen or fill texture. Since you cannot preview these types of fills, you must print out your work on a PostScript printer in order to view it. See Chapter 17, "Printing and Processing Your Images," for assistance with printing.

Defining Fill Color Defaults

Before you define fill attributes for the interior of an object, you must determine whether you want to define the attributes for existing objects or for objects not yet rendered. When defining fill attributes for an existing object, you are editing its current fill. The color or name of the fill will appear in the status line when you select the object. The changes you make apply to that object only, not to additional objects you may create later. When you set new default fill attributes, on the other hand, you are specifying how objects you create in the future will be filled automatically. In this respect, the Fill tool works like the Outline tool.

Always work with the preview window turned on when you alter fill attributes for new or existing objects. Except for PostScript textures and halftone screen patterns, the WYSIWYG preview lets you see the results of your changes instantly.

Fill Color for Existing Objects

An existing object can be either a newly created object or an object that you have drawn previously. In general, it's a good idea to define fill color for one object at a time. If you define fill colors for multiple objects that you have selected using the (SHIFT) key technique, the fill colors of all of the objects change to match the fill of the last object you selected. If you select multiple objects using the marquee, the fill colors of all the objects change to match the fill of the most recently drawn object in the group.

To begin the process of defining fill attributes for an existing object, select the object and the Fill tool in the following way:

1. Activate the Select tool ▣ and click on an object that has fill attributes you would like to edit. The current fill color of the object displays on the status line. Alternatively, if you have just drawn an object, it is automatically selected and available for further work, and you do not have to activate the Select tool.

2. Click on the Fill tool ▣ in the CorelDRAW! toolbox. The Fill tool fly-out menu appears and looks like this:

15

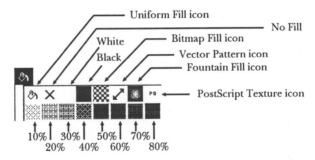

The first icon in the top row of the Fill tool fly-out menu is the Uniform Fill icon ▣. Although this icon looks just like the Fill tool icon, it has the specialized function of helping you define custom spot and process color fills and PostScript halftone screen patterns. The ⊠ icon causes an object to have a transparent (or no) fill. The two icons following the ⊠ let you specify preset fill colors of white and black. The last four icons in the top row of the fly-out menu let you access dialog boxes to customize specific types of fills, known as bitmap, vector, and fountain fills and PostScript textures. The bottom row of the Fill fly-out menu lets you specify one of eight preset shades of gray as the fill.

3. Click on the icon that accesses the desired dialog box or specifies the desired preset fill shade, as described in the previous step. To

remove the fly-out menu from the screen without making any selections, click anywhere outside the menu or press (ESC).

The major sections in this chapter offer you extensive practice in working with each dialog box and selecting fill attributes for each of the major types of fills. Whether you are setting fill attributes for selected objects or altering default attributes for objects you haven't drawn yet, the main steps involved are similar. The next section explains the minor differences in steps that change default fill attributes.

Defining New Default Fill Attributes

When you click on an option in the Fill tool fly-out menu without first having selected an object, CorelDRAW! assumes that you want to change the default attributes for objects that you will draw in the future. To begin defining new default attributes:

1. Click on the Fill tool without first creating a new object or selecting an existing one.

2. Click on the icon that accesses the desired dialog box or specifies the desired fill of black, white, or shade of gray. For any icon you select (except bitmap and vector fill patterns, which cannot be the default), the message box shown in Figure 15-1 appears, asking you whether you want to change the default settings. Only the title of the message box will differ, depending on which fly-out menu icon you select.

3. If you meant to select an existing object and edit its fill, click on Cancel; otherwise, click on OK. If you clicked on the first, next to last, or last icon in the fly-out menu (the Uniform Fill, Fountain Fill, or PostScript Textures icon), a dialog box appears. If you click on the Bitmat Fill or Vector Pattern icons (fifth and sixth from the left) you will get a message box telling you that these two fills cannot be used as defaults, like this:

If you clicked on any other icon, the next object or series of objects you draw will have the specified fill color automatically.

The major sections in this chapter describe how to set fill attributes in the respective dialog boxes. The first dialog box you will encounter is the Uniform Fill dialog box. This dialog box allows you to specify a fill color as a spot color, PostScript halftone screen pattern, or process color.

Defining Uniform Spot Color Fills

15

To fill an object with spot color, process color, or a PostScript halftone screen pattern, you use the settings in the Uniform Fill dialog box. This dialog

Figure 15-1.   *A sample 'New Object' message box for setting default fill attributes*

box appears when you click on the Uniform Fill icon, the first icon in the Fill tool fly-out menu. You can also open the Uniform Fill dialog box with the shortcut keys (SHIFT)-(F11). Its name, Uniform Fill, distinguishes it conceptually from Bitmap, Vector Pattern, Fountain, and PostScript Texture fills, which involve multiple hues or patterns rather than a single color. Except for the title, the Uniform Fill dialog box is identical in appearance and function to the Outline Fill dialog box you worked with in Chapter 14.

You will recall from Chapter 14 that spot color is the preferred color system when an image contains fewer than six colors or if you want to use PostScript halftone screen patterns. If you do not have a PostScript printer at your disposal and your work does not require spot color or four-color printing, you can use either the spot or process color system to specify fill colors.

Tip

If you have a black-and-white display adapter and monitor, you can still specify spot color fills, but your screen will not display them in color. Refer to the Pantone Color Reference Manual to see the color you have selected.

As mentioned at the beginning of the chapter, an object must be a closed path in order for you to fill it. However, a closed path does not assure a solid object. If you combine two or more objects as you learned to do in Chapter 8, "Selecting, Moving, and Arranging Objects," "holes" result where the combined objects overlap. You can then create interesting design effects by surrounding the "holes" with outline and fill colors. Perform the following exercise to create a logo with transparent text, outline it, and assign a uniform fill spot color to it. You will edit this logo throughout the chapter as you learn new ways to use the Fill tool fly-out menu. If you are working with a color monitor, you will see the example drawings come alive in living color! If you are working with a black-and-white monitor, you will see the specified colors as shades of gray.

1. To prepare the screen, set magnification at Actual Size (1:1). Activate the Snap To Grid command and set both Horizontal and Vertical Grid Frequency to 1 per pica. If the units boxes display a unit of measurement other than picas, click on it until the word "pica" displays. Activate the Show Rulers command; because of the grid settings, the rulers display in picas rather than in inches.

2. Before beginning to draw, set the default outline pen and outline fill attributes back to the original CorelDRAW! defaults. To do this, click on the Custom Outline Pen icon in the Outline tool fly-out menu. Select OK when the 'New Object' Outline Pen message box appears to ask you whether you want to set a new default value. Adjust settings in the Outline Pen dialog box as follows: solid line type, Corners sharp, butt line Cap, no arrows, width 0.003 inches, Angle 0 degrees, Stretch 100%. No checkboxes should be filled. Select OK to make these settings the default outline pen attributes.

3. To specify the default outline color as black, click on the Outline tool again and then select the black icon in the second row of the Outline tool fly-out menu. Select OK when the 'New Object' Outline Color message box asks you whether you want to set a new default.

4. Select the Ellipse tool ⬭, and position the cursor at the 24-pica mark on the horizontal ruler and the 33-pica mark on the vertical ruler. Draw a perfect circle from the center outward, starting from this point. Make the circle 22 picas in diameter or the largest circle you can draw, using the information on the status line to help you.

5. Activate the Text tool 🅐. Select an insertion point near the top of the circle, at the 24-pica mark on the horizontal ruler and the 25-pica mark on the vertical ruler. You do not have to position the cursor exactly, because you can align the text and circle later. When the Text dialog box appears, type **The World of Corel DRAW!** in the text entry window, one word per line, and select the following text attributes: Aardvark Bold, 40.0 points, Center justification. Click on the Spacing command button, set intercharacter spacing to 0.20 em and interline spacing to 115%, and then select OK twice. The text appears centered vertically and horizontally within the circle, as shown in Figure 15-2. If the text is not centered perfectly within the circle, select both the text and the circle and align them using the Align command in the Arrange menu and choosing both Horizontal and Vertical Center Options.

Depending on the type of display and display adapter you have, the diameter of the circle and the point size you can fit in the circle may differ

15

Figure 15-2.   *Centering a text string within a circle*

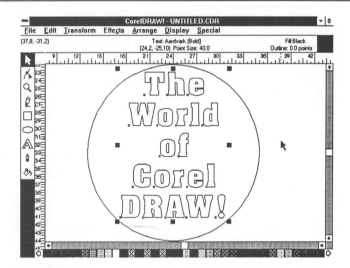

from what is described and shown here. Draw the biggest circle and use the largest type size needed to fill your screen at Actual Size magnification.

6. Click on the Show Rulers command in the Display menu again to deactivate the rulers and select fit-in-windows magnification. Turn on the preview window and adjust it to a side-by-side format. You cannot clearly distinguish the text from the circle yet, because they have the same outline and fill colors.

7. Select the Preferences command in the Special menu (or press (CTRL)-(J)). When the Preferences dialog box appears, adjust both of the numeric settings beside the Place Duplicate option to –2,0 picas and points. Make sure that you place a comma rather than a period after the 2. Duplicate objects that you create with this setting are offset from the original by the specified amount (in this case, 2 picas below and to the left of the original). Select OK to exit the dialog box.

8. Activate the Select tool, select the circle, and then click on the Duplicate command in the Edit menu. A duplicate of the circle

appears below and to the left of the original and is selected immediately.

9. Change the fill of this duplicate circle to none by clicking on the Fill tool and then on the ⊠ option in the fly-out menu.

10. Select the original circle and the text string again using the (SHIFT) key, and click on the Combine command in the Arrange menu. The message in the status line changes from "2 objects selected" to "Curve." The "Fill:" message at the right side of the status line displays a default fill of black, but the text now appears white, as shown in Full-Screen Preview ((F9)) in Figure 15-3. In combining the two objects, you have converted both the circle and the text string to curves. The area behind the text has become not white but transparent.

11. Deactivate Full Screen Preview ((F9)) and select the Save As command in the File menu. When the Save As dialog box appears, type the name **FILL-1** in the File text box, and then select Save.

15

Figure 15-3.   *Combining two objects to form a curve object with transparent "holes"*

12. With the curve object still selected, click on the Fill tool and again on the Uniform Fill icon (you can also press (SHIFT)-(F11)). The Uniform Fill dialog box appears. Click on the Spot option button, and then select the top-left color in the palette, Pantone Yellow CV, and set the tint to 55%. Your settings should match those in Figure 15-4.

13. Select OK to exit the dialog box. Now you can see some contrast between the black outline and the fill colors, even if you do not have a color monitor. The text has the same outline style as the circular shape, because CorelDRAW! treats the text curves as "holes" or edges within the single combined object. The outline is very thin, however, so you will thicken it in the next step.

14. With the curve object still selected, click on the Outline tool. Access the Outline Pen dialog box by clicking on the Custom Outline Pen icon (or by pressing (F12)). Change the Width setting for the outline pen to 5.0 fractional points. Place a checkmark in the Behind Fill option and then select OK to apply these settings to the object. Now you see a heavier outline around both the outer rim of the circle and

Figure 15-4.   *Settings for a spot color uniform fill*

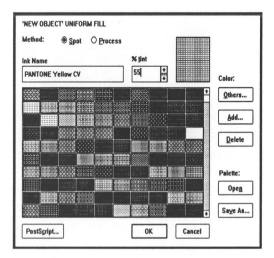

the text, as shown in Figure 15-5. Because you activated the Behind Fill option, the "ink" of the outline doesn't completely clog up the transparent spaces in the text.

15. You are ready to give the finishing touches to the curve object. Click on the Outline tool once more, and select the Custom Outline Color icon (or press (SHIFT)-(F12)) to access the Outline Color dialog box. Select the Spot option button, click on Others, and select Pantone 293 CV (in Versions 2.01 and above, type 293 in the Search Text box), and set the tint to 52%. Select OK twice to exit both dialog boxes.

16. Click on the Preview Selected Only command in the Display menu, and then select the duplicate circle. Click on the Fill tool and the Uniform Fill icon to access the Uniform Fill dialog box. Select the Spot option, click on Others, scroll to Pantone 281 CV (a dark purplish blue), and leave tint at 100%. Select OK twice to save this setting and exit the dialog boxes.

17. Deactivate the Preview Selected Only command. The image redisplays to show the background circle creating a dramatic

Figure 15-5. *Outline appearing behind fill for clearer text appearance*

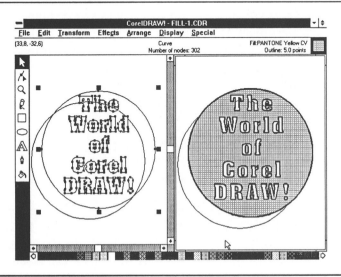

"shadow" effect against the curve object. The alignment is not quite right yet, however; white space is visible behind the upper portion of the word "The." To remedy this situation, deactivate the Snap To Grid command and adjust the position of the curve object slightly so that the background circle fills the word "The" completely. Now all of the transparent spaces behind the letters in the curve object have an apparent fill behind them.

18. To see this apparent fill more closely, select Full Screen Preview. Your screen should look similar to Figure 15-6.

19. Turn off Full Screen Preview and group the curve object and the circle behind it, and then press (CTRL)-(S) to save the changes you have made to this graphic. Leave the graphic on the screen to use in the next exercise.

Note

If you have an EGA display card and monitor, the colors you select in the Uniform Fill dialog box will not be quite as WYSIWYG as if you had a VGA or Super VGA display. Tints of less than 100%, for example, display as though they were the fully saturated color. In addition, if you select a tint of any color that is less than 51%, the color seems to disappear in the preview window completely. If you are filling an object whose outline has the ⊠ (no outline) selected, you will not be able to preview the object at all. The object is still there, however, and you can print it normally.

The kind of object you have just created makes an excellent specimen for outline and fill experiments of all kinds. You will continue to use this graphic throughout the chapter. In the next section, you will add an interesting design effect by specifying a PostScript halftone screen pattern for the background circle in FILL-1.CDR.

Defining PostScript Halftone Screen Fill Patterns

When you choose the spot color rather than the process color system in the Uniform Fill dialog box, another set of fill specifications becomes available. If you work with a PostScript printer, you can fill an object with a halftone screen pattern of the currently selected spot color. You will recall from your

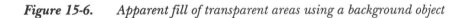

Figure 15-6. *Apparent fill of transparent areas using a background object*

15

work with outline color in Chapter 14 that the CorelDRAW! preview window displays PostScript halftone screen patterns as a solid color; to see how they actually look, you have to print them on a PostScript printer.

You define a PostScript halftone screen pattern by clicking on the PostScript command button at the lower-left corner of the Uniform Fill or 'New Object' Uniform Fill dialog box. CorelDRAW! offers ten different screen options. You can vary the frequency (number of occurrences per inch) and angle of any screen pattern to achieve dramatic differences in the appearance of a spot color fill.

In the following exercise, you will assign a PostScript halftone screen pattern of a specified angle and frequency to the background circle in the FILL-1.CDR image and save the altered image under a new name. If you have a PostScript printer, you can print this image out once you have mastered the printing techniques covered in Chapter 17.

1. With the view of FILL-1.CDR still on the screen, activate the Preview Selected Only command in the Display menu.

2. Select the image and ungroup its component objects by clicking on the Ungroup command in the Arrange menu. Deselect both objects

and then click on the outline of the curve object that you combined earlier.

3. With the curve object selected, click on the Fill tool and the Uniform Fill icon in the Fill tool fly-out menu. When the Uniform Fill dialog box appears, click on the PostScript command button at the lower-left corner of the dialog box. The PostScript Halftone Screen dialog box appears.

4. Select the MicroWaves screen type by scrolling through the Type list box until MicroWaves is highlighted.

5. Adjust screen frequency in the Frequency numeric entry box to 20.0 per inch. This is a very low frequency (the minimum is 10, the maximum 1000) and will display a dramatic pattern on a 300 dpi PostScript printer.

6. If necessary, use the scroll arrow to adjust the number in the Angle numeric entry box to 45 degrees. This will cause the screen pattern to tilt at a 45-degree angle.

7. When your settings match the ones in Figure 15-7, select OK to exit the PostScript Halftone Screen dialog box. Click on OK again to exit the Uniform Fill dialog box and return to the screen image. You will not notice anything different, because the preview window cannot display PostScript patterns.

8. Select the Save As command in the File menu and type **FILL- 2** in the File text box of the Save As dialog box. Select Save to save the file under this new name. After you complete Chapter 17, you can print this file to see the results of your settings if you have a PostScript printer.

When you assign PostScript halftone screen pattern fills to objects, base your choice of frequency on the resolution of the PostScript printer you will use. On any PostScript printer, low frequencies result in more dramatic pattern effects, while high frequencies result in the pattern being hardly visible. The resolution of the printer, not any absolute number, determines what constitutes a low or a high frequency. To achieve the same visual effect on different printers, you should vary the frequency assigned to a screen. For example, you should assign lower screen frequencies when the printer

Figure 15-7. *Defining a custom PostScript halftone screen pattern*

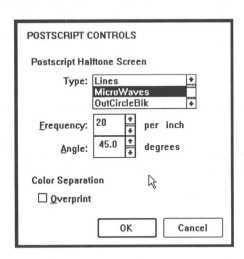

resolution is 300 dpi, and higher frequencies for Linotronic or other image-setting equipment at a resolution of 600 or 1270 dpi. Table 15-1 provides information on the number of visible gray levels for each printer resolution at a given screen frequency.

Table 15-1. *Printer Resolution and Number of Gray Levels Visible for PostScript Halftone Screen Patterns*

Selected Frequency	Number of Gray Levels		
	300dpi	600dpi	1200dpi
30 per inch	101	401	1600
60 per inch	26	101	401
100 per inch	10	37	145
120 per inch	7	26	101

You can specify a PostScript halftone screen pattern as a default fill in the same way that you would specify a normal spot color. In the next section, you will change the fill and outline colors of both of the objects in the original FILL-1.CDR file, using the process color system instead of spot color.

Defining Uniform Process Color Fills

As you will recall from Chapter 14, process color is the term used for expressing colors as percentages of other colors or color properties. CMYK Process color is the industry standard for four-color printing. In general, you should specify process color instead of spot color when your drawing includes six or more colors or when you plan to reproduce it through the four-color printing process.

CorelDRAW! supports color separation for process as well as spot color if you send your work to a PostScript printer. When you specify color in CMYK terms, your printer generates only four sheets (one each for cyan, magenta, yellow, and black percentages) for every image page, no matter how many colors the image contains. When you specify color in spot color terms, on the other hand, a separate page is printed for each color used in the drawing. Spot color is more exact for purposes of color matching than process color but also more expensive to produce.

To specify process colors for an existing object, you create or select the object, click on the Fill tool, and then click again on the Uniform Fill icon in the fly-out menu. When the Uniform Fill dialog box appears, you select the Process option button (this may not be necessary, since Process is the default) and select a color from the palette. If you want a color not on the palette, click on the Others command button, choose one of the color models (CMYK, RGB, or HSB), and select a color with the visual selector or by entering percentages of the constituent colors. You can also choose a named color from the Others command by selecting Named instead of a color model and choosing a color from the list box. All of these alternatives are explained in Chapter 14. To specify default process colors for objects that you plan to draw in the future, you access the Uniform Fill dialog box without first having selected an object.

In the next exercise, you will specify fill and outline color for the original FILL-1.CDR file using process color instead of spot color.

Assigning Process Color Uniform Fills

If you plan to generate color separations for an image in preparation for printing, remember to specify outlines and fills for all objects in terms of the same color system. In the following exercise, you will change fill color specifications for FILL-1.CDR from spot to process color.

1. Open the original FILL-1.CDR file that you created in the first exercise of this chapter. The curve object and background circle are currently grouped; to make them accessible as separate objects, select them and apply the Ungroup command from the Arrange menu.

2. Magnify the image using the fit-in-window icon in the Magnification tool fly-out menu. The preview window and Preview Selected Only should both be turned on. Deselect both objects and select the background circle.

3. With the background circle selected, press (SHIFT)-(F11) or click on the Fill tool and then the Uniform Fill icon. The Uniform Fill dialog box appears, displaying the object's current spot color fill.

4. Click on the Process option button. The contents of the dialog box change, as shown in Figure 15-8. CorelDRAW! attempts to define the spot color in terms of a process color. Here you see the same color in the display box, but the words "unnamed color" in the Color Name text box in place of the "PANTONE 281 CV," and no color is highlighted in the palette. Click on the Others command button and on CMYK, if necessary, to display the CMYK Process Color dialog box. Here you see a color definition of 100% cyan, 72% magenta, 0% yellow, and 38% black. Again, there is no name for the color.

5. Adjust the color values to Cyan 55%, Magenta 55%, and Black 75%. Leave Yellow at 0%. The color preview display box shows a royal blue. Select OK to redisplay the background circle with the new fill color.

15

Figure 15-8.   *The Uniform Fill dialog box with process color selected*

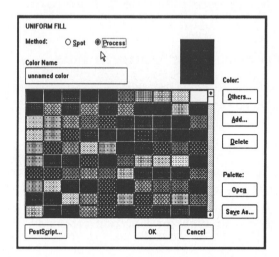

6. Select the combined curve object and access the Uniform Fill dialog box again. Select the Process Method option button, click on Others, set fill color values to Magenta 30% and Yellow 10% (leaving Cyan and Black at 0%), and then select OK.

7. Whenever you are preparing an image for four-color printing, make sure that *both* outline and fill colors are specified using the process color system. In the present illustration, the outline color for the curve object is still specified with spot color. To switch color systems for the outline of the curve object, press (SHIFT)-(F12) or select the Outline tool and the Custom Outline Color icon to access the Outline Color dialog box. Click on the Process Method option button, click on Others, and set outline fill color values to Cyan 35%, Magenta 30%, and Black 10% (leaving Yellow at 0%). Click on OK to exit the dialog box and redisplay the curve object. If you turn off Preview Selected Only and select Full Screen Preview, the image should appear similar to Figure 15-9.

Figure 15-9.   *Curve object with process color fill of 35% cyan, 30% magenta, 10% black, 0% yellow*

15

8. Deactivate Full Screen Preview and select the Save As command in the File menu. When the Save As dialog box appears, type **FILL-3** in the File text box and then click on Save.

Specifying process color uniform fills is easy; you will begin working with color separation for process color in Chapter 17, "Printing and Processing Your Images." Many CorelDRAW! applications require only black and white graphics, however. In the next section, you will learn a shortcut to specifying fill color that will be useful if you usually print to a black-and-white printer.

Filling with White, Black, or Gray

When you specified outline fill colors in Chapter 14, the second row of the Outline tool fly-out menu contained eleven preset colors (white, black, and nine shades of gray) that you could select quickly by clicking on the desired icon. The arrangement in the Fill tool fly-out menu is similar. Following the Uniform Fill tool on the top row are three icons which, in conjunction with eight icons in the second row, allow you to select a preset color without having to set attributes in a dialog box. These eleven options represent preset uniform fills in the following order: X (transparent), white, black, and 10%, 20%, 30%, 40%, 50%, 60%, 70% and 80% gray.

To select one of these preset uniform fill colors for an existing object, you simply select the object, access the Fill tool fly-out menu, and then click on the appropriate icon. If you had previously assigned a PostScript halftone screen fill to the selected object, the pattern remains the same but now has the new shade that is assigned to it.

To select one of the preset options as the default uniform fill, you click on the desired icon in the Fill tool fly-out menu, without first selecting an object. Again, if the previous default fill involved a PostScript halftone screen pattern, that pattern remains active but in the new default gray shade.

In the following exercise, you will assign black, white, or preset gray shade fills to the objects in the FILL-2.CDR file.

1. Open the FILL-2.CDR file. As you will recall, this is the file in which you assigned a PostScript halftone screen pattern to the background circle.

2. Adjust viewing magnification to fit-in-window, turn on the preview window if it isn't already, activate the Preview Selected Only command, and then select the curve object.

3. With the curve object selected, click on the Fill tool. When the Fill tool fly-out menu appears, select the 80% gray icon (the far right icon on the bottom row). After a moment, the curve object redisplays with a dark gray shade of fill.

4. Select the Outline tool and click on the 10% gray icon, the fourth icon in the second row of the Outline tool fly-out menu. The curve object redisplays with a faint gray outline around the outside and the letters.

5. Turn off Preview Selected Only. Since the background circle has a fill that contrasts poorly with the 80% gray fill of the curve object, you cannot distinguish between the circles very well.

6. Select the background circle and click on the Fill tool and then the black icon. The background circle now contrasts with the 10% gray outline of the letters and with the original circle. Make sure the Behind Fill check box in the Outline Pen dialog box is still checked and then select Full Screen Preview. You should see an image similar to Figure 15-10.

7. To save this altered image, turn off Full Screen Preview and select the Save As command in the File menu. When the Save As dialog box appears, type **FILL-** 4 in the File text window and select Save.

Although the preview window cannot show it to you, the background circle still contains a custom PostScript halftone screen fill in the MicroWaves pattern. When you reach Chapter 17, you can print out this file to see the effect of combining this pattern with the gray shades if you have a PostScript printer.

15

Figure 15-10.   *Preset fills: curve object 80% gray, outline 10% gray, background curve black*

In the next section, you will begin working with one of the most creative types of fills in CorelDRAW!: fountain fills, which involve a smooth transition of two different colors through the interior of an object.

Custom Fountain Fills

When you specify fill colors using the Uniform Fill and 'New Object' Uniform Fill dialog boxes, you are limited to one color per object. When you select the Fountain Fill icon ▓ in the Fill tool fly-out menu, however, you can define a fill that blends two different colors or shades of color. If you are familiar with state-of-the-art paint programs or business presentation slides, you have probably seen *fountain fills,* which are smooth transitions of two different colors or tints. CorelDRAW! makes the color drama of fountain fills available to you through the Fountain Fill dialog box.

By adjusting settings in the Fountain Fill dialog box, you can fill any object with two different colors or tints in such a way that the colors blend evenly from one extreme to the other. CorelDRAW! allows you to create two different types of fountain fills: *linear* and *radial.* Think of the difference between these two fills as similar to the difference between drawing a circle or rectangle from one side to the other or from the center outward. In a linear fountain fill, the color transition occurs in one direction only, determined by the angle that you specify. In a radial fountain fill, the blend of start and end colors proceeds concentrically, from the center of the object outward or from the outer rim inward. Whichever type of fountain fill you select, you can specify colors using either the spot color or process color system. If you choose spot color, you can also define PostScript halftone screen patterns to add an extra visual "punch" to your fountain fills.

The following exercises provide practice defining linear and radial fountain fills using spot color, PostScript halftone screen patterns, and process color.

Defining Linear Fountain Fills

When you specify a linear fountain fill, the start color begins at one edge of the object and the end color appears at the opposite side. In between is a smooth blending occurring along an imaginary line that extends from one edge to the other. The direction of the color blend depends on the angle of the fill, over which you have complete control.

You can use either spot color or process color to define a linear fountain fill. When you use spot color, you have the additional option of selecting a PostScript halftone screen pattern.

To control both the speed and the fineness of the display that defines the fountain fill in the preview window, adjust the Fountain Stripes setting in the Print & Preview dialog box reached from the Preferences command. A low setting (2 is the lower limit) causes the fountain fill to display rapidly with a small number of circles. A high value (100 is the upper limit) causes the filled object to redraw very slowly in the preview window, but it also results in a very finely graded transition of color. For all output devices *except* PostScript printers, the Fountain Stripes setting also determines the resolution at which the fountain fill will print. You will have the opportunity to practice adjusting this setting and viewing the results on the screen in the "Fill Tool Hints" section of the chapter.

As with the outline pen and outline fill, you can define a linear fountain fill for existing objects or set defaults for objects that you have not yet created. To define a linear fountain fill for an existing object, you first select the object and then access the Fountain Fill dialog box by clicking on the Fountain Fill icon in the Fill tool fly-out menu. To define a linear fountain fill as the default fill for the next object you create, you click on the Fountain Fill icon without first selecting an object. The exercises in the next few sections use existing objects as examples. Once you enter the 'New Object' Fountain Fill dialog box, however, the techniques for specifying the fill are the same as when you work with an existing object. To open the Fountain Fill dialog box for either future objects or existing objects, you can also use the shortcut key (F11).

Spot Color Linear Fountain Fills

Theoretically, you can select any two colors as the start and end colors when you specify a linear fountain fill using the spot color system. In practice, however, it's best to select two tints of the *same* color if you intend to send color separations of the resulting image to a commercial reproduction facility. The reason for this has to do with the way spot color is physically reproduced, which makes it difficult to blend two discrete colors evenly.

In the following exercise, you will define a spot color linear fountain fill for the objects in the FILL-1.CDR file, which you created earlier in the chapter.

1. Open the original FILL-1.CDR file you set up in the first exercise of this chapter, not one of the edited versions. Your preview window should be on. If you have a color monitor, your screen displays a curve object containing a Pantone Yellow CV spot color at 55% tint and a blue Pantone 293 CV outline at a 52% tint. A darker blue (Pantone 281 CV) fills a circle behind the object. (To check the current fill colors for an existing object at any time, just ungroup and select the object, click on the Fill tool, and click on the Uniform Fill icon to display the Uniform Fill dialog box.)

2. Adjust the viewing area to a fit-in-window viewing magnification.

3. Select the grouped objects. Apply the Ungroup command in the Arrange menu to ungroup them and then deselect both objects and reselect the curve object alone.

4. Click on the Fill tool and then on the Fountain Fill icon ✳ in the Fill tool fly-out menu or press (F11). The Fountain Fill dialog box displays, as shown in Figure 15-11.

   The upper portion of the dialog box contains controls for the type of fountain fill (linear or radial), the color method (spot or process), and the angle that determines the direction of the fill. In the lower portion of the dialog box are controls for specifying the start and end colors of the fill according to either the spot or process color system. These include a color name, percent tint, color palette, and an Others command button for both the starting color on the left and the ending color on the right. The default settings are Type of Linear, Angle 90 degrees, Color Method Process, start color White, and end color Black. These settings would result in a fill that is white at the bottom, blending gradually into solid black at the top.

5. Leave the Linear Type and 90-degree Angle. Change the Method to Spot, the start color (on the left) to Pantone Yellow CV (first color in the palette) at 100% tint, and the end color (on the right) also to Pantone Yellow CV, but at 0% tint, which will look virtually white. Remember that when you define color using the spot color method,

Figure 15-11.   *The (default) Fountain Fill dialog box*

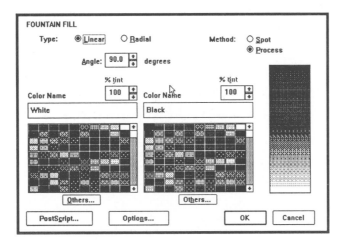

both the start and end colors should be different tints of the same color.

6. Select OK to exit the dialog box with the new settings. The curve object now shows a darker yellow fill at the bottom, with a gradual transition to white at the top. If you select Full Screen Preview, and if you have a black-and-white monitor, the transition in tones is similar to the one shown in Figure 15-12.

7. Turn off Full Screen Preview and access the Fountain Fill dialog box again ((F11)). This time, change the Angle setting to 45 degrees and then select OK to exit the dialog box. Now, the curve object redisplays with a fountain fill that is lighter at the upper right than at the lower left. With Full Screen Preview, the image should appear similar to Figure 15-13.

8. For an interesting enhancement, create a fountain fill for the background circle that runs in the opposite direction from the fill for the curve object. To do this, select the background circle and then press (F11) or click on the Fill tool and the Fountain Fill icon.

Figure 15-12.   *Spot color linear fountain fill at a 90-degree angle*

Figure 15-13.   *The same fountain fill at a 45-degree angle*

When the Fountain Fill dialog box appears, select Spot, set the start color to Pantone 281 (click on Others and use the scroll bars) at a 100% tint, and the end color to 281 at a 30% tint. Change the Angle setting to –135 degrees, the exact opposite of the 45 degree setting you chose for the fill of the curve object. This will result in a fill running in the exact opposite direction than the fill for the foreground object.

9. Select OK to exit the dialog box. When the objects are redrawn, you can see that the area behind the letters is a richer color at the upper right than at the lower left. This arrangement adds some visual tension to the mock logo. If you select Full Screen Preview, the image should appear similar to Figure 15-14.

10. Deactivate the Full Screen Preview, group the two objects, and then select the Save As command from the File menu. When the Save As dialog box appears, type the filename **FILL-5** in the File text box, and then click on the Save command button to save the altered picture under this new name.

Figure 15-14.   *Background linear fountain fill at a reverse angle from foreground*

Tip

If you plan to use a commercial process to reproduce images that contain spot color fountain fills, make the start and end colors two tints of the same color. If you do not plan to reproduce your images by a commercial process, however, this restriction does not apply.

When you select the spot color method of assigning start and end colors, you can create a fountain fill from black to white by specifying colors as 0% or 100% black. Spot color is especially useful for black-and-white linear fountain fills if you are interested in assigning a PostScript halftone screen pattern to the object at the same time. In the next section, you will review the process of specifying a PostScript halftone screen pattern with a linear fountain fill.

Spot Color Linear Fountain Fills with PostScript Halftone Screens

You will recall from your work with outline fill colors in Chapter 14 that the preview window cannot show you how a selected PostScript halftone screen pattern will look when printed. You must actually print the object with such a fill on a PostScript device in order to see the results. The same is true of PostScript halftone screens when you combine them with fountain fills, which is possible when you use the spot color system to specify start and end colors.

You cannot see the results of your work immediately when you select a PostScript halftone screen pattern with a linear fountain fill. Nevertheless, here are some tips that should help you achieve a better design on the first try:

- Set the angle of the PostScript halftone screen either at the same angle as the linear fountain fill or at an angle that complements it in a design sense. (You do not want the eye to travel in many directions at once.) Sometimes, you can determine the best angle only by experimentation; varying the angle of the halftone screen from the angle of the fountain fill can produce unexpected results.

- If you want the halftone screen to be visible when you print it, use a low frequency setting in the PostScript Halftone Screen dialog box. This is most important if the Fountain Stripes setting in the Preferences dialog box, which controls the fineness of the fountain fill itself, is high.

In the next section, you will practice defining a linear fountain fill, using the process color system instead of spot color.

Process Color Linear Fountain Fills

When you assign colors for a linear fountain fill using the process color instead of the spot color system, you can specify two discrete start and end colors, rather than just two different tints of the same color. As you will recall from the exercises in the earlier sections of this chapter and in Chapter 14, you specify the colors as percentages of other colors or color properties.

In the following exercise, you will edit the FILL-3.CDR file you saved earlier in the chapter, using the same process colors as before but this time creating a fountain fill from them.

1. Open the FILL-3.CDR file. This file contains a curve image with a uniform process fill color specified as 30% magenta and 10% yellow.

2. Adjust the viewing magnification to fit-in-window.

3. Select the curve object. Click on the Fill tool and the Fountain Fill icon in the fly-out menu to access the Fountain Fill dialog box.

4. The Process option should already be selected for process colors. The Angle setting defaults to 90 degrees, which indicates that the start color begins at the bottom and the end color appears at the top of the object. Using the Others command buttons, specify the start color as 50% magenta and 30% black, and the end color as 10% magenta. Your settings in the Fountain Fill dialog box should match the ones in Figure 15-15.

5. Select OK to exit the dialog box. The curve object redisplays with a graded fill in the specified colors at a 90-degree angle.

6. Select the background circle. To create a fountain fill behind the letters that will complement the fill of the curve object, access the Fountain Fill dialog box and keep the Process option. Set the Angle to 0 degrees (a fill from left to right). Again, using the Others command, specify the start color as 55% cyan, 55% magenta, and 75% black, and the end color to 70% cyan and 40% magenta. Select OK to exit the dialog box. If you select Full Screen Preview, the image should appear similar to Figure 15-16. The somewhat richer hues behind the letters complement the pastels of the curve object.

15

Figure 15-15.   *The Fountain Fill dialog box with Linear and Process color*
selected

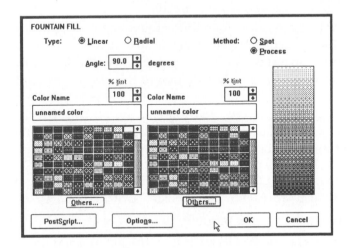

Figure 15-16.   *Linear foreground fountain fill with complementary*
background fountain fill

Even if you have a black-and-white monitor, you can see the differ-ence in tones.

7. Deactivate Full Screen Preview and select the Save As command in the File menu. When the Save As dialog box appears, type **FILL-6** in the File text box, and then select the Save command button.

To create black-and-white fountain fills using the process color system, define the start and end colors as white and black or 0% or 100% black. In the latter case, leave the percentages for all other process colors at 0.

Go on to the next set of sections to experiment with fountain fills that radiate from the center outward or from the rim inward.

Defining Radial Fountain Fills

When you specify a radial fountain fill, the start color appears all around the outer area of the object and the end color appears at its center, or vice versa. The blending of colors or tints occurs in concentric circles. Because color density in radial fountain fills changes gradually in a circular pattern, a 3-D look is easy to achieve.

You cannot specify an angle when you select a radial fountain fill, but you can control the location of the fill's apparent center. You'll see one way to change the center of a radial fountain fill in this chapter and two others—Chapters 18 and 19, "Creating Special Effects" and "Combining CorelDRAW! Features."

You can use either spot color or process color to define a radial fountain fill. When you use spot color, you have the additional option of selecting a PostScript halftone screen pattern. The tips contained in the section "Spot Color Linear Fountain Fills with PostScript Halftone Screens" apply to radial fountain fills, too.

You can control both the speed and the fineness of the display that defines the fountain fill in the preview window by adjusting the Fountain Stripes setting in the Preferences dialog box. A low setting (2 is the lower limit) causes the fountain fill to display rapidly with a small number of circles. A high setting (100 is the upper limit) causes the filled object to redraw very slowly in the preview window. It also results in a very finely graded transition of color, however. For all output devices *except* PostScript printers, the Fountain Stripes

15

setting also determines the resolution at which the fountain fill will print. You will have the opportunity to practice adjusting this setting and see the results on the screen in the "Fill Tool Hints" section at the end of the chapter.

As with the linear fountain fill, you can define a radial fountain fill for existing objects or set defaults for objects that you haven't yet created. To define a radial fountain fill for an existing object, you first select the object and then access the Fountain Fill dialog box by clicking on the Fountain Fill icon in the Fill tool fly-out menu. To define a radial fountain fill as the default fill for the next object you create, you click on the Fountain Fill icon without first selecting an object. In either case, you can press (F11) to open the Fountain Fill dialog box. The exercises in the next few sections use existing objects as examples.

Spot Color Radial Fountain Fills

Theoretically, you can select any two colors as the start and end colors when you specify a radial fountain fill using the spot color system. In practice, however, it is best to select two tints of the *same* color if you intend to send color separations of the resulting image to a commercial reproduction facility. The reason for this has to do with the way spot color is physically reproduced, which makes it difficult to blend two discrete colors evenly.

In the following exercise, you will define a black-and-white spot color radial fountain fill for the objects in the FILL-4.CDR file that you created earlier in the chapter.

1. Open the FILL-4.CDR file. As you will recall from a previous section, the curve object in this file contains a preset uniform fill of 80% black. (Remember, you can find out the current fill specifications by accessing the Uniform Fill dialog box.)

2. Adjust viewing magnification to fit-in-window. Select the curve object and access the Fountain Fill dialog box by pressing (F11), and then clicking on the Fill tool and the Fountain Fill icon in the fly-out menu.

3. Click on the Radial option button and on the Spot option button. Notice that the Angle numeric entry box is not accessible when the Radial option is selected. Specify the start color (on the left) as a 100% tint of black and the end color (on the right) as a 20% tint of

black. Then, select OK to exit the dialog box. The curve object redisplays with a brighter area (the 20% black of the color range) in its center. If you select Full Screen Preview, your screen will resemble Figure 15-17. The apparent play of light you achieve with this kind of fill creates a 3-D effect, making the surface of the "globe" appear to curve outward.

4. Deactivate Full Screen Preview and select the Save As command in the File menu. When the Save As dialog box appears, type the name **FILL-7** in the File text box and then select Save.

As long as you choose the spot color method of specifying color, you can select a PostScript halftone screen pattern with a radial fountain fill. The added 3-D effect possible with radial fountain fills can lead to quite dramatic results when you add a halftone screen.

In the next section, you will specify a radial fountain fill using the process color method.

15

Figure 15-17.   *Spot color radial fountain fill with lighter shade at center*

Process Color Radial Fountain Fills

When you assign colors for a radial fountain fill using the process color system instead of spot color, you can specify two discrete start and end colors, rather than just two different tints of the same color.

In the following exercise, you will edit the FILL-3.CDR file you saved earlier in the chapter, using the same process colors as before but this time creating a radial fountain fill from them.

1. Open the FILL-3.CDR file. The curve object in this file contains a process color uniform fill specified as 30% magenta and 10% yellow.

2. Set viewing magnification to fit-in-window.

3. Select the curve object, and then click on the Fill tool and the Fountain Fill icon to access the Fountain Fill dialog box. Make sure that the Radial and Process options are selected. Specify the start color with the Others option button as 15% cyan, 75% magenta, 10% yellow, and 0% black, and the end color as 5% cyan, 10% magenta, and 0% yellow and black. Then select OK to exit the dialog box. The curve object now displays a very light center, with the richer color at its outer rim. The apparent play of light brought about by the radial fill makes the curve object seem like a 3-D globe. To make the light seem to fall along the outer rim of the globe, you need only reverse the color combination, which you will do in the next step.

4. With the curve object still selected, access the Fountain Fill dialog box once more. This time, specify the start color as 5% cyan and 10% magenta with 0% yellow and black, and the end color as 15% cyan, 75% magenta, 10% yellow, and 0% black. Leave the other settings as before, and then select OK to exit the dialog box. The curve object now displays with the richer color at the center and the lighter color near the outer rim, as shown in Figure 15-18. This color arrangement results in a rounded appearance, but with a different play of light than before.

5. Select the background circle and access the Fountain Fill dialog box. Select the Radial and Process option buttons, and set the start color to 55% cyan, 55% magenta, and 75% black, and the end color at 50% cyan, 15% magenta, and 25% black. If you select Full Screen Preview, the image looks similar to Figure 15-18. Compare your screen with

the relative contrast of the tones in Figure 15-18. The background circle has a fill that is lighter at the center, while the foreground object has a fill that is lighter at the rim.

6. Deactivate the Full Screen Preview and select the Save As command in the File menu. Type the name **FILL-8** in the File text box of the Save As dialog box, and then select Save.

You can change the center of a radial fountain fill to create an off-center highlight for the object. You'll look at one method next. Two other methods for accomplishing this effect are available; both are included among the techniques discussed in Chapter 19, "Combining CorelDRAW! Features."

Edge Padding and Radial Offset

CorelDRAW!, in versions 2.0 and later, has a Fountain Fill Options dialog box that allows you to add edge padding and offset the center of a radial fill. This dialog box is reached by selecting the Options button in the Fountain Fill dialog box.

You may have noticed that when CorelDRAW! creates a fountain fill, it is initially rectangular, filling an object's entire boundary box. When the

15

Figure 15-18.   *Process color radial fountain fill with lighter color at rim*

creation process is complete, the excess is clipped off to fit the shape of the object, for example, the circles in this chapter. As a result, the starting and/or ending bands of the fill may be clipped off. *Edge padding* allows you to increase the percentage of an object's boundary box that is to be occupied by the starting and ending bands up to a maximum of 45%. Explore edge padding with the following brief exercise.

1. With FILL-8.CDR still on your screen and the duplicate circle still selected, select the curve object to adjust its fill.

2. Press (F11) to open the Fountain Fill dialog box and select the Options command button. The Fountain Fill Options dialog box will open as shown here:

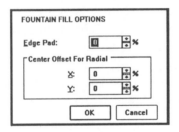

3. Type **20** in the already selected Edge Pad numeric entry box and click on OK twice to return to the drawing. At Full Screen Preview, your drawing should look like Figure 15-19. Compare this with Figure 15-18 and you will see the impact of adding 20% edge padding.

The other function of the Fountain Fill Options dialog box is offsetting the center of a radial fill—moving the center off center. Look at that next.

4. Deactivate the Full Screen Preview, press (F11) to open the Fountain Fill dialog box (be sure the Radial button is still selected), and select the Options command button.

5. In the Fountain Fill Options dialog box, press (TAB) twice, type **20**, press (TAB), type **20**, and press (ENTER) twice to set both the horizontal (X) and vertical (Y) offset to 20% and return to the drawing.

Figure 15-19. *First and last bands of fountain fill set at 20% of the object*

15

6. Again with Full Screen Preview you should see the radial fountain fill center offset to the upper-right corner as shown in Figure 15-20.

7. Deactivate the Full Screen Preview and save the current image as FILL-9.

Bitmap and Vector Fill Patterns

CorelDRAW! versions 2.0 and later, added two more ways to fill objects: bitmap fill and vector patterns. Bitmap and vector refer to two methods of forming a graphic image in a computer. Bitmap images are formed by defining each point (or bit) in an image. Vector images are formed by defining the start, end, and characteristics of each line (or vector) in an image. CorelDRAW!, 2.0 or later, comes with a number of bitmap and vector images that can be used to construct fill patterns. You can create your own or modify existing bitmap and vector images and then use them in fill patterns.

Figure 15-20.   *Center of a radial fountain fill offset 20 degrees to the right and*
20 degrees up

Bitmap and vector patterns are formed by repeating an image many times—tiling—so each image is a single tile. CorelDRAW!, in versions 2.0 and on, provides the means of selecting existing bitmap and vector images, of sizing, editing, and offsetting both kinds of images, and of creating, importing, and coloring bitmap images.

Using Bitmap Fill Patterns

Bitmap images are the most numerous and the most easily manipulated, and CorelDRAW! provides the most capability to handle them. Look at bitmap fill patterns with the following exercise.

1. FILL-9.CDR should still be on your screen with the curve object selected.

2. Select the Fill tool and the Bitmap icon ▓. The Bitmap Fill Pattern dialog box will open as shown in Figure 15-21.

Figure 15-21.   *Bitmap Fill Pattern dialog box*

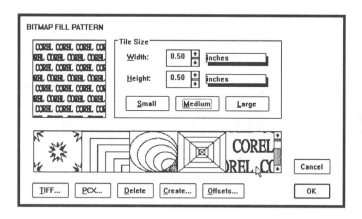

3. Take a moment to scan through the more than 45 patterns that are included with CorelDRAW!. Then select the Corel image shown in Figure 15-21.

4. Click on first Small, then Medium, and then Large to see the difference the three sizes make. Type in your own sizes in the numeric entry boxes. The height and width do not have to be the same, but for most images you probably want them to be. The maximum size is 3 inches square.

The Tile Size is the size of each tile or image in the pattern. Different sizes work for different patterns. On some patterns, Small causes the images to looked "smudged," while on others, Large causes straight lines to have jagged edges. You need to pick the size that is right for the image and for what you are trying to achieve.

5. Click on Medium and then on OK to close the dialog box. The Bitmap Pattern Color dialog box will open as shown in Figure 15-22.

Figure 15-22.   *Bitmap Pattern Color dialog box*

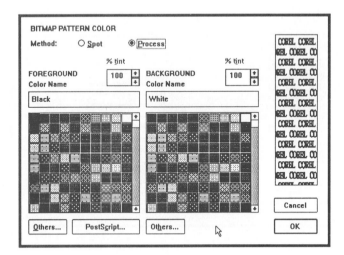

The Bitmap Pattern Color dialog box allows you to assign a color to both the foreground (the word Corel in the selected pattern) and the background. The default is a black foreground and a white background. This dialog box is very similar to other color dialog boxes you have used in both this chapter and in Chapter 14. You can select between Spot and Process color, you can select a color from a palette, specify a % tint if you are using Spot color, and use the Others command button to specify a custom process or a named color. Also, if you are using spot color you can select a PostScript halftone.

    6. Select 50% Black by clicking on the fifth color in the top row of the palette, keep the default White for the background, and click on OK. You will return to your drawing and see the bitmap pattern provide the fill for the curve object. The text in the curve object is hard to read due to the lack of contrast among the new fill, the outline of the curve object, and the fill for the duplicate circle. Change the last two to improve the contrast.

7. Select the Outline tool and select the white icon to change the outline color to white.

8. Select the duplicate circle and the Fill tool, and select the black icon to change the fill to black.

9. Press (F9) for Full Screen Preview. You screen should look like Figure 15-23.

10. Deselect Full Screen Preview and save your current drawing with the filename FILL-10.

The TIFF and PCX command buttons on the Bitmap Fill Pattern dialog box open a file selection dialog box looking for TIF and PCX files, respectively. If you select a file, the image is added to the set of images in the display box in the lower part of the Bitmap Fill Pattern dialog box. You can then select it to create a fill pattern. The Delete button deletes the selected image from the set of images in the display box and the Offset button allows you to

15

Figure 15-23. *Medium-sized bitmap fill pattern*

offset (stagger) both the horizontal and vertical starting position of each image in the pattern as well as offset two neighboring rows or two neighboring columns.

The Create button allows you to create a new bitmap image to use in constructing a fill pattern. When you activate the Create button, the Bitmap Pattern Editor opens as shown in Figure 15-24. The Bitmap Pattern Editor provides for three different sizes of drawings: 16 pixels ("dots" on your screen) square, 32 pixels square, and 64 pixels square. The more diagonal or curve elements in your image, the larger the size you will need. From a practical standpoint you should use the smallest size possible because the larger sizes take longer to draw and take more room on disk. To draw, click the left mouse button to make a pixel black and the right mouse button to make a black pixel white again. If you want to erase an unfinished drawing, change the size, say from 16x16 to 32x32. You can then change the size back, and all of pixels will be clear. When you are done with a drawing, click on OK, and the image will be saved as one of the images in the display box in the lower part of the Bitmap Fill Pattern dialog box. You can then select it to create a fill pattern.

Figure 15-24.   *Bitmap Pattern Editor*

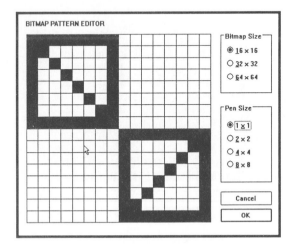

Using Vector Fill Patterns

Vector images are more clear than bitmap, but they may take more time to draw and more storage space. Change the fill in the curve object to a vector fill in the following exercise.

1. With FILL-10.CDR still on your screen and the curve object selected, open the Fill tool fly-out menu and select the Vector Fill icon ◹. The Load Vector Pattern dialog box will open as shown here:

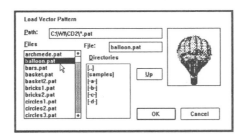

2. The Load Vector Pattern dialog box lets you open disk files with a .PAT extension. Click on a number of the files in the list box to look at the patterns that are available. You can see them in the display box on the right.

3. Select BALLOON.PAT and click on OK. The Vector Fill Pattern dialog box will open as you can see here:

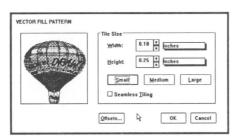

4. Select Small, Medium, and Large. Notice that the default tile sizes in the numeric entry boxes are not square like bitmap patterns were. As a result, under certain circumstances you may find that seams

appear around the tile. When that occurs, select the Seamless Tiling text box. For now, select Medium and click on OK.

5. Select Full Screen Preview and your vector filled drawing will appear as shown in Figure 15-25.

6. Turn off Full Screen Preview and save the changed drawing with the name FILL-11.CDR.

The Fill tool fly-out menu contains one more icon that you have not explored yet, but which unlocks the door to a very rich "palette" of patterns and graphic designs. This icon is the subject of the remainder of this chapter.

PostScript Fill Textures

The last icon in the Fill tool fly-out menu is the PostScript Textures icon [PS]. If you print to a PostScript printer, you can select this icon to fill selected objects with a choice of 42 different textures. This number is deceptive;

Figure 15-25.   *Vector pattern fill*

although only 42 basic patterns exist, you can alter the parameters for each texture to achieve wide variations in appearance.

When you assign a PostScript fill texture to an object, the preview window displays the object with a small gray "PS" pattern on a white background. The Fill designation in the status line, however, indicates the name of the particular texture assigned. Unfortunately, you cannot view these textures until you print them. Chapter 17 contains more information about printing these textures.

Because you cannot adequately preview an object filled with a PostScript texture, this section contains no practical exercise. It does summarize the steps involved in defining a PostScript fill texture, however: accessing the PostScript Texture dialog box, selecting a texture, and adjusting parameters.

1. To begin the process of defining a PostScript fill texture, you select the object you'd like to fill, and then click on the Fill tool and the PostScript Textures icon `PS` at the extreme right of the Fill tool fly-out menu. The PostScript Texture dialog box shown in Figure 15-26 appears.

15

Figure 15-26. PostScript Texture dialog box

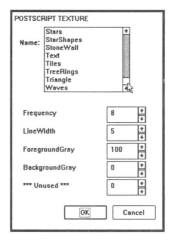

2. To select a texture, scroll down the list of texture names in the Name list box. The currently highlighted name is the selected texture.

3. Adjust each of the parameters in turn. The parameters vary, depending on the texture. You will often see references to Frequency, Foreground and Background Gray, Maximum or Minimum Size or Distance, and Random Seed (a built-in mathematical "chance" formula).

4. When you have adjusted parameters to your satisfaction, select OK to exit the dialog box and return to your drawing.

5. Print the filled object to see whether you need to adjust parameters further. Since the mathematical algorithms used to calculate the textures are very complex, some textures contain "chance" elements and may not print in a predictable way.

Working with PostScript fill textures is an adventure because of the *aleatory*, or chance, characteristics built into the mathematical formulas for the textures. Think of these textures as a way to bring more creative design elements into your drawing, even if your own drawing powers are limited.

Fill Tool Hints

The hints contained in this section by no means exhaust the many uses to which you can put the Fill tool. Rather, they represent tips to help you gain speed in your work or to introduce creative effects.

Copying Fill Styles

In previous chapters, you have learned how to use the Copy Style From command in the Edit menu to copy text, outline pen, or outline fill attributes from one object to another. You can use that same command and its associated dialog box to copy fill styles between objects, too. The following summarizes how to use this feature to best advantage:

1. Select the object or group of objects *to which* you would like to copy the fill attributes of another object.

2. Select the Copy Style From command in the Edit menu. When the Copy Style dialog box appears, activate the Fill checkbox by clicking on it. If you want to copy text, outline pen, or outline color attributes at the same time, activate those checkboxes, too.

3. Select OK to exit the dialog box. The cursor turns into an arrow containing the message "From?," indicating that you should select the object from which you want to copy the fill style.

4. Select the object whose style you want to copy to the selected object. The selected object redisplays with the new fill style.

The entire continuum of fill styles is available to you when you use this command. You can copy spot or process color uniform fills, PostScript halftone screen textures, preset shades of gray, bitmap or vector fills, or even PostScript textures. Use this command and dialog box as a handy shortcut to defining fill attributes for one or more objects.

Enhancing Preview and Printing with Fountain Stripes

You will recall that the Print & Preview dialog box (accessible from the Preferences command in the Special menu) contains many useful settings to customize the way CorelDRAW! works. One of these settings, Fountain Stripes, applies to the use of linear and radial fountain fills.

CorelDRAW! displays a fountain fill in the preview window by creating a series of concentric circles that begin at the highlighting box for the object and work their way inward. You have probably noticed this process each time the preview window redraws an object containing a fountain fill. The Preview Fountain Stripes setting in the Preferences dialog box lets you determine how many circles CorelDRAW! creates to represent a fountain fill. The number ranges from 2 to 100, with 2 representing two circles with coarse outlines, and 100 representing a high number of finely drawn circles. As you can imagine, the preview window redraws more quickly when Preview Fountain Stripes is set to a low number, and extremely slowly when the Preview

15

Fountain Stripes setting is high. Furthermore, if you print to a device other than a PostScript printer, the number of circles you select in the Preview Fountain Stripes setting represents what will actually print. You can achieve some interesting effects by varying this setting, as you will see in the following exercise.

1. Open the FILL-7.CDR file you edited in an earlier section of this chapter. The curve object in this file contains a gray-shade radial fountain fill specified with spot color.

2. Set the viewing magnification to fit-in-window and turn on the preview window, adjusting the preview and editing windows to a top-to-bottom format.

3. Open the Print & Preview dialog box from the Preferences command in the Special menu. Unless you have altered the settings since you first installed CorelDRAW!, the numeric entry box next to the Preview Fountain Stripes option contains the number 20.

4. Use the scroll bar to adjust this number downward to 2, the lowest setting possible. Select OK twice to return to the drawing.

5. Click on the preview window to cause the image to redraw. Notice how much more quickly the screen redraws now. Only two coarse concentric circles mark the fountain fill, however; as the full preview screen shows in Figure 15-27, the color transition is abrupt rather than smooth. Depending on your design, such a setting could work to your advantage.

6. Open the Print & Preview dialog box once more. Adjust the Preview Fountain Stripes setting in the Preferences dialog box upward to 100, the highest setting possible. Select OK twice to return to your drawing.

7. Click on the preview window once more to cause the image to redraw. This time, the redraw takes much longer, because of the high number of fine stripes used to recreate the fountain fill. The resulting blend of color is extremely smooth, as the full screen preview in Figure 15-28 shows.

8. Select New to clear the screen. Do not save any changes.

Figure 15-27.   *Radial fountain fill with Fountain Stripes set at 2 (coarse)*

Figure 15-28.   *Radial fountain fill with Fountain Stripes set at 100 (fine)*

If you do not have a PostScript printer, you can select a high setting for Fountain Stripes to maximize the printer output quality. If you do have a PostScript printer, you can set Fountain Stripes to a low number to speed up the redraw time in the preview window.

16

Importing and Exporting Files

As more graphics applications for IBM-compatible computers become available, the need to transfer files between different applications becomes more acute. *Connectivity*, or the ability of a software program to import and export data to and from different file formats, is rapidly becoming a requirement for graphics applications. Whether your work involves desktop publishing, technical illustration, original art, or graphic design, it is essential to be able to export your CorelDRAW! graphics to other programs, to import clipart, and to polish your work from other programs.

CorelDRAW! offers you two different methods of connectivity. In Chapter 12, you learned how to use the Windows clipboard to transfer files between CorelDRAW! and other applications that run under Microsoft Windows. The Windows clipboard is not your only option for transferring files, however. CorelDRAW! has its own independent import and export utilities specifically for transferring data between different graphics formats. These utilities allow you to import graphics from and export them to a variety of drawing, painting, desktop publishing, and word processing applications, even though some of these programs may not run under Windows. The use of the Import and Export commands in CorelDRAW! is the subject of this chapter.

CorelDRAW! imports from and exports to both bitmapped and object-oriented applications. If you are unfamiliar with the basic differences between the two graphics formats, the next section will acquaint you with the advantages and disadvantages of each.

Bitmapped vs. Object-Oriented Graphics

CorelDRAW! users come from a variety of backgrounds. Some have many years of experience with electronic drawing and design; others are experts at word processing and desktop publishing, but have little experience with graphics applications. Still others have worked with many different paint (bitmap) programs, but CorelDRAW! represents their first drawing (object-oriented) application. Whatever your background, it is important to have a clear understanding of the differences between bitmapped and object-oriented graphics. You then have a firm basis for choosing how and when to import and export graphic files.

There are many different graphics file formats, but only two kinds of graphics: *bitmapped*, also known as *pixel-based*, and *vector-based*, also known as *object-oriented*. The differences between these two kinds of graphics involve the kinds of software applications that produce them, the way the computer stores them in memory, and the ease with which you can edit them.

Paint programs and scanners produce bitmapped images by establishing a grid of *pixels*, the smallest visual unit that the computer can address, on the screen. These applications create images by altering the colors or attributes of each individual pixel. This way of storing images makes inefficient use of memory, however. The size of an image—the number of pixels it occupies—is fixed once it is created, and is dependent on the resolution of the display adapter on the computer where the image first took shape. As a result, finished bitmapped images are difficult to edit when you transfer them from one application to another. If you increase the size of a finished bitmapped image, you can see unsightly white spaces and jagged edges. If you greatly decrease the size of a finished bitmapped image, parts of the image may "smudge" because of the compression involved. Distortion can also occur if you transfer bitmapped graphics to another computer that has a different display resolution.

Object-oriented graphics, on the other hand, have none of these limitations. They are produced by drawing applications such as CorelDRAW! and are stored in the computer's memory as a series of numbers (not pixels) describing how to redraw the image on the screen. Since this method of storing information has nothing to do with the resolution of a given display adapter, line art is considered to be *device-independent*. No matter what computer you used to create an object-oriented graphic, you can stretch, scale, and resize it flexibly without distortion. Object-oriented graphics also tend to create smaller files than bitmapped graphics because the computer does not have to "memorize" the attributes of individual pixels.

How can you use each type of graphic in CorelDRAW!? As you will learn in greater detail in Appendix D, "Tracing Bitmapped Images," you can import bitmapped images in order to trace them and turn them into object-oriented graphics. Alternatively, you can simply import them and incorporate them into an existing picture. Your options for editing an imported bitmapped image do not end with the editing capabilities available in CorelDRAW!, however. When you need your finished work to issue from a paint application, or if you prefer to polish your artwork in pixel format, you can export CorelDRAW! graphics back to your favorite paint program.

If you work with other object-oriented drawing and design programs, you can import line art in order to enhance it with advanced features that only CorelDRAW! offers. You can introduce clip art and edit it flexibly. When you are finished editing, you can export CorelDRAW! artwork back to your favorite object-oriented application or to the desktop publishing application of your choice. If you have version 1.10 or later, you can even export your CorelDRAW! graphics to a format that film recorders and slide scanners will be able to use to create professional-looking presentation materials.

CorelDRAW! supports an ever-growing number of file formats that include both pixel-based and object-oriented graphics. Table 16-1 lists all of the file formats you can import into CorelDRAW!, while Table 16-2 lists the file format to which you can export CorelDRAW! graphics. Both tables categorize each file format by format type, graphics type—bitmapped (pixel) or object-oriented (line)—file extension, and the release version of CorelDRAW! in which the particular import or export option first became available.

16

Table 16-1.   *Corel DRAW! Import File Formats*

File Format	Graphics Type	Extension	Release
Corel DRAW!	line/object	.CDR	1.0
PC Paintbrush	pixel	.PCX, .PCC	1.0
TIFF (Scanners)	pixel	.TIF	1.0
Lotus PIC (graphs)	line/object	.PIC	1.0
Adobe Illustrator	line/object	.AI, .EPS	1.0
IBM PIF (GDF)	line/object	.PIF	1.02
Graphics Metafile	line/object	.CGM	1.1
AutoCAD DXF	line/object	.DXF	1.11
GEM	line/object	.GEM	1.11
Macintosh PICT	line/object	.PCT	1.2
HPGL Plotter	line/object	.PLT	1.2
Corel Trace	line/object	.EPS	2.0
Windows 3 Bitmaps	pixel	.BMP	2.0

The first half of this chapter addresses the process of importing graphics files into CorelDRAW! and special notes on importing specific file formats. The second half of the chapter covers the process of exporting graphics to other programs, as well as notes pertinent to exporting each type of file format.

Importing Graphics: An Overview

The process of importing graphics into CorelDRAW! from other file formats always involves these four steps:

1. Select the Import command from the File menu.
2. Select one of the file formats listed in the Import dialog box.
3. Decide whether you want to trace the imported graphic (this applies to bitmapped image files only).

4. Specify the directory and filename of the graphic you want to import, using the secondary dialog box that appears after you choose a file format.

Once you import the file, you have several editing options, depending on what kind of application it comes from. If the imported graphic originated in a paint program, you can trace it automatically or manually and turn it into a distortion-free, object-oriented image. You will find more information on the CorelDRAW! bitmap tracing features in Appendix D. If you use a great deal of imported clip art, you will be interested in the listing of clip art manufacturers provided in Appendix C, "Corel Connectivity: Clip Art and Fonts."

Table 16-2. *CorelDRAW! Export File Formats*

File Format	Graphic Type	Extension	Release
PostScript	line/object	.EPS	1.0
Windows Metafile	line/object	.WMF	1.0
PCX	pixel	.PCX	1.0
TIFF	pixel	.TIF	1.0
IBM PIF (GDF)	line/object	.GDF	1.02
Graphics Metafile	line/object	.CGM	1.1
SCODL (video)	line/object	.SCD	1.1
VideoShow	line/object	.PIC	1.11
WordPerfect Graphic	line/object	.WPG	1.11
AutoCAD DXF(outlines)	line/object	.DXF	1.11
GEM applications	line/object	.GEM	1.11
Macintosh PICT	line/object	.PCT	1.2
HPGL Plotter (outlines)	line/object	.PLT	1.2
CorelDRAW! 1.*xx*	line/object	.CDR	2.0
Adobe Illustrator 88	line/object	.AI	2.0
Corel Symbol & Typeface	line/object	.WFN	2.0

16

Figure 16-1.   *The Import dialog box*

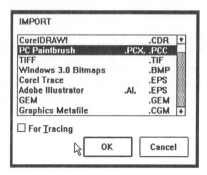

When you select the Import command from the File menu, the Import dialog box shown in Figure 16-1 appears. The list box at the top of the dialog box contains the filenames and extensions of formats available for import. Below the list box, the For Tracing checkbox lets you specify whether or not you wish to trace a bitmapped graphic. The following sections explain how to work with each of these controls.

Selecting a File Format

To select and highlight the format for the file you wish to import, click on the file format name. If the name of the file format is not visible, scroll through the list box until you can see it, and then click on it. Versions of CorelDRAW! earlier than 2.0 have a smaller number of file format options; if your dialog box contains fewer options than are shown in Figure 16-1, check your software version against Table 16-1. This table indicates which formats are available for your version.

If you want to import a file that is in an object-oriented format, the For Tracing option is gray and cannot be selected. If the file is a bitmapped graphic, however, the For Tracing option becomes available. The next section provides information about what happens to your graphic when you activate or deactivate this option.

The "For Tracing" Option and Bitmapped Graphics

You can import three different bitmapped or pixel-based file formats: .TIF files generated by scanners and software, .PCX files generated by scanners or popular paint programs such as the ZSoft PC Paintbrush and Publisher's Paintbrush family of applications, and .BMP files generated by Window 3 applications such as Windows Paintbrush and the Windows screen-capture module. CorelDRAW! handles the display, printing, and memory allocation of an imported bitmap in two different ways, depending on whether or not you activate the For Tracing option.

Memory Allocation   CorelDRAW! allocates more program memory for an imported bitmap if the For Tracing option is active. This results in a higher-resolution screen version of the bitmap in the editing window, so that you can more easily trace the bitmap to produce a curve object. The disadvantage is that program operation can slow down noticeably, particularly if the bitmapped graphic file is large or if you have an 80286-based computer.

If you leave the For Tracing option deactivated when you import a bitmap, the bitmap requires less memory, and program operation speed benefits as a result.

Displaying the Bitmap   When For Tracing is enabled, the pixel-based bitmap appears only in the editing window, not in the preview window. The preview window displays only the object-oriented curves that result after you trace the bitmap. The bitmap that displays in the editing window, however, has a higher resolution.

When you import a bitmapped graphic without enabling the For Tracing option, it is visible in both the preview and editing windows, but the screen version of the bitmap appears rather coarse. This is because CorelDRAW! allocates less memory for the bitmap in the interest of maintaining program speed.

Printing the Bitmap   When you import a bitmapped graphic with the For Tracing option active, you can print only the object-oriented curves that result from the tracing process, not the pixels in the original bitmap. When you import a bitmapped graphic without selecting the For Tracing option, the screen version of the bitmap may appear coarse, but you can print the bitmap at its full original resolution.

16

With these considerations in mind, you should activate the For Tracing option only if you are sure that you will trace the imported bitmap manually, automatically, or using the Corel Trace utility. If you plan to incorporate the bitmap "as is" into your picture, or even if you are not sure you want to trace it, leave the For Tracing checkbox blank. You can always choose to trace the bitmap later, with your only disadvantage being that Autotrace curves will be somewhat more jagged. You can edit Autotrace curves easily with the Shaping tool, however, or simply trace the curves manually instead. Appendix D describes the Autotracing process in greater detail.

The Filename and Destination Directory

After you select a file format and any other applicable options, click on the OK command button. The secondary file selection dialog box appears for you to specify the location and filename of the image you want to import. The header of the secondary dialog box varies, reflecting the file format you have chosen; the header of the dialog box in Figure 16-2, for example, reads "Import Bitmap."

Figure 16-2.   *The Import dialog box*

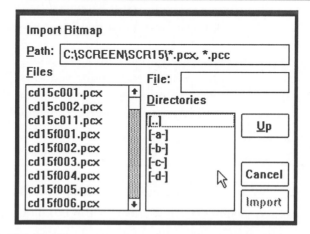

To specify the drive and directory where the import file is located, double-click on the appropriate drive or directory designation in the Directories list box at the right side of the Files list box. Use the scroll bars if the desired drive or directory name is not visible. The name of the highlighted drive and directory appears in the Path text box. To select the filename of the image you want to import, double-click on the filename in the Files list box at the left side of the dialog box. The filename will appear in the File text box. Click on the Open command button to begin the transfer of the image to the CorelDRAW! page.

What happens to the image during the import process depends on the specific file format you have chosen. The following sections offer notes on importing each file format for which a CorelDRAW! filter exists.

Importing Bitmapped Graphics

All versions of CorelDRAW! since its first release are able to import bitmapped graphics in either .PCX or .TIF format and CorelDRAW! version 2.0 added the .BMP format. The most common source of .PCX files is the ZSoft family of paint applications, although some other paint programs also allow you to save files in this format. TIFF files (extension .TIF) are generated by gray-scale scanners and by paint-and-draw programs that allow you to save bitmapped images with gray-scale information. Windows 3 Paintbrush is the primary source of .BMP files.

Bitmapped images appear inside a rectangle in the editing window after you import them. You cannot break bitmapped images down into their component parts, because CorelDRAW! treats the entire bitmapped image as a single object. You can crop a bitmap after importing it, however, so that only a specified section is visible. You can also select, move, rearrange, stretch, scale, outline, and fill a bitmap as though it were any other type of object.

In some respects, imported bitmaps behave differently from other objects when you edit them. If you rotate or skew a bitmap, you can no longer see the original image in the preview window; it becomes a gray rectangle with a white triangle in the corner to indicate its orientation. A rotated or skewed bitmap will not print unless you output it to a PostScript printer.

16

The following sections describe the limitations on importing bitmaps as they apply to a specific file format.

PC Paintbrush .PCX Files

If the file you choose to import is in .PCX or .PCC format, CorelDRAW! will accept either the original .PCX or .PCC black-and-white format or the newer color .PCX format. If you import a color, .PCX file, CorelDRAW! will print it in color on a color printer or convert it to shades of gray for a black-and-white printer.

Windows Paintbrush .BMP Files

Files imported from Windows 3 Paintbrush in the .BMP format can be either black-and-white or color but the format will not convey gray-scale information. On a color printer, files with color will print in color or they will be converted to shades of gray for a black-and-white printer.

Scanned or Gray-Scale Bitmaps (TIFF)

Scanners and some paint programs save bitmapped images in the .TIF file format. CorelDRAW! will import saved gray-scale information with the TIFF format, so if your paint application allows it, you should save gray-scale paint images in this format if you intend to import them into CorelDRAW!.

Several different versions of TIFF formats are available. CorelDRAW! supports most of these. Extra time is needed to decompress and import a compressed TIFF file, however, and you may get errors from some compressed files. Although CorelDRAW! cannot display gray-scale bitmap information on your monitor screen, it saves this information. If you use a PostScript output device, the gray-scale information will be reproduced faithfully when you print the image.

The following group of sections provides tips on importing and working with graphics files in each of the object-oriented formats that CorelDRAW! supports.

Importing Object-Oriented Graphics

The original release of CorelDRAW! allowed you to import three object-oriented graphics file formats: .CDR (the native CorelDRAW! format), Lotus .PIC graphs, and .AI and .EPS files created by Adobe Illustrator or clip art manufacturers. Since then, the ranks of supported object-oriented file formats have swelled to include .GDF, .CGM, .GEM, .DXF, .PCT, and .PLT files. Table 16-1 lists each type of object-oriented file format and the CorelDRAW! version that first supported it.

Specific notes on importing and working with each file format are provided in the following sections. Keep in mind that software applications are being upgraded continually and that process may alter the way certain file formats interact with CorelDRAW!.

CorelDRAW! Files and Clip Art

As you will recall from Chapter 12, you can copy or cut and paste objects or images between different CorelDRAW! files using the Windows clipboard. The Windows clipboard limitations render this solution less than satisfactory, especially if you attempt to transfer images that contain many nodes or complicated attributes. A better solution in such cases is to import the .CDR file into the current graphic, using the Import command.

You can also use the Import command to import clip art in .CDR format. Corel Systems and ArtRight Software Corporation are among the clip art manufacturers who provide files in this format.

A file that you import in .CDR format appears as a group of objects. You can select the group, apply the Ungroup command in the Arrange menu, and then edit the objects normally.

Lotus .PIC Files

You can import graphic images in Lotus 1-2-3 .PIC format into CorelDRAW! and modify them. When you import a Lotus .PIC file, CorelDRAW! groups the entire file. To manipulate individual objects within

16

the imported graphic, select the graphic, apply the Ungroup command, and then edit objects normally.

Adobe Illustrator Files

A wide variety of clip art files is available in either Adobe Illustrator (.AI) or Adobe Illustrator's own Encapsulated PostScript (.EPS) format, which is different from the .EPS format used by other PostScript applications. If you have a version of CorelDRAW! prior to version 1.02, you will see the extension .ART listed in the Import dialog box; later versions display the file extensions .AI and .EPS. If the extension of the file you want to import does not match the one generated automatically by CorelDRAW!, just backspace over the incorrect extension and type the desired extension instead. CorelDRAW! will recognize the correct files.

Caution

Keep in mind that the CorelDRAW! .EPS Export filter allows you to save files in a format that most desktop publishing applications can use. However, you cannot edit these files in other graphics applications that use the .EPS format. In addition, the CorelDRAW! .EPS Import filter supports only the Adobe Illustrator version of .EPS. Therefore, if you export a CorelDRAW! file in .EPS format without having saved it as a .CDR file first, you will not be able to re-import it to make changes. Always save your work in CorelDRAW! before exporting it if you think you might need to edit it later.

CorelDRAW! imports an Adobe Illustrator-compatible image file as a group of objects. To edit individual objects in the imported file, select the group, apply the Ungroup command, and then select the desired object(s).

IBM Mainframe Graphics (.PIF and .GDF) Files

Files in the Base .PIF format are most familiar to graphics users in the mainframe IBM environment. The .PIF import and export filters have been available since version 1.02 release of CorelDRAW!.

Not all information in a .PIF file transfers smoothly into CorelDRAW!. For example:

- You may sometimes need to scale and/or center the image on the page before you can edit it.

- Objects that are white in the .PIF file will not show up on the white CorelDRAW! page unless you place a page-sized colored rectangle in the background as contrast.

- Base .PIF specifications for "Set Background Mix," "Set Foreground Mix," "Call Segment," "Set Character Set," "Set Paper Color," and "Set Pattern Symbol" do not transfer into the CorelDRAW! format.

- Base .PIF "Line Types" specifications do not match CorelDRAW! outline pen line types on a one-to-one basis. .PIF line types 0 and 7 become solid; 1, 4, 2, 5, 3, and 6 become one of the dashed or dotted line styles available in CorelDRAW!; and line type 8 becomes a line type of None.

- Text strings from Base .PIF files come into CorelDRAW! as text in the font that appears at the top of the typeface list in the Text dialog box—Avalon is the default.

As with most other line-art files, a graphic imported from a .PIF application arrives in CorelDRAW! as multiple grouped objects. To edit individual objects in the graphic, select the group, apply the Ungroup command in the Arrange menu, and then select the object you wish to manipulate.

16

Graphics Metafile .CGM Files

CorelDRAW! release 1.10 was the earliest version of the software to include an import filter for the object-oriented .CGM format, which appears in the Import dialog box as the Graphics Metafile option. Unlike the other file formats discussed so far, the .CGM format has many variants because it is used by a wide variety of popular software applications, including Harvard Graphics, Lotus Freelance Plus, Zenographics Mirage, Arts & Letters, Micrografx Designer, ISSCO Display, and some CAD applications. A number of clip art libraries that make use of the .CGM format exist as well.

Since these programs all have different features, the limitations on transferring .CGM file information into CorelDRAW! vary from application to application, but two general limitations apply to all programs. The first limitation involves the size of the imported file relative to the CorelDRAW! page. As with Base .PIF files, if the imported .CGM file is larger than the page, adjust viewing magnification to fit-in-window and then select and scale the grouped image. You may then apply the Ungroup command to the image to break it into its component objects. The second general limitation with .CGM imports involves bitmapped graphics, which are supported in many applications that use .CGM file formats but which do not transfer into CorelDRAW!.

The following sections describe application-specific limitations on importing .CGM files into CorelDRAW!

Harvard Graphics

Harvard Graphics treats colors and fills differently than CorelDRAW!, and you should keep some of these differences in mind when importing a .CGM file. Specifically, a filled shape saved in Harvard Graphics transfers into CorelDRAW! as two separate objects: an outline and a fill. You will need to group these two objects in order to edit them as a single entity. In addition, colored objects created in Harvard Graphics come into CorelDRAW! darker than in their original form. This problem is due to features of the Harvard Graphics environment and has no remedy at the present time. Circles, straight lines, and curves retain their original object identity when imported, but rectangles, ellipses, and arrows transfer into CorelDRAW! as curve objects. Text transfers into CorelDRAW! as text in the Toronto typeface, but *only* if you do not save the file in Harvard Graphics with a native Harvard Graphics typeface. If you opt to use a Harvard Graphics typeface, the text turns into curves when you import it into CorelDRAW!.

CorelDRAW! uses the Windows character set for most of its native typefaces, but the extended character set for Harvard Graphics differs somewhat from the Windows set. If you use foreign-language or other special characters above ASCII 128 in Harvard Graphics, some may not transfer as expected.

Micrografx Designer

As you will recall from Chapter 12, you can transfer objects from Micrografx Designer images into CorelDRAW! through the Windows clipboard, as long as they do not run into the clipboard's limitations. If you want to transfer complex objects or entire images into CorelDRAW!, however, you can use the Import command and dialog box instead, and import the file in .CGM format.

Most file information from the .CGM format transfers into CorelDRAW! as expected. Exceptions do exist, however. For example, circles and ellipses come into CorelDRAW! as curve objects, and both fountain fills and *hatching* fills (a series of lines of varying density) transfer as solid color fills. Although Micrografx Designer can use bitmapped graphics, these do not import into CorelDRAW!.

Lotus Freelance Plus

Some text-related information in Lotus Freelance Plus .CGM files may not transfer quite as expected. As with Harvard Graphics, for example, Freelance Plus uses a character set that differs slightly from the Windows character set. If text strings created in Freelance Plus contain characters above ASCII 128, you may notice some character substitutions. In addition, text transfers into CorelDRAW! in the Toronto typeface.

Colors and fills created in Freelance Plus do not always come into CorelDRAW! as originally specified. For example, hatching fills transfer as solid color fills. More important, colors specified in the Freelance Plus .CGM file may not transfer accurately unless the printer installed for Freelance supports color printing. If a black-and-white printer was installed with Freelance Plus, colors may transfer into CorelDRAW! as gray shades.

As with Micrografx Designer, bitmapped graphics from Freelance Plus do not transfer into the CorelDRAW! file format.

Arts & Letters

Most of the file information that does not transfer well into the CorelDRAW! format has to do with object types. Circles, ellipses, and text come into CorelDRAW! as curve objects and can only be edited as such. Rectangles transfer over as connected straight line segments. And, as with other .CGM file formats, bitmapped objects saved in Arts & Letters do not transfer into CorelDRAW! at all. In addition, filled objects come into CorelDRAW! as two separate objects: an outline and a fill. This is the same situation you encounter with filled objects created in Harvard Graphics.

16

AutoCAD Data Exchange .DXF Files

Beginning with release 1.11, you can import AutoCAD files into CorelDRAW! in .DXF format. This step represents an important advance, since the .DXF format retains more AutoCAD information than any alternative format. Nonetheless, not all information resident in the AutoCAD .DXF file transfers into the CorelDRAW! format. The following sections give some examples.

3-D Information   In order to retain as much 3-D information from an AutoCAD file as possible, you should take special steps to prepare the file carefully before importing it. A recommended procedure is to save the AutoCAD 3-D file in .DXB format, then begin a new drawing and transfer the .DXB file to it, and finally save the file in .DXF format using the DXFOUT utility. You should also save the 3-D image in the specific view that you want to transfer into CorelDRAW!.

Because of the complexity of information stored in a 3-D AutoCAD image, the imported file may be much larger than will fit on the CorelDRAW! page. If this happens, adjust the viewing magnification to fit-in-window, then select the imported .DXF graphic and scale it downward.

Some precision is lost in the transfer of information, however. For example, CorelDRAW! does not support 3-D extrusion of circles, arcs, text, or polylines with dashed patterns.

Colors   When you save a 3-D file in AutoCAD according to the procedure just mentioned, color information is lost. You must respecify colors once the file has arrived in CorelDRAW!. In other cases, however, colors should match the 256-color scheme that AutoCAD uses for the IBM Professional Graphics Controller.

Lines, Outlines, and Fills   Since CorelDRAW! does not support variable widths on a single line, variable-width lines in AutoCAD are imported as single-width lines. The width of the line in CorelDRAW! is equal to the *minimum* width that the variable-width line had in AutoCAD.

Dashed lines in the .DXF file transfer into CorelDRAW! as the first dashed line pattern in the Outline Pen dialog box. You can choose another line type later.

Objects that are specified as invisible in AutoCAD come into CorelDRAW! with no outline and no fill. You can see these objects in the editing window but not in the preview window.

A point in AutoCAD transfers into CorelDRAW! as an ellipse of the smallest possible size. An extruded point (a point seeming to extend outward in 3-D format) comes into CorelDRAW! as a line segment with two nodes.

Text   Text generated in AutoCAD may appear stretched in CorelDRAW!, since CorelDRAW! attempts to keep the physical length of text the same. Some differences in text length may still occur, however.

If the point size or degree that text is skewed in the original AutoCAD file exceeds the limits allowed by CorelDRAW!, the text transfers over within the CorelDRAW! limits and may not match the original.

Non-standard characters imported into CorelDRAW! appear as a question mark (?), and some special characters are ignored. CorelDRAW! will provide some limited matching of AutoCAD fonts but most fonts are translated to the Toronto typeface.

GEM Applications .GEM Files

16

As of release 1.11, CorelDRAW! supports the import of images created in the object-oriented .GEM format. This includes artwork from GEM Draw and GEM Artline as well as files created by Ventura Publisher. You will notice a few differences between the original file and its imported version in CorelDRAW! as follows:

- CorelDRAW! does not support the custom fill patterns (grids, ball bearings, and so on) offered in GEM applications. Objects containing these fills in the .GEM format transfer into CorelDRAW! with a tinted spot color fill of the same color as the original pattern fill.

- CorelDRAW! allows only ten levels of object grouping, but GEM applications allow more. If you import a file that has more than ten levels of object groups, some objects transfer over as ungrouped. The best solution is to regroup objects after importing the file.

- In GEM applications, you can mix line cap styles in the same line. For example, a line can be rounded at one end and flat on the other.

In CorelDRAW!, however, you can mix line cap styles only if one end of the line or curve is an arrow. When you import a GEM file that contains lines with mixed line cap styles, therefore, CorelDRAW! assigns the line cap style of the starting point to both ends of the line or curve.

- Text created in GEM Artline transfers into CorelDRAW! as curve objects. Text created in other GEM applications transfers as text. The Dutch, Swiss, and System typefaces under GEM come into CorelDRAW! as Toronto, Switzerland, and Avalon, respectively. Text alignment and spacing settings are not maintained, but you can edit these features after importing the file. Text with underlines in GEM Draw, however, transfers into CorelDRAW! without outlines.

HPGL .PLT Plotter Files

Beginning with CorelDRAW! release 1.2, HPGL plotter files with the .PLT extension could be imported. HPGL files are created by various applications, notably AutoCAD, to drive a plotter.

Color is specified in HPGL files in terms of pen numbers. The CorelDRAW! CORELDRW.INI has a pen assignment list under the heading [CDrawHPGLPenColor]. An entry in this list might be

Pen3="Pen#3=Red",0,100,100,0

This assigns pen 3 to the color red, which has the CMYK color mix of 0% cyan, 100% magenta, 100% yellow, and 0% black. A pen number in an imported HPGL file not in the CORELDRW.INI file will be assigned to pen 1 (normally black). You can edit the CORELDRW.INI file and add or reassign pens.

Only HPGL objects Shade Rectangle Absolute, Shade Rectangle Relative, and Shade Wedge will be filled in CorelDRAW!.

HPGL text is imported in the first CorelDRAW! typeface (normally Avalon) and is only an outline; it has no fill. Both of these attributes can be modified in CorelDRAW!.

HPGL line types 0 through 2 are imported as dotted lines, types 3 through 6 are imported as dashed lines, and all other line types are solid lines in CorelDRAW!

Macintosh PICT .PCT Files

Files created on the Macintosh computer in either PICT1 (black-and-white) or PICT2 (color) formats can be imported into CorelDRAW! beginning with version 1.2. The Macintosh PICT format (converted to IBM PC-compatible files with a .PCT extension) can contain both vector and bitmap objects. CorelDRAW! will only import the vector objects and will ignore the bitmat objects.

PICT color will be reasonably matched, as will fills and patterns. There may be some noticeable differences, though. PICT text will transfer into CorelDRAW! as editable text with matching typefaces and typestyles where possible. Unsupported typefaces will be converted to Toronto, underlined text will not be underlined in CorelDRAW!, and there may be differences in text alignment. If text is rotated in the PICT file, it will not come into CorelDRAW! since rotated text is stored as a bitmat object.

PICT files can contain more levels of nested groups than the ten levels allowed in CorelDRAW!. If you import a file with more than ten levels, some objects will transfer ungrouped. You can regroup them in CorelDRAW!.

The CorelDRAW! import filters offer you a rich world of possibilities. But the uses to which you can put CorelDRAW!'s advanced graphics features are even richer when you consider the software applications to which you can export your images. The remainder of this chapter covers the process and pitfalls of exporting CorelDRAW! files to other applications.

16

Exporting Graphics: An Overview

Connectivity is a two-way street. The ability to import any number of different file formats would be of limited use if you could not export your work to other applications as well. CorelDRAW! has an even greater number of export filters than import filters. After perfecting a masterpiece in CorelDRAW!, you can send it to your favorite paint program, object-oriented drawing software, desktop publishing application, or film-recording device.

In some cases, you may have a choice of more than one export format. Popular desktop publishing applications such as Xerox Ventura Publisher and Aldus PageMaker, for example, accept .EPS, .CGM, .PCX, and .TIF graphics files. When several file formats are available, how do you determine which is the best for your needs? The notes on each type of export file format attempt to cover this issue, as well as to describe any features of the original CorelDRAW! artwork that transfer differently than expected.

The process of exporting a CorelDRAW! file to another application always involves these five steps:

1. Open the CorelDRAW! image file you want to transfer and save it before beginning the export procedure. If you want to export only certain objects rather than the entire file, select those objects.

2. Select the Export command from the File menu.

3. Select a file format from the choices in the Export dialog box.

4. Choose whether to export the entire file or selected objects only.

5. Specify the directory and filename of the graphic you want to export, using the secondary Export file selection dialog box that appears.

Depending on the export file format you choose, other choices in the Export dialog box may also become available to you. Each of these will be detailed in the following sections.

Preparing for Exporting

If you are planning to export an existing file, open it before you select the Export command. If the page is empty when you attempt the export procedure, you'll find you can't select the Export command.

If you are preparing to export a new file or one you have imported and edited, always save the file as a .CDR image before exporting it. This is extremely important if there is any chance that you might need to edit the image again later. In several cases, potential problems or inconveniences may occur when you try to reimport an exported file that you never saved in CorelDRAW! format:

.EPS   The CorelDRAW! .EPS import filter supports only Adobe Illustrator files. The .EPS export filter, on the other hand, supports the standard .EPS format used by desktop publishing applications such as Aldus PageMaker and Ventura Publisher. If you export a CorelDRAW! file to .EPS without saving it first, you will not be able to import it again later.

.PCX and .TIF   If you export a CorelDRAW! image to a pixel-based format without saving it first, and then re-import it, the imported image will be pixel-based as well. You would have to retrace and edit it extensively before you could make changes.

If you want to export only a part of the CorelDRAW! file rather than the entire image, select the desired objects before beginning the export procedure. An option in the Export dialog box will allow you to specify the export of selected objects only.

The Export Dialog Box

When you select the Export command from the File menu, the Export dialog box shown in Figure 16-3 appears. If you have a version of CorelDRAW! prior to release 2.0, the Export dialog box on your screen may show fewer options than shown in the figure.

At the upper-left corner of the dialog box, the file format list box contains the names and extensions of the file formats to which you can export the current file. Immediately below the file format list box are four checkboxes. These allow you to export selected objects within the file, include outline and fill attribute information, include an image header (.EPS), or use the fonts resident in the printer instead of the native CorelDRAW! fonts (extension .WFN). Not all of these checkboxes are available for selection with every file format. Below the four checkboxes are two rows of option buttons. The Resolution option buttons let you specify screen resolution when you export to a bitmapped format, while the Fixed Size option buttons let you determine the size of an image header for .EPS file exports. Again, the availability of

16

Figure 16-3.   *The Export dialog box*

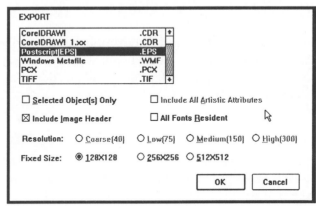

these options depend on the file format you select. The following sections explain how to work with each of the controls in the Export dialog box.

Selecting a File Format

To select and highlight the file format to which you will export the CorelDRAW! image, click on the file format name. If the name of the file format is not visible, scroll through the list box until you can see it, and then click on it. Versions of CorelDRAW! earlier than 2.0 have a smaller number of file format options; if your dialog box contains fewer options than the one in the figure, check your software version against Table 16-2.

"Selected Objects Only" Option

This option is available for any export file format that you choose. However, if you activate this option without first selecting one or more objects in the current image, the message box in Figure 16-4 appears after you specify a filename for the exported file.

Figure 16-4.   *Error message when no objects are selected for exporting*

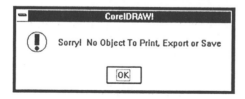

"Include All Artistic Attributes" Option

The purpose of this option is to export not only the objects in the CorelDRAW! image, but also their text, outline, outline fill, and fill attributes. This option is available only for object-oriented export file formats that CorelDRAW! introduced in versions 1.02 and later: IBM .PIF, .CGM, SCODL, VideoShow, WordPerfect, .WPG, .CGM, .DXF, and .GEM. For these formats, the Include All Artistic Attributes option is automatically activated. Due to inherent differences in the features of various software applications, however, not every format translates these attributes accurately. The "Exporting to Object-Oriented Graphics Formats" section of this chapter provides information about attributes that may not transfer well for a specific export file format.

Including an .EPS Image Header

An image header is a visual representation of a PostScript graphic on screen. The Include Image Header option is available (and automatically activated) only when you select the .EPS export file format for PostScript images. While not truly WYSIWYG, the image header helps you position or crop the .EPS image in desktop publishing applications such as Aldus PageMaker and Ventura Publisher. If you choose to deactivate the Include Image Header option, you will not have a visual representation of an .EPS image in your desktop publishing application.

Deactivate the Include Image Header option only if you plan to use the exported .EPS image in an application that cannot display an EPS image

16

header. Versions of Ventura Publisher earlier than 2.0, for example, do not support the display of EPS image headers.

"All Fonts Resident" .EPS Option

When you activate this option, which is also available only when you choose to export to the .EPS format, you tell CorelDRAW! to assume that all fonts used in your graphic are resident in the output device. Text strings in the exported graphic will be printed using the printer-resident fonts rather than the original CorelDRAW! fonts.

In versions of CorelDRAW! prior to release 1.1, the main use for this option was to create a PostScript output file for printing by a laser service bureau. Most laser service bureaus have access to all of the Adobe PostScript fonts and can substitute them for the CorelDRAW! fonts automatically. With the advent of the WFNBOSS utility that converts major manufacturers' fonts into usable CorelDRAW! fonts, the All Fonts Resident option has even wider applications. If you use the WFNBOSS utility (described in Appendix C), you can activate the All Fonts Resident option whenever you want to use the original manufacturers' fonts in printing.

Specifying a Bitmapped Graphics Resolution

The option buttons following "Resolution:" in the Export dialog box become available for selection only when you have chosen a pixel-based export file format (.PCX, .TIF). You can choose from Coarse (40 dpi), Low (75 dpi), Medium (150 dpi), or High (300 dpi) resolutions. High resolution is the option to choose if you want to give the exported image the best possible appearance.

Because of the way a computer stores pixel-based graphics, however, an image that is large in CorelDRAW! can occupy an enormous amount of memory (up to 1 MB for a full-page image) when you export it at a high resolution. Rather than export the graphic at a lower resolution, consider using the Select tool to scale the CorelDRAW! image down to the size it should be in the final application. For example, if you plan to export the graphic to a desktop publishing program and know the desired image size on the page, scale it down to that size before exporting it from CorelDRAW!. This precautionary action will also prevent you from having to resize the bitmap later, thereby causing its appearance to deteriorate.

Specifying an .EPS Fixed Size Image Header

Although an Encapsulated PostScript (.EPS) file is object-oriented, the image header that represents it is a pixel-based approximation. The Fixed Size option buttons in the Export dialog box let you specify, in pixels, the size of the visible image header in the exported file. Like the Include Image Header and All Fonts Resident options, these options become available only when you have chosen .EPS as the export format.

The image header size you select does *not* affect the size of the actual PostScript graphic. If conserving memory and disk space is a concern, you should select the 128-by-128-pixel option for the smallest image header. If accurate representation is more important to you than memory conservation, however, select the 512-by-512-pixel option to obtain an image header that is true to the proportions of the actual graphic. The size of the resulting .EPS files may exceed 64K if you select the 512-by-512 option.

16

Specifying the Filename and the Destination Directory

After you select a file format and any other applicable options, click on the OK command button. The secondary file selection dialog box appears for you to specify the destination drive and filename of the exported image. The header of the secondary Export dialog box varies, reflecting the file format you have chosen; the header of the dialog box in Figure 16-5, for example, reads "Export PostScript (.EPS)."

To specify the destination drive and directory for the exported image, click on the appropriate drive or directory designation in the Directories list box. Use the scroll bars if the desired name is not visible. The name of the highlighted drive and directory appears in the Path text box. To name the exported image file, click on the File text box. When the flashing cursor appears, type the desired filename; CorelDRAW! adds the extension for the specified file format automatically. Click on the Save command button to begin the transfer of the image to the designated file format.

Figure 16-5.   *The secondary Export dialog box*

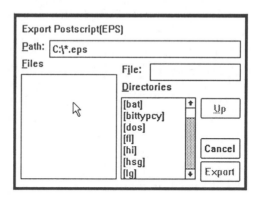

What happens to the image during the export process depends on the specific file format you have chosen. The following sections offer notes on exporting images to each available file format. Equally important, they explore the practical uses of exporting to various file formats.

Exporting to Bitmapped Graphics Formats

When you have a choice of several different export file formats, your primary concerns should be the end use to which you will put the exported graphic, the CorelDRAW! features that can or cannot be retained, and the convenience of working with the image in the export file format. The advantages of the bitmap formats supported by CorelDRAW!—.PCX and .TIF—are that they command wide support throughout the software industry and that the paint programs in which you edit them are usually easier to learn and use than most object-oriented drawing and design applications. The disadvantages are that they do not display well on monitors that support resolutions different from the resolutions in which the bitmaps were created, and that they are inconvenient to resize. If you design a bitmap on

CorelDRAW! and then export it, however, your image will not suffer from this limitation.

If you have a version of CorelDRAW! previous to 2.0, the bitmap file formats are still good choices for export to desktop publishing programs if you do not use a PostScript printer and cannot take advantage of the .EPS file format. Starting with release 1.1, however, one of the object-oriented formats such as .CGM is a better choice for desktop publishing applications. Unlike the bitmapped formats, the object-oriented formats are easy to resize without distortion and preserve more attribute information. If you have one of the more recent versions of CorelDRAW!, you should select a bitmapped file format only when one of the following conditions applies:

- Your application accepts only bitmapped graphics.
- You plan to alter the CorelDRAW! graphic, using techniques available only in the pixel-by-pixel editing environment of a paint program.

The following sections provide details on the limitations of exporting to each of the supported bitmapped file formats.

16

The .PCX Format

The .PCX format supported by CorelDRAW! describes a graphic as a collection of black-and-white dots. Since this format supports no color information, the files created when you export a CorelDRAW! image can be relatively small—*unless* the original image fills at least half of an 8 1/2-by-11-inch page. The CorelDRAW! .PCX export filter does not support the transfer of gray-scale information.

The .TIF Format

Although an image that you *import* from a TIFF file can transfer gray-scale information, the export of a CorelDRAW! image to the TIFF format cannot. Therefore, the information exported to a pixel-based file format is roughly the same, whether you choose .PCX or .TIF.

The next group of sections explores the advantages and disadvantages of exporting CorelDRAW! objects and images to each of the available object-oriented file formats.

Exporting to Object-Oriented Graphics Formats

The original release of CorelDRAW! supported export to two object-oriented file formats only: Encapsulated PostScript (.EPS) and Windows Metafile (.WMF). Since then, export filters for .CGM, VideoShow .PIC, AutoCAD .DXF, .GEM, WordPerfect Graphics .WPG, mainframe .PIF, Adobe Illustrator .AI, CorelDRAW! 1.*xx* and 2.*xx* .CDR, Corel Symbol & Typeface .WFM, and film recorder SCODL (.SCD) formats have become available as well. As mentioned earlier in this chapter, object-oriented formats transfer color, outline, fill, and attribute information more accurately than is the case with bitmapped formats. In addition, object-oriented formats are *device-independent*, which means that their images look the same despite resizing or changes in the display resolution.

Your main concerns when choosing an object-oriented export format are the final use to which you plan to put the image and the kinds of information you cannot afford to lose during the export process. The following sections provide information on the uses and limitations of each type of export file format.

CorelDRAW! and CorelDRAW! 1.*xx* .CDR Format

You can *export* files in the standard .CDR format (either 2.*xx* or 1.*xx* versions) in addition to *saving* files in the 2.*xx* format from versions 2.0 and above. You may want to do this for two reasons: First, it allows you to save just selected objects on a drawing and second, it allows you to transfer a 2.*xx* file back to an earlier version of CorelDRAW!. Note that typefaces and other features that became available in 2.0 and on are not recognized by earlier versions.

Corel Symbol and Typeface .WFN Format

CorelDRAW! versions 2.0 and above allow you to create symbols and typefaces in CorelDRAW! and export them to the symbol and typeface library with a .WFN format. This procedure allows you to incorporate an image into an existing or new typeface or symbol set. You can then retrieve and use this image as you would any character in an existing typeface.

The process of creating and storing typeface characters and symbols is fairly complex and has many considerations. See Section 2 of the *WFNBOSS Guide to Operation* for a detailed explanation.

Encapsulated PostScript .EPS Format

The .EPS file format is the export format of choice when your CorelDRAW! image contains features that are available for PostScript output devices only. Such features include PostScript halftone screen patterns and textures, and rotated or skewed bitmapped images. If you export a CorelDRAW! graphic containing both line art and bitmaps to the .EPS format, both types of graphics will transfer properly. The Graphics Metafile (.CGM) format, on the other hand, cannot accept bitmaps.

The main limitations of exporting to .EPS file format concern complex curves, the bitmapped image header, and the fact that it is a one-way export from CorelDRAW!.

Complex Graphics   If the graphic that you want to export to .EPS format contains approximately 200 or more nodes per curve object, you may have trouble printing it in your desktop publishing or other PostScript application. The same difficulty may occur if your image is laden with PostScript textures, halftone screen patterns, combined objects, and fancy text strings.

Image Header   As explained previously, the image header in an .EPS graphic is an approximate bitmap representation made available for the purposes of positioning and cropping the graphic. It is not always convenient to work with this header, because it's not truly WYSIWYG.

16

One-Way Export   The Adobe-standard .EPS import format supported by CorelDRAW! works with Adobe Illustrator files only. If you export a CorelDRAW! graphic to the *standard* .EPS format and then decide you need to make changes, you will not be able to re-import the graphic to CorelDRAW!. The importance of saving your graphic in .CDR format in CorelDRAW! before exporting it cannot be overstated.

All in all, the .EPS file format offers you the best opportunity to transfer CorelDRAW! image information if you use a PostScript printer or imagesetter and a relevant application. Other object-oriented formats work nearly as well for other applications, as you will see in the following sections.

Adobe Illustrator 88's .AI Format

As you just read, the .EPS format that CorelDRAW! exports is different from Adobe Illustrator 88 and some Macintosh-based programs. For that reason, CorelDRAW! 2.0 added the ability to export a file in the .AI format. It is *not* recommended that this format be used where you can also use .EPS, for example, with Ventura Publisher and Aldus PageMaker.

There are many limitations to the .AI format export. Among these are that fountain fills, PostScript textures, arrowheads, fitting text to a path, calligraphic pen effects, bitmaps, and individual character attributes are all not supported. Also avoid combined objects and exporting text that has been converted to curves in CorelDRAW!. If you want text as curves in the application to which you are exporting, select the "Send text as curves" option in the special .AI dialog box.

IBM .PIF Format

When you choose to export a CorelDRAW! graphic to the IBM mainframe .PIF graphics format first made available with CorelDRAW! release 1.02, two additional options in the Export dialog box become available. The first option, Selected Objects Only, allows you to transfer just a portion of your graphic rather than the whole file. The second, Include All Artistic Attributes, allows you to choose whether to transfer outline and fill attributes such as calligraphic outlines, special line caps, and fountain fills. The export filter translates these attributes into polygons and fills them accordingly. Some radial fills may not transfer exactly as they appear in CorelDRAW! and PostScript fills do not transfer at all. If you choose not to include all artistic attributes when exporting a graphic, the .PIF export filter translates custom outlines to default .PIF line thicknesses and omits fountain fills.

Color information transfers to the mainframe format regardless of whether you activate the Include All Artistic Attributes option. CorelDRAW! colors transfer over as the closest match to one of the 16 colors available in the .PIF graphic format.

Computer Graphics Metafile .CGM Format

The .CGM, or Computer Graphics Metafile format, first became an export option with version 1.10 of CorelDRAW!. In reality, .CGM represents not a single format, but rather a group of closley related object-oriented file formats. The application determines which file format will be used. Since there are so many versions available, each with its own characteristics, graphics information does not always translate in exactly the same way. The CorelDRAW! .CGM export filter cannot "know" automatically the software application to which you are planning to export a graphic.

In general, however, most color, line thickness, and fill attributes transfer well, even if you do not export a graphic with the Include All Artistic Attributes option selected. Calligraphic outlines transfer to .CGM format only if the Include All Artistic Attributes option is active. If you transfer an object containing a custom calligraphic outline and do not activate this option, the object's outline in the .CGM file will have the same width as the thickest part of the calligraphic outline in the original CorelDRAW! image.

The .CGM option is an excellent choice for exporting files to desktop publishing applications. The WYSIWYG representation of a .CGM file is much easier to work with than an .EPS header and takes the guesswork out of cropping and positioning graphics within a document. If you do not work with a PostScript printer, or if your CorelDRAW! graphics do not contain PostScript-only attributes, you might prefer the .CGM option to the .EPS format.

16

Windows Metafile .WMF Format

The .WMF format, like the .PCX, .TIF, and .EPS formats, was one of the earliest export options in CorelDRAW!. This object-oriented format makes a CorelDRAW! graphic available to a wide variety of Microsoft Windows applications. This export format does not transfer PostScript-only features, so it is best suited for graphics that do not contain such features. In addition, if the artwork in your graphic has many outline and fill attributes, many curves and nodes, or complex text, the exported .WMF file might become very large and not be acceptable to some programs. In this case, try using the .CGM export filter instead.

Exporting to Film Recorders (SCODL)

SCODL, which stands for Scan Conversion Object Description Language, is an image-description language that many popular film recorders use to create object-oriented slides at high resolution. Some ink-jet and thermal printers also make use of this language and its associated .SCD file format. The SCODL export option first became available with CorelDRAW! release 1.1. When you select the SCODL option in the Export dialog box, the additional options Include All Artistic Attributes and Selected Objects Only become available for selection.

In general, you should activate the Include All Artistic Attributes option if you want the CorelDRAW! graphic to transfer over exactly as it appears. If you do not activate this option, your export file will automatically contain sharp (miter) corners and will not support calligraphic outlines. Even if you do activate Include All Artistic Attributes, PostScript halftone screen patterns and textures translate as a shade of light gray.

After you specify the filename and destination directory of the exported graphic in the file selection dialog box, a third dialog box displays, as shown in Figure 16-6. Use this dialog box to set the background color of the slide to black, white, or none (Null Color).

If you are new to the world of film recorders and slide generation equipment, you may be interested in the following tips that will help you create a SCODL (.SCD) export file that will not produce visual surprises.

Figure 16-6. *The SCODL Background Color dialog box*

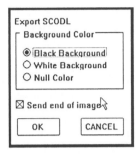

Aspect Ratio Considerations

The graphic that you plan to export to SCODL format should have the same width-to-height aspect ratio as the film that will be used to create your slide. In most cases this will be the aspect ratio of 35 mm film, which is 0.67. On an 8 1/2-by-11-inch page, this translates into 7.33-inch width by 11-inch height (or 11-inch width by 7.33-inch height in landscape format). The easiest way to ensure that a graphic will conform to the aspect ratio required for slidemaking is to define a custom page size using the Page Setup command in the File menu. Alternatively, you can activate the Show Rulers command in the Display menu to help you fit the graphic within the appropriate dimensions.

Fountain Fill Tips

The SCODL format does not support fountain fills as CorelDRAW! understands them. Recall that when you watched a fountain fill redisplay in Chapter 15, the fill began as a rectangle equal to the space occupied by the highlighting box that surrounded the object. The fill outside the object boundary disappears as the redraw of the object proceeds. SCODL does not recognize the last step in this process. As a result, linear fountain fills export to SCODL correctly *only* for rectangles. Radial fountain fills do not, however, export correctly for perfect circles.

16

If the graphic from which you want to create a slide contains fountain fills for other types of objects, there is a way to work around the problem. You can overcome this limitation by creating a *mask* that includes a background rectangle with a fountain fill. If you performed the "World of CorelDRAW!" series of exercises in Chapter 15, you are already familiar with the principles of a mask. In summary,

1. Create the object to which you want to assign a fountain fill.
2. Create a rectangle that is larger than the object you created in the last step. Place it on top of the previous object so that it covers the object completely.
3. Use the Combine command in the Arrange menu to combine both objects into one object. This creates a transparent "hole" with the shape of the first object.
4. Assign the same color fill to the combined object that you assigned to the background color of the drawing. Assign an outline of NONE to the object.
5. Create another and slightly smaller rectangle, and place it on top of the combined object so that the transparent "hole" is completely covered. Assign any desired fountain fill to this rectangle.
6. Use the To Back command in the Arrange menu to place the filled rectangle behind the combined object. The result is that the fountain fill shows through the transparent hole.
7. Apply the Group command in the Arrange menu to group the two objects and treat them as a unit.

This may seem like a complicated solution, but SCODL understands it perfectly and delivers a flawless fill in your slide if you follow the directions carefully.

Exporting to VideoShow Format (.PIC)

Beginning with CorelDRAW! version 1.11, you can export your drawings to VideoShow format to create on-screen presentations or professional slides for portfolios, business presentations, or other applications. Just use the

VideoShow option in the Export dialog box to convert your drawings to the .PIC format supported by General Parametrics Corporation's VideoShow and Slidemaker slide production equipment, and by Photometric equipment and Printmaker software.

The .PIC format supporting by slidemaking equipment is not the same as the .PIC import filter used for importing Lotus graph images.

Caution

When you select the VideoShow option in the Export dialog box, two additional options become available: Include All Artistic Attributes and Selected Objects Only. In general, you should leave the Include All Artistic Attributes option activated if you wish to preserve as many CorelDRAW! attributes as possible. If you do not activate this option, you may lose calligraphic outlines, rounded, butt, and arrowhead line caps, beveled and rounded outline corners, and dashed outlines. However, a .PIC file created with the Include All Artistic Attributes option active may be up to twice as large as a file created with this option inactive. Since the VideoShow format has a nominal size limit of 100K, you may want to consider the amount of memory you have available.

After you specify the desired slide file name in the file selection dialog box, a third dialog box appears, as shown in Figure 16-7. The three Table of Contents option buttons let you determine how VideoShow updates its catalog of pictures. If you select Append, you add the new drawing to an existing table. If you select Create New, the drawing you are about to export

16

Figure 16-7. *The VideoShow Table of Contents and Background Color dialog box*

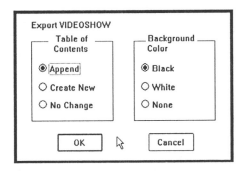

opens a new table of contents. And if you select No Change, you are telling VideoShow that you are updating an existing file and do not wish to change the order in which it appears in the current catalog.

The second group of option buttons under Background Color lets you specify a background color of white, black, or none for the drawing. If you select None (invisible), you can overlay objects in different files. Note that you may have difficulty displaying a file with an invisible background if it is the first file in the catalog.

The next two sections on exporting to VideoShow format provide guidelines for preparing your drawing before export and information about CorelDRAW! features that do not transfer exactly as expected.

File Preparation Guidelines

If you plan to use PhotoMetric equipment or PrintMaker software for multiple slide pictures, the first picture listed in the VideoShow Table of Contents should have a background color of either white or black. A picture having a different background color setting will not display. If you will be using VideoShow equipment instead, you may experience difficulties displaying a picture that has a background of NONE, unless you advance through the full cycle of files again.

The cautions about aspect ratio that apply to the preparation of pictures for SCODL export apply to VideoShow export as well. The aspect ratio of your picture should match the aspect ratio of the film used in the slidemaking equipment, or 0.67 for 35 mm film. To achieve the correct aspect ratio for your drawing, you can define a custom page size using the Page Setup command in the File menu. Alternatively, you can use the Select All command and the Select tool to stretch and scale the picture, or use the rulers as a guide when creating the artwork in CorelDRAW!.

Even when you prepare your drawing according to these guidelines, some information may not transfer, owing to the differences in software features. The next section summarizes these limitations.

Videoshow Format Limitations

The main differences between what you create in CorelDRAW! and what transfers to the VideoShow format have to do with CorelDRAW! fills, outline widths, and bitmaps. The VideoShow format does not support any PostScript halftone screen patterns or textures, and translates these into a gray shade during the export process. Fountain fills display correctly only if the object containing the fill is a rectangle, because VideoShow applies the fill to the entire highlighting box that surrounds the object. You can get around this limitation by creating a mask for fountain-filled objects, as described in the "Exporting to Film Recorders (SCODL)" section. If your drawing contains bitmapped objects, these do not appear in the VideoShow picture.

Above all, make certain that the version of the VideoShow operating system is 3.11 or later. Otherwise, the information that transfers from your drawing to the export file may differ from the preceding descriptions.

Exporting Graphics to .WPG WordPerfect Format

As of release 1.11, CorelDRAW! allows you to export images to Word-Perfect using the .WPG format. A good use of this feature is to create clip art libraries for use in WordPerfect 5.0 or 5.1.

After you select the .WPG format in the Export dialog box and specify the filename and directory in the file selection dialog box, a third dialog box containing color options displays on your screen, as shown here:

You have a choice of 16 or 256 colors. Select the option button that best matches your display adapter's capabilities, the output device you will be using, and the colors in your drawing, and then select OK.

The following kinds of information do not transfer into the WordPerfect environment:

- PostScript halftone screens and textures
- Radial or linear fountain fills
- Text as text (WordPerfect converts it to curves)
- CorelDRAW! line type settings of none
- Bitmaps

16

In addition, you cannot rotate a drawing once it is in .WPG format, or it will not print properly from within WordPerfect.

AutoCAD .DXF Format

Beginning with release 1.11 of CorelDRAW!, you can export as well as import files using the AutoCAD .DXF format. The .DXF files tend to be memory-intensive, however, so it may happen that a complex drawing that occupies only 20-30K in CorelDRAW! can take up half a megabyte or more in the AutoCAD format. Make certain that your hard drive contains enough free space to accommodate potentially large files.

A few CorelDRAW! features either export to .DXF format differently than expected, or do not transfer at all. For example, text preserves its appearance but turns into curves in AutoCAD format. Calligraphic outlines preserve their visual appearance as well, but the .DXF filter interprets them as polygons rather than as lines. Colors match fairly closely, as the .DXF format uses a 256-color scheme.

More important, the present .DXF filter supports the transfer of *outlines only*. This means that no fills at all are exported with the AutoCAD format. If you require fills for certain objects, you must add them using the CAD application.

GEM Applications .GEM Format

CorelDRAW! versions 1.11 and later allow you to import and export graphics using the .GEM graphics format. There is an important difference between the import and export filters, however. You can import .GEM files from both GEM Draw and GEM Artline, but you can export only to GEM Artline, Delvina Perform, and Ventura Publisher versions 2.0 and above. The present GEM export filter does not support export to GEM Draw. As always, save your drawing in CorelDRAW! format before exporting it if you think you might need to edit it later.

As with all object-oriented formats, you can choose whether or not to activate the Include All Artistic Attributes option. It is preferable to activate this option if you want as much visual information as possible to translate correctly. Even with this option selected, however, there are a few limitations in what kinds of features you can transfer. For example, GEM applications support only 16 colors, so colors may not match exactly. In Xerox Ventura Publisher, colored images display as black-and-white unless you have a VGA or compatible display adapter. Another limitation concerns the number of nodes in an exported file. GEM applications can handle a maximum of 128 nodes, so you should limit the size or complexity of your drawings accordingly. If your drawing contains more than 128 nodes, it may transfer, but the GEM application may segment curves into multiple sub-paths (see Chapter 10) and the object will appear differently.

HPGL Plotter .PLT Format

Beginning with CorelDRAW! version 2.0 you can export CorelDRAW! image *outlines only* in the HPGL format for plotters with a .PLT extension. When you do, a third dialog box appears as shown in Figure 16-8.

The Export HPGL dialog box allows you to make a number of choices for settings unique to plotters. These are Scale Factor for horizontal and vertical scaling in the range of 0 to 1000%; Pen Velocity in the range of 0.38 to 38.1 cm/s (centimeters per second), with increments of 0.38; Curve Resolution, which specifies the number of straight-line segments used to

16

Figure 16-8.   *HPGL export dialog box*

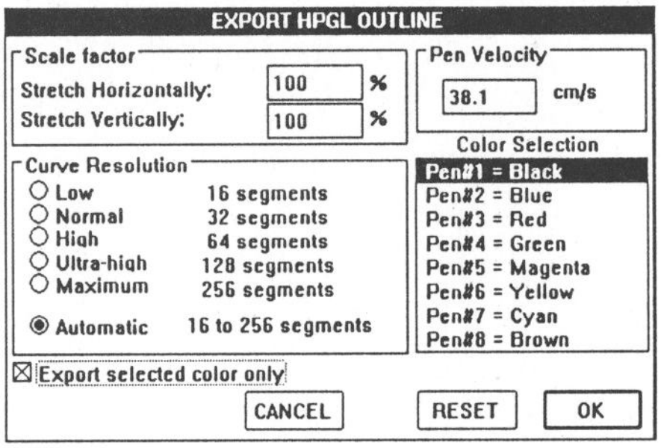

```
                    EXPORT HPGL OUTLINE
 ┌Scale factor──────────────┐ ┌Pen Velocity─────────┐
 │ Stretch Horizontally:  100  %    38.1   cm/s      │
 │ Stretch Vertically:    100  %                     │
 └──────────────────────────┘     Color Selection
 ┌Curve Resolution──────────┐   Pen#1 = Black
 │ ○ Low         16 segments     Pen#2 = Blue
 │ ○ Normal      32 segments     Pen#3 = Red
 │ ○ High        64 segments     Pen#4 = Green
 │ ○ Ultra-high  128 segments    Pen#5 = Magenta
 │ ○ Maximum     256 segments    Pen#6 = Yellow
 │                               Pen#7 = Cyan
 │ ⦿ Automatic   16 to 256 segments  Pen#8 = Brown
 └──────────────────────────┘
 ⊠ Export selected color only
              CANCEL        RESET    OK
```

approximate a curve; Color Selection, which allows you to choose from among the color pens that have been defined in the CORELDRW.INI file (see "HPGL .PLT Plotter Files" earlier in this chapter); and Export selected color only, which allows you to export only those objects with the color of the pen you have selected.

Solid lines exported in the HPGL format are given the HPGL default line thickness of 0.3 mm. A dotted line is given a 0.5 type pattern, and a dashed line is given a 3 type pattern. CorelDRAW! text is converted to line segments and is not editable. Finally, HPGL export does not support bitmaps, calligraphic pens, fountain fills, or PostScript halftone textures.

Macintosh PICT2 and .PCT Format

Beginning with CorelDRAW! 2.0, you can also export to the Macintosh in the PICT2 color file format. If you want to export calligraph pens or combined/complex objects such as text converted to curves, you must select the Include All Artistic Attributes option. If you want to have editable text in your destination program, though, do *not* select the Include All Artistic Attributes option.

Bitmaps and PostScript textures cannot be transferred to PICT, and there is no typeface correspondence between the two packages. Color transference will depend on the color capability of the Macintosh. One using 8-bit color is limited to 256 colors and will be mapped to CorelDRAW! colors as well as possible. A Macintosh with 24-bit color will be virtually identical to CorelDRAW!'s color. Radial fills and text without fill do not transfer properly to PICT.

17

Printing and Processing Your Images

No matter how sophisticated an image may look on your computer monitor, you can judge its true quality only after it has traveled from your hard drive to the outside world. The means by which graphics travel from your computer to your intended audience is a question of output, and until recently, output meant printer and paper. In today's world, however, paper is only one possible means by which your artwork can reach the outside world. As you learned in Chapter 16, film negatives, videotape, and 35 mm slides are equally valid output media. CorelDRAW! offers you your choice of all these media and their associated output devices.

If print media remain your preferred end products, you can output your images using the Print command in the File menu. CorelDRAW! allows you to print selected objects within an image, scale your image to any desired size, print oversize images on multiple tiled pages, or print to a file that you can send to a service bureau. If you work with a PostScript printer, even more advanced printing functions are available to you. You can prepare color separations for process color images, add crop marks and registration marks, print in film negative format, and add file information to your printouts. With a PostScript printing device, you can also reproduce the dotted and dashed outlines, custom halftone screens, and PostScript textures you learned to create in Chapters 14 and 15.

If you want your image produced as slides or used in presentations, refer to Chapter 16. You will use the Export command, not the Print command, to generate your output.

The first part of this chapter describes the output devices and media that CorelDRAW! supports. The middle portion of the chapter guides you step-by-step through the process of printing, using the Print Options dialog box. The concluding sections of the chapter contain tips to help you achieve satisfactory printing results, based on the type of printer you use.

Output Devices

In considering how your images will travel from your computer to your audience, you are actually concerning yourself with both equipment and the product of that equipment, or with both *output device* and *output medium*. The output device you work with determines what media you can produce, or what the end product of your work will be. For example, all printers produce paper output. PostScript printers and imagesetters, however, also allow you to prepare your images as color separations or in film negative format, so that you can eliminate costly steps in the commercial printing process. CorelDRAW! supports some printing devices better than others. As you may recall from Chapter 1, Microsoft Windows provides drivers for many different printers and plotters, but not all of them work equally well with CorelDRAW!. The following list shows the printing devices that CorelDRAW! supports best, in the order in which you are likely to reproduce the fullest range of CorelDRAW! features.

- PostScript Plus black-and-white printers, color printers, and imagesetters (Linotronic)

- HP LaserJet with Adobe-licensed PostScript controller boards and plug-in cartridges
- Older PostScript printers compatible with the original Apple Laser-Writer
- HP LaserJet printers and 100% compatibles
- HP DeskJet
- HP PaintJet

The PostScript Plus printers, older PostScript printers, and printers with genuine Adobe-licensed PostScript controller boards are the only ones in this list that let you generate output using PostScript printing options.

You can print your CorelDRAW! images with other printers, too, but the results may vary depending on the complexity of your images and the characteristics of a given manufacturer's device. With some of the following printers, your output may match your expectations exactly. With others, you may experience problems that are hard to predict because of the variety of standards in the industry.

- HP LaserJet clones that are not 100% compatible
- HP LaserJet printers, compatibles, and clones with PostScript-compatible controller boards and plug-in cartridges *not* licensed by Adobe
- Genuine HP Plotters
- HP Plotter clones and other plotters
- Dot-matrix printers

The "Hardware-Specific Tips" section of this chapter contains information about designing your images to obtain the best output results for the printer that you use. It also describes the kinds of limitations you are most likely to encounter with a specific type of printer and provides suggestions on how to solve them. The "Complex Artwork on PostScript Printers" section provides tips specific to working with PostScript printers.

In the next section, you will learn about general steps you can take before you print to ensure trouble-free output.

17

Preparing to Print

Before you select the Print command, you should make certain that your printer is correctly installed to run under Microsoft Windows. You should also adjust several other default settings in Microsoft Windows in order to customize printing for the special needs of CorelDRAW!. Two of these other settings, called *Printer Timeouts,* determine how long Windows waits before sending you messages about potential printer problems. The settings you need to review are all in the Windows Control Panel, which is available in CorelDRAW! through the Control Panel command in the File menu.

Tip

If you work with a PostScript printer, you should be using Windows' own printer driver or another viable Windows-compatible PostScript driver. Examples include the UltraScript PostScript interpreter from QMS and the PostScript driver provided with release 2.0 or later of Micrografx Designer.

Another adjustment you should make involves the disabling of the Windows print Spooler. You can make this adjustment by editing one line in the WIN.INI file. The short sections that follow will guide you through the process of reviewing and editing your printer setup.

Printer Installation and Setup

If you did not specify the correct printer and port when you installed Microsoft Windows, you will not be able to print in CorelDRAW!. To check whether your printer is correctly installed to run under Microsoft Windows, follow these steps:

1. From the main screen of CorelDRAW!, select Control Panel from the File menu. The Control Panel window appears, as shown in Figure 17-1.

2. Double-click on the Printers icon, shown in the lower-left corner of Figure 17-1. The Printers dialog box will open and display a list of installed printers. An example of a Printers dialog box appears in Figure 17-2. The Installed Printers list box should contain the name of the printer you are going to use, and this name should be

Figure 17-1.   *The Control Panel window*

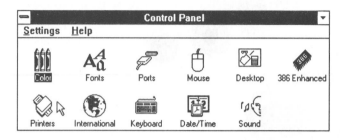

highlighted. If the name of your printer is in the list box but is not highlighted, click on it with the mouse, click on OK to return to the Control Panel, and skip to step 4.

3. If the name of your printer is missing in the Installed Printer list box, select Add Printers. An extensive list of printers appears. Use the scroll bar to find the printer you want (they are in alphabetical order) and then double-click on it (or highlight it and select Install).

17

Figure 17-2.   *The Printers dialog box of the Control Panel*

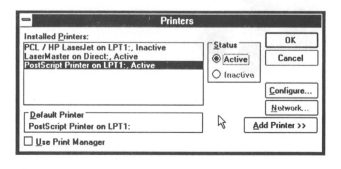

You will be asked to insert one of the original Windows Install disks so that the printer's software driver can be copied to your hard disk. When your printer appears in the Installed Printers list box, select Configure, click on the port to which the printer is attached (LPT1, COM1, and so on), and then click on OK. Repeat these steps for all the printers you have. When you are done, click on OK again to return to the Control Panel.

4. If your printer is connected to a serial port, double-click on the Ports icon in the Control Panel. Select the port the printer is connected to (COM1 through COM4), and click on Settings. The Ports-Settings dialog box will open as shown in Figure 17-3. Make sure that the Baud Rate, Data Bits, Parity, and Stop Bits are correct for your printer. Refer to your printer manual if necessary. When you are finished, click on OK to return to the Control Panel.

If you need to alter your printer installation after performing this check, refer to your *Microsoft Windows User's Guide Version 3.0.* and see the chapter that discusses the Control Panel and gives the necessary instructions. The

Figure 17-3.   *The Ports-Settings dialog box of the Control Panel*

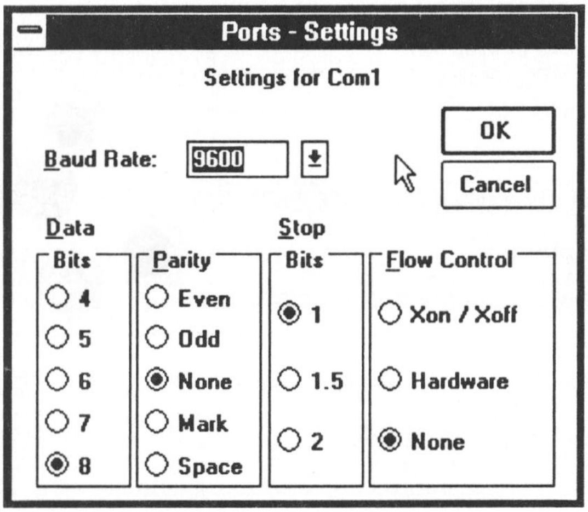

Control Panel that you access from the Microsoft Windows Program Manager is identical to the one you access from within CorelDRAW!.

Printer Timeouts

After checking for correct printer and port assignments, you should customize the Printer Timeouts settings, found under the Printers icon in the Control Panel. These settings define how long Windows waits before sending you messages about potential printer problems. The default Printer Timeouts settings installed with Microsoft Windows may be adequate for average Windows applications, but you should customize them to improve printing performance in CorelDRAW!. To edit Printer Timeouts,

1. From the Control Panel, double-click on the Printers icon again. With your printer selected, click on Configure. The Printers-Configure dialog box will open as shown in Figure 17-4.

Figure 17-4.   *Adjusting Printer Timeouts*

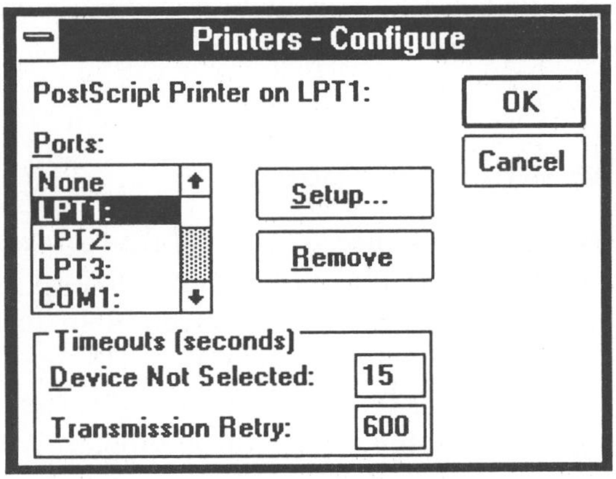

17

2. The Printer Timeouts section of the dialog box shows two settings: Device Not Selected and Transmission Retry. The Device Not Selected setting determines how long Windows waits before informing you that the printer is not connected properly, not turned on, or otherwise not ready to print. Leave this setting at its default value of 15 seconds, because if the printer is not ready to perform, you want to find out as soon as possible.

3. Adjust Transmission Retry from its default value of 45 seconds to 600 seconds (equal to 10 minutes), as is shown in Figure 17-4. The Transmission retry value determines how long the printer waits to receive additional characters before a timeout error occurs. Although 45 seconds may be long enough for most software that runs under Windows, it is not always adequate for graphics applications such as CorelDRAW!. The output file that CorelDRAW! sends to your printer can contain complex information, requiring more time to transmit.

4. Click on OK twice to return to the Control Panel, and then double-click on the Control menu box to close the Control Panel and return to CorelDRAW!.

By checking your printer setup and Printer Timeouts settings each time you run CorelDRAW!, you can prevent potential printing and communications problems before you even attempt to print. You can eliminate one more potential printing pitfall by disabling the Windows Spooler, about which you will learn in the next section.

Disabling the Windows Spooler

Microsoft Windows is installed to print all files through a Spooler. The Spooler is a program that captures printing instructions and sends them to the printer. The printer then runs in the background, so that you can continue working in your application without interruption. The Spooler doesn't always work efficiently with graphics files, however. For this reason, you can avoid printing problems if you disable the Windows Spooler. When the Spooler is disabled, the printing operation runs in the foreground; you must wait until printing is complete before you can continue with your work. Printing takes place faster this way than when the Spooler is enabled, however.

To disable the Windows Spooler, you edit a line in the WIN.INI file, as the following exercise demonstrates:

1. Exit CorelDRAW! if it is currently running.

2. From the Program Manager double-click on the Notepad icon to open the Notepad text editor.

3. When the Notepad window appears, select the Open command from the File menu. A file selection dialog box pops up.

4. The File Open Name text box shows a default file extension of .TXT. To change this to .INI so that you can access the WIN.INI file, type ***.ini** instead, and then click on the OK command button. The WIN.INI file now appears in the Files list box.

5. To open the WIN.INI file, double-click on its name. The [windows] section is at the head of the file. You will see a line that reads "Spooler=yes."

An alternative way to access the WIN.INI file is simply to double-click on the WIN.INI filename using the File Manager, without opening Notepad first. Using this method, you open Notepad and WIN.INI simultaneously.

Tip

17

6. Position the cursor after the "s" in "yes" and click once. Then backspace over the word "yes" to delete it and type **no** instead, as shown in Figure 17-5.

7. Select the Save command in the File menu to save the changes to WIN.INI, and then select the Exit command in the File menu to leave Notepad and return to the Program Manager.

8. To cause the changes you have made to take effect, exit and then restart Windows.

Now that you have customized Windows' printer settings to improve printing performance in CorelDRAW!, you are ready to explore the options in the Printer Options dialog box. The next series of sections lets you experiment with the choices available to you when printing.

Figure 17-5.   *Disabling the Windows Spooler in the WIN.INI file*

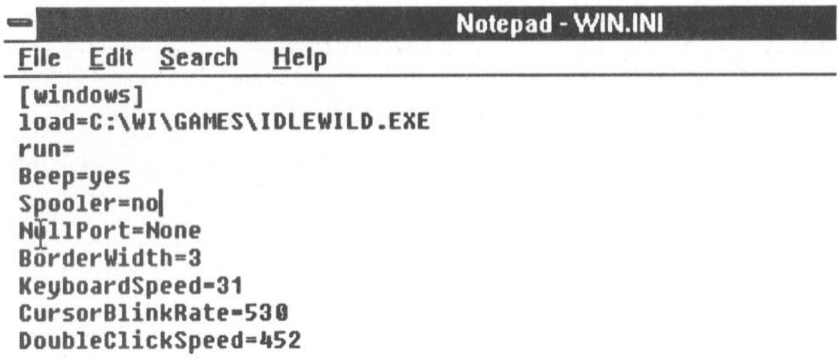

```
━  ▌                                          Notepad - WIN.INI
 File   Edit   Search   Help
[windows]
load=C:\WI\GAMES\IDLEWILD.EXE
run=
Beep=yes
Spooler=no|
NullPort=None
BorderWidth=3
KeyboardSpeed=31
CursorBlinkRate=530
DoubleClickSpeed=452
```

The Print Options Dialog Box

To begin the process of printing in CorelDRAW!, you select the Print command in the File menu. An image must be on the screen before you can select this command. The options Print Only Selected, Scale, Fit to Page, Tile, and Print to File are available for use with all printers.

If you use a PostScript printer, you can also include date and file information on the printout, prepare spot or process color separations, and print crop and registration marks with your graphic. You can also print the image in film negative format, change the default screen frequency for proofing images, or print using fonts resident in the host printer rather than the native CorelDRAW! fonts.

The following sections each explore one printing option or one aspect of the printing process. So that you can practice printing using the options in the Print Options dialog box, you will import a clip-art image in .CDR format, and then use it in the exercises that follow.

Importing an Image for Printing with Mosaic

In this chapter you will be doing a lot of printing. To have a subject worthy of that effort, you'll import one of the pieces of clip art that comes with

CorelDRAW!. In CorelDRAW! 2.0 and on, the clip art is *archived* or placed into libraries with a companion Corel product called Mosaic. Therefore, in the following steps, you will bring up Mosaic, use it to bring in a piece of clip art, and save the clip art as a normal CorelDRAW! .CDR file on your hard disk. Then you will print this file in each of the succeeding sections to practice using the options in the Print Options dialog box.

If you are using a version of CorelDRAW! prior to 2.0, you won't have Mosaic or the particular piece of clip art described here. In that case use the instructions in Chapter 16 to import a piece of object-oriented clip art (CGM or CDR extensions, not PCX or TIF). You can then adapt the steps in the exercises to fit the graphic you have chosen.

Using Mosaic

Mosaic is a separate program supplied with CorelDRAW! beginning with version 2.0. Its purpose is to provide visual access to CorelDRAW! files. Mosaic can be started from either the Windows Program Manager, by double-clicking on the Mosaic icon, or from within CorelDRAW!. In this case, you'll start Mosaic from CorelDRAW!—it is less obvious but handier for the purposes here.

To start Mosaic from within CorelDRAW!, you need to set the Use Mosaic option in the Preferences dialog box, which starts Mosaic the next time you use the File Open or File Import command. Then, for the remainder of the current session and in future sessions until you change the option in the Preferences dialog box, Mosaic is used each time you use the File Open or File Import commands.

The piece of clip art you will use, if you are using CorelDRAW! version 2.0, is named 2WOMEN. It is the first image in the business section shown on page 5 of the *Symbol and Clipart Library* manual for version 2.0. You will find it on the clip-art floppy with the business library. With the following instructions, start Mosaic and use it to bring this piece of clip art into CorelDRAW!. In the process it will be saved as a regular CorelDRAW! .CDR file and be available for the remainder of the exercises in this chapter.

1. Starting with a blank screen in CorelDRAW!, select Preferences from the Special menu. Click on Use Mosaic to turn on that capability and click on OK to close the dialog box.

17

Figure 17-6.   *Mosaic window*

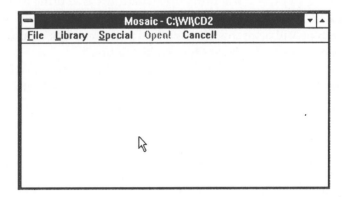

2. From the File menu, select Open. After some disk activity the Mosaic window will open as shown in Figure 17-6. You may first get an information box saying "Library File not found." This just says you will need to change the drive and/or directory to find the clip art you want to import. So, click on OK and the Mosaic window will open.

3. If your clip art is still on the original Corel floppy disks, insert the disk with the Business library on it into the appropriate drive.

4. Open the Mosaic Library menu and choose Select Library. The Select Library dialog box will open as you can see in Figure 17-7.

5. Select the drive and directory where your clip art resides, select the BUSINESS.CLB library and click on OK. A pictorial directory will open that will contain a small image for each of the images in the library as shown in Figure 17-8.

6. Double-click on 2WOMEN in the upper-left corner. When asked for the directory in which to place the expanded image, enter the directory where you keep your normal CorelDRAW! .CDR files and click on OK.

Figure 17-7. Mosaic Select Library dialog box

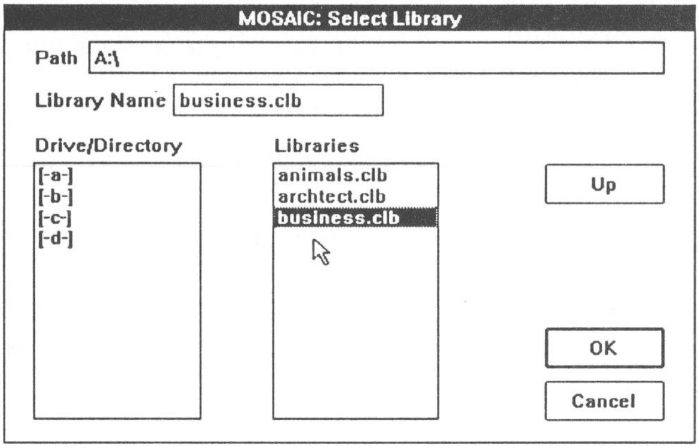

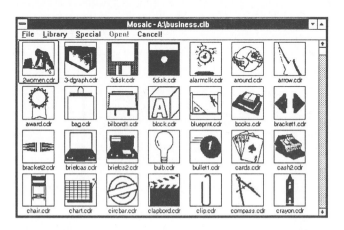

Figure 17-8. Mosaic pictorial directory

17

7. If you are getting your piece of clip art from a floppy disk, you will get a message that there is not enough space on the current drive to create the needed temporary files. If you get such a message, click on the drive you want to use and then click on OK. Then you will be asked if a temporary file can be created on your current hard drive. Click on Yes.

After a few moments, you'll see the 2WOMEN.CDR image appear in your CorelDRAW! window as in Figure 17-9. The full decompressed 2WOMEN.CDR file has also been stored on your hard disk.

Now that you have an image ready for printing, you can select the Print command and become acquainted with the Print Options dialog box.

Selecting the Print Command

Select the Print command from the File menu. The Print Options dialog box appears, as shown in Figure 17-10.

Figure 17-9.   *2WOMEN.CDR in CorelDRAW!*

The "POSTSCRIPT" designation that appears in parentheses in the title of the dialog box is misleading. Seven of the options in this dialog box—Print Only Selected, Number of Copies, Fit to Page, Tile, Scale, Fountain Stripes, and Print to File—are available for any printer supported by CorelDRAW!. The other eight options—Print As Separations, Crop Marks & Crosshairs, Film Negative, Include File Info, All Fonts Resident, Flatness, Default Screen Frequency, and For Mac—are available for PostScript printers only. In addition, you can select multiple options for any given print operation, as long as all of the ones you choose are available for your printer.

Before you experiment with the printing options, go on to the next section to learn how to check the printer setup.

Checking Printer Setup

Whenever you print, it is advisable to develop the habit of checking the printer setup *before* you select any print options. The Printer Setup dialog box,

Figure 17-10. The Print Options dialog box

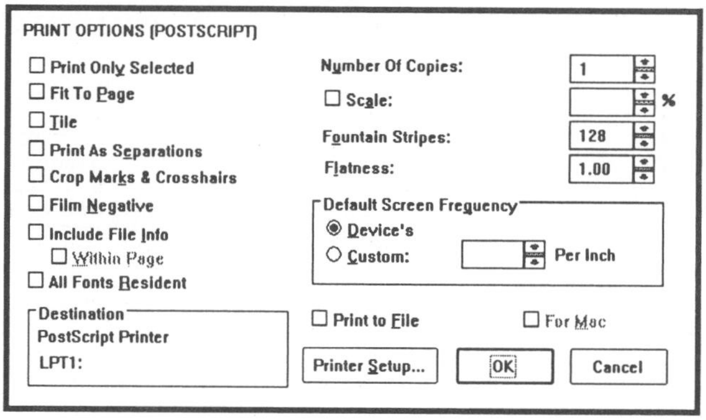

17

which you access by clicking on the Printer Setup command button in the Print Options dialog box, contains controls that allow you to define the desired number of copies, the paper size and orientation, and the brand name of your printer. The other items in the Printer Setup dialog box vary, depending on the printer you selected using the Connections command (Setup menu) of the Control Panel. For example, the Printer Setup dialog box shown in Figure 17-11 shows the controls available for a PostScript printer.

Some of the variable controls are important to know about, because they help you avoid possible pitfalls when you attempt to print complex images. Later on, in the series of sections following "Hardware-Specific Tips," you will find hints on adjusting these settings to prevent or minimize printing problems. Take a moment to explore the contents of *your* Printer Setup dialog box and of any nested sub-dialog boxes that are accessible by clicking on special command buttons. When you are ready, click on the Cancel command button of the Printer Setup dialog box. Click again on the Cancel button of the Print Options dialog box to return to the image on your screen.

Figure 17-11.   *Printer Setup options for a PostScript printer*

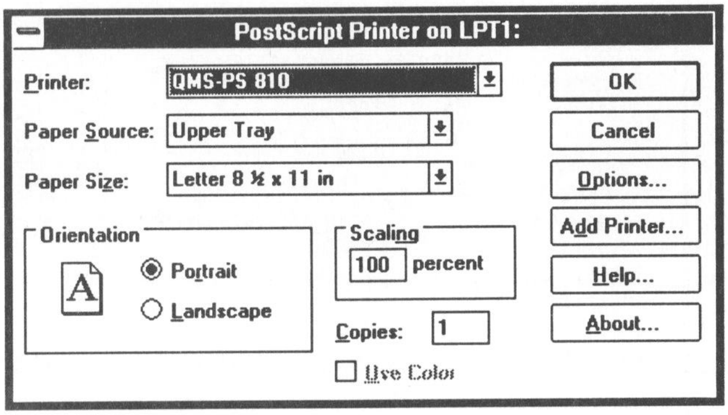

Each of the next series of sections presents a single option in the Print Options dialog box and allows you to test it using the 2WOMEN.CDR file you saved earlier in the chapter. The non-PostScript options are presented first, for the convenience of those who do not work with a PostScript printing device.

Printing Only Selected Objects

There are several reasons why you might choose to print only selected objects within a picture, rather than the entire graphic:

- You want to save printing time and need to check only a portion of the image.

- Your picture contains a great deal of fine detail, such as in a technical illustration, and you want to examine certain areas for accuracy.

- Some of your picture elements contain complex or PostScript-only features that do not display in the preview window.

- You have experienced printing problems and want to locate the object or objects that are causing the trouble.

Whatever your reason, you can print just the selected objects within a picture by activating the Print Only Selected checkbox in the Print Options dialog box. You must select the desired objects before you select the Print command, however, or you will receive an error message. Practice printing selected objects in the 2WOMEN.CDR file now.

1. If the Print Options dialog box is still on your screen, click on Cancel to exit it and return to the 2WOMEN.CDR file. Turn on the preview window. The image contains several colors in addition to black.

2. Select any object in the image; the status line shows you that all of the objects in the picture are grouped. Click on the Ungroup command in the Arrange menu to ungroup all of the objects, and then deselect all objects by clicking on any white space.

3. Magnify just the area of the image that contains the computer and monitor. Activate the Preview Selected Only command, and then

17

Figure 17-12.   *Selecting objects within the graphic for printing*

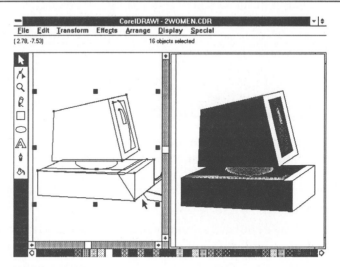

draw a marquee around the objects that make up the computer and monitor. As in Figure 17-12, you should be able to see the entire computer and monitor, and the status line informs you that you have selected 16 objects.

4. Leave the objects selected and click on the Print command. When the Print Options dialog box appears, review your Printer Setup, and then click on the Print Only Selected checkbox. An "x" appears in the checkbox.

5. Select the OK command button to begin the printing process. After a short time, the image of the terminal should emerge from your printer. Leave the 2WOMEN.CDR image on your screen for the next exercise.

As you learn about the other options in this dialog box, you will think of effective ways to combine one or more of them with Print Only Selected. Assume, for example, that you are working with a complex technical illustration and need to proof just a small area. If you activate both the Print Only

Selected and Fit to Page options, you can print the selected objects in magnified format in order to proof it more easily.

Tip

When you print complex, memory-intensive images, it is a good practice to use the Select All command in the Edit menu to select all objects before you click on the Print command, and then print with the Print Only Selected option activated. Some objects in a memory-intensive image may be left out; by using the Select All command and the Print Only Selected option, you minimize this problem.

In the next section, you will learn about a way to print proofs of a graphic that is larger than the page area.

Tiling a Graphic

You can choose from several different methods of sizing a graphic in CorelDRAW!. The most obvious method is to use rulers when creating objects. Another method involves defining a custom page size with the Page Setup command and the Page Setup dialog box. You can also use the Select tool to scale an image to the desired size *after* you have created it.

Posters and other applications, however, require images that are larger than any paper size available for your printer. Even if you print final versions of these images on a Linotronic or other imagesetter that has fewer restrictions on paper size, how do you obtain accurate proofs? The answer is through *tiling* the image. Tiling refers to the process of printing an oversize image in sections that fit together precisely to form the complete picture. If, for example, you create a poster that is 11 inches wide by 17 inches high and select Tiling as a printing option, the image will print on four 8 1/2- by-11-inch sheets (or on some multiple of whatever size paper you use for your printer).

In the following exercise, you will enlarge the page size for 2WOMEN.CDR, scale the image to fit the page, and print the entire image with the Tile option enabled.

1. With the 2WOMEN.CDR image still on your screen, deactivate the Preview Selected Only command in the Display menu, and turn off the preview window. Adjust the viewing magnification to fit-in-window.

17

Figure 17-13.   *Changing page size through the Page Setup dialog box*

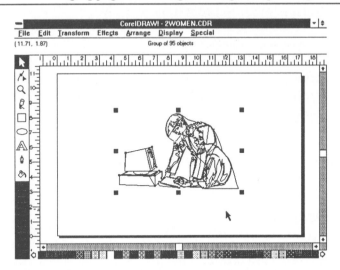

2. Click on the Select All command in the Edit menu to select all of the objects in the picture. Then select the Group command in the Arrange menu to keep all objects together.

3. Activate the Show Rulers command in the Display menu, and then select the Page Setup command in the File menu. When the Page Setup dialog box appears, click on the Landscape and the Tabloid option buttons to activate them. Selecting Tabloid will result in a page that is 17 inches wide by 11 inches high in landscape format. Click on the OK command button to exit the dialog box. Your page is now approximately twice as large as the graphic. The rulers show you the change in page size, as shown in Figure 17-13.

4. With the Select tool active, position the cursor at the upper-left corner boundary marker of the grouped image. When the cursor turns to a crosshair, drag the mouse until you have scaled the image to fit the upper-left corner area of the page. Do the same for the lower-right corner boundary marker.

5. Move the scaled image so that it is centered on the enlarged page, and then select the Print command from the File menu.

6. When the Print Options dialog box appears, deselect any options that are currently active, and then click on the Tiling option to activate it. Select OK. After a few moments, the image begins to print. Depending on the algorithm your printer uses, the number of sheets used for tiling may vary.

7. When the file has finished printing, deactivate the Show Rulers command, and then select Open from the File menu. Do not save the changes you have made to the size of the page or the picture. When the Open File dialog box appears, double-click on 2WOMEN.CDR to re-open this file in its original state. Leave this image on the screen for the next exercise.

Since most printers do not print to the edge of the page, you may need to use scissors or a matte knife to cut and paste the tiled pieces together exactly. Still, this method gives you a fairly exact representation of your image as it will print on the imagesetter. If your cutting and pasting skills are also exact, you may be able to use the tiled version of the image as the master copy for commercial printing.

Number of Copies

Beginning with CorelDRAW! version 2.0 you can enter the number of copies you want printed at one time in the Print Options dialog box. This can be a number from 1 through 100 and overrides the number entered in the Printer Setup dialog box. For versions of CorelDRAW! prior to 2.0, the Printer Setup dialog box or the front panel of the printer are the only means of entering the number of copies you want.

Scaling an Image

There is a difference in CorelDRAW! between scaling an image on the screen with the Select tool and defining a scaling value in the Printer Options dialog box. When you scale an image visually, you are altering its actual

17

dimensions. When you adjust values for the Scale option of the Printer Options dialog box, however, you change only the way the file prints, not its actual size.

Perform the following exercise to print the 2WOMEN.CDR file at a reduced size, using the Scale option:

1. With the 2WOMEN.CDR file on the screen, click on any outline within the image. As the status line informs you, the entire image is grouped.

2. Select the Print command from the File menu. When the Print Options dialog box appears, deselect any options that are currently active, and then click on the Scale checkbox. The value 100% (actual size) appears in the associated numeric entry box as soon as you enable this option.

3. Using the bottom scroll arrow, scroll to the lowest value available. This should be 10%, as shown here:

If you have a PostScript printer and are running a version of CorelDRAW! previous to 1.02, the lowest value is 29%. Selecting this value causes the image to print at the specified percentage of its original size. (You may be able to print the graphic at a percentage smaller than 29%, but part of the graphic may be cut off as a result.)

4. Click on OK to begin the printing process. If you have a PostScript printer and version 1.02 or later of CorelDRAW!, the tiny scaled-down image will appear exactly centered on your page. If you are using a PostScript printer but have a version of the software earlier than 1.02, the image will print in the lower-left corner of the page. If you have another kind of printer, the image will probably print in the lower-right corner of the page.

5. Leave this image on the screen for further work.

You have seen how you can reduce the scale of an image to a lower limit of 10% of original size. You can also increase the scale of an image to an upper limit of 1000% of original size. If you expand the scale of an image beyond the dimensions of the page, however, remember to activate the Tile option as well.

In the next section, you will experiment with another printing option that involves image size.

Fitting an Image to the Page

Like the Scale option, the Fit to Page option in the Printer Options dialog box does not affect the actual size of the graphic. When you select this option, CorelDRAW! automatically calculates how much it must increase the scale of the graphic or selected object(s) in order to make it fill the entire page. In the following exercise, you will combine the Fit to Page option with the Print Only Selected option you learned about previously.

1. Select any outline within the 2WOMEN.CDR image; since the entire image is grouped, you select all objects automatically.

2. Click on the Ungroup command in the Arrange menu, and then click on any white space to deselect all objects. As you did in the "Printing Only Selected Objects" section, select the 16 objects that make up the computer and monitor.

3. With the computer and monitor selected, click on the Print command in the File menu. When the Print Options dialog box appears, deselect any options that are currently active, and then activate the Print Only Selected Option.

4. Click on the Fit to Page option to activate it, and then select OK to begin printing. After a few moments, the computer terminal, which comprises only a small fraction of the total image, appears on the paper, filling the entire sheet as shown in Figure 17-14.

5. Leave the 2WOMEN.CDR image on the screen for the next exercise.

17

Figure 17-14.   *Computer and monitor selected and printed with Fit to Page*

As mentioned earlier, the use of the Fit to Page option with Print Only Selected is useful when you want to blow up details within a complex graphic, such as a technical illustration. In the next section, you will experiment with printing an image to a file.

Printing to a File

There are two common reasons why you might choose to print an image to a file.

- You are creating files to send to a service bureau for output on a Linotronic or other imagesetter.

- Your printer is busy and you prefer to copy the print information directly to the printer at a later time.

To print to a file, you select the Print to File option in the Print Options dialog box and name the output file. Printer output files created in applications that run under Microsoft Windows bear the extension .PRN. CorelDRAW! then displays another screen, prompting you to set printing parameters specific to the printer that will eventually print the file.

The following exercise assumes that you are going to send an output file to a service bureau for use on a PostScript imagesetter. In order to do this, you do not need to have a PostScript printer, but you must have a PostScript printer driver installed in your Windows directory. If you do not have a PostScript driver installed, use the Add New Printer command in the Installation menu of the Control Panel, which you can access from the File menu of CorelDRAW!. Refer to the discussion under "Checking Printer Setup" earlier in this chapter for assistance. Once you have the PostScript driver set up, practice printing the 2WOMEN.CDR image to a file in the following exercise:

1. With the 2WOMEN.CDR file on the screen, deselect all objects in the image, and then select Print from the File menu. When the Print Options dialog box displays, deselect any options that are currently active.

2. Click on the Print to File option. (Do not click on the Printer Setup option, because any changes you make at this point will be ignored. A dialog box similar to the Printer Setup dialog box but with a different name will pop up automatically after you finish specifying an output filename.)

3. If you are going to print on a printer or an imagesetter controlled by a Macintosh computer, select the For Mac option. Without this selection, the print files you produce will not work on a Macintosh. Select OK; a second dialog box appears with the title Print To File, as shown in Figure 17-15. This dialog box looks and operates similarly to the Open File dialog box.

4. If the filename 2WOMEN is not already in the File text box, type it, and then select Print. CorelDRAW! adds the file extension .PRN

17

Figure 17-15.   *The Print To File dialog box for specifying an output filename*

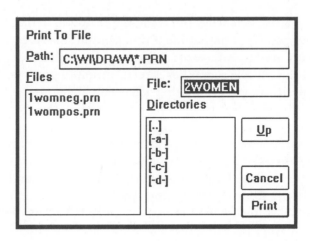

Figure 17-16.   *Printer Setup for Linotronic imagesetter (Print To File)*

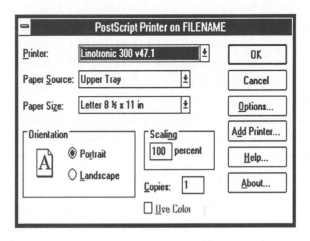

automatically to designate this as a printer output file. A third dialog box appears; the contents vary depending on the type of printer that will receive the output file. Figure 17-16 shows a dialog box set up for a PostScript printer, which is the most common case if you are sending an output file to a service bureau. If you are printing a file for use by an HP LaserJet or other printer, the dialog box you see on your screen will be different.

5. Make the changes you need in the dialog box and click on OK to begin the process of printing to a file.

6. When printing is complete, select New to clear the image from the screen without saving any changes.

When printing an image to a file, you can combine several options. For example, if you are creating color separations for commercial printing, you might choose to activate the Print As Separations, All Fonts Resident, and Print to File options at the same time.

The next group of sections introduces you to print options that apply specifically to PostScript printers. Since you may use some of these options in combination, the sections are ordered according to task, rather than according to their appearance in the Print Options dialog box.

Printing File Information with a Graphic in PostScript

17

If you are like most illustrators and designers, you probably revise a graphic several times, renaming it with each revision so that you can choose the best version later. You are therefore familiar with the bewilderment of viewing multiple printouts of the same graphic and not knowing which sheet represents which version.

CorelDRAW! provides a convenient solution to this common frustration, available to you if you print to a PostScript device. By activating the Include File Info option in the Printer Options dialog box, you can print the filename, date, and time of printing with your image. This information appears in 10-point Courier *outside* the left margin of your *page,* not of your graphic (unless you select the Within Page option). If you activate the Include File Info without the Within Page option, choose a page size in the Page Setup dialog box that is smaller than the nominal page size. For example, if your graphic fits on an 8 1/2-by-11-inch page, select a 10-by-14-inch or Tabloid page size before you print. This step is necessary because file information is visible *only* if you reduce Page Size below the size of the paper in your printer tray. If you are using 8 1/2-by-11-inch paper, for example, you must use the Page Setup dialog box to define a custom page size of smaller dimensions, and then fit the graphic within that page. You can practice defining a custom page size and printing file information in the following exercise. You'll start by separating out the sitting woman and using her as the subject for printing for the rest of the chapter. This will reduce your printing time.

1. Open the 2WOMEN.CDR file. Select any object to select the entire image, click on the Ungroup command in the Arrange menu, and then deselect all objects by clicking on any white space.

2. If necessary, turn on the side-by-side preview window and activate Preview Selected Only.

3. With the select tool, drag a marquee around the seated woman. You should get about 59 objects. You cannot help but get some of the standing women. The key is to make sure that you have all of the seated figure.

4. When you are satisfied that you have all of the seated figure and as little of everything else as possible, select Cut or Copy from the Edit menu. Then select File New, answer No to saving any of the changed 2WOMEN.CDR file, and finally select Paste from the Edit menu to paste onto the new drawing the seated figure you cut from the piece of clip art.

5. Select fit-in-window magnification and, with the Select tool, delete extraneous objects from the drawing until you have only the seated woman left. There are at least three objects that are common to both the seated and standing figures. These are the chin and neck area, the back of the head and neck, and the top of the forearm of the seated woman. If you want an image of just the seated figure, as shown in Figure 17-17, you need to use increased magnification with the Shaping tool to edit the curves associated with these areas.

6. When you are satisfied that you have a finished seated figure (you should have about 31 objects), return to fit-in-window magnification,

Figure 17-17.   *Seated woman separated from the other objects*

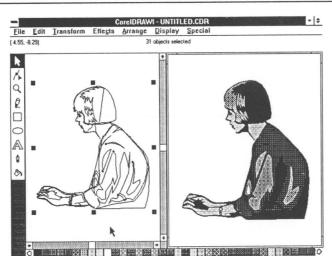

select All from the Edit menu, and then Group from the Arrange menu. Save the image with the name 1WOMAN.

7. Select the Page Setup command in the File menu. Click on the Custom option button in the Page Setup dialog box, and define a page 4.0 inches wide (the Horizontal value) and 6.0 inches high (the Vertical value). Then select OK to exit the dialog box and return to your picture, which is now larger than the new page size.

8. Scale the picture down to fit on the new page size and move the picture so that it fits entirely within the page and is reasonably centered.

9. Click on the Print command and activate the Include File Info option in the Printer Options dialog box. Check your printer setup and make sure that the settings are as you need them and then click on OK to return to the Print Options dialog box. Click on OK again to begin printing. After a few moments, the image emerges from your printer. The filename, date, and time of printing appear in 10-point Courier just beyond the left boundary of the custom page, at a 90-degree angle to the image as shown in Figure 17-18.

17

Figure 17-18.   *Seated woman printed with file information*

10. Select the Save As command in the File menu. When the Save As dialog box appears, type **1WOMAN2**, and then click on the Save command button. Leave this image on the screen for subsequent exercises.

Since CorelDRAW! generates object-oriented art, you can scale your images without distortion. It is therefore convenient to change page size so that you can print file information for your own use. Another common use for the Include File Info option is in conjunction with the Print As Separations and Crop Marks & Crosshairs options, which you will learn about in the next section.

Color Separations, Cropping, and Registration Marks with PostScript

When you began to specify outline fill and object fill colors in Chapters 14 and 15, you learned about the differences between spot color and process color in the commercial printing process. If you have a PostScript printer or plan to send output files to a PostScript imagesetter, you can reduce your commercial printing expenses by generating color separations on paper or in a file. This reduces the number of intermediary steps that commercial printers must perform to prepare your images for printing.

Put simply, *color separation* is the process of separating the colors that you specify for an entire image into the primary component colors. When you generate color separations using the process color system (CMYK), the output is four separate sheets, one each for the cyan, magenta, yellow, and black color components of the image. The commercial printer uses the four sheets to create separate overlays for each color, in preparation for making printing plates.

When you generate color separations using the spot color system, the output is one sheet for each color specified in the image, and the commercial printer creates overlays for each color. This process becomes very expensive as the number of spot colors in an image increases, so it is a good idea to use the process color system if you plan to have more than six colors in a given image.

When you generate color separations using the Print As Separations option in the Print Options dialog box, it is also important to include *crop marks* and *registration marks* (called crosshairs by CorelDRAW!). You can see examples of these marks in Figure 17-19. Crop marks are small horizontal and vertical lines printed at each corner of the image to show the exact boundaries of the image. A registration mark, two of which appear at the inside of each corner of an image, are crossed lines with a circle. Both crop marks and registration marks assist the commercial printer in aligning color separation overlays exactly; if misalignment were to occur, the final printed product would display a host of color distortions. When you activate the Include File Info option, CorelDRAW! prints the color for the page, together with the halftone screen angle and density, which appear beyond the crop marks at the left side of the image with the filename, time, and date information.

17

Figure 17-19.   *Process color separations for 1WOMAN2.CDR:*
                        (a) cyan, (b) magenta

a.

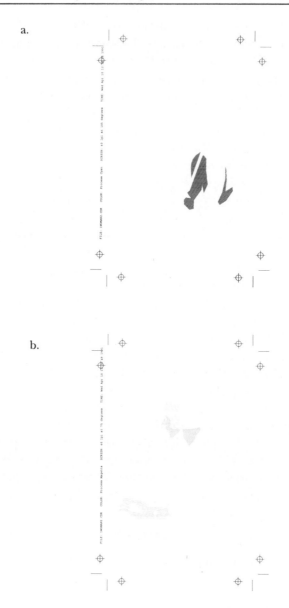

b.

Figure 17-19. *Process color separations for 1WOMAN2.CDR:*
(c) yellow, (d) black

c.

d.

Caution

Just as with File Information, you can see crop marks and registration marks from your printer only if you define a custom page size that is smaller than the size of the paper you are using unless you select the Within page option. The exception to this rule is if you are printing to Linotronic or other imagesetting equipment.

In the following exercise, you will generate PostScript color separations for the seated woman in the 1WOMAN2.CDR file using the Print As Separations, Crop Marks & Crosshairs, and Include File Info options. If you send files to a PostScript imagesetter but do not have a PostScript printer for your draft copies, you may perform this exercise with the Print to File option activated as well.

1. With the 1WOMAN2.CDR image still on the screen, turn on Preview Selected Only. Then, select various objects in turn, magnifying portions of the image if necessary for more accurate selection. When you select a color object, access the Uniform Fill dialog box and check the process color values that have been specified.

2. After you have observed the fill colors of various objects, select the Print command in the File menu. When the Print Options dialog box appears, deselect any options that are currently active. Then activate the Print As Separations options. You will see that Crop Marks & Crosshairs, Film Negative, and Include File Info get selected automatically when you select Print as Separations. Click on Film Negative to turn it off. If your own draft printer is not a PostScript printer, you can select the Print to File option, too. (If you select Print to File, do not bother to check your printer setup yet. Changes you make in the Printer Setup dialog box will not take effect until that dialog box flies out automatically later in the process. You will specify printer setup automatically after you specify an output filename.)

3. Select OK. A second dialog box, the Color Separations dialog box, now appears, as shown in Figure 17-20. In the upper-left corner of the dialog box is a list box containing the names of the four process colors. (If you were preparing to print an image using the spot color method, you would see specific color names here instead.) Under Screen Angles are four screen angle values, one for each of the process colors. Do *not* alter these values unless you are very experi-

Figure 17-20. The Color Separations dialog box

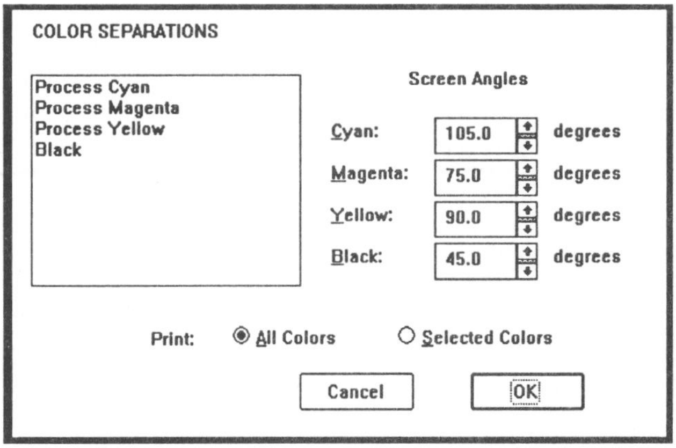

perienced in four-color printing and know exactly what you are doing. These angles are preset to ensure the best possible color alignment and registration. At the bottom of the dialog box is Print:, followed by two option buttons: All Colors and Selected Colors. For this exercise, leave All Colors selected, or click on this option if it is not selected already. For future reference, you can choose to print separations for either one color or a few colors at a time. To do so, just click on the Selected Colors option button and then on a desired color or colors in the list box. To highlight more than one color, click on the name of the first color, press and hold (SHIFT), and click on each additional color.

4. Select OK to save these settings and exit the Color Separations dialog box. If you are printing directly to your own PostScript printer, CorelDRAW! now begins printing the separations. The printing of color separation sheets takes longer than simply printing the file normally. In several minutes, four sheets of paper appear. The first shows the color values for cyan, the second for magenta,

the third for yellow, and the fourth for black. As shown in Figure 17-19, each sheet also contains a color bar, crop marks, registration marks, filename and date information, and color and screen information.

5. If you chose to print to a file, the Print to File dialog box appears when you exit the Color Separations dialog box, prompting you to name the output file. Type **COLORSEP** and select OK; CorelDRAW! adds the extension .PRN automatically. The Printer Setup dialog box now appears, bearing the title "PostScript Printer on FILENAME."

6. Adjust the file printing parameters as necessary; then click on the Options command button in the right-hand column of the Post-Script Printer on FILENAME dialog box. Make sure that the Job timeout value is 0 seconds and that Download each job is specified for the header. Then, select OK twice to begin printing the file to the specified drive and directory. You can then send the file to a PostScript service bureau for output.

7. Leave the 1WOMAN2.CDR image on the screen for the next exercise.

Caution

If you fill objects with any PostScript halftone screen pattern other than the default pattern, your custom settings will have no effect when you print color separations for the objects, because CorelDRAW! uses the halftone screen function to calculate color separation angles. This limitation applies only to the objects for which you print color separations. If you require separations for only a few objects, therefore, you are free to assign PostScript halftone screen patterns to the remaining objects. If you assign non-default screens to objects for which you must print color separations, your screen assignments have no effect.

Keep in mind that you can combine any number of options when you specify color separations. For example, you can tile separations for an oversize image, include file information, make selected objects fit the custom page size exactly, or scale the selected image for printing. If you are sure that the current image is in a final version, you can also print it in film negative format, as you will do in the next section.

Film Negative Format with PostScript

In commercial black-and-white or color printing, the transfer of the image or of color separations to film negative is one of the last steps to occur before the printing plates are made. Think of the difference between a snapshot and the negative from which it was produced: colors in the negative appear inverted and backward. The same thing happens when you activate the Film Negative option in the Print Options dialog box. White image backgrounds fill with printer toner, dark areas in the original image print as light, and the image is reversed horizontally. If you print in this format with Include File Info or Crop Marks & Crosshairs activated, even the file and color separation screen information is printed backward.

Use of the Film Negative option can save you money, but only if you are certain that the color separations in the image (if any) are in final form and will not need any further color correction or screen angle adjustments. If you intend to send a film negative file to a service bureau for output on a high-resolution imagesetter, ask the bureau management whether they can output your file in film negative format automatically. Many imagesetters can print your color separation file as a film negative just by flipping a switch. This might be preferable if your aim is to achieve a higher output resolution than that provided by your own 300 dpi laser printer.

In the following exercise, you will print one color separation screen for the 1WOMAN2.CDR file in film negative format. If you have your own PostScript laser printer, you can print this screen directly onto paper. If you use PostScript only to send files to a service bureau, steps are provided so that you can print the film negative format to a file.

1. With the 1WOMAN2.CDR file open, select the same grouped objects that you printed as color separations in the previous exercise. Then click on the Print command in the File menu.

2. Make sure that the print options that you used in the previous exercise—Print As Separations, Include File Info, Crop Marks & Crosshairs—are still active. (If you printed to a file in the previous exercise, make sure that the Print to File option is still active, too.) Then, click on the Film Negative option and select OK. The Color Separation dialog box appears, as before.

17

3. You do not need to print out all four color separation sheets to see how the Film Negative option works, so click on the Selected Colors option button at the bottom of the dialog box. Highlight the Process Yellow option in the process colors list box, and then click on the OK command button.

If you are printing directly to your printer, the color separation now begins to print. In a few moments, the color separation sheet for process yellow appears in film negative format, as shown in Figure 17-21. The image in the figure shows only the graphic and its file information, but your output sheet is covered with toner all the way to the edges of the printable page area. If you elected to print to a file, the Print to File dialog box appears, prompting you to enter a filename.

4. If you are printing to a file, type **NEG-YEL** in the File text box, and then click on the Print command button. The Printer Setup dialog box (PostScript Printer on FILENAME) now appears, as in the previous exercise.

Figure 17-21.   *Color separation sheet for process yellow printed in Film Negative format*

5. Click on OK to generate your file. When you finish printing, leave the image on the screen, with the grouped objects selected.

You need not limit yourself to printing in film negative format when you are working with a spot or process color image. You can also use this printing option with black-and-white images.

In the next section, you will learn more about the Default Screen Frequency option and how it affects your printouts.

Fountain Stripes

In CorelDRAW! version 2.0 and later, you can use the Print Options dialog box to control the number of stripes used to create a fountain fill on both PostScript and non-PostScript printers. This is a number from 2 through 250. You may want to change the number of fountain stripes for either of two reasons: to increase the smoothness of the fill and get rid of banding, you would increase the number of stripes; to increase the speed of printing, you would decrease the number of stripes. The "normal" number of fountain stripes depends on the resolution of your printer. For a 300 dpi laser printer, the normal value is 64, while for a 1270 dpi imagesetter it is 128. A value below 25, while fast to print, produces obvious banding. On the other end, around 100 for a 300 dpi laser printer, you can add fountain stripes without any gain in the smoothness of the image but with a decided increase in print time. You need to try out a series of values and see which are correct for your output device.

Flatness Setting for PostScript

The Flatness setting, which also became available in CorelDRAW! version 2.0, allows you to reduce the complexity of the curves in a drawing and thereby improve the likelihood of being able to print the drawing and also reduce the printing time. As you increase the Flatness setting, curves become less smooth with more straight ("flat") segments and, therefore, less attractive in some applications.

PostScript printers have upper limits on the number of curve segments they can handle and check for this limit. When a print image exceeds this limit, the image won't be printed. The normal Flatness setting is 1. If you are having problems printing a complex image, increase the Flatness setting in increments of 3 or 4 until you can print. By about 10 the curves are obviously less smooth. You can choose values from 0.01 to 100. Settings below 1 increase the curvature (decrease the flatness).

Screen Frequency for PostScript

The Default Screen Frequency value appears in the PostScript Halftone Screen dialog box. As you may recall from Chapters 14 and 15, you can access this dialog box whenever you assign a spot color to an outline or object fill. The frequency of the default screen pattern determines how fine the halftone resolution will appear on the printed page. Each type of PostScript printer has a default screen frequency, with the most common being 60 lines per inch for 300 dpi printers and 90 or more for high-resolution imagesetters. The standard setting for Default Screen Frequency in the Print Options dialog box is Device's, because in most cases it is best to let the printer you are using determine the screen frequency.

You can override this standard value, however, by clicking on the Custom option button and entering the desired value in the associated numeric entry box. Thereafter, *all* of the objects in your image will have the custom screen frequency. The most common reasons for altering this value are:

- You want to create special effects such as the Fill patterns that result from altering the halftone screen settings, as discussed in Chapter 15.

- You experience visible "banding" effects while printing objects with fountain fills and want the color transitions to occur more smoothly.

In the first case, you would increase the default screen value for the selected printer, while in the second, you would decrease it. If you have a 300 dpi PostScript printer, perform the following brief exercise to compare how reducing the default screen frequency alters the appearance of your output.

1. With the 1WOMAN2.CDR image open and the grouped objects selected, click on the Print command in the File menu. The Print Options dialog box appears.

2. Make sure that the Print As Separations option and the associated other options are activated. Deselect any other options that show an "x" in their respective checkboxes. Then click on the Custom option button in the Default Screen Frequency section of the dialog box. If you have a 300 dpi PostScript printer, the number 60 appears in the numeric entry box next to Custom. This is the default screen frequency for your printer.

3. Change the Custom value to 45 lines per inch, and then click on OK.

4. When the Color Separations dialog box appears, click on Selected Colors and highlight Process Yellow, as you did in the previous exercise. These settings will cause only the color separation for the color yellow to print.

5. Click on the Print command button of the Color Separations dialog box to begin printing. After a few moments, the color separation sheet appears. If you compare this output sheet with the one produced in the "Color Separations, Crop Marks, and Registration Marks with PostScript" section, you will not notice a big difference, but if you look closely you will see that the dot pattern of the 45-lines-per inch screen printout appears coarser.

6. Select New from the File menu to clear the screen of the 1WOMAN2.CDR file. Do not save any changes to the image.

17

If you alter the default screen frequency in order to proof an image, be sure to change the frequency back to Device's before sending the final output file to a service bureau. Otherwise, your image will not appear to have a much higher resolution than what your printer could offer.

Note, however, that if you assign *custom* PostScript halftone screen patterns to an object while drawing, any changes you make to the *default* screen frequency at printing time will have no effect on the screen frequency of that object. In the next section, you will become familiar with the uses of the All Fonts Resident printing option. Since the example image does not contain any text, you will not have an exercise, but the principle of the option is quite straightforward.

All Fonts Resident for PostScript

The All Fonts Resident option in the Print Options dialog box is designed with the occasional user of Adobe PostScript fonts and laser service bureaus in mind. As you are aware, CorelDRAW! comes supplied with 153 different typeface and typestyle combinations. Although these are of very high quality, they do not contain the "hints" (program instructions) that allow genuine Adobe PostScript fonts to print at extremely small sizes with very little degradation. Therefore, if you use text with a small typesize in a drawing, you might choose to substitute equivalent Adobe PostScript fonts for the Corel-DRAW! fonts at printing time. You activate the All Fonts Resident option to instruct the PostScript printer to substitute the correct fonts.

The All Fonts Resident option is intended for temporary use. If you have purchased downloadable fonts from Adobe and *always* want your printer to automatically substitute Adobe fonts for CorelDRAW! typefaces, you should alter the [CorelDrwFonts] section of your CORELDRW.INI file according to the instructions in Appendix C. If you use the All Fonts Resident option when you send output files to a laser service bureau, make sure that the service bureau has all of the necessary PostScript fonts downloaded. If you specify a PostScript font that is not in the host printer's memory, the font will print as Courier instead.

Caution

The All Fonts Resident option does not apply to fonts from other manufacturers that you have designated as substitutes for CorelDRAW! fonts through the WFNBOSS utility. Windows considers any non-Adobe fonts that you substitute through WFNBOSS as non-resident fonts.

In the final sections of this chapter, you will find tips for smooth printing based on the type of printer you are using and the features of your artwork.

Hardware-Specific Tips

Even if you closely follow all recommended printing procedures, such as checking the Printer Setup options or setting Job Timeout at 0 seconds and Transmission Retry at 600 seconds, you may encounter printing difficulties on occasion. Some difficulties involve settings for your specific printer type, while others may involve features of the artwork you are trying to print. This section deals with printing problems that could be dependent on hardware and makes suggestions for solving them. The final section, "Complex Artwork on PostScript Printers," deals with printing problems that might be related to features of the artwork itself.

Regardless of the type of printer you use, you may sometimes encounter one of several error messages indicating that you should cancel the printing process. In most cases, click on the Retry command button. Repeated attempts to print often force the data through your printer.

Caution

PostScript Printers and Controllers

CorelDRAW! is designed for the PostScript Plus type of printer, with its 11 resident typeface families and 2 or 3 MB of RAM. It also runs on older versions of PostScript printers that contain only four typeface families, but you may experience slower performance or other limitations if the memory in your printer is not sufficient. If this happens, check with your printer dealer to see whether a memory upgrade is possible. If you run CorelDRAW! with an older model of PostScript printer, you should edit your CorelDRAW! CorelDRW.INI file to notify the program that certain PostScript fonts are not available. To do this, proceed with the following steps.

1. From the Program Manager, open the Notepad application, double-click on the CORELDRW.INI filename in the directory where you installed CorelDRAW! to begin editing this file.

2. Go to the [CorelDrwFonts] section of the CORELDRW.INI file and look at the listings of fonts that are followed by the number 3 at the end of the line. These are PostScript Plus fonts, not available for the older models of PostScript printers.

3. Change each 3 to a 0. This tells CorelDRAW! always to substitute CorelDRAW! fonts for the PostScript fonts when you print the file to a PostScript printer.

4. Save these changes to the CORELDRW.INI file and exit Notepad.

17

5. Exit and then restart Windows to cause your changes to take effect.

In today's market, a number of so-called PostScript compatible controllers and plug-in cartridges are available for the HP LaserJet and compatible printers. You should be aware that there is a distinction between genuine PostScript controller boards and cartridges (licensed by Adobe), and PostScript-compatible controller boards and cartridges that are only as compatible as their interpreters. If your LaserJet printer is equipped with a genuine Adobe PostScript controller board or cartridge, you should be able to print everything that would be possible on a genuine Adobe PostScript printer. This is not necessarily true for a printer equipped with a Post-Script-*compatible* controller board or cartridge, although some of these components work extremely well.

If you have a genuine PostScript printer or if your printer has a genuine PostScript controller board or cartridge, the following tips should help you prevent printing problems when running CorelDRAW!. Potential problems are organized according to whether your printer is connected to a parallel or a serial port.

Parallel Printers

Printer or job timeout problems are common with PostScript printers that are parallel-connected. To avoid such problems, check for the following:

- The Windows Spooler should be turned off (see the "Preparing to Print" section of this chapter).

- Make sure that your printer is set up for batch processing mode, not interactive mode. Interactive mode does not permit the printing of imported bitmaps.

- See whether you can change Wait timeout directly from the printer as well as from the Windows Control Panel. Many PostScript printers provide utilities that let you specify these times independent of any software application.

- Set the Job timeout, Device Not Selected, and Transmission Retry settings as recommended in the "Preparing to Print" section of this chapter.

You will find additional tips related to printing complex artwork with PostScript printers in the "Complex Artwork on PostScript Printers" section at the end of this chapter.

Serial Printers

Although most PostScript printers attach to IBM-compatible computers with a parallel cable (the faster and preferred printing method), some printers require the use of a serial cable. To ensure trouble-free printing with a serially connected printer, compare your printer setup with the following checklist:

- Use the Ports icon in the Control Panel and make certain that the Communications settings are correct. (Refer to your printer manual.) Make sure that hardware handshaking is active.

- Make sure that hardware handshaking is also activated from the Print Options dialog box. You will find this well-hidden control by clicking on the Printer Setup command button, then on the Options command button of the Printer Setup dialog box, and finally on the Handshaking command button within the Printer Options dialog box. Some older PostScript printer models do not permit hardware handshaking; if this is the case with your printer, you may want to contact Corel Systems technical support for assistance.

- Check your printer cable. Some long or unshielded serial cables do not always transmit all available data with graphics applications.

- From DOS, check the COMM.DRV file on your Microsoft Windows disks (it is in the System directory for Windows 3). This is the serial driver for your printer. If the COM.DRV file is 4484 bytes long or shows a date of 9/07/88, you may have a faulty driver; contact Microsoft for an updated one.

HP LaserJet Printers and Compatibles

Since the HP LaserJet and compatible printers connect to your computer by means of a parallel rather than a serial cable, you should refer to the "Parallel Printers" section under "PostScript Printers and Controllers." Printers that are guaranteed to be 100% LaserJet compatible perform equally

17

with the genuine HP LaserJet. Printers that are HP LaserJet clones and that do not guarantee 100% compatibility may present erratic problems, which vary with the printer driver and manufacturer.

If your LaserJet or compatible is an older model and you have only 512K of memory, you may find that you are unable to print full-page graphics with complex features such as outlines and fountain fills. Many LaserJet-type printers split a graphic that is too large for memory and tile it over several sheets. If you plan to print large graphics regularly, see whether you can expand your printer's memory. If this is not possible, try reducing the size of the graphic on the page. Since object-oriented graphics can be scaled up or down without distortion, this should be a satisfactory solution. As a last resort, reduce the printing resolution of the graphic to 150 dpi, or even 75 dpi, in the Printer Setup dialog box.

HP DeskJet and PaintJet

The HP DeskJet is a black-and-white inkjet printer that is almost completely compatible with the HP LaserJet. There are different versions of the software driver for this printer, however. Check to make sure that you have the latest model driver when printing graphics from CorelDRAW!. In addition, avoid designing large filled objects or layered objects; the ink for the DeskJet is water-based and could run or smear if you layer it too thickly.

The HP PaintJet manifests CorelDRAW! printing problems somewhat erratically, and there are no "cookbook" solutions. It is important to keep your ink jet nozzles for each color clean and unclogged, however, to avoid smearing colors. If you have checked your Printer Setup and cannot find a solution, try printing your problem image to a file and sending it to CorelDRAW! technical support.

Hewlett-Packard has a new PaintJet driver (Spring 1991) that solves all the observed problems. To order this driver, call their Fullment number, 1-303-353-7650 and ask for the latest PaintJet driver. The cost (at time of printing) is $20 plus tax.

Genuine HP and Other Plotters   The Windows driver for plotters seems to be written specifically for the HP Plotter line. The HP Plotter supports only hairline outlines and no fills for objects that you create in CorelDRAW!. If you have a clone from another manufacturer, the Windows driver may not work well for you when you print images from CorelDRAW!. Contact your plotter manufacturer to see if a driver for CorelDRAW! is available.

Dot-Matrix Printers   The results of printing CorelDRAW! graphics on dot-matrix printers are very erratic, owing to the large number of printer types available and the many different drivers written for them. Some dot-matrix printers cannot print complex files at all, while others print part of a page and stop. Dot-matrix printers that have multicolor ribbons do not all lay colors down on the page in the same order. This can result in muddy colors that do not match what you see on your screen. Depending on the problem, you may wish to contact your printer manufacturer to see if a driver for Windows is available.

Complex Artwork on PostScript Printers

The term "complex" artwork, when applied to CorelDRAW!, can include a variety of features. Among them are curves with many nodes, multiple fountain fills in an image, PostScript halftone screens and textures, and text converted to curves. Many printing problems that are traceable to the complexity of features are encountered chiefly with PostScript printers. This happens because the PostScript language has certain internal limits. When these are exceeded, the affected object may not print at all or may print incorrectly. For example, objects that contain more than 200 to 400 nodes may cause your PostScript print job to crash. If you are having this problem, try increasing the Flatness setting in the Print Options dialog box by increments of 3. As was discussed earlier, this reduces the number of nodes in curves, and after only a couple of increments, improvement becomes noticeable.

You might not experience a problem with the same object if you are printing to an HP LaserJet printer, because the HP LaserJet does not recognize nodes; it interprets all graphic images simply as collections of pixels. Some PostScript printer manufacturers, such as QMS, allow you to run PostScript printers in LaserJet mode. If you have such a printer, try switching to LaserJet mode and printing your "problem" image again. If the file prints

17

correctly, it is safe to guess that an internal PostScript limitation is causing printing problems in PostScript mode.

Downloadable PostScript Error Handler

You may not be aware (it is undocumented) that Microsoft Windows provides an error handler that helps you diagnose PostScript printing problems. To understand how the error handler works, you need to know that PostScript prints the "bottom" or first-drawn object in the image first, followed by each succeeding layer. When you download the error handler and try to print a problem file, the printer begins with the first object and prints as far as it can. When the printer encounters an object that is problematic, it stops and prints out the objects completed so far, together with an error message. Although the messages are in PostScript code language, they are, in many cases, intelligible enough for you to decipher what the basic problem might be. The purchase of a relatively inexpensive PostScript manual, of which several are available, can help you even further.

To download the PostScript error handler to your printer and keep it resident there until you turn the printer off, follow these steps:

1. From the Print Options dialog box, click on the Printer Setup command button.

2. From the Printer Setup screen, click on the Options command button to access the PostScript Printer Options dialog box.

3. Press (ALT)-(E). The Error handler options dialog box appears as shown here:

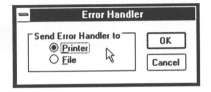

4. If you are printing to your own PostScript printer, click on the Printer option button to download the error handler directly to the

printer. This setting has no effect if you send a file to a service bureau, for most service bureaus use their own error handlers.

The Windows error handler should be helpful in fixing problems that already exist within a graphic. However, there are other measures you can take to design a graphic that will cause no printing problems. The following sections explain a few of these measures briefly.

Printing PostScript Textures

The 42 PostScript textures described in Chapter 15 were created with highly complex mathematical algorithms. Sometimes, you may not be able to make an object with a PostScript texture print correctly. If this happens, try adjusting the parameters to avoid extremely dense patterns. If the image does not print at all, try removing excess objects. PostScript textures can be so memory-intensive that they do not tolerate many other objects within the same graphic. In general, you should use these textures as fills in a limited number of objects within a given graphic. Short text strings used as headlines (but not converted to curves) are among the best applications for PostScript texture fills.

If you are a desktop publisher, you may sometimes find that a page containing a CorelDRAW! graphic with PostScript textures does not print. Try removing everything from the page except the PostScript texture graphic, and then attempt to print the page again. Sometimes a page becomes too complex for PostScript if it contains both PostScript textures and other elements.

Printing Complex Curve Objects   As previously mentioned, the current version of PostScript may give you difficulty when you try to print images that contain objects with more than 200 nodes. If you suspect that an object has too many nodes and could be causing problems, click on it with the Shaping tool. The number of nodes contained in the object appears on the status line. If the number of nodes seems too high or approaches the danger zone, reshape the object and eliminate any unnecessary nodes.

When you drag one or more control points of a curve object outward by a great distance, the boundary markers of the object may extend much further

17

outward than you can see. If you print a file containing many curve objects and some objects just do not print, it may be that you have not selected them. One remedy is to click on the Select All command in the Edit menu before you begin to print, and then activate Print Only Selected in the Print Options dialog box. This procedure ensures that all objects in the graphic are selected, no matter how extensively you may have reshaped them.

Printing Fountain Fills   A common complaint when printing fountain-filled objects on PostScript printers is that "banding" effects can occur. In other words, the edges of each fountain stripe are clearly visible and do not blend into the next stripe smoothly. This occurs more often with 300 dpi printers than with Linotronic or other imagesetters that have a higher resolution. With LaserJet and compatible printers, solving this problem is easy: you simply increase the Fountain Stripes value in the Preferences dialog box to create a smoother blend. When you alter this value with a PostScript printer, however, it affects your preview window only, not the way the image prints.

To reduce banding effects on Fountain Fills when you print to a 300 dpi PostScript printer, with CorelDRAW! versions 2.0 and above, increase the value for Fountain Stripes in the Print Options dialog box by 10 or 20. With earlier versions of CorelDRAW! click on the Custom Default Screen Frequency option button in the Print Options dialog box, and reduce the frequency to a number between 30 and 45 lines per inch according to your taste. This procedure results in a somewhat coarser dot pattern, but definitely improves the smoothness of color transition in a Fountain Fill.

Tip

If you alter the default screen frequency for a draft printout on a 300 dpi printer, remember to change the Default Screen Frequency setting back to Device's before you create an output file to be sent to a high-resolution imagesetter. Also keep in mind that when you alter the default screen frequency, your image should contain no objects that have a non-standard halftone screen pattern.

300 dpi Printers vs. High-Resolution Imagesetters

It may sometimes happen that your graphic prints on your own 300 dpi PostScript printer, but causes a high-resolution imagesetter to crash. This occurs because at higher resolutions, the amount of information in a file multiplies. It is possible that your graphic exceeds certain internal PostScript limits at these higher resolutions, but didn't at the lower resolution. To avoid such problems, try reducing the resolution at which the imagesetter prints, using the Default Screen Frequency setting in the Printer Setup dialog box. Alternatively, you can define a custom default screen frequency for the imagesetter before you create the output file. If you do so, make certain that your custom frequency is lower than that of the imagesetter. These measures help reduce the amount of data in fills and outlines.

17

18

Creating Special Effects

The Effects Menu, which is new to CorelDRAW! version 2.0, is shown in Figure 18-1. It is used to produce dramatic effects. For example, with the *Envelope* feature, you can shape an empty envelope and cause text placed within the envelope to conform to the shape. In CorelDRAW! an envelope is a box that surrounds text or graphics. You can pull the envelope in different directions, thereby distorting the shape. The text contained within will follow the shape of the envelope. Figure 18-2 shows an example.

Another special effect is the *Perspective* feature. It allows you to create depth in text or a graphic by stretching the borders of the object. The object seems to fade away into the distance. You can create a simple 3-D effect or a more complex version, such as seen in Figure 18-3.

The third special effect is the *Blend* feature. This allows you to blend one object into another, as shown here:

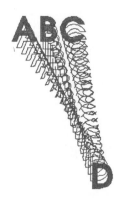

You define the beginning and ending points, and CorelDRAW! will fill in the blend steps.

Finally, the fourth special effect is the *Extrude* feature. This feature gives depth to the objects. An example of an open path extruded surface is shown here:

If your computer is not turned on, turn it on now and bring up CorelDRAW!.

You will explore these special effects beginning with the Envelope feature.

Using an Envelope

An envelope is a bounding box with eight handles on it that surrounds the text or graphic. You pull the handles to reshape the object within the envelope.

You have four editing modes available that determine how the envelope can be reshaped. Three of the modes allow you to change the shape of a side of the envelope in a specific way. The first mode allows you to pull the side

Figure 18-1.   *The Effects menu*

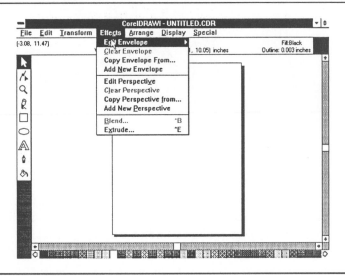

Figure 18-2.   *Example of Envelope effect*

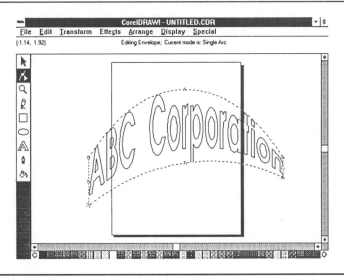

18

Figure 18-3.   *Example of Perspective effect*

in a straight line, the second in a curved line, the third in a line with two curves. The fourth envelope editing mode is unconstrained. It allows you to pull in any direction, and to change a line to a curve.

As you move the handles, the envelope changes shape. When you let go of the handle, the contents of the envelope are reshaped to conform to the new shape.

You will now create and duplicate some text to use for the first three editing modes.

Creating and Duplicating Text

To prepare for the first exercise, you need to create a piece of text and then duplicate it twice.

1. Click on the Text tool and then click on the page, at about the middle left.

2. When the Dialog Box is displayed, type **Happy Birthday.** Change the type size to 60 points. Change the typeface to Cupertino. Click on OK to return to the screen.

   Now you will copy the text twice so that there are three copies, one for each of the first three editing modes.

3. Press the (SPACEBAR) to select the text.

4. From the Edit Menu, select Duplicate for the first copy.

5. From the Edit Menu, select Duplicate again for the second copy. The three copies will be stacked on top of each other with the edges of the bottom copies peeking out, as shown here:

Now you will move them apart.

6. Place the mouse pointer on an edge of the selected text. Press and hold the mouse button while moving the box outline to the bottom of the page. Center the outline horizontally on the page. When you release the mouse button, the selected copy of the text will be moved from the stack onto the page.

7. Click on the top of the stack to select the next text object. Repeat step 6 but move the second copy from the stack to the top of the page. The last copy will remain at the center of the page.

8. Space the three text units so that you can easily work with each one. Figure 18-4 shows an example of the screen with the three copies placed on the page.

Now you are ready to work with the first envelope editing mode.

Straight Line Envelope

18

The Straight Line editing mode allows you to pull envelope handles in a straight line. You can move one handle at a time.

As in all of the first three editing modes, the handles can be moved only in a restricted way: Handles located in the center of the sides move left or right; handles located in the top- and bottom-center move up or down; corner handles move up or down, or left or right. (In the fourth mode, all handles move in any direction.)

Figure 18-4.   *Text to be used for illustrating Envelopes*

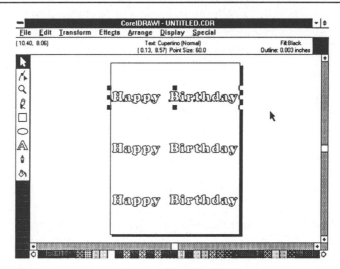

The easiest way to understand the feature is to try it out. Follow these steps:

1. If the top text object is not selected, select it by clicking on it so that the select box surrounds it.

2. Select Edit Envelope from the Effects menu.

3. Choose the first editing mode, Straight Line, as shown here:

The envelope will appear on the screen surrounding the selected text. You can see the eight handles.

3. Pull the top-center handle up, as shown here:

4. Pull the bottom-center handle up, like this:

You can see how the text conforms to the new straight line. Next you will see how the Single Arc editing mode differs.

Single Arc Envelope

The Single Arc editing mode allows you to create an arc by pulling the handles up, down, right, or left. You can only pull one handle at a time.

As above, the handles can be moved only in a restricted way: Handles located in the center of the sides move left or right; handles located in the top- and bottom-center move up and down; corner handles move up or down, or left and right.

Follow these steps to try it out.

1. Click on the Select tool, then select the second text copy by clicking on it until the select box surrounds it.

2. Select Edit Envelope from the Effects menu. Choose the second option, Single Arc, shown here:

3. Pull the top-center handle up.

4. Pull the bottom-center handle up, as shown here:

18

You can see how the Straight Line and Arc editing modes differ. Now you will try out the third editing mode.

Two Curves Envelope

The third choice allows you to create two curves by pulling one of the eight handles. You can only move one handle at a time.

Again, the handles can be moved only in a restricted way: Handles located in the center of the sides move left or right; handles located in the top- and bottom-center move up or down; corner handles move up or down, or left or right.

Follow these steps to try it out.

1. Click on the Select tool, and click on the third text object until it is selected.

2. Select Edit Envelope from the Effects menu. Then choose the third item, Two Curves, shown here:

The envelope will surround the third text object.

3. Pull the top-center handle up. Then pull the bottom-center handle up, as shown here:

You can see how two curves are created out of the line, shaping the text in an entirely different way. These three envelope editing modes have an additional feature that can be used to constrain the shapes.

Using (CTRL) and (SHIFT) with Envelopes

The above three envelope editing modes can be used with (CTRL) or (SHIFT) with surprising results. You can cause three effects to take place:

- If you hold down (CTRL) while you drag on a handle, the opposite handle will move in the same direction.
- If you hold down (SHIFT) while you drag on a handle, the opposite handle will move in the opposite direction.
- Finally, if you hold both (SHIFT) and (CTRL) while dragging a handle, all four corners or sides will move in opposite directions.

You can use these keys with any of the first three Edit Envelope options. Try the (CTRL) method now with the first text object on your screen.

1. Click on the top text image so that the envelope and handles appear on the screen.

2. Press (CTRL) while dragging the center top handle down, as shown here:

You can see two immediate effects: First, the top and bottom sides move in the same direction. You expected that. Second, and unexpectedly, the lines are *not* being shaped according to the Straight Line edit mode as was applied to this particular text object. Instead, the lines are being shaped according to the Two Curves edit mode, the last mode applied to another text object. Whenever you apply a new editing mode to any envelope on the page, *all new edits will be assigned the new mode as well.* If you need to change the shape of an object retaining the original edit mode, simply reselect that mode before making your changes.

Now you will try the (SHIFT) method with the second text object.

1. Click on the middle text object so that the envelope and handles appear on the screen.

18

2. Select Edit Envelope from the Effects Menu and then Single Arc from the submenu.

3. Press (SHIFT) while dragging the top-right handle out to the right.

The left and right sides will move in opposite directions, as shown here:

The (SHIFT)-(CTRL) method is just as easy.

1. Click on the bottom text object to select it.

2. Select Edit Envelope from the Effects menu and then Two Curves from the submenu.

3. Press (SHIFT)-(CTRL) while dragging the top-right handle to the right.

The top and bottom and both sides all move in opposite directions, as shown here:

These techniques are particularly useful when you are changing the shape of drawings, as in circles or rectangles, and you want one or all of the dimensions to be equally altered.

Now you will explore the fourth envelope editing mode.

Unconstrained Envelope

The Unconstrained editing mode is the most dynamic of the four modes. The handles can be moved in any direction, and they contain control points that can be used to fine-tune and bend the objects even more dynamically. Unlike the first three Edit Envelope options, the Unconstrained mode lets you select several handles and move them as a unit.

To experiment with this, first clear the page of its contents.

1. Select New from the File menu. Click on No when asked about saving the current screen contents.

   After the Happy Birthdays are cleared from the screen you are ready.

2. Select the Text tool and click on the center left of the page.

3. When the dialog box is displayed, type **Not Constrained**. Change the type size to 60 points and the font to Brooklyn. Click on OK.

4. Select Edit Envelope from the Effects Menu. Choose the fourth submenu option, Not Constrained:

   You will see that the text object is surrounded with the envelope and its handles. Since you are using the Shaping tool, the handles become nodes.

5. Pull the top-center handle or node up, and then the bottom-center node down, as shown here:

You can see that a pair of control points appeared first on the top and then on the bottom-center node. These control points like

18

Shaping tool control points, allow you to alter the shape by exaggerating and bending the curve.

6. Place the cursor on the left control point or bottom node and pull it down. (To experiment with it, move it down and then back up so that you will see what happens with the handle.)

7. Click on the top-center node to select it. Place the cursor on the right end node of the top-center handle and pull it up, as shown here:

Now, suppose you want the last letters to curve up at the end.

8. While holding (SHIFT), click on the bottom-center node and the bottom-right node. Now you can treat the two as a unit.

9. Hold the mouse button and pull the bottom-center node down, as shown here:

10. Press (F9) to preview the effect:

11. Press (F9) to return to the editing screen.

One way that you can use the Unconstrained edit mode is to modify text to conform to a shape, for example, text within a circle or oval. First you create the circle, oval, or whatever shape you want as a border and move the text with its envelope within the border. You then manually move the control points of the text so that they correspond with the border shape. Then if you don't want the border to appear, you can delete it.

Continue to experiment until you are comfortable with the Unconstrained edit mode. Then you can move on to more Envelope features.

Adding a New Envelope

Sometimes you may want to use more than one of the editing modes on an object. Adding a new envelope allows you to do this. You apply an envelope and then shape the object with it. You add a new envelope, which replaces the first envelope while retaining its shape. Then you select a new editing mode and change the new shape again.

To try this out,

1. Clear the screen by selecting New from the File menu. Click on No when asked if you want to save the screen contents.

2. Select the Text tool and click on the center left of the page.

3. When the dialog box is displayed, type **New Envelope**, set the type size to 60 points. and select the NewBrunswick typeface. Click on OK.

18

4. Apply an envelope by selecting Edit Envelope from the Effects menu. Choose the Straight Line editing mode.

5. Click on the top-left handle and drag it up.

6. Click on the bottom-right handle and drag it down, as shown here:

Now you will apply a new envelope and change the shape using another editing mode on top of the Straight Line editing mode. To see the effects while you are working, you will turn on Preview window.

1. Press (SHIFT)-(F9) for the Preview window. It should be in side-by-side mode.

2. From the Effects menu, select Add New Envelope.

3. From the Effects menu, select Edit Envelope. From the submenu, select the Single Arc editing mode.

   You will use (SHIFT) to move the opposite handles in opposite directions.

4. While pressing (SHIFT), drag the upper-left handle up and to the left.

5. While pressing (SHIFT), drag the bottom-right handle down and to the right, as shown in Figure 18-5.

One way that a new envelope can be used is with certain typefaces that do not bend or reshape themselves exactly as you want. You can form the basic shape with one of the first three edit modes, and then apply the Unconstrained edit mode to fine-tune the text. In this way you can manually form the letters with more precision than you might get with the typeface alone.

Figure 18-5. *Using Add New Envelope to reshape a text object within the borders of a previous envelope*

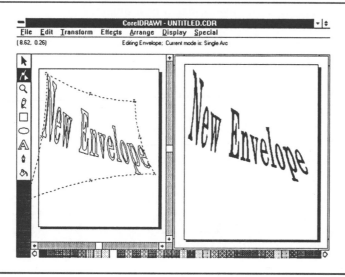

Sometimes you might want to start over again. Clearing an envelope allows you to do that.

Clearing an Envelope

The Clear Envelope command removes the current envelope and all shape changes that occurred with it. If you have applied more than one most recent, only the previous one will be removed.

To clear the last envelope from the current text object, select Clear Envelope from the Effects Menu. The drawing will be returned to the previous Straight Line edit mode. However, if you have applied a perspective (perspectives are discussed shortly) to the object after applying the most recent envelope, the perspective must be removed before you can clear the envelope.

(Note that the Clear Transformations command, found on the Transform Menu, removes all envelopes, restoring the drawing to its original shape. If

18

you have applied perspectives, they will also be removed and the original shape restored.)

Now you can copy an envelope to a new object.

Copy Envelope From

The Copy Envelope From command allows you to copy the envelope and its current shape to a new object. The new object does not need its own envelope. To try out this feature, you will first create a new object.

1. Click on the Ellipse tool. Draw a circle below the text object, using the (CTRL) key.

2. Select Copy Envelope From in the Effects menu.

   The cursor will be turned into a special "FROM?" arrow. You will move the arrow to the source of the envelope, which is the text object.

3. Move the arrow to the text object "New Envelope" contained in the envelope and click on it.

The destination object will be reshaped with the new tool, as shown in Figure 18-6.

Now you will explore another dynamic feature, Perspective.

Creating Perspective Effects

Perspective gives an object a sense of depth, as if the object were moving away from you. This effect can be applied from one- or two-point perspective views. Figure 18-7 shows the two kinds of perspective.

The one-point perspective, on the top, gives the effect of moving away from you in a straight line. The two-point perspective, on the bottom, distorts the view so that the object is moving away and being twisted in the process.

You will see how these two points are applied.

Figure 18-6. *Using Copy Envelope From to reshape a second object, in this case a circle*

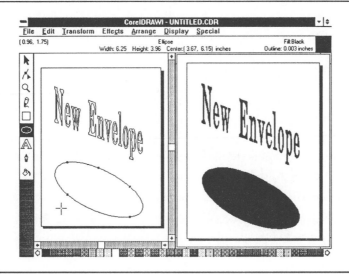

Figure 18-7. *Examples of one-point and two-point perspectives*

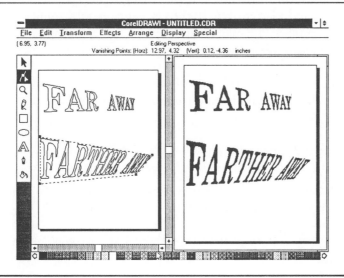

Using One- or Two-Point Perspective

You apply perspective in much the same way that you change the shape of an envelope. A perspective bounding box with handles surrounds the object. You can drag the handles to shorten or lengthen the object, giving the perspective you want.

Follow these steps to try it out.

1. Clear the screen by selecting New from the File menu. Click on No when asked if you want to save the screen contents.

2. If the rulers are not showing, click on Show Rulers in the Display Menu to display them. Place a horizontal guideline at 9 inches, and a vertical guideline at 1 inch.

3. Select the Text tool and click on the intersection of the guidelines.

4. When the dialog box is displayed, type **Moving Away** and set the type size to 60.0 points and the typeface to Toronto. Click OK when you are done.

5. Select Edit Perspective from the Effects menu.

   The cursor will change to the Shaping tool arrow. When you place it on the handles, it will change to crosshairs. You will move the handles according to the coordinates, which tell the location of the cursor. The coordinates are shown in the upper-left corner of the status line.

You will now change the shape of the text object. To change to one-point perspective, drag the handle either up, down, right or left, that is, vertically or horizontally.

6. Click on the bottom-right handle and drag it vertically straight down until the coordinates are approximately 6.4 and 7.95.

7. Drag the bottom-left handle vertically straight down until the coordinates are approximately 1.0 and 5.9, as in Figure 18-8.

Now you will alter the shape to add the two-point perspective. You do this by dragging the handles either toward or away from the center of the object:

Figure 18-8. *Example of one-point perspective created by dragging the handles straight down*

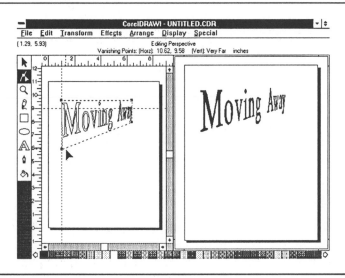

If you drag toward the object, the shape is pushed under; if pulled away from the object, the shape is pulled out toward you.

8. Drag the handles as close as possible to the following coordinates, as shown in Figure 18-9.

   Upper-right corner: 7.7, 8.96
   Bottom-right corner: 7.0, 7.28
   Bottom-left corner: 1.48, 4.77

Off the screen is an X symbol known as the vanishing point, which you will learn about next.

Using the Vanishing Point

To see the vanishing point you must press (SHIFT)-(F9) to return to the regular editing screen.

Figure 18-9.   *Example of two-point perspective created by dragging the handles diagonally toward or away from the center of the object*

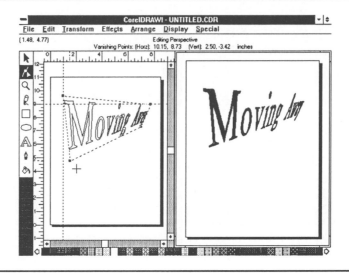

On the right, off the page, is the *vanishing point,* seen as an X. The X displayed is the horizontal vanishing point. Depending on the way the handles are moved, you may also see a vertical vanishing point, which is positioned above or below the object.

You can change the perspective by moving the vanishing point itself. By moving the vanishing point toward the object, the edge closest to the point becomes vertically shorter; the edge becomes vertically longer when the point is moved away from the edge.

When you move the vanishing point parallel to the object, the far side will remain in one place while the side nearest the point moves in the direction you drag the vanishing point.

Try these steps to see what the vanishing point can do:

1. Place the cursor on the vanishing point (it becomes a crosshair) and move it left and down, toward the text object, as shown here:

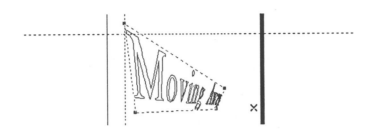

2. Press (F9) to see how moving the vanishing point has changed the view. Press (F9) again to restore the screen.

3. Move the vanishing point in the opposite direction, toward the right, away from the bounding box.

4. Press (F9) to see the effects. Press (F9) again to restore the screen.

Take a moment now to play with the vanishing point. When you are satisfied, you can explore some of the other Perspective features.

Clearing a Perspective

Clear Perspective, similar to Clear Envelope, removes the most recent perspective applied to an object. If you've applied more than one perspective, only the last one is removed.

If you've applied an envelope over a perspective, you must first remove the envelope before the perspective can be removed. Before you remove the envelope, be sure to duplicate the object in order to retain the shape you have created with the envelope. Then you can restore the shape by using the Copy Envelope From command after the perspective is removed.

Notice that Clear Transformations in the Transform menu will clear all perspectives and envelopes from an object at once. This is used when you want to restore an object to its original shape.

Now remove the perspective from the current object by selecting Clear Perspective from the Effects Menu. The perspective bounding box will be removed, and the shape will be restored. Now you will apply another perspective to the object.

18

Editing a Perspective

When you Edit a Perspective, you simply apply another bounding box to an object, or you may simply activate the Shaping tool if the object already has a bounding box.

1. Select Edit Perspective from the Effects Menu. A new bounding box will be applied, and the Shaping tool is selected.

   You will now change the shape again.

2. Drag the handles to the following coordinates, or close to them, as shown below.

   Upper-left handle: 1.0, 9.0
   Upper-right handle: 7.0, 8.0
   Lower-left handle: 1.0, 4.9
   Lower-right handle: 7.0, 5.8

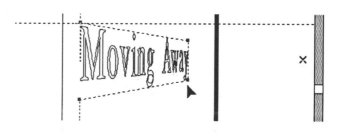

3. Press (F9) to see the effects.

4. Press (F9) again to restore the screen.

Now you will add another perspective.

Adding a New Perspective

You can add a new perspective to an object on top of one that already exists. This allows you to change the perspective, within the limits of the perspective already applied.

To see how this is done,

1. Select Add New Perspective from the Effects menu. A new bounding box will be applied to the object. Now you will change the perspective again.

2. Drag the handles to the following coordinates, or close to them, as shown in Figure 18-10.

   Upper-right handle: 5.65, 8.0
   Lower-left handle: 2.0, 6.3
   Lower-right handle: 8.15, 2.37

Figure 18-10. *Changing shape with Add New Perspective*

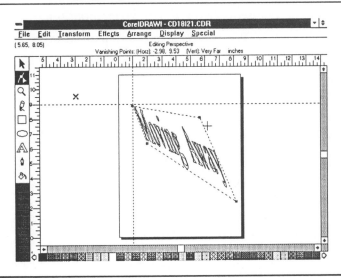

18

3. Press (F9) to see how the new perspective has changed the original:

4. Press (F9) to restore the screen.

Now you will apply the perspective to a new object.

Copy Perspective From

When you select the Copy Perspective From option, you use the shape of one object to change the perspective of another one. You will create a form to which the perspective will be applied.

1. Select the Ellipse tool and draw a circle under the text object.
2. Select the Copy Perspective From command from the Effects Menu. The From? arrow will appear.
3. Move the tip of the arrow to the outline of the text object and click on it. The circle will be redrawn with the new perspective.
4. Use the Select tool to drag the circle over the text object. (It doesn't matter if the reshaped circle isn't the same size as the text.)
5. Select No Fill (the X) from the Fill fly-out menu if necessary.
6. Press (F9). The results should look like Figure 18-11.
7. Press (F9) again to restore the editing window.

Now you will explore the Blend feature.

Figure 18-11. Preview of the circle reshaped with a copied perspective

Blending Objects

The Blend command causes one object to be blended into another by a number of connecting images. For example, you can turn a square into a circle with 20 intermediate images. You can also use this feature to create highlights and airbrush effects. The images can be of different colors, line weights, fills, and so on.

Before the objects are blended, you must fill them and place them where you want them on the screen. And, of course, first you must create the objects to be blended.

1. Select New from the File menu to clear the page. Click on No when asked whether you want to save the file.

2. Select the Text tool and click on the upper left of the page.

3. When the dialog box is displayed, type **Happy**, set the type size to 60 points, and set the typeface to USA-Black. Click on OK.

4. While the text object is selected, click on the Fill tool and select 10% gray fill for the word "Happy." If you have a color monitor, open the Custom Uniform fill dialog box, select Spot Color, and choose Pantone Yellow.

18

5. Now select the Text tool again and click on the lower center of the page.

6. When the dialog box is displayed, type **Birthday**, set the type size to 60 points, and the typeface to USA-Black. Click on OK.

7. Click on the Fill tool and select the black fill (or Spot Color Pantone Process Blue) for the word "Birthday."

Now you are ready to blend the two.

Blending Two Objects

To Blend the two objects you must first select the two objects. Then you simply select the Blend command and tell CorelDRAW! how many steps are needed between the two objects.

1. To be able to see the effects of the blend on the screen, press (SHIFT)-(F9) for the Split Preview screen.

2. Select the Select tool and then marquee-select the two objects by dragging a dotted rectangle around both objects. You must be careful that both objects are selected. If not, you will not be able to use the Blend command.

3. When both objects are selected, select Blend from the Effects menu. A second dialog box will appear:

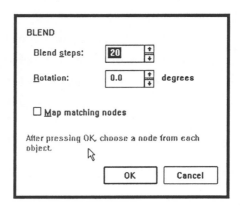

You now tell CorelDRAW! the number of intervening steps between the two objects. It assumes 20 steps, which is acceptable for this example. You can also indicate the degree of rotation and whether to map matching nodes. You'll do these in a minute.

4. Accept the 20 steps and 0 degrees of rotation by clicking on OK. You will see the two objects blended on the screen, as in Figure 18-12.

Next you will see what the rotation can do.

Rotating the Blended Objects

You can cause the figures to be rotated in two ways. First, by putting a degree of rotation in the Blend dialog box, you can cause the intervening steps to be rotated—clockwise, if a positive number is entered; counterclockwise, if a negative number is entered.

Figure 18-12.   *Blending of "Happy" into "Birthday" with no rotation*

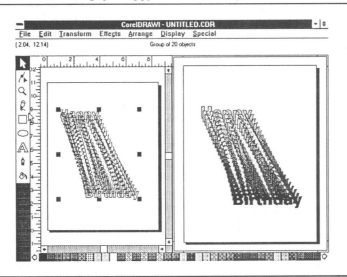

18

Second, by moving the center of rotation of the objects before they are blended, you can cause an arc to be arranged between them.

You will try both methods. First, you will see how the Blend command itself is used to create the rotation.

Rotating with the Blend Command

The Blend command, in its dialog box, allows you to specify the degrees of rotation to be used in the intervening steps. Let's see how this is used.

1. Press (DEL) to delete the current Blend effects. You will be left with the two unblended objects.

2. Select the two objects by dragging the marquee-select rectangle around them.

3. Select Blend from the Effects Menu.

4. Change the degree of rotation to 95.0. Click on OK.

The effects of the blending will appear on the screen, as shown in Figure 18-13. Now you will try out the other method of rotating the objects.

Rotating the Objects to be Blended

As you recall, you can rotate objects by double clicking on them and getting the rotation arrows to appear. If you use this technique to move the center of rotation, CorelDRAW! will create an arc between the two objects.

To see how this is done,

1. Press (DEL) to delete the current Blend effects. You will be left with the two objects.

2. Using the Select tool, marquee-select the two objects by dragging the rectangle around both of them. The highlighted box will appear. You will now cause the rotate show arrows box to appear and then drag the center of rotation to the right of the two objects.

3. Click on a letter of a word within the box so that the rotate show arrows appear. Drag the center of rotation to the right of the selected two objects, as shown here:

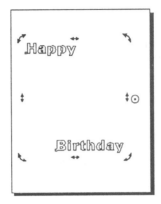

4. Select Blend from the Effects menu. Type **90.0** for the degree of rotation. Click on OK. The results look something like Figure 18-14.

One other rotation feature can be used to create interesting effects.

Figure 18-13. *"Happy" blended into "Birthday" with 95 degrees of rotation*

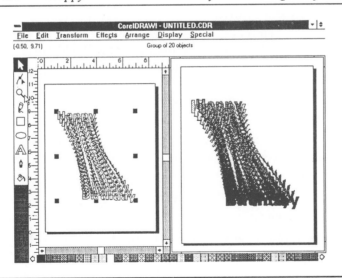

18

Figure 18-14.   *A blended arc created by replacing the center of rotation*

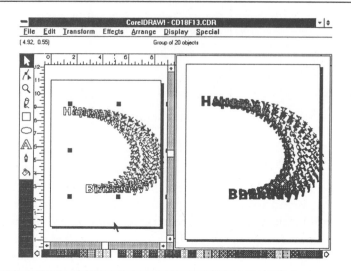

Mapping Matching Nodes

By varying the beginning nodes of both of the objects, you can create some unexpected results. The nodes identify where the blend is to begin and to end up. You will try two different ways of identifying the nodes.

1. Begin with a new screen by selecting New from the File menu. Click on No.

2. Select the Rectangle tool, and create four different-sized rectangles on your screen, as in Figure 18-15. Make sure that all four rectangles are unfilled. Select No Fill (X symbol) from the Fill fly-out menu.

3. Press (SPACEBAR) for the Select tool and marquee-select the leftmost two rectangles.

4. Select Blend from the Effects menu. Click on the Map Matching Nodes button. The 20 Blend steps and 90 degrees of rotation are acceptable. Click on OK. The cursor will become an arrow and one of the selected objects will have the nodes on each corner displayed:

5. Select the upper-left corner node by moving the arrow to that node and clicking on it. The second object's nodes will be displayed.

6. Select its upper-left corner node by moving the arrow to that node and clicking on it.

You will now see one result of Map Matching Nodes.

7. Marquee-select the second two objects. Select Blend from the Effects Menu.

Figure 18-15. *Placement of rectangles on the page*

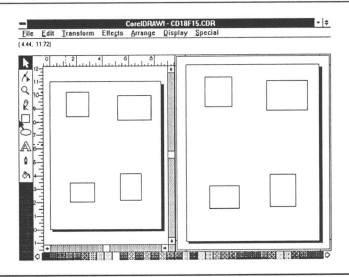

8. Click on OK to accept the Map Matching Nodes option.

9. With the arrow, click on the lower-right node of the first object.

10. Click on the upper-left node of the second object. The blend will occur as in Figure 18-16.

You can continue to experiment with Map Matching Nodes, adding a rotation degree if you want to see its effects. When you are finished you can look at the last major feature found on the Effects menu—the Extrude feature.

Extruding Objects

Extruded objects appear to have depth. You can use the Extrude feature on text, closed shapes, or open paths. The results can be very dramatic.

There are three ingredients to the extrude feature that affect the results: the X and Y Offsets, Perspective versus Parallel Extrusions, and the Scaling Factor. Each of these will be investigated separately.

Figure 18-16.   *Examples of blends with two types of Map Matching Nodes*

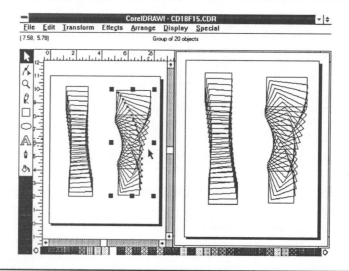

First you will create the objects to be extruded.

1. Renew the screen by selecting New from the File Menu. Click on No.
2. Click on the Text tool and click in the upper-left quadrant of the page.
3. When the dialog box is displayed, type **T**, select 120 points, and select New Brunswick typeface. Click on OK.
4. Click below the first T and to its right (Figure 18-17 shows the placement of the items). Repeat step 3.
5. Repeat the steps a third time below the second T.
6. Click on the Pencil tool and draw a wavy line in the lower part of the page. Your screen should look something like Figure 18-17.

Now you are ready to experiment with the X and Y Offsets.

Figure 18-17.   *Placement of objects for experimenting with the Extrude feature*

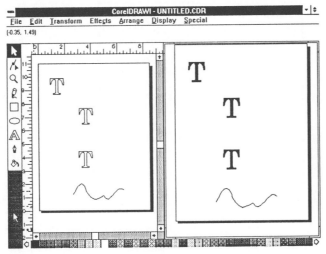

Using X and Y Offsets

The X Offset determines how far to the left or right the extrusion will occur. The Y Offset determines how far up or down it will occur. You will use the first T in the upper-right quadrant to experiment with the offsets.

1. Click on the topmost T with the arrow pointer so that the highlight box appears.

2. Select Extrude from the Effects Menu. The Extrude dialog box in Figure 18-18 will be displayed. You can see that the Extrusion Offset units of measure are currently set to "inches." You can change it to millimeters, points and picas, or points by clicking on it. For this exercise you will retain the inches units.

3. Set the X Offset to 4 inches; keep the Y Offset at zero. Click on OK.
     The T, as it is displayed, is difficult to see. You will fill the extrusions with a different fill color than T's Fill color.

Figure 18-18.   *The Extrude dialog box*

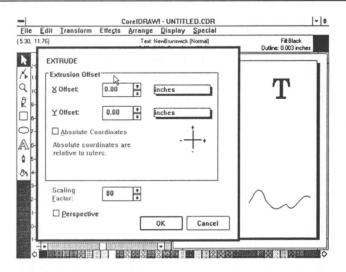

4. Select the Fill Tool and select gray as the fill. The T will look like this:

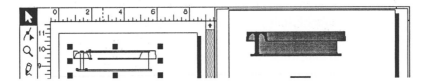

You will now see how the Y Offset changes the results. First you must delete the current extrusion. Since it is still highlighted, simply press (DEL).

1. Press (DEL) to delete the extrusion.

2. Click on the T again to select it.

3. Select Extrude from the Effects Menu. When the dialog box is displayed, keep 4 inches for the X Offset and type **1** for the Y Offset. Click on OK.

4. Select the Fill Tool and choose the 50% gray fill. Your T will look like this on the preview screen.

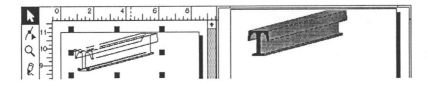

Now you will look at Parallel versus Perspective extrusions.

Parallel Extrusions and Perspective Extrusions

Parallel Extrusions show the lines drawn parallel to each other. The extrusion you created for T is a Parallel Extrusion. The way that you choose a Parallel Extrusion is to make sure that Perspective is *not* selected.

18

Perspective is used when you want the lines to look at if they were disappearing into the background. This gives a more realistic appearance to the drawings. You simply click on Perspective to get this option.

The X and Y Offsets function differently for Perspective Extrusion than they do for Parallel Extrusions. With Perspective Extrusions, X and Y represent the location of the vanishing point. If you enter the offsets, CorelDRAW! will use them to determine the depth of the extrusion. You can also enter the absolute ruler coordinates instead of the X and Y coordinates.

You will use the same coordinates as for the previous T, only you will make it a Perspective Extrusion. Follow these steps:

1. Click on the second T to select it.

2. Select Extrude from the Effects Menu. When the dialog box is displayed, keep the 4 inches for the X Offset and the 1 for the Y Offset. Click on the Perspective box. Click on OK.

3. Select the Fill Tool and choose the 50% gray fill. Your T will look like this on the preview screen:

Now you will see how the scaling factor affects the drawings.

Using the Scaling Factor

The scaling factor lets you place the vanishing point in front of or behind the object. The number assigned to the Scaling Factor determines whether the vanishing point is behind or in front of it, and how far.

Numbers between 0 and 99 place the vanishing point behind the object. The lower the number (closer to 0) the farther away the vanishing point will appear to be.

Numbers between 101 and 200 place the vanishing point in front of the object. The larger the value (closer to 200) the bigger the extrusion appears to be, that is, the closer it is.

Follow these steps to demonstrate the Scaling Factor.

1. Click on the third T to select it.

2. Select Extrude from the Effects Menu. When the dialog box is displayed, keep the 4 inches for the X Offset and the 1 for the Y Offset. Retain the check in the Perspective box. Set the Scaling Factor to 10. Click on OK.

3. Select the Fill Tool and choose the gray fill. Your T will look like this on the preview screen.

Now you will experiment briefly with how an open path can be used in a creative way with extrusions.

Using Extrusions with Open Paths

Open paths can be used to create some interesting effects with extrusions. In this case you will create a flying carpet from your wavy line.

1. Click on the wavy line.

2. Select Extrude from the Effects Menu. Set the X Offset to 1 and the Y offset to 0.5. Turn off the Perspective box. The scaling factor has no effect without the Perspective turned on. Click on OK.

3. Select No Fill (X symbol) for the open path. Your screen should look like Figure 18-19. Spend some time experimenting with the X and Y offsets and the Perspective Extrusion of this object to see how the open-path drawings can be changed.

18

Figure 18-19. *Examples of extruded objects*

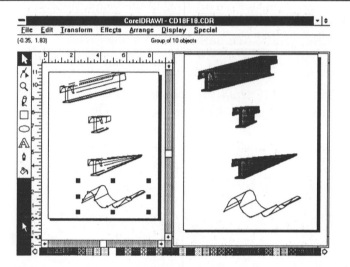

When you are finished, leave CorelDRAW without saving your test files. They can be easily created again.

You can see that the Effects Menu offers many dramatic ways to enhance your text and drawings. Chapter 19 introduces more special effects that you can use with CorelDRAW!, and combines many of the other features you've learned about CorelDRAW!.

19

Combining CorelDRAW!
Features

The previous chapters in this book concentrated on teaching you a specific set of skills. The key word is *concentrated*, for the exercises throughout the book built on skills you had already learned, even as you mastered new ones.

This final chapter, however, takes a different approach. It assumes that you have mastered all of the basic skills in CorelDRAW! and are ready to explore applications that combine many different techniques. In this chapter you will find ideas, and perhaps some of these ideas may inspire you in your own work. However, you will not find a comprehensive catalog of every possible technique or special effect of which CorelDRAW! is capable. The three major exercises that make up this chapter feature text in the sample illustrations, because no other software for the PC allows you to turn text into word pictures as magnificently as CorelDRAW!.

This chapter is composed of three major sections, each containing one exercise in designing a graphic. The title of each section describes the graphic; the introduction to each exercise describes briefly the main CorelDRAW!

techniques that help you create the graphic. If you need to review certain techniques, you can refer back to the chapter or chapters that first introduced these skills. Bon voyage!

Integrating Clip Art and Line Art

In the following exercise, you will design a poster that integrates a clip-art image with line art—in this case, text. You can use this exercise to review text editing, stretch and scale, and outline and fill techniques (Chapters 5, 9, 11, 13, 14, and 15). Since the poster format is 11 inches by 17 inches, you also can brush up on the page setup, printing, and tiling skills you learned in Chapter 17. The end result of your exercise should look similar to Figure 19-7.

Note

The instructions that follow assume that you are using CorelDRAW! version 2.0 or later. If you have an earlier version of CorelDRAW!, you cannot perform this exercise exactly as written. However, you can import the image as NEWSMAKR.PCX and try your hand at merging it with the text described here.

To create the poster:

1. Starting with a blank screen, activate the Show Rulers command in the Display menu. The Snap To Grid command should be inactive for this exercise.

2. Click on Use Mosaic in the Preferences dialog box in the Special menu. If necessary, insert the Clipart disk with the Festive library on it. Select File Open, and the Mosaic screen will appear.

3. Open the Library menu and choose Select Library. Click on the drive and directory where you store your clip art and then on the Festive library. When the visual directory appears, click on MARDIGRA. After a few moments it appears, centered vertically on the page.

4. Select Page Setup from the File menu, select Tabloid (11x17), assure that Portrait is selected, and click on OK. In the Grid Setup dialog box reached from the Display menu, type **17** in the vertical grid origin numeric box to move the vertical zero point to the top of the page, and click on OK to return to the drawing. With the Select tool,

a marquee around the entire piece of clip art and then choose Group from the Arrange menu.

5. Press (SHIFT)-(F9) to activate the preview window, which should be in side-by-side mode. Drag a horizontal guideline down to 3 inches on the vertical ruler and drag two vertical guidelines to 2 inches and 9 inches respectively on the horizontal ruler.

6. Drag the grouped object up and to the left until the upper-left corner of the dotted frame that forms when you drag the object is in the upper-left corner of the guidelines you placed. Drag the lower left boundary marker until the right edge of the object (not the boundary marker) is at 9. This scales the object about 128% (see status line). Your screen at this point should look like Figure 19-1.

7. Save and name the image. Select Save As from the File menu, and type **MASKBALL** in the file text box. Then press (ENTER) or click on the Save command button to save the file and return to the CorelDRAW! screen.

Figure 19-1.   *Incorporating a piece of clip art into a poster*

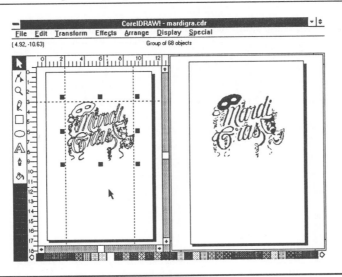

19

8. Select the Zoom-In tool 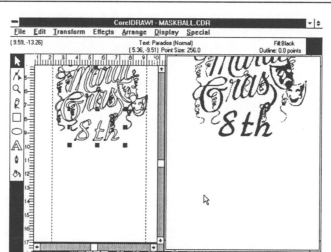 from the Magnification tool fly-out menu, and magnify just the lower half of the page, which contains a large white space.

9. Activate the Text tool and select an insertion point at 9.5 inches vertically and 5.5 inches horizontally. When the Text dialog box appears, type **8th** in the text entry window. Set text attributes to Center Justification, Paradise Normal, 256.0 points. Click on the Spacing command button and set intercharacter spacing to 0.10 em, and select OK twice. The text appears at the insertion point.

10. Activate the Select tool to select the text string automatically. Then, move it to the position shown in Figure 19-2. Press (CTRL)-(S) to save the changes you have made to the file.

11. With the text string still selected, click on the Outline tool and then on the Custom Outline Pen icon in the fly-out menu. The settings for this text string should be: solid line type, sharp corners, butt line caps, Width 0.01 inches, Angle 0 degrees, and Stretch

Figure 19-2.   *Moving "8th" into position*

100%. Both the Behind Fill and Scale With Image options should be inactive. Click on the OK command button to save these settings for the text.

12. Select the Outline tool again, and then click on the Black Fill icon ■ in the fly-out menu to make the text outline black.

13. Click on the Fill tool ⬙ and then on the 40% gray icon in the fly-out menu. This is the fourth icon from the left in the second row. The preview window shows the change in the fill color of the text. Since the outline of the text is black, however, the word stands out. Save your changes by pressing (CTRL)-(S).

14. Activate the Text tool again and select another insertion point at 11 inches vertically and 5.5 inches horizontally. When the Text dialog box appears, type **Annual** in the text entry window, and set text attributes to Center Justification, Paradise Normal, 121.0 points. Click on the Spacing command button and set intercharacter spacing to 0.10 em, then select OK twice. The text string appears at the insertion point.

15. Activate the Select tool and move "Annual" to the location shown in Figure 19-3.

16. With the "Annual" text string still selected, click on the Outline tool and again on the Custom Outline Pen icon. Make sure that the Outline Pen dialog box settings are the same as in step 11 (solid line type, Behind Fill and Scale With Image deactivated, sharp corners, butt line caps, Width 0.01 inch, Angle 0 degrees, and Stretch 100%), and then select OK.

17. Click on the Outline tool icon again, and then click on the black fill icon in the second row of the fly-out menu.

18. Click on the Fill tool icon and again on the black fill icon in the fly-out menu. The text string in the preview window now has a black fill color and a thin black outline.

19. Activate the Text tool once more and select a third insertion point at 12.5 inches vertically and 5.5 inches horizontally. When the Text dialog box appears, type **Masked Ball** in the text entry window. Set text attributes to Center Justification, Paradise Normal, 121.0 points. Click on the Spacing command button and set intercharacter spac-

19

Figure 19-3.   *Moving "Annual" into position beneath "8th"*

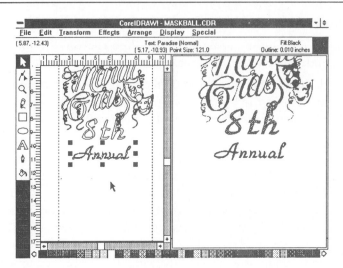

ing to 0.10 ems and interword spacing to 1.10 ems, and then select OK. The text string appears at the insertion point.

20. Activate the Select tool to select the text automatically. Move this text string to the position shown in Figure 19-4.

21. With the "Masked Ball" text string still selected, click on the Copy Style From command in the Edit menu. Activate only the Outline Pen, Outline Color, and Fill checkboxes, and then select OK. When the From? cursor appears, click on the "Annual" text string to copy its outline and fill attributes to the currently selected text string. Make certain to click on the *outline* of the object from which you want to copy the style, or you will see an error message.

22. Activate the Text tool once more and select another insertion point at 14 inches vertically and 2 inches horizontally. When the Text dialog box appears, type **Presented By:** in the text entry window. Set text attributes to Left Justification, Timpani Normal, 42.0 points. Click on the Spacing command button and set intercharacter spac-

Figure 19-4. *Aligning "Masked Ball" with the handle of the mask*

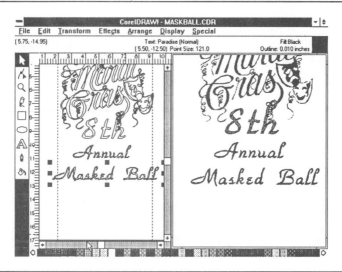

ing to 0.10 em. Reset interword spacing to 1.00 em, and then select OK twice to display the text.

23. Activate the Select tool to select the new text string automatically. Move this text string to the position shown in Figure 19-5.

24. With "Presented By:" still selected, click on the Outline tool and again on the Custom Outline Pen icon in the fly-out menu. Set outline pen attributes as solid line type, Behind Fill and Scale With Image deactivated, sharp corners, butt line caps, Width 0.01 inch, Angle 0 degrees, and Stretch 100%. Click on the OK command button to save these settings for the text.

25. Click on the Outline tool again and then on the black icon in the second row of the fly-out menu.

26. Click on the Fill tool and again on the white fill icon (the third icon from the left). The preview window shows you a white fill for this text string.

19

Figure 19-5.   *Moving "Presented By:" into position*

27. Activate the Text tool once more, and select an insertion point in the lower-right area of the page. When the Text dialog box displays, type **UPB** on the first line of the text entry window, then press (ENTER) and type **Symphony** on the second line. Set text attributes to Center Justification, Timpani Normal, 39.5 points. Click on the Spacing command button. Set intercharacter spacing to 0.10 em and inter-line spacing to 125% of point size, and then select OK.

28. Activate the Select tool to select the new text string automatically. Drag a horizontal guideline under "Presented By:" and drag the "UPB" text string to the position shown in Figure 19-6, aligning it with the line under "Presented By:".

29. Click on the Copy Style From command in the Edit menu. When the Copy Style dialog box appears, make sure that only the Outline Pen and Outline Color options are activated, and then click on OK. Then, click on the "Presented By:" text string to copy its outline attributes to "UPB Symphony."

Figure 19-6.   *Aliging "UPB Symphony" with "Presented By:"*

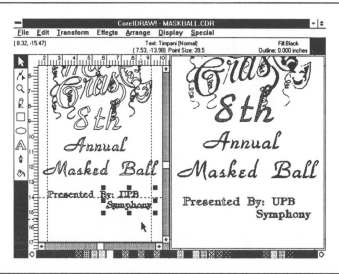

30. Click on the Fill tool and then on the Black Fill icon to fill the selected text with black.

31. Click on the Magnification Tool and again on the Show Page icon and then press (CTRL)-(S) to save your changes. Select Full Screen Preview (F9). Your final picture should look like Figure 19-7.

32. Select New from the File menu to clear the screen.

You may choose to print this oversize poster on your own printer. If you do, be sure to activate the Tile option in the Print Options dialog box. This will result in your poster being printed on four separate sheets, each containing one quarter of the graphic. If your printer does not have enough memory to print this graphic at 11-by-17 inches, try scaling the image down. Then, change the page size to 8 1/2-by-11 inches, using the Page Setup command in the File menu.

To add to your CorelDRAW! applications gallery, continue with the next exercise. There, you will create a color design that takes advantage of the CorelDRAW! features that fit text to a path and mirror images.

19

Figure 19-7.   *The completed poster illustration*

Fitting Text to a Path

If you have followed this book from the first chapter onward, you have learned nearly every available CorelDRAW! drawing technique. One important (and very creative) technique remains: fitting text to a path using the Fit Text To Path command in the Arrange menu. You can cause a text string to follow the outline of *any* object, be it a circle or an ellipse, a rectangle or a square, a line, a curve, a complex curved object, or even another letter that has been converted to curves.

Just how text aligns to a second object depends on the nature of the object. In most cases, the results are straightforward. When you fit text to a rectangle or ellipse, however, the text may appear upside down or along the bottom edge of the object. The placement of the text depends on how you drew the rectangle or ellipse. Figure 19-8 demonstrates how the "corner" from which you start a rectangular or elliptical shape determines where fitted text will appear. To summarize,

- If your starting point for a rectangle or ellipse is the *upper-left* corner or rim, fitted text appears right side up and outside the upper rim.

- If your starting point is the *upper-right* corner or rim, fitted text appears upside down and inside the upper rim.

- If your starting point for a rectangle or ellipse is the *lower-left* corner or rim, fitted text appears right side up and inside the bottom rim.

- If your starting point is the *lower-right* corner or rim, fitted text appears upside down and outside the bottom rim.

Once you have fitted text to an object, you can delete that object without causing the text to lose its newly acquired shape. If you edit text attributes later, however, the text may change its alignment. You can remedy this simply by fitting text to the same path again.

In the following exercise, you will design a stylized "rainbow" image that consists of a series of scaled and aligned wedges. You will then fit the word "Rainbow" to a curve, combine the text string with a background object to create a mask, and overlay the transparent letters on the rainbow colors. The result—after stretching and mirroring the mask and rainbow—is the illustration shown in Figure 19-19. If you have a color monitor, your results will

19

Figure 19-8.   *Starting point determines how text wraps with rectangles and ellipses*

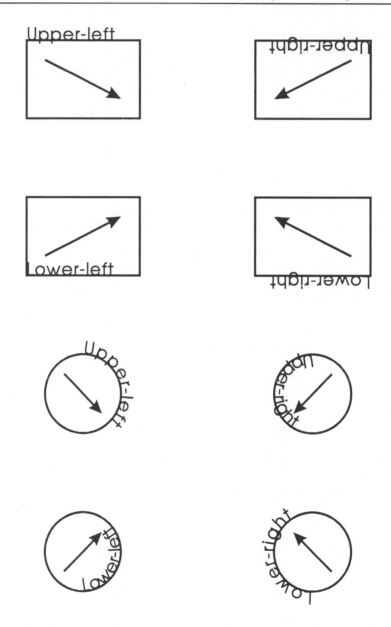

appear more vivid than the one shown in the illustration. If you have a black-and-white display adapter and monitor, you can achieve a similar "rainbow" effect by filling the wedges with the gray shades indicated in parentheses in the following steps.

1. Starting with a blank screen, select Page Setup from the File menu. When the Page Setup dialog box appears, click on the Landscape and Letter option buttons, and then select OK. This results in a page that is 11 inches wide and 8 1/2 inches high.

2. To prepare the CorelDRAW! screen for the exercise, make sure that Snap To Grid is activated and that both Horizontal and Vertical Grid Frequency is set to 8 per inch. Activate the Show Rulers command as well.

3. Set new outline and fill defaults so that all of the objects you draw will be standardized. First, click on the Outline tool and again on the X (for none) icon in the first row of the fly-out menu. The 'New Object' Uniform Fill message appears, asking whether you want to define outline pen settings for objects you haven't drawn yet. Select OK to set no outline as the new default for all objects.

4. Click on the Fill tool and then on the black fill icon. The 'New Object' Uniform Fill message box (Figure 19-9) appears, asking whether you

Figure 19-9.   *The 'New Object' Uniform Fill message box*

19

want to define fill colors for objects you haven't drawn yet. Select OK to define a default fill color of black for new objects.

5. Activate the Ellipse tool ⬭, then position the cursor at the 3 1/4-inch mark on the horizontal ruler and the 6 1/2-inch mark on the vertical ruler. Press and hold (CTRL)-(SHIFT) and drag the mouse downward and to the right until the status line shows a width and height of 3 inches. As you may recall from Chapter 4, the use of (CTRL) and (SHIFT) together results in a circle drawn from the center outward. When you release the mouse button, the circle appears with the node at the top, as shown in Figure 19-10a.

6. Create a 90-degree wedge from this circle, as you learned to do in Chapter 10. Activate the Shaping tool ⬙ and position the Shaping cursor at the node of the circle. To turn the circle into a pie wedge, press and hold (CTRL) and drag the node in a clockwise direction until you reach the 9 o'clock position (90 degrees on the status line). Hold the tip of the Shaping cursor *inside* the rim of the circle as you drag, or you will see an open arc instead of a wedge. Release the mouse button when you reach the 9 o'clock position. The wedge appears, as in Figure 19-10b.

7. Activate the Select tool to select the wedge automatically. Notice that the highlighting box is much larger than the wedge, just as in Figure 19-10c. CorelDRAW! continues to treat the wedge as though it were a full circle.

8. Click again on the outline of the wedge to enter rotate/skew mode. Position the cursor at the arrow markers in the upper-right corner, press and hold (CTRL), and rotate the wedge in a clockwise direction until the status line indicates an angle of −90 degrees. Remember to release the mouse button before you release (CTRL); otherwise, the wedge may not snap to the exact −90-degree angle. The curve of the wedge now faces upward and to the right, as shown in Figure 19-10d.

9. Click again on the wedge outline to return to stretch/scale mode. You are ready to increase the scale of the wedge and leave a copy of the original. Position the cursor at the boundary marker in the upper-right corner and scale the wedge upward and to the right, until the status line value reaches approximately 116.7%. When you

Figure 19-10.   *Creating a pie wedge from a circle and rotating it*

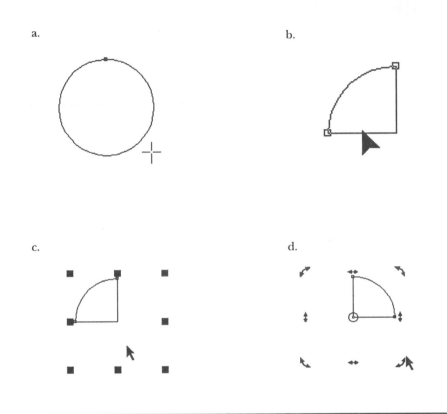

a.

b.

c.

d.

reach the desired point, continue to hold the mouse button, but press the right mouse button or the ⊙ key on the numeric keypad to leave a copy of the original. Then, release the mouse button. The original wedge remains in position, and a scaled version overlays it, as in Figure 19-11.

10. Press (CTRL)-(R) (the Repeat key combination) five times to create five additional wedges, each larger than the previous one. Your screen should show a total of seven wedges, resembling Figure 19-12.

Figure 19-11.   *Scaling a wedge and leaving a copy of the original*

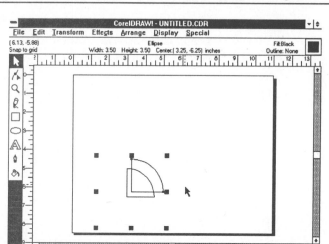

Figure 19-12.   *A series of scaled wedges created using the Repeat key combination*

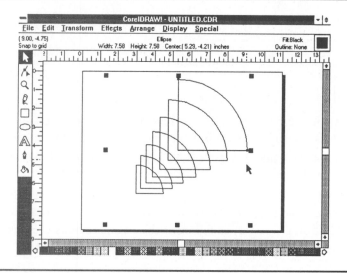

11. Your next step is to align the wedges so that they form one-half of a rainbow. Click on the Select All command in the Edit menu to select all seven wedges, and then select the Align command in the Arrange menu. When the Align dialog box appears, click on both the Horizontal Center and Vertical Center option buttons, on the Align to Center of Page checkbox, and then select OK. The wedges realign with a common corner point in the center of the page, as shown in Figure 19-13.

12. With the seven wedges still selected, click on the Reverse Order command in the Arrange menu. You will not see a visible change at this point, but you have positioned the larger wedges in the back and the smaller wedges in the front. When you turn on the preview window later in the exercise and begin to assign fill colors to the wedges, you will see each wedge as a ribbon-like band.

13. Select the Save As command from the File menu. When the Save As dialog box appears, type **RAINBOW1**, and then press (ENTER) or click on Save.

Figure 19-13. *Wedges aligned using Horizontal and Vertical Center options*

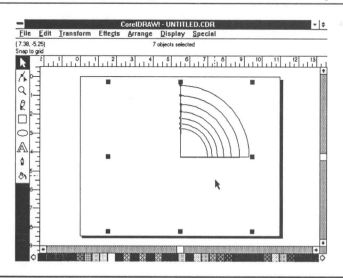

19

14. To design the other half of the rainbow, you simply create a horizontal mirror image of the currently selected image. Click on the Stretch & Mirror command in the Transform menu to access the Stretch & Mirror dialog box. Then activate both the Horz Mirror command button and the Leave Original checkbox, and then select OK. The mirror image of the seven wedges appears and fits tightly against the original group of wedges, as shown in Figure 19-14.

15. You can now begin to assign fill colors to the wedges of the "rainbow." Turn on the preview window and make sure that it is in side-by-side format; for greater convenience, activate the Preview Selected Only command in the Display menu. Adjust magnification to fit-in-window by clicking on the fit-in-window icon in the Magnification tool fly-out menu.

16. Deselect all of the wedges by clicking on any white space. Then, select both the largest wedge on the left half of the "rainbow" and the smallest wedge on the right half. To select them, click on each of their curve outlines while holding (SHIFT). Just as in Figure 19-15, the editing window looks as though all of the wedges were selected,

Figure 19-14.   *Original seven wedges with a horizontal mirror image*

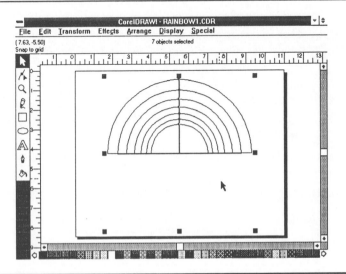

Figure 19-15.   *Selecting pairs of wedges with Preview Selected Only in effect*

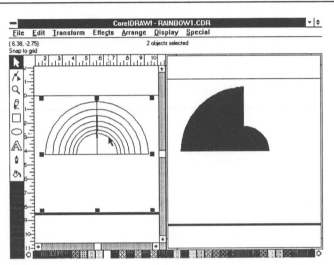

because the highlighting box of the largest wedge surrounds all of the objects. The preview window, however, shows you that only two wedges are selected.

17. With the two wedges selected, click on the Fill tool and again on the Uniform Fill icon. When the Uniform Fill dialog box displays, select Process color, click on Others if you are in the Palette, and set color values to 100% magenta, 75% yellow, and 10% black. Select OK; the two opposite wedges now redisplay with a red fill, the hue of which varies depending on whether you have an EGA or VGA display adapter. (If you have a black-and-white monitor, set black to 80% and leave all other colors at 0%.)

18. Deselect the previous wedges. Then select the second largest wedge on the left half of the "rainbow" and the second smallest wedge on the right half, and then access the Uniform Fill dialog box once more. If you have a color monitor, set process color values to 100% magenta and 100% yellow, and then select OK. The two wedges now show a bright orange fill. (If you have a black-and-white monitor, set black to 40% and leave all other colors at 0%.)

19

19. Continue in the same way with the next five pairs of wedges. If you have a color monitor, assign colors as follows: third pair, 100% yellow; fourth pair, 40% cyan and 60% yellow; fifth pair, 100% cyan, 40% yellow, and 20% black; sixth pair, 100% cyan, 100% magenta, and 10% black; seventh pair, 100% magenta and 50% black. (If you have a black-and-white monitor, assign 15% black to the third pair, 40% black to the fourth, 30% black to the fifth, 75% black to the sixth, and 100% black to the seventh.) When you are finished, turn off the Preview Selected Only feature. The two halves of the rainbow show an opposite sequence of colors, as you can see by the black-and-white representation in Figure 19-16.

20. Click on the Select All command in the Edit menu to select all 14 wedges, and then apply the Group command from the Arrange menu. This prevents you from moving or editing an individual wedge accidentally, apart from the group.

21. Press (SHIFT)-(F9) to turn off the preview window for the next few steps of the exercise. Click on the Show Page icon in the Magnification tool fly-out menu to display the full page.

Figure 19-16.   *Opposite color sequences in each half of the rainbow*

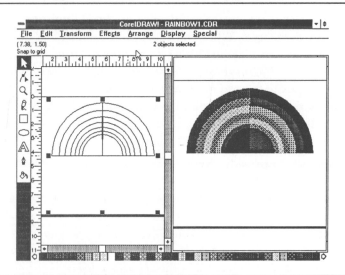

22. Now you are ready to prepare the text that will eventually overlay the rainbow as a transparent mask. First, activate the Ellipse tool and position the drawing cursor at the 2 1/2-inch mark on the horizontal ruler and the 1-inch mark on the vertical ruler. Drag the mouse downward and to the right and draw a circle 6 inches in diameter. Remember to use (CTRL) (but *not* (SHIFT)) to obtain a circle rather than an ellipse. The circle overlays most of the "rainbow" for now, but you will delete it when it has served its purpose.

23. Activate the Text tool and select an insertion point in any white space on the page. When the Text dialog box appears, type **Rainbow** in the text entry window. Set text attributes to Aardvark Bold, 105.0 points, and a Justification of None. Click on the Spacing command button and set intercharacter spacing to 0.10 em, and then select OK to display the text on the page.

24. Activate the Select tool to select the text string automatically. Use (SHIFT) to also select the circle you have just drawn. Then, press (CTRL)-(F) or click on the Fit Text To Path command in the Arrange menu. After a few seconds, the text appears right side up but on the right side of the circle, as shown in Figure 19-17.

25. Deselect the text to leave only the circle selected, and then press (DEL) to delete the circle. The text retains its new shape.

26. Double-click on the outline of the text to enter rotate/skew mode. Position the cursor over the arrow marker at the bottom-right corner, and then rotate the text counterclockwise by an angle of 67 degrees. When you release the mouse button, the text redisplays right side up but off-center from the rainbow.

27. Click again on the outline of the text string to leave rotate/skew mode and return to normal select mode. Center the text on the rainbow and then fill the text with white by clicking on the Fill tool and again on the white icon in the second row of the fly-out menu.

28. Create the rectangle that will become the background of the mask. Activate the Rectangle tool □ and position the drawing cursor at the zero point on both the horizontal and vertical rulers. From this point, draw a rectangle 7 3/4 inches wide and 3 3/4 inches high, dragging downward and to the right.

19

Figure 19-17. *Fitting text to a circle*

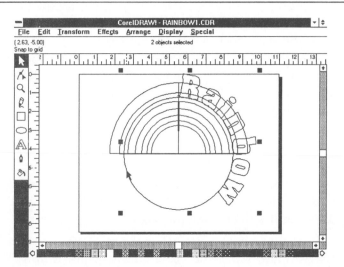

29. Press the spacebar to select the rectangle automatically. Give the rectangle a transparent fill by clicking on the Fill tool and then on the icon ⊠ in the fly-out menu. Make the edge of the rectangle also transparent by clicking on the Outline tool and again on the icon on the first row of the fly-out menu.

30. Select the text string and move it on top of the rectangle. Position it so that the bottom of the text string is 1/4 inch above the lower edge of the rectangle.

31. To center the text horizontally on the rectangle, select both objects, click on the Align command in the Arrange menu, and choose the Horizontal Center option button. Select OK to leave the Alignment dialog box and redisplay the newly aligned objects.

32. With both the text and the rectangle still selected, move both objects into the empty space at the bottom of the page, out of the way of the rainbow wedges. Then, select the Reverse Order command from the Arrange menu to place the text behind the rectangle.

33. Turn on the preview window. You cannot see the rectangle because it is transparent, and you cannot see the text because it has a white fill and is behind the rectangle. With the text and rectangle both selected in the editing window, click on the Combine command in the Arrange menu. The two objects reverse colors when they combine, and the text becomes a transparent "hole" in the white rectangle.

34. Move the newly combined object back over the grouped rainbow wedges and align the bottom edge of the curve object with the bottom edge of the wedges.

The object that is in the background when you combine two objects determines the fill color of the combined object. If you see white letters over a transparent rectangle, you forgot to place the text behind the rectangle. Select Undo from the Edit menu, use the Reverse Order command in the Arrange menu to bring the rectangle to the foreground, and then combine the two objects again.

Tip

35. Select Full Screen Preview. With the white rectangle invisible against the page, all you can see are the rainbow colors behind the transparent text string, as shown in Figure 19-18.

36. Return to a side-by-side preview window and then adjust viewing magnification to fit-in-window. Select both the combined object and the wedges and apply the Group command from the Arrange menu.

37. Create a mirror image of the grouped object. With the group still selected, click on the Stretch & Mirror command from the Transform menu. When the Stretch & Mirror dialog box appears, click on *both* the Horz Mirror and Vert mirror command buttons and make sure that a checkmark appears in the Leave Original checkbox. Select OK; an upside down and backwards version of the "Rainbow" text displays beneath the original, as shown in the full-screen preview in Figure 19-19. This object is selected automatically in the editing window.

38. Press (CTRL)-(S) to save the changes to your work, and then select New from the File menu to clear your screen.

The main emphases in this last exercise have been on fitting text to a path, working with color effects, creating a mask, aligning objects, repeating

19

Figure 19-18.   *Rainbow colors appearing as fill through the mask object*

Figure 19-19.   *Rainbow with vertically flipped mirror image*

operations, and creating mirror images. In the next and last sample application, you can achieve 3-D effects using fountain and contrasting fills, outlines, and repeated scalings.

Polishing Your Skills

The "FAX" image in Figure 19-27 has a vibrant, 3-D look; the graphic represents the power of facsimile to quite literally "broadcast" to the world. Several special effects techniques contribute to the dynamic quality of the image:

- Text fitted to a curve
- Text objects with drop shadows (shadows placed behind and offset from the original)
- A "globe" with an off-center radial fountain fill
- Repeated duplication and expansion of a text string
- Judicious use of contrasting fills
- Inclusion of a backdrop that makes the image seem to burst beyond its boundaries

You already have practiced the basic skills that make all of these special effects possible. In the exercise that follows, you will recreate this image, using the Leave Original and Repeat keys, fountain fill and node editing techniques, and the Duplicate, Fit Text To Path, Group, and Page Setup commands. For a review of shadow and fountain fill techniques, see Chapter 15.

1. Starting with a blank screen, select Page Setup from the File menu. When the Page Setup dialog box appears, make sure that Landscape and Letter options are still selected, and then select OK. Turn off the Preview Window.

2. To prepare the CorelDRAW! screen for the exercise, activate the Snap To Grid command in the Display menu, select the Grid Setup command, set both Horizontal and Vertical Grid Frequency to 8 per

19

inch and set the Vertical grid origin to 8.5 inches. Activate the Show Rulers command as well.

3. Change the default outline type to a hairline by clicking on the Outline tool and then on the hairline icon in the first row of the fly-out menu. When the 'New Objects' dialog box appears to ask whether you want this outline type applied to all future objects, click on OK.

4. Change the default outline color to black by clicking on the Outline tool and then on the black icon in the second row of the fly-out menu. The 'New Objects' dialog box appears once again; select OK as you did in the previous step.

5. Create a small circle to which you will fit text. To do this, activate the Ellipse tool and position the crosshair cursor in the center of the page at 5.5 inches horizontal and 4.25 inches vertical. Press and hold (SHIFT) and (CTRL) and draw a perfect circle 0.75 inches in diameter. When you complete the circle, remember to release the mouse button before you release (SHIFT) and (CTRL) to ensure that you create a circle rather than an ellipse.

6. Now enter the text that you will fit to this circle. Activate the Text tool and select an insertion point about an inch above the circle. The exact location does not matter, because when you invoke the Fit Text To Path command later, the text will snap to the circle no matter where it is. When the Text dialog box displays, type **FAX** in all capital letters in the text entry window. Set text attributes to a justification of None, Frankfurt Gothic Heavy, Normal, 30.0 points. Click on the OK command to display your text on the page.

7. Press the spacebar to activate the Select tool; the text string is selected automatically, since it was the last object you drew. While you press and hold (SHIFT), select the circle as well.

8. With both objects selected, press (CTRL)-(J) or click on the Fit Text To Path command in the Arrange menu. The text wraps around outside of the circle, centering itself around the upper-right segment of the rim, as shown in Figure 19-20. (The image on your screen is much smaller.)

Figure 19-20.   *Magnified view of text fitted to a small circle*

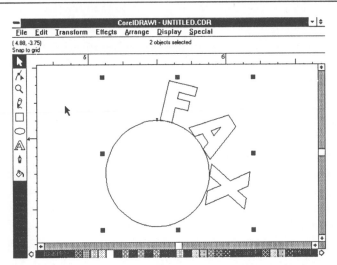

9. Deselect the text string using (SHIFT), and then press (DEL) to delete the circle. The text remains curved, even though the circle is no longer there.

10. Double-click on the text string to enter rotate/skew mode, and rotate the text by 26 degrees in a counterclockwise direction.

11. Move the text to the lower-left corner of the page.

12. Now you are ready to begin creating a text pattern. Turn off the Snap to Grid and, with the Select tool still active, position the cursor at the upper-right corner boundary marker of the text object and begin to scale the object from this point. As soon as the dotted outline box appears, click the right mouse button or press and release + on the numeric keypad (to leave a copy of the original). Continue scaling the text until the status line indicates a value of approximately 127%. Then, release the left mouse button. A larger-

19

scaled version of the text string appears on top of and offset from the original. You can see the proportions more clearly if you change magnification to fit-in-window temporarily.

13. Select the Show Page icon from the Magnification tool fly-out menu to return to a full-page view. Then press (CTRL)-(R), the Repeat key, ten times, to repeat the scaling and duplication of the text. Ten scaled replicas of the text string overlay one another, each one larger than the last. The last text string exceeds the boundaries of the page, as shown in Figure 19-21.

14. Leaving the most recently created text string selected, click on the Preference command in the Special menu. Make certain that the Place Duplicate values are both at 0.25 inches, and then select OK. These values determine the placement of a duplicate object relative to the original.

15. Press (CTRL)-(D) to create an exact duplicate of the top text string, offset 1/4 inch above and to the right of the original. The duplicate is selected as soon as it appears.

Figure 19-21.   *Scaled and repeated text strings exceeding the page boundaries*

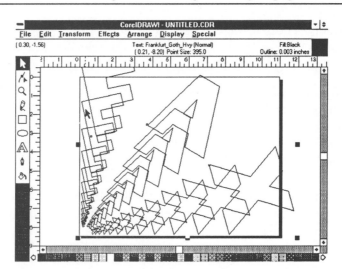

16. Turn on the preview window. All of the text strings appear with black fills. Click on the Select All command in the Edit menu and then on the Group command in the Arrange menu to group all of the text strings. Then, select the white fill icon in the Fill tool fly-out menu. The text strings redisplay in the preview window with a fill of white, making it easier to distinguish them from one another.

17. With all text strings still selected, click on the Outline tool and then on the Custom Outline Pen icon to access the Outline Pen dialog box. Change the settings to match the ones in Figure 19-22: Scale With Image active, Width 0.01 inch, Angle 0%, and Stretch 100%. Then select OK. The text strings redisplay with a fine outline of uniform width.

18. Ungroup and deselect all text strings, and then select only the last text string you created (the offset duplicate on top). Click on the Fill tool and again on the Fountain Fill icon D to access the Fountain Fill dialog box. Make sure the Spot color option button is selected and assign a start color of white (Black, Tint 0%) and an end color

Figure 19-22.   *Outline Pen settings for "FAX" text strings*

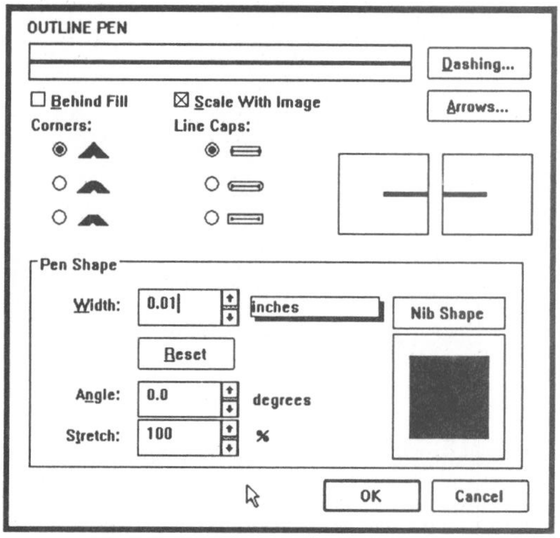

19

of black (Black, Tint 100%). Choose a linear fountain fill and an angle of 45 degrees. Click on OK to make this fill color take effect.

19. Now create a drop-shadow effect. Press (TAB) to select the text string in the layer just below the text string containing a fountain fill. Assign a fill of black to this object by clicking on the Black Fill icon ■ in the Fill tool fly-out menu. The preview window shows the result of your selection, as in Figure 19-23.

20. Continue pressing (TAB) to select each text string in the reverse order from which it was created. Fill the text strings in the following sequence, starting with the largest text string after the drop shadow: 80% black, 70% black, 60% black, 50% black, 40%, 30%, 20%, and 10% black. Fill one more text string with 10% black and the remaining (smallest) text strings with white. You can use the icons in the Fill tool fly-out menu to select these shades quickly. The resulting gradation of fills and the drop shadow make the repeated text strings seem to leap out of the screen, as shown in Figure 19-24.

Figure 19-23.   *Drop-shadow effect using duplicated text and black fill*

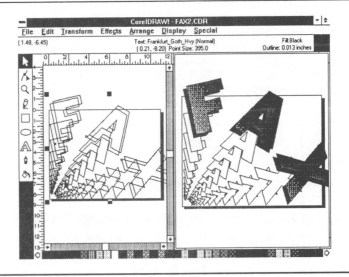

Figure 19-24. *Gradation of fills, leading to a 3-D effect*

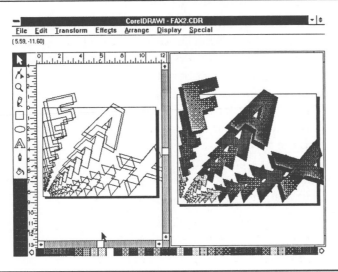

21. To group all text strings so that you cannot separate them acciden-tally, click on Select All in the Edit menu, and then on the Group command in the Arrange menu. Then, move the group upward and away from the left side of the page. You will bring the group back later, but for now you need room to create more objects.

22. Activate the Ellipse tool and position it 4 1/2 inches from the top of the page and 3/4 of an inch from the left margin. Press and hold (CTRL) and draw a circle 3 inches in diameter, starting from the upper-left area of the rim. Use the status line as a guide.

23. Turn the circle into a 3-D globe by giving it a radial fountain fill. To do this, activate the Select tool to select the circle automatically, and then click on the Fill tool and again on the Fountain Fill icon. When the Fountain Fill dialog box appears, select the Spot method, change the start color to black (Black, Tint 100%) and the end color to white (Black, Tint 0%). Select a radial fountain fill, but leave the other settings unaltered. Select OK to make the fountain fill take effect.

19

The globe reappears with a white highlight in the center and the fill gradually darkens toward the rim.

24. Prepare to create an off-center highlight so that the light source seems to be coming from above and right of the globe. Activate the Pencil tool ⎁, and draw a very short line segment above and to the right of the globe. Select both the line segment and the globe and click on the Combine command in the Arrange menu to combine these into one object. Redo the fountain fill by repeating step 23. Whenever the preview window redraws from now on, CorelDRAW! extends the first stage of the fountain fill as far as the line segment, as shown in Figure 19-25. This means that you can control the placement of the highlight on the globe by moving the nodes of the line segment with the Shaping tool.

Figure 19-25.   *Changing the center of a radial fountain fill by combining line segment with globe*

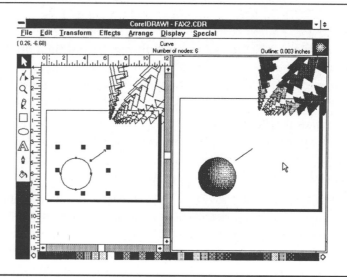

25. If you wish to change the placement of the highlight on the globe, activate the Shaping tool and move the uppermost node of the line segment in a clockwise or counterclockwise direction. You can move either or both nodes; experiment until you find the placement you want.

26. Now, make the line segment invisible. Activate the Select tool to select the combined object automatically, and then click on the Outline tool and again on the white outline fill icon in the second row of the fly-out menu. The line segment seems to disappear from the preview screen, but you can still use it to manipulate the highlight on the globe.

27. Create a rectangle that will form a backdrop for the rest of the image. Activate the Rectangle tool and begin a rectangle at the 1-inch mark on the horizontal ruler and the 1 1/2-inch mark on the vertical ruler. Extend the rectangle downward and to the right until you reach the 7 1/2-inch mark on the horizontal ruler and the 7 1/4-inch mark on the vertical ruler, and then release the mouse button. The preview window shows that this object lies on top of all the other objects, obscuring them from your view.

28. Activate the Select tool to select the rectangle automatically, and then click on the To Back command in the Arrange menu. Now, the globe appears as the top layer.

29. Assign a black outline of 2.0 fractional points and a fill of 20% gray to the rectangle.

30. To make the globe stand out in 3-D from the background, select it and assign an outline 0.01-inch wide, using the Outline Pen dialog box.

31. Select the grouped text strings and move them on top of the globe so that they seem to be emerging directly from the highlight, as shown in Figure 19-26. To make certain that the text strings are the top layer object, click on the To Front command. This also hides the line segment that you used as a "handle" to change the center of the globe's fountain fill.

19

Figure 19-26.   *Grouped text strings overlaid on the globe highlight for 3-D effect*

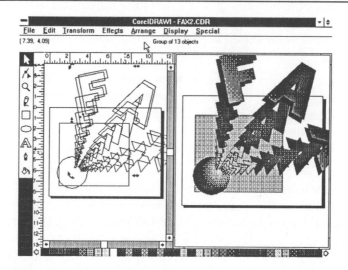

32. Adjust viewing magnification to fit-in-window by clicking on the fit-in-window icon in the Magnification tool fly-out menu. With the grouped object still selected, scale the text strings down until the status line displays a value of approximately 47%. Select Full-Screen Preview. Thanks to the insertion of the background rectangle, the text strings still seem to thrust outward in 3-D, as shown in Figure 19-27.

33. Click on the Select All command in the Edit menu and then on the Group command in the Arrange menu to group all of the objects in the image.

34. Select Save As from the File menu. When the Save As dialog box appears, type **FAXTRANS**, and then press (ENTER) or click on Save.

35. Select New from the File menu to clear the screen.

Figure 19-27.   *"FAX" illustration using fountain fill, drop shadows, and a background frame to enhance 3-D effects*

If you have performed all three of the exercises in this chapter, you are well on the way to understanding how to combine many different Corel-DRAW! features, tricks, and techniques. Perhaps these exercises have stimulated you to create your own original designs, or given you new ideas for embellishing existing ones. Whatever your field, your work in this tutorial has given you the tools to create more effective illustrations, documents, presentations, and designs. CorelDRAW! makes it all possible!

19

A

Installing CorelDRAW!

This appendix guides you through the process of installing CorelDRAW!. If you have installed your software already, you do not need to use this appendix.

This section contains detailed instructions on installing CorelDRAW!. Before you install CorelDRAW!, you must install Microsoft Windows and ensure that it is working properly. Refer to the documentation that came with your Microsoft Windows software for full instructions on installing Windows correctly.

System Requirements

Before you begin the installation procedure, review the hardware and software requirements explained in this section. You can help ensure trouble-free operation of CorelDRAW! by checking to see that your system meets all requirements.

Computers and Hard Drive Space

Your computer should be an IBM AT- or PS/2- compatible system (based on an 80286, 80386, or 80486 microprocessor) with a hard disk drive and at least one floppy disk drive. Your hard disk drive should have at least 12 megabytes (MB) of space available before you install CorelDRAW!. Of this amount, at least 3 MB should remain free *after* you have installed the software. This disk space is needed because CorelDRAW! generates large temporary files with the extension TMP each time you run the software. The size of these files can vary, depending on the complexity of your graphics and the number of bitmapped images you import (each bitmap generates a temporary file). However, you should ensure that the temporary files have plenty of room to work.

If you have less than 3 MB of hard drive space available after you install CorelDRAW!, consider removing any unneeded applications or files. Alternatively, you might choose not to install the CorelDRAW! sample files (which take about 1.1 MB) and/or the Symbol Library (which takes about 800 KB) that are provided with your software. You need a few of these files to perform some of the exercises in the book, but you can copy them to your hard drive individually as they are required. The CorelDRAW! space requirement assumes you will *not* install the clip-art library on your hard disk.

Monitors and Display Adapters

Microsoft Windows, not CorelDRAW!, determines which monitor and display adapter choices are available to you. Not all graphics adapters work well with CorelDRAW!, however. For best operation, you should have an EGA, VGA, Hercules, or other display adapter that has a vertical resolution of 350 dpi or greater. If you wish to preview your images in color, you need an EGA or VGA display adapter and compatible monitor.

Drawing Devices

You must have a mouse or another drawing device, such as a graphics tablet, in order to run CorelDRAW!. The Setup program you run when you install Microsoft Windows lists the drawing devices that Windows supports. If you use a graphics tablet instead of a mouse, choose one that has the activation button on the side rather than on the top. This type of design gives you the best results because it minimizes unwanted movement on the screen.

This book assumes that most users work with a mouse instead of some other type of drawing device. References to a mouse therefore apply to any drawing device.

Output Devices

Using the Print and Export commands in the File menu, you can output your CorelDRAW! images to paper (standard printers) or to formats used by film recorders and slide generation equipment. Chapter 16, "Importing and Exporting Files," discusses output to 35mm slide generation or presentation equipment in greater detail. If you normally print your images to paper, however, you will achieve the best results with the following types of printers:

- PostScript printers, imagesetters, and PostScript controller boards and plug-in cartridges licensed by Adobe Systems
- HP LaserJet series or 100% compatible printers
- HP PaintJet and DeskJet printers

Although Windows supports other printers as well, many of these cannot reproduce complex CorelDRAW! images exactly as expected. In addition, a few of the most complex CorelDRAW! features can be output on PostScript printers only. For more information on printer limitations, see Chapter 17, "Printing and Processing Your Images."

Memory Requirements

Unlike earlier versions, CorelDRAW! 2.0 can and does make use of extended memory. Therefore, while the minimum required memory is 1 MB, it is recommended that your system have 2 MB or more.

Operating System and Windows Requirements

You need DOS 3.1 or later and Microsoft Windows 3.0 or later to run CorelDRAW!.

Installing the Software

The INSTALL program for CorelDRAW! 2.0 installs program files, fonts, and (at your option) sample files and the Symbol Library onto your hard disk. This requires three or four disks, depending on whether you are using 5 1/4-inch or 3 1/2-inch disks. You also received four or five additional disks containing clip-art images from a variety of clip-art vendors. The INSTALL program does not install the clip art for you. If you have sufficient space available on your hard drive, you can copy the clip-art files onto separate directories, and then import the images while running CorelDRAW!. Chapter 16 discusses how to import these and other clip-art files.

The directions that the INSTALL program gives you vary slightly from version to version. The following step-by-step summary is for Version 2.0 or 2.01; if your procedure seems different, follow the on-screen instructions exactly. Before you begin, take note of the drive and directory where you have installed Microsoft Windows, and decide where you want to install CorelDRAW!. Also, make sure that you are at a DOS prompt, for example C:\>.

Caution

You should not try to install CorelDRAW! from within Windows. If you are in Windows, exit to DOS before installing CorelDRAW!

1. Insert CorelDRAW! Disk 1 into the floppy drive from which you want to install CorelDRAW!. This book assumes that you are installing the software from drive A, but you can use any drive.

2. Type **a:** and press (ENTER). (If you are installing CorelDRAW! from a different floppy drive, type that drive name instead of "a:".) Type **install** and press (ENTER). INSTALL provides some preliminary information on the screen.

3. Read the preliminary information. When you are ready to proceed, press (ENTER) to continue or type **Q** to quit without installing the program. Some versions of CorelDRAW! (not 2.0 or 2.01) have an additional information screen. You can exit the additional screen using the same commands.

4. INSTALL now asks where you have installed Microsoft Windows and proposes C:\WINDOWS as the default path. To accept

C:\WINDOWS, press (ENTER). If you have installed Windows in a different drive and/or directory, type the path name in full and then press (ENTER).

5. INSTALL asks you at this point for the name of the destination directory where you want to install CorelDRAW! and proposes a default path. To accept the pathname offered, press (ENTER). If you want to give your CorelDRAW! directory another name, type the path name in full and then press (ENTER).

6. INSTALL allows you to check to make sure you have specified the correct Windows and/or CorelDRAW! directory. In some versions of CorelDRAW!, you can type **D** if you make an error, and INSTALL will allow you to type an alternative path name. If the path name that appears on the screen is correct and you want to continue, press (ENTER).

7. Depending on your software version, INSTALL may ask you whether you are upgrading from an earlier version or installing CorelDRAW! for the first time. (Versions 1.11 and later allow you to choose whether to install the sample files only, without software.) Follow the on-screen instructions to respond properly.

8. INSTALL now asks you to specify the drive you are using as the source drive for the installation and proposes drive A. If this is correct, press (ENTER) to begin installing the software. If drive A is not correct, type the drive name you are using and press (ENTER). INSTALL first decompresses pattern files, then executable files in alphabetical order and copies them to your hard drive.

9. When INSTALL has installed the necessary files from Disk 1, it prompts you to remove Disk 1 and insert Disk 2. Insert the requested disk and then press (ENTER). Follow the same procedure when Disk 3 is requested.

10. INSTALL then asks whether you want to copy the Symbol Library and the sample drawing files from Corel Systems. If you are installing a version earlier than 1.11, these files occupy approximately 600K of hard disk space. If you are installing version 1.11 or later, the sample files require 1.1 MB of space. Version 2.0's and 2.01's Symbol Library (not available in earlier versions) takes an additional

800 KB. If you want to install the Symbol Library and you have the required space available, type **L** and press (ENTER). INSTALL will then decompress and copy a number of .WFN files to your hard disk. During this process, you will be asked to remove Disk 3 and insert Disk 4. When INSTALL has completed transferring the Symbol Library, you will again be shown the screen that asks if you want to install the Symbol Library and sample files. If you want to install the sample files (they are used in this book), type **S** and press (ENTER). INSTALL then creates a subdirectory under the CorelDRAW! directory on your hard disk, called SAMPLES, and copies the sample files there. When INSTALL has completed transferring the sample files, you will again be shown the screen that asks if you want to install the Symbol Library and sample files. Choose Exit Install by typing **E** and pressing (ENTER). You can also choose to not install either or both of the sample files and the Symbol Library and exit INSTALL by typing **E** and pressing (ENTER).

11. In some versions of the software (not 2.0 or 2.01), INSTALL now displays a screen of information about third-party clip-art images provided on separate disks and suggests how to copy them onto your hard disk manually.

12. INSTALL next asks you to reinstall Disk 1. Remove Disk 4, insert Disk 1, and press (ENTER). You will get a message that says, "The Corel Applications group will be created by installing Windows. Press any key to continue." When you do so, INSTALL loads Windows and builds the Corel Applications group. When it is complete you will get a message that says: "The Corel Applications group has been successfully created. Please exit Windows to continue."

13. Click on OK (move the mouse cursor to OK and press and release the left mouse button) or press (ENTER). Double-click on the Program Manager icon (move the mouse cursor to the icon in the lower left of your screen and press and release the left mouse button twice in rapid succession). The Program Manager window will open and you'll see the new Corel Applications window as shown Figure A-1.

Figure 1-1. *Corel Applications group window*

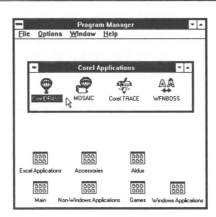

Double-click on the Program Manager's Control-menu box (upper-left corner) and then click on OK to leave Windows. Finally, you'll get a message that INSTALL is now complete.

This completes the automatic installation procedure. If you would like to install the sample clip-art images on your hard drive, you can do so manually. Make a directory for clip art, and then copy the files into that directory.

You should also decide whether you want to make automatic backup copies of your drawings when you run CorelDRAW!. If you do, use Windows Notepad to edit the [CDrawConfig] section of your CORELDRW.INI file so that a line in that section reads "MakeBackupWhenSave=1." If you do not want CorelDRAW! to make backup copies of your illustrations, edit this line so that it reads "MakeBackupWhenSave=0."

Creating a Directory

You need a directory in which to store the drawings created with CorelDRAW!. When you installed Windows and CorelDRAW!, directories were automatically created in which the program, font, and other files that came with Windows and CorelDRAW! are stored. While you could use these directories to store your CorelDRAW! drawings, it is unwise to do so for two reasons. First, when you get an update to Windows or CorelDRAW! you will want to remove the old program files and replace them with the new ones. The easiest way to do that is to erase the entire directory with a single command. If your drawing files were in the directory at the time, you would lose them. Second, if you want to do some file maintenance with either DOS or the Windows File Manager, the large number of product-related files will make looking for drawing files difficult.

Therefore, create a new directory now to hold your drawing files. You can name your directory anything you want as long as the name is from one to eight characters long and does not include the following characters:

. " / \ [ ] : | = + ; , * ?

This book will use DRAW as the example directory in which drawings will be stored. Your directory can be a full directory off of the root directory or a subdirectory off of either the Windows or the CorelDRAW! directory. For simplicity this book will assume that the DRAW directory is a full directory off of the root directory. Its path then is \DRAW. Use these instructions to create this directory:

1. Type **cd** and press (ENTER) to make sure you are in the root directory.

2. Type **md\draw** and press (ENTER) to create the new DRAW directory.

The only remaining step is to start CorelDRAW! and begin using it. Do that now by following the directions in Chapter 1, "Getting Acquainted with CorelDRAW!".

B

Keyboard and Mouse Shortcuts

This appendix contains an alphabetical listing of the CorelDRAW! operations that you can perform using keyboard shortcuts. Descriptions of the tasks you may wish to perform appear in the left column, and their keyboard shortcuts appear in the right column.

This quick reference list does not include the CorelDRAW! operations that you perform using the mouse only. However, if the word "click" or "drag" appears in the right column as part of the key combination, you must click or drag the mouse to complete the specified action. If a particular tool must be active in order to carry out the action, its icon appears within the description in the left column.

Action	Key Combination
Activate Ellipse tool	F7
Activate Fill Color dialog box	SHIFT-F11
Activate Fountain Fill dialog box	F11
Activate Outline Color dialog box	SHIFT-F12

Action	Key Combination
Activate Outline Pen dialog box	(F12)
Activate Pencil tool	(F5)
Activate previous tool (▶ active)	(SPACEBAR)
Activate Rectangle tool	(F6)
Activate Select tool (other tool active)	(SPACEBAR)
Activate Shaping tool	(F10)
Activate Text tool	(F8)
Activate Zoom-In tool	(F2)
Activate Zoom-Out tool	(F3)
Add New Envelope	(ALT)-(C) + (N)
Add New Perspective	(ALT)-(C) + (P)
Align multiple selected objects (▶ active)	(CTRL)-(A), (ALT)-(A) + (A)
Align selected text with baseline (▶ active)	(CTRL)-(Z), (ALT)-(A) + (L)
Arc, convert circle to, in 15-degree increments (◢ active)	(CTRL) + drag node outside circle
Auto-Update preview window (with preview window active)	(ALT)-(D) + (A)
Back one layer	(PGDN), (ALT)-(A) + (N)
Blend	(CTRL)-(B), (ALT)-(C) + (B)
Break apart selected combined objects (▶ active)	(CTRL)-(K), (ALT)-(A) + (K)
Clear Envelope	(ALT)-(C) + (C)
Clear Perspective	(ALT)-(C) + (L)

Action	Key Combination
Clear Transformations to selected object (⬆ active)	(ALT)-(T) + (C)
Combine selected objects (⬆ active)	(CTRL)-(C), (ALT)-(A) + (C)
Control Panel, open	(ALT)-(F) + (C)
Convert selected object to Curves (⬆ active)	(CTRL)-(V), (ALT)-(A) + (V)
Copy Envelope From	(ALT)-(C) + (R)
Copy Perspective From	(ALT)-(C) + (F)
Copy selected object to clipboard (⬆ active)	(CTRL) + (INS) , (ALT)-(E) + (C)
Copy Style From one object to another	(ALT)-(E) + (S)
Create Arrow	(ALT)-(S) + (A)
Create Pattern	(ALT)-(S) + (C)
Cut selected object to clipboard (⬆ active)	(SHIFT) + (DEL)
Delete (clear) newly drawn or selected object	(DEL), (ALT)-(E) + (L)
Dialog box, move to next field in,	(TAB)
Dialog box, move to previous field in,	(SHIFT)-(TAB)
Draw circle (⬭ active)	(CTRL) + drag
Draw circle from center outward (⬭ active)	(CTRL)-(SHIFT) + drag
Draw ellipse from center outward (⬭ active)	(SHIFT) + drag
Draw line in increments of 15-degree angles (✎ active)	(CTRL) + click

Action	Key Combination
Draw rectangle from center outward (□ active)	SHIFT + drag
Draw square (□ active)	CTRL + drag
Draw square from center outward (□ active)	CTRL-SHIFT + drag
Duplicate selected object (▶ active)	CTRL-D, ALT-E + D
Edit attributes of selected characters (▶ active)	ALT-E + H
Edit Envelope	ALT-C + D
Edit Perspective	ALT-C + V
Edit attributes of newly drawn or selected text	CTRL-T, ALT-E + T
Ellipse Tool	SHIFT-F11
Erase portions of curve as you draw (▱ active)	SHIFT + drag backwards
Exit CorelDRAW!	CTRL-X, ALT-F4, ALT-F + X
Export current selection	ALT-F + E
Extract	ALT-S + X
Extrude	CTRL-E, ALT-C + X
Fit-in-window	F4
Fit Text to a path (▶ active)	CTRL-F, ALT-A + T
Forward one layer	PGUP, ALT-A + O
Fountain Fill dialog box	F11
Full Page	SHIFT-F4
Full Screen Preview, turn on/off	F9
Grid Setup, specify	ALT-D + I

Action	Key Combination
Grid, Snap To, turn on/off	(CTRL)-(Y), (ALT)-(D) + (S)
Group multiple selected objects (▐ active)	(ALT)-(A) + (G)
Guidelines Setup	(ALT)-(D) + (L)
Import File	(ALT)-(F) + (I)
Leave Original	(+) on numeric keypad, or right mouse button in Version 2.01
Maximize CorelDRAW! window	(ALT)-(SPACEBAR) + (X)
Merge Back	(ALT)-(S) + (M)
Minimize CorelDRAW! window	(ALT)-(SPACEBAR) + (N)
Move CorelDRAW! window	(ALT)-(SPACEBAR) + arrow keys + (ENTER)
Move Object dialog box	(CTRL)-(L), (ALT)-(T) + (M)
Move selected object at 90-degree angles (▐ active)	(CTRL) + drag outline
New (clear screen)	(ALT)-(F) + (N)
Open File	(CTRL)-(O), (ALT)-(F) + (O)
Page Setup	(ALT)-(F) + (G)
Paste object from clipboard	(SHIFT) + (INS), (ALT)-(E) + (P)
Pencil tool	(F5)
Preferences, edit	(CTRL)-(J), (ALT)-(S) + (E)
Preview Selected Only, turn on/off (with preview on)	(ALT)-(D) + (O)
Preview window, turn on/off	(SHIFT)-(F9), (ALT)-(D) + (P)
Print File	(CTRL)-(P), (ALT)-(F) + (P)
Print Merge	(ALT)-(F) + (M)
Quit CorelDRAW!	(CTRL)-(X), (ALT)-(F4), (ALT)-(F) + (X)

Action	Key Combination
Rectangle tool	`F6`
Redo last undone operation	`ALT`-`ENTER`, `ALT`-`E` + `E`
Refresh Wire Screen	`CTRL`-`W`, `ALT`-`D` + `W`
Repeat last operation on selected object (active)	`CTRL`-`R`, `ALT`-`E` + `R`
Reverse Order of multiple selected objects (active)	`ALT`-`A` + `R`
Rotate & Skew selected object (active)	`CTRL`-`N`, `ALT`-`T` + `R`
Rotate selected object in 15-degree increments (active)	`CTRL` + drag corner node
Save current image	`CTRL`-`S`, `ALT`-`F` + `S`
Save As, name current image	`ALT`-`F` + `A`
Scale selected object in 100% increments (active)	`CTRL` + drag corner node
Scale selected object, leave original (active)	Drag corner, `+` on numeric keypads, or right mouse button in Version 2.01
Select All objects	`ALT`-`E` + `A`
Select multiple objects (active)	`SHIFT` + click
Select next object in picture (active)	`TAB`
Select previous object in picture (active)	`SHIFT`-`TAB`
Shaping tool	`F10`
Show Bitmaps in editing window	`ALT`-`D` + `B`
Show Color Palette, turn on/off	`ALT`-`D` + `C`

Action	Key Combination
Show Full Screen Preview, turn on/off	F9
Show Grid, turn on/off	ALT-D + I + S + Z
Show Page	SHIFT-F4
Show Rulers, turn on/off	ALT-D + R
Show Status Line, turn on/off	ALT-D + S
Show Preview toolbox, turn on/off (with preview on)	ALT-D + T
Show Preview window, turn on/off	SHIFT-F9, ALT-D + P
Size screen	ALT-SPACEBAR + arrow keys + ENTER
Skew selected object in 15-degree increments (active)	CTRL + drag middle node
Snap To Grid, turn on/off	CTRL-Y, ALT-D + S
Snap To Guidelines, turn on/off	ALT-D + G
Straighten selected text (active)	ALT-A + S
Stretch & Mirror selected object (active)	CTRL-Q, ALT-T + S
Stretch selected object in 100% increments (active)	CTRL + drag middle node
Stretch selected object, leave original (active)	+ from numeric keypad + drag middle node, or right mouse button in Version 2.01
Text tool	F8
To Back, move selected object (active)	SHIFT-PGDN, ALT-A + B
To Front, move selected object (active)	SHIFT-PGUP, ALT-A + F

Action	Key Combination
Undo last operation	(ALT)-(BACKSPACE), (ALT)-(E) + (U)
Ungroup selected group (▶ active)	(CTRL)-(U), (ALT)-(A) + (U)
Wedge, convert circle to, in 15-degree increments (⟋ active)	(CTRL) + drag node inside circle
Zoom-In	(F2)
Zoom-Out	(F3)

C

Corel Connectivity: Clip Art and Fonts

The growing number of file formats now supported for import by CorelDRAW! (14 different formats as of release 2.01) make it possible for you to edit clip art from many manufacturers. In addition, the WFNBOSS font conversion utility supplied with versions 1.1 and later gives you access to many thousands of popular commercial fonts. This appendix provides supplementary information for CorelDRAW! users who wish to take advantage of clip art and fonts produced by third-party manufacturers. It also contains tables of the character sets provided with the native CorelDRAW! typefaces. You will find the instructions at the end of this appendix useful for renaming the CorelDRAW! typefaces to correspond with their industry standard counterparts.

Table C-1.   *Major Clip-Art Vendors Providing Images in Importable Formats*

Vendor	Telephone	Formats
3G Graphics	(800) 456-0234	.EPS
ACEBO	(408) 455-1507	.CDR, .EPS
ArtRight Images	(613) 820-1000	.CDR, .EPS
Bergmoser+Höller Verlag (Germany)	241/173090	.CDR, .EPS
Casady & Greene	(800) 359-4920	.EPS
Creativ Collection Verlag (Germany)	761/42608	.EPS
Dream Maker Software	(800) 876-5665	.EPS
Dynamic Graphics	(800) 255-8800	.EPS
HAL Visual Presentation (England)	0252/622177	.EPS
Hired Hand Design	(213) 429-5653	.EPS
Image Club Graphics	(800) 661-9410	.EPS
Metro ImageBase	(800) 525-1552	.PCX, .TIF
MGI (Marketing Graphics Inc.)	(800) 368-3773	.CGM
MicroMaps Software	(800) 334-4291	.EPS
Multi-Ad Services	(309) 692-1530	.EPS
New Vision Technologies	(613) 727-8190	.CGM
Presentation Graphics Group	(800) 468-9008	.CDR, .EPS
Soft-Age Publishing	(800) 736-7103	.PCX
TechPool Studios	(216) 382-1234	.EPS
T/Maker Company	(415) 962-0195	.EPS
Totem Graphics	(206) 352-1851	.CDR, .EPS

Supported Clip Art Vendors

As of version 2.01, CorelDRAW! can import clip art in 14 different file formats: .CDR, .PCX, .TIF, Windows .BMP, Lotus .PIC, Adobe .AI or .EPS, IBM .PIF, .CGM, AutoCAD .DXF, .GEM, HPGL .PLT, and MAC PICT (.PCT).

Table C-1 provides a handy reference to vendors who have supplied clip-art samples with your software. You can use clip-art files from other vendors as well. Collectively, these vendors give you access to more than 11,000 images. The Macintosh PICT (.PCT) import option alone allows you to browse through the advertisements in any Macintosh periodical and choose from thousands of clip-art images.

CorelDRAW! Character Sets

As you may recall from Chapter 5, the 75 typefaces and 153 font combinations provided with CorelDRAW! Versions 2.0 and later include four typefaces with symbol character sets: Dixieland, Greek/Math Symbols, Geographic, and Musical. The other typefaces supplied with your software use the Corel character set.

If you are using one of the typefaces based on the Corel character set and wish to type a character not found on your keyboard, refer to Table C-2. Activate the Text tool and select an insertion point on your page. When the Text dialog box appears, select the desired typeface, press and hold (ALT), and type the three- or four-character numerical ASCII code that corresponds to the character you want. You *must* include the zero in front of the ASCII code in order for the character to be correct. Keep in mind that the Text dialog box can display only the Windows character set, which differs slightly from the CorelDRAW! character set. As a result, a few of the characters that you type in the Text dialog box look different from the characters that display in the display box of the Text dialog box and after you exit the dialog box. All Corel characters display correctly in the editing and preview windows, however. Before typing a non-alphabetic Corel character in the Text dialog box, refer to the Character Chart that came with your software or to Table C-2. As long as the ASCII code that you type matches the character you want, the character will display correctly in the editing and preview windows of CorelDRAW! and be printed correctly.

If you wish to use one of the symbol typefaces provided with CorelDRAW!, select the desired character using the appropriate character chart. Tables C-3 through C-6 show the ASCII code and corresponding characters for the Dixieland, Greek/Math Symbols, Geographic, and Musical character sets, respectively. To type any of these characters, activate the Text tool and select an insertion point. When the Text dialog box appears, select the desired symbol typeface. Then, press and hold (ALT) and type the three- or four-character numerical ASCII code that corresponds to the character

Table C-2.   *The Corel Character Set*

Code	Char	Code	Char	Code	Char	Code	Char	Code	Char	Code	Char
033	!	075	K	0117	u	0159		0201	É	0243	ó
034	"	076	L	0118	v	0160		0202	Ê	0244	ô
035	#	077	M	0119	w	0161	¡	0203	Ë	0245	õ
036	$	078	N	0120	x	0162	¢	0204	Ì	0246	ö
037	%	079	O	0121	y	0163	£	0205	Í	0247	œ
038	&	080	P	0122	z	0164	¤	0206	Î	0248	ø
039	'	081	Q	0123	{	0165	¥	0207	Ï	0249	ù
040	(	082	R	0124	|	0166	¦	0208		0250	ú
041	)	083	S	0125	}	0167	§	0209	Ñ	0251	û
042	*	084	T	0126	~	0168	¨	0210	Ò	0252	ü
043	+	085	U	0127		0169	©	0211	Ó	0253	
044	,	086	V	0128	`	0170	ª	0212	Ô	0254	
045	-	087	W	0129	^	0171	«	0213	Õ	0255	ÿ
046	.	088	X	0130	~	0172	¬	0214	Ö		
047	/	089	Y	0131	ı	0173	—	0215	Œ		
048	0	090	Z	0132	ƒ	0174	®	0216	Ø		
049	1	091	[	0133	"	0175		0217	Ù		
050	2	092	\	0134	"	0176	°	0218	Ú		
051	3	093	]	0135	‹	0177		0219	Û		
052	4	094	^	0136	›	0178		0220	Ü		
053	5	095	_	0137	fi	0179		0221			
054	6	096	'	0138	fl	0180	´	0222			
055	7	097	a	0139	†	0181		0223	ß		
056	8	098	b	0140	‡	0182	¶	0224	à		
057	9	099	c	0141	–	0183	•	0225	á		
058	:	0100	d	0142	·	0184	¸	0226	â		
059	;	0101	e	0143	ˇ	0185		0227	ã		
060	<	0102	f	0144	„	0186	º	0228	ä		
061	=	0103	g	0145	…	0187	»	0229	å		
062	>	0104	h	0146	‰	0188		0230	æ		
063	?	0105	i	0147	™	0189		0231	ç		
064	@	0106	j	0148		0190		0232	è		
065	A	0107	k	0149		0191	¿	0233	é		
066	B	0108	l	0150		0192	À	0234	ê		
067	C	0109	m	0151		0193	Á	0235	ë		
068	D	0110	n	0152		0194	Â	0236	ì		
069	E	0111	o	0153		0195	Ã	0237	í		
070	F	0112	p	0154		0196	Ä	0238	î		
071	G	0113	q	0155		0197	Å	0239	ï		
072	H	0114	r	0156		0198	Æ	0240			
073	I	0115	s	0157		0199	Ç	0241	ñ		
074	J	0116	t	0158		0200	È	0242	ò		

Table C-3. *The Dixieland Character Set*

033 ⍥	079 ★	0125 ❝	0171 ♠	0218 ⬈
034 ✄	080 ☆	0126 ❞	0172 ①	0219 →
035 ✂	081 ✳	0127	0173 ②	0220 ➡
036 ✂	082 ✺	0128	0174 ③	0221 →
037 ☎	083 ✳	0129	0175 ④	0222 →
038 ✆	084 ✳	0130	0176 ⑤	0223 ➡
039 ✳	085 ✳	0131	0177 ⑥	0224 ➡
040 ✈	086 ✳	0132	0178 ⑦	0225 ➡
041 ✉	087 ✳	0133	0179 ⑧	0226 ➤
042 ☛	088 ✳	0134	0180 ⑨	0227 ➤
043 ☞	089 ✺	0135	0181 ⑩	0228 ➤
044 ☘	090 ✹	0136	0182 ❶	0229 ➥
045 ✍	091 ✳	0137	0183 ❷	0230 ➦
046 ✎	092 ✳	0138	0184 ❸	0231 ➧
047 ✏	093 ✳	0139	0185 ❹	0232 ➨
048 ✐	094 ✻	0140	0186 ❺	0233 ⇨
049 ☜	095 ✿	0141	0187 ❻	0234 ⇨
050 ☛	096 ❀	0142	0188 ❼	0235 ⇦
051 ✓	097 ❂	0143	0189 ❽	0236 ⇐
052 ✔	098 ○	0144	0190 ❾	0237 ⇨
053 ✕	099 ✲	0145	0191 ❿	0238 ⇨
054 ✖	0100 ✪	0146	0192 ①	0239 ⇨
055 ✗	0101 ✹	0147	0193 ②	0240
056 ✘	0102 ✪	0148	0194 ③	0241 ⇨
057 ✚	0103 ✳	0149	0195 ④	0242 ⊃
058 ✚	0104 ✳	0150	0196 ⑤	0243 ➳
059 ✛	0105 ✳	0151	0197 ⑥	0244 ➘
060 ✜	0106 ✳	0152	0198 ⑦	0245 ➺
061 ✝	0107 ✳	0153	0199 ⑧	0246 ➴
062 ✞	0108 ●	0154	0200 ⑨	0247 ➴
063 ✟	0109 ○	0155	0201 ⑩	0248 ➻
064 ✠	0110 ■	0156	0202 ❶	0249 ➴
065 ✡	0111 □	0157	0203 ❷	0250 →
066 ✢	0112 □	0158	0204 ❸	0251 ↔
067 ✣	0113 □	0159	0205 ❹	0252 ➻
068 ✤	0114 □	0160	0206 ❺	0253 ➼
069 ✥	0115 ▲	0161 ❡	0207 ❻	0254 →
070 ✦	0116 ▼	0162 ❢	0208 ❼	0255
071 ✧	0117 ◆	0163 ❣	0209 ❽	
072 ★	0118 ◆	0164 ❤	0210 ❾	
073 ☆	0119 ◗	0165 ❦	0211 ❿	
074 ✪	0120 ❘	0166 ❧	0212 →	
075 ✫	0121 ❙	0167 ❦	0213 →	
076 ★	0122 ❚	0168 ♣	0214 ↔	
077 ★	0123 ❛	0169 ♦	0215 ↕	
078 ★	0124 ❜	0170 ♥	0216 ➘	
			0217 ➡	

Table C-4.   *The Greek/Math Character Set*

033	!	075	K	0117	υ	0159		0201	⊃	0243	
034	∀	076	Λ	0118	ϖ	0160		0202	⊇	0244	
035	#	077	M	0119	ω	0161	ϒ	0203	⊄	0245	
036	∃	078	N	0120	ξ	0162	′	0204	⊂	0246	
037	%	079	O	0121	ψ	0163	≤	0205	⊆	0247	
038	&	080	Π	0122	ζ	0164	/	0206	∈	0248	
039	∋	081	Θ	0123	{	0165	∞	0207	∉	0249	
040	(	082	P	0124	|	0166	f	0208	∠	0250	
041	)	083	Σ	0125	}	0167	♣	0209	∇	0251	
042	*	084	T	0126	~	0168	♦	0210	®	0252	
043	+	085	Y	0127		0169	♥	0211	©	0253	
044	,	086	ς	0128		0170	♠	0212	™	0254	
045	−	087	Ω	0129		0171	↔	0213	∏	0255	
046	.	088	Ξ	0130		0172	←	0214	√		
047	/	089	Ψ	0131		0173	↑	0215	·		
048	0	090	Z	0132		0174	→	0216	¬		
049	1	091	[	0133		0175	↓	0217	∧		
050	2	092	∴	0134		0176	°	0218	∨		
051	3	093	]	0135		0177	±	0219	⇔		
052	4	094	⊥	0136		0178	″	0220	⇐		
053	5	095	_	0137		0179	≥	0221	⇑		
054	6	096	−	0138		0180	×	0222	⇒		
055	7	097	α	0139		0181	∝	0223	⇓		
056	8	098	β	0140		0182	∂	0224	◊		
057	9	099	χ	0141		0183	•	0225	⟨		
058	:	0100	δ	0142		0184	+	0226	®		
059	;	0101	ε	0143		0185	≠	0227	©		
060	<	0102	φ	0144		0186	≡	0228	™		
061	=	0103	γ	0145		0187	≈	0229	Σ		
062	>	0104	η	0146		0188	…				
063	?	0105	ι	0147		0189	|				
064	≅	0106	φ	0148		0190	—				
065	A	0107	κ	0149		0191	↵				
066	B	0108	λ	0150		0192	ℵ				
067	X	0109	μ	0151		0193	ℑ				
068	Δ	0110	ν	0152		0194	ℜ				
069	E	0111	o	0153		0195	℘				
070	Φ	0112	π	0154		0196	⊗				
071	Γ	0113	θ	0155		0197	⊕				
072	H	0114	ρ	0156		0198	∅				
073	I	0115	σ	0157		0199	∩				
074	ϑ	0116	τ	0158		0200	∪				

Table C-5. The Geographic Character Set

033	075	0117	0159	0201	0243
034	076	0118	0160	0202	0244
035	077	0119	0161	0203	0245
036	078	0120	0162	0204	0246
037	079	0121	0163	0205	0247
038	080	0122	0164	0206	0248
039	081	0123	0165	0207	0249
040	082	0124	0166	0208	0250
041	083	0125	0167	0209	0251
042	084	0126	0168	0210	0252
043	085	0127	0169	0211	0253
044	086	0128	0170	0212	0254
045	087	0129	0171	0213	0255
046	088	0130	0172	0214	
047	089	0131	0173	0215	
048	090	0132	0174	0216	
049	091	0133	0175	0217	
050	092	0134	0176	0218	
051	093	0135	0177	0219	
052	094	0136	0178	0220	
053	095	0137	0179	0221	
054	096	0138	0180	0222	
055	097	0139	0181	0223	
056	098	0140	0182	0224	
057	099	0141	0183	0225	
058	0100	0142	0184	0226	
059	0101	0143	0185	0227	
060	0102	0144	0186	0228	
061	0103	0145	0187	0229	
062	0104	0146	0188	0230	
063	0105	0147	0189	0231	
064	0106	0148	0190	0232	
065	0107	0149	0191	0233	
066	0108	0150	0192	0234	
067	0109	0151	0193	0235	
068	0110	0152	0194	0236	
069	0111	0153	0195	0237	
070	0112	0154	0196	0238	
071	0113	0155	0197	0239	
072	0114	0156	0198	0240	
073	0115	0157	0199	0241	
074	0116	0158	0200	0242	

Table C-6.   *The Musical Character Set*

Code	Char	Code	Char	Code	Char	Code	Char	Code	Char	Code	Char
033	;	075	♪	0117	⌣	0159		0201	♪	0243	r
034	//	076	↖	0118	v	0160	▌	0202		0244	♬
035		077	∿	0119	∘	0161	Ped.	0203		0245	
036		078		0120	♪	0162	1	0204		0246	●
037	%	079	◆	0121	♭	0163	3	0205		0247	
038	♭	080	∞	0122	z	0164	6	0206	⌡	0248	
039	♪	081	⌠	0123	:	0165	8	0207	●	0249	
040	(	082	♭	0124	│	0166	7	0208	■	0250	∘
041	)	083	♪	0125	⇶	0167	⌡	0209	▲	0251	↘
042	•	084	••	0126	~	0168	♩	0210	▌	0252	
043	+	085	⌒	0127		0169	♪	0211	▌	0253	
044	,	086	8+	0128		0170	z	0212	✗	0254	
045	-	087	⊩	0129	♪	0171		0213		0255	
046	.	088	♭	0130	♪	0172	▲	0214	▯		
047	⏐	089	♪	0131	♪	0173	□	0215	8↓		
048	0	090	♪	0132		0174	▼	0216			
049	1	091	▌	0133		0175	♩	0217	tr		
050	2	092	│	0134		0176	♭	0218	♪		
051	3	093	⊩	0135		0177	△	0219			
052	4	094	∧	0136		0178	∨	0220	×		
053	5	095	_	0137		0179	⊓	0221	⊔		
054	6	096	✦	0138		0180	♭	0222	⊕		
055	7	097	⌞	0139		0181	∿	0223			
056	8	098	♭	0140	♮	0182		0224	▼		
057	9	099	c	0141	♪	0183	-	0225	◇		
058	♭	0100	DS	0142		0184	*ppp*	0226	•		
059	♪	0101	♪	0143		0185	*pp*	0227	■		
060		0102	*f*	0144		0186	♮	0228	♬		
061	☰	0103	;	0145		0187	♪	0229	♬		
062	>	0104	♩	0146		0188	o	0230			
063	𝄢	0105	♪	0147		0189	m	0231	♪		
064	;	0106	↘	0148		0190	♪	0232	▼		
065	⌐	0107	↘	0149		0191	♭	0233	♪		
066	𝄡	0108	│	0150		0192	×	0234	⌡		
067	¢	0109	∿	0151		0193	1	0235			
068	DC	0110	♮	0152		0194	↙	0236	*fff*		
069	♭	0111	∘	0153		0195	8∿	0237	⌠		
070	*mf*	0112	*p*	0154		0196	*ff*	0238	-		
071	·	0113	♩	0155		0197	♬	0239			
072	⌠	0114	♪	0156		0198	♪	0240	♭		
073	⏐	0115	♭	0157		0199	⏐	0241	⋮		
074	♪	0116	▦	0158		0200	⏐	0242	⌐		

you want. Be sure to include the zero at the beginning of the ASCII code. The Windows character set does not permit accurate representation of any of the symbol characters in the Text dialog box, but the display box in the Text dialog box and the CorelDRAW! screen displays them correctly, after you exit the dialog box. To find the character(s) you want to type, refer to the character chart that came with your software or to the appropriate table in this appendix.

An interesting use for characters in the symbol typefaces is to create your own "instant" clip art. To do this, assign a very large point size to the desired character when you type its ASCII code in the dialog box. When the character appears on the CorelDRAW! page, activate the Select tool, select the character, and convert it to curves. You can then reshape the character as a curve object, using the Shaping tool.

Tip

Renaming CorelDRAW! Typefaces

CorelDRAW! Version 2.0 is shipped with 75 different typefaces; the combination of these typefaces with the typestyles available for each yields a total of 153 fonts. Corel Systems designed these typefaces and their names to resemble popular typefaces in common use by desktop publishers and graphic designers. In many cases, the names of the CorelDRAW! typefaces will remind you of their industry counterparts, as Table C-7 shows.

If you are more familiar with the industry standard, however, you may find it too inconvenient to memorize another set of typeface names. You have the option of renaming the CorelDRAW! typefaces so that the names you see in the dialog box match the better-known industry typeface names. To do this, edit the typeface names in your CORELDRW.INI file in the following way.

1. Load Windows, load the File Manager, and change to the directory in which CorelDRAW! is installed.

2. Make a backup copy of your CORELDRW.INI file using the Copy command in the File menu. Give the copy either a different filename or a different extension to distinguish it from the original. For example, call it CORELDRW.INB.

3. Double-click on the CORELDRW.INI file to open it in the Notepad editing window.

4. Scroll through the file until you come to the [CorelDrwFonts] section (see Figure C-1). This part of the CORELDRW.INI file contains the list of typefaces used in CorelDRAW!.

5. Go to the first typeface name you want to change. Position the cursor on the far left of the line and drag across the characters until you reach the equal sign (=) character. Do not include the equal sign. Also, do not erase the characters that appear after the equal sign; these characters represent the DOS filename that CorelDRAW! refers to when identifying the typeface. Remember that you are changing the typeface name only, not the filename that contains the information about the typeface.

6. Type the name of the standard industry typeface, or an abbreviation of it. You must fit the name within 18 spaces in order to see all of it in the Text dialog box. Furthermore, you may not include any spaces in the new typeface name. If the standard industry name contains two or more words, replace the spaces between words with hyphens (-) or underline (_) characters. For example, to substitute the name Aachen Bold for the Corel name Aardvark Bold, you would type **Aachen_Bold**. To substitute the industry name New Century Schoolbook for its Corel equivalent New Brunswick, you might type **New_Century_Schbk**. Be sure not to leave any spaces between the new typeface name and the equal sign (=) character. Finally, if you are going to convert any of the CorelDRAW! fonts to Adobe Type 1 fonts, do not include a / (slash) character as in "Greek/Math_Symbols." A PostScript font name cannot include a slash.

7. Select the Save command in the Notepad File menu to save your changes.

8. Continue editing in this way until you have changed all of the names. Save the CORELDRW.INI file periodically so that you will not lose all of your changes if you make a mistake along the way.

9. If you would like to have the new typeface names in alphabetical order, reposition the lines by copying and then pasting them to the desired positions. Then you can delete the original lines that you

Table C-7.   *Commonly Used Typeface Names and Their Corel Counterparts*

Industry Name	Corel Equivalent
Aachen Bold	Aardvark Bold
American Typewriter	Memorandum
Arnold Böcklin	Arabia
Avant Garde	Avalon
Bauhaus	Bahamas
Bauhaus Heavy	Bahamas Heavy
Bauhaus Light	Bahamas Light
Benguiat	Bangkok
Bookman	Brooklyn
Bodoni Poster	Bodonoff
Brush Script	Banff
Carta	Geographic
Caslon	Casablanca
Caslon OpenFace	Casper OpenFace
Century Old Style	Centurion Old
Cooper Black	Cupertino
Cottonwood	Cottage
Dom Casual	Dawn Castle
Eras	Erie
Eras Black	Erie Black
Eras Light	Erie Light
Fette Fraktur	Frankenstein
Franklin Gothic	Frankfurt Gothic
Franklin Gothic Heavy	Frankfurt Gothic Heavy
Freestyle Script	Freeport
Friz Quadrata	France
Futura 2	Fujiyama 2
Futura Condensed	Fujiyana Condensed
Futura Condensed Extra Bold	Fujiyama Condensed Extra Bold
Futura Condensed Light	Fujiyama Condensed Light
Garamond	Gatineau
Helvetica	Switzerland
Helvetica Black	Switzerland Black
Helvetica Light	Switzerland Light
Helvetica Narrow	Switzerland Narrow
Helvetica Condensed	Switzerland Condensed
Helvetica Condensed Black	Switzerland Condensed Black

NOTE: All industry names are trademarks of their respected companies.

Table C-7.   *Commonly Used Typeface Names and Their Corel Counterparts (continued)*

Industry Name	Corel Equivalent
Helvetica Condensed Light	Switzerland Condensed Light
Helvetica Inserat	Switzerland Inserat
Hobo	Homeward Bound
Ironwood	Ireland
Juniper	Jupiter
Kaufmann	Koala
Letter Gothic	Monospaced
Linoscript	Linus
Linotext	Lincoln
Machine	Motor
Mistral	Mystical
New Baskerville	Nebraska
New Century Schoolbook	New Brunswick
Optima	Ottawa
Palatino	Palm Springs
Parisian	Paragon
Park Avenue	Paradise
Peignot	Penguin
Peignot Light	Penguin Light
Ponderosa	Posse
Present Script	President
Post Antiqua	Prose Antique
Revue	Renfrew
Sonata	Musical
Souvenir	Southern
Stencil	Stamp
Symbols	Greek/Math Symbols
Tekton	Technical
Tiffany	Timpani
Tiffany Heavy	Timpani Heavy
Times	Toronto
Umbra	Umbrella
Univers Black	USA Black
Univers Light	USA Light
University Roman	Unicorn
VAG Rounded	Vogue
Zapf Chancery	Zurich Calligraphic
Zapf Dingbats	Dixieland

copied. In repositioning the names, leave in the top or first position a font that you want used as a default. The first font is used with imported text that does not have a font specified. Figure C-1 shows part of a CORELDRW.INI typeface list with industry typeface names substituted for Corel names.

10. When you have changed and repositioned the typeface names to your satisfaction, save the CORELDRW.INI file once more and exit Notepad.

The procedure just described is handy if you want to call CorelDRAW! typefaces by the names of similar standard industry typefaces. If you regularly work with fonts from other vendors and want to use them in CorelDRAW!, however, you require a different solution. Using the WFNBOSS utility described in the next section of this appendix, you can convert fonts from other vendors into CorelDRAW! format and vice versa.

Converting Fonts with WFNBOSS

CorelDRAW! typeface files have the extension .WFN, as you know if you have browsed through the file listings in the CorelDRAW! directory or the [CDrwFonts] section of your CORELDRW.INI file. CorelDRAW! versions 1.1 and later include a utility called WFNBOSS (pronounced "Wiffen boss"), which allows you to convert other vendors' fonts into the .WFN format for use in CorelDRAW! and vice versa. WFNBOSS effectively gives you access to thousands of commercial fonts by vendors such as Adobe Systems, Agfa Compugraphic, Bitstream, ZSoft, and others. Table C-8 lists the vendors whose typeface libraries are convertible to .WFN format using the WFNBOSS utility.

Converting Fonts to Corel Format

WFNBOSS is installed automatically when you install CorelDRAW!. The process of converting a third-party vendor's fonts to Corel format (.WFN) always includes these steps in sequence:

1. Access the WFNBOSS Font Conversion Program.

2. Select the font type (Conversion Type) that you want to convert to Corel format.

3. Select the source directory where the vendor's fonts are located.

4. Choose the drive and directory where you want the Corel version of the font to reside on your hard disk.

5. Select the first font in the chosen source directory that you want to convert.

6. If desired, change the font name that WFNBOSS suggests. This is the name that will appear in the CorelDRAW! Text dialog box after you convert the font from the original vendor's format.

7. Begin the conversion process.

Figure C-1.   *Corel CORELDRW.INI font list with common typeface names substituted in alphabetical order*

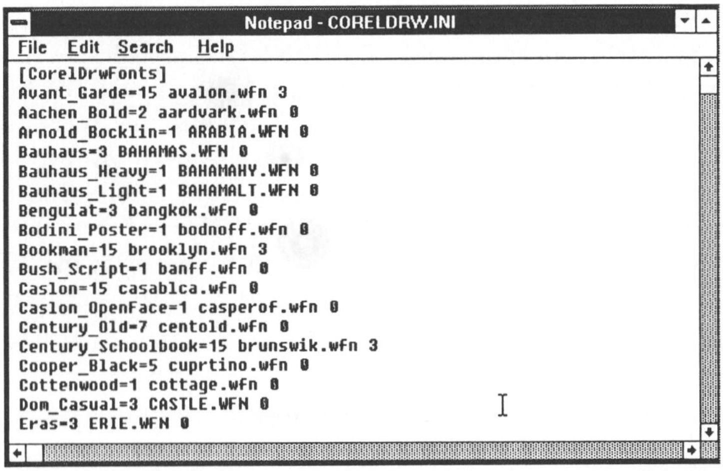

Table C-8.   *Typeface Vendors with Fonts in WFNBOSS-Convertible Format*

Vendor	Product Name	Format, Extension	Telephone Number
Adobe	Type Library	Adobe Type 1 .PFB /.AFM	(415) 961-4000 (800) 833-6687
Agfa Compugr.	Curvilinear Type Library	Type Director .FF pairs	(508) 658-5600 (800) 873-3668
Bitstream	Fontware	Bitstream .TDF, .BCO, .BEZ	(617) 497-6222 (800) 522-3668
Casady & Greene	Fluent Laser Fonts	Readable PostScript .PFA /.AFM	(408) 484-9228 (800) 359-4920
DigiFonts	Digi-Duit	DigiFont .DFI	(303) 526-2318 (800) 242-5665
HP/Agfa Compugr.	Type Director	Type Director .FF pairs	(800) 538-8787 (HP) (800) 873-3668 (Agfa)
Image Club	PS Typeface Library	Readable PostScript .PFA /.AFM	(403) 262-8008 (800) 661-9410
The Font Company	URW Type Library	Readable PostScript .PFA /.AFM	(602) 996-6606 (800) 422-3668
Treacyfaces	Treacyfaces	Readable PostScript .PFA /.AFM	(215) 896-0860
ZSoft	Type Foundry	Type Foundry .OTL	(404) 428-0008

The next section describes how to access the WFNBOSS utility and acquaints you with the contents of the WFNBOSS Font Conversion Program window.

The WFNBOSS Window

You cannot access WFNBOSS directly from within CorelDRAW!; instead, you open it from the MS-DOS Executive as a separate program in the directory where CorelDRAW! is installed. To access WFNBOSS so that you can begin the process of converting fonts, follow these steps:

1. Start Windows and if necessary, open the Corel Applications Group.

2. Double-click on the WFNBOSS icon, as shown in Figure C-2. The main window of the WFNBOSS Font Conversion Program appears, as shown in Figure C-3.

The WFNBOSS window is similar to a standard Windows dialog box. Take a moment to become familiar with the components of this window. To move between options in the WFNBOSS window, you can either press (TAB) or (SHIFT)-(TAB), or click directly on the desired option.

Conversion Type

When you open WFNBOSS, the Conversion Type is the first option you must define, as shown in Figure C-3. This option lets you determine which typeface format you are going to convert. The very first time you use WFNBOSS, the Bitstream typeface option is active. To select a different typeface family, click on the downward pointing arrow and then use the scrollbar until you see the family you want. Once you change the selected typeface, Windows remembers the last Conversion Type you selected.

Source Directory/"NewDir"

The Source Directory option shows you the drive and directory where WFNBOSS will search for fonts to convert. The very first time you start WFNBOSS, the directory where CORELDRW is installed is the default directory. To change the source drive and/or directory, you can either click on the NewDir command button, or press (TAB) until NewDir is selected and then press (ENTER). When you select NewDir, the Select New Working Directory dialog box pops up, prompting you to change the path. In Figure C-4, the path has been specified for the location of Adobe Type 1 fonts in .PFB format. The available font filenames (not the popular names of the fonts) appear in the Files list box.

Figure C-2. *Accessing WFNBOSS from the Program Manager*

Corel Applications
CorelDRAW!
MOSAIC
WFNBOSS
Corel TRACE

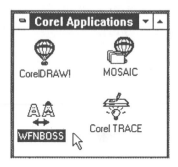

To accept the directory you have chosen, click on the OK command button or press (ENTER). The popular filenames of the fonts in the new source directory then appear in the Available Fonts box of the main WFNBOSS window, as shown in Figure C-5. The message appearing in the Status and

Figure C-3. *The WFNBOSS Font Conversion Program window*

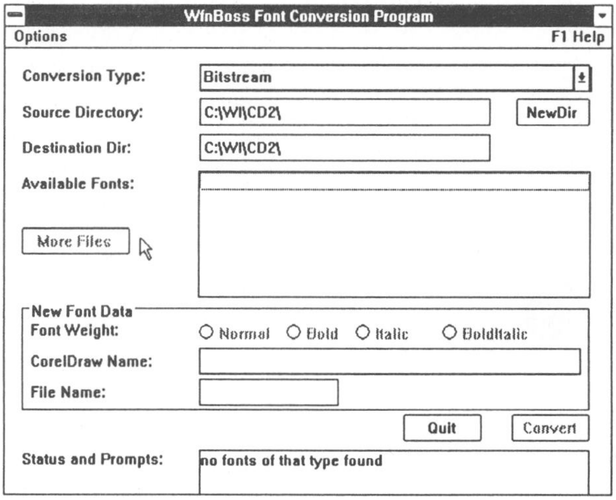

WinBoss Font Conversion Program
Options
F1 Help
Conversion Type:
Bitstream
Source Directory:
C:\WI\CD2\
NewDir
Destination Dir:
C:\WI\CD2\
Available Fonts:
More Files
New Font Data
Font Weight:
Normal
Bold
Italic
BoldItalic
CorelDraw Name:
File Name:
Quit
Convert
Status and Prompts:
no fonts of that type found

Figure C-4.   *Selecting a source directory for fonts to be converted*

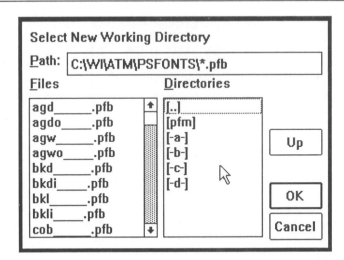

Prompts box at the bottom of the window tells you how many fonts reside in the specified drive and directory. If you have a version of CorelDRAW! earlier than 1.11, a single directory can contain only 32 fonts. If you have version 1.11 or later, you can place any number of fonts in a directory and, if there are more than 32, you can view additional font names by clicking on More.

"Destination Dir"

The Destination Dir option stands for Destination Directory, or the directory where you want the fonts to reside once they are converted to Corel format. This is always the directory where CorelDRAW! is installed, unless you deactivate the AutoInstall command in the Options menu. (Refer to the section, "The Options Menu" in this chapter.)

Available Fonts

The Available Fonts list box contains the names of fonts in the currently selected source directory that match the currently selected Conversion Type. The names that appear in this list box are the popular names of the fonts, not the filenames that contain those fonts. To select a font, simply click on it to

Figure C-5. *A listing of available fonts in the specified source directory*

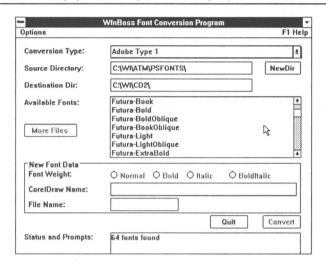

highlight it, as shown in Figure C-6. As soon as you select a font for conversion, the New Font Data options and the Convert command button become available for selection.

In most cases, you should select and convert only one font at a time. However, if you are converting four different typestyles of the same bitstream font (weights—normal, italic, bold, and bold-italic), you can convert them all at once. The resulting *merged* fonts will be stored under a single filename in the destination directory. They will also appear in the Text dialog box under one name, with four typestyle options available.

New Font Data

The three options in the New Font Data box—Font Weight, CorelDraw Name, and File Name—become available only when you have selected a font to convert from the Available Fonts list box. The WFNBOSS program suggests settings for each of these options, based on the information in the file for the font(s) you have selected. You may change any or all of these settings, however. The setting you are most likely to alter is the CorelDraw Name, which determines the font name that appears in the Text dialog box when

Figure C-6.   *Selecting a font for conversion, then altering the Corel font name*

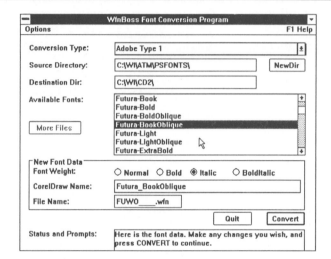

you enter new text. For example, the Futura Book Oblique font selected in Figure C-6 has been given the name Futura_BookOblique for use in CorelDRAW!.

The File Name option determines the name that the converted font is stored under in the destination directory. You should leave the suggested File Name option unaltered, because this filename is stored in your CorelDRAW! files when you save your drawing. If you need to exchange your drawing files with other users who have converted the same fonts, the filenames of the converted fonts must be the same for both users. Otherwise, CorelDRAW! will not recognize the font in the other person's computer.

The Convert Command Button

Clicking on the Convert command button begins the process of font conversion. This button becomes available as soon as you select one of the typefaces in the Available Fonts selection box. Make sure that all New Font Data information is correct before you click on Convert.

The time required to convert a particular font depends on the font manufacturer, but often ranges from three to five minutes. A single font can occupy between 10K and 25K of space on your hard drive, depending on how many ASCII characters are contained in the character set being converted. If you convert several typestyle weights of the same typestyle, merging them into one font file, the size of the font file can be much larger.

Status and Prompts

The message in the Status and Prompts box changes as you move through the font selection and conversion process. When you select a source directory, for example, Status and Prompts lists the number of fonts available in the specified format. When you select a specific font to convert, Status and Prompts reminds you to make changes to font data before beginning to convert the font to Corel format. Status and Prompts also keeps you informed about what is happening throughout the conversion process. Special message boxes also provide supplemental information.

The Options Menu

The Options menu is the only menu in the WFNBOSS program window. It contains several commands that can make the font conversion process more efficient or help you access information about fonts you have already converted. Figure C-7 shows the WFNBOSS program window with the Options menu displayed and the first command in the menu highlighted.

Font File Info

The Font File Info command allows you to change some features of font files that have already been converted to .WFN format. When you select this option, the Select Font File dialog box shown in Figure C-8 appears. This dialog box operates just like the other file selection dialog boxes within CorelDRAW!. Select the desired path and font filename; Figure C-8 shows the Corel font file AVALON.WFN selected. To confirm your selection, click on Open. The font file dialog box shown in Figure C-9 then displays. Most of the data in this second dialog box is for your information only. The Font Name option, for example, displays the name of the currently selected font file. The Fonts in File list box displays the weights of the fonts included in the selected font file. However, you can change the Default Character (the character that appears in the preview display of the Text dialog box) and the

Figure C-7.   *The WFNBOSS Options menu*

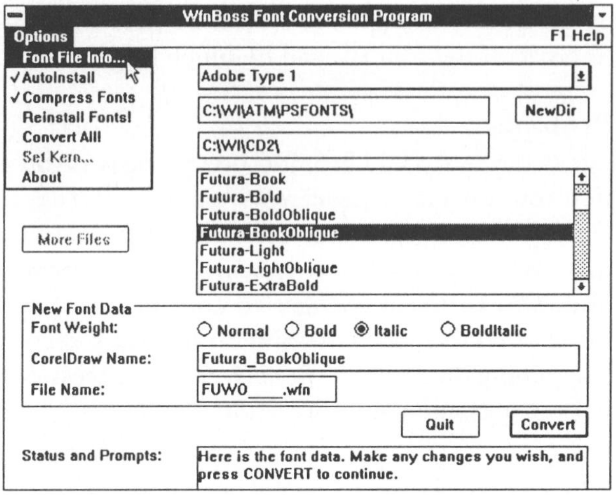

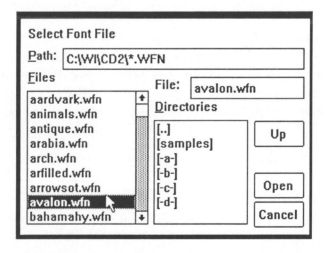

Figure C-8.   *Selecting AVALON.WFN to edit its font file information*

Figure C-9. *Editing font information in the font file dialog box*

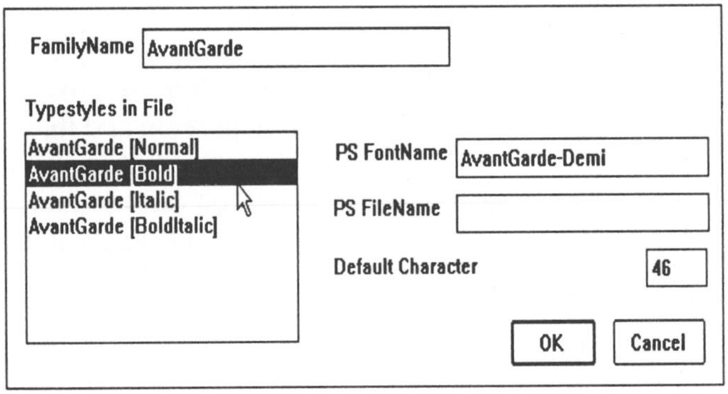

FamilyName | AvantGarde

Typestyles in File

AvantGarde [Normal]
AvantGarde [Bold]
AvantGarde [Italic]
AvantGarde [BoldItalic]

PS FontName | AvantGarde-Demi

PS FileName |

Default Character | 46

OK   Cancel

PostScript Fontname information if you desire. Remember that the PostScript Fontname refers only to the commonly used name of the font, not to the name of the file that contains the font data.

AutoInstall

The AutoInstall command is activated when you first install CorelDRAW! and remains active until you deselect it. When this command is active, the directory where CorelDRAW! is installed is automatically the destination directory for all fonts converted through WFNBOSS. If you deselect AutoInstall, you can store the converted .WFN fonts in any directory you choose.

Keep in mind that fonts stored in a directory other than the one where CorelDRAW! is installed will not appear in the CORELDRW.INI file. However, the WFNBOSS.INI file, which is located in the same directory as the one where CorelDRAW! is installed, contains a listing of those fonts. To find out which fonts you have converted and where they are located, view the contents of WFNBOSS.INI.

Tip

Compress Fonts

You can use the Compress Fonts command only if the fonts you want to convert are in Readable PostScript format (Casady & Greene, Image Club, The Font Company, Treacyfaces). This command tells WFNBOSS to compress the data in the converted font so that it takes up less space on your hard drive.

Reinstall Fonts!

The Reinstall Fonts! command is useful when you have reinstalled CorelDRAW!, thereby losing CorelDRAW! configuration and font information in the CORELDRW.INI file. WFNBOSS.INI "remembers" all of the fonts you have ever converted to CorelDRAW! format, so you can use this command to copy references to those fonts to the CorelDRAW! CORELDRW.INI file.

Convert All!

When you select Convert All!, WFNBOSS converts all of the fonts in the Available Fonts list box simultaneously. If you are converting different typestyles of the same typeface and the font manufacturer is Bitstream, WFNBOSS generates a single font file for all of the typestyles. When you convert fonts from vendors other than Bitstream, however, WFNBOSS generates a separate file and filename for each typestyle of each typeface. If this is not what you want, you should convert each font weight separately, with the Convert All command deactivated. When you convert individual weights of a single Bitstream typeface separately and in sequence, WFNBOSS merges and stores each weight in the same font file automatically.

Set Kern

Set Kern is active only for certain Type Foundry and Agfa/Compugraphic fonts. It allows you to set a percentage tolerance for finding pairs to kern. If you have a problem converting Type Foundry or Agfa/Compugraphic fonts, redo the conversion and use the Set Kern option to set a high tolerance (50%). If this works, you might want to come back and again redo the conversion with a slightly lower tolerance, until the conversion no longer works. Once you find the lowest value that works, and you have several similar fonts to convert, click on the Lock Kern value option button to maintain the value between fonts.

About

Click on the About command to see the information screen shown in Figure C-10. This screen contains information about the current version of WFNBOSS and its release date.

Figure C-10.   *The About WFNBOSS information box*

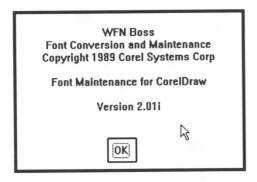

Converting Corel's Fonts to Other Formats

The 75 typefaces and 153 fonts that come with CorelDRAW! are valuable. You probably have other programs, such as PageMaker, Ventura, Word for Windows, or Ami, that could use them if they were not in the CorelDRAW! .WFM format. WFNBOSS 2.0 or later has the ability to convert the .WFM format to both Adobe Type 1 format and to ZSoft Type Foundry format. With the success of the Adobe Type Manager for Windows (ATM) and PageMaker including ATM with Version 4.0, the conversion to Type 1 is particularly valuable. Use the following exercise to see how this works (WFNBOSS 2.0 had some bugs in this area, so it is advisable that you get the 2.01 update if you don't have it already).

1. Open WFNBOSS by double-clicking on its icon from the Windows' Program Manager. The WFNBOSS Font Conversion Program window will open as shown in Figure C-3.

2. Click on the Conversion Type downward pointing arrow and use the scrollbar until you see "Corel to Adobe Type 1."

3. Your Source Directory is the directory in which you installed CorelDRAW!. It probably has already been selected.

4. You will probably need to change the Destination Directory. Do this by moving the cursor to the Destination Directory text box, drag

across the incorrect part of the path name, and type in the correct name.

5. Select the Corel typeface you want to convert by clicking on it. Remember that only 32 fonts are shown at a time. Use the More command button to see the next group of 32 and the New Directory command button followed by OK to go back to the beginning of the list. For this discussion, select Banff, whose PostScript name is "BushScript." The New Font Data will activate, as shown in Figure C-11.

The PostScript Font Name and the File Name are the standard names used by Adobe. Unless you have developed a custom font that you are converting (a very powerful capability with CorelDRAW! and WFNBOSS), you should leave these as WFNBOSS enters them. Although only the .PFB file is shown, WFNBOSS will create all three Adobe Type 1 file types, .PFB, .AFM, and .PFM.

Figure C-11.   *Converting from Corel's Banff to Adobe's BushScript*

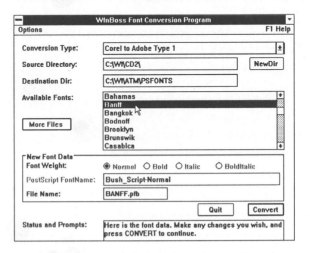

6. Click on Convert. A second dialog box opens, shown in Figure C-12, that lists the typestyles available for the typeface you have chosen. If the typeface you are converting has more than one typestyle, you must convert them one at a time. Click on the typeface/typestyle combination (font) you want to convert first and then click on OK. (Clicking on OK without clicking on a font selects the first font by default). The conversion will be carried out.

Corel's Symbol library can be converted to Adobe Type 1 fonts; but the conversion does not pick up the first 32 characters since these are not used in normal character sets.

When you have converted your Corel fonts to Adobe Type 1, you must add the fonts to the TypeManager in the normal way as described in the ATM *User Guide*. Also, if the font is not resident in your PostScript printer, you must change the WIN.INI file in the Windows directory to include the .PFB file as well as the .PFM file. For example, in the [PostScript,LPT1] section of your WIN.INI file you might have the following two lines:

softfont7=c:\atm\psfonts\pfm\tir_____.pfm

softfont8=c:\atm\psfonts\pfm\bushscri.pfm,c:\atm\psfonts\bus hscri.pfb

Softfont 7 is for Times Roman and is resident in the printer. Softfont 8 is for BushScript, not resident in the printer.

Figure C-12. *The Convert dialog box for specifying typestyles*

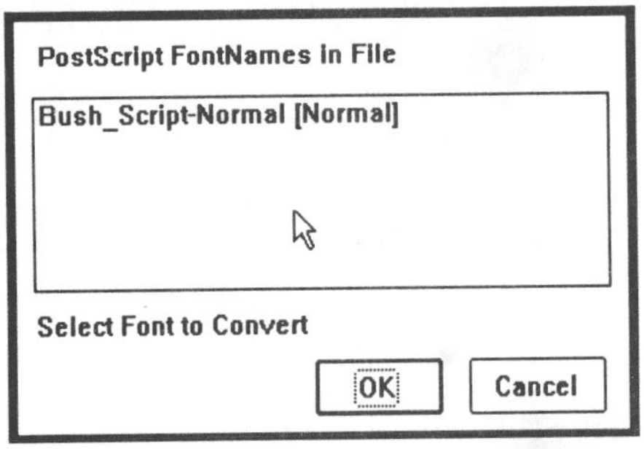

Getting Help While Converting Fonts

WFNBOSS uses the Windows on-screen Help System to give you step-by-step instructions as well as detailed information about converting each type of font format. You can access the Help System in one of two ways.

If you are running WFNBOSS, simply click on the F1 Help area of the menu line, or press (F1).

Upon clicking on the Help menu or pressing (F1), the Help Index opens as shown in Figure C-13. In the Help Index there are a number of items that are underlined. When you place the cursor on these items, the cursor turns into a grabber hand. Clicking on these items opens a new screen on the particular underlined topic, as shown in Figure C-14. You can also use the Back and Browse command buttons to work your way through the various topics and the scrollbar to move through a particular topic. The Search command button presents a list of topics you can select to see the information on that topic.

Figure C-13.   *WFNBOSS Help Index, opened with the* (F1) *key*

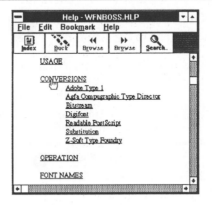

Figure C-14. *Information on a topic chosen from the Help Index*

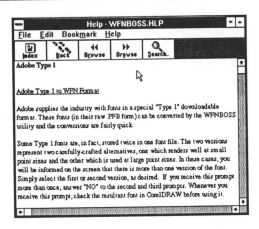

You can leave the Help system by double-clicking on Help's Control menu box, or by selecting Exit from the Help File menu.

D

Tracing Bitmapped Images

In Chapter 16, you learned about the two types of graphics that you can import into CorelDRAW!: bitmapped images and object-oriented art. When you import an object-oriented image, you can edit it just as you would any picture created in CorelDRAW!. Bitmapped images, however, contain no objects for you to select; they consist entirely of a fixed number of tiny dots, called *pixels*. If you enlarge or reduce the size of the bitmap without converting it to a CorelDRAW! object, distortion or unsightly compression of the pixels results. The solution is to *trace* the bitmap in CorelDRAW! and turn it into a curve object. You can then change the shape of its outline and the color of its fill, edit it normally, and print it, all without distortion. CorelDRAW! offers you three different methods for tracing an imported bitmap. The newest and most sophisticated of these is the CorelTRACE! batch autotracing utility, available with version 1.2 and later. You will be amazed at the speed and accuracy with which this product, similar to Adobe Streamline, can turn even the most complex bitmap into a finished curve object ready for editing. Turn to the section "Tracing with CorelTRACE!" to learn more about how to use this exciting feature.

If you have a version of CorelDRAW! earlier than 1.2, you can choose between manual tracing and the semiautomatic Autotrace feature. These methods are less rapid than the newer CorelTRACE! and require more work on the part of the user, but they offer you a high degree of control over the curves that result from your tracing.

Creating a Bitmapped Image

CorelDRAW! treats a bitmapped image as a unique object type, separate from other object types such as rectangles, ellipses, curves, and text. Unlike all of the other object types, bitmaps must be created outside of CorelDRAW!.

There are several ways to secure a bitmapped image for importing into CorelDRAW!. The easiest method is to import a finished clip-art image or a sample file having either a .PCX or .TIF extension (see Chapter 16). The next easiest method is to scan an existing image from a print source, such as a newspaper or magazine. Alternatively, you can sketch a drawing by hand, and then scan the image in .PCX or .TIF format. If you are experienced with paint software, you can create your own original pixel-based images.

Once the bitmapped image is available, you are ready to import it into CorelDRAW!. You will practice importing bitmapped images in the next section.

Importing a Bitmapped Image

You may recall from Chapter 16 that CorelDRAW! accepts three bitmapped file formats for import: .PCX, .TIF, and .BMP. The .PCX format is native to the ZSoft PC Paintbrush and Publisher's Paintbrush family of paint software, the .TIF format is the one that most scanners support, and .BMP is the Windows Paint file format. If the bitmap you want to import is in another format, you can convert it to .PCX or .TIF using an image conversion program such as Inset Graphics' Hijaak or Symsoft's HotShot Graphics.

To import a bitmap, you use the Import command in the File menu and select the appropriate bitmap file format in the Import dialog box. You also have a choice of whether or not to activate the For Tracing option when importing the image. As explained in Chapter 16, this option determines how

CorelDRAW! displays the bitmap, whether or not you can print it, and how much program memory CorelDRAW! allocates for bitmap editing operations.

The next two sections let you practice importing a bitmapped image, first with the For Tracing option selected, and then with this option inactive. The visual comparison should help you better understand how CorelDRAW! handles each type of bitmap.

Importing a Bitmap for Tracing

The standard CorelDRAW! package includes several .TIF sample files in the Sample directory. In the following exercise, you will import one of the sample .TIF files. You will select the For Tracing option in order to autotrace this image later.

1. Starting with a blank CorelDRAW! screen, pull down the Display menu and make sure that a checkmark appears in front of the Show Bitmaps command. If no checkmark appears, click on the command. This enables you to see the bitmap in the editing window after you import it.

2. Select the Page Setup command from the File menu and make certain that the page is set for Portrait format and the size is 8 1/2-by-11-inches. Click on the OK command button to save this setting.

3. Select the Import command from the File menu. The Import dialog box appears.

4. Click on the TIFF. TIF format option. The For Tracing option now becomes available for selection.

5. Activate the For Tracing option by clicking on the checkbox next to it. An X appears in the box, as shown in Figure D-1.

6. Select OK to access the secondary Import dialog box. Specify the drive and directory that contains the CorelDRAW! sample files. (If you have not installed or used the sample files, see Appendixes A and C.) Figure D-2 shows OUT_PLAY.TIF being selected.

7. To open the OUT_PLAY.TIF file, double-click on the filename in the Files list box, or highlight the filename and click on the Import

Figure D-1.   *The Import dialog box*

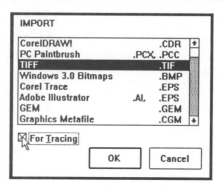

command button. After a few seconds, the image appears, centered on the screen and surrounded by a rectangular frame, as shown in Figure D-3. The status line displays the messages "Bitmap" and "For Tracing."

8. Press (SHIFT)-(F9) to turn on the preview window. The bitmapped image does not display here. When you import a bitmap using the For Tracing option, CorelDRAW! assumes that you want only the

Figure D-2.   *The secondary Import dialog box*

Figure D-3. *A bitmapped image, OUT_PLAY.TIF, imported for tracing*

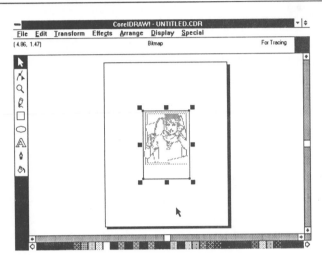

curves that result from your tracing to appear in the preview window. A bitmap imported in this way will neither print nor display in the preview window.

9. Select the Save As command from the File menu. When the Save As dialog box appears, change the directory to the one in which you save your CorelDRAW! drawings and type **AUTTRACE** in the File text box, and then click on the Save command button.

10. You will return to this image later in the chapter to autotrace it. For now, clear the screen by selecting New from the File menu.

When you first import a bitmap, it is selected automatically. At any other time, you must click on the rectangular frame surrounding the bitmap in order to select it. Clicking on any of the subjects within the bitmap has no effect and it does not select the entire bitmap object.

Tip

CorelDRAW! translates bitmaps in .PCX format into either black-and-white or color pixels, depending on the colors of the original image. The on-screen resolution of the image you have just imported is higher than if you had imported it without the For Tracing option selected. That's because CorelDRAW! allocates more program memory for a bitmap that you import for tracing, so that you can trace its curves more accurately. The disadvantage of this approach is that program operation can slow down noticeably, particularly if the bitmapped graphic file is large or if you have an 80286-based computer. Once you have finished tracing and editing a bitmap, however, you can reduce the amount of screen redraw time by deactivating the Show Bitmaps command in the Display menu. Thereafter, the bitmap itself is represented by the surrounding frame only, but the objects you have traced still continue to display in both the editing and preview windows.

When you import a bitmap for tracing, it does not appear in the preview window. Only the curves that result from your tracing operations display there. By the same token, a bitmap that you import for tracing does not print; you can print only the object-oriented curves that result from the tracing process.

In the next section, you will import the same bitmap again, but without activating the For Tracing option. You can then compare the visual differences in the way CorelDRAW! handles each type of imported bitmap.

Importing Without "For Tracing"

When you import a bitmap without activating the For Tracing option, it appears at a lower screen resolution than when you import it for tracing. You can also print the pixel-based image at its full resolution and display it in the preview window, which you cannot do with a bitmap imported for tracing.

If you want to incorporate a printable bitmapped image into an existing picture, you must import the bitmap without activating the For Tracing option. This also holds true if you are unsure whether you will trace the bitmap later. Even without tracing the bitmap, you can still crop it, change its position within the picture, and fill it with a single color. You also will save memory and you always have the option of tracing the bitmap at a later time.

In the next exercise, you will import the same bitmap that you imported in the previous section. This time, however, you will not activate the For Tracing option, and you will save the image under a different filename.

1. Select the Import command from the File menu. The Import dialog box appears.

2. Select the .TIF format option. The For Tracing option becomes available for selection.

3. Deactivate the For Tracing option by clicking on the checkbox next to it. The X disappears from the box.

4. Select OK to access the secondary Import dialog box. Specify the drive and directory that contains the OUT_PLAY.TIF image. (If you have not installed or used the clip-art samples, see Appendixes A and C.)

5. To open the OUT_PLAY.TIF file, double-click on the filename in the Files list box, or highlight the filename and click on the Open command button. After a few seconds, the image appears, centered on the screen and surrounded by a rectangular frame. The X in a square, meaning no fill with a black outline, appears on the status line instead of "For Tracing."

6. Press (SHIFT)-(F9) to turn on the preview window if it isn't already. The bitmapped image displays here as shown in Figure D-4, because you deselected the For Tracing option when you imported it. Depending on the resolution of your display adapter, the bitmap in the editing window may look somewhat coarser than the one you imported for tracing in the previous exercise. This is because of the lower amount of memory that CorelDRAW! reserves for a bitmap not intended for tracing. However, this lower on-screen resolution affects only the *display* of the bitmap. The bitmap will print at its full original resolution.

7. Select the Save As command from the File menu. When the Save As dialog box appears, type **MANTRACE** (short for "manual trace") in the Filename text box, and then click on the Save command button.

8. Clear the screen by pressing (DEL).

In a later section of this appendix, you will return to this bitmap and trace portions of it manually. First, however, you will reopen the AUTTRACE.CDR file and use the Autotrace feature to create curve objects from a bitmap.

Figure D-4.   *A bitmap imported with the For Tracing option deactivated*

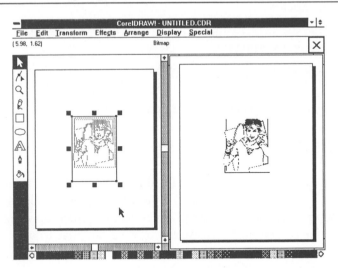

Autotracing an Imported Bitmap

As mentioned earlier in the chapter, CorelDRAW! lets you turn an imported bitmapped image into a resolution-independent curve object by tracing the image. You can trace a single bitmapped image either semiautomatically, using the Autotrace feature, or manually. (If you have version 1.2 or later, you can also use the fully automatic CorelTRACE! batch autotracing utility described later in this appendix. Manual tracing is an excellent choice if you desire total control over the appearance and placement of the outline curves. If you find it cumbersome to use the mouse for tracing long paths manually, however, use the Autotrace feature instead. You have less control over the results, but you will spend less time manipulating the mouse.

The Autotrace feature becomes available to you when the bitmap object is selected. Autotrace is semiautomatic in the sense that the software draws the actual curves for you, but you must define a number of parameters before tracing begins. You control the shape of the outline pen, the color of the outline fill, the interior fill of the object, and the smoothness of the curves.

In the following exercise, you will use Autotrace to trace portions of the AUTTRACE.CDR image that you imported earlier from the OUT_PLAY.TIF file.

1. Open the AUTTRACE.CDR file that you saved earlier in the chapter.

2. Select the bitmap object as soon as it appears, and then adjust magnification to fit-in-window.

3. All black-and-white bitmap objects are imported with a preset out-line color of black and a preset fill of None. You can adjust the Outline Pen settings as desired, but to have those settings apply to your traced objects, you must first deselect the bitmap. For the bitmap itself, the fill color applies to the background, the outline color applies to the bitmap pixels that are turned on, and outline width has no meaning. Deselect the object, click on the Outline tool and then on the hairline icon in the first row of the fly-out menu. This will result in hairline curves of a very fine width. Click on OK to apply this default to all objects. With the object still deselected, click on the Fill tool and on the X (the no fill icon). Again, accept this as the default for all objects. Now reselect the bitmap.

4. Now you will crop the bitmap just enough to tighten the frame, so that no empty space extends beyond any of the objects in the image. With the bitmap still selected, activate the Shaping tool and position it over the middle boundary marker along the bottom edge of the rectangular frame. When the cursor turns into a crosshair, press and hold the mouse button and drag the bottom edge of the boundary marker upward. As you drag, the status line displays the percentage by which your cropping is diminishing the height of the bitmap frame. Release the mouse button when the status line displays the message, "Bitmap: Crop bottom: 19%" and provides an even margin all around. When you have finished, the status line displays all four cropping percentages, as shown in Figure D-5.

5. Select the Preferences command from the Special menu and adjust the settings for the Lines and Curves options as follows: Autotrace Tracking, 10 pixels; Corner Threshold, 8 pixels; Straight Line Threshold, 3 pixels; and AutoJoin, 10 pixels. These settings will result in smoother curves, smooth (rather than cusp) nodes, curves

Figure D-5.   *AUTTRACE.CDR showing a cropped bitmap*

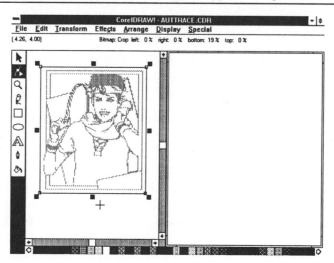

rather than straight line segments, and curve segments that snap
together when they are as far as 10 pixels apart, as shown in Table
D-1. Click on OK twice to make these settings take effect.

6. Turn on the preview window, if it isn't already. Select the Magnification tool [Q] and then the Zoom-In tool [Q] when the fly-out menu
appears. Magnify only the woman's head. Your editing window
should look similar to Figure D-6.

7. Now you are ready to begin Autotracing. Make sure that the bitmap
is still selected, and then select the Pencil tool [✐] . Notice that the
cursor looks different than usual, instead of being a perfectly
symmetrical crosshair, it has a wand-like extension on the right [✦].
This is the Autotrace cursor. It appears only when you activate the
Pencil tool with a bitmap object selected. The word "AutoTrace"
appears on the status line, indicating that you are now in Autotrace
mode.

Table D-1.   *Guidelines for Setting Lines and Curves Options in the Preferences*
              Dialog Box

Option	Determines	Settings	
		Low no. (1-3)	High no. (7-10)
Freehand Tracking	how closely Corel follows your freehand drawing	many nodes	few nodes
Autotrace Tracking	how closely the Autotrace cursor follows bitmap edges	rough curve	smooth curve
Corner Threshold	whether a node is cusped or smooth	cusp nodes	smooth nodes
Straight Line Threshold	whether a segment should be a curve or a straight line	more curves	more lines
AutoJoin	how close together two line or curve segments must be in order to join	less joining	more joining

8. Position the wand of the Autotrace cursor on the bottom of the woman's left (your right) ear, and then click once. After a moment, a closed curve object appears, completely enclosing the contours of the woman's face, as shown in Figure D-7. If you do not achieve the same result, select Undo from the Edit menu and try again.

9. Position the Autotrace cursor along the woman's hairline, but a little above the point where the woman's hair goes over the headband on the right, and click. Some seconds later, another curve appears, as shown in Figure D-8. This curve outlines something the woman is carrying.

Figure D-6.   *Magnified view of the woman's head*

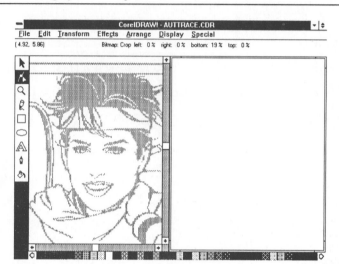

Figure D-7.   *Autotracing a closed region of the woman's face*

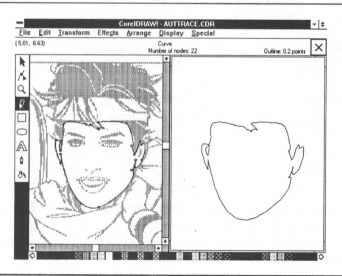

Figure D-8.   *The second Autotraced curve*

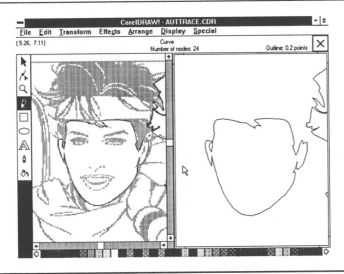

If your screen shows that a different curve was traced, select Undo and try again. Keep in mind that Autotrace does not give you the same high degree of control available with manual tracing.

10. Select the Zoom-In tool from the Magnification tool fly-out menu and zoom in on the woman's hair. Then position the intersection point of the Autotrace cursor inside one of the closed regions that represent the highlights of the hair, and click. A closed curve object appears quickly.

11. Create a few more highlighting curves in the same way. Your screen should more or less resemble Figure D-9.

12. Save your changes to the image by pressing (CTRL)-(S).

13. Select New from the File menu to clear the screen.

If you have trouble selecting a region that results in the curve you need, try pointing at the desired region using the wand of the Autotrace cursor instead of the center point of the crosshair. You will find that you can aim the wand more accurately when you are working in a magnified view.

Tip

Figure D-9.   *Creating highlights in the woman's hair with the Autotrace cursor*

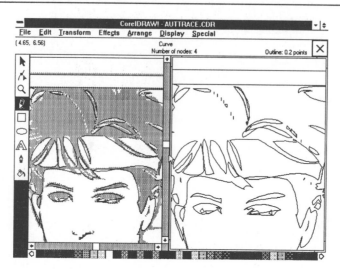

As you saw in the previous exercise, the results of the Autotrace feature depend on your choice of the area to outline and on exactly how you position the Autotrace cursor. Even if you use Autotrace in tracing the same area twice, CorelDRAW! may change the number and positions of the nodes each time. The path that an Autotrace curve takes can sometimes seem to be quite unpredictable, especially if the subjects within the bitmap have overlapping or connected pixels. With practice, you will gain skill in positioning the Autotrace cursor for the best possible results.

Tracing Manually

You don't have to be a superb drafter to trace a bitmap with precision in CorelDRAW!. By magnifying the areas you trace and adjusting the Lines and Curves settings in the Preferences dialog box, you can trace swiftly and still achieve accurate results. To trace a bitmap manually, you deselect the bitmap just before you activate the Pencil tool. This action prevents the Pencil tool from becoming the Autotrace cursor.

Manual tracing is faster and easier than using Autotrace if the imported bitmap contains multiple subjects with no clear separations between the pixels that compose these subjects. Most commercial clip art fits this description. Using the manual method avoids the problem of Autotrace curves that extend beyond the subject with which you are working. As a result, you usually need to do less editing after your initial manual tracing than when you use Autotrace.

Just as when you use the Autotrace feature, you can define the default shape of the outline pen, the outline color, the interior fill of the object, and the smoothness of the curves before you begin tracing. In the following exercise, you will trace portions of the MANTRACE.CDR image you imported earlier from the OUT_PLAY.TIF file.

1. Open the MANTRACE.CDR file.

2. When the bitmapped object appears, adjust magnification to fit-in-window.

3. Adjust the outline pen attributes of the bitmap. Deselect the object, click on the Outline tool and then on the hairline icon in the first row of the fly-out menu. This will produce hairline curves of a very fine width. Accept this setting as the default for all objects.

4. Click on the Fill tool and again on the none ⊠ icon to change the object fill color to none. This prevents any closed paths that you trace from filling with an opaque color and obscuring other traced areas that lie beneath. You can edit the fill colors of individual objects later. Again, accept this as the default and then reselect the object.

5. Crop the bitmap so that only the woman's head is visible. With the bitmap still selected, select the Shaping tool and position it directly over the boundary marker at the lower-left *corner* of the bitmap object. When the cursor turns into a crosshair, depress and hold the mouse button and drag this corner upward and to the right. Release the mouse button when the status line reads, "Bitmap: Crop left: 44% bottom 44%", as in Figure D-10.

6. The bottom of the bitmap "frame" needs additional cropping. Position the Shaping tool directly over the *middle* boundary marker

Figure D-10. *Cropping a bitmap in preparation for manual tracing*

on the bottom of the bitmap. When the cursor turns into a crosshair, press and hold the mouse button and drag this marker up. Release the mouse button when the status line reads, "Bitmap: Crop bottom 61%."

7. Position the Shaping tool directly over the top-right boundary marker. When the cursor turns into a crosshair, press and hold the mouse button and drag the marker down and to the left. Release the mouse button when the status line shows that you have cropped the top of the image 6% and the right of the image 9%, as shown in Figure D-11. Then adjust magnification to fit-in-window.

8. Select the Preferences command from the Special menu and adjust the settings for the Lines and Curves options as follows: Pencil Tracking, 1 pixel; Corner Threshold, 10 pixels; Straight Line Threshold, 1 pixel; and AutoJoin, 10 pixels. These settings will result in curves that closely follow the movements of your mouse. You will generate smooth (rather than cusp) nodes, curves rather than straight-line segments, and curve segments that snap together when they are as far as 10 pixels apart. These settings promote ease of

Figure D-11. *Cropped image of woman's head in preparation for enlarging and manual tracing*

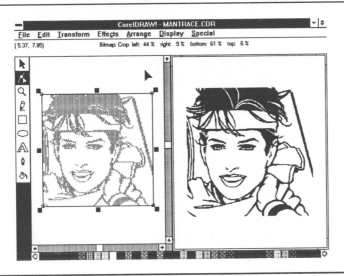

editing should you need to smooth out the traced curves later. Click on OK twice to save these settings.

9. Deselect the bitmap object, and activate the Pencil tool (if you see the Autotrace cursor instead of the regular Pencil cursor, you haven't deselected the bitmap) and with the Zoom-In tool, magnify the head so it fills the window. Position the Pencil tool anywhere along the outline of the face, then depress and hold the mouse and trace all the way around the face. End the curve at the starting point. Should you make any errors, you can erase portions of the curve by pressing the (SHIFT) key as you drag the mouse backward. If you end the curve within 10 pixels of the starting point, the two end nodes snap together and form a closed path, as shown in Figure D-12. If the end nodes are farther apart than 10 pixels, the curve remains an open path. To close the path, activate the Shaping tool and draw a marquee around the two end nodes, double-click on one of them to invoke the Node Edit menu, and select Join.

Figure D-12.   *A manually traced closed curve*

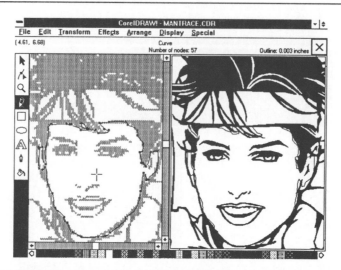

10. Trace the outline of the woman's nose as an open path. Use the preview window to help you.

11. Magnify just the area around the mouth and trace two closed paths: one around the outer lips, and the other around the mouth opening. Similarly, magnify each eye and trace them both. Don't worry about being exact; you can always reshape your curves later.

12. Use the Zoom-Out tool to return to the previous magnification showing the woman's head and neck. Then, activate the Select tool and select the entire bitmap object. Remember that unless the bitmap is selected, you cannot enter Autotrace mode.

13. To enter the Autotrace mode, activate the Pencil tool again with the bitmaps selected. Position the Autotrace cursor inside one of the highlighted areas of the hair and click to trace a curve around this tiny area automatically.

14. Using Autotrace, trace a few more highlights of the woman's hair. When you have finished, your screen should look roughly similar to Figure D-13. Save the image at this point by pressing (CTRL)-(S).

Figure D-13.   *Combining Autotracing with manual tracing to create highlights*

15. Turn on the preview window. Since you did not activate the For Tracing option when importing this bitmap, the bitmap appears in the preview window. As a result, you cannot see the traced curves clearly.

16. Activate the Preview Selected Only command in the Display menu, and then select all of the traced curves, including the highlights of the woman's hair. Now you can see the traced objects clearly in the preview window, as in Figure D-14.

17. Save the changes you have made by pressing (CTRL)-(S), and then select New from the File menu to clear the screen.

     As you have just seen, it is possible and sometimes even preferable to combine both the manual and Autotrace methods when tracing complex bitmap images. Manual tracing is best for obtaining exact control over the placement of curves in bitmaps that contain several subjects close together, as is the case with most clip art. The Autotrace method is useful for tracing small closed regions like the highlights of the woman's hair in the previous exercises. The

Figure D-14.   *Preview Selected Only showing all traced objects*

Autotrace method is also more convenient to use when the bitmap image has a single, clearly defined subject with sharp contours.

Whether you use the Autotrace feature, manual tracing, or a combination of both methods, you can always edit the curve objects you create.

Tracing with CorelTRACE!

Beginning with release 1.2 of CorelDRAW!, a third method of tracing bitmapped images became available to you—one that is more rapid, sophisticated, and efficient than either the manual or Autotrace method. The CorelTRACE! batch tracing utility, similar to Adobe Streamline, allows you to trace one or more bitmaps automatically at high speeds and save them in the Adobe .EPS format. You can choose from two default methods of tracing, or customize tracing parameters to suit your needs. CorelTRACE! is provided with sample files in which you can practice changing the tracing parameters. When you are finished tracing files, you can edit the resulting vector-based images in any drawing program that can read the Adobe .EPS file format.

The following sections provide instructions for preparing to use CorelTRACE! for selecting and tracing bitmaps, and for customizing and editing tracing parameters.

Preparing to Use CorelTRACE!

If you have version 1.2 or later, CorelTRACE! is installed in the same directory where you installed CorelDRAW!. Before you begin using CorelTRACE! for the first time, check the amount of memory available in the root directory of your hard drive C:. When you trace bitmaps using CorelTRACE!, temporary files are generated in the root directory of your hard drive unless you specify a different directory in your AUTOEXEC.BAT file. If you trace large bitmaps or more than one bitmap during a session, you are almost certain to require several megabytes of hard drive space for these temporary files. A good recommendation is to have at least 5 MB of space free, and 10 MB is not too much.

If your hard drive does not have enough space available, you can either remove unnecessary files or specify a different hard drive, if you have one, where CorelTRACE! can place the large temporary files it generates. For example, if CorelDRAW! and CorelTRACE! are installed in drive C: and you wish to locate temporary files in the TEMP directory of drive D:, edit your AUTOEXEC.BAT file and add the following line to it:

    set temp=d:\temp

This statement tells Windows always to place temporary files in the specified directory. Be sure to reboot you computer after you edit the AU-TOEXEC.BAT file in order to make your changes take effect, and be sure that the directory exists on the specified hard drive.

Never select the Windows directory as the directory in which to store the temporary files that Windows applications generate. Errors could result that might cause your system to crash unexpectedly.

Caution

Loading CorelTRACE!

Unless you have over 2 MB of memory, do not run any other Windows applications in the background while you are running CorelTRACE!. CorelTRACE! requires a large amount of memory to work efficiently. If you run other applications concurrently, CorelTRACE! may not run or may function very slowly.

To load CorelTRACE!, follow these steps:

1. Load Windows to start the Program Manager.

2. Double-click on the CorelTRACE! icon. The opening screen shown in Figure D-15 appears for a few seconds, and then is replaced by the program window depicted in Figure D-16.

The opening screen of CorelTRACE! contains five items in the menu bar: a File menu, a Tracing Options menu, the F1 Help menu, and the View Image and Preferences menus. To obtain help information on menu running CorelTRACE!, you click on the F1 Help menu or press the (F1) function key at any time after the small information box disappears from the screen. To begin the process of specifying and tracing files once the program window displays, you click on the File menu and again on the Open option.

Getting Help in CorelTRACE!

You can access CorelTRACE! help screens in one of two ways. You can press (F1) or click on the F1 Help indicator in the menu. The Index screen of the CorelTRACE! Help system window appears as in Figure D-17.

The help system for CorelTRACE! uses the standard Windows Help System and works like the WFNBOSS help system you learned about in Appendix C. To see the help information for any topic, double-click on the line that contains the topic name in the Index screen. To move to the next screen, select the Browse ahead command in the command bar. To go back to the previous *topic*, select the Browse back command in the command bar. A single topic can contain more than one screen. To go back to the previous *screen* within the same topic, use the scrollbar. You can return to the general Index screen at any time by selecting the Index command in the command

Figure D-15. *The CorelTRACE! opening screen*

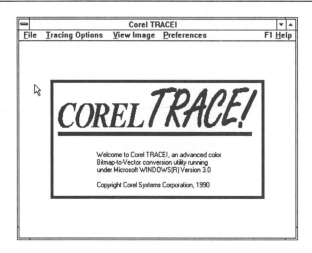

Figure D-16. *The CorelTRACE! applications window*

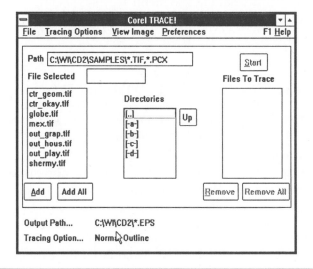

Figure D-17.   *The Index of the CorelTRACE! Help System window*

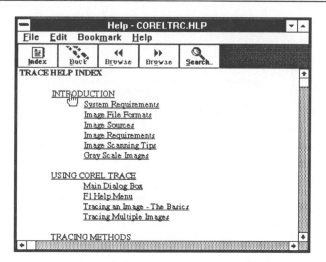

bar. To exit the CorelTRACE! help system and return to what you were doing previously, select Exit from the File menu.

Continue with the next section to learn how to work in the CorelTRACE! program window.

Selecting the "Files To Trace" Dialog Box

In order to trace one or more bitmaps, you must work with the options in the CorelTRACE! program window shown in Figure D-17. This is the main operating screen of the CorelTRACE! utility.

You can edit several of the options in this dialog box prior to tracing a file. Take a moment to become acquainted with the components of this screen.

Path, Directories   The Path text box indicates the source directory and file extension of the bitmaps to be traced. Valid input file extensions are .PCX, .TIF, and .BMP. When you first install CorelDRAW!, the default source path is the directory where either CorelDRAW! or its sample files are located. You can change the source drive and directory by double-clicking on the appropriate options in the Directories list box. This list box is located in the center of the CorelTRACE! program window.

File Selected, Files List Box   The list box just below the File Selected text box displays the names of all of the files in the specified directory that match the selected file format. To make a filename appear in the File Selected text box, click once on the desired filename in the Files list box. To select a file for tracing, double-click on the filename, or click on the Add command button, which you will learn about in a moment.

Files To Trace   With CorelTRACE!, you can *batch trace*, or trace multiple files at once. The Files To Trace list box contains the names of the files, in the specified directory, that you have chosen to trace. To make a filename appear here, select it from the Files list box in one of two ways: double-click on the filename, or click on the filename once and then click on the Add command button. To remove a file from the Files To Trace list box, click on the filename in the list box once, and then click on the Remove command button.

Add, Add All, Remove, Remove All   These command buttons work in conjunction with the list boxes above them. To add a file from the Files list box to the Files To Trace list box, click on its name once to highlight it, and then click on the Add command button. To transfer all of the filenames in the Files list box to the Files To Trace list box, simply click on the Add All command button. To remove a single file from the Files To Trace list box, click once on the desired filename, and then click on the Remove command button. To remove all of the filenames from the Files To Trace list box, simply click on the Remove All command button.

Output Path   The Output Path statement at the bottom of the dialog box specifies the directory where CorelTRACE! sends the files after tracing them. The default is the directory where you installed CorelTRACE!. You can change the output path by clicking on the Output Options command in the File menu and making adjustments to the options in the dialog box that appears.

Tracing Options   The Tracing Option statement at the bottom of the dialog box tells CorelTRACE! exactly how to trace the files. There are two default methods, Normal Outline and Normal Centerline. You can also define up to eight custom tracing methods by selecting one of the blank dotted line (. . .) options and then selecting the Edit Option command in the Tracing Options menu. Most of the time, the two default methods will be adequate for your needs. To learn more about using the default methods and customizing the tracing methods, see the "Customizing Your Tracing Options" section later in this appendix.

Start Command Button   When you have specified all of the tracing parameters using the other options in the dialog box, click on the Start command button to begin the tracing process.

Now that you are familiar with the contents of the Select Files To Trace dialog box, you are ready to practice tracing bitmapped graphics files. Continue with the next section to obtain hands-on practice.

Tracing a Bitmap with CorelTRACE!

Tracing one or more bitmaps involves several steps:

1. Specify the source directory of the files you want to trace, using the Directories list box if necessary.

2. Select one or more files to trace. To do so, either double-click on their names in the Files list box, or click on a filename and then on the Add command button.

3. Edit the Output Options—On name and output path conflict messages, use the Output Options command in the File menu.

4. Edit the tracing method options, if desired, by selecting a command from the Tracing Options menu.

5. Click on the Start command button to begin tracing the selected file(s).

In the following exercise, you will tell CorelTRACE! to batch trace (trace one after another) two bitmap files. The sample TIFF files used in the exercise were installed automatically if you installed the sample files with CorelDRAW!. If you wish, you can substitute any two bitmapped graphics files of your own.

1. If you did not install the sample files with CorelDRAW!, change to a drive and directory where .PCX or .TIF files are located. If you did install the sample files with your software, make certain that the .TIF files shown in Figure D-18 appear in the File Selected dialog box. Use the Directories list box to change the path if necessary.

2. Double-click on the OUT_HOUS.TIF and OUT_PLAY.TIF file-names in the Files list box at the left side of the dialog box. Both filenames now appear in the Files To Trace list box, as shown in Figure D-18.

3. Check the Output Path statement at the bottom of the dialog box. If you want CorelTRACE! to send the traced files to a different directory than the one specified, click on the Output Options command in the File menu. The Output Options dialog box appears, as shown in Figure D-19.

4. Check the option settings in the "On name conflict" area of the Output Options dialog box. These settings determine what happens if you attempt to retrace a bitmap for which an output file of the

Figure D-18.   *Selecting two files from the Files To Trace list box*

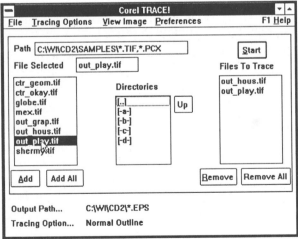

Figure D-19.   *The Output Options dialog box*

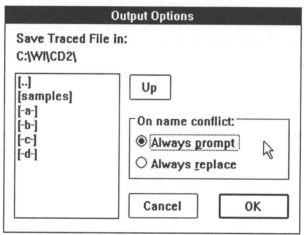

same name already exists. If you select "Always replace,"
CorelTRACE! overwrites the existing file automatically. If you select
"Always prompt," CorelTRACE! warns you about the conflict and
lets you rename the output file before proceeding.

5. Check the Save Traced File in setting. This determines the destination directory of the traced .EPS file. To change the current drive
and/or directory, backspace over the current drive and/or directory names and type the desired names in their place.

6. Select the OK command button to save your Output Options
settings and return to the CorelTRACE! application window.

7. Check the Tracing Option statement at the bottom of the dialog
box. The default tracing option is Normal_Outline. If the option
that appears in your dialog box is Normal_Centerline or something
else, open the Tracing Options menu and click on the Normal
Outline command, as shown in Figure D-20. This tells CorelTRACE!
to trace a line around each of the black or white regions of the

Figure D-20. Selecting the Normal Outline tracing method

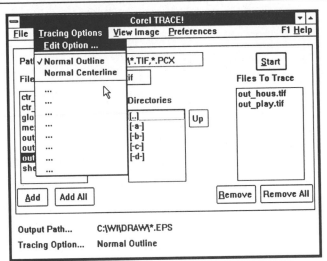

bitmap image and then fill each area with black or white to match the original bitmap. The Outline method is best for tracing bitmaps with thick lines, many fills, and a hand-sketched look. The Centerline method, on the other hand, is best for architectural or technical illustrations that have thin lines of fairly uniform thickness and no fill colors. See the next section of this appendix for more details on the differences between the Outline and Centerline methods of tracing.

8. As a last step before you click on the Start command button, open the Preferences menu shown in Figure D-21.

The Preferences menu provides five options:

- Trace Partial Area brings up an image of the bitmap after you start CorelTRACE! and allows you to identify the area to be traced by manipulating a bounding box.

- Show Progress Rate shows the percentage of the tracing that CorelTRACE! has completed.

Figure D-21.   *The Preferences menu*

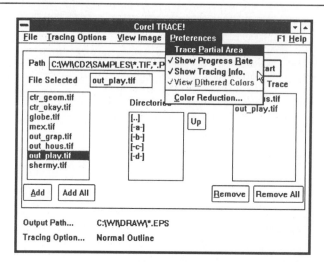

- Show Tracing Info shows the image size in pixels, the number of nodes and objects, and the time required to complete.

- View Dithered Colors lets you choose between pure colors or shades of gray and dithered colors or shades of gray for viewing purposes. This does not affect the traced image, only what you see on the screen.

- Color Reduction provides the means of reducing the number of colors or shades of gray in the traced image. This provides for faster tracing and smaller files.

9. For the work here, make sure that the Show Progress Rate is checked (that is the default), and then click on Show Tracing Info. These options provide useful information during and after tracing.

10. Click on the Start command button to begin tracing the two sample files. After a few seconds, a small window containing the first of the two bitmaps pops up at the right side of the screen. You can actually watch as CorelTRACE! traces each fine detail of the bitmap. When

the tracing is complete, the window containing the first bitmap disappears automatically and is replaced by a fly-out window that contains the second bitmap. Once more, watch as the bitmap is traced. The window containing the traced image of the second bitmap remains on the screen after the tracing is complete, as shown in Figure D-22. The information produced by Show Tracing Info is shown at the bottom of the window.

11. To make the window that contains the second traced file disappear, double-click on the control-menu icon in the upper-left corner of the window. If you quit CorelTRACE! without closing the window of the last file you traced, the window closes automatically.

12. Select the Exit command from the File menu to exit CorelTRACE! and return to the Program Manager. Now you can load CorelDRAW!, import one or both of the traced files, and edit them just as you would any other object-oriented image. Remember that when you import a .EPS file, the image takes some time to load onto the screen fully.

Figure D-22. The traced bitmap upon completion

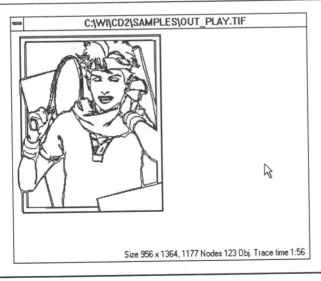

The preceding exercise gave you a brief glimpse of what CorelTRACE! can do. In the next section, you will learn more about how you can customize the options that determine the smoothness, fineness, and clarity of the curves during the tracing process.

Customizing Your Tracing Options

The Tracing Options menu in the CorelTRACE! application window contains two preset tracing options, Outline and Centerline. If you wish, you can modify the parameters associated with these two options to define up to eight custom tracing methods. When you modify a tracing option, you can save your result as a new option in the Tracing Options menu, using one of the eight blank entries shown in Figure D-20. In the following sections, you will find out more about the two preset methods, Normal Outline and Normal Centerline, and when you will want to choose each method to obtain the best results.

Normal Outline Tracing

When you select Normal Outline as the tracing method, CorelTRACE! seeks out the *outlines* of black or white areas and traces around them. Every curve becomes a closed object that is then filled with black or white, a color, or a gray shade to match the original bitmap as closely as possible. This method is most appropriate when the images that you trace contain many filled objects or have lines of variable thicknesses.

Normal Centerline Tracing

When you select Normal Centerline as the tracing method, CorelTRACE! seeks out the *center* point of lines in a bitmap and traces down the middle of those lines. No attempt is made to close paths or fill them. The resulting accuracy and attention to fine detail makes this tracing method the best choice for scanned images of technical or architectural drawings. Normal Centerline is also appropriate for tracing drawings in which line thicknesses are fairly uniform.

Defining a Custom Tracing Method

What if the image you want to trace contains both filled areas and line art? In CorelTRACE!, you can adjust a variety of tracing options by selecting the Edit Option command in the Tracing Options menu. Follow these steps to access this command and define a custom tracing option.

1. Load CorelTRACE! from the Program Manager.

2. Without selecting any files, pull down the Tracing Options menu and click on one of the blank (. . .) menu options. The Tracing Options dialog box shown in Figure D-23 appears. Using this dialog box, you can edit any of eight tracing parameters, then save them under a unique name that will appear as an option in the Tracing Options menu. You can define up to eight additional tracing options using this dialog box.

3. Position the cursor in the Option Name text box at the lower-left corner of the dialog box and type the name of the new tracing option you are about to define.

4. Edit the tracing options as desired, referring to the descriptions that appear farther on in this section.

5. When you are finished editing, select the OK command button to save the tracing option under the new name that will now appear in the Tracing Options menu, as shown in Figure D-24. The name of

Figure D-23.   *The Tracing Options dialog box*

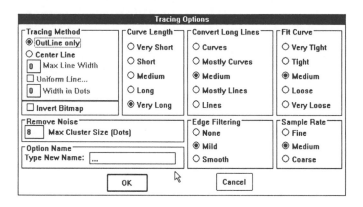

Figure D-24.   *The Tracing Options menu*

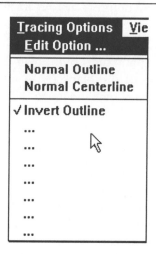

the new tracing option and the settings that define it also appear in the CORELDRW.INI file.

Information about tracing methods that you define is saved in the CORELDRW.INI file. Keep a backup copy of your CORELDRW.INI file so that you can restore your custom tracing options in the event that you reinstall Windows or lose your original CORELDRW.INI file due to some other cause.

Each of the eight parameters in the Tracing Options dialog box has a special function in the tracing process.

Tracing Method, Line Width   This tracing parameter is important only if you want to trace an image based on the Centerline rather than the Outline method. If you click on the Center Line checkbox, an X appears in the checkbox and the Line Width option becomes available. The number in the Line Width option defines the maximum width, in pixels, that you want CorelTRACE! to treat as a line. If areas in the bitmap contain higher numbers of pixels grouped together, CorelTRACE! treats them as closed objects rather than as lines. The valid range for Line Width is from 2 to 99 pixels or dots. If you select 0 or 1, the setting defaults to a value of 6.

Invert Bitmap   When the Invert Bitmap checkbox contains an X, this option is active. CorelTRACE! will convert black areas of the bitmap to white and white areas to black.

Curve Length   This parameter determines the maximum length of each curve segment within the traced image. If you select Very Short or Short, each segment may be short, but the number of nodes in each segment remains high. As a result, the curves will fit the outline of the bitmap very closely. If you select Long or Very Long, on the other hand, the traced image will have smoother curves, but they will follow the bitmap more loosely. Select the desired option based on the characteristics of your input file and the way you want the resulting object-oriented picture to look.

Convert Long Lines   Your setting for this option determines whether CorelTRACE! treats a particular curve segment as a straight line or as a curve. If you select the Curves option, for example, CorelTRACE! will convert all traced segments to curves. If you select Lines, CorelTRACE! will convert all traced segments to straight lines. The other settings permit a mixture of curve and straight line segments in the traced drawing. If you frequently trace technical illustrations or other drawings that are made up of mostly straight lines, consider creating a custom tracing option that converts all segments to straight lines.

Fit Curve   This parameter affects how closely CorelTRACE! follows the outline of the bitmap when tracing it. A Very Tight setting results in a curve that follows the bitmap closely, while a Very Loose setting results in a looser curve. You should always set this option to the *opposite* of the setting chosen for the Sample Rate option. For example, if you select Very Loose for Fit Curve, choose Fine for Sample Rate.

Sample Rate   The Sample Rate option determines how closely Corel-TRACE! matches its curve segments to the original bitmap. A setting of Fine results in a close match with many nodes, while a setting of Coarse results in a less exact match with fewer nodes per curve segment. Set this option in conjunction with the Fit Curve option, as described under Fit Curve earlier in the chapter.

Edge Filtering   Sometimes a bitmap image contains rather jagged outlines. You can select the Smooth option from the Edge Filtering selections to tell CorelTRACE! to smooth those outlines when tracing. Selecting the Mild option causes CorelTRACE! to smooth the outlines to a less extreme degree.

Remove Noise   Many scanned images contain unwanted flecks that are not truly part of the images themselves. The Remove Noise option lets you tell CorelTRACE! when to consider clumps of pixels as unwanted flecks and when to treat them as part of the picture. The number to which you set this option determines the minimum pixel cluster size that CorelTRACE! will consider to be a part of the picture. All pixel clusters smaller than or equal to the specified number will be ignored during the file conversion and tracing process. You can set this option to any number between 2 and 999. When you are tracing a poorly scanned image, set the number slightly higher; when you are tracing a "clean" file, keep the number low. You'll rarely need to set this option above 10.

Option Name   As mentioned previously, you can define and name up to eight tracing options beyond the two standard options provided with CorelTRACE!. To save a modified tracing option under a new name, you must be sure to type a name in this text box *before* you exit the Tracing Options dialog box. Otherwise,the new settings will be valid only during the current session of CorelTRACE!. Then select OK to cause this new option to appear in the Tracing Options menu.

If you trace and import many bitmaps, you probably tend to trace the same kinds of files over and over again. Defining custom Tracing Options to fit the kinds of files you trace most often can be a powerful time-saving tool.

Editing an Existing Tracing Option

Once you have defined a tracing option, you can alter its parameters permanently using the Edit Options command in the Tracing Options menu. This command always applies to the *currently selected* tracing option. You must therefore select the option you wish to edit *before* you click on the Edit Option command.

To edit an existing tracing option,

1. With the CorelTRACE! application window open, click on the Tracing Options menu and on the name of the option you wish to

edit. The name of this option appears in the Tracing Option statement at the lower-left corner of the CorelTRACE! application window, showing that it is the currently selected tracing option.

2. Now, select the Edit Option command from the Tracing Options menu. The Tracing Options dialog box for the currently selected tracing option appears.

3. Edit the tracing options as desired, then select OK to save the new settings permanently.

Editing parameters for existing tracing options, like defining new tracing options, helps you save time when you import traced graphics into CorelDRAW! and edit them. For example, if you know in advance that you need to invert colors of a particular bitmap or that you require a larger or smaller number of nodes in the traced graphic, you can change tracing parameters to give you the desired results automatically.

Index